THE NEW BOOK OF PEOPLE

Also by Christopher P. Andersen

The Name Game

A Star, Is a Star, Is a Star!: The Lives and Loves of Susan Hayward

Father

Success Over Sixty (with Albert Myers)

THE NEW BOOK OF PEOPLE

Photographs, capsule biographies and vital statistics of over 500 celebrities

Christopher P. Andersen

A Perigee Book

For my daughter,
Katharine Haines Andersen
And her grandmother,
Jeanette

G. P. Putnam's Sons
Publishers Since 1838
200 Madison Avenue
New York, NY 10016

Published simultaneously in Canada by
General Publishing Co. Limited, Toronto

Designed by James L. McGuire

Library of Congress Cataloging-in-Publication Data

Andersen, Christopher P.
The new book of people.

"A Perigee book."
1. Biography—20th century—Dictionaries.
I. Title.
CT120.A53 1986 920'.009'04 85-25862
ISBN 0-399-51223-3

Printed in the United States of America
1 2 3 4 5 6 7 8 9 10

ACKNOWLEDGMENTS

Updating this compendium of the world's most celebrated people required the assistance of many unsung superstars. First, I am grateful to my wife, Valerie, an international banker by trade but also a top-notch critic and proofreader. My thanks to Ellis Amburn, G. P. Putnam's Editorial Director, Lee Ann Chearneyi and Dan Silverman. I owe a special debt to my agent, Ellen Levine, and to Stacey Rocklyn for her help in obtaining photographs, as well as to the Memory Shop, *Movie Star News, Pictorial Parade* and *Photoreporters*. As always, my parents, Edward and Jeanette Andersen, were a tremendously valuable source of encouragement and help—particularly my mother, a walking encyclopedia when it comes to the famous and the infamous. For her part, my sister Valerie, more than a decade younger than I, made sure the new crop of superstars was not overlooked.

To the subjects of *The New Book of People* I owe another debt of gratitude. For whatever reasons, they have captured our imaginations and made us want to know all there is to know about them.

C.P.A.

A NOTE FROM THE AUTHOR

Since *The Book of People* was originally published in 1981, scores of new megacelebrities have exploded on the scene. Some are long-familiar names who, either through making a spectacular comeback (Tina Turner, Lee Iacocca, Joan Collins, Jane Wyman) or sheer perseverance (John Forsythe, Lionel Richie, Larry Hagman) transcended the barrier between mere star and superstar. Many, however, are people we had never heard of as recently as a few years ago—people such as rockers Cyndi Lauper, Prince, and Sting; TV's Tom Selleck, Victoria Principal, and Daniel J. Travanti; model Christie Brinkley and movie stars Bill Murray, Mel Gibson, Richard Gere, and Debra Winger, to name just a few. Some (Vanessa Williams, Boy George, Eddie Murphy) were still in school back when *The Book of People* first came out, and some (Gary Coleman, Emmanuel Lewis) still are.

If you ever doubted that fame is fleeting, consider some of the more than sixty celebrities dropped from this updated edition of *The Book of People*. Do you remember: Aerosmith, Tracy Austin, the Bay City Rollers, the Bottoms Brothers, Jerry Brown, the Captain and Tennille, Billy Carter, Shaun Cassidy, Steve Cauthen, Angela Davis, Kiki Dee, Mike Douglas, the Eagles, Julie Nixon Eisenhower, the Electric Light Orchestra, Emerson, Lake and Palmer, Peter Frampton, Marjoe Gortner, Brooke Hayward, Janis Ian, the Reverend Ike, Gabe Kaplan, Led Zeppelin, Meat Loaf, the Osmonds, Bonnie Raitt, Charlie Rich, Leo Sayer, Seals and Crofts, Margaret Trudeau, and Barry White?

Over these past few years since the original edition of *The Book of People,* death has also claimed a startling number of admired, respected, even beloved personalities. The following portraits are in tribute to those women and men who made a difference.

Christopher P. Andersen

New York City
1986

In Memoriam

John Belushi
(1948–1982)

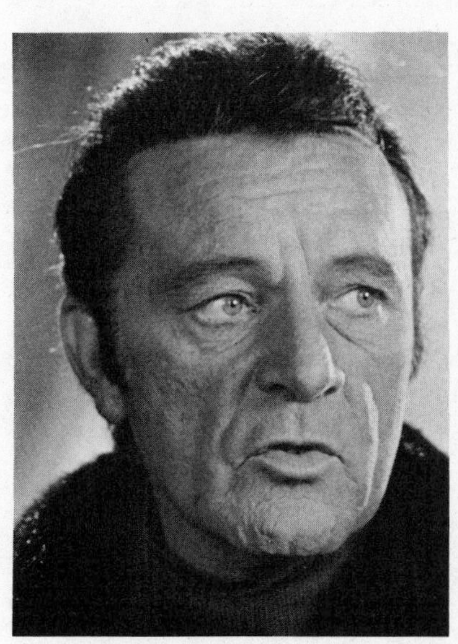

Ingrid Bergman
(1915–1982)

Richard Burton
(1925–1984)

Truman Capote
(1924–1984)

Karen Carpenter
(1950–1982)

Henry Fonda
(1905–1982)

Princess Grace
(1929–1982)

William Holden
(1918–1981)

Rock Hudson
(1925–1985)

Paul Lynde
(1926–1982)

Ricky Nelson
(1940–1986)

David Niven
(1910–1983)

Anwar Sadat
(1918–1981)

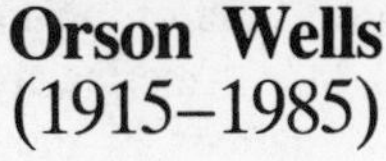

Orson Wells
(1915–1985)

Tennessee Williams
(1911–1983)

Natalie Wood
(1938–1981)

FOREWORD

The questions are as compelling as they were when the first *Book of People* was published in 1981: How much do they make? What do they spend it on? Whom do they sleep with? *How do they live?* More than ever before, America's appetite for celebrities is insatiable. *People* magazine has evolved from a publishing phenomenon to a staple of the reading public. Its spectacular success not only spawned countless imitators but also prompted almost every publication—from *Time* to *Women's Wear Daily* to *The Wall Street Journal*—to beef up its "people" coverage, not to mention paved the way for such highly rated television shows as *PM Magazine, Lifestyles of the Rich and Famous,* and *Entertainment Tonight*. Thus the purpose of *The Book of People* is to inform any avid people-watcher of what he or she needs to know about the new celebrities—those figures who in all likelihood will continue to people the columns and talk shows for years to come.

Who qualifies for inclusion in this volume? Obviously, there is no single valid method for culling celebrities. A household name need not necessarily be a household face: Sandra Day O'Connor, Norman Lear, Woodward and Bernstein, Ted Turner, and Andrew Wyeth could probably walk arm-in-arm down any Main Street without attracting attention. Certainly money alone is no criterion. America's richest private citizen (Walmart founder Sam Walton) is also one of its least visible. Still, of the more than 500 notables in this book, over 250 earn in excess of $1 million per year. The wealthiest: Christina Onassis and Paul McCartney (each with an estimated wealth of $500 million). Runner-ups include Bob Hope ($250 million), directors George Lucas and Steven Spielberg ($150 million apiece), and Michael Jackson, who raked in $70 million from his *Thriller* album alone. At the other end of the financial spectrum, the first test-tube baby, Louise Brown, hasn't yet had the opportunity to enter the job market—although her parents pocketed around $500,000 for her story rights even before Louise's historic birth in the summer of 1978. Perhaps the biggest loser of the past couple of years was Vanessa Williams, who not only lost her Miss America crown after *Penthouse* published nude photographs of her, but hundreds of thousands in lucrative endorsement contracts. Style is an important element, to be sure. Many get by on little else—take a look at Christie Brinkley, Cheryl Tiegs, Bianca Jagger, and the ubiquitous Andy Warhol.

The essential nature of fame has changed since the early 1970s. Biographies of great scientists, magnates of industry, and leading statesmen once inspired passionate curiosity and emulation. Now, with few exceptions, these are not the people celebrity-watchers watch. Instead, they want to know about superstars—and they want to know the most intimate details, served up in a no-holds-barred manner.

People arrive at "celebrity" by different paths. Some become famous by accomplishment (Meryl Streep, Ted Koppel, Mikhail Baryshnikov, Lee Iacocca), others because of power and position (Ronald Reagan, Prince Charles). A growing group is composed of those who, as was once said of Gertrude Stein, are simply famous for being famous. This generally means high visibility, although some—Garbo, for example—have managed to turn their obsessive absence from the public world into an event. An all-time master, of course, was Howard Hughes, who lived to disprove once and for all the Duchess of Windsor's dictum that you can never be too rich or too thin.

The New Book of People includes not only the powerful, rich, and accomplished, but the notorious as well. The Ayatollah Ruhollah Khomeini, Patty Hearst, and Charles Manson must surely rank as three of the world's most instantly recognizable names. With the advent of MTV and music videos, rock stars are represented in force—not only because their names and faces are known to millions of young fans, but because they manufacture the musical furniture of our lives; their influence, like it or not, is inescapable. Not that *The New Book of People* ignores Golden Oldies. Those fixtures who have been legends on the American scene for three generations are also here—some by virtue of the fact they are working now more than ever (Katharine Hepburn, Laurence Olivier, Bob Hope), others because they have reached cult status (Garbo, Cary Grant, Fred Astaire). In most cases, the selections are obvious—beginning with Michael Jackson and Princess Diana, and continuing through blazing superstars like Jacqueline Onassis, Diana Ross, Willie Nelson, Clint Eastwood, Bruce Springsteen, Joan Collins, Robert Redford, and Barbra Streisand.

The New Book of People contains the most data about contemporary celebrities ever collected in any single volume, compiled from thousands of newspaper and magazine articles, countless biographies, and hundreds of interviews. It must be emphasized that since most celebrities are more willing to talk about their sex lives than their salaries, all earnings have been estimated—albeit on the best information available.

The following pages yield some fascinating similarities among today's celebs. A disproportionate number, for example, were born under the signs of Taurus and Gemini. Many led a relatively rootless adolescence—frequently as the children of transient workers or as Army brats—and the majority claim to have survived an unhappy childhood. Most are high school graduates (although the number of dropouts is extraordinarily high), while comparatively few made it through college. Nearly 80 percent of those who have been married have also experienced at least one divorce. More than two-thirds of that number took the plunge a second time—and a significant number of those went ahead and tried yet again. Drug use of various sorts is well represented, yet drinking habits are moderate as a rule, and the nonsmokers outnumber the smokers.

There will invariably be those readers who complain that their particular idol is missing; others will challenge some of the selections. It should be remembered that timeliness is of utmost importance. The Beatles are no longer here; John Lennon is dead and three distinctly separate people with their own careers remain. Henry Ford II must bow to Lee Iacocca, while actor John Carradine takes a back seat to sons David and Keith, and Lloyd Bridges makes room for Jeff. As with all books, several months will elapse between the completion of this updated edition and its actual publication. During that period a number of births, deaths, marriages, and divorces undoubtedly will occur—not to mention the possible arrival on the horizon of one or two new superstars and equally sudden eclipse of others. But then, as Katharine Hepburn once said of the fickleness of fame: "I'm like the old Flatiron Building—maybe it hasn't been torn down yet, but I have a feeling I'm about to be any minute." Not likely!

"In the future, everyone will be famous for 15 minutes."

—ANDY WARHOL

Abba

The world's longtime number-one pop group is best known to American audiences for its million-selling singles: "Dancing Queen," "The Name of the Game," "Knowing Me and Knowing You," "Take a Chance on Me," "S.O.S.," "Fernando," and "The Winner Takes It All." Sweden's ABBA, an acronym formed from the first initials of the group's two couples, is composed of singer Agnetha Fältskog (born April 5, 1950, in Stockholm; Aries), her guitarist ex-husband Björn Ulvaeus (born April 25, 1945, in Stockholm; Taurus), key-

boardist Benny Andersson (born December 16, 1946, in Stockholm; Sagittarius) and his vocalist wife Anni-Frid Lyngstad (born November 15, 1945, in Stockholm; Scorpio). They burst on the world music scene by winning a Eurovision songfest witnessed by a half-billion viewers in 1974 with their tune called "Waterloo." Within four years they had sold over 53 million records and tapes worth well over $300 million on both sides of the Iron Curtain. Until they divorced in 1978, Björn and Agnetha lived in a modest nine-room house five miles from Benny and Anni-Frid, and both couples are still strictly family oriented; together they have six children. So far the biggest scandal involving pristine ABBA occurred onstage in a spat presaging their separation, when Agnetha hurled a herring at her husband Björn and caught him smack in the face. Despite their phenomenal global success ABBA did not make the U.S. concert circuit until 1979. "We'll go to America," said Björn, "when you're absolutely ready for us." America was ready and the tour was a moneymaker. Marital problems aside, ABBA decided to stick together and to continue to turn out hits, including their album *Voulez-Vous*. ABBA is Sweden's most profitable corporation, grossing more money than Volvo and traded on the Swedish stock exchange. Members Andersson and Ulvaeus joined lyricist Tim *(Jesus Christ, Superstar)* Rice to write *Chess,* a musical produced in London that spawned the 1985 Murray Head hit single "One Night in Bangkok."

Kareem Abdul-Jabbar

Lew Alcindor

"I can do something else besides stuff a ball through a hoop. My biggest resource is my mind."

New York-born Lew Alcindor, who would eventually change his name and his religion, grew to an astonishing height of seven feet three inches, and his brilliance as a high school basketball center attracted scores of scholarship offers. Alcindor selected UCLA, where he led his team to three consecutive national championships. Around the time he joined the Milwaukee Bucks, Alcindor converted from Catholicism to the black orthodox Hanafi sect (he considered the Black Muslims too racist) and changed his name to Kareem Abdul-Jabbar ("Generous, Powerful Son of Allah"). Kareem, who has journeyed to Mecca and bows toward it five times a day, married fellow Muslim Janice ("Habiba") Brown in 1971, but they separated after four years. Abdul-Jabbar now plays for the Los Angeles Lakers and lives on the ranch he built a few miles outside Hollywood, while his ex-wife and daughter live in Washington, D.C.—just a few blocks from the mosque Kareem bought for his church. In 1973, seven Muslims were murdered there, and four years later the mosque was used as the headquarters for a mass kidnapping that terrorized Washington for two days. At the pinnacle of his profession, Abdul-Jabbar is also cashing in on the many commercial opportunities above and beyond his $2 million salary from the Lakers, including commercials for everything from orange juice to talcum powder. In 1983, a fire destroyed his $2.5 million house along with his priceless 3,000-record jazz collection. Meantime, he bumped into secretary Cheryl Positano on an escalator, and the two had a son, Amir, in 1980. In his 1984 autobiography, Abdul-Jabbar recounted, among other things, the one time at UCLA when he snorted heroin, as well as a brief fling with cocaine that ended when he spun out on a freeway entrance ramp. The following year, his arrangement with Positano also spun out, and she filed a paternity suit.

Born: April 16, 1947, in New York City
Height: 7 ft. 3 in.
Weight: 232 lbs.
Eyes: Brown *Hair:* Black
Zodiac: Aries
Education: UCLA, B.A. in liberal arts (journalism major)
Religion: Hanafi (converted from Catholicism in 1968)
Marriages: To Habiba Brown (1971–1975)
Children: Habiba, Abdul-Kareem, Sultane, Amir
Interests: Journalism, conga drums, tennis
Personal Habits and Traits: Sleeps diagonally on a king-sized bed, is introspective
Addresses: Hollywood; Washington, D.C.
Income: $2 million+

Alan Alda

''I wouldn't live in California. All that sun makes you sterile.''

Wise-cracking Hawkeye Pierce of CBS's wildly popular *M*A*S*H* first tasted show business at the age of six when Robert Alda (best remembered for portraying George Gershwin on film) thrust his son into the act at the Hollywood Canteen. The next year, Alan almost died from polio; he recalls that his mother spent months applying hot packs to his back. While serving as a reserve Army officer, Alan married Arlene Weiss, a clarinetist with the Houston Symphony. She taught music while he scoured New York for work as an actor, appearing in an occasional Broadway hit *(The Owl and the Pussycat, The Apple Tree,* and *Purlie Victorious);* more often than not he was out of work entirely. Alda balked at taking the *M*A*S*H* role when it was offered to him—"If it was going to be just hijinks on the battlefield, I wanted no part of it"—but the series has proved to be his ticket to stardom: Alda nabbed the 1974 Emmy as Outstanding Actor in a Series. Still married to Arlene after more than two decades, Alda commutes to his wife and family in New Jersey, and as a self-described ''cross-country feminist,'' he is one of the country's foremost activists on behalf of women's rights. Alda has also managed to star in a few successful movie comedies, including *Same Time Next Year* and *California Suite.* Alda was a three-time Emmy winner by the time he appeared in *The Seduction of Joe Tynan* in 1979, the story of a U.S. senator's quest for power. His next triple-threat effort was as writer, director, and star of the film comedy *The Four Seasons* (later a short-lived

TV series) and by late 1985 he was working on a new flick called *Sweet Liberty*. The last *M*A*S*H* broadcast, in 1983, ranked as the single highest-rated program in television, watched by an estimated 106 million fanatical fans.

Born: January 28, 1936, in New York City
Height: 6 ft. 2 in.
Weight: 170 lbs.
Eyes: Brown *Hair:* Dark brown
Zodiac: Aquarius
Education: Fordham University
Religion: Roman Catholic
Marriages: To Arlene Weiss
Children: Three daughters
Interests: Feminism, chess, ecology
Personal Habits and Traits: Nonsmoker, workaholic, at times aloof
Address: Leonia, New Jersey
Income: $4 million (estimate)

Jane Alexander

Jane Quigly

''I never thought I was pretty as a child, and that is an awareness I have brought to my roles.''

The superb actress with the dour look of a country schoolmarm was 36 when she copped an Emmy nomination for her tour de force as Eleanor Roosevelt in ABC-TV's *Eleanor and Franklin* and its sequel, *The White House Years*. But she actually began her theatrical career at age 6 in her hometown, Boston, where she ''played the lead in every school play.'' Though she spent two years at Sarah Lawrence studying mathematics, Alexander switched midway through her college career to pursue dramatic arts at the University of Edinburgh. But after a year at Edinburgh, Alexander hitchhiked around Europe with a ''very close black friend'' she had met at the university. ''My father was very angry,'' she recalls, ''not because my friend was black, but because my friend was a guy. Dad didn't understand that it was much safer hitchhiking with a man.'' Appropriately, she landed her first major role—the one for which she received a Tony and then an Oscar nomination for Best Actress—as the love interest opposite James Earl Jones in *The Great White Hope*. She also received plenty of hate mail as a result. ''They called me a nigger lover, also a whore. Some came with graphic illustrations.'' Juicy roles in films *(All the President's Men,* for which she received another Oscar nod), and *Kramer vs. Kramer,* on TV *(Playing for Time),* and on stage *(Hamlet, Major Barbara, 6 RMS RIV VU, The Heiress)* ensued, but none yet so personally rewarding, says Jane, as *Eleanor and Franklin*. In 1984, she was Oscar-nominated for her poignant portrayal of a mother coping with the horror of a nuclear holocaust in *Testament*. She followed that up with a complete change of pace, first playing Calamity Jane in the TV movie of that name, then Hedda Hopper to Liz Taylor's Louella Parsons in the TV movie *Malice in Wonderland* and an autocratic WASP landowner in Hawaii in *Blood and Orchids*.

Born: October 28, 1939, in Boston, Massachusetts
Height: 5 ft. 6 in.
Weight: 127 lbs.
Eyes: Hazel *Hair:* Chestnut brown
Zodiac: Scorpio
Education: Sarah Lawrence (two years), University of Edinburgh (one year)
Religion: Protestant
Marriages:
To Robert Alexander (1962–1969)
To Edwin Sherin (1975–)
Children: Jason Edward (b. 1963, by Alexander)
Interests: Gardening, bird-watching, cleaning, photography, tennis
Personal Habits and Traits: Nonsmoker, drinks wine
Address: Putnam County, New York
Income: $275,000+

Muhammad Ali

''When you're as great as I am, it's hard to be humble.''

Cassius Marcellus Clay, Jr.

Cassius Clay spouted what was to become his trademark verse as he strutted triumphantly off the plane from the 1960 Rome Olympics. He was backed by a syndicate of wealthy Louisville businessmen and trained by Angelo Dundee, but cornerman Budini Brown gave the fighter his perfect line: ''Float like a butterfly, sting like a bee.'' Clay captured the world heavyweight crown from Sonny Liston in 1964, and the next day the brash young champ threw a left hook to black and white fans alike by announcing that he had become a Black Muslim and had changed his name—to Muhammad Ali. But it was not until he refused induction to fight in the war in Vietnam that he really drew the wrath of the American public—and of the courts. At the Houston Induction Center, Ali refused to step forward and join the Army, and four hours later the World Boxing Association stripped him of his title. Convicted of draft evasion, Ali began the arduous process of appeal, and finally on June 20, 1970, the U.S. Supreme Court overturned his conviction. But Ali had lost three and a half years of his boxing prime. Back in the role of contender, it was not until 1974 that he regained his title from George Foreman in Kinshasa, Zaire. Boxing legends like former heavyweight champs Joe Frazier and Ken Norton tried to wrest the crown from Ali, but it took a little-known underdog named Leon Spinks to topple Ali in February 1978—scoring one of the biggest upsets in sports history. Ali's reign was then only briefly interrupted; six months later he became the first boxer in history ever to seize the title three times. A fourth attempt at regaining his crown—this time from Larry Holmes—failed in 1980. Throughout his long career, Ali amassed $60 million in purses alone, and though two divorces, taxes, and a huge entourage have helped drain his coffers, Ali is still worth at least $2 million in cash and more in real estate—not to mention his income from product endorsements. A 1978 poll proved that Ali ranked above the likes of Jackie O.,

Pelé, and the Pope as the world's most famous human being. In pursuit of an acting career, Ali received rave notices playing himself in the film *The Greatest* and performed as a slave, a Union soldier, and a U.S. Senator in the NBC miniseries *Freedom Road.* Ali began the toughest fight of his life in late 1984, when he checked into the Neurological Institute at New York City's Columbia-Presbyterian Medical Center, suffering from symptoms similar to those of Parkinson's disease—persistent fatigue, lack of coordination, and slurred speech. There was little doubt that he owed his condition to his punishing career.

Born: January 17, 1942, in Louisville, Kentucky
Height: 6 ft.
Weight: 220 lbs.
Eyes: Brown *Hair:* Black
Zodiac: Capricorn
Education: High school
Religion: Muslim

Marriages:
To Sonji Roi (divorced)
To Belinda Boyd (divorced)
To Veronica Porche (divorced in 1985)
Children: Six
Interests: Acting, Islam
Personal Habits and Traits: Nonsmoker, teetotaler
Address: Chicago
Income: $3 million (minimum estimate)

Woody Allen

Allen Stewart Konigsberg

''With me, it's just a genetic dissatisfaction with everything.''

Born Allen Stewart Konigsberg (''I told the other kids my name was Frank, but they still beat me up''), Woody Allen survived a childhood in Brooklyn's Flatbush section and parents who he claims ''believed equally in God and carpeting.'' In high school Allen zipped off similar one-liners to Walter Winchell for a couple of dollars a week, and by his early 20s he was raking in over $1,500 weekly as a TV writer for Jack Paar and Sid Caesar. Mining his own angst, this Jewish Charlie Chaplin went on to thrive as a top stand-up comic, comedy recording artist (three top-selling albums), playwright (two hit Broadway shows, *Don't Drink the Water* and *Play It Again, Sam*), author of two bestsellers, and creator of many box-office bombshells—beginning with *What's New, Pussycat?* in 1965 and peaking in 1986 with *Hannah and Her Sisters.* Allen's personal life provided the grist for his comic mill. A teenage marriage to Harlene Rosen was dissolved before Allen made it big, and she sued when he sniped her in his first nightclub act; his relationship with second wife Louise Lasser (star of *Mary Hartman, Mary Hartman*) lasted 11 years. But his most fruitful collaborator was Diane Keaton, with whom he starred in *Play It Again, Sam, Sleeper, Love and*

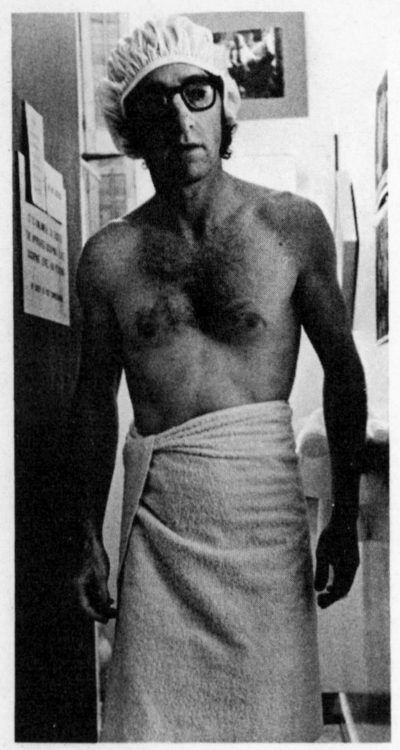

Death, and *Annie Hall* (which copped the Best Picture Oscar for 1977 and earned Allen two other Oscars—for Best Screenplay and for direction). When Allen and Keaton stopped living together in 1976, he "dated around," never living with a woman "for more than two weeks at a time." Mia Farrow, his next roommate-protegée, was one of the few who could keep up with his exhausting schedule: up at 6 A.M., two hours of clarinet practice, an hour of tennis, and up to 12 hours of writing, editing, and directing, with a late supper, usually at Elaine's, the well-known East Side bar/restaurant. And, of course, Allen allows plenty of time for analysis. After 31 years on the couch—more than half his life—the country's foremost self-described neurotic managed to cut his sessions to only three a week. Despite decidedly mixed reviews for his introspective *Interiors,* Allen garnered yet another Best Picture nomination for that film in 1979, then triumphed again with his romantic comedy *Manhattan.* His *Stardust Memories* was forgettable, but *Zelig, Broadway Danny Rose, The Purple Rose of Cairo,* and *Hannah and Her Sisters*—all featuring Farrow—helped Woody recapture his audience.

Born: December 1, 1935, in Brooklyn, New York
Height: 5 ft. 6 in.
Weight: 120 lbs.
Eyes: Blue *Hair:* Reddish brown
Zodiac: Sagittarius
Education: High school
Religion: Jewish

Marriages:
To Harlene Rosen (1954–1958)
To Louise Lasser (1966–1970)
Children: None
Interests: Clarinet, jazz, tennis, dance
Personal Habits and Traits: Nonsmoker, teetotaler, compulsive eater
Address: New York City
Income: $3 million (estimate)

Gregg Allman

"I haven't sung a lot of happy songs. The memory of pain is always there."

The beginning of the 1980s also seemed to signal the dawn of a new era for the celebrated Allman Brothers Band. Following years of booze, pills, drugs, divorce, artistic atrophy, and violent death, the South's foremost blues-rock group had finally come apart in 1976, after leader Gregg Allman (still battling heroin addiction at the time) gave testimony in court that sent his road manager and supplier, Scooter Herring, to jail (Herring's conviction was later reversed). But Allman, Dickey Betts, and the other band members could stay apart only until the summer of 1979, when they launched a resoundingly successful U.S. tour. Allman's own acquaintanceship with grief started early; when he and older brother Duane were boys back in Tennessee, their father was murdered by a hitchhiker. Gregg was a champion weightlifter and linebacker as well as a straight-A student at Castle Heights Military Academy in Lebanon, Tennessee, but when his mother moved the clan to Daytona Beach, Gregg and Duane were drawn to the rock world. Their first band was called the Allman Joys (inspired by the candy bar). It was as the Allman Brothers, however, that they went gold and platinum with albums like *Eat a Peach* and *Brothers and Sisters*. Tragedy struck again when Duane was killed in a 1971 motorcycle accident. One year later, the Allman Brothers' bassist, Berry Oakley, was struck and killed by a bus while riding his motorcycle just one block away from the spot in Macon, Georgia, where Duane's accident had occurred; Gregg turned to heroin. His first two marriages had failed (as did a live-in arrangement with James Arness's daughter Jenny, who later killed herself) by the time he was introduced to Cher by a friend backstage at Los Angeles' Troubadour in 1974. He moved into her 20-room Holmby Hills mansion one month later. Their June 1975 Las Vegas marriage was barely a week old the first time Cher walked out—initiating several such headline-making breakups that preceded their final split in 1979, when Cher filed for divorce. Their son, Elijah Blue, now lives with Cher in California. Ironically, this far-from-pure representative of rockdom (Allman was arrested for disorderly conduct even after joining Alcoholics Anonymous in 1978), was one of the biggest boosters of fellow Georgian Jimmy Carter—and vice versa.

Born: December 7, 1947, in Nashville, Tennessee
Height: 6 ft. 1 in.
Weight: 201 lbs.
Eyes: Blue *Hair:* Blond
Zodiac: Sagittarius
Education: Castle Heights Military Academy, Lebanon, Tennessee
Religion: Baptist
Marriages: Three. Last to Cher (1975–1979)
Children: Elijah Blue (b. 1976)
Interests: Cars, sports
Personal Habits and Traits: Chain-smokes, drinks, given to dark moods, a spendthrift
Addresses: Daytona Beach, Florida; Los Angeles, California

Robert Altman

''Nobody has ever made a good film. Maybe someday they'll make half a good one.''

From his Kansas City boyhood, Robert Altman retains a flat Midwestern twang as well as an informal style that has fashioned him as one of Hollywood's most innovative directors. Starting off in the mid-1950s by directing such action TV series as *Combat,* Altman later gambled his last borrowed bucks on a six-to-one shot at Hollywood Park before racking up a series of offbeat movie hits in the late 1960s and 1970s, including *M*A*S*H, McCabe and Mrs. Miller, Thieves Like Us, California Split, Nashville, Three Women,* and *A Wedding*. What makes the bearlike director so popular among his actors is his eagerness to incorporate their ideas into his films. In *Nashville,* for example, the cast often ad-libbed or wrote their own dialogue and performed their own songs. For this unparalleled freedom, Altman pays his actors modestly (in the case of *Nashville,* $10,000 apiece for ten weeks' work) and expects them to remain on the set for the entire shooting—offscreen collaboration is as important to Altman as what happens before the camera. Says Altman's third wife, Katherine Reed (they have been married since 1962): "My husband's favorite things are smoking dope and having good parties." His 1979 effort, *Quintet,* proved a dismal flop. *Popeye,* starring Robin Williams and Shelley Duvall, was released to frosty reviews in 1980. He was critically and commercially redeemed by *Come Back to the Five and Dime, Jimmy Dean, Jimmy Dean* starring Cher, Sandy Dennis, and Karen Black.

Born: February 20, 1925, in Kansas City, Missouri
Height: 6 ft.
Weight: 220 lbs.
Eyes: Blue *Hair:* Brown but balding
Zodiac: Pisces
Education: University of Missouri (three years)
Religion: Protestant
Marriages: Three. Currently to Katherine Reed (1962–)
Children: Christine (from first marriage); Michael and Stephen (from second marriage); Robert (by Reed) and Matthew (adopted, with Reed)
Interests: Poker
Personal Habits and Traits: Smokes cigars and pot, a hard drinker
Address: Los Angeles
Income: $1 million+ (estimate)

Idi Amin

"You cannot run faster than a bullet."

Idi Amin Dada Oumee

Before he was deposed in 1979 by a force of Ugandan rebels and Tanzanian troops, he was said to have a freezer in his palace stacked with the severed heads of his political enemies, so that when he felt like it he could open the door and lecture them on the folly of their errors. The "Wild Man of Africa" joined the British Army in 1943, at the age of 18. A poorly educated and impoverished member of northern Uganda's Kakwa tribe, he fought with the British in Burma during World War II and in Kenya during the bloody Mau Mau rebellion. Even then, his proclivity for mindless violence was evident; he twice faced charges of murdering prisoners, but in both cases the charges were dropped for lack of evidence. When Uganda became independent in 1962, Lieutenant Amin was one of two black officers in an army still controlled by the British, but he rose to become chief of staff of Uganda's armed forces and in 1971 led a military coup that easily overthrew President Milton Obote. The following year "Big Daddy" Amin expelled 55,000 Indian and Pakistani shopkeepers and businessmen in a fit of racist pique. Worshiping Adolf Hitler (he vowed to build a statue honoring the Führer in Kampala), Amin did his best to follow his idol's example. Between

1971 and 1979, Field-Marshall Idi Amin Dada, self-proclaimed ''President-for-Life,'' slaughtered more than 300,000 of his fellow Ugandans. In some highlights of his grotesque reign, Amin told both Queen Elizabeth of England and President Jimmy Carter to ''pull up their socks,'' threatened to crash the Queen's Silver Jubilee celebration in London, ordered all American citizens living in Uganda not to leave (withdrawing the order after several days), forced British businessmen to carry and parade him on a sedan chair through the streets of Kampala, and threatened to execute any foreigners critical of his regime. His biggest mistake, however, was allowing the hijackers of an Israeli passenger plane to land at Uganda's Entebbe airport, thus instigating the heroic raid on Entebbe by Israeli commandos. At one point married to four wives—one from each of Uganda's major tribes—Amin divorced them all under Moslem law and married new ones. Reports vary, but Big Daddy is known to have fathered at least 16 children. Since Amin's bloody reign ended, his whereabouts—and the whereabouts of several million dollars he always carried with him in suitcases—is not known for certain, though he is believed by some to be in exile in Libya. When yet another government seized power in a bloodless 1985 coup, Amin offered to return. Uganda's new leaders told him not to bother.

Born: 1925 in Koboko, Uganda (in the West Nile District)
Height: 6 ft. 4 in.
Weight: 250 lbs.
Eyes: Brown *Hair:* Black
Education: Through the fourth grade
Religion: Moslem
Marriages: Under Moslem law, he has four wives—at the same time
Children: At least sixteen (officially seven)
Interests: Rugby, swimming, boxing (from 1951 to 1960 he was Uganda's heavyweight boxing champion)
Personal Habits and Traits: Is a heavy drinker, violent, mercurial, gluttonous, carries millions of U.S. dollars with him at all times when traveling
Address: Unknown; possibly Libya
Income: $50 million (estimate of money Amin has stashed away in various banks, including a Swiss bank account)

Cleveland Amory

"I generally hate clubs, but in 1961 I formed my own. It's called the 'Hunt the Hunters Club.' After you've bagged your hunter, drape him over the hood of your car and mount him when you get home."

When he was 10 years old, Cleveland Amory experienced his first encounter with cruelty to animals—his own. "I shot a bird with a BB gun, and my father looked at me with disgust as this little bird flopped around on our porch. He said: 'You shot it, you kill it.' I had to stomp on that bird until it was dead." Interestingly enough, that incident led to his lifelong concern for animal welfare. Amory, the son of a wealthy textile manufacturer, was educated at Milton Academy and Harvard, and forever disdaining Boston's Back Bay society, he wrote a 1947 bestseller, *The Proper Bostonians,* and later *The Last Resorts* and *Who Killed Society.* For 13 years, Amory served as *TV Guide*'s resident critic, a position he resigned in 1976 to produce a syndicated gossip column ("God, I hate that word *gossip*!") and to devote more time to his 100,000-member Fund for Animals. From the Fund's headquarters in New York City, Amory spends half his time crusading against animal abuse. He engineered spectacular rescues of burros from the floor of the Grand Canyon and wild goats from an island off the California coast. His syndicated column, "Animail," appears in hundreds of newspapers across the nation. A self-confessed sports addict, he plays plenty of tennis and devotes hours to chess.

Born: September 2, 1917, in Nahant, Massachusetts
Height: 6 ft. 2 in.
Weight: 190 lbs.
Eyes: Brown *Hair:* Brown
Zodiac: Virgo
Education: Harvard University
Religion: Protestant
Marriages:
To Cora Fields Craddock (1941–1947)
To Martha Hodge (1953–separated)
Children: One stepdaughter, Gaea
Interests: Animals, chess, sports of all kinds (baseball, football, tennis, and golf in particular), world travel
Personal Habits and Traits: Smokes a pipe, does not eat red meat but will eat fish and certain types of poultry, a teetotaler
Addresses: New York City, Beverly Hills Hotel
Income: $50,000+ (minimum estimate of personal income)

Famous Amos

Wally Amos

"You can't make a living selling cookies, *right?"*

Wally Amos had tried his hand at just about everything. He spent four years in the Air Force, attended cooking school, business school, worked as a department store bookkeeper, and wound up at the William Morris Agency handling music acts like African jazz trumpeter Hugh Masakela. But Amos's attempts to set up his own talent agency never got off the ground. To alleviate his depression, Amos followed his late Aunt Della's chocolate chip cookie recipe and began baking batch after batch—as therapy it was a resounding success. "I'd go home feeling depressed and bake a batch," he recalls. "Then I'd just give them away at meetings, or on planes." Soon Amos's cookies became famous. With backing from Marvin Gaye ($10,000) and Helen Reddy and Jeff Wald ($11,000), among others, Amos set up his own Famous Amos Cookie Shop on Sunset Boulevard—and at $3 a pound (now $5 or more, no doubt, by the time you read this entry), he now sells several tons a week! Amos has opened various branches in California, Arizona, New Jersey, and Honolulu (where he settled in 1979), and has expanded his operation to include cookie T-shirts and cookie jewelry. "People are addicted to them," says the former talent agent of his new superstars. "Chocolate chip cookies are a religion."

Born: 1936 in Nutley, New Jersey
Height: 6 ft. 1 in.
Weight: 170 lbs.
Eyes: Brown *Hair:* Black
Religion: Baptist
Marriages: One
Children: Shawn (b. 1967)
Interests: Acting, rock music
Personal Habits and Traits: Does not smoke but is no teetotaler, flamboyant, a social creature, a trifle egotistical
Address: Honolulu
Income: $1.3 million (minimum estimate)

Julie Andrews

Julia Wells

"Sometimes I'm so sweet even I can't stand it!"

Julia Wells joined her family music hall act as a tot, and during World War II played the tousle-haired sidekick to Britain's Shirley Temple, Petula Clark. At age 19, Julia—now billed as Julie Andrews—scored on Broadway in *The Boy Friend,* followed in quick succession by her legendary portrayals of Eliza Doolittle in *My Fair Lady* and Queen Guinevere in *Camelot.* Walt Disney decided that the "innocence-and-light" quality she projected on stage (not to mention her bell-clear singing voice) should be a boon to the screen, and cast her in her first film role, *Mary Poppins,* for which she garnered a Best Actress Oscar in 1964. Andrews's first marriage to British stage and screen designer Tony Walton (*Tom Jones*) grew shakier with each of his wife's films—from *The Americanization of Emily* to *Hawaii* and *The Sound of Music* (the all-time top-grossing film for five years)—and they divorced in 1968. Andrews began dating movie director Blake Edwards (*Days of Wine and Roses, Breakfast at Tiffany's,* the *Pink Panther* series), and when she heard that he had once described her as being "so sweet she probably has violets between her legs," Julie sent him a purple bouquet.

They were married in 1969, and together produced two disastrous efforts—*Darling Lili* and *The Tamarind Seed*—while in 1973 her underrated TV variety series on ABC flopped. Still, Andrews proved a hit in her first Las Vegas nightclub act in 1976, and today there is plenty of time for skiing, yoga, and raising Amy Leigh and Joanna Lynne, the two Vietnamese orphans Julie and Blake have adopted. She took a back seat to bountiful Bo Derek in Edwards's top-grossing *10,* but went full-frontal, baring her breasts on screen for the first time in Edwards's *S.O.B.* Coming full circle, Andrews starred with Walter Matthau in a 1980s remake of the schmaltzy Shirley Temple Great Depression classic *Little Miss Marker,* then played a woman playing a man playing a woman in her husband's *Victor/Victoria.*

Born: October 1, 1935, in Walton-on-Thames, England
Height: 5 ft. 7 in.
Weight: 120 lbs.
Eyes: Blue *Hair:* Light brown
Zodiac: Libra
Education: High school
Religion: Protestant
Marriages:
To Tony Walton (divorced in 1968)
To Blake Edwards (1969–)
Children: Emma (by Walton); Amy Leigh, Joanna Lynn (both adopted with Edwards)
Interests: Yoga, skiing, bicycling, swimming
Personal Habits and Traits: Drinks but no longer smokes, not a partygoer, usually in bed by 11 P.M., exercises
Address: Beverly Hills
Income: $1 million+ (estimate)

Paul Anka

''It's ironic. When I had million-sellers, they didn't want me in clubs. When I was a has-been, they welcomed me with open arms. 'You're Having My Baby' *was kind of my last shot at number one.''*

This survivor of '50s rock 'n' roll became a millionaire at 19, and now stops work every year as soon as he grosses $1 million. ''Sometimes it takes three or four months,'' he allows. ''Other times, five or six.'' Anka actually started songwriting at 15 about his love for an older woman, ''Diana,'' and the single sold more than 8.5 million copies worldwide—second only to Bing Crosby's ''White Christmas.'' Over the next two decades Anka churned out such million-sellers as ''Puppy Love,'' ''You Are My Destiny,'' ''Put Your Head on My Shoulder,'' and ''Lonely Boy.'' Chucking his white bucks, Anka concentrated on writing hits for other performers during the late 1960s and early '70s. Anka wrote the theme for Johnny Carson's *Tonight Show* and gave Tom Jones's career a shot in the arm with ''She's a Lady,'' his raunchy paean to the unliberated woman. ''My Way'' became the theme of his pal Frank Sinatra. But it was not until he recorded ''You're Having My Baby'' in 1974 that Anka himself made a comeback to the number-one position on the charts. Still composing and performing (his ''The Times of Your Life'' jingle for Kodak film was a runaway single in 1977), Anka nevertheless always managed to spend several months a year with his Egyptian-born wife Anne de Zogheb (a former *Vogue* model) and their four daughters at their spectacular Carmel, California, house overlooking the Pacific. There is also the eight-acre spread 20 minutes from the gaudy center of Las Vegas, a New York town house, and a hunting lodge in Idaho. Except for his concern over losing his hair—he usually wears a cap—Anka is unabashedly pleased about his prospects. His next goal: buying his own major-league hockey team.

Born: July 30, 1941, in Ottawa, Ontario
Height: 5 ft. ½ in.
Weight: 118 lbs.
Eyes: Brown *Hair:* Dark brown
Zodiac: Leo
Education: High school
Religion: Syrian Orthodox Church
Marriages: To Anne de Zogheb (1963–)
Children: Alexandra, Amanda, Alicia, Anthea
Interests: Hockey
Personal Habits and Traits: Occasionally smokes cigars, drinks, a homebody
Addresses: Carmel, California; Las Vegas; New York City
Income: $1 million

Ann-Margret

Ann-Margret Olsson

"I'm shy—one of those people who crosses the street to avoid meeting somebody."

No less a legend than Barbara Stanwyck, picking up her Emmy for *The Thorn Birds,* took the occasion to praise the splendid performance of fellow nominee Ann-Margret in the three-hanky tearjerker *Who Will Love My Children?* But before her startling performance as the blowsy sex kitten, Bobbie, in *Carnal Knowledge* (1971), Swedish-born Ann-Margret starred in 23 barely B-grade movies—including several Elvis Presley rockers—and even did a stint as Joe Namath's motorcycle moll. Yet for 17 years, she has graced the top of the show business heap—at $285,000 per week, she remains a top draw in Las Vegas, and her annual TV specials consistently score in the Nielsens. Ann-Margret's father, Gustav Olsson, had already lived in the United States for five years when he sent for his wife and their 6-year-old daughter to join him in 1949. When Gustav became an invalid, the only way for the family to survive was for Mom to work as a receptionist in a funeral parlor, where they were given boarding privileges. For three years her parents slept on a Murphy bed in the dining room while Ann-Margret slept beside a casket in the mourning room. An excellent student, Ann-Margret went to Northwestern, but dropped out after one year. Instead, she chose to play Las Vegas as part of George Burns's act, until landing her first movie role in 1961 as Apple Annie's daughter in Frank Capra's *Pocketful of Miracles.* Then came her Elvis phase, and a downward spiral of bad film roles that continued even after she hooked up with actor Roger Smith (*77 Sunset Strip*), who quit his own acting career to become her full-time manager. On the heels of her relationship with Elvis, Smith and Ann-Margret lived together for four years, and in

1967 decided to marry. Potential tragedy struck in 1972, when Ann-Margret plunged 22 feet from a stage scaffold at the Sahara Hotel in Lake Tahoe. She suffered a brain concussion and fractured several facial bones, her left arm, and her jaw (she still hears an occasional click when she closes her mouth). When she awoke from a coma four days later, doctors refused to let her look in a mirror, but expert plastic surgery restored and even improved upon her high-cheekboned good looks; within two months she made a spectacular comeback in Las Vegas. Just three years later she peaked in her career, earning an Academy Award nomination as Best Actress for her role as Roger Daltrey's mother in the smash rock musical *Tommy*. Now sharing a seven-acre estate in Benedict Canyon (in Beverly Hills) that once belonged to Humphrey Bogart and Lauren Bacall, the Roger Smiths are free from financial worries. Smith, a shrewd investor who has sunk their earnings into everything from gold and cattle to macadamia nuts in Hawaii, estimates their worth at around $10 million. By 1985 the Smiths were still trying to have a baby. Shrugs Ann-Margret, "We must be doing something wrong." Meantime, he contracted myesthenia gravis, a frequently fatal nervous disorder. *Magic,* her 1978 screen effort, again showcased the star's considerable talents as a dramatic actress—though the response to 1980's *Middle Age Crazy* was less positive. It took *Who Will Love My Children?* and TV's *A Streetcar Named Desire* opposite Treat Williams to prove once again that she is a formidable acting talent. Recently she competed with Ellen Burstyn for the affections of Gene Hackman in *Twice in a Lifetime*. Ann-Margret remains insecure enough to continue seeing a woman psychologist.

Born: April 28, 1941, in Valsjobyn, Sweden
Height: 5 ft. 4¾ in.
Weight: 120 lbs.
Eyes: Blue *Hair:* Red blond
Zodiac: Taurus
Education: One year at Northwestern University

Marriages: To Roger Smith (1967–)
Children: None
Interests: Horseback riding, swimming, tennis
Personal Habits and Traits: Teetotaler
Address: Benedict Canyon, California
Income: $1 million+

Alan Arkin

"I've always enjoyed making a general nuisance of myself."

The little man with the eminently forgettable face has accomplished dazzling performances onstage (*Luv, Enter Laughing*) and in films like *The Heart Is a Lonely Hunter, Popi, Wait Until Dark, Catch-22,* and *Little Murders* (which he also directed). But Arkin is probably best remembered for his zany debut in *The Russians Are Coming, The Russians Are Coming*. A New York City native, he went to Franklin High School in Los Angeles and was awarded one of the few drama scholarships ever offered to men by Bennington, the women's college in

Vermont. His marriage to a Bennington girl collapsed after two years, and Arkin headed for Chicago to join Second City, the improvisational comedy group that also numbers Mike Nichols and Elaine May among its alumni; a member of the troupe, Barbara Dana, soon became Arkin's second wife. Although he has never quite made it on television—"If I weren't in movies, I don't know what the hell I'd do"—his son Adam appeared on CBS as a struggling writer cum shoe salesman in his own series, *Busting Loose*, and later in *Tough Cookies*. The elder Arkin scored again on the big screen with Peter Falk in *The In-Laws,* and in 1985 they teamed up again to film a sequel.

Born: March 26, 1934, in New York City
Height: 5 ft. 6 in.
Weight: 150 lbs.
Eyes: Brown *Hair:* Brown
Zodiac: Aries
Education: Bennington College
Religion: Jewish
Marriages: Two. Currently to Barbara Dana
Children: Three sons
Interests: Playing the guitar, directing
Personal Habits and Traits: A nonsmoker, quiet, self-effacing
Address: Los Angeles
Income: $400,000+

Beatrice Arthur

Bernice Frankel

"All this time I've just wanted to be blond, beautiful—and five feet two inches tall."

When Archie Bunker's cousin Maude dropped in for a visit to *All in the Family,* it was clear to millions of TV viewers that Archie had finally met his match. So it wasn't long before Norman Lear took the hint and launched a spinoff series about the infuriating but thoroughly infectious lady liberal from Tuckahoe, New York. *Maude* brought instant stardom for Beatrice Arthur, though her success had been a long time coming. Born Bernice Frankel, she grew up in New York City and Cambridge, Maryland, and studied acting at New York's New School for Social Research, where she met and married director Gene Saks. She first attracted attention as Lucy in a 1954 off-Broadway production of the Kurt Weill–Bertolt Brecht *Threepenny Opera,* followed by the role of a brothel madam opposite Zero Mostel in *Ulysses in Nighttown* (1958), and again as Yenta the Matchmaker with Mostel in *Fiddler on the Roof.* A Tony was bestowed on her for her portrayal of Angela Lansbury's best friend, swizzling stage star Vera Charles, in the musical *Mame,* and while Lansbury was replaced by Lucille Ball in the film version, Arthur easily made the transition to the big screen. After seven seasons to her credit as one of CBS's enduring moneymakers (*Maude* was canceled in 1977), Arthur saw her success as an actress matched by her husband's triumphs as a director. Among Gene Saks's Broadway hits are *Same Time, Next Year* and *I Love My Wife.* At home, things went less swimmingly: by 1979 their marriage

had fallen apart. Arthur returned to the small screen in the fall of 1985 as one of the stars (along with Betty White, Estelle Getty and *Maude* crony Rue McLanahan) of NBC's over-sixties comedy smash *The Golden Girls*.

Born: May 13, 1923, in New York City
Height: 5 ft. 10 in.
Weight: 150 lbs.
Eyes: Brown *Hair:* Gray
Zodiac: Taurus
Education: High school
Religion: Jewish
Marriages: To Gene Saks (1950–1979)
Children: Matthew (b. 1961), Daniel (b. 1964) (both adopted)
Interests: Politics, gardening
Personal Habits and Traits: Moderate drinker, chronic worrier
Address: Los Angeles
Income: $1.2 million+ (estimate)

Arthur Ashe

''It's an abnormal world I live in. I don't belong anywhere. It's like I'm floating down the middle. I'm never quite sure where I am.''

R. Walter Johnson, a Lynchburg, Virginia, physician whose hobby is encouraging black tennis players, could already take credit for having given Althea Gibson her start when he spotted young Arthur Ashe. Ashe, who came out swinging on a segregated court in his hometown of Richmond, Virginia, stole the National Junior Championship at 17, entered UCLA on a tennis scholarship, and became the first black ever to play on the U.S. Davis Cup team. Over the next decade he became known to his competitors as ''The Shadow'' for his unrelenting presence on his side of the net. Ashe triumphed in his second U.S. Open tournament, and was the first black man ever to win the Wimbledon title in 1975. He sank to 25th on the tour two years later, but by the end of 1978 he bounced back to 13th. He also pocketed hefty sums promoting a number of products, from Coca-Cola to Clark Gum and American Safety Razors. Married to photographer Jeanne Moutoussamy since 1977 (they met when she was assigned to photograph him at a benefit dinner), Ashe lives in a fashionable Manhattan co-op and shares all household chores. ''Marriage is very difficult for anyone,'' he says. ''You better pick your partner almost cold-bloodedly.'' In the summer of 1979, at the age of 36, Ashe walked into a New York hospital complaining of severe chest pains. Diagnosis: superconditioned athlete Ashe had suffered a heart attack. He said, however, that he planned to be back on the courts in six weeks. First, Ashe underwent a triple bypass operation. The Davis Cup captain stopped competing in 1980, and underwent a second bypass in 1983. Two years later, he was honored by *Tennis* magazine along with Bjorn Borg, Jimmy Connors, Billie Jean King, and Chris Evert Lloyd as one of the five most influential players of the last 20 years.

Born: July 10, 1943, in Richmond, Virginia
Height: 6 ft. 1 in.
Weight: 155 lbs.
Eyes: Brown *Hair:* Black
Zodiac: Cancer
Education: UCLA, B.A. in business and economics

Marriages: To Jeanne Moutoussamy (1977–)
Children: None
Interests: Race relations (an outspoken opponent of apartheid), music, art
Personal Habits and Traits: Nonsmoker, drinks little, late sleeper, follows a salt-free diet
Address: New York City
Income: $1 million+

Isaac Asimov

"Some critics say I'd write better if I'd write slower. That's like telling a sprinter he'd run better if he ran slower."

"Thinking is the activity I love best," says Isaac Asimov, "and writing to me is simply thinking through my fingers." Consequently, the Russian-born genius with the unmeasurably high IQ sits hammering away at his word processors, writing up to 50 pages a day—science fiction (his most famous sci-fi effort is probably *Fantastic Voyage*), novels, short stories, brilliantly concise scientific nonfiction, and children's books. Asimov has produced a staggering amount of work—more than 300 books in 33 years! Although his lectures (at $2,000 a shot) and his royalties finance a 33rd-floor, eight-room penthouse high above Manhattan, Asimov is no stranger to poverty. His family emigrated to the United States from the Jewish ghetto in Smolensk, Russia, when Isaac was 3, and he grew up in the slums of Brooklyn, where his father owned a candy store. Isaac helped his family endure the Depression by delivering newspapers and working behind the candy counter, and he became addicted to writing early. By the time he graduated from Columbia at 18 he had sold his first story—6,400 words at a penny a word. But it was not until the 1960s that the "Asimovalanche" began to roll. Asimov divorced his first wife, Gertrude, in 1973 and married psychiatrist Janet Jeppson, who wrote a science-fiction tale of her own, *The Second Experiment*. In 1972 Isaac and Janet faced a dual crisis. Both underwent cancer surgery—he for cancer of the thyroid, she for breast cancer. Then, in 1984, he underwent a triple bypass operation. Muses Asimov: "Someday they'll come and find me slumped over that word processor with my nose in the keys."

Born: January 2, 1920, in Petrovichi, U.S.S.R.
Height: 5 ft. 10 in.
Weight: 210 lbs.
Eyes: Blue *Hair:* Gray
Zodiac: Capricorn
Education: Columbia University, a Ph.D. (1948)
Religion: Jewish

Marriages:
To Gertrude Blugerman (1942–1973)
To Janet Jeppson (1973–)
Children: David and Robyn Jean
Interests: Everything under the sun—and beyond
Personal Habits and Traits: Quit smoking, drinks little (but loves wine), needs little sleep, is a workaholic, bluff, affectionate (a toucher)
Address: New York City
Income: $500,000 (minimum estimate)

Ed Asner

"I really wanted to be an adventurer, to lay pipeline in South America or be a cabin boy—but I didn't have the guts."

Television's newsroom toughie Lou Grant and real life's, two-term head of the Screen Actors Guild was born in Kansas City, Missouri, on November 15, 1929, and played as an all-city tackle on his high school football team. He became interested in acting while enrolled in high school radio classes, and at the University of Chicago acted in several classical productions, including *Oedipus Rex* and *Julius Caesar*. Stationed in France during World War II, Asner was drawn back to the sports world, managing an Army basketball team which ranked second best in Europe. Back home in Chicago, he joined the Playwrights Theater Club but departed for Broadway two years later, and eventually played opposite Jack Lemmon in *Face of a Hero* before heading to Hollywood in 1961. A consummate character actor, Asner appeared in dozens of popular TV series *(Medical Center, Name of the Game, Mod Squad, Peter Gunn, Ironside),* but it was not until he began bossing Mary Tyler Moore around (as the feisty news director of a Minneapolis TV station) that Asner became a bona fide star, receiving three Emmys for that role, as well as one for his portrayal of the embittered German immigrant father in the dramatic *Rich Man, Poor Man* series. Other dramatic parts followed, most notably that of captain of a slave ship in *Roots* (for which he received yet another Emmy), but in 1977, Asner returned on a weekly basis, this time as star of his own CBS series entitled—what else?—*Lou Grant*. He copped *three* Emmys for that show, as well. In 1981, he was embroiled in the controversy surrounding his portrayal of a by-the-book police official in *Fort Apache, The Bronx,* and the following year he went head-to-head with conservative Charlton Heston in a struggle for SAG. Asner prevailed. In 1985, Asner's return to the tube in *Off the Rack* was cut short when the show was canceled. Asner and his wife Nancy share a rambling Bel Air house with three children, three dogs, and two cats.

Born: November 15, 1929, in Kansas City, Missouri
Height: 5 ft. 9 in.
Weight: 198 lbs.
Eyes: Blue *Hair:* Scant
Zodiac: Scorpio
Education: University of Chicago
Religion: Jewish
Marriages: Nancy Lou Sykes (1959–)
Children: Twins Matthew and Liza (b. 1963), Kate (b. 1967)
Interests: Sports nut, collects shells, gardens, psychotherapy
Personal Habits and Traits: Overeats, moderate drinker, up at 5:30 A.M. to exercise for 30 minutes and then jog
Address: Bel Air, California
Income: $1.18 million (estimate)

Fred Astaire

Frederick Austerlitz

"When they review my shows, they don't say whether they're good or bad—they just write about how old I am."

"Can't act. Can't sing. Can dance a little." The studio executive's assessment of Fred Astaire's first screen test proved accurate on at least one count—the man could *dance*. Born the son of an Austrian beer salesman, Frederick Austerlitz and his older sister, Adele, were thrust by their stage mother onto the vaudeville stage, and from 1911 until Adele quit the stage to get married in 1932, the brother-and-sister act set box-office records in London and on Broadway. Soft-spoken, self-effacing Fred doubted that he could make it without his high-spirited sister, but in one film after another over the next 40 years, Hollywood's debonaire song-and-dance man elevated the tap dance to an elegant art. Teamed up with the likes of Rita Hayworth, Eleanor Powell, Cyd Charisse, and Barrie Chase, Astaire's most memorable collaboration was with Ginger Rogers. During his heyday in the 1930s and '40s, Astaire tapped and twirled through such classic musicals as *The Gay Divorcee* (1934), *Top Hat* (1935), *Swing Time* (1936), *Carefree* (1938), and *Blue Skies* (1946). He was called out of premature retirement in 1948 to play opposite Judy Garland in *Easter Parade* when his pal Gene Kelly injured an ankle in rehearsal. Crushed by the untimely death of his wife in 1954, he nonetheless managed to stage a comeback in such slick '50s fare as *Daddy Long Legs* (1955), *Funny Face* (1957), and *Silk Stockings* (1957). Meanwhile, the Fred Astaire Dance Studios gave Arthur Murray a run for his money in the dance instruction business. Not merely content to dance his way through a legendary show business career, Astaire gave memorable dramatic performances in such films as *On the Beach* (1959) and *The Towering Inferno,* for which he received an Oscar nomination in 1976. On television, Astaire's specials have racked up a dozen Emmys, while for two seasons he played an elder statesman among cat burglars in *To Catch a Thief.* Still, Astaire's crowning glory may turn out to be his heartrending performance opposite Helen Hayes in 1978's TV drama *A Family Upside Down.* Two years later, he turned the show business world upside down by marrying Robyn Smith, a jockey less than half his age.

Born: May 10, 1899, in Omaha, Nebraska
Height: 5 ft. 10 in.
Weight: 160 lbs.
Eyes: Blue *Hair:* White
Zodiac: Taurus
Education: High school
Religion: Episcopalian

Marriages: To Phyllis Baker (1933–1954) Robyn Smith (1980–)
Children: Fred, Ava, Peter Potter (a stepson)
Interests: Racehorses, farming, ranching
Personal Habits and Traits: Nonsmoker, moderate drinker
Address: Los Angeles
Income: $300,000+ (estimate)

Dan Aykroyd

"I'm not a homo and neither was John, but when I saw him come into a room, I got the jump you get when you see a beautiful girl. Being with him was electric, really electric."

On March 5, 1982, he was writing a line of dialogue intended for the film *Ghostbusters* when he got the news that his Blues Brother, John Belushi, died from a drug overdose. From then on, Belushi's best friend pulled out of the fast lane ("When we were young, to flirt with death was exciting, but, it's not the way to be"), married actress Donna Dixon, and concentrated on making mainstream movie comedies like *Trading Places* with Eddie Murphy and the 1984 megahit (a $200 million-plus gross) *Busters*. Like his pal Belushi, Ottawa-born Aykroyd had a strict Catholic upbringing that included occasional belt whippings. He was once kicked out of high school, then dropped out of Ottawa's Carleton University to work as a train brakeman and surveyor. Aykroyd and a friend opened their own sawdust-on-the-floor joint in Toronto in the early 1970s, and it was there that he met Belushi and Bill Murray. All of which was a walkup to New York and *Saturday Night Live,* where, in the heavily drug-oriented atmosphere described in Bob Woodward's disturbing bestseller *Wired,* Aykroyd somehow managed to create some of the most memorably hilarious characters in TV history: the huckster for "Bass-O-Matic," who takes a dead fish and liquefies it instantly; the host of "Bad Theater," Leonard Plynth Garnell; and Beldar, Connie Conehead's "parental unit"—just to name a few. When Aykroyd and Belushi first appeared on *SNL* as the black-suited, shade-wearing, briefcase-toting Blues Brothers, they caused such a sensation that they cut an album and a single, an updated version of Sam and Dave's '60s classic "Soul Man." Both became hits, as did the duo's 1980 *Blues Brothers* movie, which landed Jake and Elwood on the cover of *People* magazine. However, their other films, *1941* and *Neighbors,* were, as Leonard Plynth Garnell would say, "truly bad." Genuine soulmates off-camera ("There was no dimension of our friendship unexplored except the sexual one," Aykroyd has said), he and Belushi even bought identical cars for one another (Mercedes 280-C coupes) and two homes on Martha's Vineyard. Both had apartments in Manhattan's Greenwich Village, just a few blocks away from the private bar they built for themselves and their friends, The Blues Bar. His *Dr. Detroit* was a disaster, but with the enormous success of *Ghostbusters,* and the passable *Spies Like Us,* Aykroyd established beyond question that as a solo, he's a major box-office draw. Still, he remains as attached as ever to his old pal's memory: Whenever he drives by Belushi's grave, he always honks his horn loud and long.

Born: July 1, 1953, in Ottawa, Ontario
Height: 6 ft. 1 in.
Weight: 200 lbs.
Eyes: Brown *Hair:* Brown
Zodiac: Cancer
Education: College dropout
Religion: Roman Catholic
Marriages: Donna Dixon (1983–)
Children: None

Interests: Screenwriting, the occult, motorcycles, bars (he owns a piece of New York's Hard Rock Cafe)
Personal Habits and Traits: Workaholic, night person, smokes cigars, drinks beer, B&B, was busted in 1983 for marijuana, interested in guns
Addresses: New York City; Martha's Vineyard
Income: $5 million (minimum estimate)

Lauren Bacall

Betty Joan Perske

"I used to tremble from nerves so badly that the only way I could hold my head steady was to lower my chin practically to my chest and look up at Bogie. That was the beginning of The Look. I still get the shakes from time to time."

"You know how to whistle, don't you? You just put your lips together—and blow." With that line delivered to a transfixed Humphrey Bogart (and movie audience) in *To Have and Have Not,* a whiskey-voiced 20-year-old became one of Hollywood's most sultry sex symbols. Born Betty Joan Perske in Greenwich Village, Lauren Bacall (still "Betty" to her friends) tried professional modeling before she made the trek west. Marrying Bogart in 1945, she was sucked into the two-fisted, hard-drinking Hollywood aristocracy of which Bogie was a senior member. Over the years she made several box-office successes, including *The Big Sleep, Key Largo,* and *How to Marry a Millionaire.* Bogart died of cancer in 1957. After a brief, tempestuous affair with Frank Sinatra—"He behaved like a complete shit"—Bacall packed up her two children and returned to New York. There she tackled marriage to Jason Robards, Jr., and a Broadway career of her own. The marriage lasted a stormy eight years, reaching its nadir when Robards came to his 40th birthday party dead drunk and Bacall angrily smashed a bottle of vodka into his birthday cake! But Bacall fared considerably better on the stage. In 1965 she starred as the middle-aged love of a womanizing dentist in the smash comedy *Cactus Flower.* Five years later, the leggy, sloe-eyed beauty made theatrical history high-kicking and belting her way through the meaty role of Margo Channing in *Applause,* copping a Best Actress Tony for the musical remake of *All About Eve.* Although she clearly prefers the theater and life in New York, Bacall still grinds out an occasional film like *Murder on the Orient Express* and *The Shootist,* in which she played the landlady of dying gunfighter John Wayne. Ensconced in a cavernous, art-filled apartment in Manhattan's landmark Dakota, Bacall spent four years writing her memoirs, *Lauren Bacall: By Myself.* Almost as soon as the book became the country's number-one bestseller, she took off for Florida to start filming Robert Altman's *Health.* "I play an 83-year-old virgin. How's that for a challenge?" Bacall then took on the part of a terrorized movie queen in *The Fan,* released not long after yet another Broadway triumph in *Woman of the Year.* None of these projects gave Bacall more exposure than her High Point coffee commercials, for which she reportedly received several hundred thousand dollars each year.

Born: September 16, 1924, in New York City
Height: 5 ft. 9 in.
Weight: 134 lbs.
Eyes: Green *Hair:* Blond
Zodiac: Virgo
Education: High school
Religion: Jewish
Marriages:
To Humphrey Bogart (1945 until his death in 1957)
To Jason Robards (1961–1969)
Children: Steve Bogart (b. 1948), Leslie Bogart (b. 1952), Sam Robards (b. 1961)
Interests: The theater (particularly musical comedy), writing, art, fashion
Personal Habits and Traits: Given to colorful language, is a thorough perfectionist, kicked smoking
Address: New York City
Income: $750,000 (minimum estimate)

Burt Bacharach

"I'm not really worried about being in today and out tomorrow. The groovy thing about pop music is that it's wide open. Anything can happen."

The "Music Man of the 1970s," as *Newsweek* hailed Burt Bacharach in its cover story on the prolific songwriter, was born in Kansas City, Missouri, son of nationally syndicated columnist Bert Bacharach. Touring Army bases as a concert pianist during the Korean war preceded a decade as an accompanist to the likes of Polly Bergen, Imogene Coca, and Vic Damone (who fired him). When Marlene Dietrich decided to make her Broadway debut in a one-woman show in 1968, Bacharach filled in for her ailing conductor and wound up with a full-time job when she took her immensely popular show on the road. By then he had already established a flourishing partnership with lyricist Hal David. From the mid-1960s to the early '70s, the team created many hit songs for Dionne Warwick (including "Walk On By," "Do You Know the Way to San Jose?," "Alfie," "What the World Needs Now," "Message to Michael" and "Trains and Boats and Planes"), for Tom Jones ("What's New Pussycat"), and for many others. The Bacharach and David Broadway musical hit *Promises, Promises* left Bacharach "a sick man" despite its rave reviews and box-office magic, but Hollywood provided another challenge, and in 1970 Bacharach collected two Academy Awards—one for scoring *Butch Cassidy and the Sundance Kid* and the other for the movie's theme song, "Raindrops Keep Fallin' On My Head."

Tanned, lean, and handsome, Bacharach reached a sex symbol status of his own, and after his divorce from singer Paula Stewart married one of TV's leading bombshells, Angie Dickinson. They led a seemingly idyllic life in Bel Air with their daughter, Nikki, until the demands of Angie's hit series *Police Woman* caused the golden couple to split in 1976—and caused Bacharach to drop out of the Martini & Rossi vermouth commercials they had been doing together. Bacharach's new partner—and new wife—Carole Bayer Sager collaborated with him on their Oscar-winning theme for the movie *Arthur* and on the 1986 #1 single "On My Own."

Born: May 12, 1929, in Kansas City, Missouri
Height: 6 ft.
Weight: 160 lbs.
Eyes: Brown *Hair:* Salt and pepper
Zodiac: Taurus
Education: McGill University
Marriages:
To Paula Stewart (divorced after three years)
To Angie Dickinson (divorced in 1977)
To Carole Bayer Sager (1982–)
Children: Nikki (b. 1966)
Interests: Raising racehorses, tennis
Personal Habits and Traits: A nonsmoker, drinks Martini & Rossi, weekend athlete
Addresses: Beverly Hills; Del Mar, California
Income: $1.25 million (minimum estimate)

Joan Baez

''I've always been behind musically, but ahead politically.''

Whether she is depicted as the hypocritical ''Joany Phoney'' of the late Al Capp's *Li'l Abner* cartoons or the folksinging *La Pasionaria,* Joan Baez is undeniably one of the seminal forces in the history of modern American music. The obvious counterpart to Bob Dylan in the early 1960s, California-bred Baez brought her delicate soprano to coffeehouses from San Francisco to Greenwich Village. Linked professionally and romantically with Dylan, she did not make the transition to harder rock as Dylan did in the early 1970s, but instead became increasingly active in the antiwar and civil rights movements. Maintaining her ''Peter, Paul and Mary'' sound, throughout this musically turbulent period, Baez stuck primarily to the campus scene. She married activist David Harris in 1968, then waited for him while he served a three-year prison term for resisting the draft in 1969. No sooner was he released on parole in 1971 than Harris promptly left her, which didn't stop them from posing together for the cover of her album *Carry It On,* in which she is shown welcoming Harris home from jail. Baez finally crossed over from folk to rock in a big way with ''The Night They Drove Old Dixie Down.'' Why this desire to stand up for the underdog? ''My father was Mexican and my mother Irish,'' she explains. ''That meant that the white kids looked down on me because I was part Mexican and the Mexican kids didn't like me because I couldn't speak Spanish. So I started singing and playing—and finally I was accepted.'' Baez found herself in the unaccustomed position of being criticized by activists like Jane Fonda for attacking the inhumane policies of Vietnam's Communist government. ''I'm against all forms of oppression,'' she states, ''no matter whose flag it's under.'' Amazingly, by 1985 Baez was unable to convince a recording company to sign her.

Born: January 9, 1941, in Staten Island, New York
Height: 5 ft. 5 in.
Weight: 120 lbs.
Eyes: Brown *Hair:* Brown
Zodiac: Capricorn
Education: High school
Religion: Roman Catholic
Marriages: To David Harris (1968–1973)
Children: One son
Interests: The peace movement, cats
Personal Habits and Traits: Early riser, vegetarian
Address: San Francisco
Income: $200,000+

Lucille Ball

''Divorce is defeat.''

The greatest comedienne in the history of television and one of its few performers to attain the status of a one-name legend, Lucy was born in Jamestown, New York, to a working-class family, and quickly learned that she had the gift of making people laugh. She flunked out of John Murray Anderson's dramatic school, but managed to land several small parts in films because of her striking, redheaded good looks. Dubbed ''Technicolor Tessie'' because of her hair, she eventually appeared in more than 50 films—most often playing a tough-talking career girl. But although a full-fledged movie star, Ball discovered her real niche when she and her conga-playing husband, Desi Arnaz, exploded on television in a comedy show called *I Love Lucy* in 1951—needless to say, a watershed series in the history of TV comedy. When she timed the TV birth of little Ricky Ricardo to coincide with the birth of her son, Desi, Jr., in 1954, the event proved national news; so, too, did her divorce from Arnaz in 1960, which put a temporary moratorium on *Lucy*. She starred on Broadway in the musical *Wildcat,* then returned to TV in 1962 with *The Lucille Ball Show* (later renamed *Here's Lucy*) and was back on top in the ratings—where she remained with the help of sidekick Vivian Vance until she decided to fold the show in 1974. Far from giving up on Hollywood, Ball also made a number of movie comedies during this period: *Critic's Choice* with Bob Hope, *Yours, Mine and Ours* with Henry Fonda, and the 1974 musical *Mame*. As shrewd a businesswoman as comedienne, Lucy bought out Desi's share in their joint production company, Desilu, for $3 million. The bubble-brained redhead pulled Desilu out of the red in just three years and, for a cool $17 million, allowed the Gulf & Western conglomerate to acquire her baby in 1967. Ball shares an unpretentious Beverly Hills house with her second husband (producer Gary Morton), and keeps a keen parental eye on the show business careers of daughter Lucie Arnaz and son Desi, Jr. After a three-decade association with CBS, Lucy signed a multimillion-dollar contract with NBC, and in 1980 starred in her first comedy special for her new network. Four years later, she took an apartment in Manhattan to be closer to Lucie's kids, and wound up playing a New York bag lady in a brilliant made-for-TV movie, *Stone Pillow*. Lucy surprised even her closest friends by signing a contract with ABC to star in a new weekly comedy series planned for a fall 1986 debut.

Born: August 6, 1911, in Jamestown, New York
Height: 5 ft. 8½ in.
Weight: 120 lbs.
Eyes: Blue *Hair:* Red
Zodiac: Leo
Education: High school dropout
Religion: Protestant
Marriages:
To Desi Arnaz (1940–1960)
To Gary Morton (1961–)
Children: Lucie (b. 1951), Desi, Jr. (b. 1954)
Interests: Producing, charities, backgammon
Personal Habits and Traits: Eats a large breakfast (her main meal of the day), has quit smoking but observes the cocktail hour, is articulate but feisty
Addresses: New York City; Beverly Hills; Palm Springs
Income: $17 million (estimate of net worth)

Anne Bancroft

Annemarie Italiano

"The best thing is that I've finally gotten used to other people's inability to be me."

Darkly beautiful Annemarie Italiano was a Bronx-born ingenue when Hollywood nabbed her and ran her through the B-picture wringer. Discouraged, she headed back home to New York in 1955, attended Herbert Berghof's acting school, and finally, after three years, made her debut on Broadway opposite Henry Fonda in *Two for the Seesaw*. From then on it was relatively smooth sailing. In 1961 she claimed her Best Actress Oscar for her performance as teacher Annie Sullivan in *The Miracle Worker* (Patty Duke also won an Academy Award for her portrayal of Helen Keller in the film version), and in 1967 received another nomination for her role as Mrs. Robinson in *The Graduate*. Bancroft has kept expanding her range as an actress with Emmy-winning television specials; TV epics like *Young Winston* (1972), in which she played Churchill's mum, Jenny Jerome; and film comedies like *The Prisoner of Second Avenue* with Jack Lemmon. Since 1964 Bancroft has been half of one of show business's most unlikely duos as the wife of zany filmmaker Mel Brooks. Usually refusing to discuss one another—"It's really nobody's business but ours"—Bancroft and Brooks also refrain from

working together, though in the case of Brooks's *Silent Movie* she broke their rule with a singular cameo appearance. Bancroft's real strength, of course, remains serious dramatic roles on the big screen—which she proved once again by earning another Academy Award nomination for her portrayal of an over-the-hill ballerina in *The Turning Point*. Her first attempt at directing, *Fatso,* flubbed at the box office. She was chosen to play the part of a sadistic Joan Crawford in the movie version of Christina Crawford's controversial number-one bestseller, *Mommie Dearest,* but was replaced by Faye Dunaway. Bancroft and Brooks decided to give working together one more chance; in 1983, they played Poland's greatest acting team in a critically acclaimed remake of the Jack Benny classic *To Be or Not To Be*. Sharing top billing with Jane Fonda, Bancroft got into the habit of playing a conspiratorial mother superior in the 1985 film version of the Broadway hit *Agnes of God*. The part brought her yet another Oscar nomination (she lost out to Geraldine Page).

Born: September 17, 1931, in the Bronx, New York City
Height: 5 ft. 8 in.
Weight: 115 lbs.
Eyes: Brown *Hair:* Dark brown
Zodiac: Virgo
Education: High school
Religion: Roman Catholic

Marriages:
To Martin May (1954–1958)
To Mel Brooks (1964–)
Children: Two
Interests: Politics, Israel, ballet
Personal Habits and Traits: Smokes and drinks, an exercise nut
Addresses: Los Angeles; New York City
Income: $370,000 (minimum estimate)

Brigitte Bardot

"I wish I had invented sex. Sex is No. 1."

Though now in her 50s, the daughter of a wealthy Versailles industrialist still remains France's reigning sex kitten. She broke into films when at 15 she obtained her parents' permission to appear in a rather racy layout for the magazine *Elle.* Aspiring impresario Roger Vadim seized upon Bardot, and he set about making his new discovery "the unattainable dream of every married man"; part of his risqué campaign involved marrying her and then holding her press conferences while they lay together in bed. While BB took France by storm in the movie *And God Created Woman,* her marriage foundered and collapsed. It happened twice more to Bardot, who had a son during her marriage to Jacques Charrier, and was also briefly married to playboy jetsetter Gunther Sachs, 10 years her junior. Her marital ups and downs notwithstanding, Bardot has never faltered as a worldwide sex symbol. She is not entirely one-dimensional, though; in the mid-1970s she launched a drive to save baby seals from being slaughtered in northern Canada, and in 1976 started her own medium-priced line of ready-to-wear dresses. While her friends celebrated her 49th birthday at her beachfront hideaway at St. Tropez, Bardot took a handful of tranquilizers, washed them down with red wine, and had to be pulled from the surf.

Born: September 28, 1934, in Paris, France
Height: 5 ft. 4 in.
Weight: 118 lbs.
Eyes: Hazel *Hair:* Blond
Zodiac: Libra
Education: Dropped out of school at 15
Religion: Roman Catholic
Marriages:
To Roger Vadim (divorced)
To Jacques Charrier (divorced)
To Gunther Sachs (divorced)

Children: Nicholas Jacques (by Charrier)
Interests: Saving baby seals, the environment, travel, swimming, ballet, rock music, fashion
Personal Habits and Traits: Smokes, drinks, loves to cook, likes cards, is a bit nearsighted
Addresses: Paris; St. Tropez
Income: $100,000 (estimate), from investments

Rona Barrett

"I'm really a pussycat—with an iron tail."

Rona Burnstein

Ryan O'Neal once mailed her a live tarantula, and Frank Sinatra lambastes her regularly in his nightclub act, but that is the price for being television's answer to Hedda Hopper and Louella Parsons. She grew up in Queens, New York, as Rona Burnstein, a self-described "crippled, plain, fat kid" whose father worked as a local grocer. She overcame her childhood case of muscular dystrophy, and as a teenager changed her name to Rona Barrett when she set up fan clubs for the likes of Eddie Fisher and Steve Lawrence. After three years studying premed at NYU, Barrett abandoned the idea of becoming a doctor to spend all her time penning gossip columns for movie magazines. But after moving to California in 1958 to write for *Photoplay,* Barrett underwent a metamorphosis. She had her nose fixed, dieted off 30 pounds, and studied elocution to try to erase her Queens accent. Rona's TV break came in 1967 when ABC picked up her *Dateline: Hollywood,* and the following year Metromedia signed her to a five-year contract. By 1975 she was spewing gossip twice daily on ABC's hit *Good Morning America* show. Five years later, she defected to NBC's *Tomorrow Show*—a stint that lasted a single season. After several years of virtual invisibility, Barrett signed on with *Entertainment Tonight*. Working out of the pool house at her Beverly Hills villa—Kirk Douglas is her next-door neighbor—Barrett rises and spends each morning on the phone sleuthing for gossip. Barrett declines to name the two big Hollywood figures—one a "top male sex symbol" and the other a former LBJ aide—with whom she had long-running affairs. In 1973 she married independent film and record producer William A. Trowbridge, who oversaw her network TV specials and served as vice president of Miss Rona Enterprises—the miniconglomerate of which she is president. Unquestionably once one of the most despised women in Hollywood, Miss Rona doesn't seem to mind that she has earned the monicker "Rona Rat." Says America's number-one supersnoop: "I'm not friends with the stars, because if I was, I couldn't tell the truth about them."

Born: 1934 in New York City
Height: 5 ft. 1 in.
Weight: 96 lbs.
Eyes: Brown *Hair:* Blond
Education: New York University
Religion: Jewish
Marriages: To William A. Trowbridge (1973–)

Children: None
Interests: Medicine
Personal Habits and Traits: Nonsmoker, moderate drinker, a workaholic, hard driving
Address: Beverly Hills
Income: $600,000+ (estimate)

Mikhail Baryshnikov

"I'm not the first straight dancer or the last. Anyway, it has nothing to do with art."

Born the son of a dressmaker and an engineer in Riga, Latvia, the world's highest-paid and indisputably greatest living classical dancer was already 15 when he first witnessed rehearsals at Leningrad's famed Kirov School. On the formidable strength of his leg muscles he was accepted, and three years later accomplished the impressive leap to featured soloist with the Kirov company. A star by Russian standards—Baryshnikov enjoyed a large following, a country dacha, and the limited perks of Soviet celebrity—he nonetheless felt constrained by the classical repertoire. While touring Canada in 1974, he disappeared and within a few weeks defected to the United States, where he was able to work with choreographers Eliot Feld, Alvin Ailey, and Twyla Tharp. He has even managed to garner an Oscar nomination as Best Supporting Actor for his role as a womanizing ballet star in *The Turning Point*. Following in fellow defector Rudolf Nureyev's steps as a pop idol (Baryshnikov's own idol is Fred Astaire), Misha has cut a wide romantic swath through the West, linked at various times with most leading ballerinas (including his *Turning Point* costar, Leslie Browne), the less classical Liza Minnelli, and actresses Candy (*American Graffiti*) Clark and Jessica Lange, who gave birth to his child in the spring of 1981. But dancing remains his consuming passion. Shortly after making his debut as both director and star of *Don Quixote,* Baryshnikov made another dramatic leap from the American Ballet Theatre to George Balanchine's daring New York City Ballet. "You ask me why?" he said, after making the switch. "We're talking about Mr. B. and Jerome Robbins. It's the dream of every dancer to be around these people." Later he went back to ABT—this time as director. By that time, Lange paired off with actor-playwright Sam (*The Right Stuff, Country*) Shepard, and Misha went back to playing the field and making films like 1985's smash *White Nights*.

Born: January 27, 1948, in Riga, Latvia
Height: 5 ft. 7 in.
Weight: 147 lbs.
Eyes: Blue *Hair:* Sandy
Zodiac: Aquarius
Education: The Kirov School in Leningrad
Religion: None
Marriages: None
Children: Alexandra (b. 1981)
Interests: Szechuan food, Mozart, Broadway musicals, disco dancing
Personal Habits and Traits: Smokes cigarettes and cigars, serious drinker
Address: Park Avenue, Manhattan
Income: $500,000

Alan Bates

On his nude performance in *Women in Love (1970): "It was the first time you got to see the* actual *star's* actual *organs. Big deal!"*

The sexy painter who woos divorcée Jill Clayburgh in the 1978 hit *An Unmarried Woman* had female fans panting. Bates, the oldest of three brothers born and raised in Derbyshire, England, studied at London's Royal Academy of Dramatic Art on a scholarship, then served in the Royal Air Force before landing his first substantial role in 1956 in the English Stage Company's production of John Osborne's *Look Back in Anger*. Bates transported his sensitive acting qualities across the Atlantic in 1961, re-creating his role in Harold Pinter's *The Caretaker* for Broadway audiences. Beginning with his 1967 film performance as the *King of Hearts,* Bates became a sex symbol, and three years later caused a sensation by wrestling in the nude with Oliver Reed in Ken Russell's rendering of D. H. Lawrence's *Women in Love*. At about the same time that he brought the smash comedy *Butley* to the London stage, Bates scored a success as Julie Christie's plebeian lover in *The Go-Between,* and again as the father of a severely retarded child in *Joe Egg* (1972). He tackled a far less appealing character as Bette Midler's hard-driving manager in *The Rose*. But it was as Clayburgh's faith-restoring boyfriend in Paul Mazursky's *An Unmarried Woman* that Bates established himself decisively as an English counterpart to Warren Beatty for millions of American women.

Born: February 17, 1934, in Allestree, Derbyshire, England
Height: 5 ft. 10 in.
Weight: 178 lbs.
Eyes: Brown *Hair:* Dark brown
Zodiac: Pisces
Education: Royal Academy of Dramatic Art
Religion: Anglican
Marriages: To Valerie Ward (1970–)
Children: Twin sons
Interests: Art
Personal Habits and Traits: Smokes cigarettes, moderate drinker
Address: London
Income: $400,000 (estimate)

The Beach Boys

The eternal surfer group that inspired America to "hang 10" during pop music's California craze of the 1960s, and created a sensation in the 1980s when it was temporarily banned from playing at a Fourth of July concert in Washington, originally included Brian, Carl, and their late brother Dennis Wilson, cousin Mike Love, and high school buddy Al Jardine.

Fresh out of L.A.'s Hawthorne High School, big brother Brian Wilson masterminded the blend of traditional choral harmonies with a Presley rock beat to create the Beach Boys' first hit, ''Surfin' Safari,'' then repeated the formula with ''Surf City,'' ''Surfer Girl,'' ''Help Me, Rhonda,'' ''Fun, Fun, Fun,'' ''In My Room,'' ''California Girls,'' and their anthem ''Good Vibrations.'' But the rigors of the road, too many drugs, and creeping deafness in his right ear plunged the group's mercurial leader into an anxiety-ridden abyss. Wilson spent three and a half years in bed, venturing out only to play the grand piano he had set up in an enormous sandbox right in the middle of his dining room; Brian needed to wiggle his toes in the sand for inspiration while he sat composing at the keyboard. He also set up a tent in the den of his Bel Air estate for business meetings. Gradually, 6-foot 3-inch Wilson managed to pare down from 240 to 210 pounds through daily gym workouts, and calmed down considerably through transcendental meditation. In 1976, Wilson led a triumphant Beach Boys comeback with the album *15 Big Ones,* an SRO national tour, an NBC special honoring the Beach Boys, and a tribute from CBS's Rock Music Awards. Nominated for the Rock Hall of Fame were Elvis Presley, Bob Dylan, John Lennon, the Beatles (they won), and Brian Wilson—without the rest of the Beach Boys. Why not? Brian's compositions account for 94 percent of the group's 85 million records sold!

The only Beach Boy who ever really surfed was also the wildest and handsomest of the bunch. (At one point about a year before the Tate-La Bianca murders, Dennis Wilson put up the Manson Family at his L.A. apartment.) He went through two marriages before settling on third wife Karen Lamm, an actress who had studied with Lee Strasberg in New York. In 1977, drummer Dennis also became the first Beach Boy to turn out a solo album. Along with youngest brother Carl, Dennis managed Brother Studio, the Beach Boys' recording center in Santa Monica. In 1983, after an afternoon of heavy boozing, Dennis fell off his boat and drowned. He was 38.

The youngest Beach Boy, Carl Wilson, was only 14 when Brian launched the Beach Boys' musical wave. During the Vietnam war, he was arrested for draft evasion, although he managed to establish his conscientious objector status after a prolonged and expensive court battle. When Brian cracked up, it was Carl who fathered the group. Along with his wife, Annie, and their two sons, Jonah and Justyn, Carl lives in trendy Coldwater Canyon, renting the lavish digs of late real estate tycoon Del Webb at Trancas Beach during those California summers.

A cross between Mick Jagger and Dr. Hook, cousin Mike Love invented the puerile lyrics for ''Fun, Fun, Fun,'' but in the 1970s evolved into a vegetarian and TM freak—like the Beatles, he embarked on a pilgrimage to India to meditate with the Maharishi Mahesh Yogi. Married three times and the father of five children, Love and his lady, Sue Oliver, divide their year among homes in Santa Barbara, Lake Tahoe (the Nevada side), and Hawaii. Love has also managed to record on his own without leaving the Beach Boys.

The only nonrelative, Al Jardine, is an old buddy of Brian's—despite the fact that he broke his leg while trying to catch one of Brian's badly thrown passes during a high school football game. Singing the falsetto notes on many of the Beach Boys' records, he probably has the best voice of the group, but his main interests now are California politics and ecology. Jardine, who shares a Big Sur ranch with his wife, Lynda, and their two sons, split from the Beach Boys in 1962 to become a dentist, but came home within six months.

Group Income: $2 million+

Brian Wilson

Born: June 20, 1942, in Hawthorne, California
Zodiac: Gemini
Marriages: To Marilyn (1958–)
Children: Carnie (b. 1968), Wendy (b. 1970)
Address: Bel Air, California

Carl Wilson

Born: December 21, 1946, in Hawthorne, California
Zodiac: On the cusp of Sagittarius and Capricorn
Marriages: Currently to Annie Wilson
Children: Jonah (b. 1971), Justyn (b. 1974)
Address: Coldwater Canyon, California

Dennis Wilson

Born: December 4, 1944, in Hawthorne, California—died 1983
Zodiac: Sagittarius
Marriages: Three, the last to Karen Lamm
Children: None

Mike Love

Born: March 15, 1941, in Los Angeles, California
Zodiac: Pisces
Marriages: Four, currently to Catherine Linda Martinez (1981–)
Children: Five
Addresses: Santa Barbara; Lake Tahoe; Hawaii

Al Jardine

Born: September 3, 1942, in Lima, Ohio
Zodiac: Virgo
Marriages: Currently to Lynda Jardine
Children: Two
Address: Big Sur, California

Warren Beatty

Warren Beaty

"First they say women like me too much, then they say women don't like me at all; then they say that women like me too much again. Somewhere along the way they say that I secretly like men—but then that men don't like me! I'm old, I'm young, I'm intelligent, I'm stupid. My tide goes in and out."

"No actor of his generation, not Redford or Nicholson, has been a star half as long as Beatty has. Few in the film industry make as much money. No one can do so many of the jobs required to create a successful film as he. In the most visible function, acting, Beatty, unlike Travolta or De Niro, began at the top. He has been a sensation ever since he first appeared on the screen in *Splendor in the Grass,* seventeen years ago." Thus *Time* magazine launched its July 3, 1978, cover story on Warren Beatty and the incredible success of his romantic comedy *Heaven Can Wait.* Based on 1941's *Here Comes Mr. Jordan,* the PG-rated family film proved a marked departure from the lurid fare that had catapulted Beatty into a millionaire superstar. The son of a high school principal, Warren Beaty (he added another "t" when he invaded Hollywood) grew up in Alexandria, Virginia, with his sister, Shirley, who was three years older and destined to become a star in her own right after changing *her* last name from Beaty to MacLaine. In high school Beatty, quite a gifted student, turned his 6-foot 2-inch, 182-pound prowess to sports, sacrificing his grades to lead as captain of the football team and class president. One year at Northwestern proved enough for the ambitious Beatty, and he headed for New York to act. At 23, after a brief contract under MGM and a small part in a Broadway flop, Beatty was spotted by director Elia Kazan and signed on the spot for *Splendor in the Grass.* Notorious for his womanizing even before his first film's release—he carried on simultaneous affairs with Joan Collins, Natalie Wood, and Leslie Caron during the shooting—Beatty went on to some rather disappointing movies (*The Roman Spring of Mrs. Stone, All Fall Down, Lilith*) and more famous ladies: Julie Christie, Michelle Phillips, Carly Simon, Joni Mitchell, Diane Keaton, and others. *Bonnie and Clyde* (1968), an instant classic which he both produced and starred in, established Beatty as a major talent. With the exception of Robert Altman's *McCabe and Mrs. Miller* opposite Christie, Beatty later rejected juicy roles in such offerings as *The Godfather* and *The Sting* in order to have time to fund-raise for liberal Presidential aspirant George McGovern. But he rebounded as producer and star of 1976's box-office bonanza *Shampoo,* the story of a virile Beverly Hills hairdresser. His base since 1966 has been a suite at the Beverly Wilshire Hotel called El Escondido ("The Hideaway"), crammed with old newspapers, scripts, and magazines, not to mention half-eaten room service meals. After *Heaven Can Wait* Beatty went ahead with his long-standing plans to film a biography of author John (*Ten Days That Shook the World*) Reed. *Reds* won him his first Academy Award, as Best Director. He cracked wise with Dustin Hoffman in Elaine May's manic *Ishtar,* but Beatty's favorite on-again, off-again project is a screen bio of Dick Tracy, in which he will play the title role.

Born: March 30, 1937, in Arlington, Virginia
Height: 6 ft. 2 in.
Weight: 180 lbs.
Eyes: Brown *Hair:* Brown
Zodiac: Aries
Education: One year at Northwestern University
Religion: Protestant
Marriages: None
Children: None
Interests: Politics, reading, travel, women
Personal Habits and Traits: Does not smoke, seldom drinks, compulsive workaholic and perfectionist, loves to talk on telephone, a hypochondriac and health food nut, is always late, wears a Timex
Address: Beverly Hills
Income: $4 million +

The Bee Gees

Barry, Maurice, and Robin Gibb

Barry Gibb: *"All the crap is gone away now. We can tolerate and cope with fame without the tantrums and outbursts. There are no more glory trips."*

At one point in 1978, the Bee Gees tied the Beatles' previous record for having five singles in the same Top 10 (and at the same time boasting one of the largest-selling albums in history)—all from their celebrated soundtrack for the disco movie *Saturday Night Fever.* The Brothers Gibb—Barry and fraternal twins Robin and Maurice—had already been famous rock stars for a decade when they

accomplished the feat! Born in Manchester, England, to a bandleader and a nightclub singer, they started singing in 1955 by accident; calling themselves The Rattlesnakes, they were lip-synching a Tommy Steele tune before a live audience when the record broke, forcing them to ad-lib with their own unique, falsettolike harmony. After the family moved to Australia, they landed a record contract, but the group, by then the "B.G.s," promptly produced 14 flops. So back to England they trekked in 1967, and after knocking around several British record companies, finally persuaded an enterprising promoter named Robert Stigwood to sign them to a five-year contract. Nine major hits resulted (including "To Love Somebody" and "Words"), and soon the brothers were rolling in millions—as well as drinking too much liquor and spending too much money. At one point Maurice owned five Rolls-Royces and six Aston Martins—one of which he could be counted on to crack up and replace every week. The Bee Gees dissolved in 1969, largely due to Maurice's excessive drinking, but reunited 15 months later, and after scoring with "Lonely Days" and "How Can You Mend a Broken Heart?," both of which hit gold, the trio moved to Miami. There they wrote four hits ("Jive Talkin'," "Nights on Broadway," "You Should Be Dancing," "Love So Right") that drove their album *Here at Last—the Bee Gees Live* to sales of over 1.5 million copies. When Stigwood asked them to write and record the score for his new film, they produced the *Saturday Night Fever* album for him in just two weeks and wound up selling 27 million LPs. A year later the Bee Gees made their debut in front of his cameras, crooning 32 Beatles hits along with Peter Frampton in the unfortunately disastrous *Sgt. Pepper's Lonely Hearts Club Band.* Still flourishing in the Florida sunshine, Barry and Maurice enjoy a lavish life-style replete with sprawling oceanfront estates, speedboats, and Olympic-sized pools. But Robin is still willing to fork over 83 percent of his income in taxes for the privilege of residing in England. Whether the Bee Gees will endure through the 1980s is dubious, though Robin would like to act and Barry is producing records by fourth brother Andy, a major star in his own right. (See page 183.) At the end of a stupendously successful tour in the summer of '79, the brothers hinted strongly they might retire as performers. Explained Robin: "We want to go out on top." They did not retire, however, and in 1980 sued Stigwood for a spectacular $100 million, charging fraud and conflict of interest. They lost the battle with Stigwood and began pursuing separate interests. The most successful Gibb: Barry, who numbers among his "solo" hits two duets with Barbra Streisand, "Guilty" and "What Kind of Fool?"

Group Income: $2 million (down from $5 million in 1980)

Barry (Douglas) Gibb

Born: September 1, 1947, on the Isle of Man, England
Zodiac: Virgo
Marriages: To Lynda
Children: Stevie (b. 1974), Ashley (b. 1977)
Address: Miami

Maurice Gibb

Born: December 22, 1949, in Manchester, England
Zodiac: Capricorn
Marriages:
To Lulu (divorced)
To Yvonne (current)
Children: Adam (b. 1972)
Address: Miami

Robin Gibb

Born: December 22, 1949, in Manchester, England
Zodiac: Capricorn
Marriages: To Molly (divorced)
Children: Spencer (b. 1972), Melissa (b. 1974)
Address: Surrey, England

Saul Bellow

"The two real *problems in life are boredom and death."*

He is Augie March; he is Mr. Sammler, the aging immigrant of *Mr. Sammler's Planet;* he is Herzog the intellectual; he is Charles Coltrine, the famous man of letters who battles with Von Humboldt Fleisher in *Humboldt's Gift.* He is the protagonist of 1982's *The Dean's December.* Above all, he is perhaps the foremost American novelist of the second half of the 20th century, three-time winner of the National Book Award and recipient of the Nobel Prize for Literature. Bellow, born in Quebec to Russian immigrant parents, spoke Yiddish and then French before learning English. When he was nine, the family packed up and moved to Chicago, where his father became a bootlegger. At 20, while studying anthropology and sociology at Northwestern University, Bellow contracted tuberculosis, an experience that left him brooding about his own mortality. After years as an expatriate in Paris, the great writer is again ensconced at the University of Chicago, where he manages to teach as well as write. Beginning every morning at 6 A.M., he downs two cups of coffee, and using notes he made the night before, dictates about 20 pages a day to his typist—all to the music of Beethoven and Mozart. Paddleball, push-ups, a dietetic lunch, and a glass of gin (neat) occupy every afternoon, followed by teaching classes in Proust, Defoe, and Melville at the university. Married four times, Bellow now lives with current wife Alexandra Ionescu Tulcea, a Romanian-born theoretical mathematician. "Our society," he says, "like decadent Rome, has turned into an amusement society, with writers chief among the court jesters—not so much above the clatter as part of it." Bellow's fans found much to laugh about with the 1984 publication of *Him with His Foot in His Mouth and Other Stories*.

Born: July 10, 1915, in Lachine, Quebec
Height: 5 ft. 8 in.
Weight: 160 lbs.
Eyes: Brown *Hair:* White
Zodiac: Cancer
Education: Northwestern University, B.A. in anthropology and sociology
Religion: Jewish
Marriages: Four. Currently to Alexandra Ionescu Tulcea (1974–)
Children: Gregory (b. 1944), Adam (b. 1957), Daniel (b. 1964)
Interests: Paddleball, anthropology
Personal Habits and Traits: Early riser, moderate drinker, exercises regularly
Address: Chicago
Income: $300,000

Tony Bennett

Antonio Dominick Benedetto

"There is always a lot of pressure to change your style. But I chose to stick with what I did—and I think I made the right choice."

The "Singer's Singer" was christened Antonio Dominick Benedetto, the son of a New York tailor. During World War II he changed his name to Bennett at the suggestion of Bob Hope (who had discovered him singing in Greenwich Village under the name Joe Bari). Hope launched him on a singing career that has spanned three decades and has included two wives, three children, a nose job, and a couple of disastrous films—most notably *The Oscar*. As a recording artist and nightclub crooner Bennett has remained a consummate stylist and balladeer. From his "Boulevard of Broken Dreams" and "Rags to Riches," which made him the crew-cut idol of bobby-soxers in the 1950s, to the more musically sophisticated "I Left My Heart in San Francisco," "I Want to Be Around (to Pick Up the Pieces)," and the Beatles' "Something," Bennett has polished and refined what is indisputably a unique vocal talent. Gradually losing his battle against a receding hairline and an expanding waistline, Bennett has never ceased to draw a devoted audience. In 1971, he divorced Patricia Beech after 19 years of marriage, and married Sandra Grant—already the mother of his youngest child—shortly afterward. They split in 1980. Now devoting most of his time to nightclub dates and annual television specials (including one with Lena Horne, who periodically costars with him on the nightclub circuit), Bennett maintains an estate in Los Angeles and an apartment in Manhattan.

Born: August 3, 1926, in New York City
Height: 5 ft. 10 in.
Weight: 190 lbs.
Eyes: Blue *Hair:* Black
Zodiac: Leo
Education: High school

Religion: Roman Catholic
Marriages:
To Patricia Beech (1952–1971)
To Sandra Grant (1971–1980)
Children: Two sons, a daughter
Interests: Painting
Personal Habits and Traits: Nonsmoker, moderate drinker, soft-spoken, shy, tendency to overeat
Addresses: New York City; Los Angeles
Income: $500,000+

George Benson

''Success was a long time coming for me—and now that it's here it's that much sweeter. The wait was worth it.''

After a decade of paying dues, George Benson exploded on the pop music scene in 1976 with *Breezin'*, the first pure jazz album to go platinum, and the number-one hit single ''Masquerade'' (written by one of Benson's mentors, Leon Russell). Pittsburgh-born, Benson was a mere 7 when he began singing and dancing at ''bottle clubs,'' and by his teens could imitate jazz artist Hank Garland on the guitar his stepfather made for him. Not until 1965 was Benson ''discovered'' by legendary Columbia producer John Hammond, but he toiled in the backwaters of jazz until the unparalleled success of *Breezin'* earned him a Best New Vocalist Grammy and ''Masquerade'' was named Best Song of the Year. With a style that blends the understated grace of Wes Montgomery with the drive and soul of Stevie Wonder, Benson specializes in silky ballads, strum-humming, and scat. Now married to second wife Johnnie, whom he met at a Pittsburgh dance, Benson lives in a sprawling $500,000 estate in Englewood Cliffs, New Jersey, owns two Mercedes, a Peugeot, and two motorcycles. He prefers to work only on weekends and spends the rest of his time with his sons, Robert and Marcus. Still, there was time for a one-man show on Broadway that coincided with his 1978 smash hit called—what else?—"On Broadway,'' followed by his number-one hit ''Give Me the Night'' and ''Turn Your Love Around.''

Born: March 2, 1943, in Pittsburgh, Pennsylvania
Height: 5 ft. 9½ in.
Weight: 160 lbs.
Eyes: Brown *Hair:* Black
Zodiac: Pisces
Education: High school
Religion: Jehovah's Witness
Marriages: Two. Currently to Johnnie Benson
Children: Robert (b. 1969), Marcus (b. 1971)
Interests: The guitar, scat-singing, jazz, motorcycles, and sports cars
Personal Habits and Traits: A close-to-home family man, avoids partying, neither smokes nor drinks, is affable and low-key in both his business and professional dealings, sleeps in pajamas
Address: Englewood Cliffs, New Jersey
Income: $650,000 (estimate)

Robby Benson

Robert Segal

"I was into show business straight from the womb."

"Cute as Bambi and twice as smarmy" is the way one critic described him, but Robby Benson nonetheless managed to parlay doe-eyed good looks and a likable screen persona into stardom with films like *Ode to Billie Joe, One on One* (which he scripted with his father), *Walk Proud,* and *Die Laughing*. Dallas-born Benson took his mother's maiden name rather than his dad's, Jerry Segal, in order to avoid anti-Semitism when he auditioned for commercials. He did his first television ad at age 3, toured Japan in *Oliver* at age 8, and made his first movie, *Jory,* six years later. Benson first gained wide recognition as the misfit kid who falls in love with Glynnis O'Connor in the flick *Jeremy*. O'Connor also turned out to be the object of the 17-year-old actor's offscreen affection during the filming of *Ode to Billie Joe,* in which they costarred. Benson's first real challenge came with the title role in the TV adaptation of Thomas Thompson's *Richie,* a story about a middle-class boy whose drug addiction leads to a tragic death at the hands of his own father. More conventional, nice-kid-against-the-odds parts followed, as well as smallish roles in *Lucky Lady* and mentor Burt Reynolds's *The End.* In 1980's *Walk Proud,* Benson portrayed a Chicano gang member—a role that required the star to don brown contact lenses. Shooting on the film was delayed 10 days when the lenses proved too irritating for Benson's cobalt-blue eyes. The same year saw the appearance on the big screen of the whimsical *Die Laughing,* which Benson not only cowrote with his father, but also coproduced with Barbra Streisand's pal Jon Peters. As he moved into his mid-20s, Robby Benson had set up housekeeping with actress Merilee Magnuson in San Fernando, but wound up marrying rock singer Karla DeVito. He starred with Paul Newman in the flop *Harry and Son* at about the same time he became a father for the first time. When daughter Lyric was barely 18 months old, Dad underwent open heart surgery then bounced back to star as a charmingly callow cop in the series *Tough Cookies.*

Born: 1957 in Dallas, Texas
Height: 5 ft. 10 in.
Weight: 137 lbs.
Eyes: Blue *Hair:* Dark brown
Education: Lincoln Square Academy (high school)
Religion: Jewish
Marriages: Karla DeVito (1982–)
Children: Lyric (b. 1983)
Interests: Scriptwriting, directing, singing, songwriting and arranging, guitar, basketball and other athletics (can do 1,000 sit-ups)
Personal Habits and Traits: An incurable workaholic, a perfectionist, self-effacing
Address: San Fernando, California
Income: $700,000+

Marisa Berenson

"I can't accept that you live and die and that's it. I was born with a karma and what I make of this life will put me closer to God in the next. My ultimate goal is to become a saint."

On her own, Marisa Berenson has graced the covers of *People, Time,* and *Newsweek* as "The Girl Who Has Everything Plus." And why not? Granddaughter of legendary designer Elsa Schiaparelli and grandniece of art historian Bernard Berenson, she is the offspring of late career diplomat Robert L. Berenson and Gogo Schiaparelli, now the Marchesa Cacciapuoti di Guiliano. Along with sister Berry, Marisa attended boarding schools in England, Switzerland, and Italy, but when she arrived in New York City at 17 to visit her dying father, she never returned to school. Spotted by *Vogue* editor-in-chief Diana Vreeland, Berenson embarked on a high-fashion modeling career on both sides of the Atlantic, despite a hostile reaction from "Scap" (Berenson's grandmother). Openly envious of Berry's successful marriage to actor Tony Perkins, Marisa embarked on her own series of affairs with such highly visible notables as record mogul David Geffen (Cher's old boyfriend), Italian film star Giancarlo Giannini, Baron Arnaud de Rosnay, German actor Helmut Berger, banker David de Rothschild, and auto heir Ricky von Opel. When she finally married millionaire manufacturer James Randall in 1976, all Hollywood turned out for the Wedding of the Year, but less than 18 months later Berenson charged Randall with, among other things, heaving objects at her, stealing the Rolls-Royce Corniche he gave her as a Christmas present, and trying to lock her out of their Beverly Hills estate. Their divorce had professional repercussions as well, for since Randall was coproducing the film biography of Vivien Leigh in which Berenson had planned to star, she was unceremoniously dropped from the picture; the film was never made. She failed to rebound in the rather disappointing Carlo Ponti adventure flick *Naked Sun.* Still, she has briefly appeared on screen as the classy Jewish department store heiress of *Cabaret* and *Barry Lyndon's* all-but-mute Lady Lyndon. She is now making films in France and has published a fashion book, *Dressing Up,* with photos by sister Berry. She's now married to Manhattan lawyer Richard Golub.

Born: February 15, 1946, in New York City
Height: 5 ft. 9 in.
Weight: 117 lbs.
Eyes: Green *Hair:* Sable brown
Zodiac: Aquarius
Education: Boarding schools in Switzerland, England, Italy
Religion: Roman Catholic
Marriages: To Jim Randall (1976–1978) To Richard Golub (1983–)
Children: Daughter Starlite Melody
Interests: Movie acting, fashion, the teachings of Maharaj Ji, reincarnation, art, dance
Personal Habits and Traits: A nonsmoker (quit in 1975) and teetotaler, attends daily dance class, sleeps in satin underwear with the windows thrown open, is compulsively neat
Addresses: Beverly Hills; New York City
Income: $350,000 (minimum estimate)

Candice Bergen

"Living in L.A. is like not having a date on Saturday night."

The daughter of Edgar Bergen, America's most famous ventriloquist, Candice competed with two very famous—and very hardhearted—sibling rivals when growing up: Charlie McCarthy and Mortimer Snerd. Real childhood playmates in Beverly Hills included the likes of Liza Minnelli and Desi, Jr., and Lucie Arnaz, and at 14 Candy suddenly metamorphosed into a traffic-stopping beauty. At 19 she dropped out of the University of Pennsylvania after two years, then made her screen debut as a lesbian in Mary McCarthy's *The Group*. Initially interested only in traveling, Candy willingly accepted inferior roles so long as they led her to some exotic location. Eventually, however, she began to take her acting career more seriously, and in 1971 broke the barrier with her sensitive portrayal of a college coed in Mike Nichols's *Carnal Knowledge*. The same year she met and fell in love with producer Bert Schneider (*Easy Rider, The Last Picture Show*)—an affair that arrested her screen career for two full years, although she did do several articles for major magazines during that time. When the relationship fell apart in 1974, Candy plunged back into filmmaking and simultaneously pursued her other love, photography, with a vengeance. The *Ladies' Home Journal* ran her exclusive pictures of President Gerald Ford and the First Family, and other photographic assignments ranged from the 1976 Democratic Convention to muscleman Arnold Schwarzenegger's "Pumping Iron" show at New York's Whitney Museum. She then tried her hand at television, filming an African expedition for ABC and doing a stint on the network's *A.M. America* (renamed the following year *Good Morning, America*). Most significantly, she had managed to salvage her erratic career. Her performance in *The Wind and the Lion* was followed by *Bite the Bullet,* a western in which Candy played a hardened prostitute competing in a winner-take-all horse race. After Lina Wertmuller's forgettable *A Nightful of Rain,* Candy went back for more in 1979's *Oliver's Story,* the triumphant Burt Reynolds comedy *Starting Over, Rich and Famous,* and *Gandhi* (she played photographer Margaret Bourke-White). Her 1984 memoirs, *Knock Wood,* leaped to the bestseller lists at the same time rumors flew that her marriage to French film director Louis Malle was in trouble. The pair scotched the unfounded gossip by producing their first child, a daughter, in 1985. Like so many of her glamorous contemporaries, Bergen had already begun hawking her own line of cosmetics—"Cie is me".

Born: May 8, 1946, in Beverly Hills, California
Height: 5 ft. 9 in.
Weight: 120 lbs.
Eyes: Blue *Hair:* Blond
Zodiac: Taurus
Education: Schools in Washington, D.C., and Switzerland, dropped out of the University of Pennsylvania
Marriages: To Louis Malle (1980–)
Children: Chloe (b. 1985)
Interests: Photography, anthropology, travel, writing
Personal Habits and Traits: Has given up smoking and cut down on her consumption of alcohol; swims and runs; a night owl
Addresses: Beverly Hills; New York City
Income: $500,000 (minimum estimate)

"The theater is like a faithful wife. The film is the great adventure—the costly, exacting mistress."

Ingmar Bergman

Ernst Ingmar Bergman

Europe's gloomiest (and some say greatest) living director experienced first-hand the sort of anguish he had long depicted on screen when, in the middle of a controversy over his tax status in 1975, he suffered a nervous breakdown. Yet his family origins could not have been more stable, for as the son of a Lutheran minister, Ernst Ingmar Bergman was brought up in a parsonage in Uppsala, Sweden. This heavily spiritual background is reflected in the searing, searching quality of Bergman's groundbreaking if often baffling films. In 1944 he was accorded recognition for his brooding screenplay of *Torment,* directed by Alf Sjöberg. Two years later, Bergman launched his own career as a director with *Crisis,* and that movie's international success led to a creative outpouring unequaled by any of his European contemporaries. Among Bergman's major efforts: *Wild Strawberries, The Seventh Seal, Through a Glass Darkly, The Passion of Anna, The Magician, Persona, Cries and Whispers, Scenes from a Marriage,* and *Autumn Sonata* (his first film with another Bergman—Ingrid). Equally important are the actors and actresses who owe their start to Bergman, most notably Max von Sydow, Bibi Andersson, Ingrid Thulin, and Liv Ullmann (mother of Bergman's daughter Linn). After a stormy and scandalous affair that raised eyebrows on both sides of the Atlantic, Bergman and Ullmann split, and in 1971 the master was married for the sixth time, to Ingrid von Rosen, whom he had married once before. But domestic discord wasn't the director's only trauma. Charged with violating Sweden's income tax laws and threatened with jail, he fled to France and vowed bitterly that he would never step on Swedish soil again. When his countrymen mounted a national campaign on his behalf, the government dropped its case, and Bergman returned to his Sheep Island retreat. His brilliant 1983 film *Fanny and Alexander* won an Academy Award as Best Foreign Film.

Born: July 14, 1918, in Uppsala, Sweden
Height: 5 ft. 10½ in.
Weight: 170 lbs.
Eyes: Brown *Hair:* Dark brown
Zodiac: Cancer
Education: High school
Religion: Protestant

Marriages: Six. Currently to Ingrid von Rosen (1971–)
Children: Six
Interests: The theater, directing and writing, farming
Personal Habits and Traits: Reclusive, smokes a pipe, drinks alcohol
Address: Sheep Island, Sweden
Income: $500,000 (minimum estimate)

Leonard Bernstein

"Who do I think I am—everybody?"

The Harvard-educated protégé of Koussevitzky erupted on the music scene when he filled in for ailing conductor Bruno Walter. But the first American-born conductor of the New York Philharmonic was not content to stick to the classics. Bernstein composed the score for the film *On the Waterfront;* collaborated on hit Broadway musicals like *On the Town, Wonderful Town, West Side Story,* and *Candide;* created a controversial rock *Mass* that premiered at Washington's Kennedy Center; and even became a TV star with his musical commentaries (particularly the *Young People's Concerts*). He retired in 1970 to become the Philharmonic's Laureate Conductor, and is still best known for his furious and highly physical style at the podium. Bernstein was married for 27 years to singer-actress Felicia Montealegre, who died of breast cancer in 1978. A dyed-in-the-wool uptown liberal, Bernstein hosted a rather notorious benefit party for the Black Panthers at his elegant Manhattan residence that made history when recorded in Tom Wolfe's scathing bestseller *Radical Chic* and added a new phrase to America's social lexicon.

Born: August 25, 1918, in Lawrence, Massachusetts
Height: 5 ft. 8½ in.
Weight: 169 lbs.
Eyes: Brown *Hair:* Gray-white
Zodiac: Virgo
Education: Harvard University
Religion: Jewish

Marriages: To Felicia Montealegre Cohn (1951 until her death in 1978)
Children: Four
Interests: Art, literature, politics, fashion, tennis
Personal Habits and Traits: Chain-smokes, drinks, diets, exercises, is a social creature
Address: Manhattan
Income: $550,000+

Jacqueline Bisset

"A movie star? I sure as hell don't feel like one."

The daughter of a lawyer mother and physician father, Jacqueline Bisset grew up in England and broke into movies in Roman Polanski's *Cul-de-Sac*. Over the next decade she decorated more than 30 films, nearly all forgettable with the exception of François Truffaut's *Day for Night*. She devoted herself to two long-term love relationships, first with actor Michael Sarrazin and then with French clothing designer Victor Drai, before seeming to settle on ballet star Alexander Godunov. With the hugely successful film version of Peter Benchley's *The Deep*, Bisset at last achieved the star status that she had perhaps craved too eagerly and indiscriminately. "I'll do a part," she has admitted, "for six really good lines." That attitude (and a hefty $500,000 fee) apparently led her to film *The Greek Tycoon*, a monumental exploitation picture dealing with the love affair between Jacqueline and Aristotle Onassis (played by Onassis's friend Anthony Quinn); Jackie Onassis turned down a cool $1 million to portray herself in the film. Bisset rebounded, however, as the sassy pastry chef marked for murder in *Somebody Is Killing the Great Chefs of Europe*, the frustrated author in *Rich and Famous*, the libidinous mom in *Class*, and the boozer's wife in *Under the Volcano*. While she weighed several new offers, Bisset and Godunov rambled around a 14-room Benedict Canyon mansion, and she preferred her 1970 El Dorado to the black Rolls-Royce once owned by Clark Gable that Drai gave her as a present.

Born: September 13, 1944, in Weybridge, England
Height: 5 ft. 7 in.
Weight: 116 lbs.
Eyes: Blue *Hair:* Dark brown
Zodiac: Virgo
Education: High school
Religion: Roman Catholic
Marriages: None
Children: None
Interests: Antiques, cooking, Ping-Pong, swimming
Personal Habits and Traits: Smokes, moderate drinker, no-nonsense attitude, articulate, unaffected
Address: Benedict Canyon, California
Income: $620,000 (estimate)

Shirley Temple Black

"I was in a class with Rin Tin Tin. People were looking for something to cheer them up, so they turned to a dog and a little girl."

'The name Shirley Temple opens many doors," declared the rather dowdy matron in the African print dress. "But if you don't have something to contribute, the doors can also close very rapidly." The dimpled darling of Depression America has unexpectedly proved to her country and the world that she indeed has plenty to offer. A millionaire from her movies at the age of 3 and washed up by 20, Shirley married California shoe manufacturer Howard Black in 1950 (her brief teenage marriage to actor John Agar ended in divorce the previous year) and became active in local politics. During the 1960s she stuffed envelopes and licked stamps for Ronald Reagan and other GOP politicos, and in 1967 made her own bid for Congress in Palo Alto, California, losing by a narrow margin to Paul McClosky. As a reward for her fund-raising efforts, Mrs. Black was named by President Nixon to serve as a representative to the United Nations General Assembly, and instead of falling flat on her face as many expected, she proved to be a superb and thorough diplomat. "I do my homework," she explained simply. A two-year tour of duty in black Africa as the U.S. Ambassador to Ghana followed, and the onetime movie moppet emerged as the most popular and respected American on the African continent. In the summer of 1976, Mrs. Black returned as chief of protocol at Gerald Ford's White House—the lofty title was Assistant Secretary of State. Now out of office and working again for the GOP in California, she views her success in government with equanimity: "I was liberated when I was three. I had equal opportunity, equal education—and I certainly had equal pay!" Mrs. Black was also one of the first famous breast cancer victims to discuss her mastectomy openly—to the point of being photographed and interviewed in her hospital bed shortly after the surgery.

Born: April 23, 1928, in Santa Monica, California
Height: 5 ft. 3 in.
Weight: 137 lbs.
Eyes: Brown *Hair:* Brown
Zodiac: Taurus
Education: Westlake School for Girls
Religion: Protestant
Marriages:
To John Agar (1945–1949)
To Charles Black (1950–)
Children: Linda Susan, by Agar; Charles Alden and Lori Alden by Black
Interests: Foreign affairs, Republican politics, conservation, Africa, multiple sclerosis research, cancer research
Personal Habits and Traits: Nonsmoker, a moderate drinker, conscientious, a perfectionist, even-tempered, possesses a surprisingly wry sense of humor
Address: Atherton, California
Income: $10 million (minimum estimate of net worth)

Linda Blair

"I sometimes feel bad about how much I make as a teenager. But we do get ripped off by the government. Jeez, someday I've got to do something about that."

The devil made her do it, so audiences flocked by the millions to see 12-year-old Linda Blair throw up green vomit and bloody herself with a crucifix in William Friedkin's shocker *The Exorcist.* The daughter of a well-to-do executive head-hunter, Linda was introduced by her mother to the world of modeling at age 5,

and was soon seen in department store catalogs and TV commercials. After only two minor film roles she found her rather bizarre break in *The Exorcist,* for which she received an Oscar nomination as Best Supporting Actress. Soon she proved that demonic possession wasn't her only forte, and portrayed a hapless teenage delinquent who is raped with a broomstick in *Born Innocent,* a made-for-TV movie. Similarly excessive roles as a teenage alcoholic and a Patty Hearst–style hostage followed, but offscreen Blair led a comparatively normal life as an accomplished horsewoman (competing under the name Martha McDonald) and inveterate animal lover. But her personal life began to unravel when she started dating a series of raucous rock musicians at the tender age of 15, including Australian singer Rick Springfield, Deep Purple's Glenn Hughes, and two members of the Black Oak Arkansas band; then she moved in with rocker Ted Hartlett. Now when traveling from one equestrian event to another, Blair does so at the wheel of her luxurious customized camper, complete with CB radio, two ovens, a bathtub, and a television. Unfortunately, in 1977, after the release of the unqualified disaster *The Heretic: Exorcist II,* Blair was arrested for possession of cocaine. She skated back onto the scene in 1980's *Roller Boogie,* which was followed by a steady stream of *drek.*

Born: January 22, 1959, in St. Louis, Missouri
Height: 5 ft. 2 in.
Weight: 115 lbs.
Eyes: Blue *Hair:* Brown
Zodiac: Aquarius
Education: High school
Religion: Protestant
Marriages: None
Children: None
Interests: Horses, dogs, rock musicians, bowling
Personal Habits and Traits: Chain-smokes cigarettes, drinks Kahlua and beer, has had exposure to drugs
Address: Westport, Connecticut
Income: $200,000 (minimum estimate)

Robert Blake

Michael Gubitosi

''Every time you think you got it made, old Mother Nature kicks you in the scrotum.''

The star of television's Emmy-winning *Baretta* was born Michael Gubitosi in Nutley, New Jersey, and at age 2 was shoved into his parents' down-at-the-heels song-and-dance act. Five years later he played an extra in the *Our Gang* film series, followed by a stint as Little Beaver in the Red Ryder westerns. Washed up by his teens, Blake nosedived into drugs, booze, and violence but managed to struggle back to respectability as a stunt man in the early 1960s, then landed memorable character parts on TV's *Richard Boone Show.* Ironically, his acclaimed performance as multiple-murderer Perry Smith in the movie of Truman Capote's *In Cold Blood* marked the beginning of another downhill career plunge.

But after eight years and four film flops, Blake brought his characterization of the quirkily incomprehensible cop Baretta to television in 1975. Amassing more than $1.5 million a year from the hit series during its four-season run and from his commercials for STP, Blake was nonetheless distressed at how stardom convulsed his private life. Sondra Kerr, the actress whom he married in 1964, left him at the height of his acting career in 1977, and Blake lamented, "Fame cost me my family. Now I'm sleeping with a stranger called success." Later, despite the critical acclaim for his portrayal of Jimmy Hoffa in *Blood Feud,* it looked as if Blake might not even have success as a bedmate much longer; his *Helltown* series about a priest playing detective fizzled in '85.

Born: September 18, 1933, in Nutley, New Jersey
Height: 5 ft. 4 in.
Weight: 155 lbs.
Eyes: Brown *Hair:* Dark brown
Zodiac: Virgo
Education: High school dropout
Religion: Roman Catholic
Marriages: To Sondra Kerr (1964–1977)
Children: Noah (b. 1965), Delinah (b. 1966)
Interests: Motorcycles, dirt biking, horseback riding, hunting
Personal Habits and Traits: Two-fisted drinker, chain-smokes, a loner
Address: Los Angeles
Income: $500,000+

Blondie

Deborah Harry

"The only person I really believe in is me."

Punk's peroxide pixie was three months old when she was adopted by Richard and Catherine Harry, a solid middle-class couple who raised Debbie and their other daughter in suburban Hawthorne, N.J. By the time she was 15, Harry was making weekend trips across the Hudson to the musical haunts of Greenwich Village. After two years at an exclusive finishing school—"a reformatory for debs"—she moved to New York and at the height of the acid rock era was singing backup with a folk group called Wind in the Willows. It was while working as a Playboy Bunny and studying Indian music that she moved from amphetamine-popping to heroin—a habit she was able to kick through yoga and what she mysteriously alludes to as a "semireligious experience." In the early 1970s Harry joined the Stilettos and found herself in the vanguard of the punk rock movement. Guitarist Chris Stein spotted the group in 1973, joined the backup band, and within a year broke off with Harry to form Blondie. Blondie's other components: bass player Nigel Harrison, drummer Clem Burke, guitarist Frank Infante, and keyboardist Jimmy Destri. Riding the crest of the New Wave, Blondie and Harry became the first punkers to cross over into the AM Top 40, shattering the charts with their throbbing singles "Heart of Glass" and "One

Way or Another," and going platinum (more than 1 million copies sold) with their album *Parallel Lines*. "Call Me," the provocative theme from the film *American Gigolo*, was an even bigger success, followed in rapid succession by Blondie's suitably titled reggae rendition of "The Tide is High" and "Rapture." Harry, frequently described as the "Monroe of Punk," found her experience in movies decidedly less rapturous, however; her acting debut in *Union City* was a bust. Harry dropped out in 1984 to care for Stein when he contracted an undisclosed illness, and did not get her career back on track until she released a new album two years later.

Born: 1944 in New Jersey
Height: 5 ft. 3 in.
Weight: 107 lbs.
Eyes: Blue *Hair:* Bleached blond
Education: High school
Marriages: None
Children: None
Interests: Acting, yoga, cosmetology (has a beautician's license), health food
Personal Habits and Traits: Serious, shy, well-spoken, guzzles Perrier, neither drinks nor smokes (will leave a room full of smoke to protect her voice)
Address: New York City

Erma Bombeck

"I am not a glutton—I am an explorer of food."

This Dayton-born housewife has parlayed ring around the collar and waxy yellow buildup into several bestselling books, a syndicated column in 800 nationwide newspapers, a television career, and a reputation as one of the funniest women in America. Erma Bombeck earned a degree in English from the University of Dayton, married William Bombeck, and wrote women's-page features for the *Dayton Journal-Herald* before taking a decade off to raise her family. In 1963, she began her column "Wit's End" for a local weekly and in 1965 sold it to the *Journal-Herald*. Working at the typewriter on her column by 8 A.M. every morning, she now finds time for vacuuming and dusting as well as publishing number-one bestsellers like *The Grass is Always Greener Over the Septic Tank, If Life is a Bowl of Cherries, What Am I Doing in the Pits?, Aunt Erma's Cope Book,* and *Motherhood, the World's Second Oldest Profession* and appearing twice weekly on ABC's *Good Morning, America.* Yet her $1.3 million+ earnings have not turned Bombeck's head, and Erma and Bill, a high school principal, settled in a modest ranch house outside Phoenix, Arizona. "For someone who was never recognized by her butcher when she got the next number, all this is a really big thing for me." Bombeck's public persona blossomed even further when in 1986 she became the first woman ever to serve as Grand Marshall of the Tournament of Roses Parade.

Born: February 21, 1927, in Dayton, Ohio
Height: 5 ft. 3 in.
Weight: 129 lbs.
Eyes: Brown *Hair:* Blond
Zodiac: On the cusp of Aquarius and Pisces
Education: University of Dayton, B.A. in English
Religion: Roman Catholic
Marriages: To William Bombeck (current)
Children: Betsy (b. 1953), Andy (b. 1955), Matt (b. 1958)
Interests: Gardening, cooking, ERA, education
Personal Habits and Traits: Nonsmoker, moderate drinker, early riser, wears bifocals, diets, attends exercise class
Address: Paradise Valley, Arizona
Income: $1.3 million+

Debbie Boone

"I knew from the minute I'd started singing that I'd be doing it for a living."

Her first hit, the Oscar-winning "You Light Up My Life," not only lit up the lives of her record producer and her accountant, it instantly made Debbie the most famous Boone in the land. Although Pat is Debbie's biggest fan—and frequent partner on the nightclub circuit—all was not always harmony between father and daughter. Pulled out of L.A.'s toney Westlake School when born-again Pat caught her reading a copy of Eldridge Cleaver's *Soul on Ice,* Debbie completed her secondary education at a conservative Catholic school. Tensions mounted during the teen years, and when Dad pasted Bible stickers over the counterculture posters in Debbie's room, she responded by tearing everything off the walls in a rage. Still, Debbie joined her three sisters (Cheryl, Linda, and Laura) and mother Shirley in 1971 to back up Pat's act as the "Boone Girls." Debbie took a giant step out of the pack in 1977, however, when Joe Brook's ballad turned out to be the biggest-selling single in over 20 years—knocking the Bee Gees' *Saturday Night Fever* score off the top of the charts. It also brought her a Best New Artist Grammy. She would not be nominated for a Grammy again until 1985, this time as a gospel singer. Married to Gabriel Ferrer, handsome son of José Ferrer and Rosemary Clooney, Debbie proudly boasted on the nationally syndicated *Phil Donahue Show* that both she and her intended were virgins—and intended to remain so until their wedding night. No wonder, considering the line she has for men who try to pick her up: "I just tell them who my dad is, and that sort of takes care of it." Debbie hooked a new image playing a call girl in ABC's 1984 TV movie *Sins of the Past.*

Born: September 22, 1956, in Hackensack, N.J.
Height: 5 ft. 4 in.
Weight: 110 lbs.
Eyes: Blue *Hair:* Blond
Zodiac: Virgo
Education: Marymount High School, one year of Bible college
Marriages: To Gabriel Ferrer (1979–)
Children: Jordan Alexander (b. 1980), twins Dustin and Gabrielle (b. 1983)
Interests: Cooking, songwriting, piano, various charities, the Bible
Personal Habits and Traits: Nonsmoker, nondrinker, nonbeliever in premarital relations
Address: Beverly Hills
Income: $350,000+

Pat Boone

"I did a lot of different things to prove that I wasn't just a Johnny One-Note. But my maturity as a performer did not change my moral beliefs one bit."

Charles Eugene Boone

From "Love Letters in the Sand" to "April Love" to "Friendly Persuasion," Charles Eugene "Pat" Boone reigned in the late 1950s as an antiseptic, golden-voiced minstrel in white bucks. But when his career started to sink in the 1960s, Boone experienced an unexpected religious crisis. "My wife Shirley was the first to go into our bedroom and fall on her knees and ask God to take over her life." With that, the Boones converted into Beverly Hills' leading born-again Christians, conducting prayer breakfasts and baptizing sinners in their own swimming pool! He experienced difficulties again in the late 1970s, having to reimburse unsatisfied customers when the acne medicine he endorsed proved ineffective. Still a regular on the nightclub circuit and a blossoming country-western star with the Nashville hit "Texas Woman," Boone is also heavily involved in civic activities and politics. Not impressed with Baptist candidate Jimmy Carter's beliefs, Boone served as a Reagan delegate at the Republican National Convention in 1976. The Boone family—Pat, Shirley, and daughters—also regularly appear on holiday season TV specials. In fact, Pat may have to take a back pew to daughter Debbie. Another Boone daughter, Cheryl, wrote a book about her own battle against anorexia and her father's belief in corporal punishment. Even Mrs. Boone got into the act when she prayed at Rock Hudson's bedside as Hudson lay dying of AIDS.

Born: June 1, 1934, in Jacksonville, Florida
Height: 6 ft.
Weight: 168 lbs.
Eyes: Blue *Hair:* Dark blond
Zodiac: Gemini
Education: Columbia University (*magna cum laude*)
Religion: Church of Christ
Marriages: To Shirley Foley (1953–)
Children: Cheryl, Linda, Debbie, Laura
Interests: Religion, conservative Republican politics
Personal Habits and Traits: Nonsmoker, a teetotaler, goes to bed and gets up early, a devout Christian and family man
Address: Beverly Hills
Income: $400,000 (minimum estimate)

Bjorn Borg

"What can you do with all that money? You only need one car, one pair of jeans. My charge is Wimbledon."

The golden boy of tennis discovered the sport when his father, a clothing salesman in Stockholm, won a racket in a Ping-Pong tournament and gave the prize to his son. Seven years later, in 1971, he stole the junior championship at

Wimbledon and joined Sweden's Davis Cup team. In addition to his considerable talents on the courts—he won at Wimbledon for the fourth time in 1979—his sex appeal excited swarms of tennis groupies. Borg met Romanian tennis pro Mariana Simionescu at Wimbledon in 1975, and a year later they moved in together—but only after Borg was photographed pulling up his pants with one of his disciples in London's Hyde Park. To beat Sweden's 95 percent tax bite, Borg divides his life between a three-bedroom condominium on Hilton Head Island, South Carolina, and a swank apartment in Monte Carlo. His parents have also benefited from their top-seeded son's largesse; with the money he gave them, they fulfilled a lifetime ambition to own their own grocery store. Borg followed his 1983 retirement with a 1984 divorce.

Born: June 6, 1956, in Stockholm, Sweden
Height: 6 ft.
Weight: 160 lbs.
Eyes: Blue *Hair:* Blond
Zodiac: Gemini
Education: Dropped out of school at 17
Religion: Protestant
Marriages: To Mariana Simionescu (1980–1984)
Children: None
Interests: Pop and rock music, reads comic books, backgammon
Personal Habits and Traits: Avoids cigarettes; drinks little; has a sweet tooth; is quiet and businesslike; wears jeans, one T-shirt three days in a row, warm-up jackets, and loafers
Addresses: Monte Carlo; Hilton Head, South Carolina
Income: $1.2 million+

David Bowie

David Jones

"I'm always amazed that people take what I say seriously. I don't even take what I am *seriously."*

True to his pseudonym (Bowie is "the ultimate American knife"), British rock's spaciest bisexual superstar flashes as one of modern music's most electrifying performers. Brought up in a working-class row house in South London, David Jones often visited the orphanage where his father worked to play with the orphans. A high school dropout at 16, he tried to make it as an artist and worked as an ad designer to support himself until the legendary mime Lindsay Kemp took him under wing. In 1972 Bowie himself took to the stage as Ziggy Stardust, androgynous king of space rock, and over the next four years scored no fewer than two million-selling singles and five gold albums, including *Diamond Dogs* and *Station to Station*. Bankrupt from the excesses of his outrageous stage productions—filled with smoke bombs, sirens and fireworks—Bowie announced his retirement at the age of 28. But he was back on top of the rock world within months, this time as the closely shorn, orange-haired purveyor of slick disco sounds. Bowie is as controversial offstage as on, and in 1978 split from his wife Angela, another avowed bisexual (whom Bowie presumably met through a mutual boyfriend). They both remain close to their son, Zowie Bowie. In 1980, Bowie astounded critics with his moving performance in Broadway's Tony Award-winning *The Elephant Man*. He soon returned to the rock milieu and, with such enormous hit records as "Let's Dance," "China Girl," "Blue Jean," and (with Mick Jagger) "Dancin' in the Streets," plus an impressive performance in the film *Merry Christmas, Mr. Lawrence*, at long last landed on the cover of *Time*.

Born: January 8, 1947, in London, England
Height: 5 ft. 9½ in.
Weight: 145 lbs.
Eyes: Blue *Hair:* Reddish blond
Zodiac: Capricorn
Education: High school dropout
Religion: Protestant
Marriages: To Angela Bowie (they separated in 1978)
Children: Zowie
Interests: Art, sports
Personal Habits and Traits: Chain-smokes several packs a day, likes to drink, a night creature
Address: London
Income: $2 million

Marlon Brando

"Acting is an empty and useless profession."

"When people meet me," says America's greatest film actor, "they say to themselves, 'I hope he isn't going to be rude and uncouth.' They remember me from the days when I was supposed to be the hot-copy boy who scratched himself and spat in the potted palms." For 35 years Marlon Brando has proved one of the most controversial personalities ever to hit Hollywood. Born in Omaha, Nebraska, into a family with a strong acting tradition, Brando learned much of his craft from his mother, Dorothy, an acting coach who counted Henry Fonda among her pupils; Brando's father, Marlon, Sr., headed Brando's own Pennybaker Productions until his death in 1965. Young Marlon attended the Shattuck Military Academy in Minnesota, but was expelled in 1943 and headed for New York City and the Dramatic Workshop of the New School for Social Research. In October 1944, after studying with Stella Adler and Elia Kazan, he made his professional debut on Broadway in *I Remember Mama*. Three years later Brando staggered theater audiences as the brutish Stanley Kowalski in Tennessee Williams's *A Streetcar Named Desire*—a role that he repeated on film opposite Vivien Leigh four years later. In rapid succession he electrified movie audiences with *Viva Zapata!, The Wild One, Julius Caesar*, and *On the Waterfront*, for which he won his first Academy Award as Best Actor. By 1957 Brando had received his fifth Oscar nomination—for *Sayonara*—but over the next two decades his career foundered with no less than 15 lackluster films—most unnotably, 1962's *Mutiny on the Bounty*. Not until 1972 did he score a spectacular, Academy Award-winning comeback in the role of Don Corleone in *The God-*

father. The very next year he earned yet another Oscar nomination for the intense and steamy *Last Tango in Paris,* the first major film to show a star of Brando's caliber engaging in a variety of sexual acts. Throughout, Brando has stirred no less controversy as a political and social activist. In 1963 he marched with civil rights workers in Gadsden, Alabama, and the following year was arrested near Tacoma, Washington, on charges of illegal fishing (to dramatize Indian treaty rights). He sent an Indian messenger to the Academy Award ceremonies in 1972 to refuse his award "because of the treatment of the American Indian in motion pictures." Married to Anna Kashfi, then Movita Castenada, and finally Tarita Teripaia (his Polynesian love interest in *Bounty*), he now lives on Tetiaroa, his Pacific atoll 30 miles from Tahiti, where he is ministered to by Eddy, a Polynesian, and Eriko, a Japanese girl. So far, the greatest tragedy in his life has not been the breakup of his three marriages, but apparently the death of his close friend and onetime roommate, comedian Wally Cox. "I can't tell you how much I miss and love that man," says Brando. "I have Wally's ashes in my house. I talk to him all the time." Back in the United States to make the disappointing *Missouri Breaks* with Jack Nicholson in 1976 and *Superman* two years later, the durable legend once again rebounded as the renegade commander in Francis Ford Coppola's Vietnam saga *Apocalypse Now*. *The Formula,* in which Brando portrayed a bloated oil tycoon, lacked the chemistry for success. In 1985, Brando checked into an Arizona fat farm after blimping up to nearly 300 pounds.

Born: April 3, 1924, in Omaha, Nebraska
Height: 5 ft. 8 in.
Weight: 290 lbs.
Eyes: Blue *Hair:* White
Zodiac: Aries
Education: High school
Religion: Protestant
Marriages:
To Anna Kashfi (divorced)
To Movita Castenada (divorced)
To Tarita Teripaia (divorced)
Children: Christian, Miko, Rebecca, and Simon
Interests: The American Indian, civil rights, reading
Personal Habits and Traits: Early riser, serious drinker, binge eater, given to dark moods
Address: Tetiaroa, near Tahiti
Income: $3 million per film

Jeff Bridges

"I quickly found out that people in show business are interested in making money. If you get the work it's because you're doing the job."

A member of one of Hollywood's flourishing dynasties along with father Lloyd and older brother Beau, Jeff Bridges was eight when he was first professionally dunked on Lloyd's *Sea Hunt* television series. He did a stint in the Coast Guard Reserve before his first major screen role—the part of a Texas hell-raiser in Peter Bogdanovich's *The Last Picture Show*—landed him a Best Supporting Actor Oscar nomination in 1971, followed by another nomination from the Academy

three years later for *Thunderbolt and Lightfoot.* Other movies include *Rancho DeLuxe, The Last American Hero, Hearts of the West,* the Dino de Laurentiis remake of *King Kong,* the ill-fated *Heaven's Gate, Winterkill,* and *Against All Odds.* Counting among his long-term lovers Cybill Shepherd, Candy Clark, and Valerie Perrine, Bridges nonetheless managed to avoid the altar until 1977, when he wed Susan Geston. No less experimental was his flirtation with such drugs as LSD and marijuana, and such cultish fads as Erhard Seminar Training (est) and transcendental meditation. "The est thing was a heavy flash," says Bridges. "You can put sex in the same place. You have that orgasm and you get all blown away." A dark-horse Oscar nominee for *Starman* in 1985, he lost out to *Amadeus*'s F. Murray Abraham.

Born: December 4, 1949, in New York City
Height: 6 ft. 2 in.
Weight: 175 lbs.
Eyes: Blue *Hair:* Dirty blond
Zodiac: Sagittarius
Education: High school
Religion: Protestant
Marriages: Susan Geston (1977–)
Children: Two daughters
Interests: Carpentry, painting, composing, the guitar, gardening, the works of J. Krishnamurti, producing
Personal Habits and Traits: Occasionally goes on health food kicks, loves his digs in the Malibu Hills (including a glass-enclosed outdoor shower and Jacuzzi), runs along the beach every day, sleeps in a queen-sized bed in the nude and talks in his sleep
Address: Malibu
Income: $1 million per film

Christie Brinkley

"I was a very self-conscious teenager—chubby, 140 pounds, chipmunk cheeks. I still harbor some of those hangups."

She isn't satisfied with her hips, her derriere ("I wish my butt did not go sideways"), or her legs ("I wouldn't mind a couple more inches"). To the rest of the world, she's a perfect 10. Raised in Malibu by well-to-do parents (her stepfather, Don Brinkley, was producer of *Trapper John, M.D.*), Christie dropped out of UCLA at 17, and sold ice cream, plants, and clothes until she saved up the $1,000 she needed to fly off to Paris. There, she rented a tiny garret in Montparnasse, tried to make it as an artist, and married French illustrator Jean François Allaux. Spotted by a photographer while walking her dog in a shapeless raincoat, Christie was soon signed by the Elite Model Agency. To shed 15 pounds, she went on a starvation diet and at one point passed out in a café. Then, in 1979, she landed on the cover of *Sports Illustrated*'s swimsuit issue, and was instantly proclaimed Cheryl Tiegs's successor as the modeling game's hottest property. She switched agencies (from Elite to Ford) and loves, divorcing her French husband of eight years and becoming involved with champagne heir and race-car driver Count Olivier Chandon de Brialles. In 1983, Chandon was killed when his racecar plunged into a Palm Beach canal. Not long after, Brinkley met rocker Billy Joel while vacationing in the Caribbean. ''He was playing the piano, and I walked over to listen. Then I started singing, and he accompanied me. . . .'' He wrote a song about her, ''Uptown Girl,'' and starred her in several of his videos. Whenever they checked into a hotel, they signed the register ''Rocky and Sandy Shore.'' In March 1985, they were married in New York City aboard the 147-foot yacht *Riveranda* as it plied the Hudson. ''This isn't a marriage,'' a wedding guest said of the two multimillionaires (Christie's seven-figure deals include contracts with Russ Togs and Cover Girl) exchanging vows. ''It's a merger.''

Born: February 2, 1954, in California
Height: 5 ft. 9 in.
Weight: 125 lbs.
Eyes: Blue *Hair:* Blond
Zodiac: Aquarius
Education: High school
Religion: Protestant
Marriages: To Jean François Allaux (1973–1981)
To Billy Joel (1985–)
Children: Alexa (b. Dec. 9, 1985)
Interests: Painting, French
Personal Habits and Traits: Somewhat insecure, yet extremely ambitious
Addresses: Manhattan; Long Island
Income: $2 million yearly (minimum estimate)

David Brinkley

''The one function that TV news performs very well is that when there is no news we give it to you with the same emphasis as if there were.''

When television's top news team of David Brinkley and the late Chet Huntley bid one another goodnight, millions of American TV viewers felt satisfied that they had learned *all* the news of the day worth knowing. Indeed, the Huntley-Brinkley Report averaged 20 million viewers over their 14 years on television. They were teamed on a permanent basis after NBC executives realized that their colorful coanchoring of the 1956 Presidential conventions was far more than just a happy coincidence: Huntley provided the necessary degree of warm sobriety while the wry, often sarcastic Brinkley added a dash of vinegar. In the following years Brinkley broadcast from Washington while Huntley was based in New York. Born and raised in Wilmington, North Carolina, Brinkley was an ambulance-chasing cub reporter on the local *Star-News* before joining NBC as a newswriter in 1943. Huntley retired in 1970 (he later died of cancer), and Brinkley struck out on his own the next year with *David Brinkley's Journal*—commentary appended to the *NBC Evening News with John Chancellor*. He later became a Sunday-morning fixture as host of the ABC news program *This Week with David Brinkley*. Something of a social butterfly, Brinkley is a fixture on the Washington cocktail and embassy party scene. He has three sons by his first marriage to Ann Fischer, and after their divorce was linked to a number of well-known women—most frequently Lauren Bacall, though in fact they met only rarely. In 1972, he married divorcée Susan Adolph, currently one of Washington's leading hostesses.

Born: July 10, 1920, in Wilmington, North Carolina
Height: 6 ft. 2 in.
Weight: 180 lbs.
Eyes: Brown *Hair:* Brown
Zodiac: Cancer
Education: High school
Religion: Protestant
Marriages:
To Ann Fischer (divorced)
To Susan Adolph (1972–)
Children: Three sons
Interests: Politics, art
Personal Habits and Traits: Moderate drinker
Address: Washington, D.C.
Income: $500,000

Tom Brokaw

''TV is a fickle business. I'm only good for the length of my contract.''

''It was a very Tom Sawyeresque type of life,'' NBC anchorman Tom Brokaw recalls of his childhood in Pickstown, South Dakota. The son of a postal worker mother and construction worker father, Brokaw became a three-letter high school athlete and an A student in political science at the University of South Dakota. Upon graduation he married Meredith Lynn Auld, his high school sweetheart (a former Miss South Dakota) and the couple headed for the big city—Omaha, Nebraska. There Meredith taught school while her husband trained as a $100-a-week newscaster at the local NBC affiliate. In the mid-1960s he got his first big break covering the civil rights movement in the South for Atlanta's WSB, and turned in such notable reportage that NBC sent him to Los Angeles, followed by a stint as NBC's White House correspondent. In the summer of 1976 the network's fair-haired boy followed in the footsteps of Hugh Downs and Barbara Walters as $400,000-a-year host of the morning *Today Show.* The grueling *Today* schedule—he was in bed by 11 P.M. to be up by 5 A.M.—did not seem to bother young Brokaw, but even a Park Avenue duplex was not enough to keep him from yearning for the suburban life, especially when considering his three daughters. ''I don't want my children to grow up thinking they are better than the rest of society,'' says Brokaw. ''We're very much aware of our middle-class roots. We want to maintain those roots for the sake of the children.'' He took a giant step away from those roots when he assumed John Chancellor's seat behind the NBC News anchor desk in 1981.

Born: February 6, 1940, in Webster, South Dakota
Height: 6 ft.
Weight: 165 lbs.
Eyes: Brown *Hair:* Brown
Zodiac: Aquarius
Education: University of South Dakota, B.A. in political science
Marriages: To Meredith Lynn Auld (1962–)
Children: Jennifer, Andrea, Sarah
Interests: Jogging
Personal Habits and Traits: Nonsmoker, early riser
Address: Park Avenue, New York City
Income: $2 million

Charles Bronson

Charles Buchinsky

"I have lots of friends and yet I don't have any."

Clint Eastwood's rival as the top movie star outside the United States, Charles Buchinsky (he changed his name when Senator Joe McCarthy "made everything that sounded Russian evil") established himself in over 50 eminently forgettable westerns and war movies as a Slavic-faced heavy with a menacing scowl. However, there were several worthies along the way—*The Magnificent Seven* and *The Dirty Dozen* among them—and *le monstre sacré* (the "sacred monster," as he is known in France) zoomed from commanding $20,000 per picture to $1 million plus a percentage of the profits in one brief, six-year period. Born in a grimy Pennsylvania coal town, Buchinsky drove a delivery truck during World War II and followed his father down into the mines before escaping by bus to California and the famed Pasadena Playhouse. His nadir may have been *The House of Wax* starring Vincent Price, in which Bronson actually "played" a motionless dummy. But *Death Wish* premiered in 1974 and proved a milestone in Bronson's career. Although some critics felt the movie (in which Bronson avenges the rape-murder of his wife and daughter by systematically gunning down muggers) to be "immoral," *Death Wish* struck such a responsive chord with terrorized city dwellers that it became a top grosser that year, spawning several sequels. Less intriguing performances in movies like *Breakout* and *Hard Times* dimmed his box office luster, but Bronson continued to rack up a fortune, as well as the 36-room house in Bel Air he shares with actress Jill Ireland, his wife and costar in such films as 1976's *Breakheart Pass*. During summers they repair to a 450-acre retreat in West Windsor, Vermont.

Born: November 3, 1922, in Ehrenfeld, Pennsylvania
Height: 5 ft. 11 in.
Weight: 165 lbs.
Eyes: Brown *Hair:* Salt-and-pepper
Zodiac: Scorpio
Education: High school
Religion: Roman Catholic
Marriages:
To Harriet Tendler (divorced)
To Jill Ireland, (current) the former Mrs. David McCallum
Children: Seven
Interests: Painting, scenic design
Personal Habits and Traits: Nonsmoker, moderate drinker, early riser, inveterate dieter, exercise nut
Addresses: Bel Air, California; West Windsor, Vermont
Income: $1.6 million (estimate)

Mel Brooks

"If you got it, flaunt it."

Melvin Kaminsky

Heir to Groucho Marx as czar of zaniness in movies, Mel Brooks has matched the lunacy of *A Night at the Opera* and *Animal Crackers* with such antics as *Blazing Saddles, The Producers, Frankenstein, Silent Movie,* and *High Anxiety*. Actually, anxiety is at the root of Brooks's comedic flair. His father died of a tubercular infection when Mel was 2, and he grew up being taunted by other kids because he was puny. A comic in the Catskill resorts, he landed a $2,500-per-show contract to write for Sid Caesar's *Your Show of Shows* on television. Earning such a hefty salary plunged Brooks into frequent what-will-happen-if-it-all-goes-up-in-smoke-tomorrow? anxiety attacks, and his nightmare became reality when *Your Show of Shows* was canceled. His income immediately dropped by 95 percent. A classic comedy album called *The 2,000-Year-Old Man* (made with Carl Reiner) brought Brooks some visibility as a performer in the early 1960s, and by 1965 he had concocted a hit television spy spoof called *Get Smart*. That same year he married Oscar-winning actress Anne Bancroft. Though they refuse to discuss their marriage or each other's careers, Brooks and Bancroft are considered to be one of Hollywood's most well-adjusted couples. Their only major appearances together were on the TV special *Annie and the Hoods,* and 1983's *To Be or Not to Be*.

Born: 1926 in Brooklyn, New York
Height: 5 ft. 4 in.
Weight: 146 lbs.
Eyes: Brown *Hair:* Gray-black
Education: High school
Religion: Jewish
Marriages:
To Florence Baum (divorced)
To Anne Bancroft (1964–)

Children: One
Interests: Psychoanalysis
Personal Habits and Traits: Smokes, a moderate drinker, anxious, always "on," has a propensity to use four-letter words
Addresses: Beverly Hills; Manhattan
Income: $2 million +

Joyce Brothers

"Do I ever think of divorce? Never! Murder? All the time!"

Joyce Brothers, the daughter of two lawyers, makes the unabashed claim that she has "never failed" at anything she tried. She received a degree in home economics from Cornell University, went on to earn a Ph.D. in psychology from Columbia, then taught at Columbia and New York's Hunter College. She first attracted national attention in 1955, when she committed some 20 volumes of boxing trivia to memory in less than six weeks to score a total of $134,000 on television's *$64,000 Question,* and the show's successor, *The $64,000 Challenge.* She emerged unscathed from the scandals surrounding the shows, and soon her physician husband, Milton, was set up in a Park Avenue practice. As America's best-known psychologist, Dr. Joyce Brothers discusses everything from television violence to impotence in her daily newspaper column (syndicated to 350 papers), in her monthly column in *Good Housekeeping,* on her daily radio show syndicated by NBC, and in her books (such as 1984's best selling *What Every Woman Should Know About Men).* A regular on the lecture circuit, she delivers some 100 speeches a year at a fee of $4,000 each. Often criticized for dispensing pop psychology remedies like so much chicken soup, Brothers nonetheless strikes a responsive chord in millions of fans, adding a touch of sympathetic concern to her expert advice. Milton and Joyce divide their time between a New Jersey apartment overlooking the Manhattan skyline and an 18th-century, 210-acre farm in New York's Dutchess County. "Milton thinks that most problems are in the body and not the mind," says Joyce Brothers, "and I think vice versa. That's what's kept our marriage together since 1949."

Born: October 20, 1928, in New York City
Height: 5 ft. 3 in.
Weight: 115 lbs.
Eyes: Blue *Hair:* Blond
Zodiac: Libra
Education: Cornell University, B.A. in home economics; Columbia University, Ph.D. in psychology
Religion: Jewish
Marriages: To Milton Brothers (1949–)
Children: Lisa (b. 1954)
Interests: Politics ("I want to run for the Senate"), restoring old houses, investments, cooking
Personal Habits and Traits: Nonsmoker, moderate drinker, workaholic, nervous
Addresses: New Jersey; Dutchess County, New York
Income: $500,000 (minimum estimate)

Louise Brown

In the galaxy of recent "overnight" celebrities none has quite so instantly ascended as Louise, the world's first test-tube baby. For nine years Lesley Brown and her husband, Gilbert John, a van driver for British Rail, had futilely tried to conceive a child. Like millions of other women, Lesley Brown suffered from a fallopian tube disorder, so to bypass the tube, Oldham Hospital's Dr. Patrick Steptoe and Cambridge University physiologist Robert Edwards removed an egg from Mrs. Brown's ovary, placed it in a laboratory dish and fertilized it with her husband's sperm. Three days later, after the egg had undergone three sequences of cell divisions, the eight-celled embryo was inserted in Lesley's uterus. Hailed by many as a revolutionary medical breakthrough that would enable women with blocked or damaged fallopian tubes to bear children, it was also damned as a step toward an Orwellian society controlled by genetic engineers. Despite the enormous ethical, moral, and social implications of the event, blond-haired Louise began life like any other healthy, breast-fed baby. It was less likely, however, that the rest of her life would be as normal. Even prior to her birth, Louise was in such demand that her parents were able to close a $565,000 deal with the London *Daily Mail* giving reporters continual access to Louise and her family. Nonetheless, by 1986 Louise was attending school like any other 8-year-old.

Born: 11:47 P.M. on July 25, 1978, Oldham General Hospital in Oldham, England
Weight: 5 lbs. 12 oz. at birth
Eyes: Blue *Hair:* Blond
Zodiac: Leo
Income: $565,000 (1978)

Jackson Browne

"I still look forward to growing up—whenever that happens."

The son of Dixieland pianist Clyde Browne, Jackson picked up the guitar in high school, played clubs in Los Angeles and Greenwich Village, and easily attracted a dedicated following with his lyrical brand of country-rock. In the spring of 1976 Browne's wife, Phyllis, a former fashion model and the mother of Jackson's son, Ethan, swallowed an overdose of sleeping pills—and lived. But the day she was released from an L.A. hospital she took another overdose—and this time died. Shattered, Browne immersed himself in the creation of a poetically self-revealing album, *The Pretender,* which sold over 1 million copies. A year later his number-one *Running on Empty* sold 3 million. When he is not on the road, Browne spends as much time as possible with Ethan at his luxurious home in the Hollywood Hills.

Born: October 9, 1950, in Heidelberg, Germany
Height: 5 ft. 10 in.
Weight: 153 lbs.
Eyes: Brown *Hair:* Brown
Zodiac: Libra
Education: High school
Religion: Protestant
Marriages: To Phyllis Browne (committed suicide in 1976)
Children: Ethan (b. 1974)
Interests: Tai Chi, poetry, fiction, opposing nuclear power
Personal Habits and Traits: Smokes, drinks, is something of a loner
Address: Hollywood Hills, California
Income: $447,000 (minimum estimate)

Anita Bryant

"If God had meant to have homosexuals, he would have created Adam and Bruce."

A former Miss Oklahoma and second runner-up to Miss America in 1959, Anita would seem an unlikely candidate to provoke nationwide controversy—until in 1977, on religious grounds, she championed the repeal of an ordinance which prohibited discrimination against qualified schoolteachers who were (admitted) homosexuals in Dade County, Florida. Bryant was victorious, and from that moment on became a target of outraged gays, who mobilized politically to combat her. Bryant had made her singing debut at the age of 2 in a Baptist church, the same year her parents were divorced. By the time she was 8 Anita was singing on a local radio show, and at age 12 won a contest and landed a TV variety show of her own. The following year she cut her first record, and before graduating from high school she had become a regular on Arthur Godfrey's CBS-TV show. Her first million-seller was "Till There Was You." At a record convention she met Miami disc jockey Bob Green, and they were married in 1960. Bryant soon began to pocket millions as a spokeswoman for Kraft, Coca-Cola, Holiday Inn, and the Florida Citrus Commission, which made her its $100,000-a-year "Sunshine Girl." She also became a regular on Bob Hope's USO tours, and wrote nine bestselling inspirational volumes. But her stand against gay rights cost her $500,000 in bookings because agents were scared off by homosexuals threatening to boycott. In 1974 Bryant's grandfather and two friends died, and as a result she suffered a near breakdown. Turning to a Christian therapy group in California, she managed to pull herself together and in the process temporarily mended her strained relationship with Green. Bryant adopted a son, Bob, Jr., when she was told she could not have children, then startled her doctor by giving birth to three—a daughter and then twins (a boy and a girl). Bryant's contract with the orange growers was cancelled in 1980—the same year her marriage was squeezed dry.

Born: March 25, 1940, in Barnsdall, Oklahoma
Height: 5 ft. 4 in.
Weight: 117 lbs.
Eyes: Brown *Hair:* Brown
Zodiac: Aries
Education: One year at Northwestern University
Religion: Baptist

Marriages: To Bob Green (1960–1980)
Children: Four
Interests: The Bible, battling homosexuality, singing, writing, cooking
Personal Habits and Traits: Nonsmoker, teetotaler, disciplined worker
Address: Miami
Income: $100,000+

William F. Buckley, Jr.

"At the National Review *we spend half our time writing about the Soviet Union—and half our time writing about* The New York Times.*"*

Learning Spanish from the maids his millionaire oilman father brought back from Mexico, young Bill Buckley was trained in officer's candidate school for counterespionage work on the Mexican border, but by the time he arrived the Japanese had surrendered and World War II was over. So he returned to complete his education at Yale, where he also taught Spanish and wrote a book deriding that institution for what he perceived as creeping atheism and leftism among students and faculty alike. *God and Man at Yale* established Buckley as an articulate spokesman for the Right, but he chose to do cloak-and-dagger work for the Central Intelligence Agency for eight months before publishing yet another controversial treatise, this time defending Joe McCarthy while Buckley's fellow New York intellectuals were nearly unanimous in their outrage toward the Wisconsin senator. Relying primarily on his own family—the collective worth of Buckley and his nine siblings is estimated at an excess of $100 million—he managed to raise $375,000 to launch the *National Review* in 1955. A quarter-century later Buckley contends that the magazine is the most important thing in his life—even though he pens a daily column ("On the Right") syndicated to 300 national papers, ran against John Lindsay and Abe Beame for mayor of New York in 1965, stars in his own PBS television show *(Firing Line)*, helped elect his brother James to the U.S. Senate, and has managed to write several bestsellers in a row: *Saving the Queen* (1976), *Airborne* (1977), *Stained Glass* (1978), *Who's On First?* (1980), *Marco Polo, If You Can* (1984), and *See You Later, Alligator* (1985).

Born: November 24, 1925, in New York City
Height: 6 ft.
Weight: 167 lbs.
Eyes: Blue *Hair:* Sandy brown
Zodiac: Sagittarius
Education: Yale University, B.A.
Religion: Roman Catholic
Marriages: To Patricia Taylor (1950–)
Children: Christopher (b. 1953)
Interests: Sailing, playing the harpsichord
Personal Habits and Traits: Drinks whiskey, early riser, workaholic
Addresses: Park Avenue, New York City; Stamford, Connecticut
Income: $500,000+

Carol Burnett

"Comedy is tragedy—plus time."

As one of the triumvirate of TV Comedy Queens (along with Lucille Ball and Mary Tyler Moore), Carol Burnett recalls a family life that was anything but comic. Her parents, both alcoholics, abandoned Carol to be raised by Mae, her

powerhouse of a Christian Scientist grandmother (to whom Carol would later signal on television every week by tugging at her right earlobe) in a one-room Los Angeles apartment. Carol majored in English and theater arts at UCLA, but dropped out in 1954 after three years. In 1960 she made her debut on Broadway in the hit stage musical *Once Upon a Mattress,* and brought her knack for goofball slapstick to the *Garry Moore Show* on CBS, where she met Moore's producer Joe Hamilton, a devout Catholic with eight children. In the meantime, her marriage to actor Don Saroyan (a cousin to writer William Saroyan) had foundered, and once they obtained divorces from their respective spouses, Burnett and Hamilton were married in 1963. From that point on, Hamilton provided the power behind the Burnett phenomenon. He produced her 1964 movie flop *Who's Been Sleeping in My Bed?,* the TV version of *Once Upon a Mattress,* and a variety series called *The Entertainers* before finally hitting the jackpot in 1966 with *The Carol Burnett Show,* featuring the likes of Harvey Korman, Vicki Lawrence, Lyle Waggoner, Dick Van Dyke, and Tim Conway. Over the next dozen years the Emmy-winning show seldom dropped out of the Top 20 in the Nielsens, although only Lawrence and Conway were still regulars when Burnett folded the show in 1978. She reasons, "We had our turn, and I wanted to leave before we ran out of new ideas completely." Aside from her series, Burnett landed a much deserved Best Actress Academy Award nomination for her portrayal of a mother whose young son dies, in the tearjerker *Pete 'n' Tillie.* Her memorable TV specials include *Julie and Carol at Carnegie Hall* (with Julie Andrews), *Julie and Carol at the Palace, 6 RMS RV VU, Sills and Burnett at the Met,* and the TV version of Erma Bombeck's hilarious housewife follies, *The Grass is Always Greener Over the Septic Tank.* She also stole the show in Robert Altman's star-studded film *A Wedding.* In television's powerful *Friendly Fire,* Burnett won kudos for her role of the mother of a boy killed in Vietnam, heading a one-woman protest against the U.S. Army bureaucracy, which treats her pain as a minor annoyance. In 1980, after she had gone public about her eldest daughter's drug problems and won a $1.6 million libel suit against the *National Enquirer,* Burnett picked up with her family and moved to Maui—in part to reduce the strain on Hamilton after he suffered a mild heart attack. But within two years, their marriage was over; Burnett bought a co-op in Manhattan and sat down to pen her memoirs for Random House.

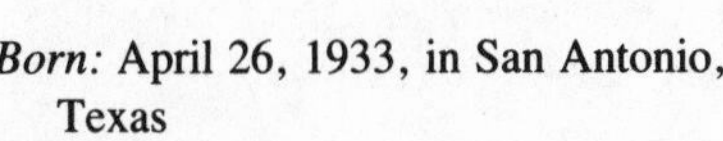

Born: April 26, 1933, in San Antonio, Texas
Height: 5 ft. 7 in.
Weight: 112 lbs.
Eyes: Brown *Hair:* Reddish brown
Zodiac: Taurus
Education: Three years studying English and theater arts at UCLA (1951–1954)
Religion: Christian Scientist

Marriages:
To Don Saroyan (divorced in 1963)
To Joe Hamilton (1963–1982)
Children: Carrie, Jody, Erin
Interests: Cancer research, yoga
Personal Habits and Traits: Nonsmoker, teetotaler, exercise nut
Addresses: New York; Beverly Hills
Income: $2.6 million

Ellen Burstyn

Edna Rae Gillooly

"I'm glad I didn't have a piece of The Exorcist. *I'd feel stupid to be a millionaire and still work, and I wouldn't know what to do if I didn't work."*

She was born Edna Rae Gillooly to a working-class Irish family in Detroit. In Dallas she worked as a fashion illustrator's model under her abbreviated name Edna Rae. Dancing in a Montreal nightclub she was known as Kerri Flynn, and she became Erica Dean when she modeled for paperback covers in Manhattan and worked as one of Jackie Gleason's sexy "Glee Girls." Then she was billed as Ellen McRae for her 1957 Broadway debut in *Fair Game* and held on to the name throughout her run on *The Doctors,* a popular NBC soap. But it was finally as Ellen Burstyn—the surname belonging to her third husband, Neil Burstyn—that this versatile actress captured audiences by portraying a series of "mothers": Cybill Shepherd's washed-out but sassy Texas ma in *The Last Picture Show,* the mother of a demonically possessed daughter in *The Exorcist,* and the widowed mom of a precocious 12-year-old in *Alice Doesn't Live Here Anymore.* Nominated for all three performances, she won the Best Actress Oscar for *Alice* in 1975, the same year she was nominated for a Tony for her smash stage role in *Same Time, Next Year* (the film version brought her yet another Academy Award nomination). She returned in *Resurrection.* Eschewing a fourth marriage (she divorced Neil in 1971), Burstyn has since shared houses in Los Angeles and New York with Bill Smith, an actor 10 years her junior, and her son, Jeff. A passionate disciple of Method guru Lee Strasberg, Burstyn succeeded him as head of the legendary Actor's Studio after his death in 1981. Burstyn was, as always, totally believable in *Twice in a Lifetime,* this time playing a wife jilted by husband Gene Hackman for Ann-Margret.

Born: December 7, 1932, in Detroit, Michigan
Height: 5 ft. 6½ in.
Weight: 120 lbs.
Eyes: Brown *Hair:* Brown
Zodiac: Sagittarius
Education: High school dropout
Religion: Roman Catholic
Marriages:
To Bill Alexander (divorced)
To Paul Roberts (divorced)
To Neil Burstyn (1960–1971)
Children: Jefferson (b. 1962)
Interests: A voracious reader
Personal Habits and Traits: Kicked smoking and drinking (replaced a glass of wine every night before bed with a glass of milk and calcium)
Addresses: New York City; Los Angeles
Income: $400,000 (estimate)

James Caan

"Everybody makes me out to be some kind of macho pig, humping women in the gutter. I do, but I put a pillow under 'em first."

This macho star *(The Godfather, Cinderella Liberty, The Killer Elite, The Gambler, Slither, Freebie and the Bean, Funny Lady, Harry and Walter Go to New York, Hide in Plain Sight, Chapter Two)* actually got his first big break portraying the dying halfback Brian Piccolo in ABC-TV's Emmy-winning tear-jerker *Brian's Song*. But until that made-for-TV movie was aired in 1972, Caan spent a decade struggling and getting nowhere, making a dozen innocuous movies (four of which were never even released). However, Caan was accustomed to toughing it out. The son of a kosher meat dealer in Queens, he won an athletic scholarship to Michigan State University, but after one week found that at a comparatively puny five feet ten and a half inches, weighing in at 165 pounds, he was definitely not suited to the rigors of freshman football. He also dropped out of Hofstra before heading toward off-Broadway, where he apprenticed in a number of plays for $37.50 a week—"If anybody said, 'There goes that faggy actor,' I'd just bust 'em in the mouth"—and occasionally played on television shows like *The Naked City*. At 21 Caan married a dancer by whom he has a daughter, Tara, but they divorced after four years, and he headed for Hollywood in 1964 to begin his long wait for stardom. After living for a time with ex-Playmate of the Year Connie Kreski, Caan unexpectedly married actress Sheila Ryan, a marriage that lasted only a few months beyond the birth of his son, Scott Andrew, in 1976. He once commanded at least $700,000 and a percentage of the gross to star in a picture. Caan (Hollywood's only New York Jewish cowboy) has spent much of his time roping steers on the professional rodeo circuit since 1970. His first attempt at directing, *Hide in Plain Sight*, excited critics. But after his string of film fiascos, beginning with 1978's *Chapter Two*, the moviegoing public's message seemed clear: No Caan Do.

Born: March 26, 1939, in Queens, New York
Height: 5 ft. 10½ in.
Weight: 165 lbs.
Eyes: Blue *Hair:* Sandy brown
Zodiac: Aries
Education: One week at Michigan State University, Hofstra University dropout
Religion: Jewish
Marriages: Two, ending in divorce
Children: Tara (b. 1965), Scott Andrew (b. 1976)
Interests: Steer roping, karate, judo
Personal Habits and Traits: Moderate smoker, heavy drinker, late riser
Address: Beverly Hills
Income: $1 million +

Michael Caine

Maurice Micklewhite

"Cockneys used to be looked upon kindly like Mickey Mouse or dwarves, but we decided to be people instead."

Typecast as the lusty, womanizing Cockney in *Alfie,* Maurice Micklewhite grew up dirt-poor, the son of a charwoman and a porter at the Billingsgate fishmarket. Contracting malaria while fighting for the British contingent in Korea, Caine later toiled in a bakery and meat market while searching for work as an actor in the West End. At the Lowestoft Repertory Theater he met and married his leading lady, Patricia Haines, but abject poverty broke up the marriage after three years, and at one point shortly after his divorce Caine was thrown in jail for failing to pay alimony. Copping a new surname from the marquee for *The Caine Mutiny,* Michael Caine was working the night shift at a laundry when asked to sub for Peter O'Toole in a road company. A small part as a patrician in *Zulu* sparked the takeoff of his film career, and Caine emerged as a major star playing the befuddled spy in *The Ipcress File.* Following a series of highly publicized romances with the likes of Bianca Jagger (before Mick) and Minda Feliciano, he wound up marrying the exotically beautiful Shakira Baksh, a former Miss Guyana (she placed third in the Miss World Contest), a few months after she became pregnant with their daughter, Natasha, in 1973. Ever conscious of his humble beginnings—Caine brags of "nicking off" (stealing) a blazer from his wardrobe for the movie *Sleuth,* for example—his life-style is distinctly "upper crust." He resides in a manor house adorned with Picassos, Modiglianis, and 16th-century antiques; a cellar stocked with over $70,000 worth of wine; and a staff of seven servants. When he is not fishing in his own trout stream, swimming in his own pool, playing tennis on his private court, or being chauffeured to Burke's, the toney men's club he helped found, Caine turns out such box office biggies as John Huston's version of Rudyard Kipling's *The Man Who Would Be King.* A shrewd businessman, he joined with *King* costar Sean Connery to sue Allied Artists for $109,000 apiece when it appeared they were not getting their fair share of the profits. In recent years, he has rivaled Laurence Olivier's reputation as a workaholic; Caine acted in more than a dozen films between 1980 and 1986, including *California Suite, Dressed to Kill, Deathtrap, Educating Rita,* Woody Allen's *Hannah and Her Sisters* and George Harrison's *Water.*

Born: March 14, 1933, in London, England
Height: 6 ft.
Weight: 175 lbs.
Eyes: Blue *Hair:* Blond
Zodiac: Pisces
Education: Dropped out of school at 16
Religion: Protestant
Marriages:
To Patricia Haines (ended in divorce after three years)
To Shakira Baksh (1973–)
Children: Dominique (b. 1958), Natasha (b. 1974)
Interests: Wines, cooking, art, antiques
Personal Habits and Traits: Starts every day with a stroll and a cigar, is a moderate drinker
Address: Near Windsor, England
Income: $2 million (estimate)

Glen Campbell

''I'm a take-me-as-I-am person. You can't change yesterday any more than you can predict what's going to happen tomorrow.''

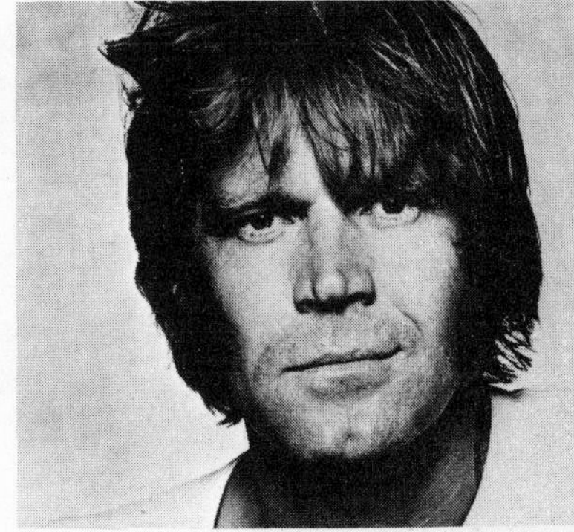

Country-rock superhits like ''By the Time I Get to Phoenix,'' ''Gentle On My Mind,'' ''Wichita Lineman,'' and ''Galveston'' catapulted Glen Campbell into $3-million-a-year TV and recording stardom by the time he was 30. The seventh son of a seventh son, Glen shared a bed with three brothers in Delight, Arkansas, and sang in the Church of Christ where his grandfather was preacher. He dropped out of school at 14, and taught himself how to play the guitar by standing outside and accompanying local gospel services. Campbell hit the road with his Uncle Boo's band in the mid-1950s, and in a decade had become one of the finest studio musicians and vocalists in the business, backing up various singers such as Frank Sinatra and Elvis Presley. All told, he performed background work on some 500 recordings, and even subbed for Brian Wilson on the Beach Boys' 1965 tour. Shorn of long hair and beard, he landed his own summer replacement series for the Smothers Brothers in 1968, and the enthusiastic reaction to his clean-cut chrome-coiffed appeal kept *The Glen Campbell Goodtime Hour* afloat on CBS for four years. A career lull coincided with the breakup of his second marriage, but in 1976 Campbell bounced back with the number-one country hit ''Rhinestone Cowboy,'' and followed it up with ''Summer Nights.'' Married that same year to singer Mac Davis's ex-wife, Sarah, Campbell rented a Beverly Hills house that once belonged to Dick Powell and June Allyson, and augmented his sizable recording income by headlining for a reported $100,000 a week in Las Vegas. After splitting with Sarah, he teamed up for a year with 20-years-younger country-western dynamo Tanya Tucker on stage and off, before ambling to the altar a fourth time, with dancer Kim Woolen. Several times Country Entertainer of the Year and winner of four Grammys, Campbell even hosts his own golf tournament, the Glen Campbell Los Angeles Open.

Born: April 22, 1938, in Delight, Arkansas
Height: 6 ft.
Weight: 158 lbs.
Eyes: Brown *Hair:* Light brown
Zodiac: Taurus
Education: High school dropout
Religion: Church of Christ
Marriages:
To Diane Kirk (1955–1958)
To Billie Jean Nunley (1959–1975)
To Sarah Davis (1976–1979)
To Kim Woolen (1982–)
Children: Seven
Interests: Golf (plays in the mid-70s, an 8 handicap), his '56 Thunderbird, tennis
Personal Habits and Traits: Does not smoke, drinks, diets
Address: Beverly Hills
Income: $1 million

Pierre Cardin

''For a woman to be loved, she usually ought to be naked.''

The fashion designer who first revived the arch Edwardian look of the 1960s ended up commanding a $250 million-plus empire encompassing womenswear, menswear, colognes, furniture, wines, linens, chocolates, and stage shows. Born in Venice but raised in France, Pierre Cardin's first love was architecture, but after joining the salon presided over by Jean Cocteau he abandoned the design of buildings for that of clothes. He headed the coat and suit shop for Christian Dior in Paris before introducing his own haute couture in 1950. Ten years later his line of men's clothes proved an instant success. Cardin, an implacable and somewhat enigmatic bachelor, presides over his far-flung interests from an apartment furnished in the Louis XVI style on the Faubourg St. Honoré. His decision to launch his own cologne in a phallic-shaped bottle signaled the beginning of a daringly aggressive marketing approach aimed at creating a Cardin ''environment,'' in which just about everything wearable, edible, drinkable, and functional imparts the mark of the master—including the fabled Paris restaurant Maxim's, which he bought and turned into an international chain with outposts as far-flung as Beijing.

Born: July 17, 1922, in Venice, Italy
Height: 5 ft. 7½ in.
Weight: 145 lbs.
Eyes: Brown *Hair:* Brown
Zodiac: Cancer
Education: High school
Religion: Roman Catholic
Marriages: None
Children: None
Interests: Politics, art, movies, music, fashion, food, health, automobiles, architecture, sports
Personal Habits and Traits: Ascetic: does not smoke, drinks wine, rises early, eats lots of salads, retires early; is somewhat antisocial
Address: Paris
Income: $50 million (estimate of net worth)

George Carlin

"In the end, I'm just the guy who thought of the stuff and got hold of the microphone. Once I'm on stage, my wits are my only defense against ignominy. That is what it all amounts to—pure self-defense."

The counterculture's Bob Hope, George Carlin dropped out of New York City's Cardinal Hayes High School to join the Air Force. During his hitch as a radar mechanic servicing B-47s, Carlin was stationed in Shrevesport, Louisiana, where the owner of radio station KJOE billed him as "America's funniest 17-year-old disc jockey." Discharged in 1955, he teamed up with Fort Worth radio newsman Jack Burns (who later became part of the Burns and Schreiber comedy team) to perform a comedy act in Boston coffeehouses. Burns and Carlin clicked, and with $400 between them they headed for Los Angeles. But the act broke up in 1962, and three years elapsed before Carlin really took off solo. Neatly dressed and generally sticking to his hilarious takeoff of Top 40 deejays, Carlin became a regular on *The Merv Griffin Show, The Mike Douglas Show, The Roger Miller Show, The Hollywood Palace,* and *The Kraft Summer Music Hall.* But Carlin was unsatisfied. "After a while," he muses, "I wasn't there—it was all just surface. And so I discovered a much better character for me—myself!" Carlin traded in the suit and tie for Levi's, a long reddish-brown beard, long hair tied in the back with a rubber band, an earring, and a whole new act geared to hip audiences. Carlin became persona non grata on the TV talk shows for several months after his sudden conversion, but eventually they welcomed him back; so much so, in fact, that Carlin frequently substituted for the often absent Johnny Carson on NBC's insomniac staple *The Tonight Show.* He was the first guest host of *Saturday Night Live* in 1975 (he was accorded the honor of guest hosting on several subsequent occasions), and Carlin's HBO comedy specials are among the cable network's most popular.

Born: May 12, 1937, in New York City
Height: 5 ft. 9 in.
Weight: 150 lbs.
Eyes: Hazel *Hair:* Brown
Zodiac: Taurus
Education: High school dropout
Religion: Protestant

Marriages: Brenda Hosbrook (1961–)
Children: Kelly Marie (b. 1963)
Interests: Music, art
Personal Habits and Traits: Smoker, nondrinker, workaholic
Address: Los Angeles
Income: $200,000 (estimate)

Princess Caroline of Monaco

Caroline Louise Marguerite

To Princess Grace:
"I can fool you, Mother. I can fool you anytime."

The jet-setting daughter of Princess Grace (Kelly) and Prince Rainier flaunted her intrepid independence even back in her schoolgirl days at the Sorbonne, where she met, pursued, and eventually landed Philippe Junot, a flamboyant Parisian financier 17 years her senior. The House of Grimaldi had banked on marrying off Princess Caroline Louise Marguerite to another noble, most particularly Britain's Crown Prince Charles. But when Caroline was caught by eager paparazzi sunbathing topless alongside Junot off the Côte d'Azur, the palace at Monaco hastily announced the couple's formal engagement. Caroline, American by temperament and taste if European by upbringing, married the man her family had initially resisted in June 1978—with Mama Grace's reluctant blessing. Within a year, the Royal Family's original misgivings about Junot were proved correct; Caroline and Philippe were *finis*. Following the tragic death of her mother in a car accident, Caroline stepped into Grace's shoes as Monaco's First Lady. And, after a much-publicized romance with Robertino Rossellini, the son of Ingrid Bergman and Roberto Rossellini, she married Italian oil scion Stefano Casiraghi—just two months before the birth of their son, Andrea.

Born: January 23, 1957, in Monaco
Height: 5 ft. 7 in.
Weight: 120 lbs.
Eyes: Blue *Hair:* Dark brown
Zodiac: Aquarius
Education: Sorbonne University, Paris
Religion: Roman Catholic
Marriages: To P. Junot (1978–1980)
To Stefano Casiraghi (1984–)
Children: Andrea (b. 1984)
Interests: Swimming, art, horseback riding, horse racing, astrology, tennis
Personal Habits and Traits: Nonsmoker, moderate drinker, late riser
Addresses: Paris, Monte Carlo

David Carradine

"I've reached a point now where I can see the limitations of Fidel Castro as easily as I can the limitations of a Rockefeller. I don't want to be either one of those guys."

He seldom wears undershorts, has allowed his pierced ear to heal, and admits to having taken no fewer than 500 acid trips; yet John Carradine's son David is one of the most disciplined actors in Hollywood today. A worshiper of his actor father, David studied composition, voice, piano, and ballet—but strangely enough, not acting. Yet after picking plums in the San Joaquin Valley and selling sewing machines, David moved to New York with his brother Keith and ultimately played Laertes to his father's Hamlet. The part of the doomed Inca king in the 1965 Broadway hit *The Royal Hunt of the Sun* established his acting credentials, and he eventually spent six lucrative seasons as the part-Chinese star of ABC-TV's *Kung Fu.* In 1976, David vied with his brother Keith for the role of Woody Guthrie in Hal Ashby's *Bound for Glory* and won; Keith was decidedly too young for the role. *Bound for Glory* bombed at the box office but was a critical success, and shortly after seeing a preview of the film Ingmar Bergman signed David opposite Liv Ullmann for *The Serpent's Egg.* Throughout, Carradine has been a perennial source of controversy within the tight-knit moviemaking community. In addition to his extensive drug experiences and his volatile temper—while on probation for wrecking a Laurel Canyon house he was fined $20,000 for assaulting a local woman—Carradine conducted a very public and tempestuous affair with Barbara Seagull (who changed her name from Barbara Hershey when she accidentally killed a seagull, then back again). They lived together for six years and costarred in 1972's *Boxcar Bertha;* the following year Barbara gave birth to their son, Free. A year later, after cutting a wide romantic swath through Hollywood, Carradine met and married Linda McGuinn, ex-wife of 1960's rocker Roger McGuinn. Grasshopper tied the knot for a third time in 1985, this time with his manager, Gail Jensen.

Born: December 8, 1936, in Hollywood
Height: 6 ft.
Weight: 175 lbs.
Eyes: Brown *Hair:* Brown
Zodiac: Sagittarius
Education: San Francisco State College, B.A.
Religion: Protestant
Marriages: Three. Currently to Gail Jensen (1985–)
Children: Calista (b. 1963), Free (b. 1973)
Interests: Race-car driving, music, dance
Personal Habits and Traits: Nonsmoker, nondrinker, stopped taking drugs
Address: Laurel Canyon, California
Income: $400,000

Keith Carradine

On father John Carradine: *"The fact that the old man did it for over fifty years cannot be ignored."*

The only Oscar-winning member of the Carradine acting dynasty, Keith Carradine was born in San Mateo, California, to patriarch John and the second of his four wives, actress Sonia Sorel. The pawn in a custody battle, he was shunted between private schools until he was 15, when his father permitted him to see his mother for the first time in seven years. He moved in with his half-brother David after a semester at Colorado State College, and they soon headed for New York to audition for *Hair*. David was too old, however, and Keith claimed the part. His first movie was Robert Altman's *McCabe and Mrs. Miller* in 1971, followed by another Altman film, *Thieves Like Us*. But it was not until 1975, when he played unscrupulous loverboy Tom Frank in Altman's *Nashville,* that Carradine succeeded on three levels—as an actor and as both composer and singer of the Academy Award-winning song "I'm Easy." Actress Cristina Raines *(The Sentinel),* his "lady" since 1971, was cast as Carradine's bedmate and backup singer in *Nashville,* and later as his wife in *The Duelists*. Overshadowed by his 12-year-old costar Brooke Shields in the controversial *Pretty Baby,* Carradine set out to recoup in *Old Boyfriends,* a film by *Nashville* scriptwriter Joan Tewkesbury. His rangy presence has been felt in the TV miniseries *Chiefs,* the 1986 TV movie *Winners Never Quit* and in a number of rock videos, including Madonna's "Material Girl."

Born: 1950 in San Mateo, California
Height: 6 ft. 1 in.
Weight: 170 lbs.
Eyes: Blue *Hair:* Brown
Education: One semester at Colorado State College
Religion: Protestant
Marriages: To Sandra Will (current)
Children: Cade (b. 1982)
Interests: Backpacking, music
Personal Habits and Traits: Nonsmoker, moderate drinker, unharried
Address: Topanga Canyon, California
Income: $300,000 (estimate)

Diahann Carroll

Carol Diahann Johnson

"It's tough to find a secure black man who doesn't feel threatened that your career might serve to deball him."

Born in the Bronx to a subway motorman and a registered nurse, Carol Diahann Johnson attended New York's High School of Music and Art and was spending her first semester at New York University when she won $3,000 on a network talent show. On her way, she soon captured a Tony for playing the lead in Richard Rodgers's touching interracial love musical *No Strings,* and by the mid-1960s was one of the country's most in-demand nightclub singers. While appearing on Broadway in *House of Flowers,* she met her first husband, white casting director Monte Kay. Divorced after a brief marriage, she conducted a nine-year-long affair with Sidney Poitier that ended when she refused to subordinate her career to his. Plunging back into work, Carroll starred in the forgettable film *Hurry Sundown,* but had considerable luck in the role of *Julia* on television.

The sitcom about a black nurse was considered a breakthrough for the medium at the time, though in retrospect many have labeled it patronizing. After several top-rated seasons, *Julia* was removed from the air and Carroll focused on her nightclub career. But the entertainer's private life made headlines when, after a long-term relationship with David Frost, she suddenly eloped with Nevada boutique owner Freddie Glusman into a marriage that lasted three months. Her third marriage, to *Jet* managing editor Robert DeLeon, occurred shortly after he interviewed her on her 1975 Academy Award nomination for *Claudine*. Less than two years later DeLeon, who was 16 years Carroll's junior, died in an automobile accident. Carroll's career peaked in the 1980s after she called up the producers of ABC's *Dynasty* and suggested that they cast her as the "first black bitch on television." She also found a new love: crooner Vic Damone. She collaborated on her memoirs with writer Ross Firestone.

Born: July 17, 1935, in the Bronx, New York
Height: 5 ft. 6 in.
Weight: 114 lbs.
Eyes: Brown *Hair:* Brown
Zodiac: Cancer
Education: High School of Music and Art
Religion: Baptist
Marriages:
To Monte Kay (divorced)
To Freddie Glusman (divorced)
To Robert DeLeon (1975 until his death in 1977)
Children: Suzanne Ottilie (b. 1960)
Interests: Fashion, cooking
Personal Habits and Traits: Smokes, drinks moderately, articulate, has given up the party circuit
Addresses: Los Angeles; Riverside Drive, New York
Income: $720,000

Johnny Carson

"The difference between divorce and legal separation is that a legal separation gives a husband time to hide his money."

The King of Late Night Television, and to many the sharpest comedy mind in America today, was born in Corning, Iowa, but raised in Norfolk, Nebraska. Carson sent away for a mail-order magic course as a youngster, later billed himself as The Great Carsoni, and entertained at local Rotary Club and Elks meetings before enlisting in the Navy at the height of World War II. Carson attended the University of Nebraska on the GI bill, worked a brief stint as an announcer with an Omaha radio station and made his comic debut quipping one-liners on an hour-long radio show mysteriously called *The Squirrel's Nest*. No sooner did he land a high-paying writer's job for *The Red Skelton Show* than Carson received the break that only happens in the movies. When Skelton injured himself diving through a prop door during rehearsals, Carson was called in to substitute, and his TV debut led to his being hired to emcee the game show *Who*

Do You Trust?, which ran for five full seasons before Carson replaced Jack Paar as host of *Tonight* in 1962. Since then, the quick-witted Carson has triumphed over such late-night rivals as Dick Cavett, Joey Bishop, and Merv Griffin, not to mention the strongest challenge of all from the *CBS Late Night Movie*. And the Nebraska boy has been rewarded accordingly. On top of his annual *Tonight Show* gross of well over $3 million for just three days' work each week, Carson plays to SRO audiences at Caesars Palace in Las Vegas for four or five weeks a year; he never plays more than a week at a time, and never more than one show a night, yet he is nonetheless paid a record $200,000 *per week!* He also has signed a deal with Paramount to produce made-for-TV movies, while his line of men's clothes grosses another $80 million per year. Not surprisingly, then, Carson's schedule is frantic. Up before 8 A.M., he breakfasts as he scans *The New York Times* and *Los Angeles Times* for monologue material, and he often swims in his oval pool or plays tennis on his backyard court before heading for work in one of his two Mercedes 450 convertibles. The *Tonight Show* airs across the country at 11:30 P.M., but is actually taped in the late afternoon. Carson had already divorced Jody Wolcott and was in the midst of shedding Joanne Copeland when he spotted top fashion model Joanna Holland across the room at New York's chic 21 Club in the fall of 1971. When Carson decided to move his show to Burbank, Joanna was reluctant to leave New York, so he flew back to her and insisted they were getting married. They did—in 1972, on the same day Carson celebrated his 10th anniversary on the *Tonight Show*. Carson stunned newly chosen NBC chief Fred Silverman in 1979 by announcing unexpectedly that he intended to leave *Tonight* with the start of the new decade. Instead, he stayed—with the proviso that the show be cut from 90 minutes down to one hour. Carson's marriage began to unravel when he was arrested for driving under the influence in 1983, and his subsequent sensational divorce from Joanna—she demanded a staggering $220,000 a *month* in temporary alimony payments—provided Karnac with plenty of fresh material: ''My cat's lawyer called, demanding $12,000 for Tender Vittles.'' A bachelor once again, Carson played the dating game with Sally Field and Morgan Fairchild before seeming to settle on onetime secretary Alexis Maas.

Born: October 23, 1925, in Corning, Iowa
Height: 5 ft. 10 in.
Weight: 170 lbs.
Eyes: Hazel *Hair:* Gray-white
Zodiac: Scorpio
Education: University of Nebraska
Religion: Protestant
Marriages:
To Jody Wolcott (divorced)
To Joanne Copeland (divorced in 1971)
To Joanna Holland (1972–1983)

Children: Chris (b. 1959), Ricky (b. 1961), Cory (b. 1962)
Interests: Flying, tennis, swimming, psychology
Personal Habits and Traits: Chain smoker, moderate drinker, early riser, quiet, reflective, exercise fanatic
Address: Malibu, California
Income: $12 to $15 million

Jimmy Carter

James Earl Carter

"Have faith in me. I am a Christian."

The first of his family to finish high school, James Earl Carter grew up in the tiny Georgia town of Plains. He was appointed to Annapolis in 1943 and selected by Admiral Hyman Rickover for the nuclear submarine program, pursuing graduate work in nuclear physics. But on the death of his father in 1953, he resigned his commission and returned to Plains to manage the family peanut business. Carter ran successfully for the Georgia State Senate, then in 1966 ran, unsuccessfully, for Governor, but triumphed four years later. Unable to succeed himself under Georgia law, Carter started campaigning for the Presidency in 1974 (by that time, the peanut business had made him a millionaire). The darkest of horses, he managed to stump the panel of the television game show *What's My Line?* Yet Carter proved himself such a tireless campaigner in the primaries that by the time the Democrats convened in New York City in the summer of 1976, the born-again Baptist had clinched the nomination. During his campaign against incumbent Gerald R. Ford, Carter managed to survive the famous "lust in my heart" *Playboy* magazine interview, as well as a series of three televised Presidential debates, to win by a relatively narrow margin and become the 39th President of the United States. Once in the Oval Office, however, Carter's popularity began to slide dramatically: Budget Director Bert Lance resigned in the midst of a scandal about his handling of bank funds; Health Advisor Dr. Peter Bourne quit after falsifying a Quaalude prescription for a secretary; United Nations Ambassador Andrew Young was chastised after charging previous Presidents with racism and claiming that there were "thousands of political prisoners" in the U.S.; and White House Chief of Staff Hamilton Jordan was investigated for allegedly snorting cocaine at Studio 54. Halfway through his term, populist "Jimmy" Carter—the first President ever to insist on being inaugurated and signing bills with his nickname—registered the lowest popularity rating of any President with the exception of Richard Nixon just prior to his resignation. Yet his deft handling of the Middle East summit at Camp David, and the subsequent peace treaty between Israel and Egypt, bolstered his standing in the foreign policy area. The reshuffling of his cabinet was a surprise to many observers, and as the 1980 election approached, Jimmy was looking over his shoulder at another Democratic Party candidate, Edward Kennedy. But Carter's handling of the Iranian Crisis in which 50 Americans were held hostage at the U.S. embassy in Teheran brought a dramatic turnabout in the polls, and once again the Georgia peanut farmer looked like the man to beat. The polls were wrong. Ronald Reagan clobbered the incumbent by a margin of two to one. Carter returned to Plains and sat down to write his memoirs, *Keeping Faith.* In 1985, he hit the bestseller lists once again with *The Blood of Abraham*—and picked up a hammer to help build housing for the poor in New York City.

Born: October 14, 1924, in Plains, Georgia
Height: 5 ft. 9½ in.
Weight: 158 lbs.
Eyes: Blue *Hair:* Sandy white
Zodiac: Libra
Education: U.S. Naval Academy (59th in a class of 820)
Religion: Southern Baptist
Marriages: To Rosalynn Smith (1946–)
Children: John "Jack" (b. 1947), James E. III "Chip" (b. 1950), Donnel Jeffrey "Jeff" (b. 1953), Amy Lynn (b. 1967)
Interests: Farming, art, literature, country music, the Bible, evangelism (he is a deacon at the Plains Baptist Church), tennis, bowling, fishing
Personal Habits and Traits: Nonsmoker, nondrinker, needs only five hours of sleep per night, methodical, watches his diet, has a "lucky" red tie. Health: excellent, though he suffers from hemorrhoids
Address: Plains, Georgia
Income: $500,000

Rosalynn Carter

"He planned to make the Navy a career, so I thought it would be exciting to get married and travel around."

The wife of the 39th President was also born in Plains, Georgia, where she and Jimmy's sister, Ruth, were best friends, and where his mother, Miz Lillian, actually nursed Rosalynn's bus driver father when he was stricken with leukemia. After his death in 1940 Rosalynn's mother, Mrs. Allie Smith, supported her four children (Rosalynn is the eldest) as a postal worker and by taking in sewing. Rosalynn was still a sophomore at Georgia Southwestern College when Midshipman Carter, home on leave from Annapolis, invited her to the movies on a double date with Ruth and her boyfriend. Several months later, over Christmas vacation, he asked her to marry him and was rejected. But by February she had changed her mind, and they were wed on July 7, 1946. For the next seven years they lived on naval bases in Norfolk, San Diego, Oahu, and New London, Connecticut. Rosalynn at first resisted Jimmy's 1953 decision to return to Plains—she dreaded the meddling of in-laws—but Jimmy prevailed. A crop failure in 1954 forced them into a $21-a-month public housing project apartment, but by the early 1960s they were well on their way to becoming millionaires. Rosalynn contributed her efforts when Jimmy ran for Governor of Georgia in 1966 and lost, and again four years later when he was victorious, so that by 1975 her political skills were honed finely enough for her to launch her own two-year trek through 40 states on behalf of Jimmy's Presidential campaign. She led a low-key but pervasive life in the White House, generally accompanying her husband on official trips abroad, and occasionally being dispatched on solo missions to deliver personal Presidential messages to foreign heads of state. Rosalynn's overriding devotion to her husband and his political ambitions throughout his career, chronicled in her 1985 autobiography *First Lady from Plains,* earned her the title of "the Steel Magnolia."

Born: August 18, 1927, in Plains, Georgia
Height: 5 ft. 5 in.
Weight: 118 lbs.
Eyes: Hazel *Hair:* Brown
Zodiac: Leo
Education: Georgia Southwestern College, B.A.
Religion: Southern Baptist
Marriages: To Jimmy Carter (1946–)
Children: Jack (b. 1947), Chip (b. 1950), Jeff (b. 1953), Amy (b. 1967)
Interests: Mental health, art, sewing, tennis, Jimmy, ERA, Southeast Asian refugees
Personal Habits and Traits: Moderate wine drinker, early riser
Address: Plains, Georgia

Johnny Cash

''I need *to be in the country. Man's instinct is to be close to nature. We haven't been out of the woods that long.''*

The Grand Old Man of Nashville's black-leather-jumpsuit set began by barely eking out a living with his five siblings on an Arkansas cotton farm, and was selling appliances in Memphis when Sun Records signed him to cut an album in 1955. But not until the early 1960s did ''Ring of Fire'' and ''I Walk the Line,'' two country-western hits, cross over onto the pop charts and indelibly impress Cash's coal-down-a-steel-shute baritone on audiences in Los Angeles and Manhattan as it already had on fans in the Deep South. Yet at the very height of his career, as ''Folsom Prison Blues'' and ''A Boy Named Sue'' topped the charts, the singer was engaged in a punishing bout with drugs and liquor (and an uncontrollable temper). Fortunately, with the help of second wife and frequent singing partner June Carter, a member of Nashville's own famous Carter Family, Cash eventually conquered his nemeses. Their daughters, Carlene Carter and Roseanne Cash, assured that the dynasty would continue when they began making names for themselves as country-rock singers in the early 1980s. He published his autobiography, *Man in Black,* and is writing a novel about St. Paul, *Man in White.*

Born: February 26, 1932, in Kingsland, Arkansas
Height: 6 ft. 1 in.
Weight: 200 lbs.
Eyes: Brown *Hair:* Black
Zodiac: Pisces
Education: High school
Religion: Baptist
Marriages:
To Vivian Liberto (1954–1967)
To June Carter (1968–)
Children: Four daughters, one son
Interests: Guitar, prison conditions
Personal Habits and Traits: Teetotaler; afraid of flying, snakes
Address: Hendersonville, Tennessee
Income: $750,000+

Dick Cavett

"I'm supposed to be wry, subtle, Midwestern, Ivy League. Sometimes I worry about it. I don't have an image of myself."

Combining the homey wit of his mentor Johnny Carson with the urban sensibility of his pal Woody Allen, Dick Cavett remains one of the most talented interviewers on television. The only child of two schoolteachers ("I was spoiled rotten"), Cavett grew up star-struck in Kearney, Nebraska, graduated from Yale, "performed" in an Army training film, and played a Shakespearean bit part at Stratford. He bombed with his own stand-up comedy routine in Greenwich Village but finally landed a job as a TV writer, first for Jack Paar, then for Carson. The lucrative position netted Cavett over $2,000 a week, yet his sudden affluence did not quench his desire to become a full-fledged TV personality in his own right. And sure enough, when Cavett was given the chance to deliver some of his own material on the *Tonight Show* he was soon offered his *own* talk show on ABC. Matching wits with the likes of Katharine Hepburn, Orson Welles, and Bette Davis, he earned the reputation as the only genuine raconteur on the tube. His ratings gradually began to slip, however, and in 1972 ABC relegated him to one week per month before canning him permanently. In the meantime, Cavett's unique talent was proclaimed on the covers of *Time* and *Life,* and his canceled show won an Emmy. Two years later he published an autobiography in the form of a straight question-and-answer interview with old Yale roommate and *Time* editor Christopher Porterfield. A bestseller, *Cavett* dealt with, among other things, the author's obsession with celebrities (he once secretly tailed Greta Garbo through the streets of New York) and his being the target of homosexual advances in men's washrooms. The sequel was also a hit, and Manhattan-based Cavett returned to the air in a half-hour nightly interview format for the Public Broadcasting Service in 1977. That show lasted five seasons. Along with Mississippi-born actress Carrie Nye, whom he met as an undergraduate at Yale and married in 1964, Cavett divides his time between a huge house in Montauk, Long Island, and a roomy New York high-rise apartment. Cavett, a former Nebraska state gymnastics champion, keeps in shape swimming and working out on the horse—his specialty, along with collecting prized American Indian arrowheads. After a stint on HBO, several commericials and another book, *Eye on Cavett,* he was back in the familiar role of interviewer—this time on cable.

Born: November 19, 1936, in Kearney, Nebraska
Height: 5 ft. 7 in.
Weight: 140 lbs.
Eyes: Brown *Hair:* Blond
Zodiac: Scorpio
Education: Yale University
Religion: Protestant
Marriages: To Carrie Nye (1964–)
Children: None

Interests: Magic, American Indian culture (a major collector of Indian arrowheads and other artifacts), the theater, gymnastics
Personal Habits and Traits: Nonsmoker, moderate drinker, has a tremendous temper, avoids parties, spends a lot of time with good friend Woody Allen
Addresses: New York City; Montauk, Long Island
Income: $280,000+ (estimate)

Richard Chamberlain

"I've learned to get angry enough to tell people to go to hell, which you've got to do. Getting out of my shell was my biggest problem."

King of the television miniseries and the first American to dare *Hamlet* in England since Barrymore—and, unexpectedly, to pull it off—George Richard Chamberlain is forever known to millions as TV's germ-free *Dr. Kildare.* The heartthrob of Blair General Hospital actually grew up in Beverly Hills surrounded by affluence; his father owned a thriving supermarket fixture business that was eventually bought by Pet Milk and is now run by Richard's older brother Bill. A track star at Beverly Hills High School, Chamberlain graduated from Pomona College in 1956 and spent 16 months as an infantry company clerk in Korea; once home, he abandoned plans to become a painter ("too lonely") and instead studied drama with Jeff Corey. He landed *Kildare* in 1961, scoring high in the Nielsens for a full five seasons, and at the height of the show received 12,000 fan letters a week. Then he decided to abandon his pop success and take a stab at the classics: the British raved about his *Hamlet* and in 1970 he repeated his triumph on NBC-TV's *Hallmark Hall of Fame.* In the mid-1970s, Chamberlain plunged himself into the world of Alexander Dumas, beginning with Richard Lester's slapstick film *The Three Musketeers* (the most-often-filmed story in movie history) and its sequel, *The Four Musketeers,* then NBC's *The Count of Monte Cristo* and *The Man in the Iron Mask.* He played the unctuous villain in 1975's box-office smash *The Towering Inferno,* and gambled less successfully in portraying Lord Byron in the film *Lady Caroline Lamb*—as well as appearing in TV shows about two colorful figures from recent history: King Edward VIII and F. Scott Fitzgerald. He would have his greatest successes, however, with purely fictional characters—the English sailor, Blackthorne, stranded in medieval Japan in the NBC miniseries *Shogun,* and the sexy priest in *The Thorn Birds.* He very nearly topped that performance with his TV portrayals of Raoul Wallenberg, the Swede who saved thousands of Jews from the Nazis, and the explorer John C. Frémont in 1986's *Dream West.* Ensconced in a high-ceilinged Coldwater Canyon manse (he also keeps a flat on Bayswater Road in London), Chamberlain runs, plays tennis, and drives fast. A semirecluse who until recently had never been seriously linked with anyone romantically, he nonetheless went to a woman psychiatrist for four years—"until she finally went crazy."

Born: March 31, 1935, in Los Angeles, California
Height: 6 ft. 1 in.
Weight: 170 lbs.
Eyes: Blue *Hair:* Brown
Zodiac: Aries
Education: Pomona College, B.A. (1956)
Religion: Protestant
Marriages: None
Children: None
Interests: Hiking, riding, tennis
Personal Habits and Traits: Early riser, semireclusive, likes to drive fast
Addresses: Coldwater Canyon, California; London
Income: $2 million

Wilt Chamberlain

The son of 5-foot 8-inch parents, 7-foot 1-inch Wilton Norman Chamberlain finally chose one of 140 athletic scholarship offers—to the University of Kansas—then spent a year as a Harlem Globetrotter before returning to his hometown as a Philadelphia Warrior. For the next 14 years the legendary ''Wilt the Stilt'' shattered one basketball record after another until his retirement in 1973. He long claimed the most baskets (12,681), the most rebounds (23,924), and the most points (31,419) of any professional basketball player in history, but undoubtedly the high point of Chamberlain's career occurred during his penultimate season, when he led the Los Angeles Lakers (he also played on the San Francisco Warriors) to the NBA championship after a 33-game winning streak. Since retiring, Chamberlain has praised the VW for its ample headroom (''More than my Rolls-Royce'') on a TV commercial and has attended to his far-flung investments, ranging from real estate and racehorses to a women's volleyball team. Nor is Chamberlain—whose spectacular $1.5 million, mirror-ceilinged aerie in the Santa Monica mountains attracted a sizable number of birds—quite ready to live down his undisputed reputation as one of the highest scorers off the court as well.

Born: August 21, 1936, in Philadelphia, Pennsylvania
Height: 7 ft. 1 in.
Weight: 275 lbs.
Eyes: Brown *Hair:* Black
Zodiac: Leo
Education: University of Kansas
Religion: Protestant
Marriages: None
Children: None
Interests: Raising thoroughbred racehorses, investing in real estate, nightclubs
Personal Habits and Traits: Semireclusive, late sleeper, swinger
Address: Los Angeles
Income: $400,000 (minimum estimate)

Carol Channing

''I am terribly shy, but of course nobody believes me. Come to think of it, neither would I.''

Almost solely on the basis of two roles—Lorelei Lee in *Gentlemen Prefer Blondes* and Dolly Levi in *Hello, Dolly!*—plus her wide-eyed wackiness, Carol Channing has somehow managed to remain a top box-office celebrity. The Seattle-born daughter of Christian Science lecturer George Channing, Carol attended high school in San Francisco before being shipped to Bennington College in Vermont. Channing dropped out, headed for four years of oblivion on the Great White Way, and finally bloomed as the Gladiola Girl in 1948's *Lend an*

Ear. When, as Lorelei, she spouted "Diamonds Are a Girl's Best Friend," her shining star status was cinched. She replaced Rosalind Russell in *Wonderful Town,* teamed up with George Burns as his Gracie foil in Las Vegas and the nightclub circuit, and arrived in *Dolly* in 1963. During the Presidential election of that year Democrat Channing repeatedly belted out President Johnson's campaign jingle "Hello, Lyndon" at the White House. Having already brought a sequel to *Gentlemen* called *Lorelei* to Broadway in 1973, Channing took a revival of *Dolly* on the road for six months before reopening on Broadway in 1977. Because of her allergy to various chemicals in food, she invariably lugs along her own organically grown food and bottled water wherever she goes, even to the best restaurants. Channing and her third husband, producer-manager Charles Lowe, spend most of the year either at their luxurious apartment in the Waldorf Towers, their house in California, or on the road—most recently in a multistar revue of *Dolly* composer Jerry Herman's songs, called *Jerry's Girls*. Channing was typecast as the whacked-out White Queen in Irwin Allen's 1985 epic television production of Lewis Carroll's *Alice in Wonderland,* and kept herself in diamonds doing ads for American Express and Oscar Mayer.

Born: January 31, 1921, in Seattle, Washington
Height: 5 ft. 11 in.
Weight: 132 lbs.
Eyes: Blue *Hair:* Blonde
Zodiac: Aquarius
Education: Bennington College dropout
Religion: Christian Science
Marriages:
To Theodore Naidish (divorced)
To Alexander Carson (divorced)
To Charles Lowe (1956–)
Children: Channing George
Interests: Democratic party politics, gardening
Personal Habits and Traits: Nondrinker, late riser, punctual and disciplined; a food allergy forces Channing to carry her own supply of organically grown food and bottled water
Addresses: New York City; Los Angeles
Income: $500,000 (minimum estimate)

Prince Charles

His Royal Highness the Prince of Wales Duke of Cornwall and Rothesay, Earl of Chester and Carrick, Baron of Renfrew, Lord of the Isles and Great Steward of Scotland

"I would have been committed to an institution long ago were it not for my ability to see the funny side of life."

The man who would be king is—with the help of his wife—the most popular member of all European royalty. Born at Buckingham Palace four years before

Elizabeth was crowned, Charles Philip Arthur George Mountbatten-Windsor was the first British heir apparent ever to be shipped off to boarding schools, which his father Prince Philip hand-picked: first Cheam in Hampshire, then Gordonstoun in Scotland, where students always begin each day—whatever the weather—with a shirtless run followed by a cold shower. Then Charles spent six months at Timbertop, a wilderness school in Australia, before entering Cambridge University's Trinity College, where he received average marks and became something of a class clown, cavorting as the star of comic revues. Yet the dedicated royal scion crammed for a crash course in Welsh to placate nationalists during his 1969 investiture at Caernarvon Castle as Prince of Wales. As a result of his military service, he is a qualified paratrooper, jet fighter pilot, and minesweeper skipper; and is also an accomplished amateur cellist, scuba diver, polo player, skier, and student of history and anthropology. Although his mother has no intention of stepping down from the throne in the near future, Charles has already embraced such royal duties as dedicating hospitals and museums, reviewing troops (he is honorary colonel of 10 regiments and patron of 147 societies), and overseeing the Prince's Trust, a charity designed principally to aid juvenile offenders. Continual speculation about a future queen ended when Charles married the delicious Lady Diana Spencer, a former kindergarten teacher 13 years his junior. Their spectacular wedding at St. Paul's cathedral was *the* event of 1981. Despite some reported tension between Mom and her willful daughter-in-law (not to mention a full-fledged feud between his sister, Princess Anne, and Diana), Charles appeared to be the model husband and—after the arrival of sons William and Harry—a model father. (See also Diana, Princess of Wales.)

Born: November 14, 1948, in London, England
Height: 5 ft. 11 in.
Weight: 154 lbs.
Eyes: Blue *Hair:* Brown
Zodiac: Scorpio
Education: Trinity College, Cambridge
Religion: Anglican Church (he is "Defender of the Faith")
Marriages: To Diana Spencer (1981–)
Children: William (b. 1982), Harry (b. 1984)
Interests: Anthropology, music (he plays the cello), flying, parachuting, world affairs, polo, sailing
Personal Habits and Traits: Does not smoke, drinks only dry white wine, eats light meals, prefers the company of a handful of close friends, is punctual, polite, jogs in Windsor Park
Addresses: Buckingham Palace; Windsor Castle; Sandringham; Balmoral; Chevening House in Kent; Highgrove, Cotswolds; Isles of Scilly
Income: $600,000+

Ray Charles

Ray Charles Robinson

"I never wanted to be famous; I only wanted to be great."

Ray Charles has wrestled with blindness (probably caused by glaucoma when he was 6), a traumatic childhood, and a 15-year addiction to heroin on his way to becoming a legend of popular music. Little Ray was raised by both his real mother (his father's mistress), Retha, and his father's wife, Mary Jane, in Albany, Georgia, but Retha died when he was 15, and two years later his father passed away. By that time Ray, who had started playing piano at 3 and nurtured his talent at the St. Augustine School for the Deaf and Blind, was already jamming professionally with small groups in the Jacksonville-Orlando area in Florida. Modeling his smooth style after the late Nat King Cole, Charles—he dropped the "Robinson" because he didn't want to be confused with boxer Sugar Ray—captured a wide audience with his very first R&B recordings for Atlantic Records in the mid-1950s. His dynamic voice and soulful rhythm established "Hit the Road Jack," "What'd I Say, Georgia," and "I Can't Stop Loving You" as R&B classics, and nearly every major contemporary musical innovator from the Beatles to Billy Joel has acknowledged Ray Charles's pervasive influence. In fact, it was Charles who emerged as first among such equals as Joel, Lionel Richie, Michael Jackson, and Bob Dylan during the landmark all-night recording session that produced USA for Africa's "We Are the World" anthem. Yet ascending to the pinnacle of the entertainment world has not been as grueling as kicking his addiction to hard drugs. Arrested on narcotics charges several times since first shooting heroin at the age of 15, Charles abruptly went cold turkey at the age of 35 because he didn't "want other kids to tell my son that his daddy is a jailbird." Married and divorced three times, Charles now lives in Los Angeles and spends two-thirds of every year on the road. "Marriage is like college," he declares. "As great as it is, it ain't for *everybody.*" In one bizarre incident, a man leapt onstage at a celebrity-packed L.A. benefit and began choking the singer with a microphone cord. "Ray Charles will see and the Lord will come tonight," the attacker yelled before being hauled off by security guards.

Born: September 23, 1932, in Albany, Georgia
Height: 6 ft.
Weight: 160 lbs.
Eyes: Brown *Hair:* Black
Zodiac: Virgo
Education: High school
Religion: Baptist
Marriages: Three, all ending in divorce
Interests: Music
Personal Habits and Traits: Drinks moderately, kicked a 20-year heroin addiction
Address: Los Angeles
Income: $700,000 (minimum estimate)

Chevy Chase

Cornelius Crane Chase

''There really wasn't any experimentation with drugs that I hadn't tried. But I was never an over-the-line guy.''

''I'm Chevy Chase, and you're not. . . .'' Any young comedian would have wanted to be in 1975, when Chase, the preppy grandson of plumbing tycoon Cornelius Crane and son of book editor Ned Chase, bumped into young Canadian-born producer Lorne Michaels while waiting in line to see *Monty Python and the Holy Grail.* Michaels asked Chase to write for his new show, and Chase was soon leading his fellow Not Ready for Prime Time Players in an invasion of network television. On NBC's irreverent *Saturday Night Live,* Chase's trademark pratfalls (usually spoofing then-President Gerald Ford), deadpan delivery of his own material, and general standing as *SNL*'s arbiter of bad taste made him the show's first standout (to be followed by John Belushi, Dan Aykroyd, Gilda Radner, Jane Curtin, Bill Murray, Eddie Murphy and others). After a single season that earned him two Emmys, Chase departed to seek movie stardom at a starting salary of $1 million per film. His first, *Foul Play,* was a hit, as was *Caddyshack* with fellow *SNL* alumnus Murray. His career fizzled with a series of flops *(Under the Rainbow, Modern Problems, Heavenly Dog, Seems Like Old Times),* and after he jokingly called Cary Grant ''a homo,'' Grant sued. The suit was dropped after Chase apologized, and not long after Chase's professional slump ended with the enormously successful *National Lampoon's Vacation.* (the sequel, *European Vacation,* was not quite so commercial), *Fletch* and *Spies Like Us.* The turnaround ended a streak of self-destructive behavior that had included drugs and a steady diet of vodka martinis. After looking at 50 houses, Chase settled with his third wife and their infant daughter into a $1.5 million Tudor-style mansion in Pacific Palisades.

Born: October 8, 1943, in New York City
Height: 6 ft. 4 in.
Weight: 185 lbs.
Eyes: Brown *Hair:* Brown
Zodiac: Libra
Education: B.A. from Bard College, Annandale-on-Hudson, New York
Religion: Protestant
Marriages: Three. Currently to Jayni Chase (1982–)
Children: Cydney (b. 1983), Caley (b. 1985)
Interests: Jazz piano and drums, tennis, swimming, cooking
Personal Habits and Traits: Does not drink or smoke, has given up marijuana, sticks to a strictly preppy wardrobe
Address: Pacific Palisades, California
Income: $2 million annually (minimum estimate)

Cesar Chavez

"Anyone who comes in with the idea that farmworkers are free of sin and that the growers are all bastards is an idealist of the first order."

The Depression-era child of migrant workers who barely earned 50 cents a day picking peas, Cesar Chavez has devoted his life to improving the economic and social conditions of Mexican-American workers and preventing California produce farmers from replacing them with cheap *braceros* from across the border. A devout Catholic with eight children, Chavez formed a powerful farmworkers union and eventually gained the admiration and support of such liberals as Robert Kennedy and Eugene McCarthy. Chavez's most effective weapon: the personal hunger strike. A modern-day Messiah to some, a possessed rabble-rouser to others, Chavez launched a five-year-long boycott against grape and lettuce growers that finally resulted in unionization. But that victory only provoked an equally bitter squabble between Chavez's United Farmworkers and the powerful Teamsters over which union would ultimately represent the pickers. The issue of representation long remained one of California's major political hot potatoes, along with Cesar Chavez himself.

Born: March 31, 1927, in Yuma, Arizona
Height: 5 ft. 6 in.
Weight: 170 lbs.
Eyes: Brown *Hair:* Black
Zodiac: Aries
Education: High school
Religion: Roman Catholic
Marriages: To Helen Chavez
Children: Eight
Interests: Theater, Democratic Party politics
Personal Habits and Traits: Does not smoke, wine drinker, early riser
Address: Delano, California

Cher

Cherylynn La Piere

"You can do the most wonderful things when you're really *close. It's hard to take showers with only one of the five men you're dating."*

"It's hard to figure how I got known as a sex symbol or brazen woman when I've been married most of my life." Well, for starters, an estimated 20 million prime-time viewers were exposed each week to the personal collapse of her 11-year marriage to Sonny Bono over her flagrant affair with record mogul David Geffen, followed by Sonny and Cher cavorting on television while she carried rock star Gregg Allman's baby. Her marriage to Allman became, in fact, a public travesty; eight days after their marriage she filed for divorce, then stuck it out another two and a half years while Allman tried to kick drugs and liquor. No sooner were they divorced in 1978 than Cher hooked up for a time with Gene

Simmons, the blood-spewing bass guitarist for the outrageous rock group Kiss. Cherylynn La Piere can trace domestic chaos back to an unstable childhood in El Centro, California. Her mother, Georgia Holt, was married eight times—thrice to the same man. Her father, toward whom she still feels intense bitterness, abandoned Cher when she was only 1 year old. By the time "Pinky" (as she was known to teenage friends) and hotshot record promoter Sonny Bono spotted each other, she was already chanting "shang-a-langs" in local clubs. Married in 1964 at just 18, she and Sonny soon coupled professionally as well. One part hippie and one part Carnaby Street, they succeeded their first hit "Baby Please Don't Go" with a string of million-sellers like "I Got You Babe," "Bang Bang," and "The Beat Goes On." But a career eclipse found them performing in roadside dives and bowling alleys until 1970, when a shot at a summer replacement series resulted in their own successful CBS variety show. However, when their marriage dissolved, so did the series. While Sonny's attempt at a solo show on ABC fizzled instantly, Cher emerged as a national phenomenon—an exotically stylish (if not overly talented) superstar. Meanwhile, her recording career flourished with "Gypsies, Tramps and Thieves," and "Dark Lady." But although the 1975 arrival of her solo TV series *Cher* was heralded on the covers of *Time* and *People* magazines, she lasted only a single season before nervous network executives lured Sonny back into the fold, and the new *Sonny and Cher Show* survived through 1976. After a year's absence from television and a trip to a New York plastic surgeon to have her breasts lifted, Cher made the first of several opulent specials for ABC, and in 1979 registered a Top 10 hit with "Take Me Home." She almost took home an Acadamy Award three years later for her portrayal of Meryl Streep's far-from-glamorous lesbian pal in *Silkwood,* and was an odds-on favorite to be among the contenders once again for her heart-wrenching role as a deformed boy's biker mom in the true story *Mask.* Overlooked by the Academy, she nevertheless stole the 1986 Oscar show by turning up in a spectacularly tasteless, navel-baring getup. Now raising both Chastity (her daughter by Bono) and Elijah Blue (her son by Allman, whom she describes as an "absolutely worthless" dad), Cher plays house alone in Beverly Hills, Malibu, and at an elaborate Egyptian-style estate in Benedict Canyon.

Born: May 20, 1946, in El Centro, California
Height: 5 ft. 8½ in.
Weight: 110 lbs.
Eyes: Brown *Hair:* Black
Zodiac: Taurus
Education: High school dropout
Marriages:
To Salvatore ("Sonny") Bono (1964–1975)
To Gregg Allman (1975–1977)
Children: Chastity Bono (b. 1969), Elijah Blue Allman (b. 1976)
Interests: est, Democratic politics, children's welfare
Personal Habits and Traits: Nonsmoker, nondrinker, late riser, perennial dieter
Addresses: Beverly Hills; Malibu, California; Benedict Canyon, California
Income: $2 million (minimum estimate)

Chicago

The most popular pop-rock group of the 1970s, Chicago was still making millions off its heavy big band brass sound well into the next decade. The result has been a slick blend of blues, rock, jazz, and overlaid symphonics on more than a dozen gold singles and LPs. At one point in 1971, all of Chicago's first four albums were on the charts simultaneously, and among the group's biggest hits are "Saturday in the Park," "25 or 6 to 4," "Feelin' Stronger Every Day," "Make Me Smile," "Wishing You Were Here," "(I've Been) Searchin' So Long," "Dialogue," and "Does Anybody Really Know What Time It Is?" Ironically, the unofficial spokesman for the group is the only member not bred in the Windy City, Brooklynite Robert Lamm. Drummer Dan Seraphine, clarinetist Walt Parazaider, Walt Perry (clarinet and other woodwinds), hornplayer Lee Loughnane, and trombonist Jim Pankow all studied at Chicago's DePaul University, and all played with a variety of bands before pooling their respective talents. Under the guidance of producer-impresario James William Guercio, Chicago moved to Los Angeles and signed with Columbia in 1969. From that point on they churned out an unbroken string of hits and made over 200 concert appearances across the country each year. Perry eventually dropped out of the group, but the arrival of Laudir de Oliveira (formerly of Brazilian group Brasil '77) added a Latin flavor to Chicago. In 1978, however, tragedy struck when group member Terry Kath jokingly put a gun to his head and pulled the trigger, ending the life of one of Chicago's most gifted songwriters and singers at the age of 31. After Kath's funeral *Tonight Show* trumpeter Doc Severinson, a close friend of the band, convinced them to continue, and they auditioned 35 musicians before hiring Texan Donnie Dacus, who had just finished playing the lead in the movie version of *Hair*. Breaking with Guercio in 1978, Chicago signed with Helen Reddy's high-powered manager (and husband) Jeff Wald and proceeded to crank out platinum album number 12: *Hot Streets,* bearing the hit single "Alive Again." They were still burning up the track in the mid-1980s with Top 10 singles like "(You're a) Hard Habit to Break," "You're the Inspiration," and "Love Me Tomorrow." The eight members of Chicago are a "family"—albeit a very rich family, where each member has pocketed at least $2 million. "If you had told me back at the beginning that we'd someday own matching Rollses," says Jim Pankow, "I'd have laughed—or puked."

Julia Child

"I'm a kind of 'what-the-hell cook'—let things fall where they may."

"I was willing to put up with all that awful cooking to get Julia," Paul Child says of his wife's first failed attempts in the kitchen. But 20 years later, the indomitable Julia Child started her decade-long reign as the fumbling *French Chef* on public television, flubbing recipes and wisecracking about the private parts of fowl in a voice reminiscent of Eleanor Roosevelt. Born Julia McWilliams in Pasadena, California, she attended Smith College, wrote advertising copy for a New York furniture store for two years, then joined the OSS during World War II. While working as a cables clerk in Ceylon she met Paul Child, and they were together in Kunming, China, and later in Paris, where she imbibed haute cuisine at the famous Cordon Bleu cooking school. As young marrieds, the Childs were posted variously in Bonn, Oslo, Marseilles, and Washington. Then Julia collaborated with Simone Beck to write *Mastering the Art of French Cooking,* which sold an astounding 2 million-plus copies since 1961. A few years later she whipped up *The French Chef* and has since frosted the cake with several more bestselling cookbooks—all of which have helped finance a Cambridge, Massachusetts, home and a villa in the south of France. Her greatest personal hurdle thus far is the radical mastectomy she underwent in 1969.

Born: August 15, 1912, in Pasadena, California
Height: 6 ft. 1 in.
Weight: 161 lbs.
Eyes: Brown *Hair:* Gray-brown
Zodiac: Leo
Education: Smith College, Cordon Bleu Cooking School
Religion: Protestant

Marriages: To Paul Child (1946–)
Children: None
Interests: Art, chamber music (plays piano)
Personal Habits and Traits: Wine drinker, workaholic, tends to overeat
Addresses: Cambridge, Massachusetts; Grasse, France
Income: $1.2 million (estimate)

Julie Christie

"I'm an incredibly selfish and insecure person. I fear the future."

The cool but ravishingly beautiful blond who was haunted by Warren Beatty in both *Shampoo* and *Heaven Can Wait* was born to a tea planter in Assam, India, and schooled in England. At 16 she went to Paris to study art and French, then spent a year at Brighton Technical College before she finally found herself in London at the Central School of Speech Training and Dramatic Art. A bit part in John Schlesinger's *Billy Liar* led to a major role as a comely colleen in *Young Cassidy,* while her next picture, Schlesinger's *Darling,* earned Christie a 1965 Best Actress Oscar. She brought her ethereal beauty to David Lean's *Dr. Zhivago* and to the memorable *The Go-Between,* but she is probably best known to American audiences for the movies in which she has shared star billing with then-offscreen-lover Beatty: *McCabe and Mrs. Miller,* in which she played a feisty Old West madam; and *Shampoo,* where Julie finally washes Warren out of her hair—until he reappears in the afterlife, in *Heaven Can Wait*.

Born: April 14, 1941, in Assam, India
Height: 5 ft. 7 in.
Weight: 116 lbs.
Eyes: Blue *Hair:* Blond
Zodiac: Aries
Education: Central School of Speech Training and Dramatic Art, London
Religion: Anglican
Marriages: None
Children: None
Interests: Cooking, transcendental meditation
Personal Habits and Traits: Smokes, drinks, but fitness-conscious, a workaholic
Address: London
Income: $400,000 (estimate)

Eric Clapton

Eric Clap

"We're all playing melody against each other. Our aim is to get so far away from the original line that you're playing something that's never been heard before."

One of the most prevalent pieces of graffiti in the late 1960s from London to New York to California was "Eric Clapton is God." Well, a rock 'n' roll god, anyway. Eric Clapton can trace his meandering career through several seminal groups of the 1960s and '70s, including the Yardbirds, John Mayall's Bluesbreakers, Cream, Blind Faith, Delaney and Bonnie, and Derek and the Dominos—not to mention his own hit-making Eric Clapton Group, formed in April 1974. Born in Ripley, Surrey, and raised by his grandparents, the Claps, Eric studied at the Kingston School of Art to become a stained-glass designer until he was expelled at the age of 17 for playing the guitar in class. Fascinated by the

music of Bo Diddley, Chuck Berry, and B. B. King, he joined the Roosters in 1963 and within three years was acknowledged to be the finest guitar player in the business. Along with George Harrison, Bob Dylan, and Leon Russell, he participated in Harrison's landmark Bangladesh Concert at Madison Square Garden in 1971, and two years later altered his career by signing a contract to record for superpromoter Robert Stigwood's fledgling RSO Records. Clapton's daring experiments with reggae in the mid-1970s resulted in the monster single "I Shot the Sheriff," and Clapton's 1978 album *Slowhand* went double platinum—selling an astounding 2 million + copies and spinning off the number-one single "Lay Down Sally." His moderately successful late-1985 LP, *Behind the Sun,* did not exactly eclipse his earlier musical achievements.

Born: March 30, 1945, in Ripley, England
Height: 5 ft. 9¼ in.
Weight: 151 lbs.
Eyes: Brown *Hair:* Brown
Zodiac: Aries
Education: Kingston School of Art
Religion: Anglican
Marriages: To Patti Harrison (1980–)
Children: None
Interests: Composing, design
Personal Habits and Traits: Soft-spoken, semireclusive, a loner
Address: Los Angeles
Income: $400,000

Dick Clark

"Get in my way when I really want to accomplish something, I can be a mean mother."

His career was no blooper. Dick Clark's *American Bandstand* has claimed two generations of bona fide teenage rockaholics. Clark started early; he was only 5 when he published his own gossip sheet (for two cents) back home in Mount Vernon, New York. Idolizing such heroes as Arthur Godfrey, young Clark secured his first part-time announcer job when his father became manager of a radio station in Utica, New York. Then Clark switched to television on Philadelphia's WFIL-TV, and soon his clean-cut good looks and self-assured delivery landed him a number of commercials. But the turning point came in 1956, when he took over a local program called *Bandstand.* An instant smash as soon as it went network a few months later, the show attracted more than 8 million viewers as the number-one daytime show in the country. Clark, who quickly established 33 different companies to capitalize on the show's success, was grossing over $1 million a year by 1960, but about that time, Congressional investigators uncovered "payola"—the hyping of certain record sales by deejays who were receiving bribes from record companies—and Clark, though everyone agreed he had broken no laws whatsoever, was persuaded by ABC to sell his own record companies at a loss of $8 million. Since then, however, he has made up for his loss many times over. Today Dick Clark Productions is a lucrative mini-conglomerate of interlocking corporations that arranges rock concerts, produces

TV programs (including the annual *American Music Awards, The $25,000 Pyramid, The $100,000 Pyramid, Bandstand,* and the made-for-TV movies, *Elvis* and *Birth of the Beatles*), and record albums (such as the million-selling anthology *Dick Clark's 20 Years of Rock*), stages Las Vegas spectaculars like *Good Ol' Rock 'n' Roll,* and operates L.A.'s radio station KPRO. Unfortunately, his *Live Wednesday* was axed with eight other NBC shows by network whiz Fred Silverman in late 1978. By the mid-1980s, prime-time audiences were gobbling up the leftovers served on his *TV's Bloopers and Practical Jokes* and *Foul-Ups, Bleeps and Blunders,* and *Puttin' On the Hits.* An international audience watched as Clark hosted 1985's spectacular Live Aid concert to benefit starving Ethiopians. After two divorces, the seemingly ageless and mercurial Clark married his executive assistant, Kari Wigton, in 1977. They share a deco-perfect 39th-floor penthouse at Manhattan's Trump Plaza and a plush Malibu beach house with a waterfall in the living room. Clark, who launched his Dick Clark's *Nitetime* show in syndication in 1985, has hinted that he plans to step down from the *American Bandstand* podium in 1987.

Born: November 30, 1929, in Mount Vernon, New York
Height: 5 ft. 8 in.
Weight: 152 lbs.
Eyes: Brown *Hair:* Brown
Zodiac: Sagittarius
Education: High school
Religion: Protestant
Marriages:
To Bobbie Mallery (divorced)
To Loretta Martin (divorced)
To Kari Wigton (1977–)

Children: Richard (b. 1957), Duane (b. 1963), Cindy (b. 1965)
Interests: Work
Personal Habits and Traits: Nonsmoker, social drinker, is an unstoppable worker
Addresses: Malibu, California; New York City
Income: $7 million. Estimated net worth: $100 million

Jill Clayburgh

"I want to be an actress—not a personality."

The rising star of the 1978 smash *An Unmarried Woman* is the granddaughter of 1920s diva Alma Clayburgh and daughter of a theatrical secretary. But Jill did not become interested in acting until a friend talked her into a walk-on role in a summer stock production of *Man and Superman.* At the Charles Street Repertory Theater in Boston she met fellow novice Al Pacino and lived with him for five years while she worked on the TV soap opera *Search for Tomorrow* before reaching Broadway in *The Rothschilds* (1970), *Pippin,* and eventually *Jumpers* (1974). Ironically, her change of boyfriend from actor Pacino to playwright David Rabe *(The Basic Training of Pavlo Hummel, Streamers)* was accompanied by a switch from stage to movies. *Gable and Lombard* was a miserable flop, though her portrayal of the endearing but foul-mouthed comedienne was admira-

ble, and she rebounded playing the love interest opposite Kris Kristofferson and Burt Reynolds in *Semi-Tough* (1977) and opposite Gene Wilder in *Silver Streak.* Occasional made-for-TV movies like *Hustling* (for which she won an Emmy nomination in 1975) kept her off the unemployment line, but with Paul Mazursky's *An Unmarried Woman,* Clayburgh stepped into the front ranks of her profession. She also quelled association with the film's title when she wed Rabe in 1979. She ended up the decade with a smash comedy *(Starting Over),* but the early 1980s proved professionally disastrous for Clayburgh, who starred in flop *(My Turn)* after flop *(First Monday in October)* after flop *(I'm Dancing as Fast as I Can)* after flop *(Hannah K.).*

Born: April 30, 1944, in New York City
Height: 5 ft. 8 in.
Weight: 121 lbs.
Eyes: Blue *Hair:* Brown/blond
Zodiac: Taurus
Education: High school
Religion: Protestant
Marriages: To David Rabe (1979–)
Children: Lily (b. 1982)
Interests: Dance, the theater, cooking, psychotherapy (in analysis beginning at the age of nine)
Personal Habits and Traits: Smokes, drinks moderately, avoids publicity, reflective, early riser, takes exercise classes
Addresses: New York City; Los Angeles
Income: $500,000+

Glenn Close

"I did it on my own."

Named after her godmother, Glenn Andrews, this Greenwich, Connecticut, native was raised on the family's 500-acre estate and as a child fantasized about being discovered by Walt Disney. After her father, a Harvard-trained surgeon, opened a clinic in Zaire (then the Belgian Congo), Glenn and her three siblings alternated among Africa, Connecticut, and boarding schools in Switzerland. As a student at toney Rosemary Hall in Greenwich, Glenn organized a theater troupe called "The Fingernails—The Group with Polish," and wound up playing Romeo in the group's first production. After graduating Phi Beta Kappa from William and Mary, Close performed in regional theater and on Broadway in the hit musical *Barnum,* then aged herself to portray Robin Williams's liberated, sex-hating mom in the film version of *The World According to Garp. Garp* marked her first Academy Award nomination; she was nominated not long after for *The Big Chill* and for *The Natural.* Long before her Broadway smash *The Real Thing,* Close proved she was.

Born: March 19, 1947, in Greenwich, Connecticut
Height: 5 ft. 4 in.
Weight: 110 lbs.
Eyes: Gray-blue *Hair:* Blond
Zodiac: Pisces
Education: B.A., William and Mary
Religion: Protestant
Marriages:
To Cabot Wade (divorced)
To James Marlas (1984–)
Children: None
Interests: Tennis, riding, reading, singing the national anthem at Mets games
Personal Habits and Traits: Outgoing, nonsmoker, light drinker, plays some raquetball, does needlepoint between scenes while working on stage
Address: New York City
Income: $400,000 per year (minimum estimate)

James Coburn

"I used to play heavies, get shot and die a lot. It was marvelous."

Continually mistaken for Lee Marvin, James Coburn is the son of a Ford auto mechanic who migrated to California at the height of the Depression. Army service, acting courses at Los Angeles City College and a stint with drama coach Stella Adler led to a Remington commercial and then his first film, a Randolph Scott western called *Ride Lonesome.* (In that same year, 1959, he experimented with LSD.) Coburn was one of the stars of 1963's *The Great Escape,* but it was not until he saddled up with Yul Brynner in *The Magnificent Seven* that he was touted as Hollywood's newest antihero. *Our Man Flint* and *In Like Flint* proved he could carry a movie himself. Coburn felt confident enough to try his hand at producing *The President's Analyst,* directing television's *The Rockford Files,* and doing second-unit work on the film *Convoy* (starring Kris Kristofferson and Ali MacGraw). At 50 Coburn starred as Dashiell Hammett's Hamilton Nash in CBS's miniseries *The Dain Curse* and shared the marquee with Sophia Loren in *Firepower;* however, Coburn, who owns two Ferraris and lives in a 22-room Beverly Hills manse was once best known and paid for ($850,000) as the mean-faced cowhand who ordered Schlitz Light on television, getting the most money for the fewest lines in the history of the medium. His salary was even higher for his series of MasterCard commercials, though in 1986 that particular gravy train was derailed when MasterCard hired on Angela Lansbury, Jackie Gleason and Robert Duvall to tout their product.

Born: August 31, 1928, in Laurel, Nebraska
Height: 6 ft. 2 in.
Weight: 173 lbs.
Eyes: Grayish green *Hair:* Salt and pepper
Zodiac: Virgo
Education: Los Angeles City College
Religion: Protestant
Marriages: To Beverly Kelly (1959–1978)
Children: Lisa (b. 1956), James (b. 1961)
Interests: Biorhythms, Sufi meditation, Chinese exercises, fasting, playing the flute, directing and producing for television and films, driving fast
Personal Habits and Traits: Chain smoker, moderate drinker, fitness fiend
Address: Beverly Hills
Income: $2 million

Joe Cocker

"I've always done me little theatricality bit of throwin' me arms about with the music. Some people think it's too much. But it's not contrived. Why would anyone want to contrive a stage routine that turns so many people off?"

The hard-drinking, unruly King of White Soul graduated from Central Tech in the English industrial town of Sheffield and worked as a gas-fitter before discovering that he could successfully emulate mentor Ray Charles—the single greatest influence on Cocker's musical development. Cocker began indulging heavily in drugs and in 1968 cut a laid-back, bluesy rendition of the Beatles' psychedelic "With a Little Help From My Friends." The album of the same name proved a smash in Europe, and in the summer of 1969 Joe Cocker's Big Blues Band made the first of several U.S. tours in which Cocker exhibited his contorted gestures and convulsive body movements—and became identified as a male Janis Joplin. Over the years his hits have ranged from the hard-driving "Delta Lady" to the breathless ballad "You Are So Beautiful." Considered one of rock's *enfants terribles,* Cocker and his Mad Dogs and Englishmen were virtually kicked out of Australia following a drug conviction, yet when he returned Down Under in the summer of 1977 Cocker enacted a repeat performance—throwing up at Perth Airport, then chugging whiskey while he badgered his hosts during a TV interview. A year later, Cocker had toned down his act enough to cut his single "Fun Time," and to tour small clubs in the United States. But it did little to raise the $400,000 he needed to buy himself out of his old record contract. His career soared again in 1982 with his number-one duet with Jennifer Warnes, the Oscar-winning love theme from *An Officer and a Gentleman.*

Born: May 20, 1944, in Sheffield, England
Height: 5 ft. 9 in.
Weight: 165 lbs.
Eyes: Blue *Hair:* Brown and thinning
Zodiac: Taurus
Education: Central Technical School, Sheffield

Marriages: None
Children: None
Personal Habits and Traits: Smokes, heavy drinker (usually whiskey), erratic, volatile, gets up at dusk and goes to bed at dawn
Address: London
Income: $200,000 (1981 estimate)

Natalie Cole

"I can't get the guilties about being an entertainer. I sing for the Lord."

Nat King Cole's talented daughter grew up in the stately Hancock Park section of Los Angeles surrounded by neighbors Harry Belafonte and Ella Fitzgerald. Like her satin-voiced father, who first started out as a musician, Natalie did not sing professionally until, while earning a degree in psychology at the University of

Massachusetts (and occasionally dabbling in acid and mescaline), she began to play small clubs in the Boston area. Blending soul and disco, she finally struck gold in 1975 with the upbeat single "This Will Be" and her first album *Inseparable*—both of which ran away with Grammys. Four more albums and two hit singles ("Love on My Mind" and "Our Love") kept her high on both the pop and rhythm-and-blues charts through 1978, when she headlined her first television special on CBS. Cole's husband, producer, chief songwriter, and preacher were the same man: Marvin Yancy, an ordained Baptist minister whom she hired in 1974 and married two years later. Dividing their time between New York, Los Angeles, and Chicago—where Yancy managed his music production offices and preached to a growing congregation every Sunday—it still wasn't all smooth sailing. Just prior to their marriage, Preacher Yancy was slapped with a paternity suit that he only settled by agreeing to pay child support. When they did get married in 1976, Cole and Yancy took their vows in the back of a white Eldorado heading for Chicago's O'Hare airport. The Cadillac dropped Cole off to fly to L.A. for a performance—and then drove back to town where Yancy had to conduct a funeral. They separated less than three years later. Cole still finds herself fielding questions about her long-standing public feud with Queen of Soul Aretha Franklin. Now, claims Cole, the war is over, as is her career-disrupting dependence on cocaine. Cole's drug problem became so acute that in 1983 her mother was named her legal steward. Two years later, having beaten her drug dependence, Cole released what may be the best album of her career: *Dangerous.* At about the same time tragedy struck again when Yancy, the father of her son, died suddenly of a heart attack.

Born: February 6, 1950, in Los Angeles, California
Height: 5 ft. 9 in.
Weight: 120 lbs.
Eyes: Brown *Hair:* Brown
Zodiac: Aquarius
Education: University of Massachusetts, B.A. in psychology
Religion: Baptist (converted from Episcopalian)
Marriages: To Marvin Yancy (1976–1979)
Children: Robert Adam (b. 1977)
Interests: Music of all kinds, songwriting, religion, human behavior, politics
Personal Habits and Traits: A nonsmoker, modest drinker, strong-willed, incisive, revels in being a mother
Addresses: Los Angeles; New York; Chicago
Income: $500,000 (minimum estimate)

Gary Coleman

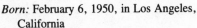

"I have four corporations. You could say I'm a conglomerate."

By 1985, this only child of Sue and Willie Coleman conceded that playing the mischievous Arnold of NBC's *Diff'rent Strokes* was "getting a little boring"—

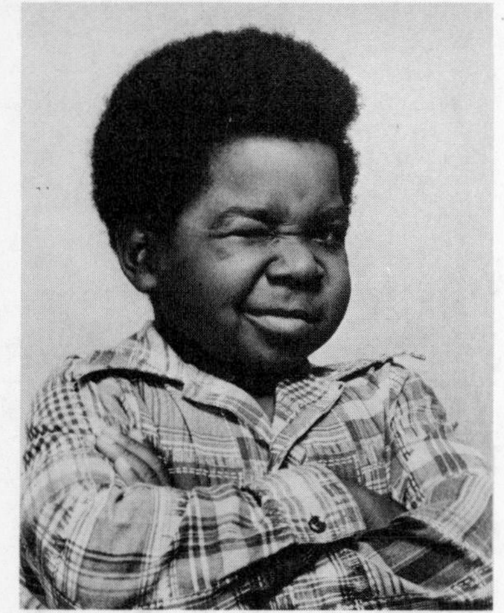

but not so boring that he wouldn't hang in for another season at $30,000+ per episode. Coleman's boundless energies seem all the more remarkable in view of his heroic battle against congenital kidney disease; he underwent one kidney transplant in 1973, and after it failed underwent years of dialysis until a second transplant in late 1984. Steroids used to treat Coleman stunted his growth (he is not likely to ever be taller than an even 5 feet) and probably puffed up his chipmunk cheeks. Undaunted, Coleman returned to the set within weeks of his second transplant, and continued to seek out projects for his own production company, Zephyr. Among his hit TV movies: *The Kid from Left Field, The Kid with the Broken Halo,* and *Playing with Fire*. Coleman divides his time between a rented West Los Angeles house and his parents' home in the Chicago suburb of Zion.

Born: February 8, 1968, in Zion, Illinois
Height: 4 ft. 7 in.
Weight: 80 lbs.
Eyes: Brown *Hair:* Black
Zodiac: Aquarius
Religion: Protestant
Interests: Electric trains (he has an extensive collection)
Personal Habits and Traits: A perfectionist ("I criticize everything"), tense, at times self-important
Addresses: Los Angeles; Zion, Illinois
Income: $30,000 per week (base salary)

Jackie Collins

"My message to men is, 'Don't screw around with women because they can turn around and screw you back.'"

They are the biggest sister act to hit Hollywood since Olivia De Havilland and Joan Fontaine, but apparently with none of the animosity. While Joan Collins steamed things up in *Dynasty,* her little sister Jackie was cranking out one torrid bestseller after another. A teenager wild enough to be one of her own characters, Jackie learned that sex sells when she started charging her pals for a peek at the torrid (and largely made-up) passages in her diary. Kicked out of school at 15 for smoking, Jackie soon thereafter accepted her movie star sister's invitation to come to California. Jackie was 18 when she wed an executive 12 years her senior. A manic depressive and drug addict, he died four years after the wedding. Three years later she married another businessman, Oscar Lerman. Her first book, *The World is Full of Married Men,* was dubbed "the most disgusting book ever written" by one British critic and promptly shot to the top of the bestseller lists. Her next literary efforts, 1977's *The Stud* and *The Bitch* (1980), served as vehicles for her sister's return to the big screen in the late 1970s. In 1983, she scored her biggest hit with *Hollywood Wives,* which was made into a TV miniseries. A stay-at-home and self-described voyeur ("I like to observe; Joan likes to participate"), Jackie promised to drop the other shoe with—of course—*Hollywood Husbands*. Her 1985 novel: *Lucky*. And that she is.

Born: October 4, 1941, in London
Height: 5 ft. 6 in.
Weight: 120 pounds
Eyes: Hazel *Hair:* Light brown
Zodiac: Libra
Education: High school dropout
Marriages:
Wallace Austin (1959)
Oscar Lerman (1966–)

Children: Tiffany (b. 1967) Rory (b. 1969)
Interests: Art deco, photography
Personal Habits and Traits: Writes her novels in longhand, nonsmoker, light drinker, up every day at 7 A.M., wardrobe consists mainly of jeans, sweaters, and men's suits
Address: Beverly Hills
Income: $2 million+ per book

Joan Collins

''Alexis is ruthless, ambitious, and pure as the driven slush.''

The Dynastiest member of ABC's hit prime-time soap family grew up the eldest daughter of a London booking agent, and made her acting debut at age 9 in a West End production of Ibsen's *A Doll's House*. She played a boy. Beginning with 1952's eminently forgettable *Lady Godiva Rides Again,* Collins fogged up the lens in more than 50 mostly mediocre films. In 1955 alone, she played the exquisitely evil Queen Nellifer in Howard Hawks's epic *Land of the Pharaohs,* stole Sir Walter Raleigh away from Bette Davis's Elizabeth I in *The Virgin Queen* and seduced architect Stanford White in *The Girl in the Red Velvet Swing*. Her sexpot days seemingly over by the 1960s, Collins paid the bills by acting in a number of horror films *(Tales from the Crypt, Empire of the Ants)*. Offscreen, however, her lovers included Nicky Hilton, Rafael Trujillo, Warren Beatty (they were briefly engaged), Ryan O'Neal, and Anthony Newley, whom she married after a drugging and sexual assault by first husband Maxwell Reed (all of which was detailed in her torrid memoirs, *Past Imperfect*). In the '70s, Collins bared all in *The Stud* and *The Bitch,* screen adaptations of little sister Jackie's novels that were produced by Joan's third husband, Ronald Kass. Although these racy movies once again made her bankable in Europe, it was not until August 1981, when she was brought in as *Dynasty*'s answer to J.R., the scheming Alexis, that Collins reached bona fide international superstar status. Krystle's nemesis was arguably television's most despised/adored character, and Collins was receiving around 12,000 love-hate letters per week. Says Collins: ''It's a great role—a larger-than-life bitch.'' Away from the cameras, Collins appears disarmingly warm, gracious, and informal. TV's toughest cookie prefers to spend her few free moments with youngest daughter Katy, who sustained severe brain injuries when she was struck by a car in 1980. Collins remained at Katy's bedside while she lay in a coma for six weeks, then took an active role in her recovery. Collins has cashed in on Alexis's mantislike persona with endorsements for Revlon's Scoundrel perfume to the tune of $2.3 million over three years, as well as commercials for a number of other products. She also proved she could rack up the ratings *sans* Alexis with the sinfully successful 1986 miniseries *Sins*. A sequel, *Monte Carlo*, was in the works a few short months later. Having ridden the show business roller coaster for decades, Collins is philosophical about it all: "I just happen to be," she told *People* magazine, "the busiest 'flavor-of-the-month brunette.'" Collins picked a decidedly unchic setting for her spur-of-the-moment marriage to Peter Holm, a Swedish pop star-turned-businessman 14 years her junior: They were wed at the Little White Chapel in Las Vegas.

Born: May 23, 1933, in London
Height: 5 ft. 6 in.
Weight: 120 pounds
Eyes: Gray-green *Hair:* Dark brown
Zodiac: Gemini
Religion: Protestant
Marriages:
To Maxwell Reed (1952–1957)
To Anthony Newley (1963–1970)
To Ronald Kass (1972–1983)
To Peter Holm (1985–)

Children: Tara (b. 1964), Sacha (b. 1966), Katy (b. 1972)
Interests: Photography, antiques, raising funds for neurological research (following her daughter's accident)
Personal Habits and Traits: Smokes, drinks moderately, witty
Address: Beverly Hills
Income: $2.5 million+

Perry Como

Pierino Roland Como

"The audience knows I'm not going to do anything after all these years to upset them."

Pierino Roland Como was born the seventh son of a seventh son, and endured a poverty-stricken childhood in Canonsburg, Pennsylvania, where his father labored as a mill hand to support 13 children. At the age of 14 Perry worked in his own barbershop, but stuck to singing for his customers until one of them suggested he audition for Freddy Carlone's band. With his relaxed, Italian crooner style, Como eventually rivaled Sinatra at the Paramount Theater when he sang his first million-seller "Till the End of Time." He may have flopped in Hollywood during the 1940s, but audiences flocked to see him in Las Vegas, and year after year over the next 20 Como always scored at least one hit record, including "Catch a Falling Star," "Hot Diggety Dog Diggety," "I Love You (and Don't You Forget It)," "Seattle," "It's Impossible," and "And I Love You So." In the late 1950s and early '60s he appeared as the cardigan-clad host of his own weekly variety series sponsored by Kraft, and when he left the series Kraft put down *$25 million* for seven Como specials. Today the singer and his wife Roselle are the most famous residents of Jupiter, Florida—well, with the possible exception of Burt Reynolds.

Born: May 18, 1912, in Canonsburg, Pennsylvania
Height: 5 ft. 6 in.
Weight: 150 lbs.
Eyes: Brown *Hair:* Silver
Zodiac: Taurus
Education: High school
Religion: Roman Catholic
Marriages: To Roselle Beline (1933–)
Children: Two sons, one daughter
Interests: Golf (a 6 handicap), fishing
Personal Habits and Traits: Nonsmoker, moderate drinker, sleeps late, inveterate dieter
Address: Jupiter, Florida
Income: $1 million+

Sean Connery

"I have always hated that damn James Bond. I'd love to kill him."

The rough-hewn son of a Scottish lorry driver—"Scotland Forever" and "Mum & Dad" are tattooed on his forearm and are camouflaged with makeup before filming—Connery rocketed to international stardom during the 1960s as the quintessential James Bond. But after films like *Dr. No, Goldfinger, From Russia with Love,* and *You Only Live Twice,* he found himself shackled by the image of the suave, sophisticated, womanizing spy created by Ian Fleming. Hounded by those who charged that he had gone to seed physically (he competed once for the Mr. Universe title), and mentally (he went to Norway to be treated by respected shrink Ola Raknes), Connery proved he could still cut the mustard by shooting one more Bond film, *Diamonds Are Forever,* in 1971. Un-Bonded thrillers like *The Next Man* failed to take off, but the famous Scot carved out a new career for himself in such lavish period flicks as *The Wind and the Lion, Robin and Marian* (in which he played an aging Robin Hood), and John Huston's film of Rudyard Kipling's *The Man Who Would Be King*. Later, Connery and costar Michael Caine sued Allied Artists for $109,000 each, profits they claimed were due them from Huston's film. Unwilling to make the move to Hollywood, Connery resides in England with his second wife, French-Moroccan portrait painter Micheline Roquebrune. He scored another triumph in Michael Crichton's *The Great Train Robbery,* then bombed in MGM's $15 million astral epic *Meteor* and Richard Lester's *Cuba*. Connery returned to the role that first made him famous in 1983's *Never Say Never Again.*

Born: August 25, 1930, in Edinburgh, Scotland
Height: 6 ft. 2 in.
Weight: 185 lbs.
Eyes: Brown *Hair:* Black
Zodiac: Virgo
Education: High school dropout
Religion: Protestant
Marriages:
To Diane Cilento (1962–1971)
To Micheline Roquebrune (1974–)
Children: One
Interests: Music, art, theater
Personal Habits and Traits: Smokes, moderate drinker, disciplined actor, mercurial
Address: London
Income: $3 million per film

Jimmy Connors

James Scott Connors, Jr.

"About every five weeks I get depressed with my life and I have to get away from the game. Hell, there has to be more to life than tennis."

Supplanted by John McEnroe as *l'enfant terrible* of tennis, James Scott Connors, Jr., is nonetheless the game's reigning comeback king. His grandmother, pro Bertha Thompson, and his stage mother, Georgia, also a teaching pro, raised Jimmy and his big brother Johnny as tennis prodigies. While Johnny exhibited the more natural talent, Jimmy practiced so doggedly that by 12 he had driven his brother out of the competition. At 16, Pancho Segura stepped in to tutor Jimmy, and within two years Connors was acknowledged to be one of the most promising young players in the country. While a freshman at UCLA, he claimed the NCAA singles title, then decided to drop out of college and turn pro. In 1974 Connors and his sometime fiancée Chris Evert—dubbed the "Love Match" of the century—swept the singles titles at Wimbledon. Later that year he also triumphed at Forest Hills and by 1976 was dating beautiful jock groupie and former Miss World Marjorie Wallace. Toppled as number one by Bjorn Borg, Connors remains one of the best players in the world and cashes in to the tune of some $1 million annually. He was also one of the least popular players on the court, despite repeated, visible efforts to restrain himself from baiting officials and fans. His most famous photograph shows Connors flipping the finger to spectators who booed his conduct during a match in Virginia. Three years later he secretly married his pregnant girlfriend Patti McGuire, *Playboy* magazine's 1977 Playmate of the Year. And in 1982 he managed to win both Wimbledon and the U.S. Open for the first time since 1974. By 1986, Connors picked up a microphone and was threatening to follow O.J. Simpson, Bruce Jenner, and other former jocks into the broadcast booth as a commentator.

Born: September 2, 1952, in St. Louis, Missouri
Height: 6 ft.
Weight: 165 lbs.
Eyes: Brown *Hair:* Light brown
Zodiac: Virgo
Education: UCLA dropout
Marriages: To Patti McGuire (1979 –)
Children: Brett David (b. 1979), Aubree (b. 1984)
Interests: Backgammon, television
Personal Habits and Traits: Does not smoke, drinks little, stays up late, is extremely close to his mother, parties a great deal
Address: Los Angeles
Income: $1 million +

Rita Coolidge

"The fame won't last forever, but we will."

Eclipsed for years by her high-flying husband Kris Kristofferson, Rita Coolidge reappeared on the pop-rock scene in the late 1970s with "Higher and Higher" and "We're All Alone." The daughter of a Baptist preacher, she harmonized in church choirs as a child and soon became a skilled piano player. Her family moved from Nashville to Florida, and at Florida State University (she majored in lithography) she formed her own band called RC and the Moon Pies, then traveled to Memphis to sing jingles on radio spots for a record company. Coolidge headed for Los Angeles and soon met Delaney and Bonnie, who signed her as a backup singer—the beginning of a new and lucrative career wailing behind the likes of Eric Clapton, Stephen Stills, David Mason, and Joe Cocker. That led to her memorable solo of Leon Russell's "Superstar" in Cocker's celebrated Mad Dogs and Englishmen tour (in which Leon Russell also starred). A sultry-voiced beauty, Coolidge toured as a team with her husband, though his heavy drinking and cavorting nude with Sarah Miles on the set of *The Sailor Who Fell From Grace With the Sea* were factors contributing to the destruction of their marriage (even though Kristofferson finally went on the wagon after filming *A Star is Born,* in which he played—appropriately enough—a boozing, self-destructive rock star). Divorce papers were filed by Kristofferson after nearly six years of often stormy marriage. Coolidge's career took a new turn when she signed on with MTV's competition, VH-1, as one of the new breed of V.J.s—video disk jockeys.

Born: May 1, 1945, in Nashville, Tennessee
Height: 5 ft. 8 in.
Weight: 120 lbs.
Eyes: Dark brown *Hair:* Black
Zodiac: Taurus
Education: Florida State University
Religion: Baptist
Marriages: To Kris Kristofferson (1974–1980)
Children: Casey (b. 1974)
Interests: Her daughter, songwriting, gardening, cooking
Personal Habits and Traits: A nonsmoker, does not drink, is ambitious, a perfectionist
Address: Los Angeles
Income: $450,000 (minimum estimate)

Alice Cooper

Vincent Damon Furnier

"The best things in life—don't make sense."

Born Vincent Damon Furnier in Detroit, he suffered from asthma and eczema as a child. But in 1971 at age 23 Furnier suddenly transformed himself into Alice

Cooper, aptly designated by *Time* magazine as the "king, queen, unicorn and Godzilla of schlock rock." Alice Cooper and his group featured simulated hangings, electrocutions, decapitations, and an assorted variety of bizarre props—including a boa constrictor that, at a high (or was it low?) point in the show, slithered down Alice's body and darted its head between his legs. Oddly enough, much of this Grand Guignol led to a rush on record counters, and beginning with *I'm 18,* he pocketed millions in record sales as the Alice Cooper phenomenon peaked with "School's Out" and "Dead Babies." Then his group began to squabble—"We began to have the same exact fights we had when we were poor, except, 'That's my tomato you're eating,' turned into, 'That's my Rolls, get your ass out of it'"—and broke up after seven albums. As a solo act, Alice barnstormed the country with his *Welcome to My Nightmare* stage extravaganza, and later reaped a television special from it. After seven years together, Cooper split from girlfriend Cynthia Lang in 1975 and married singer Sheryl Goddard in Acapulco. Lang promptly sued Cooper for $5 million. Alice now maintains a 40-room mansion in Greenwich, Connecticut, and a sprawling ranch house in Paradise Valley, Arizona, just outside his hometown Phoenix, where Alice's dad once preached. Proclaiming that "the ugly is gone for good" at the conclusion of his 1976 autobiography *Me, Alice,* Cooper cleaned up his image and recorded a ballad on his own that spun straight to the top—"Working Man."

Born: February 4, 1948, in Detroit, Michigan
Height: 5 ft. 10 in.
Weight: 170 lbs.
Eyes: Green *Hair:* Dark brown
Zodiac: Aquarius
Education: High school
Religion: Roman Catholic
Marriages: To Sheryl Goddard (1976–)
Children: Calico (b. 1981)
Interests: Cooking, writing
Personal Habits and Traits: Nonsmoker, on the wagon
Addresses: Paradise Valley, Arizona; Greenwich, Connecticut
Income: $200,000 (estimate) (net worth $10 million in 1986)

Francis Ford Coppola

"I would like to take over a major studio. It's very tempting to have real power."

The first in a new wave of big-budget epic directors that includes William Friedkin *(The French Connection, The Exorcist),* Steven Spielberg *(Jaws, Close Encounters of the Third Kind)* and George Lucas *(American Graffiti, Star Wars),* Francis Ford Coppola collected one Best Director and two Best Picture Oscars for *The Godfather* and *The Godfather, Part II.* From a close-knit Italian family (his father composed the music for the *Godfathers* and his sister, Talia Shire, launched her acting career in them), Coppola grew up in Queens and earned a bachelor of arts degree in theater at Hofstra University; his first film, the critically acclaimed *You're a Big Boy Now,* served as his master's thesis. Almost as successful a screenwriter as a director (he also won Oscars for writing *Patton* and *The Conversation*), Coppola dropped a major bomb with *Finian's Rainbow* before his now-classic *Godfather* outstripped *Gone With the Wind* as the biggest-grossing film of all time. Shunning the old Hollywood power struggle, he has become the godfather himself to Spielberg, John Milius, Lucas, and a handful of other directors and screenwriters, each encouraging one another's work and sharing ''points'' in one another's pictures. Ironically, no sooner had Spielberg's *Jaws* replaced *The Godfather* as the number-one all-time money-grosser than Lucas's *Star Wars* topped *Jaws,* and in 1978 *Close Encounters,* Spielberg's UFO saga, gave *Star Wars* a run for its money at the box office. The following year Coppola staked his entire career on the controversial Vietnam war saga *Apocalypse Now*. Plagued by storms and various disasters during filming in the Philippines, the *Apocalypse* budget soared well beyond $26 million. In the process, Coppola mortgaged his house to finance his gamble, smashed four of his five Oscars in a fit of fury, and wound up briefly separating from his wife, Eleanor Neil. *Apocalypse* opened to mixed reviews, but they were raves compared to what Coppola faced from critics and the moviegoing public alike with the release of his epic *The Cotton Club*.

Born: 1940 in New York City
Height: 6 ft.
Weight: 190 lbs.
Eyes: Brown *Hair:* Brown
Education: Hofstra University, B.A., M.F.A.
Religion: Roman Catholic
Marriages: To Eleanor Neil
Children: Three
Interests: Screenwriting, cars, urban restoration in San Francisco, opera, community theater
Personal Habits and Traits: Smokes Havana cigars, drinks moderately, is passionate when discussing his work but generally soft-spoken
Addresses: San Francisco; Los Angeles
Income: $8 million for *Cotton Club* alone

Bill Cosby

''I wasn't always black. One morning I woke up and looked in the mirror. There was this freckle, and it got bigger and bigger. . . .''

His *Bill Cosby Show* was the number-one series on television in 1986. Still, Cosby is one of the very few top stars to claim the distinction of bombing on all three major networks—although he also ranks in the '80s as the medium's favorite huckster, for Ford, Jell-O, and Coca-Cola. His roots are in Philadelphia, but Bill Cosby is one of the entire country's most sought-after comics with his characterizations of Fat Albert, Weird Harold, and Dumb Donald. He dropped out of high school to join the Navy, earned his diploma through correspondence courses, then enrolled at Temple University on a football scholarship. While tending bar at night he discovered he was so adroit at making customers laugh that he decided to perform a stand-up comic routine of his own. At the height of his nightclub career he was signed to costar with Robert Culp in the comedy

adventure series *I Spy,* for which he copped three of his five Emmys. *The Bill Cosby Show* followed, as well as a number of top-rated specials, appearances in *The Children's Theater* and *The Electric Company,* and the CBS drama *To All My Friends on Shore.* While his comedy albums continued to earn Grammys (six as of 1978), Cosby's ability to stay afloat as a prime-time attraction sank with the cancellation of *Cos* in 1976. Still, his animated Saturday CBS series *Fat Albert and the Cosby Kids,* his films *(Mother, Juggs and Speed, Uptown Saturday Night,* and *The Devil and Max Devlin),* commercials, and frequent nightclub and concert appearances continue to finance a rather lavish life-style for this son of an $8-a-day maid and her boozing husband, that includes a $1.5 million mansion and a white-jacketed butler, and blackjack forays to Lake Tahoe and Las Vegas. Cosby received his doctorate in education at the University of Massachusetts in 1977, and moved his wife Camille and their five children to New York, where he tapes *The Bill Cosby Show.*

Born: July 12, 1937, in Philadelphia, Pennsylvania
Height: 6 ft. 1 in.
Weight: 185 lbs.
Eyes: Brown *Hair:* Black
Zodiac: Cancer
Education: Temple University, B.A., University of Massachusetts at Amherst, Ph.D. in education
Religion: Protestant
Marriages: To Camille Hanks (1964–)
Children: Daughters Erika (b. 1965), Erinn (b. 1966), Ensa Camille (b. 1973), Evin (b. 1976), son Ennis (b. 1979)
Interests: Education, social work
Personal Habits and Traits: Smokes cigars, drinks moderately, weight-conscious, night person, enjoys gambling
Address: New York City
Income: $10 million+

Howard Cosell

Howard William Cohen

''They didn't give me looks, but they gave me an absolute monopoly on brains and talent.''

America's most loquacious and controversial sportscaster is the son of Polish-Jewish immigrants. Born in Winston-Salem, North Carolina, and raised in Brooklyn, New York, Cosell started talking at nine months (and has not stopped yet). Twenty years later he graduated with a degree in law from New York University, where he was Phi Beta Kappa and editor of *Law Review.* While practicing law in 1953 he was asked by ABC radio to gather and host a panel of Little Leaguers who would interview big-name athletes for a new program series. The results were so impressive that the network hired him as a sports commentator in 1956. Described as "a sufferable egotist" by one ABC executive, Cosell—the brash, arrogant inquisitor with a staccato delivery and unparalleled penchant for verbal arabesques—became something of a national institution.

Though his florid style proved a plus in interviews with Muhammad Ali (Cosell was the first announcer to stop calling the fighter Cassius Clay), Joe Namath, and other sports greats, it proved a decided disadvantage when he attempted a variety series, *Saturday Night Live with Howard Cosell.* For the most part Cosell, like his toupee, is an audacious put-on—though a shrewd one who has long earned well over $1 million a year. After a series of disappointments at ABC, Cosell vented his spleen on a variety of sports-related topics in his 1985 bestseller *I Never Played the Game.*

Born: March 25, 1920, in Winston-Salem, North Carolina
Height: 6 ft. 2½ in.
Weight: 195 lbs.
Eyes: Brown *Hair:* Brown (wears toupee)
Zodiac: Aries
Education: New York University, L.L.D.
Religion: Jewish
Marriages: To Edith (''Emi'') Abrams (1944–)
Children: Jill, Hilary
Interests: Politics and the law, his grandchildren
Personal Habits and Traits: Smokes cigars, drinks moderately, talks incessantly
Addresses: Manhattan; Pound Ridge, New York; Westhampton, Long Island
Income: $1 million

Walter Cronkite

''And that's the way it is. . . .''

Each night, every night, more than 20 million Americans sat glued to their television sets to hear Uncle Walter, who over 30 years managed to become television's most authoritative and trusted reporter. A siren-chaser for the *Houston Post* in the 1930s and later a sportscaster (he used wire-service copy and sound effects to create his own ''replays'' of games he never saw), Cronkite joined United Press as a European correspondent during World War II. CBS nabbed him in 1950, and by the 1960s Cronkite was battling for ratings against the NBC news team of Chet Huntley and David Brinkley—a war Cronkite finally won in 1967. Over the years the most popular newsman in TV history has covered every story from the assassination of President John F. Kennedy (the only time Cronkite ever cried on the air) and America's space program to Vietnam and Watergate. Ironically, his on-the-air demeanor bears little resemblance to Cronkite's off-camera escapades. Although he gave up auto racing in 1960 after his Triumph missed a curve and plunged 100 feet into a river, leaving him shaken but unhurt, Cronkite is an inveterate tennis player, yachtsman, jazz fanatic, and intrepid terpsichorean who will foxtrot or fandango at the drop of a baton. But each weekday evening he reverted to the ultimate reporter, writing his own copy and receiving updates on the telephone in a last-minute flurry before air time. His biggest worry was losing his voice, which happened rarely, but the story that he suffered a sudden attack of diarrhea while on the air is apocryphal.

Cronkite retired from his anchor spot in 1981, and was replaced by Dan Rather. His subsequent effort, a science series called *Universe,* was short-lived.

Born: November 4, 1916, in St. Joseph, Missouri
Height: 6 ft.
Weight: 190 lbs.
Eyes: Blue *Hair:* White
Zodiac: Scorpio
Education: University of Texas
Religion: Episcopalian
Marriages: To Mary Elizabeth Maxwell (1940–)
Children: Nancy (b. 1949), Kathy (b. 1951), Chip (b. 1958)
Interests: Sailing, flying, space exploration
Personal Habits and Traits: Smokes a pipe, drinks, a bit of a social butterfly, loves to dance and to sing
Addresses: New York; Martha's Vineyard
Income: $1 million (minimum estimate)

David Crosby

''I knew I needed help when drugs became more important in my life than my music.''

The son of an Oscar-winning cinematographer, temperamental David Crosby was thrown out of The Byrds in 1968 before he connected with Stephen Stills and Graham Nash during a ''family'' party at folk-rock leading light Joni Mitchell's house. Bursting on the national music scene at Woodstock in 1969, Crosby, Stills and Nash (and often Neil Young) spent the next five years churning out gold and platinum records that diluted the acid rock of the 1960s with a smooth California sound. ''Judy Blue Eyes,'' ''Marrakesh Express,'' and ''Teach Your Children'' were among their many hits, but in 1974 a clash of egos finally shattered the group. Three years later during a duo tour by Crosby and Nash, Stills leapt up on stage to chime in on ''Teach Your Children,'' and the group was reborn. Within six months they had recorded their million-selling album *CSN* and one of their biggest single hits ever, ''Just a Song Before I Go.'' Crosby was sentenced to five years for cocaine and gun possession stemming from a 1982 arrest in a Dallas nightclub. He sold his 60-foot schooner *Mayan,* and about the only asset he had left was his Mill Valley, California, house by the time he was ordered to enter a drug treatment program at Fair Oaks Hospital in New Jersey pending his Texas convictions. He skipped the program in 1985, pleading ''raw nerves.'' That same year, he managed to join Stills, Nash and Young for a reunion onstage at the internationally broadcast Live Aid concert.

Born: August 14, 1941, in Los Angeles, California
Height: 5 ft. 10½ in.
Weight: 220 lbs.
Eyes: Brown *Hair:* Brown
Zodiac: Leo
Education: High school
Marriages: None
Children: None
Interests: Collects knives and prisms, sails, studies acting, writes screenplays, loves classical music
Personal Habits and Traits: Smokes, overeats, is bluff, gregarious, a night person
Address: Mill Valley, California

Roger Daltrey

"Of course, chicks keep popping up. When you're in a hotel, a pretty young lady makes life bearable."

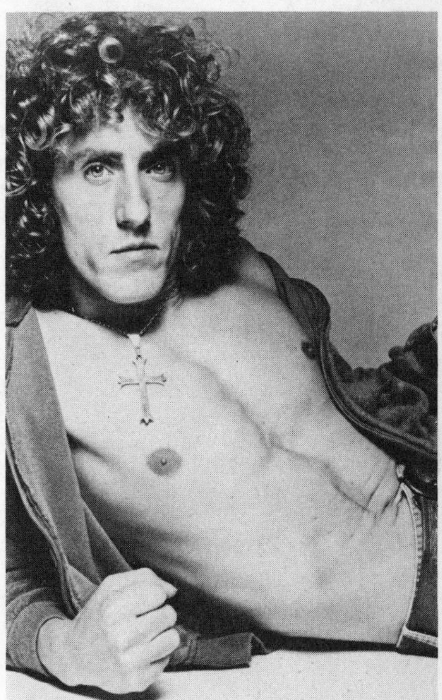

Expelled from the Acton Grammar School in West London at age 15, this son of a toilet salesman was a violent, chain-wielding "Teddy Boy" until he harnessed his explosive energy as a rock singer. With bassist John Entwistle, guitarist Peter Townshend, and the late Keith Moon on drums, Daltrey formed The Who in 1965, and over the next decade The Who carved a niche for itself as one of the longest-running supergroups in rock history, peaking with Ken Russell's kaleidoscopic 1974 film of the group's rock opera *Tommy*. Daltrey starred in the title role and followed up as a libidinous Franz Liszt in Russell's excessive movie "biography" of the Hungarian composer, *Lisztomania*. Lord of Homshurst Manor, a sprawling 17th-century estate ornate with stained glass and Persian carpets, Daltrey enjoys a lavish if generally wholesome life-style with his second wife, Heather (Daltrey married his first wife because she was pregnant, then divorced her soon afterward), and their two daughters, Rosie Lea and Willow Amber; Simon, his son by his first marriage, is a frequent visitor. Frank about his sex life, Daltrey admits to frequent liaisons on the road—a fact that Heather seems to accept grudgingly. The Who's *Quadrophenia,* based on their album of the same name, was an unqualified success. But that triumph was marred soon thereafter when 11 fans were killed in a stampede at a Who concert in Cincinnati. Daltrey eventually struck out on his own.

Born: March 1, 1945, in Hammersmith, England
Height: 5 ft. 7 in.
Weight: 134 lbs.
Eyes: Blue *Hair:* Blond
Zodiac: Pisces
Education: Dropped out of school at 15
Religion: Anglican
Marriages: Two. Currently to Heather Taylor
Children: Simon (b. 1964), by first wife; Rosie Lea (b. 1972), Willow Amber (b. 1975), by Taylor
Interests: Farming, working on his estate, playing guitar and flute, horseback riding
Personal Habits and Traits: Does not smoke, drinks in moderation, has violent temper, outspoken
Address: Sussex, England
Income: $1.33 million (minimum estimate)

John Davidson

''My face has always held me back, acting-wise, because it's very straight. Producers and casting people never felt this person inside me could go through an emotional catharsis.''

''The Boy With Nothing Extra'' as he was unjustly labeled after the demise of his TV series with Sally Field, *The Girl With Something Extra,* young Davidson wanted to follow in his father's footsteps as a Baptist minister. But fresh out of Denison University with a degree in theater arts, he headed to New York and garnered a lead role opposite Bert Lahr in Broadway's *Foxy*. The musical lasted just long enough for Davidson to be spotted by TV producer Bob Banner, who promptly signed the dimpled baritone with the-boy-next-door appeal to star in a 1964 variety series called *The Entertainers*. Later, he hosted off-season replacements like *The Kraft Summer Music Hall* and *The John Davidson Show,* as well as appearing literally hundreds of times on *Hollywood Squares* and as a frequent substitute host for Johnny Carson on *Tonight*. Yet his career as an actor was still grounded by 1973, so Davidson imitated Burt Reynolds's bravado and posed nude—appendix scar and all—for a *Cosmopolitan* centerfold. In Davidson's case, however, the gambit backfired; appalled fans wrote that it ''was like looking at your 13-year-old brother.'' Still, Davidson remains one of the best-known entertainers in America, particularly to millions of swooning over-30 housewives. Early in 1977 Davidson narrowly escaped death while his musical director was killed along with 163 others when fire swept through the Beverly Hills Supper Club in Kentucky where he was performing. Later that year he headed a benefit for children of the victims. In a subsequent effort to become the Arthur Murray of nightclub singers, Davidson set up a ''camp'' for would-be stars on Catalina Island. In 1980 he debuted on the prime time ABC hit *That's Incredible* and replaced Mike Douglas as host of a nationally syndicated talk show when Douglas's option was dropped by Westinghouse Broadcasting in a reported dispute over increasing his $2.5 million salary. *The John Davidson Show* lasted on the air several years, but after it was canceled in 1983 he returned to supper clubs, Las Vegas, and Atlantic City.

Born: December 13, 1941, in Pittsburgh, Pennsylvania
Height: 6 ft.
Weight: 170 lbs.
Eyes: Blue *Hair:* Brown
Zodiac: Sagittarius
Education: Denison University, B.A. in theater arts
Religion: Baptist
Marriages: To Jackie Miller (1969–1980)
Children: John Jr. (b. 1970), Jennifer (b. 1972)
Interests: Guitar, acting, horse breeding, horseback riding, backpacking, boating (he owns a yacht)
Personal Habits and Traits: Nonsmoker, drinks moderately, early riser
Address: Hidden Hills, California
Income: $1.5 million

Bette Davis

Ruth Elizabeth Davis

"We movie stars all end up by ourselves. Who knows? Maybe we want to."

Katharine Hepburn's closest rival for the title of greatest living American movie actress, Bette Davis has won Best Actress Academy Awards for *Dangerous* and *Jezebel,* and has starred in such Hollywood classics as *Of Human Bondage, Dark Victory, Now Voyager, The Letter, All About Eve, Elizabeth and Essex,* and *Whatever Happened to Baby Jane?* Her remarkable career has spanned a half-century and more than 83 films; and in the spring of 1977 Bette Davis became the first woman to receive the American Film Institute's Life Achievement Award (joining the likes of John Ford, James Cagney, Orson Welles, William Wyler, and Henry Fonda). On the road to that honor she also lost four husbands (one by death, three by divorce), gave birth to a daughter, B.D., and adopted two other children during her stormy marriage to Gary Merrill (Michael practices law in Germany and Margot is in a home for the retarded). The ultimate Yankee, Davis grew up the daughter of a strong-willed housewife and a lawyer father. Her parents split when she was eight and Bette was packed off to boarding school, but Davis's mother supervised her daughter's acting career and supported her in New York while she went to acting school. She eventually toured in a successful production of *The Wild Duck,* and once settled in Hollywood, made 23 dreadful films before capturing the role of Mildred in 1934's *Of Human Bondage.* She married her high school sweetheart at 24—"I was a virgin until I was married"—and divorced him six years later; was widowed when businessman Arthur Farnsworth died three years after their marriage; and divorced painter William Grant Sherry in 1950, when her career suddenly hit rock bottom. But when she was asked to replace Claudette Colbert in *All About Eve* after Colbert injured her back, the role of Margo Channing proved legendary, and she married Gary Merrill, her costar in the picture. But Davis had divorced husband number four by the time she teamed up with Joan Crawford to win another Oscar nomination for the thriller *Whatever Happened to Baby Jane?* in 1961. More chillers followed, like *Dead Ringer* (in which she murders herself) and *Hush, Hush, Sweet Charlotte,* and by the late 1970s she seemed locked into the genre. Her more recent credits include the TV miniseries *Harvest Home,* based on the Tom Tryon bestseller, and the embarrassing *Burnt Offerings.* After a few episodes, Davis was forced to bow out of the hit NBC series *Hotel* because of breast cancer and then a stroke, and her old *All About Eve* nemesis, Anne Baxter, stepped into the role (ironically, it was Baxter who suffered a stroke and died). Rocked by her born-again daughter B.D.'s tell-all book, *My Mother's Keeper,* the lady with the Bette Davis eyes suddenly found herself coping with allegations that she was a boozer and brawler who, among other things, once tore a Thanksgiving turkey apart with her bare hands and threw the parts at her astonished guests. Davis's favorite line: "I'd love to kiss you—but I just washed my hair."

Born: April 5, 1908, in Lowell, Massachusetts
Height: 5 ft. 3 in.
Weight: 129 lbs.
Eyes: Blue *Hair:* Blond
Zodiac: Aries
Education: High school
Religion: Protestant
Marriages:
To Harmon Oscar Nelson, Jr. (1932–1938)
To Arthur Farnsworth (1940–1943)
To William Grant Sherry (1945–1950)
To Gary Merrill (1950–1961)
Children: Barbara (''B.D.''), Margot, Michael
Interests: Literature, gardening, cooking
Personal Habits and Traits: Chain-smokes mild cigarettes even after her stroke and mastectomy but never inhales, has an occasional drink, outspoken, articulate
Address: Weston, Connecticut
Income: $250,000 (minimum estimate)

Mac Davis

''I stay calm for three months, then I let it out. . . . And it's over in a matter of seconds.''

His father made Mac join the church choir at the age of 10—as a soprano. After working as a ditchdigger, gas station attendant, and probation officer, he broke into show business writing songs for other artists—including Elvis Presley (''In the Ghetto,'' ''Memories''), Kenny Rogers and the First Edition (''Something's Burning''), Bobby Goldsboro (''Watching Scotty Grow''), Glen Campbell (''I'll Paint You a Song''), and O. C. Smith (''Don't Cry, Daddy,'' ''Friend, Lover, Woman, Wife''). His own theme ''I Believe in Music'' was recorded by over 50 major artists, and his own gold records include ''Baby, Don't Get Hooked on Me'' and ''One Hell of a Woman.'' All of which led to a People's Choice Award and his being selected in 1975 as the Academy of Country Music's Entertainer of the Year. One of the most even-tempered and least affected of all major country music stars, Davis led a scandal-free life until his wife, Sarah, left him and married Glen Campbell. He made his movie debut playing Nick Nolte's pro football buddy in *North Dallas 40.* At 5 feet, 10 inches tall, however, he was far smaller than the other guys in the huddle. So for several shots he used a technique perfected by Alan Ladd—he stood on a box. *North Dallas 40* was a hit. Unfortunately, Davis's later efforts, like *Sting II,* were not.

Born: January 21, 1942, in Lubbock, Texas
Height: 5 ft. 10 in.
Weight: 170 lbs.
Eyes: Blue *Hair:* Brown
Zodiac: Aquarius
Education: Emory University, Atlanta
Religion: Baptist
Marriages: Two, both ending in divorce
Children: Scotty
Interests: Songwriting, performing, comedy
Personal Habits and Traits: Nonsmoker, a beer drinker, can sleep anywhere, is messy, watches his weight
Address: Los Angeles
Income: $1 million (estimate)

Sammy Davis, Jr.

"A black person never leaves the ghetto."

From his marriage to the beautiful Swede Mai Britt to his endorsement of Richard Nixon with a kiss on the cheek, the only one-eyed black Jew in show business, "Candy Man" Sammy Davis, Jr., has been a controversial American entertainer for over a quarter-century. Sammy started out hoofing with his father and Will Mastin as part of the Will Mastin trio. When he broke out on his own in the 1950s, he instantly became a top nightclub draw and later a Broadway sensation in *Golden Boy* and *Mr. Wonderful*. Frank Sinatra initiated him into the Rat Pack, and soon Davis was shooting movies like *Porgy and Bess, Oceans 11, Sweet Charity,* and even the James Bond flick *Diamonds Are Forever*. He also made several forays into television, such as his "Here Come De Judge" slapstick on *Laugh-In,* his visit to the Bunker household in *All in the Family,* and finally his own national talk show, *Sammy & Company*. His phenomenally successful recording of the theme from *Willie Wonka and the Chocolate Factory,* "The Candy Man," shot him back on top of the recording world in 1974. For the past several years his income has averaged a tidy $3 million a year. Throughout, Davis's personal life has been a constant source of controversy. He denies it was the Mob that forced him to stop dating Kim Novak in the 1950s. "If it had only been a sordid affair, if we'd hidden and jumped into some grubby hotel bed it would have been okay, but for a black man and a white woman to be open about love was unacceptable." Davis, who described an early homosexual experience in a startling *People* interview, blames an excess of booze and drugs for the failure of his eight-year marriage to Britt.

Born: December 8, 1925, in New York City
Height: 5 ft. 3 in.
Weight: 115 lbs.
Eyes: Brown *Hair:* Black
Zodiac: Sagittarius
Education: High school
Religion: Jewish (converted)
Marriages:
To Leray White (divorced)
To Mai Britt (1960–1968)
To Altovise Gore (1970–)
Children: Tracy, Jeff, Mark (both boys adopted)
Interests: Plays a number of instruments, interested in theology, history, literature, cars
Personal Habits and Traits: Chain-smoker, wears lots of gold jewelry, golfs, rides horseback
Address: Beverly Hills
Income: $3 million+

Doris Day

Doris von Kappelhoff

"The really frightening thing about middle age is knowing you'll outgrow it."

"I knew Doris Day *before* she was a virgin" is a standard Hollywood line—and with good reason. Although she has acted in respectable melodramas *(The Man Who Knew Too Much, Love Me or Leave Me)* and memorable musicals *(Calamity Jane, Jumbo, The Pajama Game),* she became the top box-office draw in the late 1950s and early '60s because of her saccharine roles opposite the likes of Clark Gable *(Teacher's Pet,)* Cary Grant *(That Touch of Mink),* David Niven *(Please Don't Eat the Daisies),* and most often Rock Hudson *(Pillow Talk, Lover Come Back, The Thrill of It All).* No less successful in the recording studio, her top-10 hits included "It's Magic," "Lullaby of Broadway," "Secret Love," "Teacher's Pet," "Everybody Loves a Lover," and "Que Será, Será"—her theme song. Born Doris von Kappelhoff in Cincinnati, she changed her name when a nightclub owner heard her singing "Day by Day." ("Thank God I wasn't singing *Götterdämmerung,*" she says.) When Betty Hutton bowed out of *Romance on the High Seas* in 1948, freckle-faced Day won the part. After brief marriages to trombonist Al Jordon and sax player George Weidler, she wed manager Marty Melcher in 1951 and had been married 17 years when Melcher died of a heart attack (the year after Day made her long-delayed debut as the star of her own sitcom). The *Doris Day Show* ranked high in the Nielsens until the series ended in 1972, and two years later Day received a $26,396,511 windfall when the courts decided she had been defrauded over a 20-year period by her longtime legal adviser Jerome B. Rosenthal. Shortly after the publication of her frank autobiography (with A. E. Hotchner), Day married Barry D. Comden, a health-food-store owner 12 years her junior. That union lasted barely three years. Still under contract to Equinox, the record company owned by her music tycoon son Terry Melcher, Day is an unabashed animal lover ("To kill a living thing to make a coat is a crime") who always keeps a dozen stray dogs in her home. To promote her new cable TV show about animals in 1985, Day posed with old buddy Rock Hudson only days before he shocked the world by flying to Paris to be treated for AIDS, the disease that killed him only a few months later.

Born: April 3, 1924, in Cincinnati, Ohio
Height: 5 ft. 6 in.
Weight: 115 lbs.
Eyes: Blue *Hair:* Blond
Zodiac: Aries
Education: High school
Religion: Christian Scientist
Marriages:
To Al Jordon (divorced)
To George Weidler (divorced)
To Martin Melcher (1951 until his death in 1968)
To Barry D. Comden (1976–1979)
Children: Terry Melcher
Interests: Animals (specifically dogs)
Personal Habits and Traits: Nonsmoker, nondrinker, early riser, bicycles, swims
Address: Beverly Hills
Income: $500,000 + (in interests and investments)

Catherine Deneuve

"All the doors automatically open for a beautiful woman. I know it's very fashionable for good-looking ladies to say how hard it is to be beautiful, but that's not true."

"You don't have to ask for it. He knows what you want—Chanel." With that sensually whispered sales pitch, France's top movie star became television's most persuasive saleswoman (she also growled her way through TV spots for Mercury Cougar). Françoise Dorleac, already an up-and-coming star when she was killed in an auto accident in 1967, had persuaded her younger sister, Catherine, to break into films. Acting under her mother's name, the icily beautiful Deneuve left an indelible impression in *Belle de Jour, The Umbrellas of Cherbourg, Repulsion* (in which Roman Polanski cast her as a psychotic killer), *Mayerling,* and *The April Fools.* Deneuve is equally famous for her offscreen escapades: she bore a child by French director Roger Vadim between his marriages to Brigitte Bardot and Jane Fonda, married and divorced British pop photographer David Bailey, had a fling with Burt Reynolds, and gave birth to a daughter by Italian superstar Marcello Mastroianni. Her Chanel spots proved so successful that in 1986 the sexy French star launched a fragrance bearing her own name.

Born: October 22, 1943, in Paris
Height: 5 ft. 6 in.
Weight: 117 lbs.
Eyes: Brown *Hair:* Blond
Zodiac: Libra
Education: High school
Religion: Roman Catholic
Marriages: To David Bailey (divorced after five years)
Children: Christian (b. 1963, by Roger Vadim); Chiara (b. 1972, by Marcello Mastroianni)
Interests: Her children, music, art, clothes
Personal Habits and Traits: Drinks moderately, sleeps late, enjoys travel
Address: Paris
Income: $600,000 (estimate)

Robert De Niro

"There is a certain combination of anarchy and discipline in the way I work."

The son of two Greenwich Village artists, Robert De Niro was 30 and had been acting professionally for half his life when he finally attracted well-deserved attention in the role of a baseball catcher in *Bang the Drum Slowly* and as a junkie in the gritty *Mean Streets.* Only two years later he won an Oscar as Best Supporting Actor playing young Vito Corleone in *The Godfather, Part II.* Martin Scorsese's *Taxi Driver* gave him the opportunity to portray an introverted psychopath, followed by an urbane movie mogul (ostensibly Irving Thalberg) in *The Last Tycoon,* Liza Minnelli's bitter, sax-playing husband in *New York, New York,* and a young steelworker in the terrifying and brilliant *The Deer Hunter.*

With each role Robert De Niro comes closer to proving that he may be the outstanding actor of his generation. Until they split, De Niro and his exotically beautiful wife Diahnne Abbott (she stole *New York, New York* simply by singing *Honeysuckle Rose* in a Harlem scene) occupied a brownstone in Greenwich Village and a house in Los Angeles' affluent Brentwood section, where they frequented rock hangouts like the Roxy. A hard-driving perfectionist who never can get enough camera takes to be totally satisfied with a scene, De Niro gained 30 pounds, did roadwork, and sparred to prepare for his performance in Scorsese's film biography of boxer Jake La Motta, *Raging Bull.* The role earned him a second Academy Award, this time as Best Actor of 1980. His work in Sergio Leone's *Once Upon a Time in America* and in *The King of Comedy* was praised by the critics, but audiences fell out of love—at least temporarily—with De Niro and Meryl Streep when they starred in the leaden *Falling In Love.* De Niro took on the role of an 18th-century South American slave trader turned priest in *The Mission.*

Born: August 17, 1943, in New York City
Height: 5 ft. 9 in.
Weight: 148 lbs.
Eyes: Brown *Hair:* Dark brown
Zodiac: Leo
Education: High school
Religion: Roman Catholic
Marriages: To Diahnne Abbott (1975–1978)
Children: Raphael (b. 1976)
Interests: Art, music, films
Personal Habits and Traits: Is a workaholic, likes rock music, Italian food, Black Russians
Addresses: New York City; Brentwood, California
Income: $2 million+

John Denver

Henry John Deutschendorf, Jr.

"My Rocky Mountain highs have been balanced by incredible lows. When I get depressed, I question whether life is worth living."

This winsome country boy in gold-rimmed glasses and neatly pressed cowboy shirts is actually Henry John Deutschendorf, Jr., who grew up all over the United States as the son of an Air Force lieutenant colonel. Young H. J. was given his first guitar—a 1910 Gibson—by his grandfather when he was 13 and studied architecture at Texas Tech University for two and a half years before dropping out to replace Chad Mitchell as lead singer of the Chad Mitchell Trio in 1965. Changing his name to John Denver, he parlayed a knack for songwriting and his earnest though reedy tenor into a folk-rock dynamo that churns out platinum albums, number-one singles, top-rated TV specials, and multimillion-dollar concert tours. Appealing primarily to middle-class young marrieds with tunes like "Leaving on a Jet Plane" (made into a hit by Peter, Paul and Mary in 1969),

"Rocky Mountain High," "Country Roads," "Calypso," and "Fly Away" (with Olivia Newton-John), Denver managed to gather a huge following before starring in his first film, *Oh, God!*, with George Burns. A firm believer in est, this Tom Sawyer of the music world lived with his wife, Annie, and their children in a $500,000 split-level home in Starwood, near Aspen, Colorado. Yet his marriage was anything but idyllic. In 1975, he wrote the ballad "Annie's Song" after a brief separation. "It was only six days," recalls Annie, "but it felt like six months." Ironically, the causes of that brief split were Denver's moodiness and the schedule that kept him away from home for months at a time. Apparently the damage was irreparable; the Denvers divorced in 1979. Unable to father children ("People were blown away when I was willing to tell them I'm sterile"), Denver adopted Zachary John, who is part Cherokee, and Japanese-American Anna Kate. Their dad spends as much time as he can with them at their redwood-and-glass house. The steamy "Don't Close Your Eyes Tonight" video from his 1985 *Dreamland Express* album was intended to jazz up his "St. John" image. It didn't.

Born: December 31, 1943, in Roswell, New Mexico
Height: 5 ft. 9½ in.
Weight: 146 lbs.
Eyes: Blue *Hair:* Blond
Zodiac: Capricorn
Education: 2½ years at Texas Tech University
Religion: Protestant
Marriages: To Annie Denver (1967–1979)
Children: Zachary John (b. 1975), Anna Kate (b. 1977) (both adopted)
Interests: Hiking, guitar, forestry, skiing, aikido, est, pyramid power, space exploration, ERA
Personal Habits and Traits: Smokes an occasional joint, teetotaler, courteous, soft-spoken, moody, likes to garden in the nude
Address: Starwood, Colorado (near Aspen)
Income: $1.5 million (estimate)

Bo Derek

Mary Cathleen Collins Derek

"If John sees that I'm getting into a little danger, he will warn me. You are your environment, and for 24 hours a day he is my environment, as I am his."

The perfect "10" started out the oldest of four children born to a Long Beach, California, motorcycle salesman and his Hollywood hairdresser wife. Mary Cathleen Collins was a 16-year-old who had just dropped out of high school when her mother took her to Las Vegas to see a client, Ann-Margret. Bo (a childhood nickname) was spotted in the audience by an agent, who promptly sent her to see John Derek, a sometime actor *(The Ten Commandments)*, director, and photographer 30 years Bo's senior. Although Derek was married at the time to actress Linda *(Dynasty)* Evans (he had divorced his first wife, French starlet Patti Behrs, in 1955 and his second, Swiss sexpot Ursula Andress, in 1965), he took his newest find to Greece. In part to avoid the possibility of legal problems, Derek and his new love took off for Germany until she turned 18. They married soon after his divorce from Evans came through in 1974. For the next five years, Bo's film career went nowhere. Then, in 1979, she became an overnight sensation portraying the object of Dudley Moore's middle-aged sexual fantasies in Blake Edwards's *10,* in the process launching one of the bestselling posters of all time, making Maurice Ravel's *Bolero* (her theme in the picture) a *Billboard* hit, and sparking a new fashion craze, the cornrow hairstyle. *People* magazine dubbed Derek Bo's "Male Chauvinist Pygmalion," and to many it seems that his Svengali-like hold on America's love goddess of the '80s is complete. He keeps an eye on her weight, her clothes and her hair, selects her projects, clashes with her directors, answers for her during interviews. All of which is apparently fine with Bo, who showed up at Derek's 53rd birthday party with his three previous wives—all dressed in T-shirts emblazoned with his likeness on the back. Despite her $1-million-plus-a-percentage-of-the-gross price per picture, Bo and John share a modest two-room apartment in Los Angeles' Marina del Rey. After making *A Change of Seasons* with Shirley MacLaine and Anthony Hopkins, the Dereks set out to film a new, "erotic" *Tarzan* with Bo playing—who else?—Jane: a far cry from classy Maureen O'Sullivan. Her next effort, the X-rated *Bolero,* was perhaps Bo's biggest boo-boo.

Born: 1956 in Long Beach, California
Height: 5 ft. 3 in.
Weight: 110 lbs.
Eyes: Blue *Hair:* Blond
Education: 11th grade
Marriages: To John Derek (1974–)
Children: None
Interests: Horses
Personal Habits and Traits: Nondrinker, shy, defers to Derek, lifts weights
Address: Marina del Rey, California
Income: $400,000 (estimate)

Bruce Dern

"I've played more psychotics and freaks and dopers than anyone. There was a stage in my career when the first thing people asked me was where they can pick up some good grass. Actually, I don't even drink—much less take drugs."

His grandfather was the Governor of Utah, his great-uncle was Archibald MacLeish, and his parents controlled a major interest in the Carson Pirie Scott department store chain. So when Bruce Dern took first place in the Penn Relays at the University of Pennsylvania, his goal-oriented family was *not* very impressed. Nor did it approve when he saw his first James Dean movie and decided to head for Hollywood. Dern's sinister snarl made him a natural heavy, and among other roles, he was called upon to murder John Wayne in *The Cowboys* and to massacre the entire crowd at the Super Bowl in *Black Sunday* (he brought off the former, blew the latter). He slowly emerged as more than just a good-looking Ernest Borgnine, however, and in films like the sci-fi saga *Silent Running, The Great Gatsby, Middle Age Crazy, That Championship Season,* and especially *Coming Home,* Dern carved a reputation for himself as a versatile character actor. Married in 1969 to Andrea Beckett ("We both went through great tragedies—her husband had been killed in an accident and one of my two daughters had drowned in a pool"), Dern divides his time between his $1.4 million house in Malibu and a weekend retreat at Lake Tahoe. His consuming passion is running, and Dern clocks 50 miles every week. Dern was seen by more people as the spectacled scientist in the TV miniseries *Space* than the audiences of all his movies combined.

Born: June 4, 1936, in Winnetka, Illinois
Height: 6 ft. 2 in.
Weight: 175 lbs.
Eyes: Blue *Hair:* Blond
Zodiac: Gemini
Education: University of Pennsylvania dropout
Religion: Protestant
Marriages: Three. Currently to Andrea Dern (1969–)
Children: One living. Laura (b. 1966)
Interests: Running (eight miles every day—five in the morning, three at night), drug abuse
Personal Habits and Traits: Never takes drugs, claims to have never smoked a cigarette, a teetotaler (guzzles Pepsi), drives a pickup truck
Addresses: Malibu, California; Lake Tahoe, Nevada
Income: $500,000 (minimum estimate)

Neil Diamond

"I don't like to feel like the court jester, the clown. I'm not there to 'entertain' people. We're there to do something together."

Frequently ranked as the number-one male vocalist in the country, Brooklyn-born Neil Diamond dropped out of New York University to break into show business. After his first hit, 1966's "Solitary Man," Diamond continued to grind out dozens more: "Cherry, Cherry," "Sweet Caroline," "I Am, I Cried," "Holly Holy," "Song Sung Blue," "Cracklin' Rosie," "Longfellow Serenade," "Desiree"; in addition he penned smash singles for the Monkees, such as "I'm a Believer," "A Little Bit Me, A Little Bit You," and "Another Pleasant Valley Sunday." In all, he has racked up 14 gold albums. In 1972 he became the first solo performer to play Broadway's Winter Garden theater since Al Jolson in the 1930s, and five years later shattered records at Los Angeles' Greek Theater—a landmark concert also made into a prime-time TV special. At times moody, Diamond explains: "I guess to some extent I'm still tied to that kid who was not popular in school, not good-looking, not good at sports. I didn't know how to talk to people." He teamed up with a fellow graduate of Brooklyn's Erasmus Hall High, Barbra Streisand, to record 1979's number-one "You Don't Bring Me Flowers," but that particular triumph occurred only after Diamond took a four-year sabbatical from the road to undergo therapy with a clinical

psychologist. Although he is not considered part of rock's drug demimonde, Diamond was busted for possession of a half-ounce of marijuana after a mob of 50 L.A. policemen swarmed his Holmby Hills mansion on an anonymous tip. The charges were eventually dropped, though Diamond confessed to being "numbed" by the experience. For years Diamond shrugged off another numbness, in his right leg, but when he fell onstage in San Francisco and couldn't get up, he underwent delicate surgery to remove a nonmalignant tumor located dangerously close to his spine. Equally numbing was the critical response to his 1981 movie debut in a remake of *The Jazz Singer*. But "Heartlight," inspired by the movie *E.T.*, lit up the charts—and Diamond's sagging career.

Born: January 24, 1941, in Coney Island, New York
Height: 6 ft. 1 in.
Weight: 185 lbs.
Eyes: Green *Hair:* Dark brown
Zodiac: Aquarius
Education: New York University dropout
Religion: Jewish
Marriages: Two. Currently to Marcia Murphey
Children: Marjorie (b. 1965) and Elyn (b. 1967) by his first marriage; Jesse (b. 1970) and Micah (b. 1978) by Murphey
Interests: Composing, fencing (attended NYU on a fencing scholarship), movies (he and Marcia see four in a row), collecting biographies of favorite composers, motorcycles
Personal Habits and Traits: Smokes two packs a day, drinks moderately, mercurial, semireclusive
Address: Holmby Hills, California
Income: $3 million (minimum estimate)

Diana, Princess of Wales

"Royal firstborns may get all the glory, but secondborns have a lot more freedom."

"First on the list was virginity," insisted H. B. Brooks-Baker of Debrett's, the chronicler of British bloodlines, in describing the qualifications for a royal bride. "Second was the ability to do the job. Third, she must be seen to have the potential to bear heirs to the throne." Lady Diana Spencer presumably met and passed all these obstacles. Indeed, from the very beginning of her fairy-tale romance with Prince Charles, Diana has come to be an ideal for her generation—and arguably the most famous and admired woman in the world. She is strikingly beautiful and serenely regal, a future queen and wife and mother of future kings, yet human enough for women the world over to identify with her. A style-setter (when she changes her hairstyle or her hemline, millions of young women follow suit), she cannot stop chewing her nails, which are unpolished and bitten to the quick. She drops out of dance class when the steps get too rough, but at home alone she will turn on her Sony Walkman and bop around the palace to the music of Duran Duran. While pregnant with her second son, Prince Harry, Diana leapt to her feet during a Neil Diamond concert in Birmingham and swiveled her hips in time to the music. Despite these few down-to-earth characteristics, however, there is no denying that Diana, like her future husband, grew up in a cocoon of wealth and privilege. The daughter of Earl Spencer, equerry to both George VI and Queen Elizabeth, Diana was born at Park House, part of the 20,000-acre royal estate at Sandringham. She and Charles met a few times when she was a child and he a young man (there is a 12-year age difference) dating her older sister, Lady Sarah. Diana attended a boarding school, West Heath in Kent, where she was an excellent athlete but a mediocre student. At about this time her parents divorced, marrying other partners (Di's dad wed the daughter of romance novelist Barbara Cartland) and Diana enrolled at a Swiss finishing school at 16 to learn to ski as well as brush up on her typing, sewing, and cooking. Shortly after she returned, Sarah played cupid, introducing her sister to the Prince at a 1977 shoot at Althorp, the Spencers' spectacular 500-year-old home in Northamptonshire. It would be three years, however, before Charles began courting Diana, by then sharing a London flat with three other young women and teaching at a local nursery school. Constantly hounded by the press during their year-long engagement, Di was soon dubbed "Shy Di" for her bashful, downcast look. Yet she not only survived, she flourished. The July 29, 1981, royal wedding itself—unquestionably the marriage ceremony of the century—was a spectacle witnessed by a worldwide television audience of 750 million. There was cause for celebration once again one year later; on July 21, 1982, Prince William, future heir to the throne, was born in a $175-per-day, 12-foot-by-12-foot room at St. Mary's Hospital in London. His brother, Henry Charles Albert David (just plain Harry to family and friends), was born in the same room two years later. While the world delighted in Wills's antics (among other things, he tried to flush his father's shoe down the toilet), his iron-willed mum proved herself a match for her mother-in-law, the Queen. When Di went on a royal tour of Australia with her husband, for example, she overrode Elizabeth's strong objections and brought little Wills along. And during the couple's headline-making U.S. visit—Diana's first—in November of 1985, it was the Princess who made sure Clint Eastwood, John Travolta, Neil Diamond, and Tom Selleck were invited to the White House dinner held in Charles' and Di's honor. No wonder that, at Highgrove, Charles' and Diana's official residence, she is known to the household staff as "The Boss."

Born: July 1, 1961, at Sandringham, England
Height: 5 ft. 10 in.
Weight: 125 lbs.
Eyes: Blue *Hair:* Blond
Zodiac: Cancer
Education: High school, Swiss finishing school
Religion: Anglican
Marriages: To Charles (1981–)
Children: William (b. 1982), Henry (b. 1984)
Interests: Fashion, rock music, biking, skiing, swimming
Personal Habits and Traits: Nail-biter, light drinker, nonsmoker, dedicated shopper
Addresses: Highgrove; Buckingham Palace; Windsor Castle; Balmoral Castle
Income: $600,000+ (Charles's allowance) (Note: *People* magazine estimated Diana's public relations worth to Great Britain at around $500 million)

Angie Dickinson

"I dress for women—and I undress for men."

Angeline Brown

Television's leggy *Police Woman* was born Angeline Brown in Kulm, North Dakota, and took her new name when she married football star Gene Dickinson while still a coed at Glendale College. Discovered by producer Howard Hawks, she starred in *Rio Bravo, Point Blank,* and a dozen other shoot-'em-up films before arriving on television as Pepper Anderson, the hotshot female detective on NBC's hit series. Also discovered by then-Presidential candidate John F. Kennedy, Dickinson has neither confirmed nor denied rumors of a romance with the late President and merely shrugs at the story that she skinny-dipped with JFK on the night of his nomination. Before *Police Woman* (but after her affair with Frank Sinatra) Dickinson married famous pop composer Burt Bacharach. However, their storybook Hollywood marriage foundered under the strain of his comparatively stagnant career and her pressing schedule—even though she had it written into her network contract that she would return from each day's shooting in time to have dinner at home with Burt. After they split in 1976, Angie continued to do their Martini & Rossi vermouth commercials ("Say yes, yes") solo. The year 1985 marked her return to television as the agent with a secret past in the smoldering miniseries based on Jackie Collins's bestselling novel *Hollywood Wives*.

Born: September 30, 1932, in Kulm, North Dakota
Height: 5 ft. 5 in.
Weight: 115 lbs.
Eyes: Brown *Hair:* Blond
Zodiac: Libra
Education: Glendale College
Religion: Roman Catholic
Marriages:
To Gene Dickinson (divorced)
To Burt Bacharach (divorced in 1977)
Children: Daughter Nikki (by Bacharach)
Interests: Tennis, baseball, music, camping
Personal Habits and Traits: Smokes, moderate drinker, early riser, exercise nut
Address: Beverly Hills
Income: $1 million +

Jeane Dixon

"In predicting the future, I can make mistakes like anybody else. But a vision is not open to question. It is a message from God."

Jeane Pinckert

The media's favorite sibyl was only eight when a gypsy fortune-teller examined her hands and promptly handed over her crystal ball. Since then, Wisconsin-raised Dixon has served as a psychic advisor to the likes of Henry Ford, Sr. and Franklin Delano Roosevelt, and chalked up an impressive list of accurate predictions: the deaths of Mahatma Gandhi and Carole Lombard, the partition of India and, most notably, the assassination of John F. Kennedy, whom she tried to prevent from going to Dallas. Between the major historic events, Dixon has predicted floods, earthquakes, plane crashes, and illnesses by the score. Not that she is immune to mistakes: among other bloopers she prophesied that the Soviet Union would be first to put a man on the moon. In addition to being the subject of Ruth Montgomery's bestselling *A Gift of Prophecy,* Dixon herself has written, among others, *My Life and Prophecies* and *Reincarnation and Prayers to Live By*. Her annual predictions are a must for readers of the *National Enquirer* and *National Star,* and she is frequently called upon to deliver an oracle or two on TV talk shows. But Dixon, who also sells real estate for her husband's thriving Washington agency, James L. Dixon & Company, is careful to draw the distinction between predictions that emerge in her crystal ball and ''visions,'' which are ''religious experiences'' that only rarely occur and are always unsolicited. Dixon's sizable earnings as a clairvoyant help fund her nonprofit Children-to-Children Foundation.

Born: November 1918 in Medford, Wisconsin
Height: 4 ft. 11 in.
Weight: 100 lbs.
Eyes: Blue *Hair:* Brown
Zodiac: Scorpio
Education: High school
Religion: Roman Catholic
Marriages: To James L. Dixon (current)
Children: None
Interests: Real estate, politics (she is a conservative Republican), writing, broadcasting, theology
Personal Habits and Traits: Nonsmoker, teetotaler, soft-spoken but strong-willed, occasionally fasts
Address: Washington, D.C.
Income: $200,000+ personal income (more than $300,000 earned through psychic activities goes to a nonprofit charity)

Phil Donahue

''What really keeps me going is the constant belief that it could all disappear tomorrow.''

A one-time altar boy and 50-cents-an-hour window washer for a Cleveland convent, this son of a furniture salesman received straight A's in theology at Notre Dame. Although he failed his first audition as a radio broadcaster because of what he calls a ''nasal Midwest accent'' and was forced to work for a brief time as a banker, Donahue finally landed a job as a television reporter in Dayton. In eight years he advanced from calling hog prices at dawn to anchoring the 11 P.M. news. In 1967, after apprenticing with a radio phone-in series, he started his TV talk show on Dayton's WLWD. The show, *Donahue,* relocated to Chicago in 1974—a move that coincided with the breakup of his 16-year marriage to Marge

Cooney—and was soon syndicated nationally to over 100 stations and viewed by an audience of millions (85 percent women) on weekdays. One reason for Donahue's success is the boyish interviewer's tough journalistic approach. ''I think the women out there in the soap opera ghetto don't want to be treated like mental midgets,'' says Donahue, who only tackles one issue or guest per show. ''The women who watch my show don't need to be protected from controversy by male program wizards in New York.'' Donahue shares a New York apartment with second wife Marlo Thomas, and spends up to 12 hours a day scrupulously researching guests and issues. ''I couldn't live with my conscience doing a 'Goodbye, Carol Channing, and give a big welcome to Dr. Diaper Rash' kind of show,'' declares Donahue, who has joined Marlo as an ardent feminist. ''What matters to me most is my integrity as a reporter.'' His bestselling autobiography, *Donahue,* was published in 1980. Four years later, he relocated to New York City—where his ratings got stronger than ever. It remained to be seen, however, if he would be able to withstand stiff competition from another Chicago-based syndicated talkie, actress (*The Color Purple*) Oprah Winfrey.

Born: December 21, 1935, in Cleveland, Ohio
Height: 6 ft.
Weight: 174 lbs.
Eyes: Blue *Hair:* White
Zodiac: On the cusp of Sagittarius and Capricorn
Education: University of Notre Dame, B.A. in theology
Religion: Roman Catholic
Marriages:
To Marge Cooney (1958–1974)
To Marlo Thomas (1980–)
Children: Four sons, one daughter
Interests: Football, baseball, theology
Personal Habits and Traits: Nonsmoker, drinks moderately, a perfectionist, constant worrier
Address: New York City
Income: $2.3 million+

Kirk Douglas

Issur Danielovitch Demsky

''All those years I was a young actor in Hollywood, I never dreamed my son would wind up owning it.''

The only boy among six girls, Issur Danielovitch grew up the son of impoverished Russian immigrants in Amsterdam, New York. He struggled through dozens of menial jobs before Hollywood producers gambled on his clenched teeth and dimpled chin. The decision paid off as he boxed his way to success in *Champion,* the 1949 movie that established him as a major star. Douglas went on to delineate an unscrupulous moviemaker *(The Bad and the Beautiful),* the tormented painter Vincent van Gogh *(Lust for Life),* a lusty Viking sailor (*The Vikings,* which he also produced), a French colonel in World War I *(Paths of Glory),* a noble Greek slave *(Spartacus),* and a married tycoon in the throes of male menopause *(The Arrangement, Once Is Not Enough)*. The old-school matinee idol has joined many of his contemporaries who are popping up in terror films by heading Brian DePalma's horrific *The Fury,* which turned out to be one of 1978's top grossers. He wound up suing the Australian company that produced his critically acclaimed *The Man From Snowy River* for what he claimed was his $300,000 share of the profits, and stretched his talent to the limit as an abused senior citizen in television's *Amos*. But Douglas's proudest creation is son Michael, an accomplished actor in his own right and producer of the Oscar-winning *One Flew Over the Cuckoo's Nest* and *The China Syndrome*. Douglas teamed up with old buddy Burt Lancaster for the 1986 Disney comedy *Tough Guys*.

Born: December 9, 1916, in Amsterdam, New York
Height: 5 ft. 11 in.
Weight: 170 lbs.
Eyes: Blue *Hair:* Blond
Zodiac: Sagittarius
Education: High school
Religion: Jewish
Marriages: Two
Children: Four sons
Interests: International diplomacy, cultural relations, art, music, biography, tennis, swimming
Personal Habits and Traits: Nonsmoker, social drinker, early riser
Address: Beverly Hills
Income: $1 million per film

Michael Douglas

''The exciting thing about making movies today is that everything is up for grabs. And you had better grab.''

His famous father Kirk has never won a single Oscar in a career that stretches over four decades, but at the age of 30, young Michael copped one as producer of *One Flew Over the Cuckoo's Nest,* the first motion picture since *It Happened One Night* to win Academy Awards for Best Picture, Best Director (Miloš Foreman), Best Actor (Jack Nicholson), and Best Actress (Louise Fletcher). For a time it looked as though Michael was headed for a career anywhere but in Hollywood. His father and mother (British-born actress Diana Douglas) were divorced when he was 6, and Michael was educated at classy Eastern schools like Choate before enrolling in prelaw at the University of California's Santa Barbara campus. He got hooked on the theater after making his acting debut in a student production of *As You Like It* (''My dad thought I was terrible'') and acted in a number of off-Broadway roles and forgettable movies until, in the role of a rookie detective named Mike, he started to pal around with Karl Malden on ABC's hit series *The Streets of San Francisco*. He pulled out of the show in 1975 to devote himself to moviemaking full-time, and in 1976 stepped up to collect his gold statuette. The following year, he was once again in front of the camera as star of the chiller

Coma. Two years later he produced and starred in another indisputable (and frighteningly prophetic) chiller—*The China Syndrome*. Douglas's six-year relationship with actress Brenda Vaccaro went up in smoke at about the time his producing career took off, and in 1977 he married Diandra Luker. Douglas's next enterprise, *Running,* made a poor showing—as did 1981's *My Turn*. Douglas rebounded with the biggest box-office hit of his career, *Romancing the Stone,* and headed for North Africa to film a *Stone* sequel, *Jewel of the Nile*. Douglas stepped straight out of *Jewel* into one of the juiciest and most sought-after roles in Hollywood—the part of Zach in the much anticipated (if somewhat disappointing) Richard Attenborough screen version of *A Chorus Line*.

Born: September 25, 1944, in New York
Height: 5 ft. 9½ in.
Weight: 150 lbs.
Eyes: Blue *Hair:* Light brown
Zodiac: Libra
Education: University of California at Santa Barbara, B.A.
Religion: Jewish

Marriages: To Diándra Luker (1977–)
Children: Cameron (b. 1978)
Interests: Tennis, reading
Habits: Chain smoker, drinks moderately, insomniac
Address: Benedict Canyon, California
Income: $4.5 million +

Richard Dreyfuss

''The Oscar really means very little. Look at Henry Fonda—a great actor for forty years and he never won an Academy Award. I only hope I can last that long.''

This Dreyfuss Fund of acting talent has built his solid reputation with the creation of a varied group of characters: the sensitive high school senior Curt Henderson in *American Graffiti;* the hustling, Sammy Glick-like character in *The Apprenticeship of Duddy Kravitz;* the salty ichthyologist in *Jaws;* the UFO-hunter in *Close Encounters of the Third Kind;* and Marsha Mason's perennially suffering roommate in Neil Simon's *The Goodbye Girl*—the part that, against all odds, snared Dreyfuss an Academy Award as Best Actor of 1977. Born in Brooklyn and raised in Beverly Hills, Dreyfuss began acting in bit parts on television when he was still a teenager. Typecast as a ''dink'' by the time he was 15—"A 'dink' is the guy with owlish glasses who is always asking Sally Field to the school prom and is always being refused"—Dreyfuss ascended to playing psychopaths at 19, making his screen debut in 1973 as Baby Face Nelson in *Dillinger*. The real breakthrough came with *Graffiti,* which wound up as one of the Top 10 box-office grossers of all time. Having largely overcome an earlier reputation as abrasive, Dreyfuss eagerly seeks out new and challenging roles on both stage and screen, though his fee per picture has dropped from a reported $2 million—and found them in *The Competition* and *Whose Life Is It Anyway?* After recovering from injuries suffered when he slammed his Mercedes into a palm tree, Dreyfuss was arrested for cocaine possession but, rather than face a trial, voluntarily entered a drug rehabilitation program. The smash 1986 comedy *Down and Out in Beverly Hills* put Dreyfuss up and over with audiences once again.

Born: October 29, 1947, in Brooklyn, New York
Height: 5 ft. 8½ in.
Weight: 151 lbs.
Eyes: Brown *Hair:* Gray-brown
Zodiac: Scorpio
Education: High school
Religion: Jewish
Marriages: To Jeramie Rain (1983–)
Children: None
Interests: Politics (liberal, has said he would someday like to run for Congress), pro-nuclear freeze, world affairs, literature, Shakespeare
Personal Habits and Traits: Intense, drinks moderately, a night owl, workaholic
Address: Los Angeles
Income: $600,000 (estimate)

Faye Dunaway

Dorothy Faye Dunaway

"A star today has to take charge of every aspect of her career. There are no studios left to do it for you."

All eyes, cheekbones, and legs, Faye Dunaway nonetheless won her Oscar in 1976 playing a curiously sexless career woman clawing her way to the top of the ratings game in *Network*. Dorothy Faye Dunaway from Bascom, Florida, grew up an Army brat who lived at various posts from Germany to Utah and attended a dozen schools, finishing her education at the University of Florida and Boston University's School of Fine and Applied Arts. Stage roles in *A Man for All Seasons* and *After the Fall* (which she eventually re-created on television) preceded her screen debut in *The Happening*. Although the "with it" film went nowhere fast, it caught the eye of Warren Beatty, who saw in Dunaway his perfect costar for *Bonnie and Clyde*. The movie shot her to overnight stardom, and over the next decade she was seen in *The Thomas Crown Affair, The Arrangement, Little Big Man, Oklahoma Crude, Chinatown, The Towering Inferno, Voyage of the Damned,* and *Three Days of the Condor* before tackling her most challenging role in *Network*. Her next film, *The Eyes of Laura Mars,* was much less well received. Dunaway's much talked-about affair with actor Marcello Mastroianni did not lead to wedding bells, but two years after she first saw rock singer Peter Wolf (lead singer of the J. Geils Band) perform onstage, they were married and moved to Hollywood. When their marriage began to falter—"I can't grow in a company town"—Dunaway insisted they both pack up and leave California. They did, but the move wasn't enough to save their marriage, and Dunaway bounced alone between a seven-room Manhattan apartment and a flat in downtown Boston. She kicked off the 1980s with two enviable strong-woman roles—Eva Peron in TV's *Evita* and Joan Crawford in the film version of *Mommie Dearest*. While Dunaway was sinking her teeth into the role of Joan Crawford in *Mommie Dearest,* she revealed that she had given birth to a baby boy in the summer of 1980. The father: British photographer Terry O'Neill. Dunaway went on to win an Emmy as the libidinous actress in TV's *Ellis Island*.

Born: January 14, 1941, in Bascom, Florida
Height: 5 ft. 9 in.
Weight: 119 lbs.
Eyes: Brown *Hair:* Brown
Zodiac: Capricorn
Education: University of Florida; Boston University, B.F.A. in theater
Religion: Protestant
Marriages:
To Peter Wolf (divorced in 1978)
To Terry O'Neill (1983–)
Children: Liam (b. 1980)
Interests: Art, music, cooking, gardening, shopping, theater (wants to establish an American National Theater), producing, directing
Personal Habits and Traits: Smokes, drinks wine, night owl, aggressive, impatient
Addresses: Boston; Manhattan
Income: $2 million

Robert Duvall

"I'm better than Olivier."

He did not get his name over the title or an Academy Award (playing a washed-up country singer in 1983's *Tender Mercies*) until he was past 50, but at least Robert Duvall has never had to worry about being type-cast. This actor's actor has played, among other film roles: the menacing recluse in *To Kill a Mockingbird,* the pompous Dr. Frank Burns in *M*A*S*H,* John Wayne's nemesis in *True Grit,* the Mafia mouthpiece in *The Godfather* and *Godfather II,* the mentally retarded man in *The Rain People,* the corporate shark in *Network,* Dr. Watson in *The Seven Percent Solution,* Robert De Niro's older brother in *True Confessions,* and the fast-talking sports reporter in *The Natural.* For the parts of larger-than-life military men in *Apocalypse Now* and *The Great Santini,* Duvall drew on personal experience: A Navy brat, he was urged by his rear admiral father to attend Annapolis, but chose instead to study drama at Illinois' tiny Principia College. After an Army stint, Duvall headed for New York, where he studied at the Neighborhood Playhouse and palled around with other struggling young actors like Gene Hackman and Dustin Hoffman. For a time, he paid the rent sorting mail on the midnight shift at the post office. The lead in a 1957 production of Arthur Miller's *A View From the Bridge* led to TV work in dramatic series such as *Naked City, The Defenders,* and *The F.B.I.* until 1971's *The Godfather* finally made the moviegoing public sit up and take notice. In 1977, while working with actor John Savage on Broadway in *American Buffalo,* he met Savage's sister, Gail Youngs. After a stormy courtship, and before the release of *Angelo, My Love,* a documentary about gypsies which he directed, Duvall married Youngs on a small island off the coast of Maine, and the two moved into a cavernous New York City apartment that was once the home of Enrico Caruso.

Born: January 5, 1931, in San Diego
Height: 6 ft.
Weight: 180 lbs.
Eyes: Blue *Hair:* Reddish brown (balding)
Zodiac: Capricorn
Education: Principia College, B.A. in dramatic arts
Religion: Protestant
Marriages:
To Barbara Duvall (divorced in 1975)
To Gail Youngs (1983–)
Children: None
Interests: Ornithology, tennis, country music (he did all his own singing in *Tender Mercies*)
Personal Habits and Traits: Teetotaler, nonsmoker, eats out six nights a week, is politically conservative
Address: New York City
Income: $1 million per film

Bob Dylan

Robert Zimmerman

"Just because you like my stuff doesn't mean I owe you anything."

The rock-poet laureate of the 1960s was born Robert Zimmerman of Duluth, Minnesota, and took the name Dylan from his idol, poet Dylan Thomas. Landing in Greenwich Village in 1961, Dylan joined the likes of Joan Baez and Peter, Paul and Mary, playing guitar and singing in local coffeehouses. As the civil rights, drug culture and antiwar movements mushroomed, Dylan became the undisputed spokesman for a generation of protest. Starting with "Blowin' in the Wind," he composed and recorded such enduring songs as "The Times They Are A-Changin'," "Like A Rolling Stone," and "Lay, Lady, Lay" before he nearly lost his life in a motorcycle crash. That led to a two-year period of self-imposed exile which culminated in 1968 with his landmark *John Wesley Harding* album, followed in quick succession by his *Nashville Skyline* LP, signifying Dylan's conversion from a folk-rock to a country sound. The mystery man then disappeared for a second time, only to reappear in 1975 with his Rolling Thunder Revue and a hit single in defense of convicted murderer Rubin "Hurricane" Carter, called simply "Hurricane." As his spectacular, $2 million + Malibu Beach compound neared completion in 1977, Dylan split from his wife, fashion model Sarah Shirley Lownds after a dozen years of marriage and five children. One of the pop culture's most enigmatic figures, Dylan took an interest in such disparate subjects as Zionism (he has been a supporter of the militant Jewish Defense League) and ecology before inexplicably becoming a born-again Christian. He is also an aspiring filmmaker, and after much secrecy unveiled his first screen epic, *Renaldo and Clara*. It flopped, but in 1978 his album *Desire* became yet another Dylan classic—as did his subsequent *Street Legal* and *Slow Train Comin'* releases. But many Dylan fans felt Dylan's born-again zeal adversely affected his concert performances. He proved them wrong when, shortly after lending his time and talent to the creation of "We Are the World," Dylan released his 23rd album of original material—*Empire Burlesque*.

Born: May 24, 1941, in Duluth, Minnesota
Height: 5 ft. 6 in.
Weight: 130 lbs.
Eyes: Brown *Hair:* Brown
Zodiac: Gemini
Education: University of Minnesota dropout
Religion: Born-again Christian
Marriages: To Sarah Shirley Lownds (1965–1977)
Children: Jesse, Anna, Seth, Samuel, Marie
Interests: Songwriting, guitar, moviemaking
Personal Habits and Traits: Smokes, drinks, reclusive
Addresses: Malibu, California; New York City
Income: $3 million+

Clint Eastwood

"Make my day."

The archetypal screen loner, cool-eyed Clint Eastwood parlayed his soft-talking, hard-nosed cowhand image on television's *Rawhide* into the world's top male box office draw. Born in San Francisco and named after his father, Clint never stayed at one school more than a semester ("When you're a new kid in town you always have to punch it out with the kids the first day or so") and started work as a laborer when still in high school. He did a hitch in the Army as a swimming instructor at Fort Ord, and in the early 1950s signed a $75-a-week contract with Universal to do walk-ons in horror flicks like *Revenge of the Creature*. He was fired when studio executives decided his Adam's apple protruded too much for him to be star material and wound up digging swimming pools to augment what little money he could make from small parts in TV series like *Highway Patrol*. However, being cast as *Rawhide*'s Rowdy Yates in 1958 finally propelled Eastwood to the top. Between the sixth and seventh seasons of *Rawhide* Eastwood starred in his first spaghetti western, an Italian-Spanish-German production called *A Fistful of Dollars*. He established The Malpaso Company (named after a creek that crosses his Monterey property) and set out to capitalize on the resulting international spaghetti superstardom. In *Dirty Harry* (1971) he portrayed a San Francisco cop with a penchant for stepping on the civil liberties of criminals, and though the movie was extremely violent and dismissed as junk by many critics, it turned out to be Eastwood's biggest hit. After *Dirty Harry* came the sequels *Magnum Force* and *The Enforcer*, which also cleaned up at the box office. His 1978 feature *The Gauntlet*, somewhat similar to his earlier *Coogan's Bluff*, topped them all. He has also directed and starred in a Hitchcockian thriller, *Play Misty for Me*, and played the leads in the movie musical *Paint Your Wagon*, the lighthearted *Two Mules for Sister Sara*, and *Thunderbolt and Lightfoot*. A political conservative, Eastwood prefers the solitude of his magnificent Monterey estate to Hollywood. In nearby Carmel he owns and operates a popular Edwardian restaurant called, quaintly enough, The Hog's Breath Inn. Eastwood's serene marriage to Maggie Johnson was shaken, however, by rumors of his offscreen romance with *Gauntlet* costar Sondra Locke. *Escape from Alcatraz,* released in the fall of 1979, was one of the few action films of the decade well received by critics. The following year, Eastwood scored with back-to-back comedy hits *Every Which Way But Loose* and *Any Which Way You Can. Firefox,* in which he played, of all things, a Soviet pilot, was a huge hit. Eastwood's biggest year, however, was yet to come; in 1984, he ranked as the world's number-one box-office draw (for the second year in a row) with *Sudden Impact, Tightrope,* and *City Heat.* Two years later, Carmel voters made Eastwood's day by electing him mayor. Hizzoner's municipal salary: $200 a month.

Born: May 31, 1930, in San Francisco, California
Height: 6 ft. 4 in.
Weight: 198 lbs.
Eyes: Blue *Hair:* Brown
Zodiac: Gemini
Education: High school
Religion: Protestant
Marriages: To Maggie Johnson (1953–split in 1979)
Children: Kyle (b. 1969) and Alison (b. 1973)
Interests: Writing, directing, ecology, owns restaurant
Personal Habits and Traits: Golf, tennis, jogs along beach, works out in home gym, drives fast (a Ferrari Boxer), avoids parties
Address: Monterey, California
Income: $6.5 million (per film)

Werner Erhard

Jack Rosenberg

''When you drop the effort to make your life work, you begin to discover that it's perfect the way it is.''

Jack Rosenberg was born in Lower Merion, Pennsylvania, and grew up as a self-confessed schlepp who married at 18, fathered four children, and labored for a construction company before abandoning his wife and family in 1960. He then sold cars under the pseudonym Jack Frost until heading for St. Louis with his girlfriend, who later became his second wife and mother of his three youngest children. ''I wanted to get as far away from Jack Rosenberg as I could get,'' he confessed, and that included, among other things, culling a new name from the pages of *Esquire* magazine. From one article he adopted physicist Werner Heisenberg's first name and from another the surname of former West German Chancellor Ludwig Erhard. ''Freudians,'' he later mused, ''would say this was a rejection of Jewishness [his father actually converted to Christianity] and a seizure of strength.'' Erhard became the best instructor of encyclopedia salesmen in San Francisco, but one day while driving on the freeway he realized how dissatisfied he was, and set out on his own journey of self-discovery. He tried everything from Scientology to Gestalt. None of it worked, so Erhard invented an approach of his own—est, the Latin word for "it is" as well as the initials for Erhard Seminars Training. est, a blend of Zen, Transactional Analysis, Transcendental Meditation, and Dale Carnegie, has since become *the* popular middle-class therapy, boasting among its 100,000 converts across the country such celebrities as John Denver, Valerie Harper, Cloris Leachman, and activist Jerry Rubin. His "seminars" are closed-door meetings lasting four or five hours at a time during which members are subjected to a barrage of insults and no one is allowed to chat, smoke, wear a watch, or go to the bathroom. Nevertheless, San Francisco-based Erhard grossed over $36 million a year from his two-weekend, 60-hour, $250 course. Quick to point out that he technically receives a $9,000 monthly income, Erhard lives in a hilltop mansion and has access to a company Mercedes, yacht, and plane for his personal use. After 22 years of marriage, his second wife, Ellen, fed up with what she contended was his incessant adultery, filed for divorce and half ownership of Werner Erhard and Associates.

Born: September 5, 1935, in Philadelphia, Pennsylvania
Height: 5 ft. 10 in.
Weight: 170 lbs.
Eyes: Brown *Hair:* Brown
Zodiac: Virgo
Education: High school
Religion: Episcopalian

Marriages: Two, both ending in divorce
Children: Seven
Interests: Sailing, reading
Personal Habits and Traits: Nonsmoker, drinks moderately
Address: San Francisco
Income: est grosses $36 million annually, from which Erhard draws $9,000 monthly

Julius Erving

"Dr. J"

"With black kids, it's always a struggle for pride. Basketball was my way out. I worked hard to make sure it was."

Julius Erving's father, an auto mechanic, deserted his family when Julius was three, and his mother Callie worked as a maid to support her three children. Erving grew up amid the abject poverty of a housing project in Hempstead, Long Island, and at 10 was recruited to play on a Salvation Army basketball team. He acquired his nickname "the Doctor" in high school, where as an all-star player and a B student he received nearly 100 scholarship offers, finally choosing the University of Massachusetts. Three years later he signed with the Virginia Squires of the ABA for $125,000 a season, and soon met his future wife Turquoise ("Turk") Brown. Traded to the New York Nets in 1973, he established himself as the game's most astonishing player during three spectacular seasons, routinely making plays and shots that left opponents and teammates alike shaking their heads at his awesome domination of the court. In 1976, as the leading scorer in the league, he was traded to the Philadelphia 76ers for a staggering $6.5 million—half of that going to Erving over six years. An additional $500,000-plus is yielded annually from Dr. J's endorsements for Spalding basketballs, Colgate toothpaste, Converse sneakers, and Action warmup suits. Still planning on finishing that one remaining year of college (his major at the University of Massachusetts was personnel management), Erving has set his sights on a degree in tax or corporate law, and, ultimately, a business of his own. "My long-term plans," smiles the millionaire sports superstar, "are entrepreneurial."

Born: February 22, 1950, in Roosevelt, New York
Height: 6 ft. 6 in.
Weight: 187 lbs.
Eyes: Brown *Hair:* Black
Zodiac: Pisces
Education: Three years at the University of Massachusetts
Marriages: To Turquoise ("Turk") Brown (1974–)
Children: Cheo (b. 1972, by wife's first marriage); Julius III (b. 1974), Jazmin (b. 1976)
Interests: Jazz, chess, tennis, golf, weightlifting, children
Personal Habits and Traits: Moderate drinker, soft-spoken
Address: Upper Brookville, Long Island
Income: $1 million+

Linda Evans

Linda Evanstad

"I've always been protected by men. Now I feel in charge of my life."

As Krystle Carrington, the saccharine foil for Alexis Carrington Colby (Joan Collins) on *Dynasty,* Linda Evans is sort of a cross between Grace Kelly and Mother Theresa. Her sweetness comes naturally, springing from a painfully shy childhood in Hollywood, where her father was a painter and her mother a housewife. When she was 15, her father died of cancer, and for the next 20 years Evans blamed herself for "abandoning him." Evans was still a student at Hollywood High when she landed her first small part, prophetically enough, with her future *Dynasty* husband John Forsythe on *Bachelor Father.* In the mid-1960s, the statuesque blonde lent a touch of glamour to *The Big Valley* TV series—a role that attracted the attention of actor-turned-producer John *(Knock on Any Door)* Derek. He left then-wife Ursula Andress to marry Linda, and they had an idyllic marriage until 1973, when Derek announced that he had fallen in love with a 16-year-old Evans clone named Bo. Devastated, Evans put the Dereks' Hollywood house on the market and met wealthy realtor Stan Herman. When that marriage dissolved over her career ambitions, Evans immersed herself in preparations for a new ABC series tentatively called *Oil. Oil* became *Dynasty,* and evanescent Evans, at 40, became television's most glamorous blonde. The author of a bestselling beauty book and frontwoman for Crystal Light diet drinks and the Bonaventure International Hotel and Spa in Fort Lauderdale, Florida,

Evans has parlayed her ''sexy forever'' image into a solid seven-figure annual income. Her Krystle clear motto: ''Forgive yourself for the past so that you can love yourself now and tomorrow.''

Born: November 18, 1942, in Hartford, Connecticut
Height: 5 ft. 8 in.
Weight: 121 lbs.
Eyes: Blue *Hair:* Blond
Zodiac: Scorpio
Education: High school
Religion: Roman Catholic
Marriages:
John Derek (1964–1975)
Stan Herman (1976–1980)
Children: None
Interests: Cooking, meditation, and numerology; very religious (always wears a small gold and diamond cross)
Personal Habits and Traits: Nonsmoker, drinks white wine or beer, weight-trains, bikes and runs daily, loves popcorn and pasta
Address: Beverly Hills
Income: $2 million (minimum estimate)

Chris Evert Lloyd

''Winning has always been something I had *to do. I can't say I enjoy it 100 percent.''*

She had won over 500 tennis matches and earned well over one million dollars, but in 1977 at the age of 22 she suffered a traumatic emotional breakdown during a tournament in San Francisco. Chris Evert had hardly taken a break from her sport since she started playing at five at the instigation of her Fort Lauderdale tennis pro dad. At 16 she barely lost to three-time Wimbledon champion Billie Jean King at Forest Hills, and only three years later it was All-American Evert who stood victorious at center court at Wimbledon. That was also the first year she replaced King as the best woman player in tennis—and the first year she was selected by the Associated Press as the all-around top woman athlete. Still, King and Evert have remained friends and Chrissie even sought Billy Jean's advice at one point about Chrissie's on-again, off-again romance with volatile-tempered Jimmy Connors. Evert has also signed such lucrative endorsement deals as a $500,000 contract with Clairol as she racked up, among other tennis titles, no fewer than four Virginia Slims championships in six years. Taking her 1977 crisis as a signal to slow down, Evert dropped out for four months and found a new man, British tennis pro John (''Flossie'') Lloyd, though she continued to date Connors and to have a fling with Burt Reynolds. Twenty years Chrissie's senior, Burt gave her the diamond necklace spelling out BABE that she wore to all her matches. However, Evert finally wed Lloyd in 1979—the same year she was defeated by Tracy Austin at Forest Hills. In early 1980 she announced an ''indefinite leave'' from competition, then returned to recapture her U.S. Open title. Since then, Chris's career has yo-yoed as she pursued one of the great sports rivalries with Martina Navratilova. The pressures also had an impact on her marriage to Lloyd, though after a period of separation it appeared as though they had managed to get their relationship back on an even keel.

Born: December 21, 1954, in Fort Lauderdale, Florida
Height: 5 ft. 5 in.
Weight: 116 lbs.
Eyes: Brown *Hair:* Blond
Zodiac: Sagittarius
Education: High school
Religion: Roman Catholic

Marriages: To John Lloyd (1979–)
Children: None
Interests: Tennis
Personal Habits and Traits: Nonsmoker, nondrinker, soft-spoken
Address: Fort Lauderdale, Florida
Income: $1.3 million (minimum estimate)

Lola Falana

"One day I'm going to be a middle-aged lady and I don't want people to think I've got some strange disease."

Her *Dr. Jazz* lasted on Broadway a mere four days, but Lola Falana still walked away with a Tony nomination and the praise of the then-drama critic of *The New York Times,* Clive Barnes: "She's a hand grenade of a woman." Whether hawking Tigress perfume for Fabergé ("Because men are such animals"), singing and dancing on the Las Vegas strip at $100,000 per week, or causing Johnny Carson to fluff his lines on the *Tonight Show,* leggy, luscious Falana is a megawatt performer. Her parents—a Philadelphia welder and his wife—worried that Lola would wind up destitute if she pursued her wild dreams of stardom, and indeed at one point she wound up sleeping in a New York subway. She was 17 when Sammy Davis, Jr., discovered her in an Atlantic City chorus line and made her his lead dancer in 1964's *Golden Boy.* A *de facto* member of the Rat Pack in those early days, Lola remained in the background until her frequent appearances on *Tonight* helped her land a four-special package with ABC in 1976. At times exasperatingly pretentious, Falana nonetheless exudes a kind of sassy charm that has made her a most intriguing personality, both in the United States and internationally. Her brief marriage to singer Feliciano Tavares ended in divorce in 1975, and by the mid-80s Falana had added a featured role in the hit soap *Capitol* to her list of credits.

Born: 1947 in Philadelphia, Pennsylvania
Height: 5 ft. 5 in.
Weight: 110 lbs.
Eyes: Brown *Hair:* Brown
Education: High school dropout
Religion: Protestant
Marriages: To Feliciano Tavares (divorced in 1975)
Children: None
Interests: Meditation, astrology, fashion, dance
Habits: Nonsmoker, fasts
Address: Los Angeles
Income: $500,000 (minimum estimate)

Peter Falk

"I've got a weak stomach for lousy scripts."

The wearer of the world's most famous wrinkled raincoat, *Columbo* star Peter Falk grew up the only son of an Ossining, New York, dry goods merchant and the only kid in his neighborhood with a glass eye (resulting from a malignant tumor), which did not prevent him from becoming a three-letter high school athlete, a sailor in the Merchant Marine, a pool hustler, and one of Hollywood's most visceral actors. After flunking out of Hamilton College Falk completed his undergraduate degree at the New School for Social Research in New York City and went on to earn an MA in Public Administration from Syracuse; he then worked as a clerk at Connecticut's Budget Bureau. Eva Le Gallienne recognized his raw talent when Falk began to act with local New York theater groups, and urged him to pursue a theatrical career. Live television provided a tremendous opportunity for the struggling young actor when, in 1962, Falk won an Emmy (the first of three) for his portrayal of a trucker in the drama *Price of Tomatoes*. As he was becoming something of a national institution in the role of the sloppy, deceptively inept Lieutenant Columbo on NBC, Falk teamed up with John Cassavetes and Ben Gazzara to star in the critically acclaimed *Husbands*. On the stage he won a Tony as Best Actor in 1972 for his performance in Neil Simon's *Prisoner of Second Avenue*. In Cassavetes's 1975 *A Woman Under the Influence*, Falk scored again as the beer-guzzling blue collar worker who helplessly watches his wife suffer a nervous breakdown. Although Falk was nominated for an Oscar in his first film role as a vicious hit man in 1960's *Murder, Inc.*, comedy is really Falk's forte—he specialized in playing lovable gangsters like the hood in *A Pocketful of Miracles*—and in 1976 he grabbed the chance to spoof Bogart in Neil Simon's *Murder by Death*. He headed an all-star cast in Simon's *The Cheap Detective* a couple of years later, and his appearance in the real-life drama *The Brinks Job* and in the comedy hit *The In-Laws* further solidified his gumshoe image. At home, Falk's heady success took its toll; his seemingly solid marriage to Alyce Mayo went up in smoke as his career peaked in 1976, and one year later he married Shera Danese, an actress 23 years his junior. For Falk, the '80s got off to a rather lackluster start with *All the Marbles*, and after a series of flops he was betting on 1986's *Happy New Year* to pull him out of his career slump.

Born: September 16, 1927, in New York City
Height: 5 ft. 6 in.
Weight: 155 lbs.
Eyes: Brown *Hair:* Brown
Zodiac: Virgo
Education: The New School for Social Research, B.A.; Syracuse University, M.A.
Religion: Roman Catholic
Marriages: To Alyce Mayo (divorced)
To Shera Danese (1977–)
Children: One son
Interests: Pool, reading
Habits: Smokes cigars, drinks beer
Address: Los Angeles
Income: $1 million per film

Mia Farrow

"The more I am in England the more American I become. I miss it here."

The object of songwriter Dory Previn's bitter "Beware of Young Girls" (". . . of twenty and four . . .")—after conductor-husband André left Dory for her—Woody Allen's girl is descended from Hollywood aristocracy. Her mother, Maureen O'Sullivan, swung to fame alongside Johnny Weissmuller in the 1930s *Tarzan* films, and her father was the respected director John Farrow. Despite plans to become a nun, Mia was kicked out of two schools and wound up starring in the television series based on Grace Metalious's torrid *Peyton Place*. In 1968 she appeared in Roman Polanski's *Rosemary's Baby* as an affluent West Side New York matron who is impregnated by the Devil, and subsequent films *Secret Ceremony* and *See No Evil* perpetuated her horrific roles. In 1973 she lucked into the part of Daisy in *The Great Gatsby* when Paramount chief Robert Evans divorced his wife Ali MacGraw, originally slated to play the role, but critics by and large found Farrow's Daisy a fizzle. Yet Farrow's romantic life tended to be anything but lackluster, and her brief May-September marriage to Frank Sinatra provided plenty of grist for the tabloids. Farrow then broke up André and Dory Previn, and gave birth to Previn's twin sons. That marriage lasted only until 1979, however, when Farrow fell for Ingmar Bergman's cinematographer Sven Nyquist while filming a remake of *Hurricane* in the South Pacific. It flopped, but Farrow triumphed on Broadway with Tony Perkins in *Romantic Comedy,* and replaced Diane Keaton as the object of Woody Allen's affections—not to mention as the star of his *Broadway Danny Rose, The Purple Rose of Cairo,* and *Hannah and Her Sisters.*

Born: February 9, 1946, in Los Angeles, California
Height: 5 ft. 4 in.
Weight: 113 lbs.
Eyes: Blue *Hair:* Blond
Zodiac: Aquarius
Education: High school
Religion: Roman Catholic
Marriages: To Frank Sinatra (1967–1969)
To André Previn (1970–1979)
Children: Twin sons Matthew Phineas and Sascha Villiers Fletcher; two adopted daughters

Interests: Zen, ESP, yoga, TM; she paints, draws, loves music, makes patchwork quilts, sews
Personal Habits and Traits: Does not smoke or drink, sleeps no more than four hours a night, is superstitious (carries a good luck marble with her), given to long silences
Address: Manhattan
Income: $550,000

Farrah Fawcett

"Sweaty is sexy."

America's hair and teeth queen, Farrah Fawcett grew up the daughter of a wealthy Corpus Christi oil contractor and was voted one of the 10 most beautiful coeds at the University of Texas where she studied art. Later Farrah landed several minor roles on TV series and in movies (including the eminently forgettable *Myra Breckinridge* with Raquel Welch, and the less embarrassing *Logan's Run*), but she first made her mark by peddling more than 100 products on television, from Ultra-Brite and Wella Balsam to Noxzema and the Mercury Cougar. During this period she met and married a young pro football-player-turned-actor, Lee Majors, star of his own ABC-TV series, *The Six Million Dollar Man*. Once *Charlie's Angels* hit the air Farrah was splashed on the cover of just about every national magazine except *Field and Stream,* and quickly capitalized on her fame, face and figure to promote plumbing fixtures (the Farrah faucet, gold-plated for $100), Farrah Fawcett dolls, T-shirts and a new line of hair-care products for Fabergé. Fawcett dropped out of *Charlie's Angels* after only one spectacular season to tackle her first starring film role in *Somebody Killed Her Husband*. But the face and body that launched 6 million pinup posters (more than *ever* sold previously) was not unexpendable, for equally blond, beautiful, and tawny Cheryl Ladd stepped into Farrah's *Angels* slot effortlessly. "I was surprised," confessed Ms. Fawcett, "that I was so easily replaced." Coinciding with her second major film, *Sunburn,* was the breakup of her marriage to Lee Majors. During the filming of *Saturn 3* with Kirk Douglas, Fawcett (she dropped the "Majors") and actor-tennis player Vince Van Patten were linked romantically. Farrah strenuously denied the rumors: "If I were fooling around, no one would find me." They certainly found out when she took up with Ryan O'Neal, giving birth to their out-of-wedlock son in 1985. Fawcett was intent enough on becoming a serious actress to take on the punishing role of a woman who turns the tables on her attacker in Off-Broadway's graphic *Extremities*. She delivered another memorable performance as the victim of a homicidal physician in *Murder in Texas*. Her greatest career accomplishment to date: the real-life part of the abused wife driven to torching her husband in *The Burning Bed*. It was no fluke: Fawcett received more kudos as the emotionally victimized daughter-in-law in TV's superb *Between Two Women*.

Born: February 2, 1947, in Corpus Christi, Texas
Height: 5 ft. 6½ in.
Weight: 112 lbs.
Eyes: Green *Hair:* Blond
Zodiac: Aquarius
Education: University of Texas
Religion: Roman Catholic
Marriages: To Lee Majors (1973–1979)
Children: Redmond (b. 1985)
Interests: Hunting, fishing, skiing, sculpture
Personal Habits and Traits: Does not smoke, drinks little, says her rosary every night
Address: Bel Air, California
Income: $1 million

Federico Fellini

"Why do I make movies like Satyricon? *It's simple: I have always liked the world of the spectacle."*

As a teenager Fellini wanted to be a cartoonist, but before he could embark on his career he found work as a pratfalling comic for a Roman vaudeville troupe and wound up collaborating with neorealistic director Roberto Rossellini on the landmark film *Open City*. He brought his lyrical, surreal, and often grotesque vision of Rome—both ancient and modern—to his own outpouring of impressive films, including *La Strada, Nights of Cabiria, La Dolce Vita, 8½, Satyricon, The Clowns, Roma, Amarcord, Casanova* (with Donald Sutherland in the title role), and *Orchestra Rehearsal*. On every film Fellini, whose distinctive imagery has given vent to the adjective "Felliniesque," directs in a uniform of Charlie Chaplin drawers and a floppy hat. His directing style is considered a trifle lunatic, and the only movie in which the director has himself acted is *The Clowns,* in which he donned makeup to illustrate what he called the "half-magic, half-slaughterhouse" nature of the circus. He and Giulietta Masina, his wife and the star of several of his films—most notably *Juliet of the Spirits*—make their home in a villa on the outskirts of (where else?) Fellini's Roma. Released in 1986: *Ginger and Fred.*

Born: January 20, 1920, in Rimini, Italy
Height: 6 ft.
Weight: 210 lbs.
Eyes: Brown *Hair:* Brown
Zodiac: Aquarius
Education: High school dropout
Religion: Roman Catholic
Marriages: To Giulietta Masina (1943–)
Children: None
Interests: Clowns, cars, comedy, Catholicism, Italian politics, opera
Personal Habits and Traits: Smokes, drinks, needs no more than two hours sleep per day when making a film, can be abrasive, is temperamental
Address: Rome
Income: $523,000+

Geraldine Ferraro

"I didn't know what the West Bank was until I got there. It's so teeny."

The first woman to be nominated for vice-president by a major party walked at 8 months, talked at 9 months, started dancing lessons at 3, and learned to swim at 4. Raised by her dauntless mother Antonetta (her father died of a heart attack when his only daughter was 8), Geraldine Ferraro was 13 when Antonetta took her to the Queens workshop where Mom worked sewing sequins on fancy dresses. "She learned quick," Antonetta later said of her daughter. "But I didn't want her to learn. I said, 'Gerry, you better go to school and study.'" And study she did. At Marymount School in Tarrytown, New York, Gerry was in the honor society, on the debating team, and president of the literary society. She played softball, basketball, and field hockey and was—surprise!—voted most likely to succeed. Three days after passing her bar exams, Gerry Ferraro married real estate developer John Zaccaro, but kept her maiden name to honor the mother to whom she felt she owed everything. Four years and three children later, Ferraro went to work part-time in her husband's office, and stopped by the local Democratic club on her way home from PTA meetings. Her cousin Nicholas Ferraro, then district attorney of Queens, gave her a job as assistant prosecutor in 1974, and four years later she ran successfully for Congress under the slogan FINALLY, A TOUGH DEMOCRAT. Then, in 1984, she was handpicked to be Walter Mondale's running mate in the race against the unstoppable GOP ticket of Ronald Reagan and George Bush. The election proved a rough one for Ferraro, who soon found herself in the midst of a storm of controversy over her finances and those of her husband. The investigation eventually led to Zaccaro's indictment for fraud and, after plea-bargaining, a conviction on lesser charges. It killed whatever small chances for success the Democratic ticket might have had, if not Geraldine's own reputation; in late 1985 she ranked number three (behind Katharine Hepburn and Barbara Walters) in a *Ladies' Home Journal* poll of America's most admired women. Ferraro, who lives comfortably in a Tudor-style house in Forest Hills and maintains beach houses on Fire Island and in St. Croix, has in fact managed to turn political defeat into financial victory: She was given a $1 million advance to write her memoirs, began commanding $20,000 fees for her speeches, and even did a TV commercial for Diet Pepsi. The tab: $500,000. Her popularity aside, Ferraro found herself saddled with another scandal when her son John, Jr., was arrested for trafficking in cocaine at Vermont's Middlebury College.

Born: August 26, 1935, in Newburgh, New York.
Height: 5 ft. 2 in.
Weight: 120 lbs.
Eyes: Brown *Hair:* Blond
Zodiac: Leo
Education: Fordham University Law School
Religion: Roman Catholic
Marriages: To John Zaccaro (1960–)
Children: Three
Interests: Politics, clothes, cooking
Personal Habits and Traits: Although she has a live-in housekeeper, makes a weekly ritual of doing the weekly grocery shopping; nonsmoker, drinks moderately, ambitious, peripatetic
Addresses: Forest Hills, New York; Fire Island; St. Croix
Income: $2 million (estimate)

Sally Field

''In the past, I was Bob Hope's and everyone's joke. I've felt bitter because the people who laughed at me were laughing at the deepest part of me, and yet they'd never seen it.''

''You *like* me. You *really like* me!'' With that, Sally Field bared her insecurities for all Hollywood to see on the night in 1985 that she collected her second Best Actress Academy Award, for *Places in the Heart*. *The Flying Nun* flourished for three seasons on ABC, yet its star did not really take off as a serious actress until her spectacular performance as the multiple personality *Sybil* and the unionizing *Norma Rae*—she took home a Best Actress Oscar for the latter. As a high school student in the San Fernando Valley, the daughter of Paramount bit player Maggie Field dominated drama classes and was worshiped by younger schoolmates like Cindy (*Laverne and Shirley*) Williams. At 17 Sally was picked to play television's *Gidget* and shortly thereafter, when *The Flying Nun* became her winning habit, married the first man she ever dated, screenwriter Steve Craig. But after the ill-fated ESP comedy, *The Girl With Something Extra,* Field separated from Craig and enrolled in New York's famous Actors Studio, then made her first serious screen debut opposite Jeff Bridges in the iron-pumping saga *Stay Hungry,* followed by *Heroes,* with Henry (The Fonz) Winkler. The zany *Smokey and the Bandit* wound up grossing over $100 million—second only to *Star Wars* for the year 1977—and during the filming of *Smokey,* Field became the offscreen love object of costar Burt Reynolds. ''We have a very beautiful but strange relationship,'' said Field of Reynolds's continuing dalliances with old flames Dinah Shore and C&W queen Tammy Wynette. ''We don't worry about the other's dates.'' By 1980—the year she won her Academy Award for *Norma Rae*—Field and Reynolds had drifted apart, and she married producer Alan Greisman.

Born: November 6, 1946, in Pasadena, California
Height: 5 ft. 2 in.
Weight: 108 lbs.
Eyes: Brown *Hair:* Brown
Zodiac: Scorpio
Education: High school; Actors Studio
Religion: Protestant
Marriages: To Steven Craig (divorced) To Alan Greisman (1982–)
Children: Peter (b. 1970), Eli (b. 1972)
Interests: Literature, piano, quilting, sewing
Personal Habits and Traits: Early riser, moderate drinker, domestic type
Address: Laurel Canyon, California
Income: $3 million per film

Albert Finney

''Most actors make the mistake of letting press agents run their lives. I've done everything I can not to get sucked into that trap.''

The son of a Lancashire bookie, Finney spiraled to stardom portraying the kind of street-smart characters that surrounded him as he grew up. ''Albie'' was introduced to American audiences in the film *Saturday Night and Sunday Morning,* but it was as the roguish protagonist of Fielding's classic *Tom Jones* that Finney achieved bona fide star status. He produced, directed, and starred in the virtually autobiographical *Charlie Bubbles,* and triumphed on stage in the Broadway hits *Joe Egg* (later filmed with fellow British matinee idol Alan Bates) and *Luther.* Finney's best film roles include *Two for the Road,* during which he briefly wooed costar Audrey Hepburn off the set, the musical *Scrooge* and the all-star *Murder on the Orient Express,* in which he delivered a tour de force in his unrecognizable Hercule Poirot getup that garnered him a Best Actor Academy Award nomination (he lost out to Art Carney for *Harry and Tonto*). In 1970, Finney began a rocky marriage with French film actress Anouk Aimée, who has been an occasional companion of the ubiquitous Ryan O'Neal. Finney and Aimée divorced in 1978. Finney was a remarkably convincing Daddy Warbucks in the musical *Annie,* but his strongest parts dealt with the realities of divorce (*Shoot the Moon*) and alcoholism (*Under the Volcano*)—both of which garnered Academy Award nominations.

Born: May 9, 1936, in Salford, England
Height: 5 ft. 10 in.
Weight: 171 lbs.
Eyes: Blue *Hair:* Brown
Zodiac: Taurus
Education: High school
Religion: Roman Catholic
Marriages: To Jane Winham (1957–1961)
To Anouk Aimée (1970–1978)
Children: Simon (by first wife)
Interests: Travel, producing, directing, writing
Personal Habits and Traits: Chain-smokes, drinks, is independent and antisocial
Addresses: London; France
Income: $600,000 (minimum)

Carrie Fisher

"I always wanted to do what my mother did—get all dressed up, shoot people, fall in the mud. I never considered anything else."

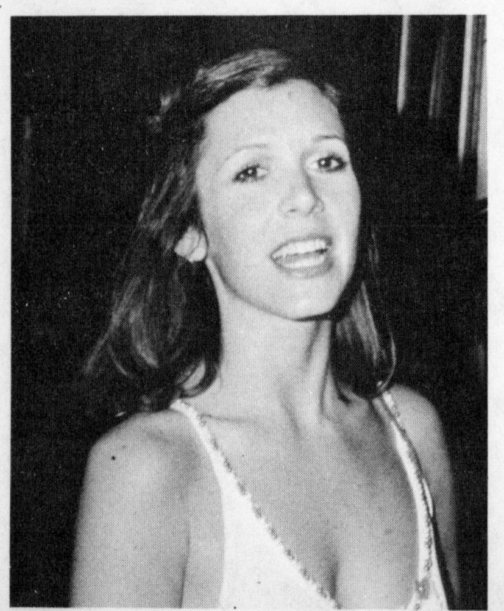

Carrie Fisher was only two when her father, Eddie, left her mother, Debbie (Reynolds), to marry dear friend Liz (Taylor). By the time she was 13 Carrie was singing at Las Vegas clubs in her mother's act, and two years later dropped out of Beverly Hills High School to study drama at London's Central School. After a brief acting career in New York, she played a teenage seductress in Warren Beatty's blockbuster sex comedy *Shampoo,* and in 1977 she snagged the starring female role of Princess Leia in *Star Wars*—the first in the spectacularly successful *Star Wars* saga that also included *The Empire Strikes Back* and *Return of the Jedi*. On good terms with both parents, Fisher and her brother Todd, a born-again Christian, can now both joke about coming from "a broken mansion." She has had her own setbacks in the marriage department. After her long-standing engagement to Dan Aykroyd dissolved amid career pressures, Fisher's marriage to Paul Simon fizzled after two years. Subsequent to the release of *Jedi* in 1984 (third in the nine-part series), Fisher left the cavernous Central Park duplex she shared with Simon and moved into a one-room log cabin in the Hollywood Hills that used to be a 1930s Twentieth Century-Fox set.

Born: October 21, 1956, in Los Angeles, California
Height: 5 ft. 1 in.
Weight: 95 lbs.
Eyes: Brown *Hair:* Brown
Zodiac: Libra
Education: High school dropout
Religion: Jewish
Marriages: To Paul Simon (1982–separated in 1984)
Children: None
Interests: Cooking, antiques and antique clothes, psychology
Personal Habits and Traits: Smokes, scrupulously watches her weight, is keen-witted
Address: Manhattan
Income: $3 million+ (mostly from the profits of *Star Wars*)

Ella Fitzgerald

"Everybody wants to know about my style and how it came about. It's no big secret. It's the way I feel."

"A-Tisket A-Tasket" established Ella's location on the musical map and since then the Virginia-born orphan who got her start as a big band canary in Harlem has sold over 30 million records. Over the years she has been backed by every legendary bandleader from Ellington to Basie to Arthur Fiedler. Still a top draw on the supper club circuit, this singers' singer is as adept as ever at the two types of music that are her forte, swing and scat, delivered with unfettered confidence. In 1977 the Grammy committee elevated Fitzgerald to the pantheon of modern musical greats, voting her a place in their Hall of Fame, and appropriately enough the award was accompanied by a musical tribute from one of the many current performers strongly influenced by Fitzgerald, Stevie Wonder. By the beginning of the 1980s, the severely myopic singer (her thick eyeglasses are ever-present) had also become a superb pitchwoman, asking millions of television viewers, "Is it live—or is it Memorex?"

Born: April 25, 1918, in Newport News, Virginia
Height: 5 ft. 8 in.
Weight: 170 lbs.
Eyes: Brown *Hair:* Black
Zodiac: Taurus
Education: High school
Religion: Protestant
Marriages: A first marriage was annulled. To Ray Brown (divorced)
Children: One son
Interests: Music, religion
Personal Habits and Traits: Nonsmoker, teetotaler, early riser, disciplined, self-effacing
Address: Beverly Hills
Income: $400,000+

Roberta Flack

"I can share with the audience the way I feel through Bach as well as pop."

An imaginary pal, Rubina Flake, would glide through Chopin concertos while Roberta Flack slogged away at piano lessons. At 13 Flack had progressed far enough in her piano lessons to perform the entire score from Handel's Messiah for her church choir; but later as an aspiring opera singer, she was crushed when her vocal coach hinted she try a pop music career. Taking the advice to heart, however, she began to mold her own unique, pop-jazz sound as folk and acid rock peaked in the 1960s. Teaching school in Washington, D.C., during the day, she moonlighted as a pianist in a Georgetown restaurant. Finally in 1972 Flack recorded her evocative blockbuster hit "The First Time Ever I Saw Your Face," followed the next year by the equally sensual "Killing Me Softly With His Song." By the time she had amassed a half-dozen gold albums and as many gold singles (including "Feel Like Makin' Love," "I Can See Clearly Now," and "The Closer I Get to You"), Flack was firmly in sole control of a flourishing music empire based in Washington, D.C.—the corporation that has produced all her albums since 1975. Chronic tonsillitis (for which she would not undergo voice-altering surgery) briefly threatened her career, as did nearly $1 million worth of IRS flak. The government charged in 1978 that Roberta Flack Enterprises owed $959,500 in back taxes and penalties for 1973 and 1974, including challenges to deductions of nearly $200,000 in pension contributions, $16,000 for travel, and $24,000 in clothes, and penalties amounting to $490,000. Flack insisted all the deductions were valid business expenses; the whole matter remained to be resolved by the courts. Not ready to abandon her classical roots, Flack, who boasted yet another hit LP with *Blue Lights in the Basement,* planned to incorporate Bach arias into her pop recordings. "I'm a serious artist," she contended. "I'm not going to be pushed into a corner and just sing soul." Flack also proclaimed that she was "trying to have a baby" with television producer Stewart Bosley, her sometime roommate at what may be New York's ritziest residential address, the Dakota. She worried, however, about "the trouble I've had in the past with miscarriages." In 1985, her duet with Peabo Bryson, "Tonight, I Celebrate My Love for You," returned her to the charts.

Born: February 10, 1940, in Black Mountain, North Carolina
Height: 5 ft. 4 in.
Weight: 136 lbs.
Eyes: Brown *Hair:* Black
Zodiac: Aquarius
Education: Howard University, B.A. in music education
Religion: Baptist
Marriages: To Steve Novosel (1965–1972)
Children: An adopted daughter
Interests: Piano, classical music, producing, composing, African culture, art, pinball (she has a $25-a-week habit)
Personal Habits and Traits: Nonsmoker, drinks little, diets frequently, a night person
Address: New York City
Income: $500,000 (minimum estimate)

Fleetwood Mac

Mick Fleetwood

"I just vibe out the situation, because a greedy drummer can ruin a band."

Self-described "mother hen" to one of the most popular groups in rock history, Mick Fleetwood grew up in Cornwall, England, the son of a Royal Air Force wing commander. His family spent three years in Egypt, then went to live in Norway during his father's stint with NATO, but when his father bought him a set of drums at 15, Mick set out to play with a series of local bands throughout England. In 1967 Fleetwood Mac was born at the height of the San Francisco sound, and moved to the U.S. to jam at the Fillmore West and other rock places of the late 1960s and early '70s. Then, shortly after Californians Lindsey Buckingham and Stevie Nicks joined Mac veterans John McVie and his wife, Chris, their new Fleetwood Mac album became the second hottest album of 1977, selling more than 4 million copies. However, domestic troubles threatened to destroy the group. Bassist John McVie and Chris were legally separated; guitarist-singer Buckingham and vocalist Nicks split after eight years together; and Mick divorced his wife Jenny. In the aftermath, the group decided to lay their troubles down on the tracks of the discreetly autobiographical *Rumours,* which became one of the biggest-selling LPs in history, remaining on the charts for well over 18 months and spinning off number-one singles like "Go Your Own Way" and "Dreams." In the meantime, Fleetwood remarried Jenny after a separation of four months. A fiend for detail, Fleetwood manages the band himself and reads all the official mail that comes to the group. At one point, he oversaw legal efforts to put an imposter "Fleetwood Mac" out of business. Now happily ensconced in a Topanga Canyon retreat with Jenny and their daughters,

Amy and Lucy, Fleetwood remains a British subject—though he pays most of his taxes in the United States as a permanent resident. The group's next effort after *Rumours, Tusk,* was over two years in the making and charged straight to the top. Amazingly, after Buckingham, Chris McVie, and Nicks split to solo success, Fleetwood filed for bankruptcy in 1985.

Born: June 24, 1942, in Cornwall, England
Height: 6 ft. 6 in.
Weight: 180 lbs.
Eyes: Brown *Hair:* Brown
Zodiac: Cancer
Education: High school dropout
Marriages: To Jenny Boyd (divorced, then remarried)
Children: Amy and Lucy
Interests: Producing, composing
Personal Habits and Traits: Smokes, drinks moderately, soft-spoken
Address: Topanga Canyon, California
Income: Filed for bankruptcy in 1985

Jane Fonda

"Being a movie star is not a purpose."

Easily the most controversial member of her unconventional family, Jane Fonda celebrated her 40th year with brilliant performances in two outstanding films—*Julia* and *Coming Home;* for the latter she received her second Best Actress Oscar in 1979. But she attained the status of a mature and outstanding actress only after several diverse incarnations—as ingenue, sexpot, and antiwar activist. When her mother, Frances Brokaw, killed herself in an asylum, 12-year-old Jane was told she died of a heart attack, and only read the true story years later in a movie magazine. After Vassar, Fonda arrived on the Great White Way in *There Was a Little Girl.* Lightweight roles in such movies as *Barefoot in the Park* (with Robert Redford) and *Sunday in New York* did little to enhance her professional reputation, and when she fled to marry French director-impresario Roger Vadim she was carelessly exploited in the tongue-in-cheek sci-fi flick *Barbarella.* However, her powerful performance in *They Shoot Horses, Don't They?,* with its deeply depressing story about the rigors of a 1930s dance marathon, established her once and for all as a major talent in 1969. Fonda received a New York Film Critics Award for the movie, and two years later copped an Oscar for her tour de force portrayal of a prostitute marked for murder in *Klute.* Then, at the height of the Vietnam war, she drew bitter national criticism for visiting Hanoi and broadcasting propaganda for the North Vietnamese. In 1973 she married a leader of the antiwar movement and former SDS chief, Tom Hayden, and stumped the state of California on his behalf when he ran unsuccessfully for the U.S. Senate in 1976. In a bizarre turn of events, Fonda's *China Syndrome,* a suspense film about a mishap at a nuclear power plant, was released the same week an actual accident occurred at the Three Mile Island nuclear power plant in Middleton, Pennsylvania. Not long after receiving her *Coming Home* Oscar, Fonda was embroiled in two controversies—a disagreement with Joan Baez over human rights in Communist Vietnam (she refused to sign Baez's newspaper ad condemning Hanoi) and the California legislature's refusal to approve Fonda's nomination to the state Arts Council. When she wasn't traveling about the country making speeches with Hayden, Fonda found time to start her own Workout gym, and costar with old *Barefoot* pal Redford in the delightful *Electric Horseman,* with Lily Tomlin and Dolly Parton in *9 to 5,* and with Kris Kristoferson in *Rollover.* In 1983, Fonda found the vehicle that earned for her father his long-deserved Academy Award—*On Golden Pond*—and wound up taking a supporting Oscar herself. Fonda also collected an Emmy for 1984's *The Dollmaker.* Yet Workout worked out to be Fonda's most lucrative venture, as she raked in royalties for two *Workout* books and the bestselling exercise video in history. For her riveting role in *Agnes of God* of a shrink uncovering secrets in a convent, Fonda had to learn to chain-smoke (in fact, she faked it with phony cigarettes).

Born: December 21, 1937, in New York City
Height: 5 ft. 7 in.
Weight: 118 lbs.
Eyes: Blue *Hair:* Brown
Zodiac: Sagittarius
Education: Vassar College
Religion: Lapsed Episcopalian
Marriages: To Roger Vadim (1965–1968) To Tom Hayden (1973–)
Children: Vanessa (named after Vanessa Redgrave) Vadim (b.1968); Troy Hayden (b. 1973)
Interests: Pro-solar power, anti-nuclear power, politics, art
Personal Habits and Traits: Cleans house, exercises rigorously
Address: Santa Monica, California
Income: $5.5 million (all sources)

Peter Fonda

"Civilization has always been a bust."

If Jane is the most controversial member of the family, the most explosive of the famous Fondas is Peter, who shot himself in the liver and kidneys when his mother committed suicide, then spent his young adulthood raising hell and damning his father. He attended the University of Omaha, made his debut on Broadway in *Blood, Sweat and Stanley Poole* in 1961, starred in his first movie, *The Interns,* and was on his way to an untainted reputation as Hank Fonda's son when he suddenly discovered LSD. Busted for possession in 1966, Fonda not only immersed himself in the drug culture, but along with Dennis Hopper tried to mystify it in *Easy Rider,* a box-office blockbuster that made them overnight multimillionaires. Married for 13 years to Susan Brewer, he divorced her in 1974 and two years later married Portia Crockett. Peter's *Dirty Larry, Crazy Mary* also stormed the screen in 1975, followed by *Futureworld,* putting him back in the chips after a series of bad investments and a rather lavish life-style that included an 80-foot yacht. After their father's death, Peter and Jane sifted through scripts in search of the right project for them to bring to the screen together.

Born: February 23, 1940, in Los Angeles
Height: 6 ft. 2 in.
Weight: 169 lbs.
Eyes: Blue *Hair:* Brown
Zodiac: Pisces
Education: University of Omaha
Marriages:
To Susan Brewer (1961–1974)
To Portia Crockett (1976–)
Children: Two
Interests: Sailing, producing, directing
Personal Habits and Traits: Does not smoke, does drink, a night person
Address: Los Angeles
Income: $350,000+

Betty Ford

Elizabeth Bloomer Ford

''They've asked me everything but how often I sleep with my husband. And if they asked me that I would have told them, 'As often as possible.' ''

Rated in one national poll as the most popular First Lady in U.S. history, the onetime Martha Graham student and John Robert Powers model was born in Chicago and grew up as Betty Bloomer in Grand Rapids, Michigan. After a brief career studying modern dance with Graham, she gave up her Greenwich Village apartment and returned home to Grand Rapids, where she worked as a fashion coordinator for a local department store. A five-year marriage to furniture salesman William Warren ended in divorce on grounds of incompatibility. When Betty met young Gerald Ford she recalls that he crossed his legs and nearly knocked over all the flowers on her coffee table. Married in the midst of his first campaign for Congress in 1948, they found that the hectic pace of their lives increased after Ford became the Republicans' House Minority Leader in 1965—he wound up spending as many as 200 nights a year on the road. A severely pinched nerve in her neck and a painful case of arthritis were intensified by emotional stress, and on the advice of her doctor Betty began seeing a psychiatrist. After Vice President Ford's ascension to the Presidency upon Richard Nixon's August 9, 1974 resignation, the new First Lady quickly earned a reputation for being outspoken and candid. She did not hesitate to sip a drink occasionally in front of reporters, and following her radical mastectomy, openly discussed her battle with breast cancer in the hope of educating other women on the need for early diagnosis. On the subject of her own children she was no less forthright, admitting that she would not be shocked if her daughter Susan, then 18, had told her she was having an affair. Even after Ford's defeat by Jimmy Carter in the 1976 Presidential election, Betty Ford often commanded more attention than her successor Rosalynn Carter. In the spring of 1978 she openly checked into a hospital to overcome an increasing dependency on painkillers and alcohol, then had a facelift—"a new face to go with my marvelous new life.'' After penning her dramatic history in her bestselling autobiography *The Times of My Life,* Ford lent her name to a Palm Springs alcohol and drug-abuse clinic that would become a magnet for the likes of Elizabeth Taylor and Liza Minnelli.

Born: April 8, 1918, in Chicago
Height: 5 ft. 6 in.
Weight: 108 lbs.
Eyes: Blue-green *Hair:* Auburn blond
Zodiac: Aries
Education: Bennington College School of Dance
Religion: Episcopalian (taught Sunday School from 1961 to 1964)
Marriages:
To William C. Warren (1942–1947)
To Gerald R. Ford (1948–)
Children: Michael (b. 1950), Jack (b. 1952), Stephen (b. 1956), Susan (b. 1957)
Interests: Dance, art, fashion, music, sports (gave up skiing because of neck injury), women's rights, Republican politics, cancer research, psychotherapy
Personal Habits and Traits: Smokes occasionally, has cut down on her drinking (vodka and tonics) and her consumption of painkillers for her arthritis and the nerve in her neck, exercises 15 minutes every morning
Addresses: Palm Springs, California; Vail, Colorado
Income: Gerald and Betty Ford have combined earnings of around $1.5 million yearly

Gerald R. "Jerry" Ford

"Eating and sleeping are a waste of time."

With the unprecedented resignation of Richard Nixon, Gerald R. Ford became the 38th President of the United States. Born in Omaha, his parents were divorced when he was less than a year old, and taking the name of his stepfather (his real name was King), Ford was raised with his stepbrothers in Grand Rapids, Michigan. He worked his way through the University of Michigan as a busboy at a local coffee shop while leading the school's Wolverine football team to two Big 10 championships in 1932 and 1933. From there he entered Yale Law School, and although he graduated in the top third of his class, Ford was later scathingly characterized by longtime political foe Lyndon Johnson as "playing without a helmet" and not being "able to walk and chew gum at the same time." Ford briefly worked as a male model in New York—one *Look Magazine* spread depicted him modeling ski clothes with an attractive blonde—before running for Congress in 1948. During the campaign he married a divorced dancer and occasional model named Betty Bloomer, then immediately continued his barnstorming after the ceremony. Such single-minded determination paid off, leading to his election by a sound majority, and for the next quarter-century the conservative Republican pursued his ambition to become Speaker of the House. In 1973 Nixon tapped him to replace Spiro Agnew as Vice President after Agnew was forced to resign because of a bribery scandal surrounding his term as Governor of Maryland. A year later, on August 9, 1974, Watergate catapulted Gerald Ford into the Oval Office. During his two and a half years in the White House, Ford exercised fiscal restraint while relying on Secretary of State Henry Kissinger to administer foreign policy. Up against a then relatively unknown Jimmy Carter, Ford led a feverish campaign to overcome the aftereffects of

Watergate and to dilute his subsequent unpopular decision to pardon Nixon. Despite a sudden surge at the finish, Ford lost to Carter by about 1 percent of the popular vote. After the election Ford retreated to the impressive house he had built on a golf course in Palm Springs, and in 1980 passed up the chance to try to seize the GOP nomination from former California Governor Ronald Reagan.

Born: July 14, 1913, in Omaha, Nebraska
Height: 6 ft. 2 in.
Weight: 180 lbs.
Eyes: Blue *Hair:* Blond
Zodiac: Cancer
Education: University of Michigan, B.A.; Yale University, LL.D
Religion: Protestant
Marriages: To Betty Bloomer (1948–)
Children: Michael (b. 1950), Jack (b. 1952), Steve (b. 1956), Susan (b. 1957)
Interests: Golf, tennis, swimming, football (a self-confessed sports nut)
Personal Habits and Traits: Smokes a pipe, drinks martinis, up at 5:30 A.M. (needs only four hours sleep per night), works out on stationary bicycle, diets, wears pajamas
Addresses: Palm Springs, California; Vail, Colorado
Income: The Fords have a combined income of about $1.5 million yearly

Harrison Ford

''I am very, very rich. That's what people want to hear, isn't it? People would like to know exactly how rich I am, but it's none of their goddamn business.''

After his first film, 1966's emminently forgettable *Dead Heat on a Merry-Go-Round,* a Columbia executive told him, ''Kid, you ain't got it.'' It took more than a decade, but Harrison Ford proved he had plenty of ''it'' by starring in half of the Top 10 grossers in motion picture history: *Star Wars, Return of the Jedi, The Empire Strikes Back, Raiders of the Lost Ark,* and *Indiana Jones and the Temple of Doom.* Part Russian-Jewish and part Irish Catholic, Ford grew up with ''a real fear of facing people'' in the suburbs around Chicago. Ford overcame that fear by acting in class productions at Wisconsin's Ripon College, and actually dropped out in his senior year to pursue an acting career. After *Merry-Go-Round,* bit parts in flops like *Luv,* and an occasional job on TV shows *Gunsmoke* and *Ironside,* Ford took up carpentry as a reliable means of supporting his family. For seven years, he virtually dropped out of the business, turning down nearly all the parts he was offered until the right one came along in 1973—the role of an out-of-town hot-rodder in George Lucas's *American Grafitti.* Parts in *The Conversation* and *The Trial of Lieutenant Calley* followed, but it wasn't until he blazed a trail across the galaxy as Hans Solo in Lucas's *Star Wars* that Ford felt safe turning down carpentry jobs. Ford also turned in memorable performances as an inscrutable army colonel in Francis Ford Coppola's *Apocalypse Now* and as a 21st-century cop in *Blade Runner,* but it took 1985's enormously successful thriller *Witness,* in which Ford plays a Philadelphia detective hiding out among the Amish, to help him at least momentarily break free from his Hans Solo-Indiana Jones-swashbuckling-antihero image. A tremendous stickler for detail, Ford calls himself a "technical actor." That means knowing everything about a character he is to portray—from how and where he would live to the kind of shoes he wears. Ford, who shuns publicity, has put his skill as a builder to work on the house in the Santa Monica mountains where he lives with his second wife, Melissa Mathison. Mrs. Ford herself is no stranger to blockbusters of the interstellar variety; she wrote the screenplay for *E.T.*

Born: July 13, 1942, in Chicago
Height: 6 ft. 1 in.
Weight: 175 lbs.
Eyes: Blue *Hair:* Brown
Zodiac: Cancer
Education: Four years at Ripon College, but dropped out before earning a degree
Marriages: Two. Currently to Melissa Mathison (1983–)
Children: Benjamin (b. 1967), Willard (b. 1969)
Interests: Carpentry, literature
Personal Habits and Traits: Intensely private, sometimes abrasive, smokes occasionally, moderate drinker
Addresses: Los Angeles; Wyoming
Income: $5 million+

John Forsythe

John Lincoln Freund

"It's rather amusing at my advanced age to become a sex symbol."

From *Bachelor Father* to the disembodied voice of Charlie on *Charlie's Angels* to *Dynasty* patriarch Blake Carrington, John Forsythe has managed to sustain his remarkable television career for nearly three decades. The son of a Wall Street executive, he was raised in New Jersey and the suburbs of Connecticut, where he dreamed of being a sports announcer. Instead, he acted on radio soap operas like *Stella Dallas* and *Helen Trent* and, while waiting on tables at Schrafft's, finally landed a role on Broadway in the short-running farce *Vickie*. At least it got him noticed by Warner executives, who cast him in 1943's *Destination Tokyo* and *Northern Pursuit*. After serving as a counselor for shell-shocked Air Force pilots during the war, he returned to the stage and soon replaced Henry Fonda in the role of *Mr. Roberts* on Broadway. For five years beginning in 1957, Forsythe found himself the sole charge of his willful teenage niece, Noreen Corcoran, in *Bachelor Father*—a formula he repeated with far less success in the *John Forsythe Show* (1965–1966) and *To Rome With Love* (1969–1971). There were also a few memorable parts in movies—like the determined detective in *In Cold Blood,* and the CIA agent in Alfred Hitchcock's *Topaz*—before he agreed to do the heard-but-never-seen Charlie as a favor to old pal Aaron Spelling. Forsythe, who is also the voice of Michelob beer, predicted the series would flop, and went on to act on it for its entire six-year run. In 1979, he underwent a risky quadruple heart bypass operation that left him with a new outlook: ''I thought the hummingbird that drinks outside my window was routine, but now I find it miraculous.'' Previously an intensely competitive, driven man, Forsythe decided to ease up somewhat, and within months was offered the juiciest part of his career—that of *Dynasty*'s intensely competitive, driven oil tycoon, Blake Carrington. Although he was soon pulling down $100,000 per episode, Forsythe at one point became so angry about Blake's unremitting ruthlessness that he threatened to leave the show if Carrington wasn't softened up a bit. He was. Married for more than 40 years to former Broadway actress Julie Warren, Forsythe lives in a Bel Air colonial filled with the antiques both he and his wife collect. But his real passion is for horseflesh; he owns shares of several thoroughbred stallions. The Silver Fox's assessment of his own talent is measured: ''I don't think I'm Olivier or Brando, but I do think I'm a better actor than I've been given credit for.''

Born: January 29, 1918, in Carney's Point, New Jersey
Height: 6 ft.
Weight: 170 lbs.
Eyes: Blue *Hair:* Gray
Zodiac: Aquarius
Religion: Protestant
Marriages: To Paula McCormick (1938–1940)
To Julie Warren (1943–)
Children: Dall (b. 1939), Page (b. 1950), Brooke (b. 1954)
Interests: Women's rights, mental health, liberal politics, antiques, music and painting, horses, sailing, reading, the environment (he narrates a TV wildlife series called *The World of Survival*)
Personal Habits and Traits: Has given up smoking, drinks vodka, runs two miles a day
Address: Bel Air, California
Income: $3 million (estimate)

Bob Fosse

''My friends know that to me happiness is when I am merely miserable and not suicidal.''

In a scene requiring Marisa Berenson to register horror at the sight of her butchered dog in *Cabaret,* she received no instructions from her director, Bob Fosse. She merely opened a door and looked down; what she saw was a pile of raw animal entrails that elicted exactly the proper response. Such tricks have always helped choreographer-director Bob Fosse get results. He began as a hoofer in nightclubs and vaudeville at age 13. A benign deception landed him his first big opportunity as a choreographer when he fabricated a list of credits on the spur of the moment so that producer George Abbott would hire him to choreograph the dance numbers for *Pajama Game*. Abbott did, and Fosse won the first of several Tonys for the hit musical. He married and divorced two of his dancing partners—first Mary-Ann Miles and then Joan McCracken—before settling into a director-to-star relationship with third wife Gwen Verdon in such musicals as

Damn Yankees and *Redhead*. *Pippin,* for which he won two Tonys as Best Director and Best Choreographer, premiered just as the Fosse-Verdon marriage foundered, though shortly after their 1973 divorce he directed her once again in *Chicago*. The film version of *Cabaret,* based on Christopher Isherwood's stories of decadent, prewar Berlin, netted him an Academy Award as Best Director. Acclaim for his *Lenny* soon followed, and by 1976 Fosse was an Oscar, Tony, *and* Emmy winner. His romantic interest, Ann Reinking, became something of a Fosse protégée. She ultimately replaced Verdon in *Chicago* after three years, then was tapped to star in Fosse's Broadway smash *Dancin'* (which earned him yet *another* Tony in 1978). By that time, however, Fosse and Reinking had finished their lengthy pas de deux. Fosse then launched the production of his self-indulgent autobiographical movie musical *All That Jazz,* which for some reason was greeted with raves when it was released in late 1979, and a short-lived romance with Jessica Lange. It was a quantum leap from *Jazz* to Fosse's gory and gruesome film biography of murdered *Playboy* Playmate Dorothy Stratten, *Star 80*.

Born: June 23, 1927 in Chicago
Height: 6 ft.
Weight: 172 lbs.
Eyes: Blue *Hair:* Brown
Zodiac: Cancer
Education: High school
Religion: None
Marriages: To Mary-Ann Miles (divorced)
To Joan McCracken (divorced)
To Gwen Verdon (divorced)
Children: Two
Interests: Films, theater, nightclubs, television
Personal Habits and Traits: Still smokes despite heart attack, drinks moderately, nail biter
Address: New York City
Income: $700,000 (estimate)

Jodie Foster

"I still think of myself as a kid. I like being a kid. I liked filming Bugsy Malone *because I got to throw pies in people's faces. Can I be hurt by this business? Judy Garland was one in a thousand."*

Tatum O'Neal's only competition as *the* child actress of the 1970s, Jodie Foster actually started her career in the 1960s when Jodie's older brother, Buddy (then 8 years old), became determined to act professionally. Their mother Brand Foster, a former Hollywood press agent, took Buddy to audition for a TV commercial and he was soon shooting job after job. Jodie accompanied him when she was 3 and landed her own part in a commercial for Coppertone. Managed by her mom, Jodie switched from commercials to TV drama roles at age 10, and when Peter Bogdanovich's *Paper Moon* was translated into a TV series, Foster easily nabbed the Tatum O'Neal lead. Her film breakthrough came at 12 as a drug-addicted child prostitute in Martin Scorsese's *Taxi Driver,* for which she was nominated for an Academy Award as Best Supporting Actress. Among Foster's other film

credits are *Bugsy Malone, The Little Girl Who Lives Down the Lane* and *Candleshoe,* yet despite the fact that she is one of the most sought-after young actresses in Hollywood, Jodie was determined to complete her education at Los Angeles's chic Lycée Français and remained content with a $5-a-week allowance until she graduated. In 1980 Foster scored with her portrayal of an L.A. high school senior in *Foxes,* then enrolled at Yale. In 1981, Foster was at the center of the firestorm created by the attempted assassination of Ronald Reagan. John Hinckley's morbid obsession with the star apparently led to his decision to "impress" her by shooting the President. Four years later, after reappearing on the screen in the unfortunate *Hotel New Hampshire,* she graduated magna cum laude from Yale.

Born: November 19, 1962, in Los Angeles
Height: 5 ft. 5 in.
Weight: 115 lbs.
Eyes: Blue *Hair:* Blond
Zodiac: Scorpio
Education: Lycée Français, Los Angeles; Yale
Religion: Protestant
Marriages: None
Children: None
Interests: Skateboarding, swimming, horseback riding, rock music, French
Personal Habits and Traits: Early riser, modest, unaffected
Address: Los Angeles
Income: $260,000 (minimum estimate)

Michael J. Fox

Michael A. Fox

"I got sick of turning on the TV and seeing my face. The television turned into a mirror for a while."

He had lost twenty pounds on a diet of macaroni, was operating out of a phone booth near a Pioneer Chicken outlet and had resorted to selling off parts of his sectional couch to pay for the $30,000 of debts he had piled up when the call came to audition for a new sitcom about the Reaganaut son of two '60s liberals. Fox helped make *Family Ties* one of the '80s most successful series (routinely behind No. 1 show Bill Cosby in the ratings), and Steven Spielberg's *Back to the Future*, a box-office blockbuster. Growing up on a series of military bases as the son of a career man in the Canadian signal corps, Fox learned to adapt and make friends quickly. The family eventually settled in Vancouver, and after some success on Canadian television Fox moved to Los Angeles to pursue his acting career. After a few jobs—like a supporting role in an ill-fated series called *Palmerstown, U.S.A.*—Fox found himself out of work at twenty and scraping by until *Family Ties* came along in 1982. Since then, Fox (his *Teen Wolf* racked up around $35 million on his name alone) has earned a reputation as one of the most articulate and likeable young talents in the business—not to mention one of its most promising. No lesser judge than the late James Cagney recognized that promise: Cagney wanted Fox to play the title role in his life story. Fox (he changed his name from Michael A. to head off fanzine headlines like "Michael, A Fox") lives in a tastefully decorated house in Brentwood, drives a $20,000 Nissan 300ZX Turbo and has maintained and on-again, off-again relationship with *Facts of Life* star Nancy McKeon. There is little chance of Fox having to return to his old phone booth outside of the Pioneer Chicken store: He was paid a high six figures to do a commercial for Pepsi, his *Family Ties* salary is estimated at $30,000 per episode, and his asking price per film is $1.5 million. Producers were more than happy to ante up the full amount to have Fox star as a struggling rocker in (*Just Around the Corner to*) *The Light of Day* and as a business school grad in *Private Affairs*.

Born: June 9, 1961, in Edmonton, Alberta
Height: 5 ft. 4 in.
Weight: 120 lbs.
Eyes: Blue *Hair:* Light brown
Zodiac: Gemini
Education: High school
Religion: Protestant
Marriages: None
Children: None
Interests: Hockey, fishing, a number of charities
Personal Habits and Traits: Chain-smokes, optimistic, unassuming
Address: Brentwood, California
Income: $2 million+

Redd Foxx

John Elroy Sanford

"There ain't nuthin' in the whole world worse than an ugly white woman."

This black-and-blue comedy king was already becoming a millionaire on the basis of X-rated albums and nightclub appearances when Norman Lear tapped him to play junkman Fred Sanford in the Americanized version of the BBC comedy *Steptoe and Son*. *Sanford and Son* (the character's name was taken from Foxx's real surname) proved an overnight success that topped the Nielsens and made Foxx as heralded a star to a mostly white family audience as he had been to Harlem and Vegas crowds for over 30 years. St. Louis-born, Foxx chose his stage name from both the red fox in children's books and from baseball legend Jimmy Foxx (hence the two x's). Foxx, nicknamed "Chicago Red," and "Detroit Red" Malcolm Little were fast friends in Harlem during the 1940s. Detroit Red later changed his name too—to Malcolm X. Several top-rated seasons and an annual take that reportedly exceeded $2 million did not constitute much of a lesson in humility, and in 1977 Foxx left NBC after a long contract dispute during which, among other things, Foxx complained that the network brass had "insulted" him with a gift of two bottles of wine on the occasion of his third marriage. A year after *Sanford* folded, Foxx flopped terribly with *The Red Foxx*

Show on ABC. Reruns of *Sanford* continue, however, and Foxx continues to accumulate healthy residuals as well as collecting a healthy salary in Atlantic City, Reno and comedy clubs around the country.

Born: December 9, 1922, in St. Louis, Missouri
Height: 5 ft. 8 in.
Weight: 158 lbs.
Eyes: Brown *Hair:* White
Zodiac: Sagittarius
Education: High school dropout
Religion: Baptist
Marriages:
To Evelyn Killibrew (divorced)
To Betty Jean Harris (divorced)
To Yun Chi Chung (1977; split in 1979)
Interests: Cars, dogs
Habits: Chain-smokes, drinks, is not punctual, late sleeper
Address: Beverly Hills
Income: $1 million+

Aretha Franklin

"At the core of all *my singing is just good old gospel music. I can't get away from it—and I don't want to."*

The Memphis-born Queen of Soul grew up in musically rich Motown, was barely 10 when her mother died, and was raised by her father, a minister who used family members to wail the gospel hymns that helped fill collection plates. Unsuited to the polished rhythm-and-blues style of neighbors Diana Ross and Marvin Gaye, Aretha did not seem to fit into the pop music mold until the mid-1960s, when she decided to plunge headlong into unsullied soul. A string of chartbusters—"R-E-S-P-E-C-T," "Chain of Fools," "The House That Jack Built," "Natural Woman"—soon landed her on the cover of *Time* magazine in 1968. Although she evoked a new sound in her lilting 1975 ballad "That's What I'm Gonna Do," Aretha has not strayed far from her gospel roots; she still occasionally solos as a member of her father's Sunday choir. Her religious faith helped pull Franklin through a rough marriage with real estate agent Ted White, who slapped her around in public, and after their 1972 divorce, she gave birth to a son by road manager Ken Cunningham. Looking like a young Mahalia Jackson for much of her career, Aretha dieted off more than 50 pounds in the early 1970s, though much of the weight returned. In 1978 she married actor Glynn Turman, five years her junior—after he proposed to her in the motel room where he was staying while on location shooting a TV movie. They lasted less than two years. She was brilliant in a vignette in the otherwise uneven Belushi movie *Blues Brothers*. Following a brief slump, Franklin's career was reignited with her gold LP *Almighty Fire,* and in 1985 she teamed up with Annie Lennox of the Eurythmics to create a soulful New Wave sound. Her "Freeway of Love," "Who's Zoomin' Who?" and "Another Night" cuts from Franklin's electric *Who's Zoo-*

min' Who? album varoomed to the top of the charts, as did the accompanying videos. The Soul Queen also picked up some extra cash doing commercials, most notably for Dial soap and (there's gold in them there arches) McDonalds.

Born: March 25, 1942, in Memphis, Tennessee
Height: 5 ft. 7 in.
Weight: 131 lbs.
Eyes: Brown *Hair:* Brown
Zodiac: Aries
Education: High school
Religion: Baptist
Marriages: To Ted White (divorced)
To Glynn Turman (divorced)

Children: Three sons by White and one by road manager Ken Cunningham
Interests: Religion, gospel singing, meditation
Personal Habits and Traits: Chain-smokes, does not drink alcohol, is a diet fanatic, a fearful flier
Address: Encino, California
Income: $2.2 million (estimate)

Betty Friedan

"Man is not the enemy here, but the fellow victim."

Betty Goldstein, the loudest, brassiest and most abrasive of feminists, comes from Peoria, Illinois. She ensured her position in the history of the women's movement by penning its manifesto, *The Feminine Mystique,* in 1963. Her bestseller proved only the first step in a nonstop career of lobbying, speechmaking and writing that has earned her the unofficial title of feminist Godmother and in the process cost her a 22-year marriage to Madison Avenue executive Carl Friedan. Founder and first president of the National Organization of Women (NOW), Betty Friedan "womaned" the barricades in the battle for passage of the Equal Rights Amendment, and delivered a keynote speech at the historic Houston Conference in 1977. Friedan thrives in the thick of the good fight and was ranked by author Michael Hart (*The 100*) as one of the 25 most influential Americans of all time. Friedan shocked many of her fellow feminists with the publication of her 1982 have-we-gone-too-far? volume, *The Second Stage*.

Born: February 4, 1921, in Peoria, Illinois
Height: 5 ft. 4 in.
Weight: 130 lbs.
Eyes: Brown *Hair:* Gray
Zodiac: Aquarius
Education: High school
Religion: Jewish
Marriages: To Carl Friedan (1947–1969)

Children: David, Jonathan, Emily
Interests: Democratic Party politics, art, music
Personal Habits and Traits: Chain-smokes, not a teetotaler, tends to overeat
Address: New York City
Income: $80,000+

William Friedkin

"By the time a film makes it into the theaters, I have a love-hate relationship with it. There is always something I could have done to make it better."

Before *The French Connection* claimed five Academy Awards—including one for Best Director—and before the horrific *The Exorcist,* Billy Friedkin had, unbeknown to all but diehard trivia addicts, already directed dozens of television shows and four major films. Beginning at the bottom as a mailboy at a local Chicago TV station while still in high school, the future Oscar-winner got his first chance to direct a feature film with *Good Times* in 1966. Determined to direct a movie a year, he turned out *The Night They Raided Minsky's* (starring Elliot Gould and Jason Robards), *The Birthday Party* and *Boys in the Band,* but Friedkin's winning streak that had begun with *The French Connection* expired with 1976's *The Sorcerer*—one of the industry's biggest critical and commercial turkeys in memory. He consoled himself by marrying Jeanne Moreau, the French superstar 11 years his senior. Their union lasted less than three years. Friedkin made headlines once again with the release of his 1980 film *Cruisin'*, which so incensed the gay community that riots threatened to halt on-location shooting in New York City. Freidkin's marriage to British actress Lesley-Anne *(Upstairs, Downstairs)* Down ended in an acrimonious 1985 divorce, and a bitter battle for custody of their son Josh. At the same time, Friedkin, who of late has taken to directing videos for Barbra Streisand and others, called it a wrap on his film *To Live and Die in L.A.*

Born: August 29, 1939, in Chicago
Height: 6 ft.
Weight: 175 lbs.
Eyes: Brown *Hair:* Brown
Zodiac: Virgo
Religion: Jewish
Marriages: To Jeanne Moreau (1976–1979)
To Lesley-Anne Down (1982–1985)

Children: Josh (b. 1982)
Interests: Writing, producing, directing
Personal Habits and Traits: Smokes, drinks, is quiet and blunt, needs little sleep
Addresses: Los Angeles; Paris
Income: $1 million (estimate)

David Frost

"Success is a crappy, trendy word. Don't aim for success if you want it, just do what you love doing and it will come naturally."

The French proverb "Even a stopped clock is right twice a day" is David Frost's favorite because, as he interprets it, "You can learn something from everybody—if you just take the time to listen." Frost has listened to some of the world's most celebrated figures on his Emmy-winning *David Frost Show,* and on his *Headliners* series that was aired on NBC in 1978. Unquestionably his most riveting interview of all was with ex-President Richard Nixon—a singular broadcasting coup that generated headlines of its own and resulted in Frost's bestselling account of the interview, *I Gave Them a Sword.* The son of a Methodist minister, Frost graduated with honors in English at Cambridge in 1961, and immediately inaugurated a TV satire called *That Was the Week That Was. "TW3,"* as it came to be called, scored considerable success both in England and in the United States, but the topical show was cancelled after a couple of seasons. Now a one-man miniconglomerate zipping across the Atlantic on a weekly basis, Frost not only interviews celebrities (a roster including Prince Charles, Noel Coward, Spiro Agnew, Golda Meir, Jackie Gleason, and Frost's friends Elizabeth Taylor and Richard Burton), but also hosts a *Guinness World Book of Records* show on ABC, collects royalties from earlier books *(The English, The Americans),* produces movies *(The Slipper and the Rose),* and heads an English TV syndicate. Back home he was often boosted as a possible Prime Minister, but although rumpled and baggy-eyed as a result of his grueling schedule, Frost remains content with what he is doing. For a time he evaded marriage—he came extremely close with black singer Diahann Carroll before she decided instead to marry a Nevada boutique owner—but finally plighted his troth to Peter Sellers's widow, Lynne Frederick. Less than a year after their 1982 divorce, he wed Lady Carina Fitzalan-Howard, daughter of the Duke of Norfolk. Frost's run-in with NBC over editorial content of his Henry Kissinger interview spawned yet another tell-it-all book.

Born: April 7, 1939, in Tenterden, England
Height: 6 ft.
Weight: 174 lbs.
Eyes: Blue *Hair:* Sandy
Zodiac: Aries
Education: Cambridge University, an English Degree at Gonville and Caius College
Religion: Methodist
Marriages: To Lynne Frederick (1981–1982)
To Carina Fitzalan-Howard (1983–)
Children: None
Interests: Politics, international relations, soccer, publishing, producing
Personal Habits and Traits: Does not smoke, drinks moderately, a nail biter, needs little sleep
Address: London
Income: $1 million

Greta Garbo

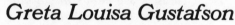

"I want to be let *alone."*

Greta Louisa Gustafson

"I want to be *let* alone," was her actual plea, but since she went into seclusion in 1941 very few people have been willing to accommodate her. Nearly four decades after she abandoned movies forever, Garbo is the world's most elusive celebrity—and as such, one of its most sought after. Ironically, back in the days when she lathered patrons in a Stockholm barber shop, Greta Louisa Gustafson yearned for such attention. She got it at 17, her second year at the Swedish Royal Dramatic Academy, when director Maurice Stiller spotted her and promptly set out to change her name. He toyed with the pseudonym of Greta Gabor, then decided to transpose two letters. At first she was dismissed by MGM's moguls, but then they suddenly noticed a remarkable face that was perfectly sculpted for the camera, and she soon became a top silent star in movies like *The Temptress* (1926). Even after the Svengali-like Stiller died in 1928 she continued to command a staggering $300,000 per picture. When she ordered a whiskey in her first talkie, *Anna Christie,* headlines blared GARBO TALKS! Nine years later in 1939, GARBO LAUGHS! became the headline when the star cracked up opposite Melvyn Douglas in her first comedy, *Ninotchka.* One of the most personally revealing films she made was the silent *Flesh and the Devil,* a 1926 melodrama in which her torrid lovemaking with John Gilbert on screen was inspired by a raging offscreen romance. Later, Garbo conducted a well-publicized affair with Leopold Stokowski and then paired up with nutritionist Gayelord Hauser, who remained close to her until his death in 1985. Garbo can frequently be seen strolling through the stores on Manhattan's Upper East Side. Incredibly, one of her favorite pastimes is picking people out of the crowd at random—and following them!

Born: September 18, 1905, in Stockholm, Sweden
Height: 5 ft. 8 in.
Weight: 121 lbs.
Eyes: Blue *Hair:* Brown
Zodiac: Virgo
Education: Sweden's Royal Academy of Dramatic Art
Religion: Protestant
Marriages: None
Children: None
Interests: Antiques, nutrition, reading, art, classical music
Personal Habits and Traits: Smokes, drinks an occasional whiskey, walks several miles a day
Address: New York City
Income: $300,000 (minimum estimate, from investments)

Art Garfunkel

"I have no priorities; I like all the things I'm into—acting, teaching, singing, and composing. I think an individual should—must—experience all types of growth."

The frizzy-haired half of Simon & Garfunkel grew up just three blocks away from future collaborator Paul Simon in Queens, and their professional association commenced when Paul played the White Rabbit and Art the Cheshire Cat in a grammar school production of *Alice in Wonderland.* Years later, recording under the name Tom and Jerry, they scratched the charts with a forgotten tune, "Hey, Schoolgirl," then reverted to their real names just in time to claim national recognition with "Sounds of Silence." With Simon as composer and Garfunkel as arranger, the duo laid down such enduring, lyrical 1960s hits as "The 59th St. Bridge Song," "Feelin' Groovy," "At the Zoo," "Cecilia," "Parsley, Sage, Rosemary and Thyme," and "The Boxer," as well as coo-coo-ca-chooing their way through the soundtrack of *The Graduate* with their Grammy-winning song "Mrs. Robinson." Following *Bridge over Troubled Waters,* a platinum album that amassed six Grammys, Garfunkel split to prove himself a movie star, appearing in Mike Nichols's *Catch-22* in 1969 and a year later in Nichols's highly controversial *Carnal Knowledge.* He did not exactly storm the acting front however. After a hit single ("All I Know") he recorded a smash LP, *Watermark,* containing Top 10 remakes of the old standard "I Only Have Eyes for You" and Sam Cooke's classic "Wonderful World." His 1979 effort, "Fate for Breakfast," was notably less successful. A math and music major at Columbia, Garfunkel also enjoys teaching math at a private school in Connecticut. After his marriage dissolved, Garfunkel struck up a long-lasting romance with Penny *(Laverne and Shirley)* Marshall.

Born: November 5, 1941, in Newark, New Jersey
Height: 6 ft. 1 in.
Weight: 170 lbs.
Eyes: Blue *Hair:* Blond
Zodiac: Scorpio
Education: Columbia University, B.S. in mathematics and music
Religion: Jewish
Marriages: To Linda Grossman (1972–1980)
Children: None
Interests: Teaching, composing, acting, horses
Personal Habits and Traits: Does not smoke, is introspective, methodical, apolitical
Address: New York City
Income: $500,000 (minimum estimate)

James Garner

James Baumgarner

"If you have any pride in your work, you don't go on TV."

This handsome actor from Norman, Oklahoma, may be one of the richest men in show business. James Garner grew up the son of a carpet layer, served in the Army and Merchant Marine, and modeled bathing suits until he stumbled into acting, making a less than spectacular Broadway debut as one of the silent judges in *The Caine Mutiny Court Martial.* In the late 1950s Garner became a high-salaried star as the dashing hero of TV western *Maverick,* then made a number of films, including *The Great Escape, Grand Prix, Boys Night Out,* and *The Americanization of Emily.* But in movies he could not shake his public image as a poor man's Rock Hudson, so he eventually returned to the medium he has been most critical of, starring in another hit series—this one a tongue-in-cheek detective show called *The Rockford Files.* In the late 1970s Garner experienced a sudden surge in his popularity (and the fattening of his wallet) as a result of a lucrative series of Polaroid commercials. He parlayed all the profits from his various enterprises to finance his Cherokee Production Company (he is part Cherokee) and now has far-flung investments that include oil wells and apartment buildings. Although ill health forced him to discontinue *The Rockford Files* at its ratings peak in 1980, Garner remained in the public eye with the help of Polaroid. He returned to the big screen in *Victor/Victoria* and the unfortunate *Tank,* but Garner fared better on TV's *Heartsounds* and *Space. Murphy's Romance,* in which he starred with Sally Field, brought Garner his first Academy Award nomination, but no Oscar. That went to William Hurt for *Kiss of the Spider Woman.*

Born: April 17, 1928, in Norman, Oklahoma
Height: 6 ft. 1 in.
Weight: 206 lbs.
Eyes: Brown *Hair:* Brown
Zodiac: Aries
Education: High school
Religion: Protestant
Marriages: To Lois Clark (split in 1980)
Children: Two daughters
Interests: Finance, real estate, race-car driving
Personal Habits and Traits: Smokes cigarettes, not a teetotaler, aloof, something of a recluse
Address: Beverly Hills
Income: $2.15 million (minimum estimate)

Crystal Gayle

Brenda Gail Webb Gatzimos

"Loretta and I fight a little bit, but that's just sisters. And we never fight over the music business."

Loretta Lynn's baby sister Brenda Gail (Loretta nicknamed her Crystal for the Krystal hamburger chain located in the South) grew up in Wabash, Indiana, where her mother worked as a nurse's aide and her coal miner father waged a losing battle against black lung disease. Loretta was virtually queen of country music by the time Crystal began touring with Loretta's show, but with the help of husband Vassilios ("Bill") Gatzimos, who postponed law school for three years to manage her career, Gayle began to plug along on the concert circuit as a solo act. When Loretta wrote a tune for Brenda Lee, "I've Cried the Blue Right Out of My Eyes," it turned out that Lee had blue eyes, so the tune went to Gayle and became a modest C & W hit. Then a spin-off of that song, "Don't It Make My Brown Eyes Blue," crossed over from country-western to pop charts and zoomed to number one—a hit bigger than any of Loretta's. Sibling rivalry only intensified when Crystal beat out Loretta for the 1977 Country Music Association's Best Female Vocalist Award and topped off the year with a Grammy. While Lynn is tough, shrewd and outspoken, her sister is soft-spoken and somewhat self-effacing. She lives with Gatzimos on a five-acre spread near Nashville, just 70 miles from Hurricane Mills, a town Loretta actually owns. Gayle's trademark is her hair, which measures nearly five feet in length.

Born: January 9, 1951, in Paintsville, Kentucky
Height: 5 ft. 6 in.
Weight: 117 lbs.
Eyes: Blue *Hair:* Auburn
Zodiac: Capricorn
Education: High school
Religion: Protestant
Marriages: To Vassilios ("Bill") Gatzimos (1971–)
Children: None
Interests: Mine safety, motion pictures, reading
Personal Habits and Traits: Nonsmoker, drinks
Address: Nashville
Income: $800,000+

Boy George

B. George Alan O'Dowd

''OK, I've experimented with both sexes, but I'm not a limp-wristed floozy and I'm not a transvestite. I'm a very masculine person.'' On winning a 1984 Grammy: ''It's nice to see that America can appreciate a good drag queen.''

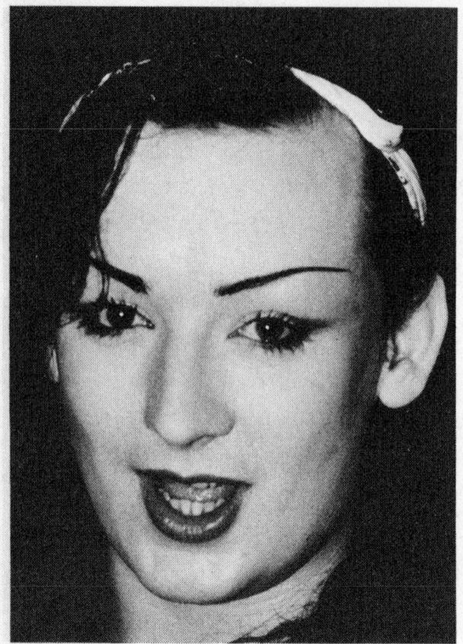

Success is a drag for rock's George O'Dowd. Wearing bag-lady dresses, a rabbi's black felt hat, and enough Pan-Cake, lip gloss and mascara to make even the Happy Hooker wince, George proved himself not only to be *the* gender-bender of the '80s, but one of the decade's most formidable talents as well. He was born the third of six children to working-class parents in London, but George was never exactly the boy next door. He played dress-up early, flouncing off to Catholic school in Mum's high heels, scarves, and floppy hats. When he showed up at 15 with dyed orange hair and white pegged pants, *People* noted that they finished off the outfit—they gave him the boot. Variously working as a fruit picker, window dresser, and printer, George spent nights prowling London's gay clubs, where weird costumes provided instant entree. His hair went from greaser to punk to fright locks to bouffants, his outfits from Teddy Boy to heavy metal to femme fatale (one favorite ensemble from this period was a harem-girl outfit, complete with feathered turban). George found steady work in the late 1970s at the Foundry, an offbeat London clothing store, but in 1981 he split to sing with the New Wave group Bow Wow Wow. A young black bass player, Mikey Craig, was so impressed by George's voice that he suggested teaming up with drummer John Moss and guitarist-keyboardist Roy Hay to form a group of their own. They called it Culture Club, to reflect the blend of various styles and cultural influences they hoped to achieve. They did, and spectacularly, with their debut album *Kissing to Be Clever,* off which the group released three hit singles: ''Do You Really Want to Hurt Me?'', ''Time (Clock of the Heart),'' and ''I'll Tumble 4 Ya.'' Their next LP, *Colour by Numbers,* sailed to platinum on the strength of more hit tunes written by the group: ''Karma Chameleon,'' ''Church of the Poison Mind,'' and ''It's a Miracle'' among them. By the time their *Waking Up With the House on Fire* album was released, there were rumblings of discontent among band members who felt eclipsed by the Mascaraed One, and rumors of a breakup. For his part Boy, who admits to being bisexual (''I'm as gay as I am heterosexual''), takes his global celebrity in stride: ''I'd sooner be in *Dynasty* than be a rock star.''

Born: June 15, 1961, in London
Height: 6 ft.
Weight: 200 lbs.
Eyes: Blue *Hair:* Naturally brown, but at various times streaked orange, blue, blond, purple, etc.
Zodiac: Gemini
Education: High school dropout
Religion: Roman Catholic
Marriages: None
Children: None
Interests: Clothes, kitsch
Personal Habits and Traits: Visits Mum and Dad once a week when he can, shuns drugs, nonsmoker, articulate, ambitious
Address: London
Income: $3 million (his share of Culture Club's $12 million gross)

Phyllis George

''I like to entertain, to flash teeth and turn people on, or I wouldn't do what I do.''

There she was, Miss America, and the First Lady of Kentucky, *and* the host of the CBS morning news show. Spoon-fed on the Dallas Cowboys and the Texas Longhorns in her native state, Phyllis George entered the Miss Dallas contest on a lark and wound up being crowned by Bert Parks in 1971. When her reign as Miss America was over, George seized any available TV opportunity: commercials, game shows and even co-hosting *Candid Camera* with Allen Funt. Picked by CBS president Robert Wussler to invade the locker rooms of America, George soon became TV's top female sports commentator and achieved national recognition for her news-making interviews. In one exchange Dallas Cowboys quarterback Roger Stauback, Mr. Clean of the National Football League, blurted out to George that he ''likes sex as much as Joe Namath, but with one person—my wife.'' Married to Hollywood superproducer Robert Evans in 1977, Manhattan-based George was reluctant to have children as long as she had to travel more than 40,000 miles a year covering football and basketball games. ''I'm really a small-town girl who was raised to sit and chat in people's living rooms,'' George explained. ''And that's what I do on Sunday afternoons.'' Split from Evans after less than one year of marriage, George took on husband number two—Kentucky Fried Chicken tycoon-turned-team owner (the Boston Celtics) John Y. Brown—in 1979. He went on to run for Governor of Kentucky against Louis Nunn—and won. After Brown served out his term, George was free to move north to New York and replace Diane Sawyer on the morning news show. After several on-air gaffes—like asking a man falsely accused of rape to hug the woman who had sent him to prison—George was replaced by Maria Shriver.

Born: 1949 in Denton, Texas
Height: 5 ft. 8 in.
Weight: 119 lbs.
Eyes: Blue *Hair:* Auburn
Education: North Texas State College, B.A.
Religion: Methodist
Marriages:
To Robert Evans (1977–1978)
To John Y. Brown (1979–)

Children: One
Interests: Tennis, piano
Personal Habits and Traits: Churchgoer, incessant dieter
Addresses: New York City; Frankfort, Kentucky
Income: $500,000

Richard Gere

"I will not become a piece of meat just so some jerk will pay $5 to look at an image on a screen."

Yet another oft-touted heir to the throne of Marlon Brando, Gere grew up on a farm, went to church, competed on the high school gymnastics team, and played the trumpet with a dance band at bar mitzvahs and weddings. After stints at the University of Massachusetts (he dropped out after two years), doing summer stock and joining a commune of rock musicians in Vermont, he landed a role in the London production of the long-running Broadway musical *Grease*. Returning to New York in the mid-1970s, Gere dazzled audiences and critics alike as a violent hustler who terrorizes Diane Keaton with a nearly-naked saber dance in 1977's brilliant and gruesome *Looking for Mr. Goodbar*. With the moviegoing public Gered up, Richard mumbled and brooded his way through the arty *Days of Heaven* and such disappointments as *American Gigolo* (originally intended for fellow *Greaser* John Travolta) and *Yanks,* before yanking fans back into the theater with the tremendously successful *An Officer and a Gentleman*—sort of a *Rocky Goes to Flight School* that showed Gere was still in his prime as Hollywood beefcake. His on-set feud with *Officer* costar Debra Winger was so intense, however, that they refused to travel together to promote the movie. In the mid-1980s, Gere was on a downslide again with *Breathless* and the back-to-back disasters *Cotton Club* (for which he cut his own tracks on the coronet) and *King David*. Gere, who portrayed a concentration camp homosexual in the Broadway play *Bent,* has dated the likes of Tuesday Weld, Barbara Carrerra, Diane Von Furstenberg, and Diana Ross. But his long-standing love is Brazilian painter Sylvia Martins, who in 1979 placed several breathy but unsolicited calls to Gere over the phone, then walked up to his table at Elaine's in New York one night and introduced herself. After a parking lot attendant accused Gere of striking him (the court dismissed the charges), Gere embraced respectability by taking a seat on the board of his co-op.

Born: August 29, 1949, in Philadelphia
Height: 5 ft. 9 in.
Weight: 155 lbs.
Eyes: Brown *Hair:* Brown
Zodiac: Virgo
Education: Two years at the University of Massachusetts
Religion: Protestant
Marriages: None
Children: None
Interests: Music (plays the trumpet, piano, guitar, and banjo), German cinema, t'ai chi
Personal Habits and Traits: Chain-smokes, does not eat red meat, night owl, and late sleeper, works out daily with weights, is at times sullen with the press, somewhat reclusive
Addresses: New York City; Los Angeles
Income: $2 million per film

Andy Gibb

"I don't see myself as a teenybopper idol. I don't even like to dance."

The baby Gibb, young Andy was unleashed on the music scene at age 19 with his falsetto "I Just Want to Be Your Everything," and within a year vied with his brothers' smash *Saturday Night Fever* score by releasing two more bubblegum hits: "Love Is Thicker Than Water" and "Shadow Dancing." Wandering with his nomadic family from the Isle of Man to Ibiza and then Australia, he was for the most part raised in Brisbane, then dropped out of school at 13 and bummed around Ibiza. After his brothers reunited and settled in the Miami area, he married Kim Reeder, a former receptionist, and joined his brothers in acquiring an 80-foot houseboat previously owned by a mobster who was gunned down in the mirrored master bedroom. Gibb's teenage marriage came to an abrupt end before the release of his fourth hit, "Our Love, Don't Throw It Away." Gibb tried Broadway but missed so many performances as the replacement star of *Joseph and the Amazing Technicolor Dreamcoat* that he had to be replaced himself by David Cassidy. Gibb's personal life eclipsed his career when Victoria Principal left him over his drug use—a problem that forced him to check into the Betty Ford Clinic in 1985.

Born: March 5, 1958, in Manchester, England
Height: 5 ft. 10 in.
Weight: 149 lbs.
Eyes: Brown *Hair:* Blond
Zodiac: Pisces
Education: Grammar school dropout (at 13)
Religion: Protestant
Marriages: To Kim Reeder (1976–1978)
Children: A daughter, Peta
Interests: Scuba diving, tennis, fishing, boating, composing, guitar
Personal Habits and Traits: Nonsmoker, drinks, a TV addict, congenial
Address: Miami
Income: Down to $300,000 from a 1977 high of $1.9 million

Mel Gibson

"It's all happening too fast. I've got to put the brakes on or I'll smack into something."

Proclaimed "The Sexiest Man Alive" on the cover of *People* magazine, the dish from Down Under was in fact born in Peekskill, New York, the sixth of a railroad worker's 11 kids. The family picked up and moved to Australia when Mel was 12, and though he retains his U.S. citizenship, Gibson still thinks of himself as "an Aussie." He attended the National Institute of Dramatic Art and—though his face was battered from a ballroom dust-up the night before—successfully auditioned for *Mad Max* in 1977. The hot-buttered success of *Mad*

Max spawned a series of sequels *(Mad Max II: Road Warrior, Mad Max III: Beyond Thunderdom),* but Gibson also found time to play a World War I soldier in the critically acclaimed *Gallipoli,* Mr. Christian in *Mutiny on the Bounty,* a reporter in the steamy *The Year of Living Dangerously* (he wore lifts to work with 5-foot 11-inch costar Sigourney Weaver), Diane Keaton's lover in *Mrs. Soffel,* and an embattled farmer in *The River*. Gibson does not appear to have handled his newfound fame all that well. He was fined $240 for drunk driving during the filming of *Mrs. Soffel* in Toronto, and has repeatedly proved his own worst enemy in his dealings with the press. When a woman reporter wrote an unflattering story about him, for example, he complained, "If she discredited a 5-year-old mongoloid it wouldn't mean a lot, but I have an image with the public." Between such foot-in-mouth episodes and his hectic schedule on location, Gibson, his wife, Robyn, and their four children share a sprawling house near Sydney that once was a beachside boarding house; the bathroom doors are still marked His and Hers.

Born: January 7, 1956, in Peekskill, New York
Height: 5 ft. 10 in.
Weight: 160 lbs.
Eyes: Blue *Hair:* Brown
Zodiac: Capricorn
Education: National Institute of Dramatic Art at the University of New South Wales
Marriages: To Robyn (1980–)
Children: Hannah (b. 1980), Edward and Christian (b. June 1982), Will (June 1984)
Interests: Sports, running
Personal Habits and Traits: Chain-smokes, drinks beer, hates interviews, given to sarcasm
Address: Sydney, Australia
Income: $1.5 million per film

Eydie Gorme

"I think the music of the last fifteen years is horrendous—I can't stand the ridiculous, asinine lyrics coming out of human beings' throats. Radio stations insist on playing computerized crap."

Big bandleaders Tommy Tucker and Tex Beneke gave Bronx-born belter Eydie Gorme her start, and in 1953 she settled in with a singer named Steve Lawrence as a regular on Steve Allen's old *Tonight Show*. She subbed for an ailing Billy Daniels at the Copacabana, wound up with her own show at the Copa and in 1957 married Lawrence. While Steve and Eydie worked their way toward becoming first-name legends with a hit Broadway show (1968's *Golden Rainbow*), their own TV show and an SRO Las Vegas act, they each pursued separate recording careers. On her own, Grammy-winning Gorme spun out gold singles like the upbeat "Blame It on the Bossa Nova" and the powerful ballads "If He Walked Into My Life" and "Send in the Clowns." Gorme and Lawrence were dealt a personal blow then their son Michael died of natural causes in 1986 at the age of 23.

Born: August 16, 1932, in the Bronx, New York
Height: 5 ft. 4 in.
Weight: 115 lbs.
Eyes: Brown *Hair:* Dark brown
Zodiac: Leo
Education: High school
Religion: Jewish (Sephardic)
Marriages: To Steve Lawrence (1957–)
Children: David (b. 1960), Michael (b. 1962–1986)
Interests: Cooking
Personal Habits and Traits:
Nonsmoker, moderate drinker, a night owl, perfectionist, fast-talker, giggler
Address: Beverly Hills
Income: $280,000 (minimum estimate)

Elliott Gould

Elliott Goldstein

"Success didn't change me. I was distorted before *I was a star."*

"Mr. Streisand," as he was often called during his marriage to Flatbush's favorite superstar, was also born and raised in Brooklyn. He had reached the point of pawning his father's jewelry when he landed his first bit part in *Hit the Deck*. The musical comedy *I Can Get It for You Wholesale* introduced him not only to Broadway but to his future bride, who was making her mark in the show-stealing role of Miss Marmelstein. As Barbra's career soared, his ground to a halt, picked up with *The Night They Raided Minsky's,* and climbed dramatically when he was given the chance to play Trapper John in Robert Altman's flick *M*A*S*H*. This was quickly followed by *Bob & Carol & Ted & Alice,* in which he romped as the klutzy, would-be wife-swapper Ted. His appearance several years after Streisand's on the cover of *Time* proved that he had overcome his professional inferiority complex. Whether he is the ultimate antihero or just a *shmuck* the average moviegoer can relate to, Gould scored similar successes in *California Split* and *Little Murders*. Ingmar Bergman singled him out as the first major American actor to star in one of his films, *The Touch,* though with disappointing results. Gould returned in 1978's suspenseful *Capricorn One*. After divorces from both Streisand (in 1967) and his second wife, Jennie Bogart, Gould remarried Bogart two years later, in 1977. They made their home in Los Angeles, where Gould taped his short-lived 1984 series, *E.R.*

Born: August 29, 1938, in Brooklyn, New York
Height: 6 ft. 1 in.
Weight: 174 lbs.
Eyes: Brown *Hair:* Black
Zodiac: Virgo
Education: High school
Religion: Jewish
Marriages:
To Barbra Streisand (1963–1967)
To Jennifer Bogart (1971–1975), (1977–)
Children: Jason (b. 1967) by Barbra Streisand; Molly Safire (b. 1972), Sam Bazooka (b. 1973) by Jennifer Bogart
Interests: Card-playing, music

Personal Habits and Traits: Smokes cigars and cigarettes, drinks, is a night owl
Address: Los Angeles
Income: $500,000 (estimate)

Billy Graham

William Franklin Graham

''If I didn't have spiritual faith, I would be a pessimist. But I'm an optimist. I've read the last page in the Bible. It's all going to turn out all right.''

Aside from the Pope, the best-known (and best-dressed) preacher in the world was born in Charlotte, North Carolina, and became a convert himself at 16. Forsaking the Presbyterianism of his parents for the Southern Baptist Church, he attended Wheaton College, then found a job as a radio preacher in Chicago. However, not until he caught the eye of William Randolph Hearst during a Los Angeles tent crusade was Graham touted nationwide as another Billy Sunday. The message Hearst sent out to his newspapers: PUFF GRAHAM! The first evangelist to capitalize on the electronic immediacy of television on a grand scale, he formed the Billy Graham Evangelical Association and began beaming ''Decision for Christ'' crusades to all corners of the globe, from Bangor to Bombay. Graham now conducts five major crusades each year, and has personally preached to more than 85 million people. Often criticized for a lavish lifestyle that includes $700 suits, private jets, and plush hotel suites, Graham is a longtime friend of Richard Nixon and has been a favorite guest at the White House during the Truman, Eisenhower, Kennedy, Nixon, and Ford administrations. Ironically, Graham was *not* a favorite of Jimmy Carter, a Southern Baptist whose own religious zeal was unprecedented among U.S. Presidents. Graham, nicknamed ''Billy Frank,'' consistently ranks as one of the 10 most admired men in the world. His column *My Answer* is syndicated to well over 160 newspapers, his magazine *Decision* boasts 4 million readers, and his books *Angels* and *How to Be Born Again* were instant number one bestsellers. Graham even produced a movie, 1975's *The Hiding Place* starring Julie Harris, which proved a critical and commercial success—as was his doom-and-gloom 1984 tome *The Four Horsemen.*

Born: November 7, 1918, in Charlotte, North Carolina
Height: 6 ft. 2 in.
Weight: 190 lbs.
Eyes: Blue *Hair:* Pale blond
Zodiac: Scorpio
Education: Wheaton College
Religion: Southern Baptist
Marriages: To Ruth Bell (1943–)
Children: Three daughters, two sons
Interests: Theology, the Bible, broadcasting, writing, golf
Personal Habits and Traits: Nonsmoker, teetotaler
Address: Montreat, North Carolina
Income: $30 million (annual gross of the Graham organization)

Cary Grant

Archibald Leach

When a magazine editor wired him "How old Cary Grant?" he replied, "Old Cary Grant fine. How you?"

Father Goose with Leslie Caron was his last picture, and ever since that delightful 1964 comedy he has contented himself with serving on the board of directors of Fabergé and managing his own company, Granox Productions. And despite a constant barrage of film offers, Archibald Leach from Bristol, England, seems less and less likely to make movie number 72. As it stands now, his is an incomparable career. Running away from home at 15, young Archie started in show business as a stand-up entertainer (yes, he can sing) in dives from London to Coney Island. He racked up four years as chorus boy before heading West to break into movies. There, the image makers promptly decided that Leach should change his name to Cary Grant and be groomed as an urbane and witty love interest opposite Hollywood's leading ladies. His first major film was 1932's *Blonde Venus* with Marlene Dietrich. *Sylvia Scarlett,* with Katharine Hepburn, was terrible, but enough of the Grant charm showed through to give him his pick of properties. He shared name-over-the-title billing with Mae West, Rosalind Russell, and Marlene Dietrich in those early years, and by 1937 was easily considered the screen's top romantic comedian. His best movies, several of which were directed by Hitchcock, include *Bringing Up Baby* and *The Philadelphia Story* (both with Hepburn), *Topper* (with Constance Bennett), *Gunga Din, Arsenic and Old Lace, Suspicion, Notorious* (with Ingrid Bergman), *North By Northwest, An Affair to Remember* (with Deborah Kerr), *To Catch a Thief* (with Grace Kelly), and *Charade* (with Audrey Hepburn). Married first to actress Virginia Cherrill, then to Woolworth heiress Barbara Hutton, actress Betsy Drake, Dyan Cannon and finally Barbara Harris, he shares custody of his only child, Jennifer, with Cannon. During the rather spectacular legal proceedings between Grant and Cannon, she charged that his personality had altered for the worse after taking LSD.

Born: January 18, 1904, in Bristol, England
Height: 6 ft. 1 in.
Weight: 184 lbs.
Eyes: Brown *Hair:* White
Zodiac: Capricorn
Education: High school dropout
Religion: Church of England
Marriages: To Virginia Cherrill (divorced)
To Barbara Hutton (divorced)
To Betsy Drake (divorced)
To Dyan Cannon (divorced)
To Barbara Harris (1981–)

Children: Jennifer (b. 1966)
Interests: Baseball, swimming, reading, tennis, riding
Personal Habits and Traits: Smokes, is generally unflappable, retires early, a physical fitness nut
Address: Beverly Hills
Income: $1.35 million (estimate)

Lee Grant

Lyova Haskell Rosenthal

"If a guy comes up to me and says 'I know you,' the first thing I think is—'Did he and I make it once?'"

Lee Grant became a skillful actress in movies and on television long before she topped off her career with a Best Supporting Actress Oscar for *Shampoo* in 1976. Thrust by a stage mother into the chorus of the Metropolitan Opera when she was 3, she received a New York Drama Critic's Award as the shoplifter in *Detective Story* on Broadway by the time she was 18, and for the film version she received her first Academy Award nomination. When her playwright husband Arnold Manoff was blacklisted during the McCarthy era, she was barred from all studio work because she would not testify against him. She continued to be blacklisted even after they divorced and until he died in 1965. Her first major assignment after the showbiz witchhunt ebbed was in TV's controversial *Peyton Place* series; and a decade later she attempted an ill-fated sitcom of her own, NBC's *Fay*. Married since 1965 to adman Joseph Feury, whom she met on the road when he danced in the chorus of *Silk Stockings,* Grant has a daughter, actress Dinah *(Grease)*, by her marriage to Manoff and together she and Feury have adopted a Thai refugee. As her *Omen II* was being edited in January 1978, the Feurys' uncompleted mansion on the Southern California coast was demolished by a raging storm and they were forced to await reconstruction in a rented $500,000 ranch house overlooking Zuma Beach, near Malibu. An aspiring director, Grant did not exactly give Steven Spielberg any trouble with such forgettable films as *Tell Me a Riddle, The Willmar 8, When Women Kill,* and *A Matter of Sex*.

Born: October 31, 1930, in New York City
Height: 5 ft. 4 in.
Weight: 114 lbs.
Eyes: Blue *Hair:* Reddish blond
Zodiac: Scorpio
Education: High school
Religion: Jewish
Marriages:
To Arnold Manoff (divorced)
To Joseph Feury (1965–)
Children: Dinah (b. 1958), Belinda (b. 1971, adopted)
Interests: Painting, cooking, directing
Personal Habits and Traits: Smokes, drinks, diets, is demanding and a perfectionist
Address: Malibu, California
Income: $480,000+ (estimate)

The Grateful Dead

lead singer *Jerry Garcia*

"I like Crosby, Stills and Nash, Neil Young, the Beatles, The Band, country-western stuff, Freddie King. Elton John doesn't do it for me."

The Grateful Dead, the Hell's Angels' favorite band, is largely the brainchild of rock legend Jerry Garcia. The son of a Spanish-born musician-cum-bartender and a Swedish-Irish mother, Garcia was born in San Francisco and at 13 was by his own account a hoodlum. When his mother gave him an accordian for his 15th birthday Garcia traded it in for an electric guitar. After a nine-month stint in the Army he traveled up and down the San Francisco peninsula playing coffeehouses and hanging around with future stars like Jimi Hendrix and Janis Joplin. Strongly influenced by the Beatles in the mid-1960s, Garcia teamed up with conga drummer-harpist-vocalist Ron "Pig Pen" McKernan and guitarist Bob Weir as Mother McGree's Jug Band. With the addition of bassist Phil Lesh and Bill Kreutzmann on drums, they transmogrified into the Warlocks and played Bay Area pizza parlors for enough spare change to eat and buy drugs. Since there existed another group called the Warlocks, they assumed various new names—"The Mythical Ethical, Icicle Tricycle" was one tongue-twister—before Garcia opened up an Oxford English Dictionary and randomly picked out The Grateful Dead. Marriage and a child did not keep Garcia from exploring the San Francisco drug scene in the heyday of the Haight-Ashbury, paying particular attention to pot, coke and LSD. The Grateful Dead concerts in Golden Gate Park elevated them to one of the most popular San Francisco groups, but their first three albums—*The Grateful Dead, Anthem to the Sun,* and *Aoxomoxoa*—were unqualified failures that plunged them $180,000 in debt to Warner Brothers Records. Their fourth LP, *Live Dead,* helped pull them out of the red, as did *Working Man's Dead* and *American Beauty,* featuring vocals by Pig Pen (who died in 1973). Eventually, Garcia cut his own successful solo album. An accident in his youth cost Garcia part of a finger on his left hand. As a result, he is known as the best nine-fingered guitarist in the business.

Jerry Garcia

Born: August 1, 1942, in San Francisco
Height: 5 ft. 9 in.
Weight: 155 lbs.
Eyes: Brown *Hair:* Brown
Zodiac: Leo
Education: High school dropout
Religion: Roman Catholic (lapsed)

Marriages: One. Ended in divorce
Children: One
Interests: Guitar, philosophy, filmmaking
Personal Habits and Traits: Drinks, smokes cigarettes, smokes "lots of pot"
Address: San Francisco
Income: $200,000 (minimum estimate)

Al Green

"People say I've always been a preacher."

One day in 1974, Al Green is said to have returned from one of his SRO concerts with a young female fan and to have been soaking in the bathtub of his Memphis mansion when an ex-lover burst into the bathroom, poured scalding grits on him, then shot herself to death with a revolver. Perhaps in atonement for his wild career days, three years later soul's "Velvet Funk" bought Memphis's Full Gospel Tabernacle from the Assembly of God for $350,000 and became the tabernacle's ordained pastor. He now preaches there three out of four Sundays, and with his backup group the Angels offers his 400 members an inspired gospel show that would rival any raucous concert act. The sixth in a family of 10 children, Green lived with his sharecropping parents in Arkansas until his family picked up and moved to Grand Rapids, Michigan. Green started singing gospel hymns with his brothers in local churches, but eventually left the fold to record his decidedly secular *Back Up Train.* What followed was a string of singles and albums—both gold and platinum—that always scored high on the R&B charts and frequently crossed over to the big money pop charts; his "Let's Stay Together," for example, not only made it to the Top 10 on both charts, but also sold more copies than any other single in London Records' history, outselling the Stones' "Satisfaction." Most recently, he has found a new audience for his gospel recordings, several of which have been Grammy-nominated. Married to divorcée Shirley Ann Kyles, who once sang for a group called the Revelations and now directs his church choir, Green unquestionably disappointed the 200 Memphis women who actually petitioned him to remain single.

Born: April 13, 1946, in Forest City, Arkansas
Height: 5 ft. 9 in.
Weight: 149 lbs.
Eyes: Brown *Hair:* Black
Zodiac: Aries
Education: High school
Religion: Nondenominational pastor of the Full Gospel Tabernacle in Memphis
Marriages: To Shirley Ann Kyles (1977–)
Interests: Religion, producing records
Personal Habits and Traits: Nonsmoker, teetotaler
Address: Memphis, Tennessee
Income: $478,000 (minimum estimate)

Merv Griffin

"I'm not an actor. I like to do the kind of show I do, with real people doing real things."

A dyed-in-the-wool Californian, Mervyn Griffin grew up in San Mateo and studied music at San Mateo Junior College and the University of San Francisco.

Griffin became the overweight boy singer for Freddie Martin's big band during the 1940s and captured international attention with the tongue-in-cheek hit "I've Got a Loverly Bunch of Coconuts." A contract player in such Hollywood turkeys as *The Boy from Oklahoma,* Griffin appeared on television in the 1950s series *Saturday Prom* but soon discovered his knack for hosting or producing game shows like *Play Your Hunch, Talent Scouts, One in a Million,* and the hugely successful *Jeopardy* and *Wheel of Fortune*. But Griffin is best known as the boyish-faced and facile host of his own talk show, where he favors "theme" programs in which he moderates a panel of experts or celebrities. Divorced from former radio comedienne Julann Wright in 1976 after 20 years of marriage, Griffin lives on the San Francisco peninsula and flies his own plane to Los Angeles to tape his nightly show. Among his current consuming passions: tennis and breeding quarter horses. Griffin added another moneymaker to his video stable in the '80s with the hugely successful syndicated show *Dance Fever*. But as *Wheel of Fortune* took its place as the most profitable game show in history, Griffin seized the opportunity to sell his production company to Coca-Cola for $200 million.

Born: July 6, 1925, in San Mateo, California
Height: 5 ft. 10 in.
Weight: 170 lbs.
Eyes: Brown *Hair:* Salt and pepper
Zodiac: Cancer
Education: San Mateo Junior College, Stanford University, the University of San Francisco
Religion: Roman Catholic
Marriages: To Julann Wright (1956–1976)
Children: Anthony Patrick
Interests: Producing, raising quarter horses, flying, tennis
Personal Habits and Traits: Has quit smoking, usually drinks wine, is an inveterate dieter
Address: San Mateo, California
Income: $4.5 million (minimum estimate)

Sir Alec Guinness

"Acting is happy agony."

More people will have seen him as Obi-Wan Kenobi in *Star Wars* than in any of his other motion pictures, but devoted Guinness fans will always remember this fine British actor for his multiroled *Kind Hearts and Coronets* (1950) and as the driven British Colonel leading fellow POWs in 1957's *The Bridge on the River Kwai,* for which he won an Academy Award. By no means forgotten are his dapper Pocket in *Great Expectations* (1946), his malicious Fagin in *Oliver Twist* (1949), his disdainful Disraeli in *The Mudlark* (1950) and his elderly crook in *The Lavender Hill Mob* (1951). Born into a reasonably well-to-do banking family, he endured an unhappy childhood followed by a frustrated early manhood as he tried for years to break into theater. His first role, playing three parts in a play called *Queer Cargo,* foretold the frequent comparisons that would be made to

Lon Chaney as a master of disguise, and he apprenticed a while longer with John Gielgud and the Old Vic before *Great Expectations* established him as an international star. Guinness, knighted by Queen Elizabeth in 1959, managed to win a Tony for his 1964 portrayal of Dylan Thomas in the Broadway hit *Dylan,* and 14 years later at age 64 he uttered *Star Wars'* now famous salutation: "May the force be with you." Guinness delivered another tour de force performance in the title role of miniseries *Smiley's People,* but his portrayal of an Indian in David Lean's *A Passage to India* was disappointing to critics and audiences alike. His *Macbeth* on the London stage, though original and powerful, failed to impress reviewers; nor did costar Simone Signoret, whose Lady Macbeth was scarcely intelligible through a thick French accent. Far more entertaining were his 1986 memoirs *Blessing in Disguse.*

Born: April 2, 1914, in London, England
Height: 5 ft. 10 in.
Weight: 173 lbs.
Eyes: Blue *Hair:* Gray
Zodiac: Aries
Education: High school
Religion: Roman Catholic
Marriages: To Merula Salaman (1938–)
Children: Matthew
Interests: Writing, acting
Personal Habits and Traits: Smokes, drinks, is self-effacing and withdrawn
Address: Petersfield, England
Income: $452,000

Arlo Guthrie

"I haven't sung Alice's Restaurant *since 1969. Can't remember the words."*

The son of socially conscious Depression troubadour Woody Guthrie ("This Land Is Your Land"), Arlo attended a select private school in Stockbridge, Massachusetts, then headed for Montana's Rocky Mountain College where he lasted barely six weeks. Greenwich Village was his next stop; then his song "Alice's Restaurant" launched his folk-singing career at the Newport Folk Festival. That tune and Arthur Penn's 1969 spinoff film dealt with the period when Arlo and his hippie-commune-oriented friends descended on and frolicked with Stockbridge librarian Alice Brock. After eight solid-selling albums, a number of memorable singles ("Coming Into Los Angeles") and several cross-country tours, Guthrie became a Catholic convert and was invested as a lay brother in the Third Order of St. Francis; now when he travels he often prefers to check into monasteries instead of motels. One of the reasons for such religious fervor may be Guthrie's acute sense of his own mortality; after 15 bedridden years his father died in 1967 from Huntington's chorea, a rare hereditary neuromuscular disorder that usually develops after age 30. Arlo's grandmother also died of Huntington's, as did one of Arlo's half sisters from an earlier marriage. Despite warnings from doctors not to have children of his own who might inherit the always fatal disease, Guthrie and his wife Jackie have three—Abe, Cathy and Annie—and they all live on a 260-acre farm outside Stockbridge.

Born: July 10, 1947, in Brooklyn, New York
Height: 6 ft.
Weight: 162 lbs.
Eyes: Hazel *Hair:* Brown
Zodiac: Cancer
Education: High school
Religion: Roman Catholic convert (a member of the Third Order of St. Francis)

Marriages: To Jackie Hyde (1969–)
Children: Abe (b. 1970), Cathy (b. 1972), Annie (b. 1975)
Interests: Plays mandolin, banjo, guitar, harmonica and keyboards; theology; farming
Personal Habits and Traits: Chain smoker
Address: Stockbridge, Massachusetts
Income: $200,000+

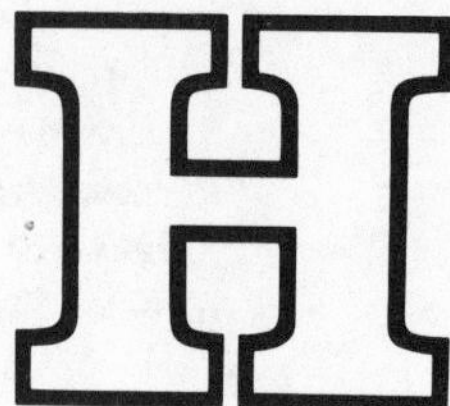

Gene Hackman

"I'm disappointed that success isn't a Himalayan feeling."

"Unlike others who play mediocre men," wrote Pauline Kael in *The New Yorker,* "Gene Hackman is such a consummate actor that he illuminates mediocrity." Mediocre may be too kind a word to describe Hackman's early days. As a Marine he achieved the rank of corporal and then was busted back to private. Once out of the service he barely eked out a living as a Times Square doorman. He met his future wife, a bank secretary named Faye Maltese, when he was locked out of his room at the YMCA for failing to pay his bill. He studied commercial drawing on the GI Bill, then contemplated a career behind the TV cameras before he dived into serious acting at the Pasadena Playhouse. Returning to New York he scored his first Broadway hit opposite Sandy Dennis in *Any Wednesday,* then appeared with Warren Beatty in the screen bomb *Lilith.* Beatty must have seen something because he tapped Hackman to play his brother in *Bonnie and Clyde,* for which Hackman received a Best Supporting Actor nomination. The moving *I Never Sang for My Father* with Melvyn Douglas meant yet another Oscar nomination, but it wasn't until the role of Popeye Doyle in *The French Connection* that Hackman got to deliver an acceptance speech for the top prize as Best Actor. Hackman starred in the sequel, *French Connection II,* as well as in the blockbuster *The Poseidon Adventure,* the grade-A western *Bite the Bullet,* and Francis Ford Coppola's masterful *The Conversation.* Ironically, the film for which he was paid the most money—$1,350,000 plus a percentage of the profits (*Lucky Lady,* with Burt Reynolds and Liza Minnelli)—turned out a major embarrassment and Hackman's most forgettable attempt. He bounced back as Christopher Reeve's endearingly rotten nemesis in *Superman,* then fell flat with Barbra Streisand in the inexplicable *All Night Long.* Hackman was squeezed between screen wife Ellen Burstyn and screen mistress Ann-Margret in

1985's drama *Twice in a Lifetime*—the critically acclaimed movie that finally pulled his career out of a decade-long nosedive.

Born: January 30, 1931, in San Bernardino, California
Height: 6 ft. 2 in.
Weight: 184 lbs.
Eyes: Blue *Hair:* Brown
Zodiac: Aquarius
Education: High school dropout
Religion: Protestant
Marriages: To Faye Maltese
Children: Christopher (b. 1960), Elizabeth (b. 1962), Leslie (b. 1966)
Interests: Stunt-flying, tennis, art
Personal Habits and Traits: Quit smoking, drinks moderately, is antisocial and blunt
Address: Beverly Hills
Income: $1.84 million

Larry Hagman

"I don't know why, but I think maybe people are sick of good guys."

An estimated 200 million viewers worldwide waited the long hot summer of 1980 to find out *Who Shot J.R.?*—and whether everybody's favorite S.O.B. would survive. He did, and Larry Hagman went on to rack up more top-rated seasons playing the rottenest Ewing on *Dallas*. Hagman's own roots are in Texas, where his father was a small-town lawyer and his mother an aspiring singer. She split for Broadway and conquered it under the name Mary Martin. Larry, meanwhile, had trouble coping with his parents' divorce and the round-robin living arrangements it imposed; in the course of a year, he would live with his father in Texas, his mother in New York, and his grandmother in Los Angeles. Hagman was also unhappy growing up in his mother's sizable shadow; he would later spend years in analysis trying to come to terms with her fame. Hagman performed off-Broadway in a brilliant cameo role as a young soldier in *Career,* which caught the critics' eyes in the 1950s, and though he went on to Broadway, stardom elude him there. He did a two-year stint on the soap *Edge of Night* before he stumbled upon the role of a harried astronaut visited by a comely 2,000-year-old genie in *I Dream of Jeannie*. After the show's five-year run on NBC, Hagman had two unsuccessful series—*The Good Life* and *Here We Go Again*— until the juicy part of J.R. came along ("The time is ripe for a real bad guy, and I'm it!"). All of which has allowed him to moonlight as pitchman for a number of products such as B.V.D. underwear. Off-camera, Hagman, who married Swedish designer Maj Axelsson in 1959, is known throughout Malibu as something of an eccentric. He never speaks at all on Sundays, dresses up in wild costumes, organizes parades on the beach, and gives his wife power tools instead of furs for Christmas. A banner flutters from the deck of his house: *Vita Celebratio Est* ("Life is a celebration").

Born: September 21, 1931, in Weatherford, Texas
Height: 6 ft. 1 in.
Weight: 190 lbs.
Eyes: Blue *Hair:* Reddish-gray
Zodiac: Virgo
Education: One year at Bard College, Annandale-on-Hudson, N.Y.
Marriages: To Maj Axelsson (1954–)
Children: Heidi (b. 1958), Preston (b. 1962)
Interests: Zen, crusading against cigarette smoking (he carries a battery-powered hand fan to blow smoke back at offenders)
Personal Habits and Traits: Reformed smoker, fasts, never talks on Sundays, runs daily, practices t'ai chi
Address: Malibu, California
Income: $4 million (minimum estimate)

Alex Haley

''Roots *is not just the saga of my family. It is the symbolic saga of a people.*''

He was so heavily in debt and so many years overdue on the deadline for his manuscript that at one point Alex Haley stood at the railing of a freighter sailing home from Africa and contemplated suicide. It was then, according to the college dropout who had spent 20 years as an enlisted man in the Coast Guard, that the voices of his slave ancestors pleaded with him to continue. The work-in-progress, *Roots,* ultimately required nine years to complete. The Pulitzer Prize–winning book grew out of the stories Haley used to hear at his grandmother's knee in Henning, Tennessee, where his father taught at Alabama A&M University and his mother was an elementary school teacher. Haley was not suited to the academic life and dropped out of college after two years to enlist in the Coast Guard. Starting out as a steward he worked his way up to the position of cook—all the while penning his shipmates' love letters and an occasional short story on his portable typewriter. He sold his first fictional piece to a Sunday supplement in 1948 and two years later was named first Chief Journalist of the U.S. Coast Guard. Retiring at the age of 37, he moved to New York and began writing freelance articles for *Reader's Digest* and *Playboy,* where he conducted the first of that magazine's now famous interviews—with jazz giant Miles Davis. Haley's first book, 1965's *The Autobiography of Malcolm X,* sold 6 million copies. Then, as he worked on *Roots,* Haley spent 65,000 hours in 57 libraries and explored remote villages in Gambia. He also retraced the steps of his slave forebears, trying to simulate the conditions of a slave ship by stripping and spending the night on a freighter belowdecks lying on a cold girder. *Roots,* made into a miniseries by ABC, had the largest audience in television history. Despite lawsuits from two authors who claimed that he plagiarized their books (the suits were settled out of court) and criticism that he distorted black history, Haley was absolutely assured of yet another blockbuster when he sat down to write *My Search for Roots,* the story behind one of the most successful commercial books of the century, brought to television with James Earl Jones playing Haley. As just one indicator of the impact Haley's historical drama had on American blacks, hospitals across the country reported that hundreds of children have been named after main character Kunta Kinte and his daughter Kizzy since the book and series appeared.

Born: August 11, 1921, in Ithaca, New York
Height: 5 ft. 10½ in.
Weight: 195 lbs.
Eyes: Brown *Hair:* Black
Zodiac: Leo
Education: College dropout
Religion: Methodist
Marriages: Two, both ending in divorce
Children: Lydia (b. 1945), William (b. 1948), Cindy (b. 1964)
Interests: Jazz, history, biography, education (he is a consultant to Miami-Dade Community College in Florida), slow-oven cooking, the sea
Personal Habits and Traits: Nonsmoker, drinks, works at night until daybreak, is not a particularly social person
Addresses: Cheviot Hills, California; Jamaica
Income: $1.5 million (estimate)

Daryl Hall and John Oates

''We are not cute. The ones who always say, 'Ooh, they're sooo cuuute,' wouldn't like us if they knew us.''

Both halves of the biggest duo in musical history went to school in the suburbs of Philadelphia. But it wasn't until 1967 that they met, when Hall's band, The Temptones, and Oates's group, The Masters, squared off in a battle of the bands at Philly's Adelphi Ballroom. They became roommates in New York, brought their blend of R&B and soft-rock to school dances and sleazy joints, and even tried to capitalize on the androgynous look before finally clicking in 1976 with the ballad ''She's Gone'' and their first number-one record, ''Rich Girl.'' A four-year slump followed, until the release of Hall & Oates's *Voices* album in 1980, and *Private Eyes* in 1981 catapulted them to the top of the charts once again with such hits as ''Kiss on My List,'' ''Private Eyes'' and ''I Can't Go for That.'' The next year's LP, *H20,* yielded ''Maneater,'' while 1985's *Big Bam Boom* contained ''Adult Education,'' ''Out of Touch,'' ''Method of Modern Love,'' and ''Some Things Are Better Left Unsaid"—all Top 10 singles. John, the swarthy, mustachioed guitarist, seems perfectly willing to allow Daryl, the Blue-Eyed Dreamer, to monopolize center stage—literally—as lead vocalist, which is undeniably one of the reasons the pair managed to survive so long as a unit. Though rumors persisted that they are gay—unfounded gossip fueled in part by the 1975 *Silver Album* showing them in full cover-girl makeup—Oates is married to model Nancy Hunter and Hall, once divorced, lives near his partner in Greenwich Village with lyricist Sara Allen. Hall and Oates were among the legion of rock superstars assembled as USA/Africa to record 1985's hugely successful single ''We Are the World.'' They surely ranked as the business's highest-paid backup singers when they oo-ooed behind other stars onstage at 1985's historic Live Aid concert.

Born: Hall (October 11, 1949, in Pottstown, Pennsylvania) Oates (April 7, 1949, in New York City)
Height: Hall (6 ft. 3 in.) Oates (5 ft. 4 in.)
Eyes: Hall (Blue) Oates (Brown)
Hair: Hall (Blond) Oates (Brown)
Zodiac: Hall (Libra) Oates (Aries)
Education: Hall (three years studying music at Temple University) Oates (B.A. in journalism, Temple University)
Marriages:
Hall (one, to Bryna Lublin, ended in divorce)
Oates (one, to Nancy Hunter, 1979–)
Children: Hall (none) Oates (none)
Personal Habits and Traits: Hall (smokes, drinks Moët, considered somewhat moody), Oates (smokes, drinks dark rum, upbeat and cheerful)
Addresses: Both live in New York City
Income: $8 million (minimum estimate, joint annual)

Halston

Roy Halston Frowick

"We only suggest things. It is fashionable people who make fashion."

It all began with a red Easter hat which Roy Halston Frowick designed for his mother when he was 13. He attended the University of Indiana for two years, then transferred to the Art Institute of Chicago, while the hats he fashioned in his spare time were displayed at Chicago's Ambassador Hotel (home of the famous Pump Room). As soon as he graduated from the Art Institute, Halston, as he began calling himself, opened a millinery shop at the Ambassador. Like all would-be major American designers, Halston headed for New York and an apprenticeship in the salon of milliner *par excellence* Lilly Daché. Before moving uptown to his own boutique at Bergdorf Goodman, he began selling to Jacqueline Kennedy in the late 1950s. On the occasion of the inauguration of her husband in 1961, the future First Lady turned to Halston for the perfect hat. He produced an off-white pillbox, and for the next four years his pillbox was *the* hat to wear. A pal of Mrs. Onassis, Elizabeth Taylor, Liza Minnelli, and Lauren Bacall among others, the tall, boyishly handsome designer bestrides an empire of clothes, perfumes, linens and furniture that by the mid-1980s was still grossing around $100 million—enough to make Halston a profitable subsidiary of the Norton Simon conglomerate. Halston lives alone in a minimally furnished black-sheathed town house off Park Avenue and frequents discos like Regine's, just three blocks from his home. After 11 years as part of the Norton Simon conglomerate, which in the early 1980s was absorbed by Esmark and then Beatrice Foods, Halston bought back his company in 1984. "I feel great," he said of the bold business move. "It's like a whole new frontier."

Born: April 1932 in Des Moines, Iowa
Height: 6 ft. 1 in.
Weight: 169 lbs.
Eyes: Blue *Hair:* Dark brown
Zodiac: Aries
Education: University of Indiana, the Art Institute of Chicago
Religion: Protestant
Marriages: None
Children: None
Interests: Smokes, drinks, diets, is an exercise nut
Personal Habits and Traits: Stays out late, gets up late, is a supersocial, disco-dancing New Yorker
Address: New York City
Income: $2.5 million (minimum estimate)

Dorothy Hamill

"I don't mind the celebrity status, and I don't mind signing autographs either. When I was a little girl, I missed getting Peggy Fleming's autograph, and I never forgot that."

"Every time she got on the ice," Carol Hamill recalls of her daughter Dorothy, "we just couldn't say, 'Sorry, honey, we can't afford it, you'll have to quit.'" So starting at the age of 8 Dorothy Hamill practiced every morning before going to school in suburban Greenwich, Connecticut. As soon as her sisters Sandy and Arci left home for college, Mrs. Hamill and Dorothy moved to Denver to be closer to her skating coach, Carlo Fassi. It definitely paid off, because at 19 Dorothy copped a gold medal for figure skating at the 1976 Winter Olympics at Innsbruck, and soon the real gold appeared when she signed a $2 million contract to star in the Ice Capades. America's sweetheart on ice, she even inspired her own haircut—the short, pageboyish "Hamill" that resulted in her landing a hefty $500,000 contract to promote Clairol hair products. Since Innsbruck, Dorothy has been criticized for acting haughty and aloof, and her romance with Dino Martin somewhat tarnished her image. In 1974, Martin, divorced from British actress Olivia Hussey, was convicted for possession of firearms and sentenced to a year's probation and a $200 fine. Still, Martin competed with the rink for Hamill's attention. Landing off balance during Ice Capades rehearsals, she was furious with herself. "Oh, piss!" she screamed. "I can't seem to get this right. I need a cigarette." The world's number-one figure skater has come a long way since the days when she refused to skate unless her stuffed animals—a tiger, a turtle, and a bear—were propped on a chair at ringside. A half-pack-a-day smoker since she was 15, Hamill resists indulging her passion for ice cream to retain her 115 pound figure.

Born: 1956, in Greenwich, Connecticut
Height: 5 ft. 3 in.
Weight: 115 pounds
Eyes: Brown *Hair:* Brown
Education: High school
Marriages: Dino Martin (1982–83)
Children: None
Interests: Ballet, teaching blind skaters, interior decorating
Personal Habits and Traits: Smokes, ice cream addict, early bird
Address: Riverside, Connecticut
Income: $500,000 (minimum estimate)

Mark Hamill

"I'm waiting for my body to catch up with my age."

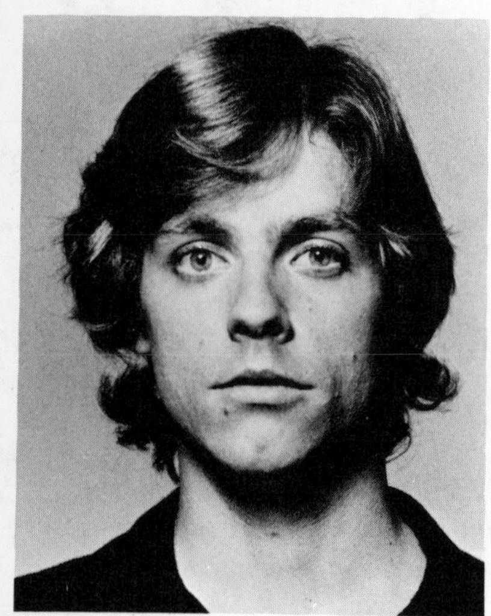

Star Wars' Luke Skywalker was played by a rambunctious Navy brat who grew up in 10 cities (including Yokohama) before settling in California. He enrolled in L.A. City College, but dropped out after his sophomore year. Over the next few years Hamill filmed 89 guest shots in various TV series and performed in the soap *General Hospital* before signing a contract to act in ABC's sitcom *Eight Is Enough*. When offered the potential star-making role of Luke Skywalker, he asked to be released from his television contract and ABC threatened to sue. To complicate matters Hamill drove his spanking new BMW over a 30-foot cliff, injuring himself and rearranging his boyish features. "My nose," he sadly recalls, "was wiped right off," but three operations later his face was good as new—though not his psyche. It took a pep talk from *Eight Is Enough* mom Diana Hyland, who visited him in the hospital just three weeks before she died of cancer, to convince him to continue his career. A millionaire as a result of his share in the biggest box office bonanza of all time, Hamill followed *Star Wars* with *Corvette Summer* and *The Big Red One*. Known affectionately as "Motor-Mouth" to his friends, bachelor Hamill lives in Malibu and amuses himself with marathon Monopoly games, baking cakes, and engaging in food fights. Along with the rest of the original *Star Wars* cast, Hamill gladly returned to shoot the sequels, *The Empire Strikes Back* and *Return of the Jedi*. His Broadway musical debut in *Harragan and Hart* was a catastrophe of intergalactic proportions.

Born: September 25, 1952, in Oakland, California
Height: 5 ft. 8 in.
Weight: 147 lbs.
Eyes: Blue *Hair:* Dark blond
Zodiac: Libra
Education: Two years at Los Angeles City College
Religion: Protestant
Marriages: To Mary Lou
Children: Nathan (b. 1979)
Interests: Politics, women's rights (a supporter of ERA), Monopoly, cake-baking
Personal Habits and Traits: A rapid-fire talker, intelligent, articulate, ambitious, drives fast
Address: Malibu, California
Income: $2 million (estimate)

Marvin Hamlisch

"My whole life revolves around dessert."

At six he had already begun composing and by seven was enrolled as the youngest student in the history of the prestigious Julliard School of Music. At 17 he wrote "Sunshine, Lollipops and Rainbows" for Lesley Gore, and the following year was composing for up-and-coming Liza Minnelli. When playing the piano at a party given by Hollywood producer Sam Spiegel, Marvin Hamlisch was matter-of-factly informed by his host that he was looking for someone to write the theme for his new Burt Lancaster film *The Swimmer*. Three days later Hamlisch presented him with a composition, and Spiegel was so impressed he hired Marvin on the spot. In 1974 he rocked the music world by collecting no fewer than three Oscars—for Best Original Song ("The Way We Were"), Best Original Score (also *The Way We Were*) and Best Scoring (for his adaptation of Scott Joplin's "The Entertainer" in *The Sting*). Two years later he shared a Tony and a Pulitzer Prize for Broadway's *A Chorus Line,* and in 1977 he received yet another Academy Award nomination for "Nobody Does It Better," the suggestive title theme from the James Bond flick *The Spy Who Loved Me*. He did not win the award, but Carly Simon turned the song into one of the Top 10 singles of the year. Manhattan-born, Hamlisch has parlayed his success at the keyboard into a successful Las Vegas and concert circuit act as well, but he remains an unrepentant bachelor. His former living arrangement with Carole Bayer Sager was the inspiration for the Broadway smash *They're Playing Our Song,* crafted by Hamlisch, Sager, and Neil Simon. After Sager married Burt Bacharach, Hamlisch's new muse was Cindy Garvey, pitcher Steve Garvey's leggy ex.

Born: June 2, 1944, in New York City
Height: 6 ft. 2 in.
Weight: 174 lbs.
Eyes: Brown *Hair:* Brown
Zodiac: Gemini
Education: The Julliard School of Music; Queens College, B.A. in music
Religion: Jewish

Marriages: None
Children: None
Interests: Motion pictures, ice cream
Personal Habits and Traits: Nonsmoker, nondrinker, a workaholic
Address: Beverly Hills
Income: $1.7 million+

Valerie Harper

"I used to get some ego thing out of saying I wasn't a star, just an actress. Forget it. I'm a star. I wanted it. I worked for it. I got it."

Although born in upstate New York, onetime Radio City chorine Valerie Harper grew up all over America (her dad was a traveling salesman) and did not hesitate to move out west as a member of the *Li'l Abner* chorus in 1958. When she later contracted hepatitis, her doctor prescribed candy—the main reason she ballooned to the 155-pound chub who was perfect a decade later for the role of Mary Tyler Moore's dateless pal Rhoda. She became a national star as the dieting, kvetching sidekick in the MTM superhit, and in 1974 embarked on her own spinoff sitcom. Within weeks it was number one in the Nielsens; for each of the annual 22 episodes of *Rhoda* Harper received $17,000. In 1964 she married *Second City* alumnus Dick Schaal, who also costarred in *Rhoda's* sister show *Phyllis,* but by 1978 she and Schaal had come to the end of the road—as did *Rhoda,* canceled after two years of steadily falling ratings. Perhaps through her

lucrative commercials for Total cereal and est, of which Harper is an avid devotee, the four-time Emmy winner found adequate consolation. She certainly couldn't find comfort in movies like *Chapter Two* and *Blame It on Rio*. In late 1985, she returned to the tube with her own series, *Valerie,* at the same time old pal M.T.M. returned to the small screen with *her* show called—uh-huh—*Mary*.

Born: August 22, 1940, in Suffern, New York
Height: 5 ft. 4 in.
Weight: 118 lbs.
Eyes: Brown *Hair:* Brown
Zodiac: On the cusp of Virgo and Leo
Education: High school
Religion: Roman Catholic
Marriages: To Dick Schaal (1964–1978)
To Tony Cacciotti (1984–)
Children: None of her own, but raised Wendy, Schaal's daughter by a previous marriage
Interests: est
Personal Habits and Traits: Nonsmoker, dieter
Address: Beverly Hills
Income: $300,000 (minimum estimate)

Emmylou Harris

''Too many record producers slick you up, and you wind up losing the home feel.''

A Marine brat who moved with her family from Virginia to Alabama to North Carolina, Emmylou Harris made it through three semesters at the University of North Carolina in Greensboro before she floated up to New York's Greenwich Village coffeehouses. While singing Dylan folk songs and country tunes like ''It Wasn't God Who Made Hony-Tonk Angels,'' she caught the eye of ex-Byrd Gram Parsons, then singing with the Flying Burrito Brothers. He asked her to become the only Burrito Sister, but the group broke up before she could join. So Harris backed Parsons's solo efforts on the stage and on two albums until his death from a heart attack at the age of 26. Eventually ascending to the level of country-rock royalty like Linda Ronstadt and Dolly Parton, Harris recorded the number-one country LP *Pieces of the Sky* in 1975, then crossed over into the more lucrative AM rock market with her *Elite Hotel* the following year. A decade after she started singing his songs in the Village, Harris was asked by Bob Dylan to collaborate with him on his 1977 classic album *Desire*. Her early marriage to an unnamed songwriter lasted less than a year, and Harris has been a solo parent to her daughter Hallie since her birth in 1970. Although she makes it a rule to spend at least one week of every month with her daughter even if she is on tour, Harris has managed to become one of country-pop's biggest moneymakers with hits like her bluesy ''Blue Kentucky Girl,'' and the remake of the 1950's hit ''Mr. Sandman.''

Born: April 2, 1948, in Birmingham, Alabama
Height: 5 ft. 4 in.
Weight: 115 lbs.
Eyes: Hazel *Hair:* Brown
Zodiac: Aries
Education: University of North Carolina (dropped out after three semesters)
Religion: Protestant
Marriages: One. Divorced.
Children: Hallie (b. 1970)
Interests: Songwriting, singing, cooking
Personal Habits and Traits: Smokes occasionally, does not shun alcohol, is a night person, needs little sleep
Address: Los Angeles
Income: $250,000 + (minimum estimate)

Richard Harris

''I call my approach 'the secret world of an actor.' After all, people don't have babies right out in the street.''

This hard-drinking, two-fisted Irishman declined to go into the family flour business and instead studied at London Academy. His first movie was an I.R.A. potboiler with James Cagney, *Shake Hands With the Devil.* His face became more familiar in *The Guns of Navarone, This Sporting Life* (for which he received an Academy Award nomination) and *Mutiny on the Bounty,* but he did not play the lead in a big-budget film until the role of King Arthur in *Camelot.* That singing part evolved into a major recording career that peaked with his number-one recordings of Jim Webb's eerie ''MacArthur Park'' and ''Didn't We?'' In the late 1970s Harris's career went into something of a stall with such bombs as *Orca* (the *Jaws* ripoff that replaced the shark with a whale) and *The Cassandra Crossing.* He went through a controversial divorce from the former Elizabeth Rees-Williams (who went on to marry Rex Harrison) and soon after wed comely actress Ann Turkel, one of his *Cassandra Crossing* costars. ''After ten years of Rabelaisian drunkeness and boudoir folly,'' said Harris, who was drinking up to two quarts of vodka a day and earned his reputation as a pub brawler, ''I met somebody who said, 'Hey, stop!'" Easier said than done; in frustration, Turkel once stood on a cliff near their Bahamas home and tossed every liquor bottle she could find onto the rocks. Eventually, that's where the marriage ended up.

Born: October 1, 1933, in Limerick, Ireland
Height: 6 ft.
Weight: 184 lbs.
Eyes: Blue *Hair:* Brown
Zodiac: Libra
Education: London Academy
Religion: Roman Catholic
Marriages: To Elizabeth Rees-Williams (divorced in 1972)
To Ann Turkel (1975–1983)
Children: Three sons
Interests: Poetry, songwriting, singing
Personal Habits and Traits: Smokes, admittedly hot-tempered, sips mineral water
Address: Los Angeles
Income: $400,000 (estimate)

George Harrison

"Anywhere is paradise."

The quietest and most spiritual Beatle, gaunt George Harrison dropped out of the Liverpool Art Institute while a teenager to work as an electrician's assistant. He soon discovered, however, that he was inept at the job and found himself spending more and more time playing guitar in Liverpool clubs with his friends John and Paul (Ringo eventually joined them in Germany). Between 1963 and 1971 the Beatles ranked as the most popular pop group in history, establishing sales records that have yet to be broken, while their movies—*A Hard Day's Night, Help, The Yellow Submarine, Let It Be*—all scored as big moneymakers. The first of the Beatles to embrace the teachings of the Maharishi Mahesh Yogi and to latch onto sitar virtuoso Ravi Shankar, Harrison pursued a post-Beatles period heavily saturated with musical influences from the East (his "My Sweet Lord," for example, employs the Hari Krishna chant). Second to Paul McCartney in his success after the group's 1971 breakup, Harrison gathered together the cream of 1960s musicians—Bob Dylan, Eric Clapton, Leon Russell, Billy Preston, and Ringo Starr among them—to perform a benefit concert for Bangladesh at Madison Square Garden that later became a landmark triple album. But it was eventually disclosed that much of the money raised by the concert never arrived in Bangladesh—a revelation that left Harrison discouraged and bitter. Another disappointment: a 1976 court ruling that Harrison fork over $587,000 because he "subconciously" employed the melody from 1963's "He's So Fine" in writing "My Sweet Lord." After his eight-year marriage to former model Patti Boyd dissolved, Harrison, clean-shaven and slicker than ever, returned to the charts in 1977 with his nutty "Crackerbox Palace." After John Lennon's murder, Harrison was not eager for a reunion of the survivors. Instead, he went into the movie business; his Handmade Films has bankrolled a number of features, including the 1986 Sean Penn–Madonna pic *Shanghai Surprise*. Married to former secretary Olivia Ariás (they wed five weeks following the birth of their son, Dhani), Harrison stays out of the limelight at his thirty-room Victorian mansion outside London. The 35-acre estate, Friar Park, boasts elaborate formal gardens and three private lakes.

Born: February 25, 1943, Liverpool, England
Height: 5 ft. 8½ in.
Weight: 141 lbs.
Eyes: Brown *Hair:* Brown
Zodiac: Pisces
Education: High school dropout
Religion: Anglican
Marriages: To Patti Boyd (1966–1974)
To Olivia Ariás (1978–)
Children: Dhani (b. 1978)
Interests: Yoga, meditation, the sitar, automobiles
Personal Habits and Traits: Smokes two packs a day, drinks, quit drugs (used to take LSD), no longer a vegetarian—eats fish, chicken
Address: Henley-on-Thames, England
Income: $4.5 million (minimum estimate)

David Hartman

"This whole TV business is someone counting. You got twelve seconds! You got nine! You got six! It's like something out of The Music Man.*"*

During his senior year in high school young David Hartman was offered contracts to play with both the Boston Braves and Philadelphia Phillies; he had by that time also mastered the clarinet, flute, violin and saxophone. Ultimately Hartman pursued neither sports nor music, although he did graduate from Duke University with a straight-A average in economics while playing on the baseball team, singing in campus chorale groups and announcing on local radio and TV stations. Following a stint in the Air Force as a second lieutenant, Hartman studied at the American Academy of Dramatic Arts in New York, gained experience in off-Broadway musicals and summer stock, toured with the Harry Belafonte singers and appeared in *Best Foot Forward* with another newcomer named Liza Minnelli. That led to 800 performances in the original Broadway production of *Hello, Dolly!* and a part with the national road company of *My Fair Lady*. A role in a made-for-TV movie, *I Love a Mystery,* brought him to the attention of the producers of *The Virginian,* where he spent a season, and led to the part of a surgeon on *The Bold Ones*. That in turn landed Hartman the title role in NBC's *Lucas Tanner*. Following the demise of that series he signed with ABC as host of the *Good Morning, America* show, and largely because of Hartman's facile manner and his considerable skills as an interviewer, *Good Morning, America* gave NBC's *Today* its first serious competition. But it was not the first time Hartman had made his mark in television news; the documentary *Birth and Babies,* which he produced and narrated, brought to the home screen network television's first coverage of childbirth.

Born: May 19, 1935, in Pawtucket, Rhode Island
Height: 6 ft. 5 in.
Weight: 200 lbs.
Eyes: Blue *Hair:* Brown
Zodiac: Taurus
Education: Duke University, B.A. in economics
Religion: Protestant
Marriages: To Maureen Downey (current)
Children: Sean (b. 1975), Brian (b. 1977)
Interests: Golf, tennis, baseball (trained with the Giants), Muscular Dystrophy Association, medicine, music
Personal Habits and Traits: Nonsmoker, moderate drinker, inexhaustible worker, goes to bed by 10 P.M. for early morning taping of *Good Morning, America,* eats scrambled eggs and a cheeseburger for lunch every day
Address: New York City
Income: $1.9 million

Goldie Hawn

"What makes me different from an electrician? We're all gifted, all trained."

Jobs as a can-can dancer at the 1964 New York World's Fair, as a caged go-go dancer in New Jersey, and as a Las Vegas showgirl preceded the three-year *Laugh-In* stint that made Goldie Jean Hawn from Takoma Park, Maryland, the 1960s line-blowing answer to Judy Holliday and Gracie Allen. Anything but dumb—she worked her way through Washington's American University by teaching dance classes—Goldie won an Academy Award as Best Supporting Actress for *Cactus Flower* and delivered convincing performances in *Sugarland Express, Butterflies Are Free,* and *Shampoo* (of which she owns 7 percent); not so impressive were *There's a Girl in My Soup, $,* and *The Duchess and the Dirtwater Fox.* After waiting a year for divorce from director Gus Trikonis to be finalized, Goldie married singing Hudson Brother Bill (four years her junior) just three months before their child was born in 1976. Complications set in after the cesarean birth of young Oliver Hudson and he developed pneumonia. But Oliver recovered, and after three years away from films and a six-year absence from the medium that made her famous, Goldie returned with a CBS prime-time special of her own and her 10th movie, *Foul Play* with Chevy Chase. Number 11: *Private Benjamin,* for which she received another Oscar nomination. A few years passed before Hawn's career swung back into high gear starring opposite new beau Kurt Russell in *Swing Shift.* Her 1984 effort, *Protocol,* flopped. *Wildcats* didn't.

Born: November 21, 1945, in Washington, D.C.
Height: 5 ft. 6 in.
Weight: 119 lbs.
Eyes: Blue *Hair:* Blond
Zodiac: Scorpio
Education: American University in Washington, D.C., B.A. in drama
Religion: Jewish
Marriages:
To Gus Trikonis (1969–1976)
To Bill Hudson (1976–1982)
Children: Oliver (b. 1976), Kate (b. 1979)
Interests: Cooking, sewing, knitting, music, antiques, producing her own TV projects
Personal Habits and Traits: She smokes occasionally, does not drink, loves to eat, a self-described homebody, loathes parties
Address: Malibu, California
Income: $2 million

Patty Hearst

"I was nineteen when all this happened, and now I'm not nearly so naive."

The fresh-scrubbed granddaughter of publishing tycoon William Randolph Hearst certainly seemed the perfect all-American girl. She was a cheerleader in high school and like many of her contemporaries of the early '70s she met a

young man at college, became engaged, and moved in with him. She had just finished picking out her china pattern when, on the night of February 4, 1974, her life was changed forever. Dragged screaming from her apartment wearing only a blue bathrobe, Patty was kidnaped by three members of the Symbionese Liberation Army, who kicked her fiancé Steven Weed and struck him with a bottle before stuffing Patty in the trunk of a car and speeding off. Randolph Hearst and his wife Catherine, a University of California regent, met the S.L.A.'s ransom demand by giving away $2 million worth of food to the poor in the San Francisco Bay Area. The result was full-scale rioting (with full-scale media coverage) as mobs fought for tons of supplies tossed off trucks into the city streets. Nine weeks later, Patty boldly declared on a tape that she had joined the S.L.A.; two weeks after that "Tania" Hearst, along with other S.L.A. members, strolled into a branch of San Francisco's Hibernia Bank brandishing a rifle. The ensuing robbery was clearly filmed by the bank's automatic cameras and the robbers fled with $10,960, needlessly spraying the bank with gunfire during their getaway. Later, when the S.L.A.'s Bill and Emily Harris were spotted shoplifting at a sporting goods store in Los Angeles, Patty peppered the store with rifle bullets. Millions of viewers (including the Hearsts) watched live television coverage of the climactic shootout on May 17, 1974, when police cornered six S.L.A. members in a small house in L.A. As it burned to the ground amid a hail of gunfire, all six died—but Patty, it turned out, was not among them. Still, she remained underground until September 1975 when an FBI agent and a policeman climbed the back stairs to a top-floor San Francisco apartment in which she was staying. Inside, Patty Hearst surrendered quietly, bringing to an end one of the longest, most intensive manhunts in history. She went on trial in federal court for bank robbery in San Francisco on February 4, 1976—two years to the day after she was abducted by the S.L.A. Her defense was conducted by celebrated attorney F. Lee Bailey, but he could not convince the seven women and five men on the jury that her actions were the result of S.L.A. brainwashing and psychological torture (among other things, she had been locked in a closet for days). On March 20, 1976, she was convicted for bank robbery and misuse of a firearm. The sentence: seven years in federal prison—far more than the usual sentence for bank robbery and even more than the prosecution suggested. In 1978, as she served her time by doing dishes for two cents an hour in the federal women's prison at Pleasanton, California, Hearst filed suit against attorney Bailey and sought a new trial, claiming that her defense had been bungled. Meanwhile, such diverse figures as Cesar Chavez, William F. Buckley, Louisiana congresswoman Lindy Boggs, and Ronald Reagan called for her release. As the public outcry for commutation grew, Patty became engaged to Bernie Shaw, the divorced cop who once worked as her bodyguard. Inside prison, however, stress continued to take its toll. The rough treatment she received at the hands of other inmates contributed to her deteriorating physical condition, which included bouts with pleurisy and pneumonia and a collapsed lung. Finally released under an executive clemency order signed by President Carter in early 1979, she promptly married Shaw. In a strange twist of fate Patty's return to a relatively normal life also signaled the demise of her parents' marriage. In the mid-1980s, the Shaws moved to Connecticut, where Patty Hearst blended into the scene as the typical suburban housewife and mother of two.

Born: February 20, 1954, in San Francisco, California
Height: 5 ft. 3½ in.
Weight: 100 lbs.
Eyes: Brown *Hair:* Light brown
Zodiac: Pisces
Education: High school
Religion: Episcopalian
Marriages: To Bernard Shaw (1979–)
Children: Gillian Catherine (b. 1981), Lydia Marie (b. 1984)
Interests: Horseback riding, the outdoors, art, dogs, jogging, touch football
Personal Habits and Traits: Has quit smoking, does not drink, rises at 6 A.M., reads, avoids television
Address: Westport, Connecticut
Income: Her share of the Hearst fortune is at least $3 million

Hugh Hefner

"Playboy *is sex, closely linked to great business success—and those are the two great Puritan hangups.*"

Stag Party was the original name for his new magazine, but when *Stag* magazine objected Hugh Hefner had to settle for *Playboy*. "Hef," who had quit his subscription department job at Esquire when they refused to raise his salary from $60 to $85 per week, eventually pyramided *Playboy* magazine into a global empire of bunny-stocked Playboy clubs, a Playboy Press and Book Club, a Playboy theater chain, a Playboy production company, a Playboy limousine service and even a spinoff magazine, *Oui*. Before he put together the first issue of *Playboy* on a shoestring in 1953, Hefner had served in the Army, worked as a clerk, studied psychology at the University of Illinois, married his high school sweetheart, Millie Williams, and fathered two children. Since *Playboy,* however, Hefner has definitely embraced the hedonistic lifestyle his so-called "philosophy" prescribes. After 20 years spent operating his business from the bed of the famous Playboy Mansion in Chicago—where he hosted his *Playboy After Dark* and *Playboy's Penthouse,* a TV variety series—Hefner hopped aboard his all-black Big Bunny DC-9, and set up shop in the $2 million Playboy Mansion West in Beverly Hills; that pleasure dome, replete with indoor grotto and private zoo, is staffed by 40 full-time servants. In 1974, an unauthorized biography by former Playboy employee Frank Brady threatened trouble in paradise. The book described an alleged homosexual affair in Hefner's distant past and a ritual where ten bunnies massaged the boss nude. Brady estimated that Hef has slept with over 2,000 women. Hefner has denied the allegations. A number of business setbacks, particularly the heavy losses chalked up by the Playboy Clubs and the movie division, caused Playboy stock to plummet from $23.50 in 1970 to around $9 in 1978. Not that Hefner has all that much to worry about; his private fortune is estimated at well over $200 million. At one point, it looked as if longtime live-in Barbi Benton, an aspiring country singer-starlet, would snag the desirable role of Mrs. Hugh Hefner. But they drifted apart and the one woman that Hefner then concentrated on most was his daughter and corporate heir apparent, Chris. After the publication of director Peter Bogdonavich's explosive book about murdered Playmate Dorothy Stratten, *Death of the Unicorn,* Hefner suffered a stroke. Several weeks later, Hefner responded to Bogdanovich's charges that he exploited Stratten by holding a press conference and accusing Bogdonavich of seducing not only Stratten but also her underage sister. The sister replied with a lawsuit, and Hefner conceded that he had made a huge mistake. The suit was later dropped, leaving Hef free to enjoy turning 60 with 23-year-old model Carrie Leigh at his side.

Born: April 9, 1926, in Chicago
Height: 5 ft. 8 in.
Weight: 154 lbs.
Eyes: Brown *Hair:* Brown
Zodiac: Aries
Education: University of Illinois, B.S. in psychology
Religion: Agnostic
Marriages: To Millie Williams (1949–1959)
Children: David and Christine
Interests: Books, movies, backgammon
Personal Habits and Traits: Smokes a pipe, swizzles Pepsi, is a chronic insomniac
Addresses: Beverly Hills; Chicago
Income: $18 million annually (minimum estimate). Hefner is worth more than $200 million

Jim Henson (The Muppets)

"I still have trouble believing that puppeteering is the sort of thing one does for a living."

To millions of *Sesame Street* and *Muppet Show* addicts of all ages and nationalities, the foam rubber figments of Jim Henson's fertile imagination—including Kermit the Frog, Miss Piggy, Oscar the Grouch, Big Bird, Ernie, the Cookie Monster, and Gonzo—are bona fide superstars. Born in Mississippi and raised in Hyattsville, Maryland, a suburb of Washington, D.C., Henson grew up the son of an agronomist with the Department of Agriculture. He never played with puppets as a child, but when it looked like that might be a way to break into television he joined his high school puppet club. Henson met his wife Jane in a puppetry class at the University of Maryland, and soon they landed a five-minute late-night puppet show on local TV called *Sam and Friends.* One of the stars was Kermit the Frog, a rather articulate amphibian made out of an old coat with Ping-Pong balls for eyes. In 1962 the Hensons moved their Muppets (a combination of marionette and puppet) to New York and were soon performing routines on the *Today* show. Eight years later, after hundreds of appearances on numerous TV shows, they signed with *Sesame Street.* It was not until he could convince Lord Lew Grade to back him in England that Henson launched *The Muppet Show.* Taped in London with guest stars ranging from Bob Hope to Rudolf Nureyev, the series was syndicated to 163 American cities and 103 foreign countries. At a

Jubilee performance in November 1977, Kermit (along with Bob Hope and Frank Sinatra) was presented to Queen Elizabeth. Astonishingly, the *Muppet Show's* "cast" record album topped the charts in England. There are now over 500 Muppets (most of whom owe their voices to Henson), and hundreds of spinoff books, dolls, toys, and games that gross an estimated 30 million annually. To top it off, the first *Muppet Movie* became a monster hit, as did the *The Great Muppet Detective Caper* and *The Muppets Take Manhattan* (climaxed by the long-awaited marriage of Miss Piggy and Kermit). Henson's ambitious *Dark Crystal* fared less well, but his HBO series *Fraggle Rock* was an unqualified success, and Henson was able to pull enough strings to guarantee that the first Sesame Street movie, *Follow That Bird,* would not lay an egg at the box office.

Born: September 24, 1936, in Greenville, Mississippi
Height: 6 ft. 1 in.
Weight: 175 lbs.
Eyes: Blue *Hair:* Brown
Zodiac: Libra
Education: University of Maryland
Religion: Protestant
Marriages: To Jane Nebel (1959–)
Children: Lisa (b. 1960), Cheryl (b.1961), Brian (b. 1963), John (b. 1965), Heather (b. 1971)
Interests: Sailing, skiing, traveling, education
Personal Habits and Traits: Nonsmoker, drinks moderately, a workaholic
Addresses: New York City; Bedford, New York
Income: $5 million+ (minimum estimate of personal net)

Audrey Hepburn

Audrey Hepburn-Ruston

"My responsibilities to my family come first. If I have to make a choice, acting loses out."

This daughter of a Dutch baroness was born in Belgium and grew up during the Nazi occupation. Svelte to the point of emaciation and holding her head almost disconcertingly erect on her swanlike neck, Audrey Hepburn-Ruston studied ballet in Amsterdam and dropped half her surname before aiming at London and a West End acting career in 1948. Three years later she was tapped by Colette to play *Gigi* on Broadway, and in 1953 won a Best Actress Oscar for her U.S. movie debut *Roman Holiday* (with Gregory Peck). Commanding a half-million dollars per movie—between 1953 and 1968 she shared honors with Liz Taylor as the world's most highly paid female star—she went on to star in a series of splashy extravaganzas like *Sabrina, War and Peace, The Nun's Story, Breakfast at Tiffany's, Charade,* and *My Fair Lady. Two for the Road* with Albert Finney became something of a cult film, and 1967's shocker *Wait Until Dark* marked a superlative contribution to the suspense genre. After a 10-year absence from films during which she lived in quiet semiretirement with psychiatrist Dr. Andrea Dotti (her second husband, after Mel Ferrer), Hepburn staged a comeback playing Robin Hood's middle-aged love interest in *Robin and Marion,* and then the pursued heiress in *Bloodline*. That film roughly coincided with the impending breakup of her marriage to Dotti. ''She gives the distinct impression,'' director Billy Wilder once observed, ''that she can spell 'schizophrenia.''' Notwithstanding constant rumors to the contrary, Hepburn, who received a standing ovation when she materialized like Holly Golightly at the 1986 Oscar show, seemed not to be interested in marrying longtime post-Dotti beau Rob Wolders, Merle Oberon's much-younger widower.

Born: May 4, 1929, in Brussels, Belgium
Height: 5 ft. 7 in.
Weight: 100 lbs.
Eyes: Brown *Hair:* Brown
Zodiac: Taurus
Education: High school, ballet school
Religion: Roman Catholic
Marriages:
To Mel Ferrer (1954–1967)
To Andrea Dotti (1969–1981)
Children: Sean (b. 1960) by Ferrer; Luca (b. 1970) by Dotti (suffered 5 miscarriages)
Interests: Dance, music, literature, fashion, skiing
Personal Habits and Traits: Chain smokes Kents, high-strung, does not exercise, is semireclusive
Address: Rome
Income: $300,000 + (minimum estimate)

Katharine Hepburn

''Sometimes I wonder if men and women really suit each other. Perhaps they should live next door and just visit now and then.''

''My greatest strength is, and always has been, common sense. I'm really a standard brand—like Campbell's tomato soup or Baker's chocolate.'' To moviegoers of three generations, Katharine Hepburn is anything but ''a standard brand.'' In fact, Hepburn, whose career over five decades has careened from box office poison to unparalleled superstardom, is considered by many to be the greatest actress in the history of the movies. The only actor nominated for a dozen Academy Awards, she was also the only one to win four times in the Best Actress category—for *Morning Glory* (1933), *Guess Who's Coming to Dinner* (1968), *The Lion in Winter* (1969) and *On Golden Pond* (1983). A legendary personality the American public cannot seem to get enough of, she continually ranks in polls as one of the world's most admired women. In recent years two national bestsellers, Garson Kanin's *Tracy and Hepburn* and Charles Higham's *Kate,* have been written about her, but she refuses to read them. Born the daughter of a leading Connecticut urologist and a women's liberationist mother, Hepburn grew up in a household where everyone started the day with a cold shower and ended it with heated dinner table debates. After Bryn Mawr, the angular-featured hellion scored her first Broadway success playing a leggy Amazon in 1932's *The Warrior's Husband.* The part landed her a contract with RKO, and Hepburn achieved immediate screen stardom in *Bill Of Divorcement, Little Women, Alice Adams, Mary of Scotland,* and *Stage Door*—the classic in which she intoned her famous ''the calla lilies are in bloom again.'' A five-film slump ended with her triumph on stage and screen in Philip Barry's *The Philadelphia*

Story (1940), but after that smash, Hepburn's career sank again. Then came *Woman of the Year* (1942), the first of nine Hepburn and Spencer Tracy films. Their lifelong collaboration (both onscreen and off) flourished with such comedies as *Without Love, State of the Union, Adam's Rib, Pat and Mike, Desk Set,* and of course *Guess Who's Coming to Dinner*. In between, she triumphed opposite Humphrey Bogart in *The African Queen* and returned to Broadway in 1950 as Rosalind in Shakespeare's *As You Like It.* In the 1962 screen adaptation of Eugene O'Neill's wrenching classic *Long Day's Journey Into Night,* Hepburn turned in what many consider one of the greatest performances in screen history as the morphine-addicted Mary Tyrone. After Tracy's death in 1967, she plunged into *The Lion in Winter,* in which she played Eleanor of Aquitaine to Peter O'Toole's Henry II. Two years later she recaptivated Broadway in another hit, *Coco,* her first musical. Turning then to the medium of television, Hepburn starred in *The Glass Menagerie* and *Love Among the Ruins,* for which she and costar Laurence Olivier easily won Emmys. It marked the first time she worked with Lord Olivier, just as *Rooster Cogburn and the Lady* was her first pairing with John Wayne and 1981's *On Golden Pond* her first with Henry Fonda. After a successful tour in Enid Bagnold's *A Matter of Gravity,* Hollywood's number-one legend was reunited with George Cukor (her director on *The Philadelphia Story* and *The African Queen*) for a TV remake of *The Corn Is Green.* Astonishingly, she had never even met Henry Fonda before the two acted opposite one another in the film that earned Fonda his very first Oscar and Hepburn her fourth, *On Golden Pond.* She returned to Broadway as a crippled pianist in *West Side Waltz* and misfired with Nick Nolte in *Grace Quigley,* but it seemed a miracle that she made that film, followed by TV's top-rated *Mrs. Delafield Wants to Marry,* at all—Hepburn and her secretary, Phyllis Wilbourn, were nearly killed in a 1984 automobile accident, and at one point it seemed almost certain that Kate would at very least lose her foot. She didn't. Following the death of Tracy's widow Louise, Hepburn for the first time talked movingly about Tracy the actor and the man as host of a PBS special entitled *The Spencer Tracy Legacy*. Next up: a movie about Hepburn's relationship with Wilbourn called—what else?—*Me and Phyllis*. "It deals with my life today," smiles Hepburn. "Sort of a Life Among the Ruins."

Born: November 8, 1909, in Hartford, Connecticut
Height: 5 ft. 4 in.
Weight: 110 lbs.
Eyes: Blue *Hair:* Reddish brown
Zodiac: Scorpio
Education: Bryn Mawr
Religion: Protestant
Marriages: To Ogden Smith (1928–1934)
Children: None
Interests: Painting, reading, the theater, bicycling, driving
Personal Habits and Traits: Neither smokes nor drinks, gets to bed by nine, takes several cold showers a day, is a perfectionist, loves risks (her only real fear is fire) and Baker's chocolate, studies for all her parts in Central Park
Address: New York City; Old Saybrook, Conn.

Charlton Heston

"I have played three presidents, three saints and two geniuses. If that doesn't create an ego problem, nothing does."

He parted the Red Sea as Moses in *The Ten Commandments,* but Charlton Heston struggled to put new life into his movie career after *Planet of the Apes* in 1967. In *Soylent Green* he stumbled through a futuristic society where people are converted into the staple food; in 1974's *The Three Musketeers* he appeared in a cameo as Cardinal Richelieu; in *Airport 1975* he saved a 747 from disaster; and four years later he played Henry VIII in *Crossed Swords.* But the era of the DeMille epic is over, and Heston may have to look back on the monumental characters he has portrayed rather than ahead to an active future in films. In addition to Moses, Heston became the valiant Spanish hero of *El Cid,* Andrew Jackson in *The President's Lady,* John the Baptist in *The Greatest Story Ever Told,* Michelangelo in *The Agony and the Ecstasy,* and Judah in the blockbuster *Ben-Hur* (which garnered him an Academy Award as Best Actor in 1959). More than ever, the congenial, intelligent, tennis-playing Heston is a bastion of the Hollywood establishment. Seven-term president of the Screen Actors Guild, he received the Jean Herscholt Humanitarian Award in 1978 for his numerous charitable activities and published his personal journals in *Charlton Heston: An Actor's Life.* After years of leading SAG's conservative forces in a continuing struggle with liberal Edward Asner for control of the union, Heston weighed the possibility of seeking the GOP nomination for U.S. Senator from California. Instead, he accepted an offer from superproducer Esther Shapiro to play John Forsythe's patriarchal counterpart on *The Colbys: Dynasty II.*

Born: October 4, 1924, in Evanston, Illinois
Height: 6 ft. 3 in.
Weight: 200 lbs.
Eyes: Blue *Hair:* Brown
Zodiac: Libra
Education: Northwestern University, B.A. in drama
Religion: Protestant
Marriages: To Lydia Clarke (current)
Children: Two
Interests: Tennis, horses, politics, a wide variety of charities, the American Film Institute, directing
Personal Habits and Traits: Nonsmoker, teetotaler, exercise and health fiend
Address: Beverly Hills
Income: $1.15 million (minimum estimate)

Dustin Hoffman

"In my room as a kid, I used to create an atmosphere of the ring. I'd play a fighter and get knocked to the floor and come back to win."

The son of a Columbia Pictures assistant set decorator who eventually became a furniture designer, Dustin (named by his starstruck mother after silents cowboy star Dustin Farnum) Hoffman grew up the perennial class misfit with the big nose, terrible acne, and braces. Hoffman studied drama at Santa Monica City

College and directed community theaters in North Dakota, New Jersey, Connecticut, and New York's Lower East Side before tackling classes at Lee Strasberg's Actors Studio. During this period he slept on Gene Hackman's kitchen floor, and worked at everything from waiting on tables to typing entries for the Yellow Pages. Mike Nichols grabbed the unknown Hoffman for the plum role of Benjamin in *The Graduate,* and sure enough, Dustin Hoffman became an overnight star. Next came *John and Mary* (with Mia Farrow), the landmark *Midnight Cowboy, Little Big Man, Straw Dogs, Papillon, Lenny, All the President's Men, Marathon Man, Agatha,* and his Oscar-winning part in *Kramer vs. Kramer.* Hoffman also found enough time between films to create the title character *Jimmy Shine* on Broadway and to direct Murray Schisgal's hit 1974 comedy *All Over Town.* Residing in an Upper East Side town house in Manhattan, Hoffman enjoys startling nosy fans with embarrassing retorts (''Do you like sex?'' or ''You have a lovely bosom''). In 1969 he married Ann Byrne, a ballet dancer who is three inches taller than he is, and they have two children. The Hoffmans briefly separated in 1978, reconciled, but finally went ahead with a divorce. He married lawyer Lisa Gottsegen in 1980. Hoffman came very close to winning another Academy Award for *Tootsie,* and a Tony for his portrayal of Willie Loman in *Death of a Salesman.* But no cigar. He returned to comedy opposite Warren Beatty in Elaine May's *Ishtar.*

Born: August 8, 1937, in Los Angeles, California
Height: 5 ft. 6 in.
Weight: 135 lbs.
Eyes: Brown *Hair:* Brown
Zodiac: Leo
Education: Los Angeles Conservatory of Music, Santa Monica City College
Religion: Jewish
Marriages: To Ann Byrne (1969–1979)
To Lisa Gottsegen (1980–)
Children: Four, including son Max (b. 1984)
Interests: Piano, dance, sculpture, painting, tennis, antiques, boxing, toy clowns, gardening, reading, directing
Personal Habits and Traits: Does not smoke, drinks moderately, gets up at 6:30 A.M. (needs only five hours of sleep), is given to artistic rages
Addresses: New York City; Woodbury, Connecticut
Income: $25 million from his share of *Tootsie* alone.

Bob Hope

Leslie Townes Hope

''I was in this crowded elevator, and this little old lady turned around and stared in my face. 'Bob Hope,' she said. 'Say something cute.' So of course I said 'Avocado.' It's pretty hard to say something cute unless you have your cute writers right beside you.''

Known to his classmates as ''Les,'' British-born Leslie Townes Hope changed his name to Bob when his nickname became ''Hopeless.'' At age four he moved with his parents and six brothers to Cleveland, where he eventually pursued a short-lived career as a prizefighter before turning to vaudeville and then Broadway. The 1933 hit *Roberta* defined Bob Hope as a unique entertainer, and provided him with his perennial theme song, *Thanks for the Memories.* That same year he met and married singer Dolores Reade, and over the next half-century the possessor of the notorious ski-jump nose established himself as *the* ultimate stand-up comic on radio, television, and in more than 50 movies. With Bing Crosby, his inseparable sidekick both on and off the screen, and often accompanied by Dorothy Lamour, he cavorted in more than seven gold-paved "road" pictures including *The Road to Morocco, The Road to Singapore, The Road to Hong Kong* and *The Road to Utopia.* Other films include: *Monsieur Beaucaire, The Paleface* and *How to Commit Marriage.* Although he relied heavily on visual sight gags in his movies, Hope is best known as master of the speedy quip. His irreverent humor satirizes even the gravest issues—a technique he employed to best advantage on his annual overseas trips to entertain American troops between 1940 and 1972. During that period he also became a pal to every occupant of the White House from FDR on. Continually on the road, Hope rarely relaxes either at his Palm Springs estate or his spacious Beverly Hills home. At one point *Fortune* magazine estimated Hope's personal wealth at $500 million, but the true figure may be closer to half that amount. He didn't need the money, but royalties rolled in from his best-selling memoir *Confessions of a Hooker.*

Born: May 29, 1903, in Eltham, Kent, England
Height: 5 ft. 10 in.
Weight: 170 lbs.
Eyes: Blue *Hair:* Gray-white
Zodiac: Gemini
Education: High school
Religion: Protestant
Marriages: To Dolores Reade (1933–)
Children: Four, all adopted
Interests: Golf, investments, politics (a conservative Republican), charities
Personal Habits and Traits: Does not smoke, drinks little, diets, has been treated for recurrent eye problems, is meticulous about his dress and work, a workaholic
Addresses: Palm Springs, California; Beverly Hills
Income: $7.5 million+ annually (worth approximately $250 million)

Lena Horne

"All those years I was made into a symbol, whether I liked it or not. I had to be careful not to step out of line, not to make a fuss. It was all a lie. The only thing that wasn't a lie was that I made money. If I didn't they wouldn't have kept me."

In 1978, at the age of 60, she was ranked alongside Elizabeth Taylor and Farrah Fawcett as one of the 10 Most Beautiful Women in the world by *Harper's Bazaar.* Three years later, she was the undisputed Queen of Broadway as the star of her sellout one-woman show. The great-granddaughter of a slave woman and her Caucasian master, Lena Horne was born in Brooklyn, then shunted to relatives in the South at age 13 when her parents divorced. She came back up North as a teenager and hoofed in the chorus at Harlem's famous Cotton Club in the mid-1930s. A stint with Charlie Barnet's band followed, then a movie contract—the first that Hollywood ever offered to a black woman. Many of her scenes in movies like *Cabin in the Sky, Stormy Weather* (her theme song), and *Ziegfeld*

Follies were edited out for white audiences in the South, and often when touring that part of the country Horne was forced to sleep in segregated hotels. Prior to being a star she married Louis Jones, and they had two children before splitting in 1938. Nine years later she secretly wed white horn player Lennie Hayton in Paris, and the couple waited several years before publicly acknowledging their married status. In the turbulent 1960s Horne's past bitter experiences gave rise to a delayed reaction, and she became a committed civil rights activist. During one highly publicized incident she responded to one man's racist epithet in a restaurant by hurling an ashtray at him across the room. Then tragedy dealt a double blow to Horne when her son Teddy died of kidney disease in 1970, followed a year later by Hayton's fatal heart attack. Settled into the role of grandmother to the children of her daughter Gail and Gail's ex-husband, director Sidney Lumet, Horne did not abandon a career that includes numerous television specials, frequent concerts (solo or with Tony Bennett; their 1975 Broadway show proved a continual sellout), and occasionally even movies. She played a controversial role as a madam in the Richard Widmark western *Death of a Gunfighter,* and gave Diana Ross's Dorothy some wise advice in Lumet's film version of the Broadway hit *The Wiz*. Horne's phenomenal comeback on Broadway landed her on *People's* list of the intriguing personalities of 1983.

Born: June 17, 1917, in Brooklyn, New York
Height: 5 ft. 5½ in.
Weight: 116 lbs.
Eyes: Brown *Hair:* Black
Zodiac: Gemini
Education: High school dropout
Religion: Protestant
Marriages:
To Louis Jones (1934–1938)
To Lennie Hayton (1947 until his death in 1971)
Children: Teddy (b. 1936–died in 1970); Gail Lumet (b. 1937)
Interests: Fashion, health, civil rights
Personal Habits and Traits: Nonsmoker, moderate drinker, early riser
Address: New York City
Income: $600,000+

Ron Howard

"I'm at home in front of the camera. After all, I grew up with it."

He made such a *Splash* that Ron Howard became one of Hollywood's most in-demand directors—though not exactly overnight. Born to a family of show business troupers, Howard literally grew up on television—15 seasons in two different sitcoms. Howard appeared in his first film, *The Journey,* at age 5, and by 6 he was already a TV star as Opie on *The Andy Griffith Show.* In 1963, he won critical acclaim for his performance as Eddie in MGM's *Courtship of Eddie's Father* with Glenn Ford. A couple of seasons playing Henry Fonda's kid on the tube followed, but his watershed role—the part that allowed him to trade in "Ronny" for the more mature "Ron"—occured with the smash film *American Graffiti.* When the 1950s nostalgia craze overtook television with *Happy Days,* wholesome Howard was the logical fresh-scrubbed foil for The Fonz. Now operating out of a three-bedroom house in the San Fernando Valley where he lives with his psychologist wife Cheryl, Howard pursues a career that includes acting (opposite John Wayne in *The Shootist,* for example) and director (1977's predictable *Grand Theft Auto*). The transition from child star to mature actor-director has not been easy for Howard, but he says, "You reach a point where you say you're not going to do juveniles any longer. You have to put your foot down." Howard's delightful tale of a modern-day mermaid swept away all doubts about his maturity—along with much of the Disney Studio's debt. He also directed the first Gray Power sci-fi flick—the 1985 summer hit *Cocoon,* and continued his winning streak with the next year's smash comedy *Gung-Ho*.

Born: March 1, 1954, in Duncan, Oklahoma
Height: 5 ft. 10 in.
Weight: 145 lbs.
Eyes: Hazel *Hair:* Red
Zodiac: Pisces
Education: High school
Religion: Protestant
Marriages: To Cheryl Alley (1975–)
Children: One, a daughter.
Interests: Directing, screenwriting, acting, automobiles
Personal Habits and Traits: Does not smoke, drinks beer, eager, a perfectionist, sticks close to home
Address: San Fernando Valley, California
Income: $4 million (estimate)

Rock Hudson (1925–1985)

Roy Scherer, Jr.

"What do I see when I look in a mirror? A lie."

The cinematic cynosure of heterosexual masculinity stunned even those who had long known he was gay when in the summer of 1985 he announced to the world that he was locked in a life-and-death battle with AIDS. Really close friends still call him Roy—he was born Roy Scherer, Jr., in Winnetka, Illinois—but since the mid-1950s he has been known to millions of swooning female fans as Rock Hudson. In typical Schwab's drugstore fashion, he was driving a truck around Hollywood when agent Henry Willson spotted him behind the wheel and wangled him a part in *The Magnificent Obsession.* When the film with Jane Wyman grossed a hefty $8 million Hudson's face landed on the cover of *Life* magazine. *Giant,* with James Dean and Elizabeth Taylor, followed in 1956, and in the late 1950s Hudson became Doris Day's main man in comedies like *Pillow Talk* and *Lover Come Back.* Despite occasional adventure thrillers (Alistair MacLean's *Ice Station Zebra*), period pieces *(Darling Lili)* and offbeat dramas

(Pretty Maids All in a Row, Seconds), Hudson's career stalled until the tremendous success of NBC's *McMillan and Wife* with Susan Saint James and Nancy Walker. In 1978 he also ventured out to play a disillusioned auto company president in the TV miniseries based on Arthur Haley's bestseller *Wheels,* and three years later starred with old *Giant* buddy Liz Taylor in *The Mirror Crack'd.* Offscreen he has sung in several in-the-round stage musicals and in 1977 toured the country playing King Arthur in Lerner and Loewe's *Camelot.* Hudson underwent open heart surgery in 1982, but managed a stint on *Dynasty* before returning to a semireclusive life on his Beverly Hills estate. A studio arranged marriage to his former secretary, Phyllis Gates, was of course a total sham, but for years Hollywood's star-making machinery managed to keep Hudson's homosexual life-style largely hidden from the adoring multitudes of moviegoers. At one point at the height of Hudson's career, when a fan magazine threatened to expose the superstar, studio execs reportedly bought them off by handing over damaging information on a less important "property." Only days after posing for photographers alongside old pal Doris Day, Hudson, looking shockingly gaunt and dissipated, sought AIDS treatment in Paris. He chartered a 747 a week later and returned to L.A., only to die three months later. Hudson's death triggered what amounted to nationwide hysteria over AIDS, and especially a concern among actors and actresses that they might contract the disease during love scenes. That in turn led the actors' union to decree that no performer would be required to engage in heavy kissing for the camera. In 1986, Dionne Warwick joined with Elton John, Stevie Wonder and Gladys Knight to record the stirring "That's What Friends Are For" for AIDS relief.

Born: November 17, 1925, in Winnetka, Illinois
Height: 6 ft. 3 in.
Weight: 200 lbs.
Eyes: Brown *Hair:* Gray
Zodiac: Scorpio
Education: High school
Marriages: To Phyllis Gates (1955–1958)
Children: None
Interests: Chess, music, poetry, astronomy, crossword puzzles, sailing
Personal Habits and Traits: Chain-smokes, drinks, does not exercise, is calm and articulate
Address: Beverly Hills
Income: $10 million+ (estimate)

Engelbert Humperdinck

Arnold Dorsey

"When I was an utter flop, I kept having the same dream—that all my teeth were falling out. I don't have that dream any more."

Gordon Mills, who turned Thomas Jones Woodward into Tom Jones and Raymond O'Sullivan into Gilbert O'Sullivan, did the same thing for one Arnold

Dorsey, the ninth of ten children born to a British Army officer stationed in Madras, India. The young lad had already embarked on a singing career as Gerry Dorsey, but repeated failures had driven him into a nervous breakdown when Mills got hold of him and gave him the name of *Hansel and Gretel's* German composer. Within a year Engelbert Humperdinck had a five-million-seller, "Release Me"—the first in a string of hit ballads including "Les Bicyclettes du Belsize," "The Last Waltz," "Lonely Is a Man Without Love," and "After the Loving." He is also Tom Jones's main competition in Vegas and on the nightclub circuit. All this success finances a princely life-style that includes a Surrey estate, three Rolls-Royces, and a sizable personal entourage.

Born: May 3, 1936, in Madras, India
Height: 6 ft. 1 in.
Weight: 186 lbs.
Eyes: Brown *Hair:* Black
Zodiac: Taurus
Education: High school
Marriages: To Patricia Healey (1963–)
Children: Louise, Jason, Scott
Interests: Swimming, reading
Personal Habits and Traits: Drinks moderately, smokes
Address: Surrey, England
Income: $1.8 million (minimum estimate)

Lauren Hutton

Mary Laurence Hutton

"They told me to fix my teeth, change my nose, even get out of the business. But I stayed, and learned and didn't give up."

She has a bumpy nose, dishwater blond hair and a gap-toothed grin, but by the time she was 30, Mary Laurence Hutton had become the highest-paid model up to that time—with earnings of over $300,000 per year. The stepdaughter of a Borden's executive in southern Florida, Lauren grew up a gawky, unpopular adolescent who emulated her comic strip idol Sheena of the Jungle by communing with the lizards and snakes in her tropical backyard. Dropping out of college at 18, she worked as a cocktail waitress at the New York Playboy Club and later at a Bahamas casino, finally landing a $50-a-week modeling job for Christian Dior on the basis of an impressive (albeit phony) list of modeling credits. Eileen Ford soon signed her, and 22 *Vogue* covers later, Lauren was signed by Revlon tycoon Charles Revson to endourse his high-priced Ultima II line of cosmetics at an annual $200,000 salary. The husky-voiced Hutton also tried to crack the movies, but in *Paper Lion, Pieces of Dreams, Little Fauss and Big Halsey, Gator,* and *The Gambler* (with James Caan), she failed to capture the interest of either critics or moviegoers; her best efforts to date are the NBC miniseries *The Rheinman Exchange* with Stephen Collins and José Ferrer, and the part of a murderous Nazi spy in the movie *Lassiter*. An avid safari-goer—a throwback to her Sheena days—Hutton nevertheless for years called home a Greenwich Village apartment that she shared with "mystery man" Bob Williamson. Only her

closest friends ever met the intensely private, publicity-shy stock speculator, who lost her to rock manager Malcolm McLaren in 1986. Hutton herself is anything but shy; she loves to carry on conversations from her doorless bathroom, and during the shooting of a scene from *The Gambler* in a men's lavatory she stunned the crew by pulling up her skirt and relieving herself in one of the stalls.

Born: November 17, 1943, in Charleston, South Carolina
Height: 5 ft. 8 in.
Weight: 118 lbs.
Eyes: Brown *Hair:* Dark blond
Zodiac: Scorpio
Education: High school
Religion: Protestant
Marriages: None
Children: None
Interests: Safaris, wildlife, travel, acting, knitting, antique clothes
Personal Habits and Traits: Smokes, drinks, is unrestrained in her use of explicit sexual language
Address: Los Angeles
Income: $500,000 +

Timothy Hutton

''I never wanted or needed a shrink. For a while you can get off on being complex and broody: it's cool. But boy, I don't believe that anymore. That's what can destroy you.''

The lanky son of Jim *(Walk, Don't Run)* Hutton made his feature-film debut in *Ordinary People,* and proved that he was anything but ordinary in the role of a suicidal teenager. At age 20, he walked home with a Best Supporting Actor Oscar. The triumphant moment came too late for Hutton, Sr. When Tim was 3, his parents divorced, and the boy grew up with his schoolteacher mom in Connecticut and Berkeley. At 15, father and son started getting to know one another again: Jim got Tim started in the business, and in 1979, the two sat in Dad's hospital room and watched young Hutton's moving performance in the TV drama *Friendly Fire.* Not long after, just four months prior to the shooting of *Ordinary People,* Jim Hutton died of liver cancer at age 45. ''We just,'' Tim still says tearfully, ''got to know each other.'' Soon viewed as a cross between Tony Perkins and Holden Caulfield, Hutton made a quick succession of hits—*Taps, Iceman, The Falcon and the Snowman*—but he also flopped in *Daniel* and 1985's abysmal *Turk 182.* Finally coming to terms with his stardom (''Two years ago, you wouldn't have felt restful with me. I was angry, moody, cynical, sarcastic''), the Tim Hutton of 1985 had come to accept his teen idol status and consoled himself playing the field with the likes of Diane Lane, Rosanna *(Desperately Seeking Susan)* Arquette, Brooke Shields, and his *Ordinary People* costar Elizabeth McGovern. But in early '86, he stunned just about everyone by eloping with Debra (*Urban Cowboy, Officer and a Gentleman*) Winger.

Born: August 16, 1960 in Malibu, California
Height: 6 ft. 1 in.
Weight: 170 lbs.
Eyes: Blue *Hair:* Brown
Zodiac: Leo
Education: High school
Marriages: To Debra Winger (1986–)
Children: None
Interests: Riding, rock, basketball and chess
Personal Habits and Traits: Angry when crossed, drinks beer, night owl, enjoys morning rides on the beach, drives a red Porsche
Address: Malibu, California
Income: $1 million+ per film

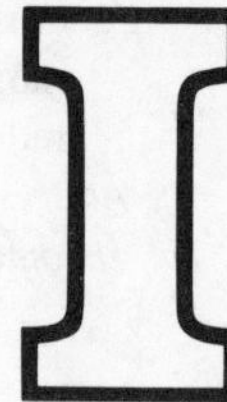

Lee Iacocca

''If a guy is over 25% jerk, he's in trouble. And Henry Ford was 95%.''

Lido Iacocca

The best-known businessman in the world was not the first in his family to make a million. Nicola Iacocca made and lost several fortunes dabbling in a variety of enterprises, from hot dog stands to car rental agencies. His son, classified 4-F during World War II because of a childhood case of rheumatic fever, earned an engineering degree from Lehigh University and a master's from Princeton. Young Lido started with Ford in 1946, selling trucks in Chester, Pennsylvania, and a decade later was a Detroit-based marketing manager under whiz kid Robert McNamara. He became known with the company for dreaming up a $56-a-month credit plan and a slogan to go with it: ''$56 for '56''. As the acknowledged father of the Mustang in 1964, he made it to the top of the corporate ladder—and onto the covers of both *Time* and *Newsweek*. Iacocca became Ford president in 1970, only to be fired by Henry Ford II eight years later. Ford's explanation to Iacocca: ''I never liked you.'' The episode, recounted by Iacocca in his blockbuster 1984 autobiography, the fastest-selling nonfiction book ever, marked the beginning of another remarkable phase in his career. He accepted the challenge of rescuing Chrysler from the brink of bankruptcy in 1979 and lobbied to obtain the federal loan guarantees that permitted the car company to survive. He also took his case direct to the public through a series of television commercials, quickly becoming the medium's hottest corporate huckster. All told, his 30-second spots have made it into 97 percent of all U.S. households an average of 63 times apiece. After three years, Chrysler was healthy enough to pay back all the government loans right on schedule. Every inch the tycoon in appearance, Iacocca wears $700 suits and smokes three Monte Cristo Havanas a day. He enjoys duck hunting in Canada and hanging out with fellow Italo-American Frank Sinatra at "21," but Iacocca is still most comfortable playing cards in the family room (dubbed "Lido's Lounge") of his less-than-overwhelming home in Bloomfield Hills, Michigan. In addition to running Chrysler, Iacocca also heads up the Statue of Liberty–Ellis Island renovation commission and the Lee Iacocca diabetes foundation (his wife Mary, a diabetic, died in 1983). He is also entertaining making a career switch—to politics. Iacocca, a Democrat, is touted by the savvy likes of House Speaker Tip O'Neill as one of the strongest contenders for that party's 1988 Presidential nomination. In 1986, he picked his potential First Lady, marrying former airline stewardess Peggy Johnson.

Born: October 15, 1924, in Allentown, Pennsylvania
Height: 6 ft. 1 in.
Weight: 194 lbs.
Eyes: Brown *Hair:* Gray
Zodiac: Libra
Education: Bachelor's degree in engineering, Lehigh University; masters from Princeton ("I wasn't interested in a snob degree. I was after the bucks")
Religion: Roman Catholic
Marriages: To Mary (1956 until her death in 1983)
To Peggy Johnson (1986–)
Children: Two daughters: Kathi and Lia
Interests: Diabetes research, crossword puzzles, the Statue of Liberty and Ellis Island, Democratic politics
Personal Habits and Traits: Drinks Scotch, is blunt, conversation liberally sprinkled with four-letter words, every weekday at 11:15 begins a 45-minute workout, uses a rowing machine at home on weekends, is something of a hypochondriac—every night takes Metamucil, a fiber laxative
Address: Bloomfield Hills, Michigan
Income: $9 million (estimate)

Julio Iglesias

Julio Iglesias de la Cueva

"Why did you discover me so late? I'm not so young anymore!"

He managed to sell 100 million albums in six languages (more than any other recording artist), amass 350 platinum discs and 965 gold ones—and still be virtually unknown in the United States. That all changed in the mid-1980s, when the vibrato-voiced Spanish Sinatra blitzed the United States with a 33-city tour and his first American-made, all-English album, *1100 Bel Air Place,* featuring duets with Willie Nelson, Diana Ross, the Beach Boys, and the Pointer Sisters. The second child of a prominent Madrid gynecologist, he studied law at Madrid University and eventually qualified for the bar, though he chose instead to pursue a soccer career. Sidelined by an auto accident that injured his vertebra, Iglesias went through nearly two years of painful therapy—a period during which a nurse gave him a cheap guitar to occupy his time. He began writing songs, and his first hit, "Guendoline," put him on the map in Europe. Over the next decade, the suave Spaniard with the perpetual tan (he picks his concert dates around the world so that he spends most of each year basking in the sun) and the megawatt grin became a global phenomenon except in the United States. However, even though he quickly became popular with Hispanics on this side of the Atlantic, it took *1100 Bel Air Place* to give him a shot at becoming a familiar name in the United States. The jury is still out. In 1981, Julio, who still walks with a slight limp, spent 19 tense days before his father was rescued from Basque terrorist kidnappers. Iglesias's marriage to Isabel Preisler was annulled after eight years in 1979, and when he's not zipping around the world in his private Mystère-Falcon 20 jet, he spends most of his time alone at his homes in Bel Air and on an island off Miami Beach (his contract with CBS stipulates that he spend several months each year in the United States), in Tahiti, Madrid, and Majorca.

Born: September 23, 1943, in Madrid
Height: 6 ft. 1 in. *Weight:* 167 lbs.
Eyes: Brown *Hair:* Grayish-brown
Zodiac: Libra
Education: Law school
Religion: Roman Catholic
Marriages: To Isabel Preisler (1971–annulled in 1979)
Children: Two sons—Julión José and Enrique—and a daughter, Chaveli
Interests: Swimming, bicycling, sailing, dogs
Personal Habits and Traits: A workaholic, quiet, self-effacing yet impatient (when the water was too warm in his Miami pool, he could not wait for the thermostat to be turned down; he had trucks dump five tons of ice in it instead); very superstitious (if salt is spilled he leaves the table, or if he hears very bad news, he immediately sends his clothes, underwear included, to be burned)
Addresses: Bel Air, California; Miami Beach; Tahiti; Madrid; Majorca
Income: $15 million +

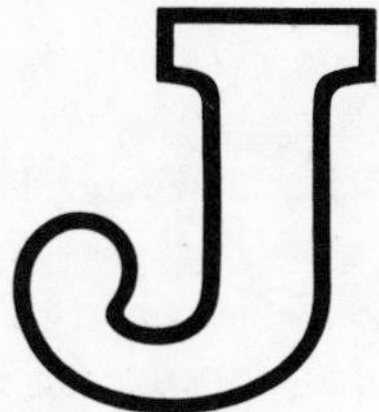

Glenda Jackson

"I had no real ambition about acting, but I knew there had to be something better than the bloody chemist's shop."

This two-time Oscar winner (for *Women in Love* and *A Touch of Class*) was the eldest of a bricklayer's four daughters. She performed in a number of offbeat plays before commanding center stage as Charlotte Corday in the Royal Shakespeare production of Peter Weiss's *Marat/Sade*. She went on to portray Tchaikovsky's nymphomaniac wife Nina in Ken Russell's *The Music Lovers,* a sex-crazed nun in *The Devils,* a career woman competing with a physician (played by the late Peter Finch) for the love of a bisexual young artist in *Sunday, Bloody Sunday,* Walter Matthau's lover in the comedies *House Calls* and *Hopscotch,* and the tormented poetess in *Stevie*. Jackson was also a convincing Nora in one screen version of Ibsen's *A Doll's House* and excelled in the difficult role of *Hedda Gabler* on stage. However, she is probably most closely associated with a very real historical figure, Queen Elizabeth I, whom she brought vividly to life in a six-part BBC television biography and then on the big screen opposite Vanessa Redgrave in *Mary, Queen of Scots*. In 1976 she divorced actor-turned-art dealer Roy Hodges after 18 years of marriage and one child. Jackson was pure laudanum in 1985's *five-hour* Broadway production of Eugene O'Neill's *Strange Interlude,* and little better in the following year's *Turtle Diary*.

Born: May 9, 1936, in Birkenhead, England
Height: 5ft. 6 in.
Weight: 118 lbs.
Eyes: Brown
Hair: Reddish brown
Zodiac: Taurus
Education: Two years at the Royal Academy of Dramatic Art

Religion: Anglican
Marriages: To Roy Hodges (1958–1976)
Children: Daniel (b. 1969)
Interests: Art, music, gardening, literature (Jane Austen), cooking
Personal Habits and Traits: Smokes, drinks, is afraid of flying
Address: London
Income: $400,000 (minimum estimate)

Jesse Jackson

"Many of us allow our children to eat junk, watch junk, listen to junk, talk junk, play with junk—and then we're surprised when they come out to be social junkies."

When Reverend Martin Luther King, Jr., was assassinated in 1968, Jesse Jackson—the footballer-turned-preacher that King had chosen two years before to head his Operation Breadbasket in Chicago—was by his side. A decade later Jackson had clearly become one of the country's most influential black leaders, spreading his hard-work gospel ("Nobody can save us but us") among black teens all over the country. His project EXCEL, a tough self-help regimen, is, according to *Time* magazine, "turning the old ghetto battle cry of 'Burn, baby, burn!' into 'Work, baby, work!'" No one better understands that virtue than the Greenville, North Carolina–born Jackson. Raised on collard greens and chitterlings, he went to work delivering stovewood at age six. An activist during the early 1960s, he joined King's Southern Christian Leadership Conference in 1966, but quit in 1971 to devote his energies to Operation PUSH—People to Save Humanity. One of the black movement's most impassioned and charismatic orators, Jackson rejected the near-radicalism of his earlier years for more traditional values in order to attack what he considers to be the main obstacle to progress in the black community: the decline of discipline and standards in U.S. schools. "When the doors of opportunity swing open," he exhorts his young audiences, "we must make sure that we are not too drunk or too indifferent to walk through." Not that he is without his detractors; Jackson was lambasted for his trip to the Middle East in late 1979, and is frequently criticized for exploiting his dramatic personality and (though he is the married father of five) for having a freely wandering eye. None of which dampened the spirits of his admirers during Jackson's unsuccessful bid for the 1984 Democratic Presidential nomination in San Francisco, nor negated the fact that his was easily that convention's most stirring speech.

Born: October 8, 1941, in Greenville, North Carolina
Height: 6 ft. 2 in.
Weight: 220 lbs.
Eyes: Brown
Hair: Brown
Zodiac: Libra
Education: North Carolina A & T
Religion: Baptist (ordained a minister in 1968)
Marriages: To Jacqueline Lavinia Brown (1964–)
Children: Five
Interests: Football, education, upgrading all aspects of the black community, music art
Personal Habits and Traits: A nonsmoker, teetotaler, workaholic, at times brusque
Address: Chicago
Income: $60,000 (minimum estimate)

Kate Jackson

"I can't go on playing Holly Golightly all my life."

The tomboyish ex-member of ABC's *Charlie's Angels,* Kate Jackson is the daughter of a building materials wholesaler in Birmingham, Alabama and attended Birmingham University. Although she considered a career as a professional tennis player, a stint in summer stock whetted her appetite for acting, and two years on the hit horror soap opera *Dark Shadows* followed. Jackson's first prime-time exposure came with the role of a nurse in ABC's *The Rookies,* and as that show completed its fourth season Kate came up with the idea of a series about three karate-chopping women detectives. Kate was cast as Sabrina, while Farrah Fawcett landed the role of Jill and Jaclyn Smith the part of Kelly. Jackson was paid twice as much as the other angels under her contract terms ($10,000 per episode compared to their $5,000), but she still earned nowhere near what her TV partners raked in from commercials, endorsements and movie deals. She was romantically involved with Edward Albert, Jr., for a while and later dated Burt Reynolds, but her love life stalled when the nearly round-the-clock demands of filming *Charlie's Angels* overwhelmed her life. It thus came as an absolute surprise to her fans when in 1978 Jackson eloped with young Andrew Stevens, son of Stella Stevens and then a handsome new face in the movies (*The Fury*) and on television (*The Bastard, Emerald Point, Hollywood Wives*). Three years later, the marriage was over. She starred with Michael Onthean and Harry Hamlin in the first major male homosexual movie, *Making Love*. Jackson bobbed up again in prime time, playing an almost-middle-aged widow in the hit comedy spy series *Scarecrow and Mrs. King*. As her career took off again, her second marriage, to New York businessman David Greenwald, went kaput.

Born: October 29, 1948, in Birmingham, Alabama
Height: 5 ft. 9½ in.
Weight: 124 lbs.
Eyes: Brown
Hair: Brown
Zodiac: Scorpio
Education: University of Mississippi, Birmingham University, American Academy of Dramatic Arts in New York City
Religion: Protestant
Marriages:
To Andrew Stevens (1978–1981)
To David Greenwald (1982–84)
Children: None
Interests: Skiing (her favorite sport), tennis
Personal Habits and Traits: Nonsmoker, a teetotaler, health food nut
Address: Beverly Hills
Income: $75,000 (minimum estimate)

Michael Jackson

"I am very uncomfortable around others in a social situation; people don't treat me like a person. I'm really only at home on the stage."

It took his spectacular 1983 album *Thriller* (sales: 20 million and still counting) to make him indisputably the world's top entertainer, but it seemed as if The Gloved One had been around forever. Indeed, Michael and his brothers Tito, Marlon, Jackie, and Jermaine (who left the group to pursue his own successful career in 1977 and was replaced by Randy) had sold an estimated 100 million records and harvested a peck of Grammys after the Jackson Five exploded on the entertainment scene in a blaze of sequins in 1969. Yet the rest of the family was always quick to concede that its staggering and enduring success was always due to the formidable talents and bottomless energy of Brother Michael. The sons of a Gary, Indiana, crane operator and sometime jazz musician, the Jacksons were discovered by Diana Ross, who saw to it that little Michael, then only 10, and his brothers got a poolside audition with Motown record mogul Berry Gordy, Jr. Ross produced the group's first album, and within months the LPs were racking up bubble-gum hit singles with Michael as the lead—including "I Want You Back," "ABC," "The Love You Save," "I'll Be There," "Never Can Say Goodbye," "Ben," "Dancing Machine," and "Enjoy Yourself." Michael shot up to an impressive 6 feet 2 inches, but never outgrew his hitmaking little-boy voice. At 20, he made an unimpressive movie debut with mentor Ross as the Scarecrow in *The Wiz,* and capitalized on disco the following year by laying down several hits—including his own "Don't Stop Till You Get Enough" and "Dance the Night Away"—on his triple-platinum, number-one *Off the Wall* album. None of which even came close to *Thriller*'s record-smashing success; nearly every cut of the album made it into the Top 10, including "Billie Jean," "Beat It," "You Wanna Be Starting Something," "PYT," "Human Nature," and the title song featuring Vincent Price, which was also werewolfed down by the video-buying public. Before embarking on the controversial Victory Tour with his brothers in 1984, Jackson also collaborated with old-timers Paul McCartney and Mick Jagger on several chartbusters—"The Girl Is Mine" and "Say, Say, Say" (with McCartney)—and "State of Shock" with Mick. A stadium-packing performer who has spent half his life on the road, Jackson nonetheless continues to live in the protective cocoon of his parents' estate in Encino, California, with sisters La Toya, also a singer and actress, and equally precocious Janet, who at 12 was a star of CBS's *Good Times* comedy series and in 1984 signed on with the TV show *Fame* (hitting the charts on her own two years later with "What Have You Done for Me Lately?"). So painfully shy that he did not date until he was 20 (with Tatum O'Neal), the post-*Thriller* Michael emerged as a sort of Howard Hughes recluse, hiding behind dark glasses and a ton of makeup. Although Jackson did have his nose refashioned surgically, he angrily denied rumors that his family had kept him on hormones to maintain his breathless falsetto. An unabashed showbiz buff who spends much of his time watching old movies on television and reading Hollywood biographies, Jackson likes to tool around

Beverly Hills alone in the Rolls-Royce he bought himself with proceeds from *The Wiz.* His tight circle of friends includes Brooke Shields and tiny Emmanuel (*Webster*) Lewis, who stood on the chair next to him at the 1984 Grammy Awards and whispered in Jackson's ear throughout the televised ceremony. Before stepping before the cameras to star in a Steven Spielberg remake of *Peter Pan,* Jackson collaborated with Lionel Richie on writing "We Are the World," the all-star megahit that raised more than $30 million for Ethopian famine relief. Michael established himself as a force in music publishing by anteing up $50 million (outbidding Yoko Ono and McCartney) for the rights to 210 Beatles songs.

Born: August 29, 1958, in Gary, Indiana
Height: 6 ft. 2 in.
Weight: 150 lbs.
Eyes: Brown
Hair: Black
Zodiac: Virgo
Education: High school (private tutors)
Religion: Jehovah's Witness
Marriages: None
Children: None
Interests: Old movies, songwriting, acting, stuffed animals (has huge stuffed animals collection)
Personal Habits and Traits: Nonsmoker, teetotaler, does not take drugs of any kind, very religious, very reclusive
Address: Encino, California
Income: $70 million from *Thriller* alone; estimates are that from T-shirts, sequined gloves, and other Jackson spinoffs, he could earn as much as $1 *billion*

Reggie Jackson

"I'd rather hit than have sex."

The son of an impoverished tailor from Wyncote, Pennsylvania, Reggie Jackson broke into the big leagues when Charlie Finley tapped him for the Oakland A's outfield. And though he played a major role (with teammates Catfish Hunter, Rollie Fingers, Sal Bando, Gene Tenace, et al.) in the team's copping an unprecedented three World Series in a row, Jackson was launched as a superstar only after the Yankees lured him away with a five-year, $2.9 million contract. Jackson batted in five homers—three in a single game—during the 1977 World Series, the first the Yankees had won in 15 years. Egotistical, temperamental, and unpopular among Yankee fans and teammates, Jackson repeatedly battled catcher Thurman Munson (who tragically died in a small plane crash in 1979) and team manager Billy Martin. He makes frequent appearances on television, and has made good his prediction that some day a candy bar would be named after him—in 1978 kids across America rushed out to buy the Reggie, a two-ounce chocolate bar. The market for it soon melted, however. From his various lucrative endorsements, Jackson is able to afford an art-filled Fifth Avenue apartment in Manhattan, a condominium outside Oakland, a San Francisco auto

dealership of his own, and a private pool of Rolls-Royces and antique cars. One year after Jackson switched to the California Angels, his memoirs were published by the Villard Books division of Random House.

Born: May 18, 1946, in Wyncote, Pennsylvania
Height: 6 ft. 2 in.
Weight: 184 lbs.
Eyes: Brown
Hair: Black
Zodiac: Taurus
Education: High school
Religion: Protestant
Marriages: Divorced since 1972
Children: None
Interests: Automobiles, Reggie Jackson
Personal Habits and Traits: Does not smoke, drinks moderately, is brusque
Addresses: Oakland, California; New York City
Income: $1.8 million

Bianca Jagger

Bianca Perez Morena de Macias

"Homosexuals make the best friends because they care about you as a woman and are not jealous. They love you but don't try to screw up your head."

"Mick screws many," shrugs the dark-eyed lookalike ex-wife of the Rolling Stones' Mick Jagger, "but has few affairs." She forgave his affair with Linda Ronstadt and he forgave hers with Ryan O'Neal, but the real strain in the couple's relationship occurred when Bianca no longer felt content to be famous simply as the First Lady of Rock and International Fashion (she is history's youngest member of the best-dressed Hall of Fame). Bianca Perez Morena de Macias grew up the daughter of a Nicaraguan diplomat-cum-coffee baron, and after the "sexual repression" of convent schools (an experience she later made up for with a vengeance) won a scholarship at age 15 to the Institut d'Etudes Politiques in Paris. Her "almost first" lover was British movie star Michael Caine ("Caine was unkind, superficial and kept me like a geisha"), and in 1970 she met Jagger at a Stones party. They were married in St. Tropez in 1971 when Bianca was four months pregnant with their daughter Jade. By her own account she was "servile and subservient" during the first four years of their marriage, but Bianca would nonetheless fly into Latin rages and tear up all Mick's shirts whenever she learned that yet another groupie had hit the jackpot. Maintaining several residences—including a villa in St. Tropez, a sprawling country estate outside London, a house in Malibu, and a four-story Manhattan town house packed with African sculptures and Indian paintings—they also rented Andy Warhol's $5,000-a-month beach house on Montauk, Long Island, every summer. Domesticity aside, Mick and Bianca Jagger had wild reputations—both were widely rumored to be bisexual. When Mick finally left her for model Jerry Hall, Mrs. Jagger launched her dubious screen career playing the icy, unfaithful wife of a Mafia don in the French-English production *Flesh Color*. Shortly before Anastasio Somoza fell from power in Nicaragua, Bianca visited her civil war-torn homeland. She toured several refugee and prison camps while in Nicaragua, but the main object of her concern was her divorced mother, who runs a diner in a rundown section of Managua and has always refused to leave the country.

Born: 1945 in Managua, Nicaragua
Height: 5 ft. 4 in.
Weight: 120 lbs.
Eyes: Brown
Hair: Black
Education: Institut d'Etudes Politiques in Paris
Religion: Roman Catholic
Marriages: To Mick Jagger (1971–1979)
Children: Jade (b. 1971)
Interests: Acting, fashion, nutrition, acupuncture, South American and Vietnamese cooking
Personal Habits and Traits: Chain-smokes, jogs, swims, parties regularly, drinks vodka martinis
Address: Manhattan
Income: Her share of the Jagger fortune would, it is estimated, be well in excess of $5 million.

Mick Jagger

"I'd rather die than be forty-five and still singing 'Satisfaction.'"

The overtly sexual, sometimes sinister King of Spastic Rock had very conventional beginnings as the son of a physical education professor near London. A superb and disciplined student, Jagger majored in European history and literature at the prestigious London School of Economics before dropping out to form the Rolling Stones. The Beatles' major competitor for title of the greatest rock group of the 1960s, Jagger and the Stones bumped and ground their way through such powerfully gripping hits as "Satisfaction," "19th Nervous Breakdown," "Lady Jane," "Ruby Tuesday," "Sympathy for the Devil," "Midnight Rambler," "Honkytonk Woman," "Jumpin' Jack Flash," "Brown Sugar," and "Angie." Along the way, guitarist Brian Jones was found dead at the bottom of his swimming pool in 1969, drugged and, possibly, according to Jones's ex-lover Nicholas Fitzgerald of the Guinness brewing family, a murder victim; the Stones' disastrous concert in Altamont, California, resulted in four deaths (and the chilling documentary *Gimme Shelter*); and pivotal group member, Keith Richards, was charged with possession of heroin in Toronto in 1977. Jagger and Bianca, the daughter of a Nicaraguan diplomat whom he married in 1971, flitted from one tax haven to another until he finally left her in 1978. Now in the company of stunning blond model Jerry Hall (he has two children by Hall and another daughter by black model-actress Marsha Hunt). Jagger eludes Britain's 94 percent tax bite by hopping from New York to Cannes to Paris to a 52-acre country estate in England, thereby avoiding taxable-resident status and holding onto the bulk of his $3 million+ annual haul from such revenue-producing singles as "Emotional Rescue" and "Lucky at Love." Jagger's "State of Shock"

duet with Michael Jackson left their fans in a state of ecstasy—as did his sexy "State of Shock" duet with Tina Turner onstage at the 1985 Live Aid Concert and his *Harlem Shuffle* hit a few months later.

Born: July 26, 1943, in Dartford, Kent, England
Height: 5 ft. 10 in.
Weight: 149 lbs.
Eyes: Blue
Hair: Brown
Zodiac: Leo
Education: London School of Economics dropout
Religion: Protestant
Marriages: To Bianca Perez Morena de Macia (1971–1979)
Children: Jade (b. 1971) by Bianca Jagger, Karis (b. 1971) by Marsha Hunt, Elizabeth Scarlett (b. 1984) and James Leroy August (b. 1985) by Jerry Hall
Interests: African art, acting, investments
Personal Habits and Traits: Chain-smokes, drinks alcohol, a night animal (gets up at 4 P.M., retires at dawn)
Addresses: New York; Cannes; Paris; Surrey, England
Income: $15 million +

Bruce Jenner

"The whole ballgame is to preserve your credibility and not do something that makes you look like a fool. I don't want to end up like Mark Spitz."

A native of New York State, Bruce Jenner trained in California on his way to the Decathlon gold medal at the Montreal Olympics in 1976. He was supported by his wife Chrystie, who worked as a United Airlines stewardess for four years so Jenner could perfect his athletic prowess. No sooner had he won the Decathlon than the Montreal press dubbed him an "instant millionaire." Jenner bided his time, but in the end he was that and more. The Jenners soon set up their own corporation named after his world-record decathlon score—8618 Inc.—and set out to collect. ABC signed him for two years of sportscasting and special assignments on *Good Morning, America,* Buster Brown manufactured a line of Bruce Jenner sneakers and—in his biggest catches—Wheaties and Minolta groomed him as their primary TV pitchman. The Jenners lived in a Malibu beachhouse, and during the ten days a month he wasn't on the road Bruce zipped around the colony on one of his three dirt bikes. The Jenners' marriage fell apart during Chrystie's pregnancy and shortly before his inauspicious movie debut with the Village People in Allan Carr's disastrous *Can't Stop the Music*. In 1981 he wed Elvis's ex-love Linda Thompson—a move that presaged General Mills' decision not to renew Jenner's contract as its Wheaties spokesman. Yet he kept going for the gold and getting as pitchman for Minolta and Tropicana orange juice. He also maintained a high profile as a sportscaster, and even launched his own fitness magazine. Jenner, who split from Thompson in 1985, owns a house in the Malibu foothills is called "The Knest," inspired by a nearby estate once owned by Kenny Rogers, "The Knoll."

Born: October 28, 1949, in Mt. Kisco, New York
Height: 6 ft. 2 in.
Weight: 193 lbs.
Eyes: Hazel
Hair: Brown
Zodiac: Scorpio
Education: San Jose State College
Religion: Protestant
Marriages:
To Chrystie Jenner (1972–1980)
To Linda Thompson (1981–1985)
Children: Burton (b. 1978) and Cassandra (b. 1979)
Interests: Broadcasting, motorcycles, swimming
Personal Habits and Traits: Nonsmoker, nondrinker, needs seven hours' sleep, workaholic, swims in his three-tiered pool, bikes rather than runs
Address: Malibu, California
Income: $500,000

Waylon Jennings

"I'm outside of the system."

Born the son of a truck driver in Littlefield, Texas, Waylon Jennings dropped out of school at 14 and within months was the country's youngest deejay, based in legendary Lubbock. Young Waylon was taken under wing by rock 'n' roll giant Buddy Holly, who produced Jennings's first country record, and in a macabre coincidence Jennings gave up his seat at the last minute in the chartered plane crash that killed Holly, Richie Valens, and the Big Bopper in 1959. Shaken, Waylon was coaxed to Nashville by guitar great Chet Atkins and over the next two decades roughhoused and womanized his way to the point where he was known in C&W circles as "The Outlaw." He won a Grammy in 1969 for his countrified version of Jim Webb's "MacArthur Park," but Jennings had a hard time handling success and went through a bout with amphetamines and three stormy marriages before discovering his fourth wife, singer Jessi Colter. Although he "inspired" her 1975 hit "I'm Not Lisa" by calling out another woman's name in the middle of the night, Jennings seems happy in his current marriage. He and Colter make their home in Nashville with his three children by earlier marriages and Jessi's daughter by her first husband, Duane Eddy. He may be best known as the balladeer of *The Dukes of Hazzard*.

Born: June 15, 1937, in Littlefield, Texas
Height: 6 ft. 1 in.
Weight: 180 lbs.
Eyes: Blue
Hair: Brown
Zodiac: Gemini
Education: High school dropout
Religion: Protestant
Marriages: Four. Last to Jessi Colter (1969–)
Children: Terry (b. 1957), Julie (b. 1958), Buddy (b. 1960)
Interests: Writing, producing, guitar, cars
Personal Habits and Traits: Smokes, hard drinking, reclusive, wears dark glasses
Address: Nashville
Income: $550,000 (minimum estimate)

Billy Joel

"I have matured to the point where I don't kick over garbage cans."

Whether performing the lyrical "Just the Way You Are" or the plaintive "Piano Man," the driving "Only the Good Die Young" or the rebellious "I'm Moving Out," the moving "Honesty" or the whimsical "It's Still Rock and Roll to Me," Billy Joel created a hit-making 1980s sound that veers between slick pop and hard rock. Joel's father was an Alsace-born engineer who left the family when Billy was a tot. Young Joel grew into a street thug in his hometown of Hicksville, New York—a chain-wielding gang member (though he was often taken to the opera as a child and took classical piano lessons) who was refused a high school diploma because of his behavior. There was perhaps some poetic justice when, at the time of his 10th reunion, Joel declined the invitation from his high school and instead performed selections from his double platinum album *The Stranger* on NBC's *Saturday Night Live.* A self-described draft-dodger during the Vietnam war and at one time a burglary suspect (he was later cleared), Joel moved to Los Angeles, continued to record his songs of urban desperation, and scored with the hit single "Piano Man" (chronicling the six months he spent playing under the name "Bill Martin" at an L.A. bar) and several albums. "Just the Way You Are" soared to number one and established Joel as a king-sized talent in 1977, followed by his smash *52nd Street, Glass Houses,* and *Innocent Man* L.P.s—the last of which spun off such hit singles as the title cut, "Tell Her About It," "The Longest Time," "Leave a Tender Moment Alone" and "Keeping the Faith." Another *Innocent Man* single, "Uptown Girl," was inspired by supermodel Christie Brinkley. After leaving his manager-wife Elizabeth (who had been married to his drummer), Joel was wed to Brinkley in a highly publicized ceremony aboard the yacht *Riveranda* as it plied the Hudson. Confessing that he had once contemplated taking his own life, Joel did what he could to try and turn the rising tide of teenage suicides with his reassuring 1985 hit single "You're Only Human (Second Wind)."

Born: May 9, 1949, in Hicksville, New York
Height: 5 ft. 8 in.
Weight: 152 lbs.
Eyes: Brown
Hair: Brown
Zodiac: Taurus
Education: High school
Religion: Jewish

Marriages:
To Elizabeth Joel (1973–1982)
To Christie Brinkley (1985–)
Children: Alexa (b. Dec. 29, 1985)
Interests: Boxing
Personal Habits and Traits: Smokes, drinks, night owl, reclusive
Address: New York City
Income: $7 million (minimum estimate)

Elton John

(Reginald Kenneth Dwight)

"I don't want to end up my life like Elvis. I want to be active and involved with people—and that means going outside."

Reginald Dwight—better known to legions of fans as Elton John—is balding, chubby, shy, and unhappy enough to have attempted suicide twice. Yet he pulled down over $7 million per annum as he strutted and romped around concert stages all over the world in feather boas, foot-high platform shoes and sequined capes, flashing his trademark—$50,000 worth of eyeglasses, ranging from a simple rhinestoned pair to solid gold-and neon-rimmed varieties. Not that John's superstardom is based solely on flash, for beginning with the poignant ballad *Your Song,* John and his lyricist-partner Bernie Taupin are responsible for such instant rock classics as "Daniel" (about a blind Viet vet), "Rocket Man," "Candle in the Wind" (a tribute to Marilyn Monroe), "Benny and the Jets," "Philadelphia Freedom" (a musical nod to Billie Jean King's tennis team), and "Goodbye, Yellow Brick Road." Resentful of his father, an RAF squadron leader, young Reg pounded away on the family piano at the age of 5 and wound up studying Chopin and Bach at the Royal Academy by the time he was 11. Two weeks before finals he quit to join an R&B group called Blues Elegy, where he chose his new pseudonym from sax player *Elton* Dean and lead singer Long *John* Baldry. When Blues Elegy dissolved in the late 1960s, John answered a Liberty Records newspaper ad for new singers and composers. He was paired with Lincolnshire farmer-turned-lyricist Bernie Taupin, and after three years of collaborating in a dingy London flat—it was during this period that Elton made a halfhearted attempt to gas himself—John was discovered at L.A.'s trendy Troubadour club in 1970. Since then he has sold some 50 million albums and 20 million singles worldwide, was named Rock Personality of 1975 on the annual Rock Awards telecast, played the part of the Pinball Wizard in Ken Russell's film *Tommy,* became the artistic force at Rocket Records (among other things, Rocket resurrected Neil Sedaka's career), and bought his hometown soccer team, the Watford Hornets. John also made headlines in late 1977 by announcing that he would no longer be giving live concerts and declaring that he was a bisexual and had sex three times a week—"more female than male." His sybaritic lifestyle includes a mansion in Benedict Canyon, an English manor house in Windsor, 17 cars worth $750,000, and plenty of Magritte and Rembrandt etchings. Yet John, who underwent a hair transplant after attempts to color his hair blue, green, pink, and orange resulted in a bald spot, remained unhappy and alone. His depression was so great that in 1977 he swallowed 83 sleeping pills, admitting afterward, "I have no close friends and I am not happy. I'm a prisoner of success." A year later, he suffered an apparent heart attack. He rebounded in 1979 with the soul-baring "Mamma Can't Buy You Love," and with a wildly received series of concerts in Moscow—the first rock shows ever in the U.S.S.R. "Little Jeannie," which climbed to number one in late 1980 after his smash Central Park concert, as well as subsequent hits like *Sad Songs* and *Nikita,* confirmed Reginald Dwight as a talent still to be reckoned with in the new decade. John's set during the globally televised Live Aid concert with George Michaels of Wham! singing "Don't Let the Sun Go Down on Me," was a show stopper. So was John's unexpected marriage to an Australian named Ranate on St. Valentine's Day, 1984.

Born: March 25, 1947, in Pinner, Middlesex, England
Height: 5 ft. 8 in.
Weight: 145 lbs.
Eyes: Brown
Hair: Brown
Zodiac: Aries
Education: Royal Academy of Music
Religion: Protestant
Marriages: To Ranate (1984–)
Children: None
Interests: Songwriting, soccer, art, clothes
Personal Habits and Traits: Nonsmoker, nondrinker (used to drink a bottle and a half of Scotch a day, now sticks to fruit juice, tea and Perrier), a cleanliness freak (he dusts and vacuums), collects dolls, cars
Addresses: Los Angeles; Windsor, England
Income: $5 million (estimate)

Pope John Paul II

Karol Wojtyla

Only days before his election: *"It is too early for a Polish Pope."*

At one time he wanted to be an actor, but settled for a higher calling. He is an expert skier, volleyball ace, strong swimmer and ardent canoer; and he loves to sing in a rich baritone ("Home on the Range" is a favorite) and joke with his colleagues. The first thoroughly modern Roman Catholic pontiff, John Paul II is the youngest Pope (58 at his election in 1978) in 132 years, the first non-Italian to sit on the Throne of St. Peter in 455 years and the first Polish Pope ever. His election climaxed a series of events that had rocked the Church: Pope Paul VI's death, the selection of dark horse John Paul I and John Paul I's sudden death after a reign of only 34 days. When the College of Cardinals met for a second time in just over a month to choose the 264th Pope, it seemed likely they would select one of the leading candidates and not another unknown. They cast seven hotly contested ballots during a 50-hour session in the Sistine Chapel before the stream of white smoke signified that the Princes of the Church had agreed on Cardinal Karol Wojtyla (pronounced Voy-tih-wa), Archbishop of Krakow. The choice stunned and delighted the world—with the exception of the Eastern-bloc governments that Wojtyla had been battling all his life. Born to a working-class family in the sooty industrial town of Wadowice, he was three when his mother died, a teenager when his older brother died and twenty-one when his father died. Known as "Lolek" to his friends, young Wojtyla played goalie for his school soccer team, studied Greek and Latin, and charmed his fellow students—particularly the young girls who were not oblivious to his rugged good looks. During

World War II he studied for the priesthood in an underground seminary and fulfilled his dream of becoming an actor by joining the Rhapsodic Theater, a group that performed dramatic readings in private homes. He also distributed anti-Nazi newspapers as a young seminarian and was placed on a wanted list that forced him to hide out in the home of Krakow's archbishop until Poland was liberated. Ordained in 1946, he received a philosophy degree at Rome's Anglicum and later became a professor of theology at the Catholic University of Lublin. Awarded a cardinal's biretta in 1967, he and Poland's senior cardinal, Stefan Wyszynski, constantly criticized the Communist government. Since being chosen to lead the world's 720 million Roman Catholics, John Paul II has already left an indelible mark on the Vatican, and his daily schedule is nothing less than exhausting. Up at 5 A.M., he attends mass at 5:30, meditates for an hour and then breakfasts on a soft-boiled egg, cheese and sausages. He spends three hours on paperwork, starts his round of audiences, breaks for soup and a sandwich at 2:30, naps for fifteen minutes, walks two miles around the Vatican gardens, meditates for another two hours, then reviews his calendar with the Prefect of the Apostolic Palace and the Vatican Secretary of State. His evenings are often reserved for cocktails (he prefers beer to wine) and dinner with close friends before listening to classical music on the stereo system installed by Pope Paul VI. No doubt destined to become one of the most beloved religious leaders in history, John Paul II enjoys his pastoral duties, dispensing with profuse ring-kissing to plunge headlong into the throngs that await him wherever he goes. Yet, when it comes to work he is no-nonsense, and literally rolls up his sleeves in his office. His dramatic visits to Mexico and Poland in mid-1979 and to the United States in October of that year, proved what many had expected—that, like John XXIII, John Paul II is a "Pope of the People" (although his conservative stands on birth control, abortion, women's participation in the church, and other issues irk many liberals). In May 1981, the world was stunned when John Paul II was shot by a would-be assassin. After abdominal surgery the Pope made a speedy recovery, then visited his intended killer in jail and forgave him.

Born: May 18, 1920, in Wadowice, Poland
Height: 6 ft.
Weight: 175 lbs.
Eyes: Blue
Hair: White
Zodiac: Taurus
Education: Rome's Anglicum and the Catholic University of Lublin, degrees in philosophy and theology
Religion: Roman Catholic
Interests: Music, art, theology, philosophy, poetry, skiing, volleyball, swimming, boating, the outdoors, languages (speaks German, French, English, Italian, Latin and Polish)
Personal Habits and Traits: Does not smoke, drinks beer, in bed at 11 P.M.
Address: Vatican City
Income: None, but has unlimited expense account

Don Johnson

"I still like to party. I just do it without the mind-altering substances."

Voted prime time's Numero Uno Hunk by *TV Guide* in 1986, this blond Beau Brummell with the rolled up jacket sleeves and perpetual 5 o'clock shadow shot right to the top as detective Sonny Crockett on NBC's embattled *Miami Vice.* The Missouri farmer's son got off to a rocky start: at 12, the same year he lost his virginity by seducing his 17-year-old babysitter, Johnson was arrested for stealing a car. Four years later, he moved in with a 26-year-old cocktail waitress. After playing the lead in a high school production of *West Side Story* Johnson was hooked on acting, and wound up attending the University of Kansas on a drama scholarship. After a brief affair with his professor, Johnson married Tippi Hedren's daughter, Melanie Griffith, in 1976. That lasted a little over a year, and in 1980 Johnson became involved with actress Patti D'Arbanville. Both drank heavily and did drugs, but when D'Arbanville became pregnant with their son Jesse in 1982, she joined Alcoholics Anonymous. The following year, Johnson climbed aboard the wagon right behind her, giving up not only liquor, marijuana and cocaine but cigarettes as well. Nevertheless, they split up in 1985. Johnson, an aspiring guitarist and singer-songwriter, planned to record an album for CBS in 1986—the same year he picked up a spare $1 million endorsing Pepsi on television.

Born: 1950 in Crane, Missouri
Height: 5 ft. 11 in.
Weight: 160 lbs.
Eyes: Blue *Hair:* Blond
Education: University of Kansas
Religion: Protestant
Marriages: To Melanie Griffith (1976–1977)
Children: Jesse (b. 1982 by Patti D'Arbanville)
Interests: Music, directing
Personal Habits and Traits: Quit drugs, drinking and smoking; mercurial
Address: Miami, Florida
Income: $2 million

James Earl Jones

"The last thing I want to be is a rich black superstar. I just want to act."

Like Alec Guinness, this fine actor who has performed more than his share of Shakespeare, may wind up being best known for his part in a film called *Star Wars*. Though never seen on screen in that movie, and its blockbuster sequels *The Empire Strikes Back* and *Return of the Jedi,* Jones provided the cultivated baritone of helmeted arch-villain Darth Vader. Born on a farm near Arkabutla, Mississippi, Jones's family later moved to Michigan where he was raised on a farm. He attended Michigan State University, served a hitch in the Army and then joined his actor father in New York. Nearly 15 years' apprenticeship off-Broadway culminated in his brilliant portrayal of Jack Johnson, the first black heavyweight boxing champion, in *The Great White Hope* both onstage and onscreen. Jones's bellowing, rageful performance earned him an Oscar nomination, and he went on to star in such movies as *The Man* (playing America's first black President) and *Claudine*. He returned to Broadway in the highly controversial one-man show *Paul Robeson*. Jones and his wife Julienne Marie Hendricks, who once played Desdemona to his *Othello,* reside in New York City. He joined the ranks of TV detectives as the star of CBS's short-lived *Paris,* portrayed Alex Haley in *Roots II* and the bad guy in *Conan*.

Born: January 17, 1931 near Arkabutla, Mississippi
Height: 6 ft. 1½ in.
Weight: 210 lbs.
Eyes: Brown
Hair: Black
Zodiac: Capricorn
Education: Michigan State University, B.A. in drama
Religion: Protestant
Marriages: To Julienne Marie Hendricks (1967–)
Children: None
Interests: Off-Broadway, politics, history, biography
Personal Habits and Traits: Smokes, drinks, is soft-spoken, affable, polite, a night owl, sleeps in pajama bottoms
Address: New York City
Income: $500,000 (minimum estimate)

Tom Jones

Thomas Jones Woodward

"If I'm a release valve for women's pent-up feelings, that's great. It's as much a release for me as it is for them."

To avoid following his father down into the mines, Welshman Thomas Jones Woodward tried everything else he could to make a living, from digging ditches and laying bricks to singing in local pubs. Rock impresario Gordon Mills, who would later package two other recording stars, Engelbert Humperdinck and Gilbert O'Sullivan, discovered Woodward singing under the name Tommy Scott, and persuaded him to change it again, this time to Tom Jones. Capitalizing on the hit movie of the same name, the hip-swiveling Tom Jones soon reached a number-one position with "It's Not Unusual," and followed up with other hits like "What's New Pussycat," "Delilah," and "The Green Green Grass of Home." Jones, a Sinatraesque dandy in open ruffled shirt and pants that fit like spray paint, has taken Elvis Presley's pelvic gyrations a step or two further. Jones and Elvis met in Hawaii, where Elvis caught Jones's nightclub act and came backstage to congratulate him. Elvis had been convinced, from listening to Jones's records that Tom was black. The two remained friends until Elvis's death. Aside from causing some minor riots at his shows, Jones, who became a grandfather in 1984, can always count on having several hotel-room keys thrown at him by ladies in the audience during his sweat-drenched performances. One of Jones's other greatest pleasures is cigar smoking, and he prefers the Havanas he purchases from vendors in Canada.

Born: June 7, 1940, in Pontypridd, Wales
Height: 6 ft.
Weight: 178 lbs.
Eyes: Brown
Hair: Brown
Zodiac: Gemini
Education: High school dropout
Religion: Protestant
Marriages: To Linda Jones (1956–)
Children: Mark (b. 1957)
Interests: Boxing
Personal Habits and Traits: Smokes cigars, drinks whiskey
Address: London
Income: $1.4 million

Erica Jong

"Many, many people have done a lot more sexual experimentation than I have. Yet it's the one who writes about it who is thought to be weird."

The author who unzipped women's sexual fears and fantasies with her number-one bestseller *Fear of Flying* (more than 6 million copies sold) is the daughter of a designer and her importer husband. Growing up on Manhattan's Upper West Side, Erica attended the High School of Music and Art, Barnard College, and Columbia University. After ending a brief college marriage, she walked to the altar with Chinese-American psychiatrist Allan Jong—an emotionally tumultuous relationship that provided the grist for *Fear of Flying* and ended in a quickie Dominican Republic divorce in 1975. Jong then settled in New York City with science-fiction writer Jonathan Fast and completed a volume of poetry and a second bestselling novel, *How to Save Your Own Life*. Fleeing from Manhattan, Jong and Fast lived in Weston, Connecticut, where, having completed her master's thesis on Alexander Pope, she wrote a randy novel set in 18th-century England, *Fanny*. The bitterness of Jong's divorce from Fast became evident when he sued to prevent her from publishing *Molly's Book of Divorce,* using their daughter's name in the title. She changed it to *Megan's Book of Divorce*.

Born: March 26, 1942, in New York City
Height: 5 ft. 7 in.
Weight: 126 lbs.
Eyes: Brown
Hair: Blond
Zodiac: Aries
Education: Barnard College, Columbia University
Religion: Jewish
Marriages: Three. Last to Jonathan Fast (1977–1983)
Children: Molly Miranda (b. 1978) by Jonathan Fast
Interests: Poetry, history, classical music, yoga, George Gershwin and Cole Porter
Personal Habits and Traits: Chain-smokes, drinks beer
Address: Weston, Connecticut
Income: $300,000+

Madeline Kahn

"I've played all the crazies. I could ride bareback down Broadway and nobody would recognize me."

One of Hollywood's most talented and wackiest character actresses started out in Queens and began singing opera when she was an undergraduate at Hofstra University. As a lyric soprano she was better than average, but Kahn soon discovered her undeniable ability to crack people up with her neurotic comedy routines. In her first major film role, she played Ryan O'Neal's featherbrained fiancée in *What's Up, Doc*? Later she received Oscar nominations for *Paper Moon* and Mel Brooks's *Blazing Saddles,* as well as a Tony nomination for *On the Twentieth Century*. A hit of the 1978 season, that show was also a crucible of sorts for Kahn, who was finally paid $100,000 to leave the part to her understudy. Kahn's best-known work continues to be with Mel Brooks, who also featured her in *Young Frankenstein* and *High Anxiety,* and with Neil Simon. Starring in Simon's crime comedy *The Cheap Detective,* she donned five wigs and wound up bald. Understandably altar-shy because of wealthy parents who tallied five divorces between them, Kahn broke off with her longtime steady Ted Bentell in 1978 and set up house alone in a spanking new Park Avenue co-op. For all her film success, Madeline Kahn't seem to make it in prime time; her 1984 sitcom *Madeline* did not last a single season.

Born: September 29, 1942, in Boston, Massachusetts
Height: 5 ft. 7in.
Weight: 117 lbs.
Eyes: Brown
Hair: Blond
Zodiac: Libra
Education: Hofstra University, B.A.
Religion: Jewish
Marriages: None
Children: None
Interests: Opera, human behavior, comedy, literature
Personal Habits and Traits: Nonsmoker, drinks moderately, workaholic
Address: New York City
Income: $350,000 (estimate)

Diane Keaton

"Oh, wow. Oh, God, well . . . Oh, well . . . La-de-dah."

Diane Hall

Woody Allen's favorite clown not only snagged a Best Actress Academy Award for *Annie Hall* but created the Annie Hall "look"—floppy hats, baggy trousers, and men's tweedy blazers. The daughter of a prosperous engineer and a former "Mrs. Los Angeles," Diane Hall grew up a stone's throw from Disneyland in the windy town of Santa Ana. She played the second lead in a high school production of *Little Mary Sunshine* and after graduation sampled Santa Ana College and Orange Coast College for a few months. At the suggestion of her high school acting teacher, Diane moved to Manhattan and studied at the Neighborhood Playhouse School of the Theater, adopting her mother's maiden name of Keaton. She auditioned for *Hair* and was on her way out the door when the director inexplicably changed his mind and decided to hire her as an understudy. When the star left the production, she took over the lead (she was the only cast member in *any* of the many *Hair* companies to refuse to shed her clothes), and after the musical's run Keaton tried out for a role in *Play It Again, Sam,* Allen's first Broadway attempt. Between the stage and movie versions of Allen's hit, she donned a track suit for "Hour after Hour" underarm deodorant commercials, and appeared in the films *Lovers and Other Strangers, The Godfather* (Parts I & II), and *I Will, I Will for Now.* But Keaton's befuddled Gracie Allen image blossomed in Woody's futuristic slapstick *Sleeper* and his *War and Peace* takeoff, *Love and Death.* Meanwhile, she moved in with the neurotic young comic. Straight from her triumph as *Annie Hall,* which loosely traced her relationship with Allen, Keaton tested her mettle in Richard Brooks's grisly interpretation of Judith Rossner's bestselling *Looking for Mr. Goodbar* and in Allen's *Interiors.* Reviews for *Goodbar* were mixed, but Keaton was almost universally praised for her disturbing portrayal of an alienated young schoolteacher who prowls singles bars at night. Though Keaton and Allen have not been a twosome since before *Annie Hall,* they remain the closest of friends. ("There's something utterly guileless about her," he muses. "She's a natural.") Keaton starred with him in *Manhattan* while exploring a relationship with actor Warren Beatty offscreen. Between her firebrand roles in *Reds* and *Little Drummer Girl,* Beatty did the one thing he had never done before: he asked Keaton to marry him. She said no.

Born: January 5, 1946, in Los Angeles, California
Height: 5 ft. 7 in.
Weight: 118 lbs.
Eyes: Green
Hair: Brown
Zodiac: Capricorn
Education: High school
Religion: Methodist
Marriages: None
Children: None
Interests: Psychoanalysis (has seen a shrink several times a week since 1972 at the suggestion of Woody Allen), her cat Buster Keaton (Diane is no relation to the famous Buster Keaton), photography
Personal Habits and Traits: Insecure about her looks, her acting, her singing; gets up late; is something of a night person
Address: New York City
Income: $3 million per film (minimum estimate)

Gene Kelly

"I got started dancing because I knew that was one way to meet girls. Then I found out that it was good for a hell of a lot more—like being a movie star!"

Rediscovered by a new generation when the hit musical montage *That's Entertainment* spotlighted his celebrated *Singin' in the Rain* and *An American in Paris* dance routines, Gene Kelly experienced a remarkable comeback in the mid-1970s. Eugene Curran Kelly studied economics at Pennsylvania State University and the University of Pittsburgh, yet found that giving dance lessons in his basement, augmented by ditchdigging, was the only way to make ends meet during the Depression. *The Time of Your Life* and Rodgers and Hart's *Pal Joey* established him as a Broadway star by 1940, and during the next two decades he turned out movies like *For Me and My Gal* (his first, with Judy Garland), *Brigadoon, Les Girls, On the Town, Marjorie Morningstar* and *What a Way to Go*. After collecting a special Academy Award in 1951 for his contribution to the art of cinema choreography, Kelly tried his hand at directing, first with Rodgers and Hammerstein's *Flower Drum Song* and then with *Hello, Dolly*! starring Barbra Streisand. For the most part, however, Kelly faded from the public eye until the tremendous resurgence of interest in his craft generated by *That's Entertainment* and its sequel, *That's Entertainment, Part II*. With the exception of Fred Astaire, no hoofer ever made it bigger in the movies. Not willing to let Saturday night fever pass him by, Kelly was back on celluloid after the death of his wife, with Olivia Newton-John in 1980's disco disaster *Xanadu*. His sloppy *That's Dancing* montage was little better. In 1984, Kelly narrowly escaped death when his son saved him from the fire that destroyed his Beverly Hills home.

Born: August 23, 1912, in Pittsburgh, Pennsylvania
Height: 5 ft. 10 in.
Weight: 173 lbs.
Eyes: Brown
Hair: Dark brown
Zodiac: Virgo
Education: High school
Religion: Roman Catholic

Marriages:
To Betsy Blair (divorced)
To Jeanne Coyne (died)
Children: Two daughters and one son
Interests: Directing, literature, art, music
Personal Habits and Traits: Smokes, drinks, exercise nut, early riser
Address: Beverly Hills
Income: $200,000 (minimum estimate)

Edward M. Kennedy

"I'm only interested in getting reelected to the Senate."

The last surviving Kennedy brother, Edward "Ted" Kennedy seems destined to haunt the American political landscape for some time to come. Far more controversial than either John or Robert while they served in the Senate, Ted was once

caught cheating on a Spanish exam at Harvard (he had a classmate take it for him), but nonetheless, he graduated and went on to the University of Virginia Law School. Even before graduating from law school, he managed JFK's reelection campaign for the Senate; two years later he participated in his brother John's quest for the Presidency. As soon as he reached the required age of 30, he launched his own campaign for John's former Massachusetts Senate seat. Running against the son of Henry Cabot Lodge and the nephew of House Speaker John McCormack, he won easily, and then set out aggressively to earn a reputation as one of the Senate's most liberal members. His pet issues include national health care (for which he is Congress's number-one backer) and civil rights. In the hallowed tradition of the Kennedy clan, Teddy is also well known as one of the Hill's most accomplished skirt-chasers, and perhaps destroyed his chance of ever occupying the White House when a car he was driving plunged off the bridge at Chappaquiddick and drowned his passenger, attractive campaign worker Mary Jo Kopechne. Rose Kennedy's youngest child has also been frequently ticketed for speeding, narrowly escaped death while climbing in the Alps, and was nearly killed in the crash of a private plane. Yet political insiders knew that under the right circumstances, Kennedy would eagerly run for President. And he did. His wife, Joan, whose drinking problem escalated when their eldest son Ted, Jr., was diagnosed as having cancer and had his leg amputated, checked into Silver Hills sanitarium, but credited her actual rehabilitation to Alcoholics Anonymous. As for Ted, he later went on a highly publicized holiday with ski champion and Chapstick-endorser Suzy Chaffee. When he finally announced his candidacy on November 7, 1979, Kennedy led incumbent Jimmy Carter in the polls—until the President's handling of the Iran crisis gave Carter the boost he needed. After years of speculation, Teddy was unable to wrest the nomination for himself in 1980, much less the election. He was virtually invisible during the quest for the Presidency four years later, embarking instead on a book entitled *My Brother Jack.*

Born: February 22, 1932, in Boston, Massachusetts
Height: 6 ft. 2 in.
Weight: 200 lbs.
Eyes: Blue
Hair: Grayish brown
Zodiac: Pisces
Education: Harvard University, University of Virginia Law School
Religion: Roman Catholic
Marriages: To Virginia Joan Bennett (1958–1981)
Children: Kara Ann (b. 1960), Edward Jr. (b. 1961), Patrick (b. 1967)
Interests: Politics, skiing, swimming, reading, music, art
Personal Habits and Traits: Smokes cigars, drinks, enjoys frequent female company
Addresses: Washington, D.C.; Boston; Hyannis, Massachusetts; Palm Beach, Florida
Income: $1 million (minimum estimate)

Ayatollah Ruhollah Khomeini

"Americans are Satan's people. . . . Rub America's snout in the dirt!"

No one is certain if he actually was born, as Iranian officials claim, on May 17, 1900, in the town of Khomein (from which he takes his name). Nor do they know if his wife of over a half-century—alternately spelled Khadijah and Quesiran—is his first or second. What is certain is that Iran's fanatical Ayatollah Khomeini, as *Time* pointed out when it proclaimed him its "Man of the Year" for 1979, "seized his nation and shook all Islam. Rarely has so improbable a leader shaken the world." The incident that made Khomeini a household name on this side of Mecca was the seizure by Iranian students of the U.S. Embassy in Teheran and the Americans inside. The students would release the hostages, they declared, only in exchange for the exiled Shah, then undergoing cancer treatment in a New York City hospital. Instead of pressing for the release of the hostages, Khomeini not only backed the mob but threatened to try some of the Americans as spies. This flouting of centuries-old international conventions providing immunity for all diplomats—rules that even Adolf Hitler observed during World War II—incensed not only Americans, who took to the streets in support of the hostages, but the entire world. The UN soundly condemned the action and voted economic sanctions against Iran. Egyptian President Anwar Sadat railed against the Ayatollah as "a lunatic and a disgrace to Islam." But no matter; the ruler of 35.2 million Iranians, totally confident of the righteousness of his position, merely called for the whole of the Moslem world to rise up against America and the West—the "infidels." Khomeini himself had literally grown up with violence. He was barely five months old when his father, a minor leader of Islam's Shi'ite sect (of which 93 percent of all Iranians are members), was murdered. Austere and fiercely uncompromising in his desire to bring Iran under a Shi'ite theocracy, Khomeini frequently declared that the five-year reign of Muhammad's son-in-law Ali over the Arabian Peninsula ending in 661 A.D. was the ideal Islamic government. He slowly built his own constituency among Iran's 1,200 *mullahs*—religious leaders—and in 1941 began his relentless attacks against the westward-leaning Pahlavi dynasty. When the Shah paid a visit to the mullahs in the holy city of Qum, Khomeini was the only one who refused to stand. Khomeini was exiled in 1964, and in Turkey and, later, in Iraq, he recorded taped sermons against the Shah that were smuggled into hundreds of mosques throughout Iran. The Ayatollah showed virtually no signs of emotion when his small daughter drowned, or when his son Mustafa was murdered in 1977, supposedly by SAVAK, the Shah's secret police. The following year, due to further pressure from the Shah, Khomeini was expelled from Iraq, and he landed outside Paris. From there he stepped up his campaign against his old nemesis, and when the Pahlavi dynasty came to its abrupt end in the spring of 1979, the embittered, vengeful Ayatollah returned as the conquering hero. Within months, some 600 Iranians who had been loyal to the Shah faced firing squads, as did countless more adulterers, usurers, homosexuals and other "defilers of the faith." Women returned to wearing black *chadors,* and music and free speech were banned. As his first full year in power came to an end, Khomeini faced total isolation from the rest of the world, provincial uprisings against his regime by the Kurds and the Azerbaijanis—and a very real threat from the Soviet Union, which became critical when Russian troops invaded Afghanistan. Yet Khomeini continued in his efforts to pull his people back into the 7th century. In one of his books, he outlines rigid rules of conduct that describe in detail the "right" way for everything from sexual intercourse to defecation. Though he displays no emotion publicly—part of his well-choreographed effort to maintain an ascetic mystique—the Ayatollah is said to laugh and even tell jokes in the company of his surviving son Ahmed and his 14 grandchildren. Khomeini's holy war against Iraq had cost the lives of more than 1 million of his countrymen as of 1986.

Born: May 17, 1900 (?) in Khomein, Iran
Height: 5 ft. 10 in.
Weight: 190 pounds (estimate)
Eyes: Brown
Hair: White
Zodiac: Taurus (?)
Education: ?
Religion: Shi'ite Muslim
Marriages: Currently to Khadijah (or Quesiran), 1930?—
Children: One surviving son, Ahmed (b. 1945?)
Interests: Islam
Personal Habits and Traits: Moody, sullen, vindictive, egocentric, given to periods of irrationality and disorientation, martyr complex
Address: Qum, Iran
Income: Unknown

Billie Jean King

"I used to get out of bed ready to tear people apart on the court. Now it just doesn't happen."

The female sports personality of the 1970s, Billie Jean King picked up a tennis racket at the age of 11 and developed a razzle-dazzle killer style that led to her coronation as Queen of the Courts by the time she was 28. Having won virtually every major tennis title on both sides of the Atlantic (at Wimbledon she captured six singles, nine mixed doubles, and four doubles titles), Billie Jean fought to establish the women's tennis tour and became first president of the Women's Tennis Association. She signed on as coach and player of the Philadelphia Freedoms and then the New York Apples of World Team Tennis, founded the magazine *WomenSports* with her manager-husband Larry King, and became a $200,000-a-year television sports commentator. King struck a blow for feminism when she overpowered male chauvinist Bobby Riggs at the much-ballyhooed showdown in the Houston Astrodome. In 1974, King was suddenly dethroned when upstart Chris Evert was named the year's top woman athlete. In spring 1981, when her former secretary Marilyn Barnett brought a palimony suit for lifetime support, King rocked the tennis world by admitting they had had an affair. Though the scandal may have cost her endorsements, she rebounded and devoted her prodigious energies to resurrecting team tennis.

Born: November 22, 1943, in Long Beach, California
Height: 5 ft. 5 in.
Weight: 123 lbs.
Eyes: Blue
Hair: Dark brown
Zodiac: Sagittarius
Education: University of California at Los Angeles
Religion: Protestant
Marriages: To Larry King (1965–)
Children: None
Interests: Tennis, broadcasting, publishing
Personal Habits and Traits: Nonsmoker, teetotaler, a rotten loser
Addresses: Berkeley, California; Hilton Head Island, S.C.; New York City
Income: $2 million (estimate)

Carole King

"I'm not that great a singer. What's important are the songs."

Her 1971 Grammy-winning album *Tapestry* was the largest-selling LP in history (13 million copies) until Fleetwood Mac's *Rumours* and the score from *Saturday Night Fever*. She also earned Grammys for her album *It's Too Late* and her song "You've Got a Friend" before zooming to the top of the charts with the smash singles "I Feel the Earth Move," "Where You Lead," "So Far Away," "Jazzman," and "Hardrock Cafe." Yet long before record buyers knew her as a performer, Brooklyn-bred Carole King was touted in the music business as one of the best and most prolific rock songwriters around. Starting with "Will You Still Love Me Tomorrow?" for the Shirelles in 1961, she and her husband, Gerry Goffin, composed an avalanche of hits for a variety of performers, including "The Loco-Motion" (first made into a hit by their maid, Little Eva, in 1962 and again a dozen years later by Grand Funk), "A Groovy Kind of Love," "He's a Rebel," "Go Away Little Girl," "A Natural Woman" (made into a classic by Aretha Franklin), and "Up on the Roof." Carole wrote the music while Goffin penned the lyrics, but she took on both jobs after the breakup of their marriage in 1968. Now based in California, she lived a hermitic existence with her second husband, musician Charles Larkey, before divorcing him and being momentarily struck by Ryan's Express—Malibu neighbor Ryan O'Neal. Third husband Rick Evers cowrote two tunes on King's 1978 *Welcome Home* album, but died of a drug overdose two months after the recording session. Although King was repeatedly named as the top female vocalist in *Playboy*'s annual jazz poll, her rare concerts are vintage musical events—such as her appearance with James Taylor and Barbara Streisand at a 1972 campaign benefit on behalf of Democratic Presidential candidate George McGovern. Continuing the family tradition, daughter Louise Goffin recorded her first LP at age 19, "Kid Blue." Aiming at even younger audiences, King wrote a modestly successful Broadway musical, *Really Rosie,* and several songs for 1985's animated *Care Bears Movie.*

Born: February 9, 1941, in Brooklyn, New York
Height: 5 ft. 5 in.
Weight: 117 lbs.
Eyes: Blue
Hair: Blond
Zodiac: Aquarius
Education: High school
Religion: Jewish
Marriages:
To Gerry Goffin (1960–1968)
To Charles Larkey (1968–1976)
To Rick Evers (1977 until his death in 1978)
Children: Louise, Sherry (by Goffin); Molly (by Larkey)
Interests: Meditation, reading
Personal Habits and Traits: Smokes, drinks moderately, reclusive, uneasy as a performer (would rather write and remain in the background)
Address: Laurel Canyon, Los Angeles
Income: $700,000

Stephen King

"We make up horrors to help us cope with the real ones."

He calls his books "fearsomes," and with good reason. This master of the macabre began his profitable reign of terror with the hugely successful *Carrie,* and at one point in 1980 became the only American writer ever to have three different books—*Firestarter, The Dead Zone,* and *The Shining*—on the best-seller lists at the same time. The following year, with *Firestarter* climbing to number one on the paperback lists, he simultaneously had the number-one hard-cover, *Cujo.* (*Cujo,* predictably, would also hit number one in paperback.) Stephen Edwin King's merchant seaman father deserted his family when Stephen, a native of Portland, Maine, was 3, and Stephen's mother was forced to take a series of low-paying jobs to support her family. An introverted boy, Stephen lost himself in the pages of blood-curdling comics like *Tales From the Crypt* and *Tales of the Vault,* and never missed a Vincent Price offering at the local movie house. King's addiction to the horror fare of the 1950s—most notably such classics as *The Invasion of the Body Snatchers, The Creature From the Black Lagoon,* and *The Thing*—evolved into a taste for terrifying novels when he came upon his father's pulp collection of fantasy-horror fiction, including several stories by H. P. Lovecraft. While still in high school, King began jotting off wild stories of his own and submitting them to magazines, though not a single one sold. By then a more sociable creature, King also found time to play tackle on the football team and play rhythm guitar for a local rock band called the MooonSpinners. While majoring in English at the University of Maine, King sold his first two stories to *Startling Mystery Story* magazine for $35 each. He made so little money as a writer for the next several years that he had to make ends meet by working as a janitor and gas station attendant before finally landing a job teaching English at the Hampden Academy in Hampden, Maine. Writing on a child's desk in the school's boiler room, he produced two novels that were never published and became so depressed by the Everest of rejection slips that he had accumulated that he threw away the manuscript of his third book; fortunately King's wife, Tabitha, retrieved the pages from the wastebasket and convinced him to send the manuscript to Doubleday, where he was advanced $2,500 for *Carrie,* which went on to become not only King's first bestseller but a hit movie as well. *Carrie* was followed by *Salem's Lot, The Shining, The Stand, The Dead Zone, Firestarter, Dance Macabre, Cujo, Different Seasons, Christine, Pet Sematary,* and *Skeleton Crew.* He also collaborated with fellow horror novelist Peter Straub (*Ghost Story*) on *The Talisman,* and by 1985 flooded the market with another bestseller, *Thinner,* published under the pseudonym "Richard Bachman." All of which has added up to total sales in excess of 40 million copies. In addition to *Carrie,* several of King's novels—including *The Shining, The Dead Zone, Firestarter, Cujo,* and *Christine*—have made it to the screen, and King wrote the screenplay for and acted in another profitable horror movie, *Creepshow.* The incredibly prolific author sits down to work at his word processor each morning to blaring rock music. King, his wife, Tabitha, and their three children divide their time between a 23-room Bangor mansion and a summer house in the White Mountains. The houses appear quite normal, save for King's collection of grotesque masks, many of them sent by fans. In 1981, Tabitha published a thriller of her own, *Small World.* Despite the bizarre nature of his work, King has been personally disturbed by only one of his tales—*Pet Sematary.* "You never know when an idea will turn mean," he explained. "My wife read it and cried and said, 'You can't publish this.'" He put it in a drawer for three years until he was legally obligated to supply a book to Doubleday to fullfill his multimillion-dollar multibook contract. *Pet Sematary* evolved from what could have been a fatal accident to one of King's three children. In 1979, his cat was run over by a truck, and his son was very nearly killed in the same accident. "If things had changed by five seconds," King recalled, "we would have lost one of our children." Even those few remaining souls who have never read one of his thriller-chillers know King from his scarifying performance on one of those "Do you know me?" American Express commercials.

Born: September 21, 1947 in Portland, Maine
Height: 6 ft. 3 in.
Weight: 225 lbs.
Eyes: Blue
Hair: Black
Zodiac: Virgo
Education: University of Maine
Religion: Protestant
Marriages: To Tabitha Jane Spruce (1971–
Children: Three: Naomi, Joe Hill, and Owen
Interests: Rock music, video, bowling, cross-country skiing, poker
Personal Habits and Traits: Drinks beer, nonsmoker, shuns the trappings of celebrity, frequents local fast-food hangouts, easygoing, a fearful flyer
Addresses: Bangor, Maine; White Mountains, Maine

Henry Kissinger

"Power is the ultimate aphrodisiac."

America's modern-day Metternich during the Nixon and Ford administrations, Henry Kissinger was one of the very few top public officials not to be splashed by the Watergate scandal. During the eight years that preceded Watergate he accomplished more foreign diplomatic miracles than any previous secretary of state in U.S. history: detente with Moscow, the opening of Red China, an end to the Vietnam war, and vast improvement of relations with most countries in the Middle East. Not that he was without his critics; Kissinger's support of the bombing of Cambodia in 1970, his backing of the junta that overthrew Chilean President Salvador Allende and his support of the Shah all stirred controversy and debate. The only factor that prevents him from seeking the Presidency is Constitutional—he is not a native U.S. citizen. Born in Fürth, Germany, to a Jewish family, he attended an all-Jewish school and was frequently beaten or harassed by the Nazis until his family finally fled to New York in 1938. He served in Europe as an army sergeant during World War II; returned to attend Harvard, where he graduated *summa cum laude;* and then obtained his master's and doctoral degrees. As a Harvard professor he earned a distinguished reputation through his writings, which attracted the attention of Presidential hopeful Nelson Rockefeller. He served as Rockefeller's foreign policy adviser during the 1968 Presidential campaign, and when Richard Nixon won the election, the President-elect was quick to tap the brilliant Kissinger to officiate as director of his National Security Council. While William P. Rogers served as Nixon's figurehead secretary of state, Kissinger actually dictated all foreign policy, jetting from one high-level round of negotiations to the next. In 1973—the year Kissinger was awarded the Nobel Peace Prize for his Vietnam peace efforts—Rogers resigned and Nixon made it official: Kissinger became the first Jewish secretary of state. Urbane, witty, and cosmopolitan (though also pictured as egocentric and power-obsessed in William Shawcross's *Sideshow*), the divorced Dr. Kissinger (his 1949 marriage to Ann Fleischer ended after 15 years) dated glamorous stars like Jill St. John and Raquel Welch. But in 1974 he retired as "Playboy of the Western Wing" and married Rockefeller foreign policy staffer Nancy Maginnes, who shared his *realpolitik* philosophy and proved a decided asset on his nonstop rounds of shuttle diplomacy. Pocketing close to $4 million for his various book and TV contracts (with NBC), Kissinger now lives quietly in New York, surrounded by his rich and famous pals. By 1980 he was contemplating a run for the U.S. Senate (he decided against it) and watching his *White House Years* soar to number one on the bestseller lists—only to be topped after a few weeks by Erma Bombeck's *Aunt Erma's Cope Book.* Seymour Hirsh's devastating 1984 biography of Kissinger portrayed the former secretary as an obsessive self-promoter.

Born: May 27, 1923, in Fürth, Germany
Height: 5 ft. 10½ in.
Weight: 184 lbs.
Eyes: Brown
Hair: Brown
Zodiac: Gemini
Education: Harvard University, B.A., M.A., and Ph.D.
Religion: Jewish
Marriages:
To Ann Fleischer (1949–1964)
To Nancy Maginnes (1974–)
Children: Elizabeth, David
Interests: Foreign policy, politics, fiction, classical music
Personal Habits and Traits: Does not smoke, does drink, has weight problem, needs only four hours sleep per night, demanding, a workaholic
Address: New York City
Income: $1.3 million

Calvin Klein

"Before the showing of a new collection I'll go four days without sleeping at all. I don't need it. It's like being on drugs—an incredible high."

The youngest designer ever to be inducted into the Coty Hall of Fame, Calvin Klein always knew exactly what he wanted to do, even back in the days when he rode the school bus with Bronx neighbor and fellow future fashion giant Ralph Lauren. Idolizing Coco Chanel, Klein graduated from New York's Fashion Institute of Technology in 1962 and borrowed $10,000 from partner Barry Schwartz to create his first collection. Bonwit Teller instantly ordered $100,000 worth of his designs—and Klein took off. Within five years the boyishly handsome designer controlled a $30 million fashion empire based on a moderate-priced ready-to-wear women's line featuring classic skirts, blazers and turtlenecks—"real fashions for real women." On the way, Klein spent two years in psychotherapy and divorced his wife, Jayne, in 1973. Klein's name was splashed across the front page five years later when his young daughter, Marci, was kidnapped. After a tense day-long wait, both Klein's daughter and the sizable ransom that he had paid were recovered. Deciding to enter the already-glutted designer jean market, Klein clobbered the competition—largely because of a controversial ad campaign starring Brooke Shields. Klein kept up the sensational commercials for his men's and women's underwear lines, as well as his perfume Obsession. He summers in Fire Island Pines in a house designed by Horace Gifford, featuring a black swimming pool. In 1985, Hurricane Gloria literally raised Klein's roof—an event that was recorded on the front page of the *New York Times*.

Born: November 19, 1942, in the Bronx, New York
Height: 5 ft. 9 in.
Weight: 152 lbs.
Eyes: Brown
Hair: Brown
Zodiac: Scorpio
Education: Fashion Institute of Technology
Religion: Jewish
Marriages: To Jayne Klein (1964–1973)
Children: Marci (b. 1967)
Interests: Swimming, horseback riding, sailing, reading
Personal Habits and Traits: Smokes, drinks, a workaholic (13 hours a day minimum), a chronic worrier, soft-spoken and polite
Address: New York City
Income: $8 million yearly

Jack Klugman

"I'm a loner. I like a good meal, a good script, and a good BM. That to me is a great life."

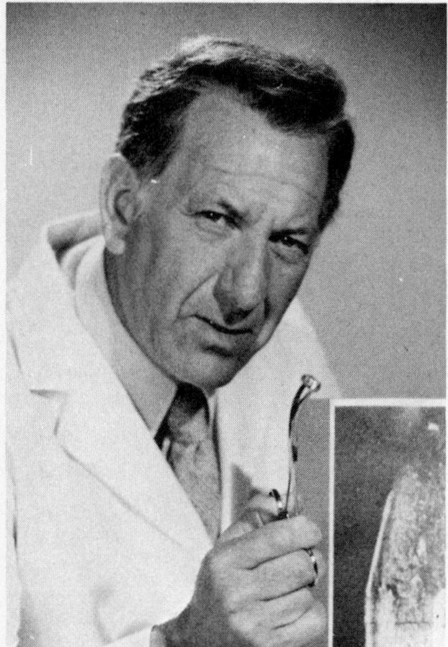

The youngest of six children born to poor Russian immigrants in South Philadelphia, Jack Klugman grew up knowing he lacked the looks and appeal of a matinee idol. But after drifting from one odd job to another, he decided while studying at Carnegie Tech to give acting a try. He shared a $14-a-month New York apartment with Charles Bronson while both actors searched desperately for stage parts, and after a decade in summer stock, finally got his break playing second fiddle to Henry Fonda in *Mr. Roberts* on Broadway. Movie roles in which he was invariably cast as the homely schmo made his face if not his name recognizable. After films like *Twelve Angry Men* and *Goodbye, Columbus,* Klugman emerged from the shadows as Oscar Madison, the unrepentant slob who bedevils finicky Felix Unger (played by Tony Randall) in ABC's *The Odd Couple.* At the very height of the series' popularity, Klugman was stricken with throat cancer and was suddenly faced with the agonizing choice of either having his larynx removed or undergoing cobalt treatment with its unpleasant side effects. He gambled on having the tumor removed—though not the voice box—in a risky operation performed by Frank Sinatra's specialist, Dr. Max Som. The experience prompted Klugman to look for the role of a doctor, and in 1976 he brought *Quincy,* a dramatic series about an irascible and uncorruptible medical examiner, to TV. Within a year it became NBC's second-highest-rated show and made the three-time Emmy-winning character actor into a major star. More closely resembling Oscar Madison offscreen, Klugman split with his actress wife, Brett Sommers (*Match Game*), in 1974. Klugman got another shot at a potential hit series with 1986's *You Again,* but while his annual income (he moonlights as spokesman for Minolta copiers) exceeds $1 million, Klugman lives modestly in a two-bedroom condominium overlooking Malibu Beach. His twin passions are playing the horses and popcorn; he even started his own nationwide popcorn chain.

Born: April 27, 1922, in Philadelphia, Pennsylvania
Height: 5 ft. 10 in.
Weight: 181 lbs.
Eyes: Brown
Hair: Brown
Zodiac: Taurus
Education: Carnegie Tech
Religion: Jewish
Marriages: To Brett Sommers (1956–1974)
Children: David (b. 1958), Adam (b. 1962)
Interests: Gambling on the horses, raising his own racehorses (he owns two), writing, music
Personal Habits and Traits: Kicked his five-pack-a-day smoking habit, drinks moderately, popcorn freak
Address: Malibu, California
Income: $1 million (minimum estimate)

Evel Knievel

Robert Craig Kneivel

On assaulting Sheldon Saltman with a baseball bat:
"I got out of jail, looked in the mirror and was proud of what I'd done."

A consummate hustler who claims he once sold 110 insurance policies to patients at an insane asylum in Warm Springs, Georgia, Evel Knievel proudly boasts that he spent only two weeks in jail during a youth devoted to conning, stealing, and cheating at cards. But after he had already made a name for himself as the legendary daredevil who jumps over 19 cars at a time on a motorcycle, Knievel was sentenced to six months in prison for bashing *Evel Knievel on Tour* author Sheldon Saltman with a baseball bat. Saltman, who incurred a broken wrist, hip, and arm, sued—bringing the total in lawsuits against Knievel to over $2 million. The experience in prison left its mark on Knievel physically and emotionally—even though he had nearly killed himself more than a dozen times in outlandish acts of daring. His most famous mishaps occurred in Las Vegas, where he jumped the fountains at Caesars Palace only to crash-land at the other end; and at Idaho's Snake River Canyon, where in 1974 Knievel failed to ride a rocket across the canyon, parachuting instead to its floor. Despite the abysmal failure of two films, *Evel Knievel* (in which he was portrayed by George Hamilton) and *Viva Knievel*! (in which his improbable costar was Gene Kelly), Evel consistently drew large audiences for his stunts and his annual income easily passed the half-million-dollar mark before he landed in jail.

Born: October 17, 1938, in Butte, Montana
Height: 6 ft.
Weight: 184 lbs.
Eyes: Blue
Hair: Light brown
Zodiac: Libra
Education: High school dropout
Religion: Protestant
Marriages: Linda Joan Bork (1959–)
Children: Kelly Michael, Robert Edward, Tracy Lynn
Interests: Automobiles, motorcycles, boats, skiing, cards
Personal Habits and Traits: Smokes, drinks, irascible, prone to violence
Address: Los Angeles
Income: $200,000 (estimate)

Gladys Knight

"I'm not afraid to stand alone professionally. I simply don't want to."

This child prodigy of the rhythm and blues world could not have surged to the top of the music business without her Pips—brother Merald and cousins William Guest and Edward Green—spinning their elaborate choreography behind her. At the age of four Gladys was already harmonizing with the adult choir of Atlanta's Mt. Moriah Baptist Church, and four years later she won the $2,000 first prize

singing on Ted Mack's *Original Amateur Hour.* She headed out on the road with the Pips in 1953 at the age of nine. The group was so vulnerable to unscrupulous club owners that on one occasion when they tried to collect payment after two performances in Paducah, Kentucky, they wound up being rejected at gunpoint. Gladys Knight and the Pips cut their first hit single, "Every Beat of My Heart" in 1961, but did not manage to land a Motown recording contract until 1966. While Motown's favored acts—Diana Ross and the Supremes, Marvin Gaye, the Temptations, and Smokey Robinson—obtained first choice of all promising songs, groups like the Four Tops and Gladys Knight and the Pips had to settle for whatever remained. Nevertheless they broke through with "I Heard It Through the Grapevine" in 1967 (a jazzy R&B number that Marvin Gaye made into an even bigger smash one year later) and topped themselves with "Neither One of Us" before signing with Buddah Records as soon as their Motown contract expired in 1973. Then followed a string of monster hits which coincided with their $1 million suit against Motown for nonpayment of royalties: "I've Got to Use My Imagination," "I Feel a Song," their soundtrack from the movie *Claudine,* "Midnight Train to Georgia" (which won two Grammys), and a soulful version of Marvin Hamlisch's Oscar-winning "The Way We Were." In 1977, Knight starred in the movie *Pipe Dreams.* Along the way from one-night shows to selling 15 million records and earning $50,000 per concert, she shed 30 pounds and two husbands: James Newman, whom she married at 16 and divorced four years later, and movie producer Barry Hankerson. She tried her luck on television as a star, opposite Flip Wilson, of 1985's *Charlie and Co.* Hedging her bets, Knight joined with Dionne Warwick, Elton John and Stevie Wonder to produce the No. 1 single for AIDS relief, *That's What Friends Are For.*

Born: May 28, 1944, in Atlanta, Georgia
Height: 5 ft. 4 in.
Weight: 118 lbs.
Eyes: Brown
Hair: Black
Zodiac: Gemini
Education: High school
Religion: Southern Baptist
Marriages:
To James Newman (1960–1964)
To Barry Hankerson (1974–1978)
Children: Daughter Kenya, son James (by Newman); daughter Shanga-Al (by Hankerson)
Interests: Movies, fashion, politics
Personal Habits and Traits: Nonsmoker, moderate drinker, a night person, tireless worker, unyielding perfectionist
Addresses: Detroit; Los Angeles
Income: $520,000 (minimum estimate)

Ted Knight

Tadeus Wladyslaw Konopka

"I won't do a Ted Baxter spinoff for television. I love the guy, but who could stand him for thirty minutes a week?"

The son of a Polish bartender in Terryville, Connecticut, Tadeus Wladyslaw Konopka is known to millions of MTM fans as Ted Baxter, the flea-brained TV anchorman with an ego as big as all Minneapolis. Knight won two Emmys for his role on the *Mary Tyler Moore Show* and when Moore decided to fold the series, Knight tried his luck on the Broadway stage in a comedy called *Some of My Best Friends*. It closed after one night and Knight returned to CBS with his own *The Ted Knight Show*. Although he clearly wanted to shed his "double-breasted moron" image by playing the clever boss of a New York escort service, the series lasted less than one season. He tried TV again in 1981 with *Too Close for Comfort;* when it was dropped by the networks, the show's producers syndicated *Too Close* to an even wider audience. Knight—whose nightclub act included impersonations of Bela Lugosi and James Cagney as well as his "Good evening, this is Ted Baxter" routine—is not worried about his finances. "We'll all be senile," he comments, "and the MTM residual checks will still be coming in."

Born: December 7, 1923, in Terryville, Connecticut
Height: 5 ft. 10 in.
Weight: 168 lbs.
Eyes: Blue
Hair: White
Zodiac: Sagittarius
Education: High school
Religion: Roman Catholic
Marriages: To Dorothy Knight (1949–)
Children: Ted Jr. (b. 1954), Elyse (b. 1960), Eric (b. 1963)
Interests: Antiques, sketching and painting, baseball (a Dodgers fan), hiking, driving his Jaguar
Personal Habits and Traits: Does not smoke, teetotaler, avoids coffee, eats health foods, chugalugs vitamins (30 a day)
Address: Pacific Palisades, California
Income: $510,000 (minimum estimate)

Ted Koppel

"I'll balance a dog biscuit on my nose if it causes enough people to tune us in."

The thinking-man's anchor with the Kennedy coif did not set foot in the United States until he was 13. His parents, Jewish refugees from Hitler's Germany, had moved to England, where Ted was born in Lancashire and attended a boarding school where corporal punishment was meted out to by older students to younger ones like Koppel. He went on to a bachelor's degree in speech from Syracuse and a masters in journalism from Stanford, then joined ABC News in 1963 and served as correspondent in Vietnam, Hong Kong, and Miami. In 1977, he was widely praised for putting his career on hold for almost a year to be a househusband while his wife Grace Anne started law school. In fact, he continued to anchor the Saturday night news, do a daily ABC radio commentary from his home, and work with fellow newsman Marvin Kalb on a bestselling novel, *In the National Interest*. After resuming his regular duties at ABC, he quit for a month in a dispute with ABC news chief Roone Arledge, then resumed his job covering the State Department. When American diplomats were held hostage in Iran in 1979, Koppel began anchoring a special late-night series, beginning at 11:30, called *The Iran Crisis: America Held Hostage*. In March 1980, after the hostages were returned, the program was recast as *Nightline*, and Koppel the cool, don't-let-them-off-the-hook interrogator established himself as the news junkie's alternative to Johnny Carson and reruns of *Magnum, P.I.* He is given so much time (even though an expanded, hour-long *Nightline* had to be cut back, he is still permitted to frequently run over his 30-minute allotment) and control over the program's content, he turned down an offer to succeed Frank Reynolds as anchor of *World News Tonight* (Peter Jennings took the job). The Koppels, including Ted's father-in-law, live in a modern, six-bedroom house in Potomac, Maryland, and eschew the Washington party scene. Because he is Jewish and his wife Roman Catholic, they were married three times: first in a civil ceremony, then in a Unitarian service, and finally, with two of their children serving as bridesmaids, in a Catholic church in Hong Kong. Koppel is famous in news circles for his merciless impressions of his good friend Henry Kissinger, Richard Nixon, and Cary Grant. On *The David Letterman Show* he also impersonated William F. Buckley, Jr., and balanced a dog biscuit on his nose.

Born: February 8, 1940, in London
Height: 5 ft. 9 in.
Weight: 155 lbs.
Eyes: Blue
Hair: Reddish
Zodiac: Aquarius
Education: Syracuse University, Stanford School of Journalism
Religion: Jewish
Marriages: To Grace Anne Dorney (1963–)
Children: Andrea (b. 1964), Deirdre (b. 1966), Andrew (b. 1971), and Tara (b. 1972)
Interests: Reading, skiing, water-skiing, tennis (he plays weekly at 1 A.M., after *Nightline* broadcast), running
Personal Habits and Traits: Does not smoke, moderate drinker, is supremely confident, droll, day begins around 9 A.M. and ends around 2 A.M.
Address: Potomac, Maryland
Income: $900,000

Kris Kristofferson

"Freedom's just another word for nothing left to lose."

When he played the part of a boozing, pill-popping rock star in the 1976 remake of *A Star Is Born,* Kris Kristofferson could not have been better cast. Each day on the set he consumed over a quart of tequila and two 6-packs of beer. After witnessing a rough cut of the film Kristofferson realized that the self-destructive character he was portraying was himself. He switched there and then from alcohol to coffee (and pot)—and in the process saved his marriage to second wife Rita Coolidge, at least temporarily. An Air Force brat (his father was a general) born in Brownsville, Texas, Kristofferson played football and rugby at Pomona College in California, and as a Phi Beta Kappa graduate studied English literature at Oxford University on a Rhodes scholarship. He quit two years later, however, and joined the Army, where he learned to pilot a helicopter. Having already tried a solo country-western singing career as "Kris Carson," he resigned his captain's commission to work as a gofer at Columbia Records in Nashville. During the early 1970s he wrote a number of hit C&W tunes for singers like Janis Joplin ("Me and Bobby McGee"), Sammi Smith ("Help Me Make It Through the Night") and Johnny Cash ("Sunday Mornin' Comin' Down"). Throughout this prolific period as a gravel-voiced songwriter-troubadour, Kristofferson dated Joplin, Carly Simon, and Barbra Streisand (later his costar and producer in *A Star Is Born*). An aspiring actor, he appeared in *Cisco Pike, Blume in Love,* and *Pat Garrett and Billy the Kid,* but his first major role was in *Alice Doesn't Live Here Any More.* In the R-rated *The Sailor Who Fell from Grace with the Sea,* he regularly arrived on the set drunk for his steamy nude scenes with costar Sarah Miles—scenes that drove his marriage with Coolidge to the brink of divorce. Kristofferson's reviews for *A Star Is Born* were mixed, but he rallied in the macho part supplied by the football flick *Semi-Tough.* After appearing opposite Jane Fonda as a clean-shaven banker in *Rollover,* his career almost did. Sharing his Pacific Coast home with a Mexican gardener and three dogs, Kristofferson, who drew praise as the tenacious detective in the TV miniseries *Blood and Orchids,* says: "I'd forgotten what it was like to think without alcohol." But this change of heart was too little and too late to save his marriage.

Born: June 22, 1936, in Brownsville, Texas
Height: 5ft. 11 in.
Weight: 175 lbs.
Eyes: Blue
Hair: Gray-black
Zodiac: Cancer
Education: Pomona College, Oxford University (a Rhodes scholar)
Religion: Baptist (converted from Catholicism)

Marriages:
To Fran Beir (1960–1972)
To Rita Coolidge (1973–1979)
Children: Tracy, Kris (by Beir); Casey (by Coolidge)
Interests: Poetry (particularly Blake), songwriting, movie acting, guitar
Personal Habits and Traits: On the wagon in 1977 after 20 years of very heavy drinking, no longer smokes tobacco (but hasn't given up marijuana)
Address: Los Angeles
Income: $400,000 (estimate)

Stanley Kubrick

"All a filmmaker can do is either pose questions or make truthful observations about human behavior. The only morality is not to be dishonest."

Born in New York, Kubrick started out as a photojournalist working primarily for *Look* magazine but ended up one of the world's top directors largely on the basis of sheer grit. Stanley Kubrick works 18 hours a day when filming, then overseas every aspect of the package from scoring to publicity. The director of *Star Wars'* spacy forerunner *2001: A Space Odyssey,* he has created a half-dozen other film classics, including *Paths of Glory, Lolita, Spartacus, Dr. Strangelove, A Clockwork Orange,* and *Barry Lyndon.* A sometimes maddening perfectionist, he personally inspected the first 17 prints of *A Clockwork Orange,* his ultraviolent portrait of futuristic society, before allowing them to be shipped to theaters. "From start to finish," Kubrick explains, "the only limitations I observe are those imposed on me by the amount of money I have to spend and the amount of sleep I need." Kubrick, who among other things is deathly afraid of flying, is now living with his third wife Suzanne at their home in England while at work on a project to top the box-office hit *The Shining*. By mid-1986, Kubrick was filming a Vietnam epic, the oddly titled *Full Metal Jacket*.

Born: July 26, 1928, in New York City
Height: 5 ft. 9 in.
Weight: 165 lbs.
Eyes: Brown
Hair: Dark brown
Zodiac: Leo
Education: High school
Religion: Jewish
Marriages: Three. Currently to Suzanne Harlan
Children: Anya, Vivian, Katherine
Interests: Work
Personal Habits and Traits: Chain smoker and moderate drinker, a fiendish worker, demanding
Address: Borehamwood, England
Income: $2 million per film (minimum estimate)

L

Cheryl Ladd

"There is only one Farrah Fawcett, and how do you replace a phenomenon?"

Farrah Fawcett's hair apparent, Cheryl Stoppelmoor, was the daughter of a train engineer operating out of Huron, South Dakota, and an ex-waitress who fostered her child's dreams of making it in Hollywood. Cheryl became the class drama nut and in high school divided her off hours between carhopping at a neighborhood drive-in and singing with a local group called The Music Shop. She later provided the voice of one of the Pussycats in the TV cartoon series *Josie and the Pussycats* and shot 100 commercials before her unsuccessful screen test for the hit series *Family* (Meredith Baxter Birney got the part) caught the eye of *Charlie's Angels* producer Aaron Spelling. When Farrah decided to leave the show for bigger things, Spelling chose the shapely Cheryl to replace her. More intelligent and talented than her predecessor, Cheryl easily settled into the Angel role and in addition found time and energy to pursue, with little success, a recording career. Meanwhile, she married actor David Ladd, handsome son of Alan and brother of Twentieth Century-Fox chief Alan, Jr. Ever-conscious of the strain her sudden stardom could put on the Ladd's marriage, Cheryl posted a sign in their kitchen: LOVE IS EATING OUT SO YOUR HUSBAND DOESN'T HAVE TO COOK DINNER. That notwithstanding, their marriage lasted barely two years after she hit the jackpot. In 1981, Ladd married her ex-husband's best friend, Scottish-born songwriter Brian Russell. Her lackluster credits for the '80s include a TV bio of Princess Grace and the TV movie *Death in California*.

Born: April 2, 1950, in Huron, South Dakota
Height: 5 ft. 4 in.
Weight: 100 lbs.
Eyes: Blue
Hair: Blond
Zodiac: Aries
Education: High school
Religion: Protestant
Marriages:
To David Ladd (1973–1979)
To Brian Russell (1981–)
Children: Daughter Jordan (b. 1975)
Interests: Exercise, music, art, swimming
Personal Habits and Traits: Nonsmoker, drinks Perrier, loves Hershey bars
Address: Hollywood Hills, California
Income: $370,000 (estimate)

Burt Lancaster

On why he doesn't do more films:
"I'm too rich to bother."

The burly Irishman from East Harlem started out a scrappy dead-end kid, won a scholarship to New York University and dropped out after two years to join the circus as a trapeze artist—an experience that proved invaluable when he filmed *Trapeze* two decades later. Disappointed because he was not succeeding as an acrobat, he tried selling ladies' lingerie in a department store and shortly thereafter was discovered in an elevator by Hollywood agent Harold Hecht. An instant star in 1946's *The Killers,* he grinned and grimaced his way through *Brute Force, From Here to Eternity, Sweet Smell of Success, Birdman of Alcatraz, Seven Days in May, The Swimmer, Twilight's Last Gleaming, Buffalo Bill and the Indians* and Bernardo Bertolucci's controversial *1900.* Along the way he claimed an Oscar for *Elmer Gantry.* To prepare for his role in CBS's six-part *Moses the Lawgiver,* Lancaster immersed himself in the writings of Jewish philosopher Martin Buber. After a brief marriage to another circus acrobat, he met Norma Anderson while entertaining troops on a USO circus tour during World War II. They produced five children before their divorce in 1969, and since then he has kept company with Jackie Bone, in whose custody he was released after being arrested for drunken driving in 1971. He reciprocated four years later by bailing Bone out of a Rome jail after her dispute with a traffic cop. In film dramas like *Atlantic City* and *Some Kind of Hero,* Lancaster reaffirmed his status as one of his generation's most underrated actors, though he is best known to a whole new generation as the TV pitchperson for MCI.

Born: November 2, 1913, in East Harlem (New York City)
Height: 6 ft.
Weight: 200 lbs.
Eyes: Blue
Hair: Brown
Zodiac: Scorpio
Education: New York University (two years)
Religion: Roman Catholic
Marriages: Two (both ended in divorce)
Children: Five
Interests: Literature, politics, theology, acrobatics, animals
Personal Habits and Traits: Gave up smoking, hard drinker, early riser, a perfectionist, scrapper
Address: Los Angeles
Income: $400,000+

Ann Landers

Esther "Eppie" Pauline Friedman Lederer

"After years of advising other people on their personal problems, I was stunned by my own divorce. I only wish I had someone to write to for help."

Sprouting up in Sioux City, Iowa, Esther ("Eppie") Pauline Friedman and her identical twin sister Pauline ("Popo") Esther Friedman were so used to being stared at as youngsters that "it never seemed any different" when they both became national celebrities in their own right. In school they dressed alike and sometimes attended each other's classes, but once out of college Eppie and Popo became one another's fiercest professional competitors—Eppie as Ann Landers and Popo as Abigail ("Dear Abby") Van Buren. As Ann Landers, a name and column Eppie assumed at the *Chicago Sun-Times* in 1955, she maintains a slight readership edge (she is syndicated in more than 1,000 papers) over her sister. In 1966, Landers was presented with the President's Citation of the National Council on Alcoholism, and two years later was named by the Gallup Poll as one of the 20 most admired women in the world. After more than 20 years of marriage, she found herself in need of advice when her marriage to Budget Rent-a-Car tycoon Jules Lederer crumbled. Their daughter, Margot, who married actor Ken (*White Shadow*) Howard, recounted the whole painful affair in her bestselling biography of Mom, entitled *Eppie*. Happily based in Chicago, Landers lives in a luxurious high-rise and is ferried from home to office by Rolls-Royce limousine. One of her more surprising polls, conducted in 1985, revealed that most women prefer "dinner at a nice restaurant" to sex.

Born: July 4, 1918, in Sioux City, Iowa
Height: 5 ft. 5½ in.
Weight: 118 lbs.
Eyes: Brown
Hair: Dark brown
Zodiac: Cancer
Education: Morningside College (1936–1939)
Religion: Jewish
Marriages: To Jules Lederer (divorced)
Children: Margo
Interests: Charities, Combating alcoholism and drug abuse, fashion, theater
Personal Habits and Traits: Does not smoke or drink, a perfectionist and a workaholic
Address: Chicago
Income: $900,000 (estimate)

Michael Landon

Eugene Orowitz

"If Michael Landon bombs, I don't want anyone else to take the blame but Michael Landon."

Little House on the Prairie it wasn't. Growing up a skinny kid in the blue-collar town of Collingswood, New Jersey, Eugene "Oogie" Orowitz and the only other

Jewish kid in his 8th-grade class were forced to clean the chalkboard and erasers while their Christian classmates were let out of school early to attend their weekly services. There were no dates in high school—Christian fathers would not let their daughters go out with a Jew—and his parents' loveless marriage created enough anxieties to keep him wetting the bed well into his teens. A track scholarship got him to USC at 17, and after he dropped out the next year he worked as a blanket salesman, process server, warehouse stock boy, factory hand, and car washer. He eventually changed his name to Michael Landon, toured the country as a teen singer with Jerry Lee Lewis and made his movie debut growling the title role in *I Was a Teenage Werewolf.* At 22, Landon began a 13-year stint as Little Joe in *Bonanza.* One year after hanging up his Stetson, Landon was in a hit show again, this time as the solid-as-a-rock character of Charles Ingalls in *Little House on the Prairie,* for which he would also serve as executive producer, frequent writer-director and story editor over the show's 11-year run. Almost as soon as *Little House* closed its doors for good, Landon was back—this time playing a guardian angel in the critically panned but top-rated series *Highway to Heaven.* There were, however, many painful personal detours along the way. His first two marriages ended in divorce, and at one point he not only battled his own dependence on Miltowns, but watched helplessly as his then-19-year-old stepdaughter Cheryl nearly died of a drug overdose. Landon reacted by becoming an outspoken crusader against drug abuse. As he entered his 50s, Eugene Orowitz from Collingswood, N.J., ranked as one of the most powerful men in television—and one of the wealthiest. His not-so-little $10 million Beverly Hills house features a library, a projection room, 13 bathrooms, two maids' quarters, an English pub room, and a *Bonanza* room filled with mementos from the Ponderosa, including the outhouse.

Born: October 31, 1936, in Forest Hills, New York
Height: 5 ft. 11 in.
Weight: 165
Eyes: Green
Hair: Brown
Zodiac: Scorpio
Education: One year at the University of Southern California
Religion: Jewish
Marriages:
To Dodie Fraser (divorced in 1962)
To Lynn Noe (1962–1981)
To Cindy Clerico (1983–)
Children: Eight: Mark, Josh, Cheryl, Mike J., Leslie Ann, Shawna Leigh, Christopher Beau, and Jennifer
Interests: Writing, directing, producing, Republican politics, combating drug abuse, golf, cooking (favorite recipe: Texas chili)
Personal Habits and Traits: Workaholic (works 16 hours a day), guarded, considered abrasive and temperamental, works out daily
Addresses: Beverly Hills; Malibu, California
Income: $665,113 per *month*

Jessica Lange

"When you learn not to want things so badly, life comes to you."

Playing second banana to a big ape in the 1976 remake of *King Kong* practically did in her career—and her life (when one of Kong's 1,650-pound mechanical arms caressed Lange and almost broke her neck). The Cloquet, Minnesota-born actress was left with small roles in Bob Fosse's autobiographical *All That Jazz* and in *How to Beat the High Cost of Living*. Lange fared little better with another remake, *The Postman Always Rings Twice*. But she finally rebounded in 1982 with *Frances,* the gut-wrenching story of Frances Farmer, the 1930s actress whose leftist politics and fierce independence led to alcoholism, mental problems, and, finally, a lobotomy. The same year, Lange also appeared on the big screen in the Dustin Hoffman transvestite smash *Tootsie*. Receiving Academy Award nominations for both, she won in the Best Supporting category for *Tootsie*. With the monkey at last off her back, Lange returned to her $90,000 "log cabin" near her parents' Minnesota home to savor her success. Split from Spanish-born photographer Paco Grande, she followed up Fosse with ballet superstar Mikhail Baryshnikov (father of Lange's daughter, Alexandra) and actor-playwright Sam Shepard. The self-described ugly duckling with the "boxer's nose" (the result of banging it into a parking meter) took her passion for her rural roots to the moviegoing public with 1984's *Country,* for which she won yet another Academy Award nomination. No sooner was filming on *Sweet Dreams,* her screen bio of country singer Patsy Cline completed, than work on her second child, this time by Shepard, had begun.

Born: April 20, 1949, in Cloquet, Minnesota
Height: 5 ft. 7½ in.
Weight: 120 lbs.
Eyes: Hazel
Hair: Blond
Zodiac: Aries
Education: High school
Marriages: To Paco Grande (1970–1981)
Children: Alexandra (b. 1981)
Interests: Art, antiques
Personal Habits and Traits: Nearsighted (nickname: "Blinky"), introspective, light drinker, early riser
Addresses: New York City; Los Angeles; Nickerson, Minnesota; Taos, New Mexico
Income: $2 million (minimum estimate.)

Angela Lansbury

"I just stopped playing bitches on wheels and people's mothers. I have only a few more years to kick up my heels!"

During the London blitz, she was evacuated to the United States with the rest of her family in 1940. By the time she landed her first screen role—as the petulant Cockney maid in the classic 1942 film *Gaslight,* Angela Lansbury had already performed in nightclubs in Montreal and Manhattan, worked in the wrapping department at Bullock's and knocked on every studio door in Hollywood. And she was not yet 18. During a remarkable film career that spanned the next four decades, she invariably played, as she puts it, "venal bitches" or somebody's mother. For example, she portrayed Laurence Harvey's Machiavellian mom in *The Manchurian Candidate* even though, at 34, he was only three years younger. No matter. The part, one of her favorites, earned Lansbury a third Academy Award nomination (in addition to the ones she had already received for *Gaslight* and *The Picture of Dorian Gray*). At the age of 41, she tried out for and won the lead in *Mame,* the smash musical version of *Auntie Mame,* and managed to cop a Tony for herself in that role and for *Dear World* two years later. Then—in the space of a single year—her mother died of throat cancer, the family house burned down in one of the most devastating fires to hit Malibu, and her children became casualties of the drug scene. Dropping out for a time, she moved the entire family to a 150-year-old farmhouse in Ireland. She describes that period as "fabulous," and by 1974 Lansbury was ready to return to the Great White Way in a triumphant revival of *Gypsy* (Tony No. 3). Before undertaking Stephen Sondheim's *Sweeney Todd,* for which she won yet another Tony, the star of *Dark at the Top of the Stairs, All Fall Down* and *Death on the Nile* substituted for six weeks as Anna in the 1978 revival of *The King and I.* At 59, Lansbury reinvented herself once again, making a career switch to the medium she had for the most part avoided. Ironically, as Down East supersleuth Jessica Fletch in the prime time mystery series *Murder, She Wrote,* Lansbury achieved her greatest popularity. The show proved such a hit that it trounced Steven Spielberg's much-ballyhooed *Amazing Stories* in the ratings, routinely landing in the top three—right behind Bill Cosby and *Family Ties.* Lansbury, who does her own make-up and cuts and dyes her own hair, says her show owes its phenomenal international popularity (*Murder, She Wrote* is also a major hit in Europe) in large part to the appeal of the character she plays. "There are a lot of middle-aged women out there," she explains, "who are thrilled to see someone in their age bracket depicted in a positive up-beat way."

Born: October 16, 1925, in London
Height: 5 ft. 9 in.
Weight: 140 lbs.
Eyes: Blue
Hair: Reddish-blond
Zodiac: Libra
Religion: Anglican
Marriages: Peter Shaw (1949–)
Children: Anthony (b. 1952), Deidre Angela (b. 1953)
Interests: Gardening, family violence (she supports a shelter for battered wives in Chicago)
Personal habits and traits: Quit smoking and drinking, early riser, cat lover, leans toward "English shabby" furniture
Address: Los Angeles
Income: $1 million +

Louise Lasser

"In California, they confiscate everybody's books at the airport—to see if they can make a movie out of them."

After 15 years of therapy and four years of marriage to Woody Allen, Louise Lasser trundled her heavy load of neuroses onto the set of a daring new Norman

Lear soap opera spoof called *Mary Hartman, Mary Hartman.* The spaced-out Mary, in puffed sleeves and braids, coped—or didn't cope—with everything from her husband's impotence to ring around the collar. The series rescued Lasser from shooting Nyquil commercials ("You're a good wife, Mildred") and an occasional movie role (Allen's *Bananas, Slither*) and propelled her into TV superstardom and cult-figure status. At the height of the show's popularity in 1976 she was busted for cocaine possession while shopping for an antique doll house and was sentenced to spend six months in a special drug program; she satisfied that requirement by merely continuing to see her own psychiatrist. The pampered only child of millionaire tax expert S. Jay Lasser—after her parents divorced, her mother committed suicide—Louise spent three years at Brandeis, then dropped out to study acting. After an Elaine May revue and a couple of Broadway musical flops, Lasser married Woody Allen, and they lurched along for four years until their split in 1970. Lear canned *Mary Hartman* after one hit season, and Lasser, avoiding such spinoffs as *Forever Fernwood* and *Fernwood 2-Nite,* channeled her energy back into movies—and into eating; she ballooned in weight, then became the voice of Weight Watchers on the organization's television spots. Having nervously adjusted to a Southern California life-style, Lasser shared rented homes in Benedict Canyon and Malibu with her mongrel Kefir. Appropriately enough, Kefir's previous owner was the late Wally Cox.

Born: 1941 in New York City
Height: 5 ft. 7½ in.
Weight: 135 lbs.
Eyes: Blue
Hair: Reddish blond
Education: Three years at Brandeis University
Religion: Jewish
Marriages: To Woody Allen (1966–1970)
Children: None
Interests: Singing, acting
Habits: Still chain-smokes, is a sometimes maddening perfectionist, a starer—"I stare at the fireplace, the ocean, the dog."
Addresses: Benedict Canyon, California; Malibu, California
Income: $100,000+

Cyndi Lauper

"My gift to society is not getting a driver's license."

It's a rags-to-rags success story. Cyndi Lauper's aptly named 1984 debut album, *She's So Unusual,* thrust this Queens-bred belter with the Betty Boop voice and multicolored coif onto center stage as the Clown Princess of Rock—and brought her $4 million in the process. Impressive, considering that not long before, after cutting a record with a group called Blue Angel that promptly "went lead," she declared personal bankruptcy and had to work behind the counter of a vintage clothing store to pay the rent. Her parents were divorced when Cyndi was 5, and Lauper remembers a lonely childhood waiting for her mother to return home from her series of waitressing jobs. By the time she ran away from home at 17, Lauper had been through booze, drugs, malnutrition, dehydration, and a series of auto accidents. She spent a year at a small college in Vermont ("It was like *Walt Disney Presents*"), then began singing with a number of bands before forming

Blue Angel. After filing for bankruptcy in 1981, she met David Wolff, who became her manager and boyfriend, and the two shrewdly planned to capitalize on Cyndi's thrift-shop chic in a series of videos for the newly popular MTV cable channel. The scheme worked: Singles like "Girls Just Want to Have Fun," "Time After Time," "She Bop," "Money Changes Everything," and "Goonies 'R' Good Enough" went to the top of the charts, won Lauper a Best New Artist Grammy, and netted several video music awards as well. As if she weren't visible enough, Lauper also hyped the wrestling craze by sponsoring her own lady wrestler in a series of grudge matches against another female wrestler managed by her alleged nemesis, "Captain" Lou Albano. Now that she's got plenty of it, does Lauper believe that "Money Changes Everything"? "After watching *Lifestyles of the Rich and Famous,* said the girl who once cleaned out kennels and worked in a Japanese nightclub, "I decided on all linoleum floors, maybe even the kind that look like brick. Forget parquet. Linoleum you wax and it shines. You don't get splinters."

Born: June 20, 1953, in Brooklyn
Height: 5 ft. 3 in.
Weight: 108 lbs.
Eyes: Blue
Hair: Indeterminate
Zodiac: Gemini
Education: One year of college
Religion: Roman Catholic
Marriages: None
Children: None
Interests: Wrestling, vintage clothes, laundry, old movies, cards, miniature golf
Habits: Night person, doesn't smoke or drink
Address: New York City
Income: $5 million+

Steve Lawrence

Sidney Liebowitz

"There really isn't a Steve Lawrence, you know. Eydie's a ventriloquist."

The son of a Brooklyn cantor, Sidney Liebowitz sang at his father's synagogue. "Discovered" (after three unsuccessful auditions) on Arthur Godfrey's *Talent Scouts,* Lawrence made his acting debut in a summer stock production of *Pal Joey,* played the driven Mr. Glick in *What Makes Sammy Run*? and met Eydie Gorme when they both were signed as TV regulars on Steve Allen's *Tonight Show.* It was not exactly love at first sight, but after four years the two singers warmed to each other and were married in 1957. They performed together in a Broadway hit called *Golden Rainbow,* then set out on the nightclub trail. By the late 1960s, Steve and Eydie had become a show business institution and one of Las Vegas's top headline acts. While Gorme racked up several gold records and a Grammy of her own (in 1967 for "If He Walked into My Life"), Lawrence scored with the smash single "Go Away, Little Girl" and became a fixture on TV's *The Carol Burnett Show.* The "Steve 'n Eydie" image continues to charm the over-40 set, and if the pipes have gotten a little rusty, his easy professional style remains. There was an outpouring of sympathy from friends and fans alike when the couple's younger son, Michael, died in 1986 at the age of 23.

Born: July 8, 1935, in Brooklyn, New York
Height: 5 ft. 9 in.
Weight: 140 lbs.
Eyes: Brown
Hair: Brown
Zodiac: Cancer
Education: High school
Religion: Jewish
Marriages: To Eydie Gorme (1957–)
Children: David (b. 1960), Michael (1962–1986)
Interests: Cars, tennis, various charities
Personal Habits and Traits: Smokes, a social drinker and partygoer
Address: Beverly Hills
Income: $500,000+ (minimum estimate)

Cloris Leachman

"I think husbands and wives should live in separate houses. If there's enough money, the children should live in a third."

"Of course it's my real name. Would anyone in his right mind change it *to* Cloris Leachman?" The wacky star of her own spinoff TV series in the mid-1970s, *Phyllis,* Leachman was 11 when she hitchhiked with her parents' blessing from her childhood home in Des Moines to nearby Drake University. There she won her first part—in a children's radio show. She enrolled at Northwestern on a drama scholarship at 15, and six years later competed as Miss Chicago in the 1946 Miss America Pageant in Atlantic City. The Actors Studio followed, as well as a long series of minor roles on stage and television that even included a brief stint as one of Lassie's many TV mothers. Genuine stardom arrived only at 46, when Leachman was awarded an Oscar for her portrayal of the desperate, affection-starved wife of a high school basketball coach in 1972's *The Last Picture Show.* At about the same time, she received one Emmy as Mary Tyler Moore's rotten neighbor Phyllis and another for the made-for-TV drama *A Brand New Life.* Her *Phyllis,* one of several successful spinoffs from *The Mary Tyler Moore Show,* soared straight to the top of the Nielsens in 1975. On film Leachman played Cybill Shepherd's social-climbing mother in Peter Bogdanovich's *Daisy Miller* and a sadistic frau in Mel Brooks's zany *Young Frankenstein.* Off camera she is one of Hollywood's certifiable crazies. Her rollercoaster marriage to producer George Englund (they were married in 1953 and experienced a series of separations) finally rolled to a stop when they filed for divorce in 1978, and personal tragedy struck when—like former costar Mary Tyler Moore—Leachman confronted the untimely death of her actor son.

Born: April 30, 1925, in Des Moines, Iowa
Height: 5 ft. 7 in.
Weight: 115 lbs.
Eyes: Grayish-green
Hair: Blond
Zodiac: Taurus
Education: Northwestern University
Religion: Protestant
Marriages: To George Englund (1953–1978)
Children: Four sons and a daughter
Interests: Music, cooking, gardening, five kids and a basset-schnauzer named Captain Bobby Snout
Personal Habits and Traits: A strict vegetarian, vehemently antismoking, does drink moderately
Address: Mandeville Canyon, California
Income: $300,000 (minimum estimate)

Norman Lear

"I never forgave my father for being a bigot."

Born and raised in New Haven, Connecticut, this television mogul based the character of Archie Bunker on his own father, and Beatrice Arthur's Maude bears more than a passing resemblance to Lear's own liberated spouse, Frances. Lear dropped out of Emerson College to join the Army during World War II and was already a top writer for comics like Danny Thomas, George Gobel, and the Martin & Lewis team when his first marriage collapsed. In 1955 he met Frances, a twice-divorced sportswear buyer for Lord & Taylor who called to invite him out, and as soon as his divorce became final in Las Vegas they were married. After writing movies like *The Night They Raided Minsky's,* he borrowed a concept from a BBC sitcom called *Till Death Do Us Part* and Americanized it. *All in the Family* satirized bigotry and burning issues, and it changed the face of prime time. It also led to a virtual outpouring of hit shows by Lear and his partner, Bud Yorkin: *Sanford and Son, Maude,* an *All in the Family* spinoff called *The Jeffersons,* a *Maude,* spinoff called *Good Times, One Day at a Time, All's Fair, Mary Hartman, Mary Hartman,* and spinoffs *Fernwood 2-Nite* and *America 2-Nite.* After a series of disappointments—most notably the series *a.k.a. Pablo*—Lear bought Embassy Pictures. Constantly battling network censorship, Lear is a confessed knee-jerk liberal who heads the American Civil Liberties Foundation in Southern California. His proudest political moment came with his inclusion on a Richard Nixon enemies list. Frances, in turn, runs her own executive placement agency for minorities and women.

Born: July 27, 1922, in New Haven, Connecticut
Height: 5 ft. 9 in.
Weight: 163 lbs.
Eyes: Brown
Hair: White
Zodiac: Leo
Education: Dropped out of Emerson College
Religion: Jewish
Marriages: Two. Currently to Frances Lear
Children: Ellen (by first wife); Kate (b. 1958), Maggie (b. 1960)
Interests: Civil liberties, women's rights, Democratic party politics, tennis, travel (always takes a vacation without his wife)
Personal Habits and Traits: Smokes, moderate drinker, unflappable
Address: Beverly Hills
Income: $3 million (minimum estimate)

Jack Lemmon

"Nobody deserves this much money—certainly not an actor."

Nervous Mr. Niceguy in Billy Wilder comedies like *Some Like It Hot, The Apartment,* and *Irma La Douce,* Jack Lemmon won a Best Supporting Actor Oscar as Ensign Pulver in Mr. Roberts. But it was chiefly as the lush in *Days of Wine and Roses* and the opportunistic garment company owner in *Save the Tiger* (for which he won the Best Actor Oscar in 1973) that Lemmon established himself as one of the highest-powered dramatic talents of his generation. Lemmon was born in a hospital elevator, suffered from a painful hernia as an infant, developed jaundice and grew up chronically anxious and skittery. New England-bred, he released his nervous energy in music and acting at Andover and Harvard. Once in New York, he worked as a singing waiter at a beer parlor before doing radio soaps, live television, and a part in the film *It Should Happen to You*. After his string of lighthearted Billy Wilder hits he experienced a fallow two-year period in the early 1970s during which he made no movies at all. *Save the Tiger* catapulted Lemmon back on top, although he didn't abandon comedies altogether; he exhibited his old and very flappable self in a 1974 remake of *The Front Page* and two movies by Neil Simon, *The Out-of-Towners* and *Prisoner of Second Avenue*. Married to second wife Felicia Farr since 1963, Lemmon lives in a $1 million Beverly Hills mansion, drives a Rolls-Royce, and finds time for an occasional weekend at his $200,000 beach house in Trancas. In 1978 Lemmon made a triumphant return to the Broadway stage playing a doomed actor in *Tribute* (a role he would recreate on film), and turned in harrowing performances as a distraught nuclear plant foreman in the prophetic *China Syndrome* and a father hunting for his murdered son in Costa-Gavras's controversial *Missing*. Lemmon was true to form as the had-it-up-to-here-with-hypocrisy priest in *Mass Appeal*, and returned to Broadway in a 1985 production of Eugene O'Neill's *Long Day's Journey into Night*.

Born: February 8, 1925, in Newton Center, Massachusetts
Height: 5 ft. 10 in.
Weight: 160 lbs.
Eyes: Blue
Hair: Gray-brown
Zodiac: Aquarius
Education: Phillips Andover and Harvard University
Religion: Protestant
Marriages:
To Cynthia Stone (1950–1956)
To Felicia Farr (1962–)
Children: Christopher (by Stone); Courtney (by Farr)
Interests: Piano (he recorded an album of Gershwin and Cole Porter tunes), composing
Personal Habits and Traits: Smokes cigars, not exactly a teetotaler, is full of nervous tics, faultlessly polite
Addresses: Beverly Hills; Trancas
Income: $1.5 million+

David Letterman

"I just keep waiting for someone to tap me on the shoulder and say, 'Okay, buddy, give us the money back.' "

More than half his audience was born after World War II—the sort of Baby Boomer demographics that give advertising agency executives everywhere a rush. The fans who show up in NBC's Studio 6A applaud wildly when Paul Shaffer's band strikes up the show's R&B theme and announcer Bill Wendell says, "And now, a man who is frightened by the slightest change in air temperature, David Letterman." The gap-toothed crown prince of late night then

proceeds to engage in such stunts as dropping watermelons off the tops of buildings, dressing up in a Velcro suit and sticking himself to a wall, and using a megaphone to summon passersby on the street below to come up and appear on the show. Indeed, Letterman's guests (not to mention regulars like New York accountant cum comic Larry "Bud" Melman) are hard to outclass in the weird department. In addition to his "stupid pet tricks" segments, Letterman has interviewed the likes of a man who flew to an altitude of 15,000 feet in a lawn chair and a woman who claimed to have gone shopping on Venus. All of which earns him in excess of $1 million per year. Not bad for a guy who as recently as 1974 was fired from his $15,000-a-year job as an Indianapolis weatherman for, among other things, reporting that the city was being pelted by hailstones "the size of canned hams." Born in Indianapolis, where his father owned a flower shop and his mother was a secretary at the Second Presbyterian Church, Letterman was not yet out of high school before deciding his lifetime ambition was to become a talk-show host. Majoring in radio and television at Ball State University in Muncie, Indiana, he joined a fraternity and married his sweetheart before graduating in 1970. After the weatherman stint, he spent a year as a local radio talk jockey before making the decision to split for L.A. There, Jimmy "J.J." Walker" spotted him onstage at the Comedy Store, and hired Letterman as a writer at $150 a week. Bob Hope and Paul Lynde followed suit, but as Letterman's career took off, his marriage deteriorated, ending in a 1978 divorce. Then came a fateful appearance on *The Tonight Show,* and within months Letterman was being touted as a permanent replacement for Johnny Carson. Instead, he got a morning show of his own, which failed miserably. Enter Fred Silverman, then head of NBC, who offered Letterman a staggering $650,000 a year just to wait around for the right slot to open up. It did, late in 1981, when Tom Snyder's *Tomorrow* show was cancelled. *The David Letterman Show* was launched, and was an immediate success. So too has been his relationship with the show's longtime head writer, Merrill Markoe. They divide their year between homes in Malibu and Connecticut. A favorite pastime: Watching the Jerry Lewis telethon. "A volatile guy with no sleep in front of a live Las Vegas audience—you just don't get that kind of excitement anywhere else." Least favorite guest: Andy Rooney.

Born: April 12, 1947, in Indianapolis
Height: 6 ft.
Weight: 165 lbs.
Eyes: Blue
Hair: Brown
Zodiac: Aries
Education: Ball State University
Religion: Presbyterian

Marriages: To Michelle Cook (1969–1978)
Children: None
Interests: Baseball, carpentry
Personal Habits and Traits: Drinks beer, messy, chronic worrier
Addresses: Connecticut; Malibu, California
Income: $1 million +

Emmanuel Lewis

"If it's right for me to grow, it'll come. Even if you rushed it, you'd still have to wait, because God already planned it."

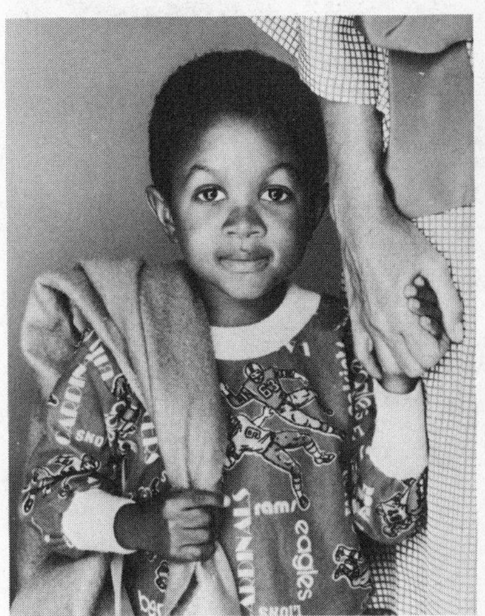

Gary Coleman's successor as the cutest kid on the Nielsen block was raised in Brooklyn by his divorced mother, an ex-computer programmer. When Emmanuel was nine, an actor friend suggested to his mother that he get into the business. Soon he was chosen over 150 other kids for a Campbell's soup ad, the first of his more than 40 commercials. An NBC executive caught one of Lewis's Burger King spots, and cast him in the title role of an orphaned 7-year-old adopted by Alex Karras and Karras's real-life wife Susan Clark in *Webster*. Lewis attends a public junior high in Brooklyn for kids involved in the arts, but his best pal has been out of school for some time now—Michael Jackson and Lewis met during the taping of Jackson's *Thriller* video, and from then on the Gloved One would frequently be seen dandying little Emmanuel on his knee like his very own flesh-and-blood Charlie McCarthy. Though he veers between acting Webster's age ("Mommy says . . .") and his own ("Be cool, Mom, just keep on walkin' and smilin'"), Lewis was tiny enough at 3 feet 6 inches and a little over 40 pounds to convince TV viewers that he was an eternal imp. His mother, who is about 5 feet tall, insists that there is no medical reason for her son's height; Emmanuel's brother Roscoe was Emmanuel's size until age 13, when he shot up to 6 feet 1 inch. Meantime, Lewis is making the most of his diminutive stature. "If I'm small right now," he shrugs, "it's got to be for a reason."

Born: March 9, 1971, in Brooklyn, New York
Height: In 1985, 3 ft. 6 in.
Weight: 40 pounds
Eyes: Brown
Hair: Black
Zodiac: Pisces
Religion: Baptist
Personal Habits and Traits: Takes afternoon nap before taping *Webster*, collects teddy bears
Address: Brooklyn, New York
Income: $1 million

Jerry Lewis

Joey Levitch

"When the light goes on in the refrigerator, I do 20 minutes."

When on his 29th wedding anniversary in 1973 Jerry Lewis stood in the bathroom of his Bel Air mansion and put the muzzle of a .38-caliber revolver in his mouth, only the sound of his children laughing kept him from pulling the trigger. Lewis had been driven to the verge of suicide by his addiction to the pain-killer Percodan, which he began to rely on after chipping a bone in his upper

spinal column while taking a Vegas pratfall in 1965. Fourteen years elapsed before Lewis, also suffering from a potentially fatal ulcer, confronted and kicked his addiction with the help of heart specialist Michael DeBakey, but it came as no surprise to many that Lewis had been suffering from severe emotional problems. Manic, abrasive, and shouldering massive insecurities, Jerry Lewis is clearly not one of the best-loved members of the Hollywood community. Born Joey Levitch in Newark, he started out at five singing on the Borscht Belt circuit with his vaudevillian father. While a cheerleader at Irvington High he developed his loony stand-up routine in one joint after another until it all came together at Brown's Hotel in the Catskills. In 1946, while working in Atlantic City, Lewis met an Italian singer named Dean Martin, and the act they put together became one of the most successful partnerships in show business history. It lasted a decade before differences busted up the pair in 1956. Although Lewis was expected to soar solo while his straight-man partner floundered, it was Martin who fared spectacularly well on his own. After some 40 movies—with and without Dean—Lewis set up the Jerry Lewis/Network Cinema Corporation, a chain of some 200 automated movie houses in the United States and France (where he is worshiped as a comedy genius second only to Charlie Chaplin). In 1976, Lewis's attempt to revive *Hellzapoppin* on Broadway folded before it ever got to the Great White Way. Still one of Las Vegas's biggest headliners and a top draw on the concert circuit, the master mugger is also perhaps the most effective fundraiser ever; his annual Muscular Dystrophy Telethons had drawn over $300 million in donations by 1980. Among his better-known films are *My Friend Irma, The Nutty Professor, Geisha Boy, Cinderfella, The Caddy, The Family Jewels,* and *Hook, Line and Sinker.* Yet the performance that rang truest was undoubtedly *King of Comedy,* in which Lewis played an obnoxious talk-show host who is kidnapped by a crazed would-be comic named Rupert Pupkin (played by Robert De Niro). Following emergency open heart surgery (he was clinically dead for seconds), Lewis returned to work, this time behind the camera directing episodes of HBO's hit series *Brothers.*

Born: March 16, 1926, in Newark, New Jersey
Height: 5 ft. 11 in.
Weight: 175 lbs.
Eyes: Brown
Hair: Black
Zodiac: Pisces
Education: High school dropout
Religion: Jewish
Marriages:
To Patti Palmer (1944–1980)
To Sandra "Sam" Pitnick (1983–)
Children: Gary, Ronnie, Scott, Christopher, Anthony, Joseph
Interests: Muscular Dystrophy (a building bears his name at the UCLA Medical Center), music, producing and directing, yachting
Personal Habits and Traits: Quit smoking, not a teetotaler (prefers Scotch), chronic worrier, perfectionist, a night person
Address: Beverly Hills
Income: $1.3 million (minimum estimate)

Liberace

Wladziu Valentino Liberace

"Wisecracks lifted my income from $150 a week to more than $2 million a year. You know the bank I used to go crying to? Now I own it."

Wladziu Valentino Liberace had an Italian father who played the French horn and a Polish mother with whom he remained extraordinarily close. Starting out on the piano as Walter Busterkeys, he combined a hammy style of performing with a natural flair for outlandish costumes (blinding sequins, gold lamé, and mink are particular favorites) and parlayed them into one of the highest-paying acts in show business. His candelabra (used "for inspiration"), white Steinways (he later graduated to clear plastic), a piano-shaped swimming pool, and saccharine delivery caught the imagination of over-40 female fans. A veritable matinee idol during his hit television show in the 1950s, Liberace switched to concerts and Las Vegas, where he routinely packs them in. He smashed house records when he appeared at Radio City Music Hall in 1983, but the triumph was tarnished somewhat when his ex-bodyguard filed for palimony, claiming they had been lovers. Always an easy target for ridicule, Liberace resorted to a classic riposte early in his career: "They've got me crying—all the way to the bank."

Born: May 16, 1919, in West Allis, Wisconsin
Height: 6 ft.
Weight: 180 lbs.
Eyes: Brown
Hair: Brown
Zodiac: Taurus
Education: High school
Religion: Roman Catholic
Marriages: None
Children: None
Interests: Cooking, reading, films, composing, automobiles, dogs
Personal Habits and Traits: Nonsmoker, teetotaler, a workaholic, needs little sleep, lavishes gifts on friends, has a sweet tooth, has undergone several face-lifts
Address: Beverly Hills; Palm Springs, California; Las Vegas; New York City
Income: $2.5 million+

Hal Linden

Hal Lipshitz

"It was so easy to raise my family when I was not a 'success.' It took so long—about 20 years—but I'm not complaining."

ABC-TV's *Barney Miller* was actually Hal Lipshitz from the Bronx, who earned a college business degree, but preferred singing and playing saxophone with several big bands (including Sammy Kaye's) in the late 1940s and early 1950s. Though he proved a hit in 1958's *Bells Are Ringing on Broadway,* Linden's next major triumph did not occur until his Tony Award-winning performance in 1971's *The Rothschilds.* After doing dubbing for foreign films (like the X-rated *I*

Am Curious Yellow and *Z*), Linden landed the Barney Miller role in 1975. Unconvinced that the show would survive, he maintained his family in a five-bedroom Manhattan co-op while he commuted to Hollywood. The following summer, Linden took his wife, Fran, and their four children on a photographic safari in South Africa—and landed in the middle of the Soweto race riots. The Lindens made it to Kenya safely, where—as in other parts of Africa—he was continually asked for his autograph. After ABC closed up the precinct house in 1981, Linden acted in a few made-for-TV movies and hosted the daily FYI news feature spots on CBS before returning to episodic television with Harry (M*A*S*H) Morgan in NBC's *Blacke's Magic*.

Born: March 20, 1931, in New York City
Height: 6 ft. ¼ in.
Weight: 184 lbs.
Eyes: Brown
Hair: Gray
Zodiac: Pisces
Education: City College, B.S. in business administration
Religion: Jewish
Marriages: To Fran Martin (1958–)
Children: Amelia, Jennifer, Nora, Ian
Interests: The saxophone, singing, acting, movies, theater, photography, travel
Personal Habits and Traits: Nonsmoker, moderate drinker, early riser, easygoing
Address: Brentwood, California
Income: $1.8 million (estimate)

Rich Little

"Finding the right person wasn't that easy. Who wants to marry 135 different people?"

Back in his hometown of Ottawa, Rich Little used to crack up his classmates by imitating his teachers to their faces. "But none of the teachers ever caught on," he recalls, "because most people don't recognize themselves when they're being imitated." Fellow old-movie buff Mel Torme brought Little to Hollywood in the late 1960s, and from then on his staple impressions of John Wayne, Truman Capote, Paul Lynde, Richard Nixon, Johnny Carson, Cary Grant, Kirk Douglas, and Carol Channing earned him a million-dollar Las Vegas contract, countless guest shots on TV talk and game shows, and a short-lived NBC comedy hour of his own. Now up to 160 impressions, Little is always adding new personalities to his repertoire, and his working day often includes carefully examining videotapes of new personalities he wants to impersonate. Then he will walk along the beach near the Malibu home he shares with wife Jeanne and sheepdog Dudley, to practice his routine—like Capote giving his play-by-play rundown of a World Series game. As with many impressionists, Little will sometimes lapse into character inadvertently. When a car cut him off on the freeway, Little rolled down his window and in his best Paul Lynde manner clucked, "You're disgusting. Why don't you go report yourself?" A favorite pastime is answering the phone in anyone's voice but his own, from Jack Benny to Rod Steiger to Ronald Reagan.

Born: November 26, 1938, in Ottawa, Ontario
Height: 6 ft.
Weight: 175 lbs.
Eyes: Brown
Hair: Dark brown
Zodiac: Sagittarius
Education: High school
Religion: Protestant
Marriages: To Jeanne Worden (1971–)
Children: None
Interests: Old movies, trivia, pool
Personal Habits and Traits: Workaholic, social drinker
Address: Malibu, California
Income: $400,000 (estimate)

Kenny Loggins

"Sure, sadness can spark creativity. But so can happiness and love."

They had produced a number of hits like *Your Momma Don't Dance,* but after seven years the collaboration of Kenny Loggins and Jim Messina was no longer paying off for them creatively. So the rangy Loggins took off on his own in 1977, opening Fleetwood Mac's act until his first solo album, *Celebrate Me Home,* sold close to a million copies and established him as a stadium-filling headliner. Teaming up with Fleetwood's Stevie Nicks on "Whenever I Call You Friend," he recorded a second platinum LP, *Nightwatch.* Then came the rambunctious *This Is It,* and the biggest hit of his career: the Oscar-nominated title song from the movie "Footloose" (the soundtrack also yielded other Loggins hits, "Heart to Heart" and "I'm Free"). Born in Everett, Washington, Loggins's musical training consisted of three lessons with a Lawrence Welk guitarist and writing songs for the girls in his Catholic high school. Yet he eventually became one of the rock world's most talented songwriter-performers, composing "Please Come to Boston" (sung by his brother, David Loggins), and crafting two hits for Anne Murray, "Danny's Song" and "Love Song." Loggins, whose "Dangerzone" single from the film *Top Gun* soared into the top ten, kicked his habit of drinking an eight-ounce glass of tequila before each concert after finding domestic bliss with his Swedish-born wife, six-footer Eva Ein. The groupies that Loggins used to entertain must now look elsewhere—"except for the ones who only want to talk and not to go to bed."

Born: January 7, 1948, in Everett, Washington
Height: 6 ft. 4 in.
Weight: 170 lbs.
Eyes: Blue
Hair: Blond
Zodiac: Capricorn
Education: One semester at Pasadena City College
Religion: Roman Catholic
Marriages: To Eva Ein (current)
Children: Two boys
Interests: Guitar, composing
Personal Habits and Traits: Does not smoke, has cut down on his once heavy drinking
Address: Encino, California; Santa Barbara
Income: $3 million (estimate)

Sophia Loren

Sofia Scicolone

"Everything you see, I owe to spaghetti."

The world's wealthiest and (many believe) most beautiful actress was the illegitimate daughter of a would-be actress. A street waif in Naples during World War II, Sofia Scicolone was 14 when she and her mother moved to Rome to work as extras. There Sofia, known as Sofia Lazzaro, was spotted by producer Carlo Ponti, who changed her name to Loren and molded her career. *The Gold of Naples* boosted her to international star status in 1954, and after turning down a marriage proposal from *Houseboat* costar Cary Grant, three years later she wed Ponti—21 years her senior and four inches shorter—by proxy in Mexico. The Italian government and the Vatican refused to recognize Ponti's Mexican divorce from his first wife, and over the next nine years the Pontis expended some $2 million in legal fees to become French citizens and legally marry once and for all under French law. Starring in successful Ponti productions like *Marriage Italian Style* and *Yesterday, Today and Tomorrow,* she won an Oscar for her spellbinding performance in 1961's *Two Women.* With her acting career and his film company booming, they moved into a 16th-century Roman palace that they transformed into a spectacular 50-room villa. After an attempt to kidnap Ponti was thwarted by his bodyguards, and two heists totaling $1.07 million in jewelry (one in London and the other in New York, where two holdup men held a gun to Sophia's head and threatened her son), Loren and Ponti packed up and moved to a Paris penthouse. Shortly after he left Italy, Ponti was accused of illegally transferring millions of dollars out of the country, and eventually an Italian court fined him $50 million in absentia; she later returned to Italy to serve out a brief prison sentence. Loren, who had four miscarriages before giving birth to Carlo, Jr. ("Cipi") and Edoardo ("Dodo"), most enjoys playing mother to her family at their apartments in Paris, Switzerland, and New York City, and on their farm in Tuscany and in their chalet in the French Alps. After an 18-month absence from films, she returned to the screen in 1977 in *The Cassandra Crossing* and the critically acclaimed *A Special Day* with old pal Marcello Mastroianni. In 1979, Loren's autobiography (*Sophia: Living and Loving,* written with A. E. Hotchner) was an international bestseller and reaffirmed her stature as one of filmdom's most intelligent, articulate stars. NBC plunked down $3 million for television rights to Sophia's story, in which Loren played both her mother and herself as an adult. While trying to get her long-planned movie biography of Maria Callas off the ground, Loren hawked her own line of designer eyeglasses, "Sophia" perfume, and a resort island off Florida—in return for which she received one of the resort's choice villas.

Born: September 20, 1934, in a Pozzuoli, Italy, charity ward
Height: 5 ft. 8½ in.
Weight: 125 lbs.
Eyes: Brown
Hair: Brown
Zodiac: Virgo
Education: Grammar school
Religion: Roman Catholic
Marriages: To Carlo Ponti (1957–)
Children: Carlo, Jr., "Cipi" (b. 1968), Edoardo, "Eli" (b. 1971)
Interests: Poker, literature, art, music, cooking
Personal Habits and Traits: Is so superstitious she always wears something red and carries a packet of salt with her. Does not smoke, sips wine, goes to bed at 9 P.M., gets up at 6:30; enjoys household chores, exercises every morning, drinks espresso continually
Addresses: Paris; Switzerland; Tuscany; Rome; New York
Income: $2 million (minimum estimate)

George Lucas

"Star Wars *is about 25 percent of what I wanted it to be.*"

He is "The Force" behind some of the biggest-grossing pictures of all time—*Star Wars, The Empire Strikes Back, Return of the Jedi*—and his *American Graffiti,* long ranked in the Top 10. George Lucas had intended to become a race-car driver, but that dream was shattered when he was nearly killed in a crash just two days before his high school graduation. After attending the University of Southern California, he was taken under wing by Francis Ford Coppola, who bankrolled Lucas's 1971 debut *THX 1138* and *Graffiti,* and helped Lucas become one of the industry's most in-demand young directors by age 28. With his 1977 space saga alone Lucas stands to pocket $50 million—a figure definitely not reflected in the modest home and life-style he once shared with his film editor wife, Marcia (*Star Wars, Taxi Driver*), in the San Francisco suburb of San Anselmo. Unlike the intensely competitive moguls of old Hollywood, Lucas shares not only advice but percentage points with Coppola, Steven Spielberg (Lucas produced his *Raiders of the Lost Ark*), and John Milius (*The Wind and the Lion*). Lucas suffers from diabetes and often feels the strain of directing is too much, but it could not compare with the stressful breakup of his marriage—and his wife's claim to an estimated $50 million in community property. He was consoled by Linda Ronstadt.

Born: May 14, 1944, in Modesto, California
Height: 5 ft. 9 in.
Weight: 151 lbs.
Eyes: Brown
Hair: Brown
Zodiac: Taurus
Education: University of Southern California
Religion: Catholic
Marriages: To Marcia Lucas (divorced)
Children: None
Interests: Movies, comic books, tennis
Personal Habits and Traits: Does not smoke, drinks moderately, likes to drive fast, is semireclusive
Address: San Anselmo, California
Income: $50 million (minimum estimate)

Loretta Lynn

"My attitude toward men who mess around is simple: If you find 'em, kill 'em."

This *Coal Miner's Daughter*—the title of her 1976 bestselling autobiography, the hit movie it spawned, and the song for which she is most famous—was born the second of eight children in the Appalachian hamlet of Butcher Hollow, Kentucky. Her father died of black lung disease in 1959. Married at 13 to philandering moonshiner Oliver "Mooney" Lynn, Jr., she became a mother within a year and a grandmother by the time she was 29. Country music's first female millionaire by the time she was 30, Lynn learned as a youngster to play on a guitar bought at Sears. She drew upon her colorful life in songs like "Out of My Bed and Back in My Bed" and "Fist City." A regular at Nashville's Grand Ole Opry, she teamed up with Conway Twitty and they became C&W's super duo in the 1970s. Lynn's sister Crystal Gayle threatened to snatch her crown with "Don't It Make My Brown Eyes Blue," but Lynn still outdraws her sister among hard-core Nashvillians. Having conquered through psychotherapy a dependency on sedatives that often landed her in the hospital, Lynn logs around 150,000 miles a year in her $200,000 customized van. In between her rigorous concert tours and tapings of her Crisco commercials, she returns to her mansion in Hurricane Hills, Tennessee (population 120), the town she literally owns. Her property includes the Loretta Lynn Museum and the Loretta Lynn Dude Ranch. Lynn was dealt another emotional blow in 1984, when her eldest son was killed while riding his horse.

Born: April 14, 1935, in Butcher Hollow, Kentucky
Height: 5 ft. 3½ in.
Weight: 130 lbs.
Eyes: Blue
Hair: Brown
Zodiac: Aries
Education: High school dropout
Religion: Baptist
Marriages: To Oliver "Mooney" Lynn, Jr. (current)
Children: Six
Interests: Farming, horses, mine safety
Personal Habits and Traits: Does not smoke, does not drink to excess, nervous, underwent psychotherapy to overcome her dependence on barbiturates
Address: Hurricane Hills, Kentucky
Income: $2 million (minimum estimate)

Paul McCartney

"While I accept that I was with a group called the Beatles—they were very famous—'Beatle' is really just like a nickname now."

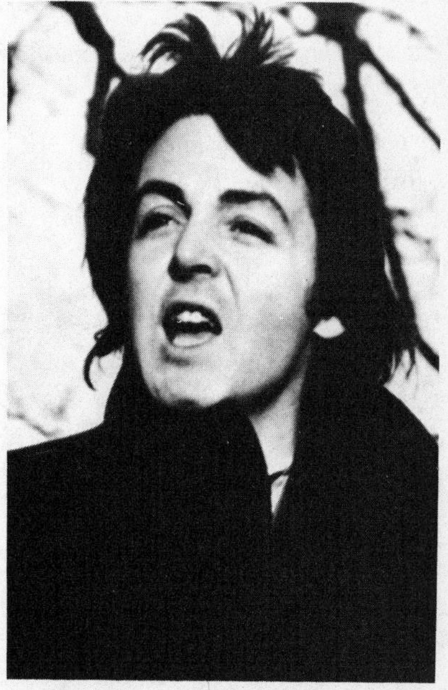

The Green Giant of show business—he is easily pop music's richest performer—Paul McCartney is the son of a Liverpool cotton salesman and a midwife. In 1956, 16-year-old John Lennon and 14-year-old McCartney started playing music together, and after several months Paul's school chum George Harrison joined them. Calling themselves the Quarrymen, they began to attract a following at a local Liverpool nightclub; then the group passed through several incarnations as the Moondogs, the Moonshiners, the Beatles, and the Silver Beatles. They settled on the Beatles for their first paying gig in Hamburg, Germany, and later traded in drummer Pete Best for a fellow named Ringo Starr (born Richard Starkey). Beginning on October 5, 1963, with the release of their first single, "Love Me Do," the Beatles established themselves as *the* preeminent group in rock history. Nearly all their many hits during the next decade were written by lyricist Lennon and composer McCartney. When the Beatles ceased to exist in 1970 amid Lennon's charges that McCartney was trying to usurp creative control, Paul and his wife, American Linda Eastman, launched their own debut album *McCartney,* followed by *Ram.* Both were unequivocal hits, earning gold records and spinning off a number-one single entitled "Uncle Albert-Admiral Halsey." During the summer of 1971 Paul and Linda formed a new band called Wings, and remained at the top of the charts with songs like "Mary Had a Little Lamb/Little Woman Love," the McCartney composition "My Love," the theme from the James Bond thriller *Live and Let Die,* "Band on the Run," "Silly Love Songs," the number-one tunes "With a Little Luck" and "Comin' Up." After clipping Wings, he recorded "Say, Say, Say" with Michael Jackson and the aptly titled hit song "Don't Say It" from his dismal 1985 film *Give My Regards to Broad Street.* Maintaining a home in London and a farm in Scotland, Mc-

Cartney, who was busted in Japan for marijuana possession and booted out of the country, is now a devout family man. Eschewing nannies, Paul and Linda usually take their four children along on concert tours. McCartney enjoyed teaching them how to read, though his personal taste in literature runs to comics and science fiction. He stunned Beatles fans worldwide by referring to his late songwriting partner John Lennon in an interview as a "maneuvering swine."

Born: June 18, 1942, in Liverpool, England
Height: 5 ft. 9 in.
Weight: 158 lbs.
Eyes: Brown
Hair: Dark brown
Zodiac: Gemini
Education: High school
Marriages: To Linda Eastman (1969–)
Children: Heather (b. 1962), Eastman's by her first marriage, has been adopted by Paul; Mary (b. 1969), Stella (b. 1971), James (b. 1977)
Interests: Composing, reading science fiction and comics, raising his children
Personal Habits and Traits: Hates being on the road, a nervous flier, disciplined, introspective
Addresses: London; Scotland
Income: $500 million (estimate of net worth)

Ali MacGraw

"I'm confident for one reason: I lived in the country and we were a close family who liked each other a lot."

Much like Jennifer Cavalleri of *Love Story,* one of the biggest-grossing movies of all time and the role for which she is best known, Ali MacGraw is the product of the elite college Wellesley, where she received a degree in art history in 1960 and stayed married to her Harvard sweetheart for 18 months. Unlike Cavalleri, however, MacGraw was born in New York State (on April Fool's Day) to upper-middle-class parents in affluent Westchester County. Her first job in Manhattan was as an editorial assistant at *Harper's Bazaar*. Within a few months she found she could make more money as a model and had become a top cover girl by the time the part of Brenda opposite Richard Benjamin in *Goodbye, Columbus* came along. Initially producers rejected MacGraw because she was definitely "not the type" to portray a libidinous Jewish princess, but they changed their minds several months later and MacGraw's riveting performance won critical acclaim while *Columbus* cleaned up at the box office. During the filming she met and married powerful Paramount production chief Robert Evans in 1969. Four years later she left Evans for her costar in Sam Peckinpah's *The Getaway,* Steve McQueen. Subsequently she yielded the prize role of Daisy in Paramount's *The Great Gatsby* to Mia Farrow, and in 1974 became Mrs. Steve McQueen. For the next few years she could not find any work in the movies. It was only after the breakup of her third marriage in 1977 that MacGraw returned to the screen with Kris Kristofferson in Peckinpah's *Convoy,* then played opposite Dino Martin in

Players. Through it all, she has refused to have a crooked front tooth fixed. She held her own with Robert Mitchum in TV's *Winds of War*. After a single season flirting with Blake Carrington on *Dynasty,* McGraw landed on the cover of *People* talking about the abortion she underwent back in her modeling days.

Born: April 1, 1939, in Westchester, New York
Height: 5 ft. 9½ in.
Weight: 128 lbs.
Eyes: Brown
Hair: Brown
Zodiac: Aries
Education: Wellesley College, B.A. in art history
Religion: Roman Catholic
Marriages:
To a college sweetheart
To Robert Evans (1969–1973)
To Steve MacQueen (1974–1977)
Children: Joshua (b. 1970), by Robert Evans
Interests: Fashion, art, music, reading
Personal Habits and Traits: Nonsmoker, drinks moderately
Address: Los Angeles
Income: $420,000 (estimate)

Rod McKuen

"I always had a father complex. Now maybe I'm at a point where I can be a father figure for somebody else."

Traveling with his mother, a dance-hall hostess, from town to town, Rod McKuen would search for his unknown father by looking for the name McKuen in every town's phone book. After Army service in Japan this grammar school dropout got his start in 1954 at San Francisco's Purple Onion under the wing of Phyllis Diller, reading his own poetry and singing his own songs. Hardly an instant hit, he spent the next several years working as a lumberjack, disc jockey, and even blood salesman (he sold nine pints of his own at $5 a pint). In 1957 McKuen acted in the beach epic, *Rock, Pretty Baby,* and the next year in *Summer Love* and *Wild Heritage*. By the late 1960s, however, he was selling millions of Whitmanesque (*Listen to the Warm*) volumes. His best-known composition is not a poem but the pop ballad "Jean," the title song for the film *The Prime of Miss Jean Brodie*. McKuen finally concluded his search for his father in 1976 at age 43, when he found the grave site of an ice salesman named Rodney Marion McKuen who had died in 1963. The long journey is chronicled in McKuen's prose book, *Finding My Father: One Man's Search for Identity*. Although he never knew his father, McKuen might well have understood him; the poet also sired a son out of wedlock. The boy, whom McKuen occasionally visits, lives with his mother in France.

Born: April 29, 1933, in Oakland, California
Height: 5 ft. 11 in.
Weight: 178 lbs.
Eyes: Blue
Hair: Blond
Zodiac: Taurus
Education: Grammar school dropout
Religion: Roman Catholic
Marriages: None
Children: One son
Interests: Composing, singing, poetry, music, adoptees' rights
Personal Habits and Traits: Smokes, drinks, a night person
Address: Beverly Hills
Income: $300,000+ (estimate)

Shirley MacLaine

Shirley Beaty

"I've always felt that I would never develop into a really fine actress because I care more about life beyond the camera than in front of it."

From her days with Frank Sinatra's Rat Pack to George McGovern's 1972 Presidential campaign to her highly publicized odyssey as the leader of the first American women's delegation to China, Shirley MacLaine has provoked controversy—though apparently not to the detriment of her career. She has received one Oscar (for *Terms of Endearment*) and five nominations, written three best-selling memoirs (*Don't Fall Off the Mountain, You Can Get There From Here,* and *Out on a Limb*), produced an Oscar-nominated documentary on China called *The Other Half of the Sky,* starred in several Emmy-winning TV specials, and headlined a knock-'em-dead nightclub act. All in all she has given her brother Warren Beatty (he kept the family name but added an extra *t*) a run for his money. Brought up in a fractious Virginia household, Shirley was sent to dancing school to correct her ducklike walk. She shot up to 5 feet 9 inches by the time she was a teenager and channeled her prodigious energy into becoming a hoofer. Taking her mother's maiden name, MacLaine headed for Broadway, where in 1954 she was whisked from the chorus of *Pajama Game* to center stage after Carol Haney injured her ankle. In typical Ruby Keeler style, she was spotted by a movie producer, and within a year walked on the set of her first film. Invariably cast as a carrot-topped pixie or a wide-eyed hooker—"I've played more prostitutes than anyone in movies"—MacLaine sparkled in such films as *The Apartment, Irma La Douce, What a Way to Go,* and *Sweet Charity.* Next to *Terms* and *The Turning Point,* her best dramatic role was as a teacher driven to suicide in Lillian Hellman's *The Children's Hour.* Boasting a trans-Pacific open marriage with Tokyo-based producer Steve Parker, MacLaine began playing the field after the breakup of her very public relationship with New York columnist Pete Hamill. MacLaine's year was definitely 1984, when she finally won her Oscar, saw *Out on a Limb* rise on the bestseller lists, opened on Broadway, made the cover of *Time*—all in time for her 50th birthday.

Born: April 24, 1934, in Richmond, Virginia
Height: 5 ft. 9 in.
Weight: 118 lbs.
Eyes: Blue
Hair: Reddish brown
Zodiac: Taurus
Education: High school
Religion: Protestant
Marriages: To Steve Parker (1954–)
Children: Sachi (b. 1957)
Interests: Writing (fiction and nonfiction), producing, China, politics (a liberal Democrat), women's rights
Personal Habits and Traits: Stopped smoking, drinking, and overeating; runs three miles a day
Addresses: New York City; Malibu
Income: $3 million

Ed McMahon

"Idleness is one thing I cannot stand. The busier I am, the happier I am."

Johnny Carson's second banana was born in Detroit, but spent most of his youth in Lowell, Massachusetts. His father had once been the interlocutor for a minstrel show, but had become a professional fund-raiser by the time Edward Lee came along. Young McMahon worked his way through the Catholic University of America selling vegetable slicers on the Atlantic City boardwalk and hosted a children's show on Philadelphia television shortly after graduating with a B.A. in speech and drama. McMahon flew as a Marine fighter pilot during the Korean war and later as a flight instructor. After his discharge he reentered broadcasting and linked up with Johnny Carson in 1958 on the *Who Do You Trust?* game show. When Carson succeeded Jack Paar as the host of *The Tonight Show* on October 1, 1962, McMahon went along as his sidekick. McMahon has also proven himself to be a solid actor in several films, most notably in the roles of a terrorized subway rider in *The Incident* and an unscrupulous businessman in the comedy *Dick and Jane*. He has also augmented his considerable income by several millions as pitchman for Budweiser, host of *Bloopers and Practical Jokes*, *Star Search* and several NBC specials, and as a Las Vegas headliner. At a time when most men think of settling down to become a grandpa, McMahon jumped at the chance to become a new dad. He and second wife Victoria, 23 years his junior, adopted five-day-old Katherine in December 1985.

Born: March 6, 1923, in Detroit, Michigan
Height: 6 ft. 4 in.
Weight: 210 lbs.
Eyes: Hazel
Hair: Brownish gray
Zodiac: Pisces
Education: Catholic University, B.A.
Religion: Roman Catholic
Marriages: Two. Currently to Victoria Valentine (1976–)
Children: Claudia (b. 1946), Michael (b. 1949), Linda (b. 1954), Jeffrey (b. 1960), adopted daughter Katherine (b. 1985)
Interests: Boating, photography, flying, a number of charities
Personal Habits and Traits: Does not smoke, drinks, partygoer, workaholic
Address: Beverly Hills
Income: $5.5 million +

Kristy McNichol

"I want to work on becoming a good actress. For a kid, I can't think of a better life."

The fresh-faced tomboy who made "Yucka!" part of every preteen's lingo copped an Emmy in 1977 for her third hit season as the sassy Buddy on ABC's dramatic series *Family*. Her parents were divorced when she was 3, and Kristy's secretary/movie-extra mother introduced her to commercials by the time she was 8. She appeared in bit parts on *The Bionic Woman* and *Starsky and Hutch* before landing a regular role in the deservedly short-lived *Apple's Way*. *Family* came along when she was 12, and Kristy left public school to be tutored between takes on the Twentieth Century-Fox lot. Dividing her time between the three condominiums and seven houses into which her mother invested the sizable combined earnings (at least $500,000) of Kristy and her big brother, Jimmy (*The Fitzpatricks, California Fever*), Kristy zipped around the sets on an electric golf cart and her XR-75 Honda dirt bike. She made her movie debut with Burt Reynolds, Sally Field, Dom DeLuise, and Joanne Woodward playing Burt's daughter in *The End,* and floored critics with her sensitive portrayal of a young girl from Georgia in love with a Nazi POW in NBC's *Summer of My German Soldier*. Yet it all proved too much too soon for McNichol, who suffered a "chemical imbalance" that temporarily halted the production of *I Won't Dance* (later retitled *Just the Way You Are*). In 1985, McNichol graduated from the California College of Hair Design with a degree in cosmetology. She planned to open a beauty parlor with good friend Ina Liberace, you-know-who's niece.

Born: September 9, 1962, in Los Angeles, California
Height: (as of 1981): 5 ft. 3 in.
Weight: 103 lbs.
Eyes: Blue
Hair: Sandy
Zodiac: Virgo
Education: High school (so far); cosmetology training
Religion: Roman Catholic
Marriages: None
Children: None
Interests: Skateboarding, dirt bikes, swimming, rock music
Personal Habits and Traits: Candid, articulate, unpretentious
Addresses: Tarzana, California; New York City
Income: $410,000 (estimate)

Madonna

Madonna Louise Ciccone

"Mouthing off comes naturally to me."

The Pop-Tart of the '80s, her dark-at-the-roots blond hair tied up in floppy rags, wriggled onto the scene in black lace and ankle boots, fluorescent rubber bracelets, a suggestive "Boy Toy" belt buckle (slung below a winking belly button), and cross-shaped earrings—and was immediately mimicked by millions of

"Wanna Be's," pubescent girls who wanna be like Madonna. Her voice has been likened to Minnie Mouse on helium, but—thanks largely to MTV—her first album (containing hits like "Holiday," and "Lucky Star") went triple platinum, and her second, "Like a Virgin," went quadruple platinum with nearly 5 million copies sold in the United States alone. And even as her "Material Girl," "Crazy for You," "Into the Groove," and "Dress You Up" singles zipped up the charts, she made an impressive screen debut in the title role of *Deperately Seeking Susan*. Madonna was 7 when her mother died of cancer, and her father, a General Dynamics engineer, became the single strongest influence in his daughter's life. She took dance lessons in high school, and, prodded by ballet school owner Christopher Flynn to pursue her show business aspirations, saved up enough money for a one-way ticket to New York. There she moved from one East Village dive to the next, surviving on little more than popcorn ("I still love it. Popcorn is cheap and it fills you up"). She auditioned for and won a scholarship to the Alvin Ailey dance school, and became a decent rock guitarist and drummer during those knockabout years in Manhattan. She resents the intimation that she slept her way to the top, though she certainly passed through the lives of a number of musicians and disc jockeys on her way up the ladder. Mark Kamins, deejay at New York's trend-setting Danceteria, is credited with discovering Madonna in 1982. Three years later, Madonnamania was in full blossom, and so was her romance with actor Sean (*The Falcon and the Snowman*) Penn. In the midst of her record-smashing North American tour, the newest exemplar of trash with flash landed on the covers of *two* issues of *People* magazine—not to mention the cover of *Time*. Both *Penthouse* and *Playboy* ungallantly featured nude spreads of her, using old photos from Madonna's early days. Her much ballyhooed wedding to the rambunctious Penn took place in August 1985 in Malibu, on a cliff overlooking the Pacific. They then embarked on their first joint screen venture, in George Harrison's *Shanghai Surprise*.

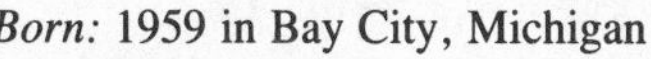

Born: 1959 in Bay City, Michigan
Height: 5 ft. 4½ in.
Weight: 118 lbs.
Eyes: Blue
Hair: Dirty blonde
Education: One year at the University of Michigan
Religion: Roman Catholic
Marriages: Sean Penn (1985–)
Children: None
Interests: Dance, songwriting, acting ("I aspire to be a great actress")
Personal Habits and Traits: Determined, ambitious, straightforward, smokes, does not take drugs, has few possessions
Address: New York City
Income: $5 million (minimum estimate)

Norman Mailer

"Economics is half of literature."

More journalist than novelist, Norman Mailer was a Brooklyn boy who at 16 went to Harvard to study aeronautical engineering and 24 hours after Pearl

Harbor decided to write the Great American War Novel. The result was *The Naked and the Dead,* and by 25 he was a national literary celebrity. Over the next quarter-century he wrote about American socialism in *Barbary Shore,* dissected Hollywood in *The Deer Park,* indulged in self-analysis in *Advertisements for Myself,* described the political turmoil of the 1960s in *Armies of the Night* (for which he was awarded a Pulitzer and a National Book Award), decried bourgeois shallowness in *The American Dream,* mused on the meaning of the lunar landing in *Of a Fire on the Moon,* crafted a biography of Marilyn Monroe with *Marilyn,* gave a blow-by-blow account of the 1974 heavyweight championship in *The Fight,* and chronicled the death of Gary Gilmore in *The Executioner's Song* (another Pulitzer). He indulged his fantasies by acting in, directing and producing three underground film flops. He left his first wife, stabbed his second with a penknife, then left wives three and four, siring a total of eight children—the last out of wedlock with girlfriend Norris Church. But when his divorce from fourth wife Beverly Bentley came through, he did not marry Church. Instead, he wed Carol Stevens, a jazz singer who bore him a daughter before he and Church became pals. After a "civilized" divorce, Mailer—who said he wanted to give his daughter by Stevens parents who at some point had been married—made arrangements for his sixth marriage, to Norris Church. Once a New York mayoral candidate with Jimmy Breslin ("Vote the Rascals In"), Mailer is first to admit he commits many of his antics for the money; he must earn $150,000 a year just to make his alimony and child-support payments. Mailer's Egyptian epic, *Ancient Evenings,* read like a bad LSD trip, but it made it onto the best-seller lists, as did his subsequent *Tough Guys Don't Dance.*

Born: January 31, 1923, in Long Branch, New Jersey
Height: 5 ft. 4 in.
Weight: 170 lbs.
Eyes: Blue
Hair: Salt and pepper
Education: Harvard University
Religion: Jewish
Marriages:
To Bea Silverman (divorced)
To Adele Morales (divorced)
To Lady Jean Campbell (divorced)
To Beverly Bentley (divorced)
To Carol Stevens (divorced)
To Norris Church (1980–)
Children: Eight
Interests: Existentialism, technology, politics, religion, violence, sports (particularly boxing), movies
Personal Habits and Traits: Does calisthenics every morning, writes 1,500 words daily
Address: Brooklyn Heights, New York
Income: $500,000 (minimum estimate)

Lee Majors

"I like my wholesome image. Somebody else can be on dope, a boozer and divorced 14 times."

No longer in real danger of being known to the world as "Mr. Farrah Fawcett," Lee Majors became the bionic beefcake star of ABC's hit *The Six Million Dollar*

Man series long before his wife scored her own triumph on the tube with *Charlie's Angels*. Kentucky-bred Majors was orphaned before he was two years old, attended Eastern Kentucky on a football scholarship (his nose was broken five times) and as a prospective high school coach, headed to Los Angeles, where he latched onto the notion of acting. Two years later he was playing a bastard son on the ABC show *The Big Valley* starring Barbara Stanwyck. Divorced from his first wife, Majors ran across an agent's glossy of Hollywood newcomer Farrah Fawcett and called her up for a date. In 1973 they were married. Majors costarred in *The Men From Shiloh* and *Owen Marshall* before being offered his own series. *The Six Million Dollar Man* was canceled in 1978 after a five-year run. Majors then joined his wife in the hunt for film properties. Boasting joint earnings well in excess of $1.5 million Majors and Farrah could easily afford their Bel Air chateau and his-and-hers Mercedes—until they split in the summer of 1979. While she pursued more heavyweight dramatic projects, Majors stuck to what he knew best, playing a stuntman on the hit ABC series *The Fall Guy*. His commercials for Diet-Rite cola made only his wallet fatter.

Born: April 23, 1940, in Wyandotte, Michigan
Height: 6 ft. 2 in.
Weight: 200 lbs.
Eyes: Blue
Hair: Light brown
Zodiac: Taurus
Education: Eastern Kentucky State College
Religion: Protestant
Marriages: Two. The second to Farrah Fawcett (1973–1979)
Children: Lee, Jr. (b. 1962)
Interests: Football, hunting, fishing, art, motion pictures, directing
Personal Habits and Traits: Nonsmoker, moderate drinker, early riser, quiet, introspective
Address: Bel Air, California
Income: $800,000 (minimum estimate)

Melissa Manchester

"Writing and singing for me are like sharing secrets. They're an obsessive thing."

Like Barry Manilow, silken-voiced Melissa Manchester emerged from the group that backed Bette Midler in the early 1970s. Unlike Manilow, it took Manchester nearly five years after splitting from the Divine Miss M to establish herself as a vital force in the music world. The Bronx-born daughter of a bassoonist with the Metropolitan Opera Orchestra, Manchester wrote and sang commercial jingles at 15, and upon graduation from New York's famous High School of Performing Arts was hired as a staff writer for Chappell Music. While studying drama at New York University she auditioned for a music class taught by Paul Simon, and he not only helped her improve her songwriting but nudged her into performing. During her first appearance at a small club called Focus, she met the up-and-coming Bette and accepted her backup offer. Bell Records signed Melissa soon after, and when Clive Davis took over the company and changed its name to

Arista, her career as a recording artist started to rise. In 1975 she scored with the hit ballad "Midnight Blue," but despite success on the road and a number of respectable albums, she remained a notch below the top until her number-one hit "Don't Cry Out Loud." Residing in Los Angeles for eight years with her manager-husband Larry Brezner, Manchester looked forward to mellowing with age: "I'm going to make a fabulous middle-aged lady!" Before she was out of her 20s, however, Manchester split from Brezner and returned to New York. She married her stage manager the same year she collected a Grammy for her jazzy "You Should Hear How She Talks About You."

Born: February 15, 1951, in New York City
Height: 5 ft. 4 in.
Weight: 129 lbs.
Eyes: Brown
Hair: Dark brown
Zodiac: Aquarius
Education: New York High School of Performing Arts
Marriages:
To Larry Brezner (1971–1979)
To Keven DeRemer (1982–)
Children: None
Interests: Songwriting, performing
Personal Habits and Traits: A nonsmoker, drinks moderately
Address: Los Angeles
Income: $800,000 (minimum estimate)

Chuck Mangione

"Most of what I do came out of the TV theme for The Cisco Kid."

This consummate jazzman had every right to toot his own flugelhorn with the gold-plated success of 1978's "Feels So Good," but it marked the end of an arduous struggle to the top of the charts. The son of an Italian immigrant grocer, Mangione was taken by his father to listen to jazz greats like Dizzy Gillespie. Mangione went on to attend the prestigious Eastman School of Music in Rochester, New York, and in 1968 he formed his first group and turned out Latino-influenced LPs like "Land of Make Believe." He appealed primarily to hard-core jazz fans until "Feels So Good" crossed over to the much broader and more lucrative pop audience. A Grammy winner for his 1976 album *Vellavia,* Mangione still spends nine months of the year on the road performing one-nighters at $15,000 a shot. But periodically he will dash back to his modest suburban house in Rochester, New York, to spend time with his wife of 13 years, Judi, and their daughters, Nancy and Diana. When he is away, Chuck receives homemade "care packages" containing his mother's spaghetti sauce, while his dad Frank sells "Feels So Good" albums and T-shirts in the lobby wherever his immensely popular son is performing. His unmistakable musical themes are inevitably simple, repetitious, and frequently reminiscent of movie scenes where caballeros are riding off into the sunset.

Born: November 29, 1940, in Rochester, New York
Height: 5 ft. 6 in.
Weight: 130 lbs.
Eyes: Brown
Hair: Brown
Zodiac: Sagittarius
Education: Eastman School of Music
Religion: Roman Catholic
Marriages: To Judi Mangione (1964–)
Children: Nancy (b. 1968), Diana (b. 1970)
Interests: Baseball, football, basketball, his family
Personal Habits and Traits: Does not smoke, drinks moderately, demanding perfectionist
Address: Rochester, New York
Income: $500,000 (minimum estimate)

Barry Manilow

"I grew up wanting to be Nelson Riddle."

Before he had recorded his first hit, the current King of the Middle Road had already made himself rich by composing and sometimes performing commercial jingles for, among other products, McDonald's, Band-Aids, Dr Pepper, Chevrolet, Kentucky Fried Chicken, Pepsi, and Stridex. An only child, Manilow grew up tough in Brooklyn, raised by his mother after his father, a truck driver, deserted the family. Barry was playing the accordion by the age of 7, and for his bar mitzvah was given a piano. His marriage to a high school sweetheart lasted one year, and after putting himself through college and a year at Juilliard by working in the CBS mailroom, he received his first break on local TV by coming up with a new theme for *The Late Show*. In 1972 he became the house pianist at Manhattan's Continental Baths, a famous gay bathhouse in the basement of the Ansonia Hotel, and several weeks later an unknown singer named Bette Midler came to wow the boys. Manilow went on to coproduce her Grammy-winning *The Divine Miss M* album and arrange her hit singles "Do You Wanna Dance?" and "Boogie Woogie Bugle Boy" before laying down a monster hit of his own, "Mandy." In addition to turning out three or four Top 10 hits every year (including "I Write the Songs," "Looks Like We Made It," "Weekend in New England," "It's a Miracle," "American Bandstand," "I Just Can't Smile Without You," "The Copacabana," "Even Now," and "Some Kind of Friend"), Manilow has garnered two Emmys for his television specials and a special Tony for his one-man show on Broadway. Still, he appears far from happy—a recluse who shares his life only with platonic roommate–agent Linda Allen and close friends like singer Melissa Manchester. He ruefully points out that when he was awarded his Tony the only congratulatory telegram he received was from old partner Bette Midler. He is currently writing his autobiography for, according to agents Eric and Maureen Lasher, a record advance.

Born: June 17, 1946, in Brooklyn New York
Height: 6 ft. 3 in.
Weight: 150 lbs.
Eyes: Brown
Hair: Dark blond
Zodiac: Gemini
Education: Juilliard School of Music
Religion: Jewish
Marriages: One (divorced)
Children: None
Interests: Theater, movies, writing his memoirs
Personal Habits and Traits: Smokes, a moderate drinker, a virtual recluse, protected by bodyguards and a sizable number of go-betweens
Addresses: New York City; Beverly Hills
Income: $3 million+

Charles Manson

No Name Maddox

"Mr. and Mrs. America—you are wrong. I am not the King of the Jews nor am I a hippie cult leader. I am what you have made of me and the mad dog devil killer fiend leper is a reflection of your society. In my mind's eye my thoughts light fires in your cities."

Born "No Name Maddox" when his mother bore him out of wedlock, he became Charles Manson when his promiscuous mother finally married. Married twice himself and an abysmal failure as a musician, Manson has spent more than 23 years of his life behind bars on convictions for homosexual rape, car theft, forgery, and finally murder. In 1971, he was convicted of masterminding the gruesome slaughters of actress Sharon Tate and eight others. Operating out of the Spahn Ranch on the outskirts of L.A., Manson instructed his LSD-drugged and freaked-out "family" of misfits, psychotics and runaways to go on a bloody rampage through Bel Air and Beverly Hills that culminated in what many have deemed "the crime of the century." Manson is now serving out a life sentence (as are his codefendants Susan Atkins, Patricia Krenwinkel, and Leslie Van Houten) in a cramped, maximum-security cell at San Quentin, and, presumably because he is a marked man among his fellow prisoners, refuses to perform any work or take the customary daily hour of outdoor exercise. Manson, who sometimes sports a beard and Fu Manchu fingernails, automatically became eligible for parole in 1978 and was rejected. Californians who have had to cope with Zebra, Zodiac, and—if Woody Allen is correct—wheat-germ murderers, all sleep a little better because he's tucked away. In 1985, he joined a host of other notorious criminals seeking the literary limelight by offering his memoirs to New York publishers.

Born: November 12, 1934, in Cincinnati, Ohio
Height: 5 ft. 5 in.
Weight: 125 lbs.
Eyes: Brown
Hair: Brown
Zodiac: Scorpio
Education: Dropped out of school at 16
Marriages:
To Rosalie Jean Willis (1955–1958)
To Leona Manson (1959–1963)
Children: One son by each of his marriages, plus several more children out of wedlock
Interests: The guitar, mind control, writing
Address: San Quentin
Income: None

Penny Marshall

"When you start this high, you've got to tumble down."

Laverne and Shirley was number one the morning after it premiered in 1976 and remained there for years, thanks in large part to this talented New Yorker who plays Laverne, lady lug to Cindy Williams's demurely scatterbrained Shirley. Marshall grew up on the Grand Concourse in the Bronx, directly across from where her future husband, Rob Reiner (*All in the Family*), spent his early childhood. Her father made industrial films while mom, who taught dance classes, had her daughter hoofing on the *Ted Mack Amateur Hour* and the original *Jackie Gleason Show* in the mid-1950s. The University of New Mexico and a brief marriage preceded Penny's decision to join up with her producer brother Garry in Hollywood. There she bumped into Reiner at a repertory group called The Committee, and lost out in *All in the Family* auditions to Sally Struthers. After 18 months of living together, he and Marshall were married in 1971. Commercials kept her career afloat—Marshall was the "before" in shampoo commercials where Farrah Fawcett was the "after"—and occasional appearances on *The Odd Couple, The Mary Tyler Moore Show,* and *The Paul Lynde Show*. After Penny and Cindy Williams double-dated with Henry "The Fonz" Winkler and Ron Howard on *Happy Days,* ABC concocted a spinoff series about two girl bottlers for the mythical Shotz Brewery. Insecure and nervous about her looks, Marshall is a compulsive worrier, and one way for her to cope with her constant anxiety is needlepoint. So far she has embroidered a virtual mountain of needlepoint pillows. With good reason: Success took its toll at home, precipitating the breakup of the Marshall-Reiner marriage. Marshall, who recalled dropping LSD with pals Carrie Fisher and Judy (Mrs. John) Belushi in Robert Woodward's John Belushi biography, *Wired,* subsequently became Art Garfunkel's love.

Born: October 15, 1945, in New York City
Height: 5 ft. 6 in.
Weight: 123 lbs.
Eyes: Green
Hair: Brown
Zodiac: Libra
Education: University of New Mexico
Religion: Protestant
Marriages: Two. The last to Rob Reiner (1971–1979)
Children: Tracy (b. 1965)
Interests: Dancing, needlepoint, sports
Personal Habits and Traits: Chain smoker, not a teetotaler, a compulsive worrier
Address: North Hollywood, California
Income: $1 million (estimate, mostly from residuals)

Dean Martin

Dino Crocetti

"I'd hate to be a teetotaler. Imagine getting up in the morning and knowing that's as good as you're going to feel all day?"

When double-downing Dino split from partner Jerry Lewis in 1957 after nine years of goofy comedy, it was generally presumed that Lewis would soar and straight man Martin would sink. Amazingly, it was Martin who succeeded as recording artist ("Houston," "Everybody Loves Somebody Sometime"), movie star (the popular Matt Helm series), and ultimately as host of one of the most successful variety series in television history. Most of Martin's comedy is predicated on his laid-back image as a boozer, though Martin in fact is a solid, disciplined professional. With the cancellation of *The Dean Martin Show* after a seven-year run, the onetime day laborer and hustler from gritty Steubenville, Ohio, now hosts NBC's enormously popular celebrity "roasts." Along the way he accumulated three marriages (his second marriage to Jeannie Martin provided the grist for many of Martin's jokes during the late 1960s) and seven children. His handsome son Dino, Jr.—married for a short time to actress Olivia Hussey and then to skater Dorothy Hamill—belonged to the rock group Dino, Desi and Billy before embarking on an ill-fated film career of his own. Trying his hand at television, Dino flubbed in the misunderstood series *Misfits of Science*.

Born: June 17, 1917, in Steubenville, Ohio
Height: 6 ft.
Weight: 178 lbs.
Eyes: Brown
Hair: Gray-brown
Zodiac: Gemini
Education: High school dropout
Religion: Roman Catholic
Marriages:
To Elizabeth Ann MacDonald (1940–1949)
To Jeanne Biegger (divorced)
To Catherine Mae Hawn (current)
Children: Craig, Claudia, Gail, Deana (with MacDonald); Dino, Jr., Ricci, Gina (with Biegger)
Interests: Golf, motion pictures, automobiles
Personal Habits and Traits: Chain-smokes, drinks but is not quite a heavy boozer, is punctual, polite
Address: Beverly Hills
Income: $500,000

Steve Martin

"There's got to be order for my comedy to work, because chaos in the midst of chaos isn't funny, but chaos in the midst of order is."

This "wild and crazy guy" started out the soft-spoken son of a Garden Grove, California, realtor. Martin spent eight years selling Mouseketeer ears and Davy Crockett coonskin hats at Disneyland, but a profession in comedy wasn't in the offing until his senior year at UCLA. Switching his major from philosophy to theater, he wrote a stand-up routine that he performed at local nightspots, then broke into show business as a $1,500-a-week writer for the Smothers Brothers, John Denver, Glen Campbell, Dick Van Dyke and Sonny and Cher. He began appearing as an opener for rock acts in the early 1970s, and in 1973 traded in his beads and beard for a Pierre Cardin wardrobe and a spot on Johnny Carson's *Tonight Show*. Strumming the banjo while delivering his lines like a crazed disc jockey, Martin honed his trademark patter ("Well, excuuuuuse me") on other talk and variety shows before recording his first gold comedy album, *Let's Get Small*. He played the fiendish Dr. Maxwell Edison in *Sgt. Pepper's Lonely Hearts Club Band* in 1978, then wrote and starred in his first film for Universal, *The Jerk*, followed by *The Muppet Movie*, the disastrous *Pennies from Heaven, The Man With Two Brains, Dead Men Don't Wear Plaid, The Lonely Guy*, and *All of Me*. Martin, an expert skier, calls Aspen his home, but maintains a two-bedroom bachelor apartment in Los Angeles; he kept company for several years with actress-singer Bernadette Peters (his movie wife in *The Jerk*) before switching to Victoria Tennant (the seductress in *All of Me*). He meshed easily with the regulars on *Saturday Night Live* and his book, the number-one bestselling *Cruel Shoes*, ran up plenty in royalties through 1980. Martin shrugged off the controversy surrounding the Motion Picture Academy's failure to even nominate Martin or Lily Tomlin for their hilarious performances in *All of Me* .

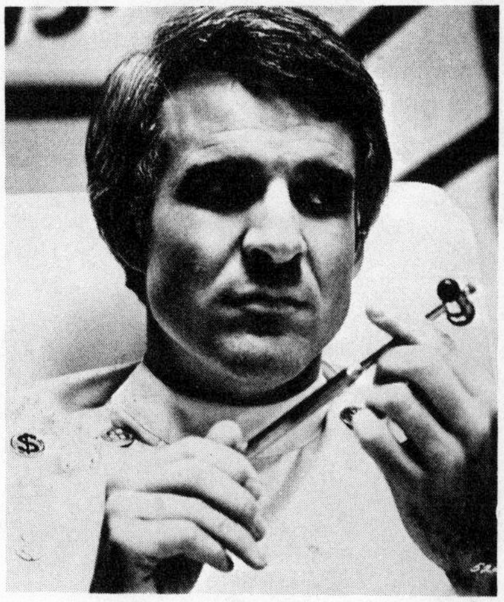

Born: 1945 in Waco, Texas
Height: 5 ft. 9½ in.
Weight: 150 lbs.
Eyes: Blue
Hair: White
Education: University of California at Los Angeles
Religion: Protestant
Marriages: None
Children: None
Interests: Painting, skiing, short-story writing
Personal Habits and Traits: Never cooks, eats fish but no meat, an avid museum goer, drives a Ford, something of a recluse, very serious offstage, never wears jeans
Addresses: Aspen, Colorado; Los Angeles
Income: $2 million (estimate)

Lee Marvin

On the court-mandated settlement with his ex-lover: *"It's just a mishmash decision. It's part of my dead life."*

Ironically, this tough guy's tough guy came from the family of a wealthy Madison Avenue executive and his socialite–fashion editor wife. Marvin kept getting kicked out of private schools until he joined the Marines, and was shot in the spine while fighting in the Pacific during World War II. He started acting in the theater, but switched to movies and won an Oscar in 1965 for playing the dual role of over-the-hill-and-off-the-wagon Kid Shelleen and his no-good, metallic-nosed brother ("It got bit off in a fight") in the "antiwestern" comedy *Cat Ballou*. The TV series *M Squad* made him a household face if not a household name. *The Dirty Dozen* and movie version of Lerner and Loewe's *Paint Your Wagon* followed, as did a hit single from the musical ("I Was Born Under a Wandering Star"). By the mid-1970s, however, Marvin's star had faded and he was slapped with a precedent-setting lawsuit by his ex-lover, Michelle Triola. She lived with Lee between 1964 and 1970, and claimed she was entitled to half of his earnings (around $4 million) under California's community property laws,

even though they were never legally married. The suit, masterminded by attorney Marvin Mitchelson, initially netted Michelle an award of $104,000, but was later overturned. Nevertheless, the "palimony" decision provoked profound repercussions across the country.

Born: February 19, 1924, in New York City
Height: 6 ft.
Weight: 180 lbs.
Eyes: Blue
Hair: White
Zodiac: Pisces
Education: High school dropout
Religion: Protestant
Marriages:
To Betty Edeling (1952–1965)
To Pamela Feeley (1970–)
Children: Three
Interests: Sailing, the theater, music
Personal Habits and Traits: Chain-smokes, drinks considerably
Address: Los Angeles
Income: $400,000 (minimum estimate)

Marcello Mastroianni

"I have a problem: I only really exist when I am working on a film."

La Dolce Vita made him not only a first-name legend in 1960—but the sexy, flawed, and funny prototype for every Italian movie star who would follow. His life, like that of his frequent costar Sophia Loren (*Yesterday, Today and Tomorrow, A Special Day*), was shaped by poverty and World War II. The son of a carpenter, he spent his childhood mostly in Turin and Rome. Sent to a labor camp in 1943, he escaped to Venice just before the liberation of Italy, and managed to survive the postwar years by selling paintings to tourists. He joined a theatrical company in 1948 and apprenticed onstage and in mediocre Italian films until *La Dolce Vita,* whereupon he appeared in a torrent of movies that include *Divorce, Italian Style, 8½* and *The Stranger*. This world-weary antihero also believes in extolling *la dolce vita,* not merely portraying it. His controversial private life includes devoted wife Flora Carabella, a longtime Italian mistress, and frequent liaisons with the likes of Faye Dunaway and Catherine Deneuve (the mother of his second daughter, Chiara). A poor command of English was mistaken for a lack of decorum when, while promoting *A Special Day* with Sophia Loren, he freely used a choice four-letter Anglo-Saxon word for sexual intercourse on *The Dick Cavett Show*.

Born: September 28, 1924, in Fontana Liri, Italy
Height: 5 ft. 9 in.
Weight: 155 lbs.
Eyes: Brown
Hair: Brown
Zodiac: Libra
Education: High school
Religion: Roman Catholic
Marriages: To Flora Carabella (current)
Children: Two daughters (one by Carabella, the other with Catherine Deneuve)
Interests: Theater, art, music, sports cars
Personal Habits and Traits: Chain-smokes, not a teetotaler, speaks poor English
Addresses: Paris; Rome
Income: $630,000 (minimum estimate)

Johnny Mathis

"I'm scared to death of audiences. Every time I go out, the people seem to be saying, 'Prove it! Prove it!' I still have the feeling of not being good enough."

"Too Much Too Little Too Late" certainly was not Johnny Mathis's real life problem, though it became the title of his phenomenal number-one 1978 hit with Deniece Williams. Astonishingly, after 76 albums (eight of them gold), Mathis had never before made it to number one. The fourth of seven kids born to a valet-chauffeur and a maid, Mathis was a record-breaking track star and basketball player at San Francisco State College, where he prepared himself for a career as a physical education teacher. Johnny wanted to sing, but his parents were unable to afford singing lessons for their son. So they brought him to a singer named Connie Cox, who trained him for six years without charging a fee. Helen Noga, who owned San Francisco's 440 Jazz Club, heard Mathis sing during a jam session with friends and instantly became his manager. Within a year Mathis recorded a hit—"All the Way"—for Columbia, and began turning out dozens of million-selling singles and albums. "Wonderful, Wonderful" climbed to the Top 10 in 1957 and became his theme song, though Mathis is almost as strongly associated with "It's Not for Me to Say," "Chances Are," and "Misty." Always popular with pop music fans—anthologies of his early hits gross millions every year—it nonetheless took "Too Much Too Little Too Late" to put him back on top of pop after a long absence. Unmarried, Mathis shares his Hollywood Hills house (once owned by Howard Hughes's wife Jean Peters) with two Oriental exchange students, while his main charity is the L.A. Health Clinic for Gay People. He also maintains a ranch in Santa Barbara. For years, *Johnny Mathis' Greatest Hits* was the longest-charting record of any kind at an astonishing 490 weeks.

Born: September 30, 1935, in San Francisco, California
Height: 5 ft. 8 in.
Weight: 148 lbs.
Eyes: Brown
Hair: Black
Zodiac: Libra
Education: San Francisco State College
Religion: Roman Catholic

Marriages: None
Children: None
Interests: Golf (a 9 handicap), basketball, tennis, swimming, track, dance, gardening, cooking, drama, gay rights
Personal Habits and Traits: Nonsmoker, bites fingernails
Addresses: Hollywood; Santa Barbara
Income: $1.5 million

Walter Matthau

"My first wife never complimented me on the way I look, but Carol says I am the handsomest man in the world. Believe it or not, that made a big change in my life."

Always looking as if he just spent the night on tumble dry, the perennially disheveled Walter Matthau is unsurpassable when it comes to portraying the tough but soft-on-the-inside average guy. Growing up dirt-poor and Jewish on New York's Lower East Side, Matthau made his first stage appearance in a

religious play when he was four. In middle age he wound up playing the sloppy Oscar Madison in both the stage (with Art Carney) and screen (with Jack Lemmon) versions of Neil Simon's comedy classic *The Odd Couple*. There were some serious roles, such as the villain in the Cary Grant–Audrey Hepburn spellbinder *Charade,* but Matthau mainly kept hunting for laughs—and got them. He undertook three parts in Neil Simon's *Plaza Suite,* tried to rub out Elaine May in *A New Leaf,* was Horace Vandergelder to Barbra Streisand's Dolly Levi in *Hello, Dolly!,* received an Oscar for Billy Wilder's *The Fortune Cookie,* married Carol Burnett in the touching *Pete 'n' Tillie,* coached Tatum O'Neal in *The Bad News Bears,* kept George Burns hopping in Simon's *The Sunshine Boys,* played doctor with Glenda Jackson in *House Calls* and buccaneer in Roman Polanki's *The Pirates*. Matthau was divorced when he met Carol Grace Saroyan, twice married to playwright William Saroyan, and he remembers her as looking "like one of those women who come out of the Algonquin Hotel with yak dew on their faces." Nevertheless he married Carol, and with their son, David, the Matthaus comprise one of the closest and strongest families in filmdom.

Born: October 1, 1920, in New York City
Height: 6 ft. 2 in.
Weight: 181 lbs.
Eyes: Brown
Hair: Brown
Zodiac: Libra
Education: High school
Religion: Jewish
Marriages:
To Grace Johnson (1948–1958)
To Carol Grace Saroyan (1959–)
Children: David, Jenny (by Johnson); Charles (by Saroyan)
Interests: Gambling; plays the horses
Personal Habits and Traits: Quit smoking, he drinks his share, a late sleeper, not particularly neat
Address: Beverly Hills
Income: $1 million

Menudo

Roughly translated, the name means "small change." But there's nothing small about their bank accounts, or the noise made when 100,000 frenzied adolescents turn one of their concerts into a screamathon. The five boys who make up Menudo must savor the moment; once a member turns 16 or his voice changes, he is contractually obligated to leave the group. The man who makes the rules for Menudo is the man who conceived of the group in 1976, Puerto Rican businessman Edgardo Diaz Melendez. A onetime singer in the clean-cut Up With People organization, Edgardo says he "got the idea for a group of young singers who would be healthy kids without vices, who didn't take drugs, who had good grades at school and good family relations, and would project a positive image."

Their sound is bland, and their lyrics banal, and the boys' onstage moves won't put Glady Knight's Pips out of business, but Melendez was right. In addition to the albums, their syndicated Spanish-language television program, their lucrative endorsement contract with Pepsi, and their Saturday-morning spots on ABC, in 1985 the group brought Menudo Mania to 36 cities in the United States and Latin America.

Income: $20 million gross for the group (an estimated annual net income of $300,000 for each member)

Melina Mercouri

Maria Amalia Mercouri

"My supporters didn't consider me a star. They saw me as a woman who has made a long march."

Born Maria Amalia Mercouri (Melina is a nickname, the Greek word for honey), her grandfather was a mayor of Athens for 30 years and her father a respected member of Parliament. But when the military junta of General Papadopoulos came to power, she fled and was stripped of her citizenship. By then she had already established her credentials on stage in Greece and was known for her movies *Never on Sunday, Phaedra, Topkapi,* and *Promise at Dawn*—all of which were made with her second husband, American filmmaker Jules Dassin. With the return of democracy in Greece in 1974, she returned triumphantly and made her first bid for Parliament as standard-bearer of the leftist Panhellenic Socialist Movement—only to lose by 33 votes. In the next election three years later she ran as a candidate from the port city of Piraeus, winning easily despite a recurrence of bleeding ulcers that threatened to end her campaign prematurely. When her party finally did come to power, it wasted no time in making Mercouri its Minister of Culture. Among her many controversial demands: returning the Elgin Marbles to Greece from the British Museum.

Born: October 18, 1925, in Athens, Greece
Height: 5 ft. 7 in.
Weight: 125 lbs.
Eyes: Brown
Hair: Blond
Zodiac: Libra
Education: High school dropout
Religion: Atheist

Marriages:
To Pan Gharocopos (1942–1965)
To Jules Dassin (1966–)
Children: None
Interests: Politics, socialism, theater
Personal Habits and Traits: Chain smoker, drinks her share
Address: Athens
Income: $70,000 (minimum estimate)

Freddie Mercury

Frederick Bulsara

"The whole point is to be pompous and provocative, to prompt speculation and controversy."

The androgynous king of Queen, Britain's platinum-edged answer to Kiss, Freddie Mercury was born Frederick Bulsara to Persian parents in Zanzibar, where his father worked as an accountant in the British Colonial Office. He attended private school in Bombay, India, and played keyboard with a group called The Hectics at 18. Mercury enrolled in London's Ealing College of Art with the idea of becoming an illustrator, but soon dropped out to found Queen with drummer Roger Taylor. For all its blatantly crass bisexual appeal, Queen boasts some of the best-educated musicians anywhere. One member holds a degree in biology, another in astronomy, and yet another in electronics. In spite of his supertight spandex jumpsuits and outrageous posturing, snaggletoothed Mercury (he avoided the dentist for 15 years) is serious about his work and is personally rather straight: since 1970 he has lived with Mary Austin, a clerk-turned-bookkeeper. Queen's—and Mercury's—million-selling anthem, "We Are the Champions," established the rock group as big-time moneymakers. Their number-one single, "Another One Bites the Dust," proved that—unlike many other groups—Queen wasn't about to. Mercury went solo in 1985, quickly scoring with "I Was Born to Love You."

Born: September 8, 1946, in Zanzibar
Height: 5 ft. 11 in.
Weight: 174 lbs.
Eyes: Brown
Hair: Brown
Zodiac: Virgo
Education: Dropped out of Ealing College of Art
Marriages: None
Children: None
Interests: Oriental antiques, art
Personal Habits and Traits: Afraid of dentists (he put it off for 15 years), smokes, drinks tea, has violent temper (throws things)
Address: London
Income: $450,000 (estimate)

Bette Midler

"I wouldn't say I invented tack, but I definitely brought it to its present high popularity."

The Lilliputian Divine Miss M owes her rather peculiar first name to the fact that her movie buff mother thought Bette Davis's first name was pronounced the way it looked. Growing up Jewish and unhappy in Honolulu, where her father labored as a house painter for the Navy, Midler had finished her first year at the University of Hawaii when her very best friend from high school died in a car crash. Five years later Midler's sister Judith was also killed in an automobile crash, and

Bette's first album was dedicated to her. A tiny part in 1965's *Hawaii* was enough to send Midler on the road to Los Angeles and then New York, where, after scraping along as a file clerk and a go-go dancer, she worked her way up from the chorus to a leading role as Tevye's eldest daughter in *Fiddler on the Roof.* When she learned that the Continental Baths, Manhattan's subterranean gay mecca, was beginning to feature entertainment, Midler donned her platforms and knocked them out with her act. While she became a cult figure at $50 a night, her accompanist, a young composer-arranger-singer named Barry Manilow, began producing her first album. Since winning a Grammy and a Tony in 1973 for her "trash with flash" and "sleaze with ease," the "last of the tacky ladies" (as she bills herself) has been anything but in the pits. Two gold singles—"Do You Wanna Dance" and an overdubbed version of the Andrews Sisters' "Boogie Woogie Bugle Boy"—preceded Midler's triumphant *Clams on the Half Shell Revue* and a TV special of her own. A grueling concert tour several years before had left Midler physically drained, but in the winter of 1977–1978 she decided to hit the road again, touring smaller clubs, and no sooner had the successful tour ended than Midler began filming the first movie in which she had a starring role—*The Rose,* a fictional account of the rise and fall of a rock singer à la Janis Joplin. No sooner did *The Rose* open to ecstatic reviews (the title song was also a superseller and earned her a 1981 Grammy as female vocalist of the year) than Bette bowled 'em over again with a new album, *Thighs and Whispers,* and *Divine Madness* on Broadway and on film. Midler's raunchy memoir, *A View From a Broad,* was published in 1980, and she followed that up with the less successful *Baby Divine*. Her movie *Jinxed* definitely was, but she proved she could still steal a show as one of the hosts of the first MTV Awards show. Midler ended her bachelorettehood in late 1984, trading 2 A.M. vows at Las Vegas's Candlelight Wedding Chapel with Argentine commodities trader Martin Rochus Sebastian von Haselberg. After making *Down and Out in Beverly Hills*, Bette followed with the second in her three-film deal with Disney, *Ruthless People*. Two years after her marriage to von Haselberg, following the release of *Down and Out*, Midler announced that she would soon be a mommy.

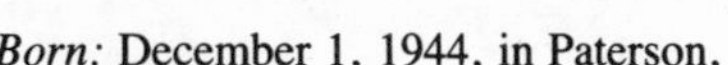

Born: December 1, 1944, in Paterson, New Jersey
Height: 5 ft. 1 in.
Weight: 110 lbs.
Eyes: Blue
Hair: Reddish blond
Zodiac: Sagittarius
Education: University of Hawaii
Religion: Jewish

Marriages:
To Martin Rochus Sebastian von Haselberg (1984–)
Children: None
Interests: Acting, gardening, antique clothing
Personal Habits and Traits: Chain smoker, a hard drinker, compulsive, night animal
Address: Los Angeles
Income: $750,000 (minimum estimate)

Sarah Miles

"Before I fall in love again, he will have to be superior to me in every way. It will never happen—unless I meet a madman."

She unself-consciously bared her breasts for 1972's *Lady Caroline Lamb* and smoldered on the screen in nude love scenes with Kris Kristofferson in *The Sailor Who Fell From Grace With the Sea,* yet Sarah Miles somehow manages to present herself as quite refined and woefully shy. A descendant of the man who owned Britain's very first railway line, Miles stayed far away from the family engineering business and headed straight for the Royal Academy of Dramatic Art. She burst onto the acting scene as the less-than-demure love of Dirk Bogarde in *The Servant,* then cinched it with the role of Rosie in David Lean's *Ryan's Daughter*. Married for 10 years to Oscar-winning screenwriter Robert Bolt (*A Man for All Seasons, Ryan's Daughter*), Miles became enmeshed in scandal when her young business manager killed himself in her motel room while she was shooting the 1973 *The Man Who Loved Cat Dancing* with Burt Reynolds in Arizona. After rumors of a tempestuous affair with Reynolds and a merciless inquest into the bizarre circumstances of her manager's death, Miles returned home to England but not to Bolt—her marriage officially ended four years later. Though still vividly remembered, Miles's career seemed barely extant by the mid-1980s.

Born: December 31, 1943, in Essex, England
Height: 5 ft. 5 in.
Weight: 120 lbs.
Eyes: Blue
Hair: Brown
Zodiac: Capricorn
Education: Royal Academy of Dramatic Art
Religion: Anglican

Marriages:
To Robert Bolt (1967–1977)
Children: Thomas
Interests: Horses, men
Personal Habits and Traits: Smokes, drinks, is a loner, wears Winchester prep school pajamas to bed, a nonstop talker
Address: Los Angeles
Income: $50,000 (estimate)

Steve Miller

"I want to lead a normal life, to walk into the grocery store and go unnoticed. I'm a musician, not a rock personality."

His *Fly Like an Eagle* album did just that—gliding in the Top 20 for no less than 42 weeks and selling 3 million copies. The son of a pathologist, Steve Miller was born in Dallas where his mother and all three brothers were musicians; it was only natural for Steve to form his own band at the age of 12. With an eye on becoming a comparative literature professor, he enrolled at the University of Wisconsin and then studied at Copenhagen University before being lured to San Francisco's acid-rock scene in the 1960s. Not until 1973's *The Joker* did he strike platinum at age 30. Shunning the trappings of success in the rock world, Miller hung his gold record for *The Joker* above the washing machine in his house so he could look at it every time he washed his underwear. He retains neither a manager nor a publicist, and spends most of his time on his 312-acre farm in a remote part of central Oregon. There he keeps house with his Australian girlfriend, Jennie, whom he met at a Pink Floyd concert. Their crops include wheat, corn, alfalfa, oats, rose hips, and more hits recorded at Miller's own 24-track studio.

Born: 1944 in Dallas, Texas
Height: 5 ft. 10½ in.
Weight: 170 lbs.
Eyes: Brown
Hair: Brown
Education: University of Wisconsin, Copenhagen University
Religion: Protestant
Marriages: One (divorced)
Children: None
Interests: Literature (particularly Proust), fishing, driving his $18,500 Dino Spyder Ferrari, farming
Personal Habits and Traits: Does not drink, smokes, does not take dope, consumes lots of coffee
Address: Central Oregon
Income: $300,000 (estimate)

Liza Minnelli

"I think it's neat that a lot of people are still making money off my mother. Bone-picking was never my bag."

The multitalented daughter of Judy Garland and Vincente Minnelli, Liza Minnelli was still an infant when carried in her mother's arms into the happy ending of the 1946 musical *In the Good Old Summertime.* By the time she was 6 her parents split, and by 11 she was running a household in the absence of any authority from her severely troubled mother—hiring and firing servants, keeping creditors at bay, and dealing as best she could with Garland's frequent suicide attempts. Liza had attended 20 schools in Europe and the United States by the time she broke away at 19 to win a Tony for *Flora the Red Menace*—a feat she repeated a dozen years later when she copped a second Tony for *The Act.* Her first major movie was Albert Finney's *Charlie Bubbles.* The second time at bat she won an Academy Award nomination for *The Sterile Cuckoo,* and finally copped a Best Actress Award for 1972's *Cabaret,* the same year she won an Emmy for her TV special *Liza With a Z.* She repaid *Cabaret* director Bob Fosse several years later by subbing for the ailing Gwen Verdon as star of Fosse's Broadway hit *Chicago,* and her entire five-week run was sold out within 12 hours—without any advertising. She was not so lucky with her subsequent movies, however. She bombed in her father's dreadful *A Matter of Time* in 1976, while her *Lucky Lady* of the same year was a major fiasco, and even her singing could not save Martin Scorsese's pretentious big-band saga *New York, New York.* Minnelli's romantic life has been no less varied—and no more successful. Her 1967 marriage to songwriter and cabaret performer Peter Allen ended after five years. For two years she was engaged to Desi Arnaz, Jr., then had flings with a Parisian aristocrat, a Brazilian playboy, and Peter Sellers before marrying producer Jack Haley, Jr. (*That's Entertainment, I and II*). Haley, Sr. was the Tin Man who escorted Liza's mom on the yellow brick road in *The Wizard of Oz*. The Haleys were divorced in 1978. A year later, she married sculptor Mark Gero, and a week after the wedding suffered a miscarriage. She promptly declared her intention to try again: "I'm going to keep doing it," she joked, "till I get it right!" She suffered yet another miscarriage in December 1980. Minnelli became increasingly dependent on booze and pills to get her through *The Rink* on Broadway, and in late 1984 checked herself into the Betty Ford Clinic at the urging of close friend (and clinic alumna) Elizabeth Taylor.

Born: March 12, 1946, in Los Angeles, California
Height: 5 ft. 6 in.
Weight: 124 lbs.
Eyes: Brown
Hair: Black
Zodiac: Pisces
Education: High school
Religion: Roman Catholic

Marriages:
To Peter Allen (1967–1972)
To Jack Haley, Jr. (1974–1978)
To Mark Gero (1979–)
Children: None
Interests: Ballet, fashion
Personal Habits and Traits: Smokes, bites her fingernails
Address: New York City
Income: $1 million (estimate)

Joni Mitchell

Roberta Joan Anderson

"If I were to write the words I'm feeling now, it would probably read something like 'Zsa Zsa's got her jewels/Minnie's got her chicken to go/I've got my corporations/I'm a capitalist so-and-so.'"

Born to an RCAF officer-turned-grocery-store-manager and his schoolteacher wife, Roberta Joan Anderson started life at the edge of the Canadian prairie in Alberta's rolling foothills. By the time the family settled in Saskatoon, Saskatchewan, the rugged beauty of central Canada had inspired her to become an artist. Literally kept on a leash as a child, Joni eventually rebelled by becoming fiercely independent. She took off for art school in Calgary, then decided that her guitar and ukulele strumming were good enough for her to try make it as a musician. Playing clubs in Toronto, she ran into a cabaret singer named Chuck Mitchell and married him a month later. A duo onstage as well as off, they moved to Detroit's Wayne State University campus and after their nightly act at local spots would engage in all-night poker with the likes of Gordon Lightfoot and Buffy Sainte-Marie. Joni left Mitchell after less than a year (but kept his name), and headed for New York City where she composed and recorded one of her first hits, "Chelsea Morning." The decline of the San Francisco sound signaled the rise of L.A. as the country's rock-music capital, and Joni brought her effortlessly lyrical music to the West Coast in 1968. Mitchell's ethereal, poetic quality attracted a number of famous rockers who eventually became her lovers—James Taylor, Jackson Browne, Leonard Cohen, David Crosby, Graham Nash—not to mention Warren Beatty and record tycoon David Geffen. She also packed coliseums with her penetrating soprano and created million-sellers like "Yellow Taxi" and "Help Me." Joni, seldom alone in her 16-room Bel Air mansion, still makes a twice-annual pilgrimage back to Saskatoon. She joined countrymen Anne Murray, Gordon Lightfoot, and others to record "Tears Are Not Enough," Canada's answer to Britain's "Do They Know It's Christmas?" and USA for Africa's "We Are the World."

Born: November 7, 1943, in Ft. McLeod, Alberta
Height: 5 ft. 8 in.
Weight: 128 lbs.
Eyes: Blue
Hair: Blond
Zodiac: Scorpio
Education: High school
Religion: Protestant
Marriages: To Chuck Mitchell (1965–1966)
Children: None
Interests: Picasso, poker and cribbage, skiing
Personal Habits and Traits: Smokes, drinks, is a night owl
Address: Bel Air, California
Income: \$1 million+ (from her two corporations and real estate)

Robert Mitchum

"What was it like in jail? Just like Palm Springs—without the riffraff, of course."

The "shark with a broken nose" spent time on a Georgia chain gang for vagrancy and was busted in 1948 for possession of marijuana just as his career was getting off the ground. None of it hurt Mitchum's popularity, however, predicated as it is on the image of a sullen outsider. After an itinerant childhood bumming around the country during the Depression, Mitchum worked at Lockheed until the noise from the machinery threatened to ruin his hearing and shatter his nerves. He rode as an extra or bit player in several Hopalong Cassidy flicks until *The Story of G.I. Joe* made him a top box-office draw in 1945. Of more than 45 films, some of his best include *Heaven Knows Mr. Allison, Crossfire, The Night of the Hunter, Two for the Seesaw, What a Way to Go!, Ryan's Daughter, The Friends of Eddie Coyle,* and *The Long Goodbye*. Mitchum's worst include *The Last Tycoon,* in which he played a philandering Hollywood mogul, the pointless *Yakuza,* and a disastrous remake of the Raymond Chandler classic *The Big Sleep*. He switched to television for the miniseries based on Herman Wouk's *Winds of War* and did an unfortunate piece of work portraying William Randolph Hearst in an amateurish TV movie on the Hearst–Marion Davies affair. Mitchum was nonetheless excited by the prospect of working with his son Chris and grandson Bentley in a CBS-TV movie, *Fathering*.

Born: August 6, 1917, in Bridgeport, Connecticut
Height: 6 ft.
Weight: 200 lbs.
Eyes: Blue
Hair: Brown
Zodiac: Leo
Education: High school dropout
Religion: Protestant
Marriages: To Dorothy Spence (1940–)
Children: Three
Interests: Theater, music, art, books, horseback riding
Personal Habits and Traits: Smokes, a hard drinker, articulate
Address: Beverly Hills
Income: $1.1 million (estimate)

Dudley Moore

"I try to seduce."

His "gamey" left leg is a half-inch shorter than his right, he is slightly pudgy, and he stands barely 5 feet 2 inches. No matter. In hit movies like *10* and *Arthur,* cuddly Dudley Moore emerged as one of Hollywood's most engaging romantic leads. The son of a secretary and a British Railways electrician (Dudley still wears his dad's retirement watch), Moore learned early that the best way to blunt the taunts of his peers (they called him "Hopalong") was to become the class clown. He also lost himself in music, starting lessons at 6 and later attending Oxford's Magdalen College on a music scholarship. After a couple of years touring with an orchestra and composing his own tunes, Moore teamed up in 1961 with Peter Cook and several other Oxbridge grads to create a satiricial revue called *Beyond the Fringe. Fringe* was a huge success, as was the subsequent Dudley Moore–Peter Cook collaboration, *Good Evening,* which ran almost continuously in London and New York for five years. After Moore and Cook split up in 1977, Dudley costarred with Goldie Hawn and Chevy Chase as a libidinous loser in *Foul Play,* which led to his part in *10*. Moore spent more than 17 years in analysis trying to come to terms with his insecurities, but he's been anything but shy around women; he talks relentlessly and unselfconsciously about his sexual history. Married twice, to English actress Suzy Kendall and to Tuesday Weld, Moore dates the likes of actress Brogan Lane, 28 years his junior, but spent most of his time in 1985 with 5-foot, 11-inch singer Susan Anton. Their song: "I've Got You Under My Chin."

Born: April 19, 1935, in Dagenham, Essex, England
Height: 5 ft. 2 in.
Weight: 136 lbs.
Eyes: Brown
Hair: Brown
Zodiac: Aries
Education: Oxford University
Religion: Protestant

Marriages:
To Suzy Kendall (1968–1970)
To Tuesday Weld (1970–1975)
Children: Patrick (b. 1975)
Interests: Classical and jazz piano, composing, movies
Personal Habits and Traits: One of Hollywood's few admitted partygoers, night owl, drinks moderately
Address: Marina del Rey, California
Income: $1.5 million per film

Mary Tyler Moore

"I'm not an actress who can create a character. I play me. I'm scared that if I tamper with it I might ruin it."

She started out as the legs (her face was never seen) on TV's *Richard Diamond* series in the 1950s and wound up 20 years later as a multimillionaire television tycoon. Brought up by Irish parents in Brooklyn, she was 9 when her family picked up and moved to Los Angeles. Mary attended Immaculate Heart High and right after graduation marched down the aisle with CBS sales representative Richard Meeker; later she gave birth to a son, Richie. It took six years—during which she played three-inch "Happy Hotpoint" in a TV appliance commercial and divorced Meeker—before the role of Laura Petrie on *The Dick Van Dyke Show* materialized in 1961. Moore had collected two Emmys and a new husband, producer Grant Tinker, by the time Van Dyke closed down the show after five tremendously successful seasons. A stab at movies (*Thoroughly Modern Millie*) and a stage musical version of *Breakfast at Tiffany's* with Richard Chamberlain (it closed out of town) set back Moore's career drastically, but a CBS special with Van Dyke in 1969 signaled her return to the tube. The following year she was launched in the role of Mary Richards, the 30ish single woman who works in a Minneapolis newsroom. *The Mary Tyler Moore Show* was the biggest comedy hit since *I Love Lucy,* and soon MTM Productions (with its pussycat put-on of the MGM lion) was an assembly line of sitcom hits, including *The Bob Newhart Show* and the spinoffs *Rhoda, Phyllis,* and *Lou Grant,* as well as *The White Shadow*. With Mary as chairman and Tinker as president, the MTM lot hummed, and although Moore made the decision to close down *The Mary Tyler Moore Show* at its peak in 1977, MTM grosses well over $25 million annually and is constantly turning out new series, including *Bob Newhart, Remington Steele,* and *St. Elsewhere*. MTM's sole stockholders, separated for five months in 1974, were headed for divorce six years later. Moore proved herself to be a first-rate dramatic actress playing cancer-stricken TV reporter Betty Rollin in *First You Cry,* and again as the mother in the Robert Redford–directed *Ordinary People*—the role for which she was nominated for an Academy Award (but lost to Sissy Spacek). Marring that was a deeply felt personal tragedy; not long after the release of *Ordinary People,* Mary's only child, Richie, accidentally shot and killed himself. Moore married Dr. Robert Levine, 16 years her junior, and was soon drinking heavily enough to alarm her husband; she then joined the celebrity parade into the Betty Ford Clinic. Her attempt to update the Mary Richards image on a new series, *Mary*, didn't make it after all. *Just Between Friends*, a movie about a woman whose best friend unwittingly becomes her husband's mistress, fared better.

Born: December 29, 1937, in Brooklyn, New York
Height: 5 ft. 7 in.
Weight: 118 lbs.
Eyes: Brown
Hair: Brown
Zodiac: Capricorn
Education: High school
Religion: Roman Catholic
Marriages:
To Richard Meeker (divorced)
To Grant Tinker (1963–1980)
To Robert Levine (1983–)
Children: Richie (1957–1980)
Interests: Diabetes (she is a diabetic), ballet, the Fund for Animals, Los Ranchos Amigos Children's Hospital, needlepoint
Personal Habits and Traits: Chain-smokes, an exercise nut
Addresses: New York City; Los Angeles
Income: $35 million (estimated annual gross of MTM)

Roger Moore

"My biggest fault is my humility. I'm really a very humble person. For somebody who's 6 feet 2 inches, with blue eyes, rich and talented and charming, I'm terribly modest!"

While not the Bonded original, this once-chubby London copper's son, who dropped out of school at 15 to become an artist, has just as much claim on the movies' best-known fictional character as the first 007. In fact, when he was asked to take over the role of Ian Fleming's urbane alter ego from Sean Connery, the situation was very familiar to Moore; much of his career had been spent taking over parts made famous by other actors. He replaced James Garner in the hit western series *Maverick,* and then followed George Sanders and Louis Hayward as debonair Simon Templar in the TV version of *The Saint.* His movie career, which began with 1954's *The Last Time I Saw Paris* (Moore played the young tennis player who loses Elizabeth Taylor to Van Johnson), stalled until he went into Bondage with *Live and Let Die,* followed by *The Man With the Golden Gun, The Spy Who Loved Me, Moonraker, Octopussy,* and *A View to a Kill.* Once an extravagant gambler, he claims he retired from the backgammon tables feeling like one of James Bond's martinis—"bruised, stirred, but still definitely unshaken." After one teenage marriage and another to popular British singer Dorothy Squires, Moore married Italian actress Luisa Mattioli, whom he met on the set of *The Rape of the Sabine Women.* They and the three children divide their time among homes in Switzerland, Italy, and the south of France.

Born: October 14, 1928, in London
Height: 6 ft. 2 in.
Weight: 195 lbs.
Eyes: Blue
Hair: Light brown
Zodiac: Libra
Education: High school dropout
Religion: Protestant
Marriages:
To Doorn Van Steyn (1947–1951)
To Dorothy Squires (1953–1969)
To Luisa Mattioli (1969–)
Children: Three: Deborah (b. 1963), Geoffrey (b. 1966), Christian (b. 1973)
Interests: Painting and sketching, music (guitar), backgammon
Personal Habits and Traits: Up at 6 A.M. and exercises 20 minutes, watches what he eats but doesn't diet, smokes, moderate drinker, a self-confessed workaholic, charming to a fault
Addresses: Switzerland, Italy, France
Income: $3 million per film

Eddie Murphy

"I think in 20 years I'll be looked at like a Bob Hope. Doing these President jokes and golf shit. It scares me."

"I had a potbelly, brown frame glasses, and a bald head," the decade's standout comedy star says of that fateful day back in the third grade. "One day, Mr. Wunch came into class and said that whoever made up the best story would win an Eskimo Pie. I cracked the kids up with a story about rice and Orientals. It was my first performance. And guess who won the pie!" A dozen years later, at 20, he brought his own cast of memorable characters to the revived *Saturday Night Live:* Mister Robinson, the ghetto version of Mister Rogers ("Can you say 'scumbucket,' boys and girls?"), TV con man Velvet Jones pushing a book called *I Wanna Be a Ho,* a carping Gumby, and a growed-up Buckwheat—not to mention his on-the-mark impressions of Jerry Lewis, Stevie Wonder, Mr. T, and James Brown. Soon he was a quadruple threat, adding records (Grammys for gold comedy albums), concerts, and movies (*48 Hours, Trading Places,* and the phenomenally successful *Beverly Hills Cop*—part of his $15 million deal with Paramount). Although he has a very strong attachment to his family and appears level-headed in the wake of his meteoric rise, Murphy liberally sprinkles his conversation and his stage act with obscenities. (Gays and women in particular have been offended by jokes that smack of sexism and bigotry.) Has he been spoiled by success? "Johnny Carson said that you don't change," says Murphy, "the people around you do. It's *true.*"

Born: April 3, 1961, in Brooklyn, New York
Height: 5 ft. 10 in.
Weight: 160 lbs.
Eyes: Brown
Hair: Black
Zodiac: Aries
Education: High school
Marriages: None
Children: None
Interests: Luxury cars, clothes, jewelry
Personal Habits and Traits: Eschews alcohol, tobacco, drugs; is a junk-food junkie
Address: Alpine, New Jersey
Income: $12 million annually (estimate)

Anne Murray

"Las Vegas isn't for me. I'm just a turntable person."

The former physical education teacher from Springhill, Nova Scotia, who once sang for beer money in Halifax's Monterey Lounge, was for years the biggest pop entertainer in her native Canada before she clicked south of the border. After her first gold record "Snowbird" took flight both in the United States and Canada in 1970, she made several appearances on network television and teamed up with Glen Campbell to record an album that sold more than 350,000 copies. Still, her career stalled until she connected with Shep Gordon and Allan Strale, the New York music promoters whose Alive Enterprises also managed Alice Cooper. Gordon arranged an appearance at the Troubadour in Los Angeles during Murray's 1973–1974 tour, and for the occasion a doorkeeper blew fanfares on a hunter's horn as guests arrived bearing parchment invitations, hand-delivered by messengers in pilgrim costumes. Grammy-nominated that year for her Capitol hit "Danny's Song," she followed up with "Oklahoma Crude" (nominated for an Oscar), "A Love Song" (which earned Murray her first Grammy), and a remake of the Beatles's "You Won't See Me." In 1979 "You Needed Me," delivered in her characteristic husky contralto, garnered yet another Grammy and made it to the top of the pop charts, followed by "I Fall in Love Again," "Shadows in the Moonlight," "A Little Good News," and "Tears Are Not Enough," the joint effort of several Canadian artists to benefit Ethiopian famine relief. As for her own image, Murray gravitated away from country and even closer to pop-rock with her slick "Now and Forever (You and Me)."

Born: June 20, 1945, in Springhill, Nova Scotia
Height: 5 ft. 6 ½ in.
Weight: 127 lbs.
Eyes: Blue
Hair: Blond
Zodiac: Gemini

Marriages:
To David Langstruth (1975–)
Children: William and Dawn
Interests: Sports, songwriting
Personal Habits and Traits: Nonsmoker, drinks beer, not overly sociable
Address: Nova Scotia
Income: $1.2 million (estimate)

Bill Murray

"I'm a nut, but not just *a nut."*

Bill Murray a movie star? Get outta here. In truth, Chicago-bred Murray did not get off to an auspicious start. A self-described "screw-off" in Catholic boys school, he was also kicked out of the Boy Scouts, Little League, and the altar boy society. As a teenager, this fifth of a working-class couple's nine children helped pay the bills by caddying (experience he would later use in the film *Caddyshack*) and by working in a pizzeria. A short-lived premed student at Denver's Regis College, Murray dropped out and returned to his hometown to join older brother Brian Doyle-Murray as part of Chicago's Second City improvisational group. Later, along with fellow wild and crazies John Belushi, Chevy Chase, Dan Aykroyd, and Gilda Radner, Murray joined the cast of the *National Lampoon Radio Hour,* and in 1976 was tapped to join his old buddies as a Not Ready for Prime Time Player on the hit NBC series *Saturday Night Live*. Murray's best *SNL* bits: a sleazy, off-key lounge singer, an overly hip movie critic/gossip ("Love you, Baby—don't ever change"), and the ultimate nerd, Todd Loopner. Murray's first starring role in a movie was that of a sarcastic summer camp counselor in the hugely profitable *Meatballs,* followed by the equally off-the-wall *Stripes*. He also played Dustin Hoffman's friend in *Tootsie* without a screen credit. This was all merely a walkup, however, to one of the biggest-grossing films of all time: *Ghostbusters,* in which Murray, Aykroyd, and fellow *Lampooon*er Harold Ramis play spook-removers battling the forces of darkness with electronic spirit-zappers and an air of professional detachment. Although *Ghostbusters* pushed Murray into the top ranks of Hollywood money-earners, he in fact had only agreed to do the film provided that Columbia would allow him to play the dramatic lead (his first) in a remake of *The Razor's Edge*. The critics cut him to ribbons, but that didn't stop American theater owners from voting him 1984's number-one male star. Murray, who married his high school sweetheart, Mickey Kelley, in 1981, shares a penthouse pied à terre on New York's Upper East Side and a large rented house at Sneden's Landing on the Hudson with Mickey and their son, Homer.

Born: September 21, 1950, in Chicago
Height: 6 ft.
Weight: 185 lbs.
Eyes: Blue
Hair: Brown, thinning
Zodiac: Virgo
Education: College dropout
Marriages: To Mickey Kelley (1981–)
Children: Homer (b. 1982)
Interests: Baseball, spiritual questions
Personal Habits and Traits: A dedicated sloppy dresser, broods occasionally, but not sullen or difficult, drinks moderately, is a devout Elvis Presley fan; favorite foods are yogurt and peanut butter and mayonnaise sandwiches with lettuce
Addresses: New York City; Sneden's Landing, New York
Income: $7.5 million asking price per picture

Jim Nabors

As Gomer Pyle on *The Andy Griffith Show* Jim Nabors was required to drawl little else than "Gaawwllee!", but it proved more than enough to catapult the policeman's son from Sylacauga, Alabama, into a career as a million-dollar-a-year entertainer in nightclubs, on records, and on television. Nabors obtained a degree in business administration from the University of Alabama, moved to New York to work as a clerk at the United Nations, and finally headed for L.A. and a job as a junior film cutter for NBC. After hours Nabors brought his powerful though untrained operatic voice and a flair for down-home humor to The Horn, a Santa Monica showcase for raw talent. Comic Bill Dana (creator of José Jiménez) caught his act, and Nabors was soon appearing on Steve Allen's late-night show. Andy Griffith asked him to audition for the role of a naive gas station attendant, and though it was intended as a one-shot appearance, Gomer Pyle proved so popular that he became a regular with Griffith and eventually landed his own separate sitcom—*Gomer Pyle, USMC*. A top draw in Las Vegas and Lake Tahoe, Nabors has also recorded a number of albums, including one that went gold, and upon the cancellation of *Gomer Pyle, USMC* after four successful seasons, the country boy with the booming baritone tried his own midday syndicated talk show in 1978. It lasted less than a year. Nabors's closest pal over the years was Rock Hudson—until false rumors of a "marriage" between the two brought an abrupt end to the friendship.

Born: June 12, 1932, in Sylacauga, Alabama
Height: 6 ft.
Weight: 175 lbs.
Eyes: Brown
Hair: Brown
Zodiac: Gemini
Education: University of Alabama, B.A. in business administration

Religion: Protestant
Marriages: None
Children: None
Interests: Opera
Personal Habits and Traits: Nonsmoker, moderate drinker, not a partygoer
Address: Sherman Oaks, California
Income: $500,000 (minimum estimate)

Ralph Nader

"Obviously, the answer to oil spills is to paper-train the tankers."

Ever since he wrote *Unsafe at Any Speed* in 1965—the bestselling exposé of the auto industry that launched him on a career as Detroit's "number-one enemy" and as America's number-one consumer advocate—Ralph Nader and his young cadre of Raiders have investigated everything that influences the quality of American life from dirty air and water to unsafe toasters and Congressional tax reform. But for a man who demands openness on the part of business and government, Nader remains one of the most secretive of public figures. No one is certain exactly where he lives (his permanent quarters may be the elegant Washington town house of his bachelor brother, Shaffak Nader, an education consultant), or whether he has any romantic or social life. And when General Motors launched a controversial investigation into the private life of its nemesis, Nader easily won his invasion-of-privacy suit against the company for $425,000. Nader—who speaks Arabic as well as some Chinese, Russian, Portuguese, and Spanish—was raised by Lebanese immigrant parents who owned the Highland Arms Restaurant in the factory town of Winsted, Connecticut. In the afternoons after private school, he worked behind the counter at his parents' restaurant. Nader's mother posted a reading list for her children on the kitchen wall; *The Jungle,* Upton Sinclair's classic indictment of working conditions in Chicago meat-packing houses, was included. Nader headed for Princeton, where one former classmate remembers him as an "intellectual who never had a date." Harvard Law School followed, as did six months in the Army. When he was discharged, Nader traveled in South America and wrote pieces for the *Christian Science Monitor*. Later, while compiling investigative reports in Washington about the automobile industry, Nader formulated the idea for *Unsafe at Any Speed.* Today Nader directs his Public Citizen, Inc. (an umbrella organization including the Tax Reform Research Group, the Health Research Group, the Aviation Consumer Project and Congress Watch) from offices only six blocks from the White House. Though shunned by Presidents Johnson, Nixon, and Ford, he at last found an ally of sorts in Jimmy Carter, who consulted Nader occasionally and even appointed two of his Raiders to important subcabinet positions. Many consider Nader to be an arrogant and intolerant do-gooder, yet Nader seems content to remain remote. He needs only four hours sleep each night, has not owned a car for more than 25 years, and reaps his only recreation from reading and watching sports programs on television. He keeps in close touch with boyhood friend David (*The Best and the Brightest*) Halberstam.

Born: February 27, 1934, in Winsted, Connecticut
Height: 6 ft. 2 in.
Weight: 180 lbs.
Eyes: Brown
Hair: Dark brown
Zodiac: Pisces
Education: Princeton University, Harvard Law School

Marriages: None
Children: None
Interests: Consumerism, ecology, economics, reading, watching sports on television
Personal Habits and Traits: Nonsmoker, does not drink alcohol, a vegetarian
Address: Washington, D.C.
Income: $300,000 (estimate)

Joe Namath

"I couldn't do anything I didn't enjoy. You can't fool yourself."

Joe Willie Namath, the steelworker's boy from Beaver Falls, Pennsylvania, was once paid $1 an hour to tend the baseball field at the University of Alabama. When he later signed to play football for the New York Jets, it was for no less than $400,000—at that time the most ever shelled out for a rookie. And although he became an instant playboy cum pop idol, Namath proved to be well worth his salary. Easily the finest passer in the game (he threw a record 4,007 yards during the 1967 season), Joe made sports history the following year by leading the Jets to a spectacular 16–7 upset over the Baltimore Colts in the Super Bowl. By the time his recurring knee injuries forced him to retire from his team in 1978 after an unlucky 13th season—his first with the L.A. Rams—Namath was earning $500,000. He also established himself as one of Madison Avenue's most effective pitchmen, pocketing at least $250,000 for endorsing Fabergé's Brut products for men, and perhaps another half-million a year for peddling Presto hamburger and popcorn makers and La-Z-Boy chairs. Paid $10,000 to shave off his mustache for a razor company, he later shaved his legs for a pantyhose commercial. After his retirement from football, Namath, who has pyramided his fortune into a personal worth of perhaps $10 million, turned his sights to the movies. He had already tried his hand as a cycle jockey in the tongue-in-cheek *C.C. Rider & Company* with Ann-Margret, and in a spaghetti western called *The Last Rebel*, but Broadway Joe plunged headlong into acting lessons—though they did nothing to prevent his disastrous *Waverly Wonders* from being canceled after only a few weeks on TV. Namath was intercepted at the altar by actress Deborah Mays. A few days later, he unveiled his own line of underwear. In August 1985, Namath joined the *ABC Monday Night Football* broadcast crew, replacing Don Meredith and joining Frank Gifford and O. J. Simpson.

Born: May 31, 1943, in Beaver Falls, Pennsylvania
Height: 6 ft. 1 in.
Weight: 200 lbs.
Eyes: Blue
Hair: Brown
Zodiac: Gemini
Education: University of Alabama
Religion: Protestant
Marriages: To Deborah Mays (1985–)
Children: Jessica Grace (b. 1985)
Interests: Golf (shoots in the 80s), fishing, reading, acting
Personal Habits and Traits: A nonsmoker but does drink beer, not punctual, can be rude
Addresses: New York City; Fort Lauderdale, Florida; Tuscaloosa, Alabama
Income: $1.2 million

Graham Nash

"We're not a group. We're three individuals making albums together. I don't want to feel as if I have to be in a certain place at a certain time, to arrange my life to suit anyone but me. I've always been kind of selfish that way."

The driving force behind Crosby, Stills and Nash, British-born Graham Nash commenced his musical career by playing a banjo-tuned guitar in Manchester, where his father labored as a machine shop engineer. The elder Nash's death at the age of 46 left the would-be rock star "wanting to use my life and talents to the fullest," and at 22 he founded the Hollies, an enormously successful group that spun off several hits before dissolving in 1967. Nash met Stephen Stills and David Crosby in 1969, and the trio became an almost instant success with songs like "Judy Blue Eyes" and "Marrakesh Express." Their mellow folk sound kept them at the top of the charts—often accompanied by talented Canadian guitarist Neil Young—until what seemed to be the demise of the group in 1974. But CS&N regrouped in 1977, and found their following had not diminished. Now living with his second wife Susan in a three-story Victorian San Francisco town house, Nash collects rare photographs (his collection is valued at nearly $800,000), W.C. Fields memorabilia, and antiques. He also sculpts, plays chess with a computer, and scuba dives. And he composes songs, like "Teach Your Children"—the folk-rock classic that lured Stephen Stills back into the fold. Their *Southern Cross* video and their crowd-pleasing performance at 1985's Live Aid concert introduced Nash and friends to a new generation of fans.

Born: 1942 in Blackpool, England
Height: 6 ft. 1 in.
Weight: 159 lbs.
Eyes: Brown
Hair: Brown
Education: High school
Marriages: Two. Currently to Susan Nash
Children: None
Interests: Rare photographs, an amateur photographer himself, collects antiques, sails and scuba dives, is a soccer and chess nut, sculpts
Personal Habits and Traits: Smokes, drinks little, forceful, articulate, independent, never seems to gain weight
Address: San Francisco
Income: $350,000 (minimum estimate)

Willie Nelson

"I've had so many ups and downs over the last 30 years, I've learned to live with both."

The ponytail, the on-again, off-again beard, the bandanna, and the quavering, whispered falsetto add up to one of show business's most unlikely legends. Given his first guitar at the age of 5 by his blacksmith grandfather, Willie learned to play by imitating the Grand Ole Opry tunes he heard over the radio. After high school, Willie enlisted in the Air Force and a year later, after being discharged with a back injury, landed a job as a disc jockey in Waco, Texas. He lasted one semester at Baylor University, but dropped out in the late 1950s to play in local

honky-tonks for 50 cents a night. He moved to Nashville with the first of his three wives, a full-blooded Cherokee, and became so despondent over his failure to sell his songs that he sprawled in a drunken stupor outside a Nashville bar and waited for a car to run over him. The last night of their marriage, he passed out drunk and woke up to find that his wife had sewn him up in a sheet. She then beat him up with a broomstick, took their children, and left with her clothes *and* his clothes so he couldn't follow her. From then on, he began selling his bittersweet laments to be performed by established country singers, and by the mid-'60s was one of Nashville's most successful composers. His next stormy marriage—to country singer Shirley Collie—gave him even more material. After years of boozing, drugs, and adultery, they split—but even before their divorce was final, Willie went ahead and married factory worker Connie Koepke. Willie was still unable to get his performing career off the ground when, in 1970, his house caught afire. He ran in to save a pound of marijuana, but more than 100 tapes of his songs went up in smoke. Nelson moved his family to Austin, Texas, bought a used Greyhound bus, and started touring county fairs and sawdust-on-the-floor bars. At long last, he broke from the pack with his 1973 album *Shotgun Willie,* followed up by *Red Headed Stranger* and a C&W hit that would become his theme song: "On the Road Again." And on the road he usually is, averaging 250 days a year on tour (he gets $1.5 million, for example, just to play Caesars Palace). Then there are movies (*The Electric Horseman, Honeysuckle Rose*) and holdings that include a country club, an apartment complex, a music publishing company, several ranches, and the Austin Opry House.

Born: April 30, 1933, in Fort Worth, Texas
Height: 5 ft. 8 in.
Weight: 145 lbs.
Eyes: Blue
Hair: Gray-brown
Zodiac: Taurus
Education: One semester of college
Religion: Baptist
Marriages:
To Martha Mathews (1952–1960)
To Shirley Collie (1961–1970)
To Connie Koepke (1970–)

Children: Five: Lana (b. 1954), Susan (b. 1957), Billy (b. 1959), Paula Carlene (b. 1970), Amy Lee (b. 1973)
Interests: Running, golf
Personal Habits and Traits: Heavy marijuana smoker, drinks Jack Daniel's, easygoing and accessible
Addresses: Austin, Texas; Denver, Colorado; Evergreen, Colorado; Utah; Hawaii
Income: $7 million

Bob Newhart

George Robert Newhart

"I was a lousy accountant. I always figured that if you came within eight bucks of what you needed you were doing okay. I made up the difference out of my own pocket."

An instant success with the release in 1960 of his album *The Button-Down Mind of Bob Newhart,* this accountant-turned-comic was rewarded with a television series of his own in 1961 that won both an Emmy and a Peabody Award, but lasted only a single season. Newhart fared much better 11 years later, when his MTM-produced *Bob Newhart Show* nearly reached the top of the Nielsens and remained there until he decided to quit the show in 1978. He returned a few years later with yet another *Bob Newhart Show*—this one about a writer-turned-New-England-innkeeper—which turned out to be even bigger in the ratings. Born George Robert Newhart, he was educated at Chicago's St. Ignatius High School and earned a bachelor's degree in commerce at Loyola University. Following a two-year hitch in the Army and a brief attempt at law school, Newhart worked as a copywriter, a clerk and finally as an accountant before landing a job as host of a Chicago-based morning TV show. The show lasted only five weeks, but it brought Newhart to the attention of Warner Brothers Records, which signed him to record his now classic album. In addition to frequently substituting on the *Tonight Show* for Johnny Carson and appearing on numerous variety and comedy series, Newhart has been featured in such movies as *Hot Millions, Catch-22* (playing Major Major), *Cold Turkey, Thursday's Game,* and *First Family.* Even while *Bob Newhart Show* Number 3 was maintaining its hold in the Top 10, *Bob Newhart Show* Number 2 was developing a cult following in reruns. An avid golfer, Newhart lives on a lavish Beverly Hills estate with his wife, Ginny, and their three children, while his best friend is none other than the "Sultan of Insult," Don Rickles.

Born: September 5, 1929, in Chicago, Illinois
Height: 5 ft. 8 in.
Weight: 148 lbs.
Eyes: Blue
Hair: Sandy
Zodiac: Virgo
Education: Loyola University, B.S. in commerce
Religion: Roman Catholic
Marriages: To Virginia "Ginny" Quinn (current)
Children: Robert (b. 1963), Timothy (b. 1967), Jennifer (b. 1971)
Interests: Golf, acting
Personal Habits and Traits: Quit smoking, drinks moderately, late sleeper, a social animal
Address: Beverly Hills
Income: $2.5 million+

Paul Newman

"You don't stop being a citizen just because you have a SAG [Screen Actor's Guild] card."

Since the mid-1950s Paul Newman has been *the* premier Hollywood sex symbol—not to mention the owner of the most famous blue eyes in show business

(with the possible exception of Frank Sinatra). Newman, who intensifies the blue with imported French eye drops, is the scion of a well-to-do family in the sporting goods business—"If I'm close to any of the characters I've played I'm closest to the wealthy young businessman in *From the Terrace*." He served during World War II in the Navy Air Corps as a radioman (partial colorblindness kept him out of flight training). Graduating with a B.A. in economics and dramatics from Kenyon College, he studied drama at Yale and then the Actors Studio until his first small role on Broadway in William Inge's *Picnic*. A biblical epic called *The Silver Chalice* provided his movie debut in 1955, and he soon triumphed in the meaty part of Brick in Tennessee Williams's *Cat on a Hot Tin Roof*. Though several times an Oscar nominee (*Cat on a Hot Tin Roof, The Hustler, Hud, Cool Hand Luke, the Verdict*), he has yet to win the coveted award for a single performance. Instead, in 1986 the Academy bestowed a special lifetime achievement Oscar. Indeed, his output has been impressive: Williams's *Sweet Bird of Youth, Butch Cassidy and the Sundance Kid, The Sting,* and, in 1981, *Fort Apache: The Bronx*. An accomplished director, he copped a New York Film Critics Award for *Rachel, Rachel,* in which his wife, Joanne Woodward, starred; he also directed her in the absorbing film version of *The Effect of Gamma Rays on Man-in-the-Moon Marigolds*. Away from the cameras Newman races Formula One cars professionally and has proved an outspoken advocate on behalf of many liberal causes. He actively supported Presidential aspirants Eugene McCarthy and George McGovern, and claims he is proudest of having wound up on one of Richard Nixon's enemies lists. Newman was appointed by President Jimmy Carter as a U.S. delegate to the UN Conference on Nuclear Disarmament in 1978. Tragedy struck in November of that year, when Newman's stunt man–actor son Scott (from his first marriage) died after mixing pills and alcohol at age 28. While Newman's film career stalled a bit with *Harry and Son,* he embarked on a new career as an entrepreneur, marketing his own salad dressing, popcorn, and "industrial strength" spaghetti sauce—the profits from which go to charity.

Born: January 26, 1925, in Cleveland, Ohio
Height: 5 ft. 9 in.
Weight: 150 lbs.
Eyes: Blue
Hair: Gray
Zodiac: Aquarius
Education: Kenyon College, B.A. in economics and dramatics; Yale University Drama School
Religion: Protestant
Marriages:
To Jackie Witte (divorced)
To Joanne Woodward (1958–)
Children: Three by Witte; three by Woodward
Interests: Auto racing, politics and international relations, directing, literature
Personal Habits and Traits: Chugalugs beer, drives fast, won't sign autographs, a popcorn addict, eats watermelon in the shower
Addresses: Westport, Connecticut; Beverly Hills; Malibu, California
Income: $2.6 million (minimum estimate)

Randy Newman

"I didn't expect 'Short People' to go over big in Japan."

In his brief but decidedly vitriolic song about short people, boldly stating that with their grubby little fingers and dirty minds they have no reason to live, songwriter-singer Randy Newman finally chalked up his first number-one single—and infuriated innumerable shorties in the process. The son of a Los Angeles physician and nephew of Oscar-contending composers Alfred, Emil, and Lionel Newman, Randy studied music at UCLA and in the early 1970s started composing offbeat songs like "Love Story (You and Me, Babe)," "Sail Away," and a number of anti-Archie Bunker cuts on his *Good Ole Boys* album. Newman's *Little Criminals* LP was his first to become gold, but it was recorded only after a three-year dry spell during which he holed up with his wife and children at his spacious home in the Pacific Palisades. He finally overcame his writer's block when he rented an office in Santa Monica and treated the task of songwriting like a regular nine-to-five job. It worked: Newman's "I Love L.A." became that city's new anthem.

Born: November 28, 1943, in Los Angeles, California
Height: 5 ft. 11 in.
Weight: 180 lbs.
Eyes: Brown
Hair: Brown
Zodiac: Sagittarius
Education: University of California at Los Angeles, B.A.
Religion: Jewish
Marriages: To Roswitha Newman (1967–)
Children: Three
Interests: Piano, drums
Personal Habits and Traits: Smokes, drinks, wears thick glasses (he is myopic), is a TV addict
Address: Pacific Palisades, California
Income: $500,000 (minimum estimate)

Wayne Newton

"You really grow up fast in a nightclub."

This cherub-faced Virginian started taking music lessons when he was 6, and by the time he was 16 had become a regular on the Jackie Gleason, Jack Benny and Ed Sullivan television shows. His high-pitched rendition of "Danke Schoen," in which he sounded not unlike Patti Page, marked Newton's first hit single and was produced by his good friend Bobby Darin, who also signed Newton to his new T.M. Music label. Newton's subsequent million-sellers included "Red Roses for a Blue Lady," "Summer Wind," "Dreams of the Everyday Housewife," and "Daddy Don't You Walk So Fast." Having appeared on every major television show and nightclub in the country, Newton ultimately snagged the biggest performing contract in Las Vegas history—$8 million a *year* for performing at the Summa Corporation's Desert Inn, and the Sands and Frontier hotels. Stints in Reno and Tahoe bring in another $2 million. Now making his home in Las Vegas, Newton, who divorced former airline stewardess Elaine Okamura in 1984, lives at Casa Shenandoah, his 458-acre ranch complete with two artificial lakes. There Newton raises prize Arabians, as he does at his enormous spread in Prescott, Arizona. He also gives frequent fund-raising benefit performances on behalf of the St. John's Indian Mission and School in Laveen, Arizona, and for the Nat King Cole Cancer Foundation. Newton, who has had a running feud with Johnny Carson over Carson's cracks about his high-pitched voice, blocked Carson from buying Las Vegas's Aladdin Hotel-Casino, but his own plans to buy the Aladdin, the Stardust, and the Fremont fell through. At one point, he testified before a government committee investigating organized crime that his life had been threatened by underworld figures.

Born: April 3, 1942, in Norfolk, Virginia
Height: 6 ft. 2 in.
Weight: 175 lbs.
Eyes: Brown
Hair: Brown
Zodiac: Aries
Education: High school
Religion: Protestant
Marriages: To Elaine Okamura (1968–1984)
Children: Daughter Erin (b. 1977)
Interests: Breeding Arabian horses, a variety of charities, flying his jet helicopter, motion pictures, antique cars
Personal Habits and Traits: Does not smoke, drinks little, workaholic, early riser, needs little sleep
Addresses: Las Vegas; Prescott, Arizona
Income: $25 million

Olivia Newton-John

"Singing has always come naturally to me. I don't even know what key I sing in."

Nashville raised a ruckus when she was named the Country Music Association's Top Female Vocalist, but there was little doubt that the English-Australian singer deserved it. Olivia's grandfather was Nobel Prize–winning German physicist Max Born; her father yielded to family pressure and became an eminent professor instead of an opera singer, but continued to collect thousands of records—from Chopin to Tennessee Ernie Ford. When Liv was 5, her father moved the family to Australia, where he was made headmaster of Melbourne's University College. At 15 she quit school, won a trip back to England on a talent show, and hooked up with a group called Toomorrow. Then came a tour with popular British crooner Cliff Richard, her European hit "If Not for You," and a string of American gold singles: "Let Me Be There," "If You Love Me Let Me Know," "I Honestly Love You," "Have You Never Been Mellow?," and "Please Mr. Please (Don't Play B-17)." Grammy-winner Newton-John cashed in on her All-American, blond looks and countrified Anglo charm playing opposite John Travolta in

the smash film version of the musical *Grease*. Months before the film's June 1978 release, Newton-John and Travolta shared a million-selling hit with their duo "You're the One That I Want," quickly followed up with her solo hit from the movie, "Hopelessly Devoted to You." Newton-John tried a new, more sophisticated sound with the hit "Will a Little More Love?" Throughout, Olivia's off-and-on boyfriend has been her manager, Lee Kramer. The arrangement was off for good at the time she twirled before the cameras with Gene Kelly in the discomaniacal *Xanadu*. Newton-John and Travolta could not repeat their *Grease* success in 1984's *Two of a Kind,* but she kept cranking out the hits—most memorably "Physical" and its logical follow-up, "Heart Attack." In 1984 she wed Matt Lattanzi, an actor (he played the hustler in *Rich and Famous*) 11 years her junior, and the following year their first little Lattanzi arrived. Her name: Chloe.

Born: September 26, 1948, in Cambridge, England
Height: 5 ft. 5 in.
Weight: 113 lbs.
Eyes: Blue
Hair: Blond
Zodiac: Libra
Education: High school dropout
Marriages: To Matt Latanzi (1984–)
Children: Chloe (b. 1985)
Interests: Animals, motion pictures, television, classical music, swimming, clothes
Personal Habits and Traits: Smokes occasionally, early riser, polite, punctual
Addresses: Malibu, California; London
Income: $2 million+

Mike Nichols

Michael Igor Peschkowsky

"I was fired from my job at a Howard Johnson's when somebody asked me the ice cream flavor of the week and I said chicken."

In the late 1950s and early 1960s Mike Nichols and another engagingly neurotic comic genius named Elaine May teamed up to conquer nightclubs, television, and the Broadway stage. By the 1970s Nichols had reached the summit of his career in yet another incarnation—as the Tony and Oscar-winning director of hit plays (*The Odd Couple, Plaza Suite, The Prisoner of Second Avenue, Streamers, Comedians, The Real Thing, Hurlyburly*) and movies (*Who's Afraid of Virginia Woolf?, The Graduate, Catch-22, Carnal Knowledge*). Berlin-born Michael Igor Peshkowsky, the son of a Russian-Jewish doctor, was 8 when his family fled the Nazis in 1939. After attending private schools in New York City and Connecticut, Nichols dropped out of premed classes at the University of Chicago in 1951 to try his wings as an actor. He supported himself as a Howard Johnson's busboy in New York while attending Lee Strasberg's drama classes, then returned to Chicago to join an improvisational group called Second City. There he met May, and for the next eight years they evolved a unique and wry comedy style as the country's number-one satirical duo, until amicably parting in 1961—she to pursue a writing career and he to make his way as a director. Nichols divorced his first wife, singer Pat Scott, to marry Margot Callas in 1974. Now Nichols and his third wife, Annabel, live with their daughter, Jenny, and son, Max, in a spacious, art-filled Connecticut farmhouse replete with private lake, 60 acres of farmland, and stables for over 90 prize Arabian horses. Nichols auctioned off 31 of them for $913,000.

Born: November 6, 1931, in Berlin
Height: 6 ft. 1 in.
Weight: 182 lbs.
Eyes: Blue
Hair: Blond
Zodiac: Scorpio
Education: Two years at the University of Chicago
Religion: Jewish
Marriages:
To Pat Scott (divorced)
To Margot Callas (divorced)
To Annabel Davis-Goff (current)
Children: A daughter by Margot; a son and a daughter by Annabel
Interests: Directing, acting, writing, psychotherapy, raising Arabian horses, art, music
Personal Habits and Traits: Chain-smokes, a worrier
Address: Connecticut
Income: $850,000 (estimate)

Jack Nicholson

"A star on a movie set is like a time bomb. That bomb has got to be defused so people can approach it without fear."

"With James Dean dead and Marlon Brando middle-aged, Jack Nicholson is creating a new model of the American antihero." With that, *People* magazine proclaimed the belated arrival of a high-voltage actor with few equals in today's Hollywood firmament. Nicholson's father left before Jack was born and (like Sylvester Stallone's mom) Nicholson's mother made ends meet by running a beauty parlor in the living room. Growing up fat, Jack used his caustic humor to overcome his weight problem, and rather than attend college he traveled to Los Angeles and a job in MGM's mailroom. After appearing in several low-budget flicks he scored a breakthrough in *Easy Rider,* then began running in the company of his high-flying costars Dennis Hopper and Peter Fonda. Nicholson openly admits to smoking pot, snorting cocaine, and dropping LSD: to the latter he attributes the tapping of the inner resources of his talent. He is also a firm believer in psychotherapy and claims that during one session with his therapist he discovered that he had always suffered from a classic, paralyzing fear of castration. After *Easy Rider* and a supporting part in the Barbra Streisand version of *On a Clear Day You Can See Forever,* he tackled the role of a disaffected pianist in *Five Easy Pieces* and then equally demanding roles in *The Last Detail, The King of Marvin Gardens, Carnal Knowledge, Chinatown,* and finally *One Flew*

Over the Cuckoo's Nest, for which he won an Academy Award. His forgettable efforts include *The Missouri Breaks* with Marlon Brando, a small character part in *The Last Tycoon,* and his *Goin' South.* After filming the shocker *The Shining,* he took on the John Garfield role in a 1980 remake of *The Postman Always Rings Twice* and then the lead in Tony Richardson's *The Border.* He won a second Oscar, this time for Best Supporting Actor, for *Terms of Endearment.* Despite the rumors that proliferate about his predilection for the orgy scene, Nicholson has conducted basically long-term affairs since his four-year marriage to actress Sandra Knight broke up in 1966, and his closest companions have included model Mimi Machu, singer-actress Michelle Phillips (the surviving Mama of the Mamas and the Papas), and Anjelica Huston. Nicholson's winning streak continued with *Prizzi's Honor,* for which longtime love Anjelica won a Best Supporting Oscar. After losing out to dark horse William (*Kiss of the Spider Woman*) Hurt, Nicholson was hit with a case of *Heartburn*—the eagerly awaited movie version of Nova Ephron's novel, costarring Meryl Streep.

Born: April 22, 1937, in Neptune, New Jersey
Height: 5 ft. 9 in.
Weight: 160 lbs.
Eyes: Blue
Hair: Brown
Zodiac: Taurus
Education: High school
Religion: Protestant
Marriages: To Sandra Knight (1962–1966)
Children: Jenny (b. 1964)
Interests: Directing, reading, rock music, psychotherapy, skiing
Personal Habits and Traits: Chain-smokes cigarettes, drinks, smokes grass, has occasionally snorted cocaine
Address: Los Angeles
Income: $3 million (minimum estimate)

Jack Nicklaus

"I've been competitive ever since I can remember. I always wanted to be the best at whatever I did."

He is claimed by many to be the greatest golfer in the history of the game, and with good reason—in over 20 years on the PGA tour, he has won more than 20 major tournaments and amassed at least $3 million in purses. Nicklaus's father, the owner of a drugstore chain in Columbus, Ohio, pushed his son to undertake every sport from football to basketball and tennis before young Jack was taken under wing by Jack Grout, golf pro at the Scioto Country Club. At 13 his natural talent had developed to the point where he easily stole the Ohio State Junior Championship. By the end of his senior year in high school he rejected a basketball scholarship and set out to conquer the amateur golf world. He did, shattering records along the way, and turning pro two months before his 22nd birthday. He quit Ohio State University because he was spending so much time on the road, and supported his wife Barbara and their infant son Jack, Jr., selling insurance. Pocketing just $33.33 for his first professional golf effort, it looked as if he was consigned to be a salesman for life—until he won his first U.S. Open five months later. Since then he has been elevated to the pantheon of sports greats as the stolid "Golden Bear" of golf, while off the fairways Nicklaus has hit the jackpot in the area of product endorsements. In addition to peddling Hathaway shirts, Hart, Schaffner and Marx clothing, and American Express, he also presides over Golden Bear Inc.—his miniconglomerate of real estate companies employing over 50 people, with offices in North Palm Beach, Columbus, Madrid, Geneva, and London. He has been on the cover of *Sports Illustrated* more often than any other sportsman, but Nicklaus tried to get the 1985 cover on his then-16-year-old son Gary, an aspiring golf star, killed. "Gary," Dad explained, "doesn't need this kind of pressure—not now, anyway." For his part, Nicklaus, Sr., seems to have the situation well under control: in 1986, at age 46, he drove his way to a sixth Masters victory.

Born: January 21, 1940, in Columbus, Ohio
Height: 6 ft. 2 in.
Weight: 200 lbs.
Eyes: Blue
Hair: Blond
Zodiac: Aquarius
Education: Three years at Ohio State University
Religion: Protestant
Marriages: To Barbara Bash (1960–)
Children: Jack, Jr. (b. 1962), Steve (b. 1963), Nan (b. 1965), Gary (b. 1969), Michael (b. 1973)
Interests: Tennis, investments, building golf courses (like the 6,978-yard Muirfield Village course in Dublin, Ohio), football
Personal Habits and Traits: Occasionally smokes a cigarette, drinks vodka and tonics, a devout family man (never stays away from home more than 15 days at a time)
Addresses: Palm Beach, Florida; Columbus, Ohio
Income: $3.8 million (minimum estimate)

Stevie Nicks

Stephanie Nicks

The seductively slinky lead singer of Fleetwood Mac started out the daughter of a Greyhound-Armour executive. After high school in Arizona, she worked as a waitress before accompanying her boyfriend Lindsey Buckingham when he decided to join Fleetwood Mac. The group regularly played San Francisco clubs for years as a minor act—until 1976, when the 4-million-selling *Fleetwood Mac* album set the music industry on its ear. The following year *Rumours* clung to the number-one spot for an astounding eight months, selling no less than 9 million copies, and both albums spun off several Top 40 singles, including "Sound of a Heartbeat" and "Dreams," which Nicks herself composed. Their next LP, *Tusk,* was another blockbuster. The group's romantic entanglements proved trying for Nicks but not nearly so much as the nodules on her vocal cords that threatened to end her singing career. Surgery was not required, but to this day Nicks does not smoke and drinks no more than two glasses of wine a night. "Whenever I Call You Friend," recorded with Kenny Loggins, marked her first number-one single without the assistance of her Fleetwood Mac cohorts. Another memorable duet followed—"Stop Dragging My Heart Around," with Tom Petty sans the Heartbreakers—and solo hits like "Stand Back." Nicks's personal life took a bizarre turn when her close friend Robin Anderson died of leukemia in 1982. Nicks, having promised she would raise her friend's newborn daughter after Robin's death, married her widower, record promoter Kim Anderson. But that brave gesture lasted barely eight months. Nicks's *Rock a Little* album brought the "White Witch" of pop music back to the charts with singles like "You Can Talk to Me" and "I Can't Wait."

Born: May 26, 1948, in Phoenix, California
Height: 5 ft. 6 in.
Weight: 120 lbs.
Eyes: Brown
Hair: Blond
Education: High school diploma
Religion: Protestant
Marriages: To Kim Anderson (1982–1983)
Children: None
Interests: Composing
Personal Habits and Traits: Nonsmoker, limits alcoholic intake to two glasses of wine
Address: Hollywood
Income: $2.5 million (minimum estimate)

Richard Milhous Nixon

"Let me make one thing perfectly clear . . ."
"You won't have Dick Nixon to kick around anymore."
"I am not a crook."
"I gave them a sword."

The 37th President of the United States can rightfully claim to be the most enigmatic figure in modern American political history—reelected to the White House in 1972 by the largest margin ever, only to become the first President ever forced to resign. In exile Nixon is no less a constant source of fascination for the American people. Born to Quakers in Yorba Linda, California, Richard Milhous Nixon was 9 years old when his family moved from their lemon farm to Whittier, California, where his father ran a combination gas station and grocery store. At Whittier College he became president of the student body and played football (without much success). At Duke University Law School he was again elected student body president and after his graduation in 1937 returned to private practice in Whittier. Nixon married schoolteacher Thelma Catherine Patricia

(Pat) Ryan in 1940 and worked briefly as an attorney for the Office of Price Administration in Washington before obtaining a commission in the Navy in 1942. A Lieutenant Commander by the time he returned home in 1946, Nixon was urged to seek the Congressional seat held by New Deal Democrat Jerry Voorhis. Nixon won after a bitterly debated campaign. He then played an important part in the passage of the Taft-Hartley Act and the Marshall Plan before gaining national prominence by pressing the investigation of accused spy Alger Hiss. The same year Hiss was convicted of perjury by a federal district court, Nixon trounced Democrat Helen Gahagan Douglas in a nasty 1950 election battle for the U.S. Senate. Two years later Republicans nominated him as Dwight Eisenhower's running mate. In a brilliant stroke of political strategy Nixon saved himself from being bounced off the ticket—for having accepted $18,000 from some California businessmen—by delivering his now-famous "Checkers" speech. After eight years as Vice President he ran against John F. Kennedy for the Presidency and was defeated by one of the narrowest margins in history. Two years later he lost against incumbent Edmund G. "Pat" Brown for the governorship of California—the occasion for his "You won't have Dick Nixon to kick around anymore" speech. That was also the year he published his political memoirs, *Six Crises*. Nixon subsequently spent the years 1962–1967 earning over $200,000 a year as a lawyer, living in a spacious Fifth Avenue apartment, and faithfully campaigning on behalf of GOP candidates. Entering a crowded field of candidates in 1968, he walloped his opponents and, despite 11th-hour competition from conservative challenger Ronald Reagan, landed a first-ballot victory. The "new Nixon" went on to score a narrow victory over Democrat Hubert Humphrey and American Independent Party nominee George Wallace, and as President proceeded to take bold steps in the area of foreign policy: deploying Henry Kissinger on shuttle diplomacy missions to end the Vietnam war (though his bombing of Cambodia outraged many), opening up trade with the People's Republic of China, signing a Strategic Arms Limitations agreement with the Soviet Union, and courting previously unfriendly Arab states without alienating Israel. Domestically there were fewer surprises—four conservative Supreme Court appointees, cuts in expensive welfare programs, an attempted crackdown on crime—though his imposition of wage and price controls to fight double-digit inflation proved less in keeping with Republican policies. Nixon claimed a spectacular reelection victory over George McGovern in 1972 with his slogan "Four More Years," but it all began unraveling as two young *Washington Post* reporters named Bob Woodward and Carl Bernstein pressed their investigation of a supposedly "third-rate" break-in at the Democratic National Committee Headquarters. As Watergate gradually mushroomed into the most explosive American political scandal of the century, a separate bribery scandal involving Vice President Spiro T. Agnew forced Agnew's resignation, and he was replaced by House Minority Leader Gerald Ford. Then on August 9, 1974, after months of countless revelations concerning laundered money, bribes, and payoffs, a crucial 18-minute gap in Nixon's White House tapes, and many other ethically (and legally) questionable activities, the combined forces of a Senate investigation committee, a special Watergate prosecutor, and the press compelled Nixon to resign rather than face a protracted impeachment trial. Not long after his tearful farewell Nixon nearly died as a result of complications from phlebitis. Fully recovered by 1976, he resumed his familiar position center stage by journeying on his own to China, where he and Pat were accorded full official honors. The following year he was dubiously watched by millions of TV viewers during the long-awaited broadcast of a series of in-depth interviews with David Frost. Nixon's equally long-awaited $2 million autobiography also proved a disappointment. Finally quitting Casa Pacifica in San Clemente (for tax reasons) with the former First Lady—she bounced back from a stroke suffered in 1975—Nixon bought a smaller house nearby and ventured forth occasionally to attend ceremonial functions (the funeral of Hubert Humphrey in 1978, for example), and to record his own foreign policy observations. He became a grandfather for the first time in August 1978, when his younger daughter Julie, married to Ike's grandson David Eisenhower, gave birth to a daughter, Jenny. Tricia and her husband Edward Cox soon followed suit; their son Christopher was born in 1979—a blessed event that prompted the Nixons' attempt to purchase a New York apartment. Co-op owners refused to allow him to buy in, so the Nixons ended up buying a brownstone on East 65th Street, next door to the David Rockefellers. Nixon sold the town house and moved to toney Saddle River, New Jersey, where Pat suffered a second stroke. His book *The Real War* was a modest bestseller, but few Nixon-watchers were aware that his advice was sought by Reagan campaign advisers during the 1984 Presidential campaign—and that Nixon eagerly gave it.

Born: January 9, 1913, in Yorba Linda, California
Height: 5 ft. 10 in.
Weight: 174 lbs.
Eyes: Brown
Hair: Gray-brown
Zodiac: Capricorn
Education: Whittier College, Duke University Law School
Religion: Quaker
Marriages: To Thelma "Pat" Ryan (1940–)
Children: Tricia (b. 1946), Julie (b. 1948)
Interests: Foreign affairs, history, biography, football, golf, bowling, classical music, plays the piano
Personal Habits and Traits: Does not smoke, does drink cocktails, is reflective, verbally facile, perspires profusely
Address: Saddle River, New Jersey
Income: $1.5 million (minimum estimate)

Nick Nolte

"If you feel you have a film that's valid, you stick your ass on the line."

An instant star after his television appearance as the poor half of Irwin Shaw's original *Rich Man, Poor Man* miniseries, Nick Nolte—the son of an irrigation engineer—was a jock at five different colleges before latching onto acting at Pasadena City College. After 15 years spent learning his craft at regional the-

aters, the surly, blond antihero exploded on the scene in *Rich Man,* but disdained the sequel TV series and instead starred in Peter Benchley's lucrative treasure-hunting saga *The Deep.* That movie, in which he shared billing with Robert Shaw and Jacqueline Bisset, established Nolte as a competent talent. So did his performances in *Who'll Stop the Rain?* (based on Robert Stone's National Book Award–winning *Dog Soldiers*) and the gridiron yarn *North Dallas Forty.* Speculation linking Nolte with Bisset and his *Rain* costar Tuesday Weld was apparently baseless, but in 1978 Karen Ecklund, his companion of eight years, split and filed for $4.5 million of her roommate's earnings under California's new precedent-setting court award to partners in live-in relationships. Nolte nonetheless became a legal husband that same year, marrying nightclub singer Sharyn "Legs" Haddad. Nolte's rollercoaster career has recently had almost as many lows (*Cannery Row, Grace Quigley*) as highs (*48 Hours,* with Eddie Murphy, *Teachers* and *Down and Out in Beverly Hills*)—and so, too, has his private life: After divorcing Legs, Nolte took Becky Linger, a West Virginian 19 years his junior, as his bride. Becky got him to slow down on his drinking in preparation for fatherhood (she gave birth to a stillborn baby girl). Barely two years after their marriage, Becky and Nick split.

Born: 1940 in Omaha, Nebraska
Height: 6 ft. ½ in.
Weight: 171 lbs.
Eyes: Blue
Hair: Blond
Education: Pasadena City College
Religion: Roman Catholic
Marriages:
To Sheila Paige (divorced)
To Sharyn Haddad (1978–1984)
To Becky Linger (1984–1986)
Children: None
Interests: An all-around jock (football, baseball, scuba diving, swimming, etc.), theater, rock music, ranching and horses
Personal Habits and Traits: Smokes cigars, drinks moderately, eats no meat, fasts twice a week
Address: Santa Monica, California
Income: $1 million+ (estimate)

Rudolf Nureyev

"My feet are dogs."

Before his spectacular defection from the Soviet Union (in 1961 he hurled himself into the arms of the French police at a Paris airport, proclaiming, "I won't go back!"), Rudolf Nureyev endured the hardship of growing up in a peasant family 250 miles from the Siberian border. His father despised Rudolf's ambitions to become a dancer, but fortunately for balletomanes, at 16 Nureyev was selected to tour with a local dance troupe. Thus encouraged, he scraped together enough money for a one-way ticket to Leningrad, where he auditioned for the Kirov Ballet School. Instantly accepted into the elite school, he soon became its star pupil. He danced with the Kirov troupe for two years before his dramatic airport scene. Then, just four months after his defection, Nureyev teamed up with British prima ballerina Dame Margot Fonteyn, and their very first performance together proved a milestone in the history of dance. A self-described loner who shuns any talk of his personal life, the Russian star nonetheless loves to make the rounds of Manhattan parties, and after an increasingly rare performance will frequently take in a disco or film. Nureyev's first stab at movie stardom in 1977, playing the lead in Ken Russell's *Valentino,* was a decided embarrassment—particularly in light of competitor Mikhail Baryshnikov's first-time-out Oscar nomination the same year for *The Turning Point*. Still, as he reached his late 40s, Nureyev remained ballet's highest-priced artist at a reported minimum $10,000 per performance. His two closest friends are Fonteyn and underground star Monique Van Vooren, with whom he often stays in New York when visiting from his spectacular residence in Paris. His biggest disappointment: being unable to obtain an exit visa from the Soviet Union for his mother, whom he has not seen since his defection. Like Baryshnikov, with whom he planned to team up for an historic onstage performance in 1986, Nureyev prepared for the day he would hang up his toeshoes by taking on the job of running a ballet company—the Paris Opera Ballet.

Born: March 17, 1938, on a train near Irkutsk, U.S.S.R.
Height: 5 ft. 10 in.
Weight: 170 lbs.
Eyes: Brown
Hair: Brown
Zodiac: Pisces
Education: Kirov School of Ballet, Leningrad
Marriages: None
Children: None
Interests: Discos, clothes (he owns several lizard skin outfits and many mink coats), rock music
Personal Habits and Traits: A night person, needs little sleep, practices six hours a day, eats two pounds of rare steak at a sitting washed down with heavily sweetened tea
Addresses: Paris; New York City; London
Income: $450,000+

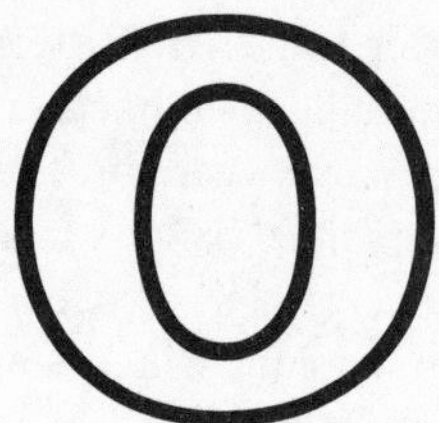

Carroll O'Connor

"Bogart once said that all an actor owes the public is a good performance. I say an actor owes the public as many good performances as possible."

The bluff, 210-pound actor boasted 27 movie and 120 television credits before being pegged by Norman Lear to rant as blue-collar bigot Archie Bunker in CBS's superhit *All in the Family*—and by the mid-1970s the meat(head)y role had beefed him into America's number-one Nielsen star, grossing around $3 million annually. Offscreen, Archie's alter ego is intelligent, articulate, and politically liberal, although equally irascible at times. Carroll O'Connor grew up in the quasi-intellectual New York home of his lawyer father and retired school-teacher mother. He wrote crusading college editorials while attending the University of Montana, and it was during a school production of *Life With Father* that Nancy Fields, the wardrobe and set designer, slyly cornered him under a campus tree to measure his chest for a costume. She followed him to National University in Dublin, where they were married for the first time in her Episcopal Church. A decade later, after she had converted to O'Connor's Catholicism, they were wed once again in Los Angeles. Returning to his native city, O'Connor landed his first Broadway role as Buck Mulligan in 1958's *Ulysses in Nighttown,* and today O'Connor will occasionally step out of his lucrative TV role to appear in a play, a movie, or a special—like his TV remake, with Cloris Leachman, of George and Ira Gershwin's 1930s classic *Of Thee I Sing*. Sharing a hacienda with "Nance" in the affluent Westwood section of Los Angeles, O'Connor retains his grandfather's diamond ring on the middle finger of his right hand for sentimental reasons and drives a silver-blue Rolls-Royce with the license plate UGO PRD—for Ugo Productions, named after his adopted Italian son. In June 1978, the mercurial superstar invited the L.A. press to the opening of his new restaurant, then proceeded to lambaste them from atop a chair. Although *All in the Family* is finally off the air, Archie's popularity did not diminish—and O'Connor held forth at *Archie Bunker's Place* for another five years. O'Connor's 1984 Broadway production *Brothers* closed after a single performance; he fared little better in the following year's *Home Front*.

Born: August 2, 1924, in New York City
Height: 5 ft. 10 in.
Weight: 210 lbs.
Eyes: Blue
Hair: White
Zodiac: Leo
Education: National University, Dublin
Religion: Roman Catholic
Marriages: To Nancy Fields (1951–)
Children: Hugh (adopted)
Interests: Baseball, football, producing, directing
Personal Habits and Traits: Smokes, no teetotaler, drinks gallons of coffee, prone to rages, goes to mass every Sunday
Address: Westwood (L.A.), California
Income: $3 million+ (minimum estimate)

Sandra Day O'Connor

"As far as I'm concerned, the best place in the world to be is on a good cutting horse working cattle."

By the age of 10, the towheaded tomboy who would one day become the first woman to sit on the Supreme Court could drive a tractor and truck, mend fences and windmills, ride horses, and rope steers—all talents that came in handy growing up on the family's Lazy B Ranch that straddles the New Mexico–Arizona border. Graduating from high school at 16, she went straight to Stanford and zipped through her undergraduate and law studies in only five years. She was on the *Stanford Law Review* and ranked in the Top 10 of her class. When she got out, she was offered her first job—as a legal secretary. With her husband John, whom she had married in 1952, she eventually settled in Phoenix, where she held several state offices before being elected a Republican state senator and then made Senate Majority Leader in 1972. Two years later, she donned judicial robes for the first time as Maricopa County Superior Court Judge, and sat on the Arizona Court of Appeals only 18 months before being appointed to the nation's highest court by Ronald Reagan in 1981. Although a she is a conservative, the selection of then-51-year-old O'Connor to become the Brethren's First Sister was generally hailed by left and right alike. With good reason: O'Connor's attention to legal detail (as a legislator, she once amended a bill because she discovered an all-important comma missing) transcends her personal political views. Not easily pigeonholed, she voted with the conservative majority on scores of issues ranging from Presidential immunity to criminal law. But she split with them on certain civil rights issues, sex discrimination, and freedom of information. O'Connor, who gets more mail than any other justice (1,200 letters a week) and puts in a good 12 hours a day on the job, also surprised Washington by becoming a regular on the party circuit. During one brief period, the O'Connors attended a White House dinner, several gala receptions and openings, a party for Donny Osmond, and a ball where they even won the door prize—round-trip tickets for two to Morocco.

Born: March 26, 1930, in El Paso, Texas
Height: 5 ft. 6 in.
Weight: 120 lbs.
Eyes: Blue
Hair: Blond
Zodiac: Aries
Education: Stanford University and Stanford Law School
Religion: Episcopal
Marriages: To John Jay O'Connor (1952–)
Children: Scott (b. 1958), Brian (b. 1960), Jay (b. 1962)
Interests: Tennis, golf, skiing
Personal Habits and Traits: Witty, affable, talkative, likes to socialize (belongs to several exclusive private clubs and attends several functions a week), excellent dancer, seemingly tireless, methodical in her work, drinks moderately, nonsmoker, superb cook specializing in Mexican dishes, likes country music
Addresses: Washington, D.C.; Paradise Valley, Arizona
Income: $104,100 Supreme Court salary

Laurence Olivier

Baron Olivier of Brighton

"A friend of mine told me, 'I think you've become one of the stately homes of England. You're hired for those two-week cameo performances the way they hire the exterior of a castle in Scotland.'"

Unanimously regarded as the greatest living actor in the English-speaking world, Lord Laurence Olivier made his debut at Stratford at the age of 15 in a plum Shakespearean role he was not likely ever to repeat—that of Katherine in an all-schoolboy production of *The Taming of the Shrew*. His legendary Heathcliff in 1939's classic film *Wuthering Heights* established the young actor as a formidable talent as well as a certified box-office draw, and he proved his extraordinary versatility over and over again through outstanding performances in *Rebecca* (1940), *Pride and Prejudice* (1940), *Henry V* (1945), *Richard II* (1956), *The Entertainer* (1960), *Othello* (1965), *Three Sisters* (1970), and *Sleuth* (1972), and in TV productions ranging from *Long Day's Journey Into Night* to a highly controversial version of *The Merchant of Venice* to the juicy part of Big Daddy in Tennessee Williams's *Cat on a Hot Tin Roof*. He directed his own 1948 screen version of *Hamlet,* for which he received an Academy Award as Best Actor (he would later receive a life achievement Oscar). Knighted in 1947 by George VI, he was finally made Baron Olivier of Brighton by Queen Elizabeth in 1970. He still continues to be one of his profession's most prolific actors, and does not shy from secondary character parts (he has appeared in smaller roles in *Nicholas and Alexandra, A Bridge Too Far, Marathon Man,* and *The Boys From Brazil*). Interspersed between his countless films has been his singular devotion to Britain's National Theater, of which he was a longtime director. Married first to Jill Esmond, Olivier often costarred with his second wife, Vivien Leigh (as in *That Hamilton Woman,* in which he played Lord Nelson), and is currently married to actress Joan Plowright (*A Taste of Honey, Equus*). His 1983 biography, *Confessions of an Actor,* recounted, among other things, Leigh's mental illness, both of their extramarital affairs, and his bout with premature ejaculation. More recently, he has been beset with a litany of ailments: prostate cancer, an obstructed kidney, thrombosis, pneumonia, appendicitis, and, since 1974, dermatopolymyositis, a muscle-wasting disease that Olivier sees as his most formidable opponent.

Born: May 22, 1907, in Dorking, Surrey, England
Height: 5 ft. 10½ in.
Weight: 177 lbs.
Eyes: Brown
Hair: White and balding
Zodiac: Gemini
Education: High school
Marriages:
To Jill Esmond (divorced)
To Vivien Leigh (divorced)
To Joan Plowright (current)
Children: Simon Tarquin (by Esmond), Richard Kerr, Tamsin Agnes Margaret, and Julie Kate (by Plowright)
Interests: Directing, producing
Personal Habits and Traits: Quit smoking, still drinks quite a bit, scrupulously polite
Address: London
Income: $1 million per film

Christina Onassis

"Sometimes when you have everything, you can't really tell what matters."

At 27 she stunned society by marrying a balding, one-eyed Soviet shipping clerk named Sergei Danyelovich Kauzov, whose only gold was in his cap-toothed smile. But it was certainly not the first time that Christina Onassis, star-crossed heiress to a $500 million shipping fortune, defied convention. Aristotle called his only daughter "Chryso Mou" (my golden one), but when 20-year-old Christina defiantly wed a Los Angeles real estate broker 27 years her senior, Ari withdrew his coming-of-age gift of 21 ships. Nine months later the marriage, punctuated by reports (denied by the family) that she had attempted suicide, ended in divorce. In 1973, her brother Alexander was killed in a plane crash. The following year her mother, Tina (then married to Onassis's shipping rival Stavros Niarchos), died unexpectedly in Paris—just five months before Aristotle Onassis's death from a heart attack. Shattered emotionally, Christina embarked upon another dubious marriage, this time to Greek banking scion Alexander Andreadis, which lasted just two years—a period during which Christina, who was expected to shun the responsibilities of running her father's far-flung empire, instead revealed herself a canny businesswoman, consolidating her control of the Onassis cartel. Now Christina, who speaks five languages fluently, spends half her time at her late father's headquarters overlooking Monte Carlo harbor. She divides the rest between New York, Paris, the island of Skorpios, and a villa in Glifadha, an Athens seaside resort. To placate stepmother Jacqueline Kennedy Onassis, Christina agreed to a $26 million settlement with Ari's widow in which

Jackie waived any future claims on the Onassis estate. Christina's startling decision to wed Kauzov led to speculation that the Communist bridegroom might be working for the KGB, and their union left Western espionage experts worrying, despite assurances from Christina that control of Olympic Maritime would remain out of Soviet hands. The newlyweds then moved into a two-and-a-half-room Moscow apartment with Sergei's mother while searching for a larger flat of their own. "I've had so much luxury," she shrugged, when asked if she could survive her spartan Moscow life-style, "that it won't be such a problem." It was. She returned to New York one year later, after paying off Sergei with a tanker of his very own. Onassis gave birth in 1985 to a daughter one year after marrying French pharmaceutical heir Thierry Roussel. One month later, she was offering him a settlement of $50 million to depart.

Born: December 11, 1950, in New York City
Height: 5 ft. 6½ in.
Weight: 174 lbs.
Eyes: Brown
Hair: Dark brown
Zodiac: Sagittarius
Education: A number of private schools in the United States and Europe
Religion: Greek Orthodox
Marriages:
To Joseph Bolker (1971–1972)
To Alexander Andreadis (1975–1977)
To Sergei Danyelovich Kauzov (1978–1979)
To Thierry Roussel (1984–1985)
Children: Athina (b. 1985)
Interests: Finance, shipping, fashion, loves the Beatles and Frank Sinatra
Personal Habits and Traits: A nonsmoker, nondrinker, takes tranquilizers, never carries cash (charges everything to the company), binges on cheeseburgers and junk food, constantly battles weight, semireclusive, temperamental, moody
Addresses: Monte Carlo; Paris; New York; Glifadha (Athens); Skorpios
Income: $500 million (approximate net worth)

Jacqueline Onassis

Jacqueline Bouvier Kennedy Onassis

"For a while I thought history was something bitter old men wrote. But Jack loved history so . . . for Jack history was full of heroes."

The single most famous woman in the world since the assassination of her husband on November 22, 1963, Jacqueline Bouvier Kennedy Onassis was born in fashionable Southampton, Long Island, to stockbroker/gambler John "Blackjack" Vernou Bouvier III and socialite Janet Lee Bouvier. Following her parents' divorce she and younger sister Lee were raised by her mother and stepfather Hugh Auchincloss in Newport, Washington, D.C., and Virginia. Vassar-educated Jackie was working as a newspaper photographer when she met young Senator John Fitzgerald Kennedy, and in 1953 they were married by Archbishop (later Cardinal) Cushing near the Auchincloss's family manse in

Newport. With Jack's election to the Presidency in 1960, Jackie plunged into the hectic pressures of serving as a First Lady at the age of 31, redecorating the White House with her inspired sense of style and presiding as one of its most talented and imaginative hostesses. After "Camelot" was shattered in Dallas, Jackie became the universal object of seemingly endless speculation until four months after the assassination of Robert Kennedy in 1968, when she stupefied the world by marrying Greek shipping tycoon Aristotle Onassis on his private island of Skorpios. Following Onassis's death in 1975 at the age of 69, Jackie once again became the object of unrelenting speculation, yet she kept the international press at bay and simply went back to work—first as a $10,000-a-year editor for Viking Press (her first book, the emphatically unsuccessful *In the Russian Style,* lavishly displayed costumes of Imperial Russia), and then for Doubleday. Now ensconced in her Fifth Avenue apartment, Mrs. Onassis makes the rounds of openings and parties more frequently than ever. As for financing her lavish life-style, Jackie O has no worries since Onassis's daughter and primary heir, Christina, agreed to pay her stepmother a $26 million hunk of Onassis's estate. Mother of Caroline and John, Jr., Jackie hit the campaign trail in 1980 on behalf of brother-in-law Ted's Presidential aspirations. One of her acquisitions as an editor: rock-'n'-roller Michael Jackson's autobiography. Although she shows no sign of wanting to marry a third time, Jackie appeared to have settled on an escort—financier Maurice Tempelsman. With his help, she reputedly upped her personal estate to $50 million plus.

Born: July 28, 1929, in Southampton, Long Island
Height: 5 ft. 7 in.
Weight: 115 lbs.
Eyes: Brown
Hair: Dark brown
Zodiac: Leo
Education: Vassar
Religion: Roman Catholic
Marriages:
To John Fitzgerald Kennedy (1953–until his assassination November 22, 1963)
To Aristotle Onassis (1968 until his death in 1975)

Children: Caroline (b. 1957), John, Jr. (b. 1960)
Interests: Art, music, fashion, publishing, horses, antiques, restoration of historic buildings, ballet, theater, photography
Personal Habits and Traits: Smoker, drinks moderately, is generally inaccessible
Address: New York City; Martha's Vineyard, Massachusetts
Income: $50 million (minimum personal worth)

Ryan O'Neal

In imminent danger of being overshadowed by his Oscar-winning daughter Tatum, this often pugnacious actor received his big break on television's *Peyton Place* in the role of bratty scion Rodney Harrington. Not that he was exactly an

"The greatest moment of my career was on the set of Barry Lyndon. *After a difficult take, Stanley Kubrick found a way to walk past me, giving instructions to the crew—but as he passed me, he grabbed my hand and squeezed it. It was the most beautiful and appreciated gesture in my life."*

overnight success, for the son of actress Patricia Callaghan and playwright-novelist Charles O'Neal climbed his way up the show business ladder as a stunt man on TV's *Tales of the Vikings,* and then did numerous bit parts on shows like *Dobie Gillis, Bachelor Father,* and *My Three Sons.* When he left *Peyton Place* in 1969 after five seasons, he embarked on a three-hit winning streak with *Love Story, What's Up, Doc?,* and *Paper Moon* before testing his acting limits with Stanley Kubrick's ambitious *Barry Lyndon* and filming another Bogdanovich comedy (*Nickelodeon*), a dismal World War II adventure (*A Bridge Too Far*), and an inane sequel to *Love Story* called *Oliver's Story.* Divorced twice—first from Tatum's mom, Joanna Moore, and then from Peyton Place costar Leigh Taylor-Young—O'Neal has cut a wide romantic swath through Hollywood with the diverse likes of Joan Collins, Barbra Streisand (his costar in *What's Up* and *The Main Event*), Ursula Andress, Anouk Aimée, Bianca Jagger, and Farrah Fawcett, the mother of his son Redmond. A hardworking actor generally accepted by Hollywood society as an amiable offscreen pal, O'Neal is not always Mr. Nice Guy, and once spent 51 days in jail for punching the entertainment editor of the *New Orleans Times-Picayune.* He also flattened his son Griffin, also a talented actor, before sending the boy to a drug rehabilitation clinic in Hawaii. Appropriately, O'Neal's best-received film in the mid-1980s was about a child who sues her self-absorbed parents, *Irreconcilable Differences.*

Born: April 20, 1941, in Los Angeles, California
Height: 6 ft. 1 in.
Weight: 170 lbs.
Eyes: Blue
Hair: Blond
Zodiac: Taurus
Education: High school
Religion: Roman Catholic
Marriages:
To Joanna Moore (divorced)
To Leigh Taylor-Young (divorced)
Children: Tatum (b. 1963), Griffin Patrick (b. 1964) by Moore; Young Patrick (b. 1967) by Taylor-Young; Redmond by Farrah Fawcett
Interests: Surfing, handball, horseback riding, fencing, running, working out, discos
Personal Habits and Traits: A nonsmoker, does drink, something of a night owl
Address: Malibu, California
Income: $2 million (minimum estimate)

Tatum O'Neal

"I had some bad lives when I lived with my mother."

The youngest Oscar winner in history (at 10, for her supporting role as a chain-smoking Depression-era con artist in *Paper Moon*) experienced a childhood that would have made even Judy Garland blanch. Seven months after her father, Ryan, married Joanna Moore, an aging starlet eight years his senior, Tatum was born in Los Angeles; her Southern name originally belonged to Moore's mother. When Tatum was 3, her father, by then the star of TV's racy *Peyton Place,*

divorced Moore and on the same day married his *Peyton Place* costar, Leigh Taylor-Young. Partly because of Ryan's many affairs (with Ursula Andress and Barbra Streisand, among others) plus an early jail record for assault and battery, O'Neal lost custody of Tatum to her mom. Tatum ran away to her father when she was 8, and the resulting custody battle featured courtroom allegations of drug addiction and child abuse that was said to have occurred while Tatum and her younger brother Griffin lived with their mother in a hippie commune. When O'Neal went to pick up his daughter he discovered that she had stashed away $1,200 in cash from leading a ring of bicycle thieves, and even after director Peter Bogdanovich tapped her for *Paper Moon,* she did little to dispel her growing image as a detestable brat, abusing waitresses in restaurants and throwing occasional temper tantrums. Despite a sometimes frightening precocity off camera, Tatum wisely stuck to such lighthearted movie fare as *Nickelodeon, The Bad News Bears, International Velvet,* and *Little Darlings.* By 1985 Tatum was playing doubles with another *enfant terrible,* John McEnroe, and gave birth to their child the following year.

Born: November 5, 1963, in Los Angeles, California
Height: 5 ft. 4½ in.
Weight: 117 lbs.
Eyes: Blue
Hair: Brown
Zodiac: Scorpio
Education: Private school
Marriages: None
Children: Kevin Jack (b. 1986)
Interests: Horses, chess
Personal Habits and Traits: Quit smoking cigarettes
Address: Los Angeles
Income: $250,000

Yoko Ono

"We never claimed that we walked on water."

Once the eulogies for her slain husband were over, once a portion of Central Park had been renamed Strawberry Fields in his honor, Yoko Ono had to begin her life without John Lennon. When the former Beatle was gunned down before her eyes in 1980 by a crazed fan named Mark David Chapman, the world was stunned; yet Yoko (which means "Ocean Child" in Japanese) was probably better equipped than most to cope with the emotional trauma. The daughter of a Tokyo banker father and heiress mother who warned her never to smile in public, she moved with her family to San Francisco at age 3, only to return to Japan at the outbreak of World War II. After the war they resettled in the United States, this time in the affluent New York City bedroom community of Scarsdale. She attended toney Sarah Lawrence College, but dropped out after three years to plunge into the Greenwich Village Beat scene of the late 1950s. She married avant-garde composer Toshi Ichiyanagi and began staging "conceptual" art shows—placing her paintings on the floor to be stepped on, for example, or digging "a shallow hole for the moonlight to make a pond." Divorcing Ichiyanagi in 1964, Yoko then wed filmmaker Tony Cox, and the two began collaborating on such epic movies as one 1967 study of 365 bare derrières—one for each day of the year. At about this time, Lennon wandered into one of her London exhibits, and the two struck up a relationship that was consummated in 1969 with a tape recorder running beside the bed; they used the tape in their first joint album, *Two Virgins,* for which they posed nude on the cover. Lennon divorced his wife of six years, Cynthia Powell, Ono shed Cox, and John and Yoko were married on Gibraltar. In 1972, Cox defied a court order and vanished with daughter Kyoko, then 8. Their whereabouts remain a mystery. The Beatles, meantime, were breaking up, and many blamed Yoko. All of which took its toll, and beginning in 1973, the two separated for 18 months while Lennon drank heavily, took drugs, and lived with his secretary, May Pang. John and Yoko reconciled, and though they were repeatedly told that they could not have children, at 42 she gave birth to their son, Sean. Ironically Lennon, who had long sought happiness as a Beatle, a disciple of the Maharishi, and a heavy user of drugs, found it in his new role of househusband. While he stayed at one of the several apartments they maintained at New York's fashionable Dakota, she took over the handling of Lennon's formidable finances. By the time he was shot outside the Dakota, Lennon's fortune was estimated at more than $50 million. After his death, an album of songs from the Lennons, *Milk and Honey,* was released; it rocketed to the top of the charts despite widespread objections to the cover photo of John's blood-splattered eyeglasses. Incredibly, even more drama lay ahead for Yoko, when it was revealed that over three years she was the victim of threats against her life, blackmail, exploitation, burglary, and buggings—all part of an alleged scheme, code name "Project Walrus," hatched to betray and discredit Lennon's widow.

Born: February 18, 1933, in Tokyo
Height: 5 ft. 4 in.
Weight: 120 lbs.
Eyes: Brown
Hair: Black
Zodiac: Pisces
Education: Three years at Sarah Lawrence
Marriages:
To Toshi Ichiyanagi (1964)
To Anthony Cox (1964–1969)
To John Lennon (1969 until his assassination in 1980)
Children: Kyoko (b. 1964), Sean (b. 1974); Yoko has also grown close in recent years to stepson Julian Lennon
Interests: Art, photography, poetry, music
Personal Habits and Traits: Seldom smiles, nearly always wears dark glasses and dark colors, speaks in a shy whisper but is often perceived as ambitious and temperamental, begins her day at 4 A.M., tries to stick to a macrobiotic diet but has fatal weakness for ice cream; Yoko and Sean are generally accompanied by bodyguards
Address: The Dakota, New York City
Income: $50 million (estimate of net worth)

Peter O'Toole

Peter Seamus O'Toole

"For me, life has either been a wake or a wedding."

Aside from a lucky pair of emerald green socks that he *always* wears—even though he dons nothing else for bed—Peter Seamus O'Toole is one of the most quirky and talented actors on stage and in films. The son of a bookie, O'Toole attended a Catholic school in Leeds, where the nuns beat him to correct his left-handedness. Leaving school at 13, he packed cartons in a warehouse until he found a job as a copyboy with the *Yorkshire Evening News*. Two years in the Royal Navy preceded a scholarship to the Royal Academy of Dramatic Arts in London. O'Toole played with the Old Vic in Bristol for a number of years before testing for the title role in the movie *Lawrence of Arabia*. Producer Sam Spiegel balked when a pint of liquor inadvertently fell out of O'Toole's pocket, but director David Lean hired O'Toole anyway. Never an Oscar winner, he has nonetheless been nominated six times—as the heroic *Lawrence,* as the meddlesome priest in *Beckett,* as Katharine Hepburn's ranting husband in *The Lion in Winter,* as a loony lord in *The Ruling Class,* as the director in *The Stunt Man,* and as the perennially soused matinee idol patterned on Errol Flynn in *My Favorite Year*. His other films include a musical version of *Goodbye, Mr. Chips* with Petula Clark, *How to Steal a Million, Lord Jim, Man of La Mancha, Svengali* (for television), *Supergirl,* and *Kim*. Married in 1959 to Welsh actress Sian Phillips (they split in 1979) and the father of two girls, the outspoken, hard-drinking Irishman married California model Karen Brown in 1981. She gave birth to their son, Lorcan (Gaelic for Lawrence, after O'Toole's greatest film role), in 1983, but their marriage broke up 18 months later.

Born: August 2, 1933, in County Galway, Ireland
Height: 6 ft. 3 in.
Weight: 175 lbs.
Eyes: Blue
Hair: Blond
Zodiac: Leo
Education: School dropout (at 13)
Religion: Lapsed Roman Catholic
Marriages:
To Sian Phillips (1959–1979)
To Karen Brown (1981–1985)
Children: Kate, Pat, Lorcan
Interests: Theater, literature, horses, gambling, music
Personal Habits and Traits: Smokes, a hard drinker (mostly beer), moody, antisocial, a perfectionist, chronic worrier
Address: London
Income: $1 million+

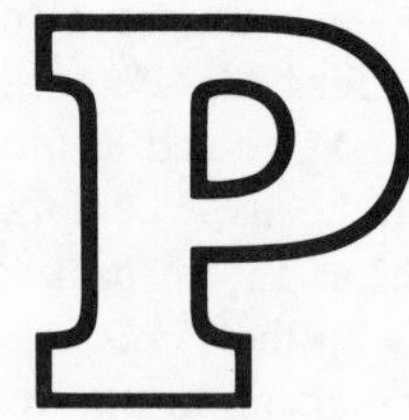

Al Pacino

"An actor becomes an emotional athlete. The process is painful—my personal life suffers."

Deliberately cast in the Brando mold, this devoted student of the Actors Studio earned his bankable status in a variety of highly taxing roles: the ruthless mafioso (*The Godfather*, I and II), the earnest cop (*Serpico*), the bungling bank robber (*Dog Day Afternoon*), and the race-car playboy with a dying girlfriend (*Bobby Deerfield*). Born Alfredo Pacino in East Harlem and raised in the South Bronx by his divorced mother and her parents, Pacino liked to act out roles in movies as a kid—Ray Milland in *The Lost Weekend* was his favorite—often leaping from tenement roof to tenement roof. Pacino quit high school after two years and got his off off-Broadway start in William Saroyan's *Hello Out There*. Unnerved by the fact that the audience laughed at his lines (it was a comedy), he did not return to the stage for over a year. When he did, however, he was an overnight sensation as the toughie, Murph, in *The Indian Wants the Bronx*, and electrified film audiences in his role as a junkie in 1971's *Panic in Needle Park*. In 1972 he received his first Oscar nomination playing Brando's son in the first *Godfather*, and five years later returned to Broadway and collected a Tony for his moving performance in the antiwar drama *The Basic Training of Pavlo Hummel*. An elusive loner dubbed by columnist Earl Wilson as "the male Garbo," Pacino lived in a small New York apartment rented from Candice Bergen, and for protection his downstairs buzzer was marked "Goldberg." Pacino has remained a bachelor despite long-term affairs with actresses Jill Clayburgh (*An Unmarried Woman*) and Marthe Keller (*Marathon Man, Bobby Deerfield, Fedora*). He starred in the late 1979 release *. . . And Justice for All,* where he played a Serpico-like attorney, not long after he had found himself at the center of a violent controversy when New York City gays tried to stop the filming of *Cruising,* in which Pacino portrayed a homosexual cop. Audiences were not shouting *Author, Author* after his appearance in that lackluster film, either, but they seemed drawn to his portryal of a Cuban immigrant hood in the ultraviolent *Scarface*. His *Revolution* Struck even diehard Pacino fans as, well, revolting.

Born: April 25, 1940, in East Harlem, New York
Height: 5 ft. 7 in.
Weight: 140 lbs.
Eyes: Brown
Hair: Brown
Zodiac: Taurus
Education: High school dropout
Religion: Roman Catholic

Marriages: None
Children: None
Interests: Acting and actors
Personal Habits and Traits: Chain-smokes, drives fast cars, is reclusive
Address: New York City
Income: $1.2 million +

Dolly Parton

"I don't want to leave the country, but to take it with me wherever I go."

Like fellow country-western star Loretta Lynn, Dolly Parton grew up in a two-room shack in Tennessee's Great Smoky Mountains. The fourth of a toiling farmer-laborer's dozen children recalls that rats would skitter across the floor at night—a memory that persists so strongly she can even now only sleep with a night light. Parton was just 6 years old when she fashioned her first impromptu guitar from an old mandolin and two bass strings, and started singing in her preacher grandfather's Church of God choir. An astonishingly prolific songwriter even though she never learned to read music, she began her flow of autobiographical songs at the age of 7 and by 10 was singing them on Knoxville radio and television. When she finished high school Parton headed for the country-western Mecca—Nashville. Her big break came three years later in 1967, when established singing star Porter Waggoner picked Parton to replace his newly married partner, Norma Jean. Parton stopped singing with Waggoner in 1974 and as a soloist has recorded over 500 of her own songs, including the folk hymn "My Tennessee Mountain Home" and her deeply moving tribute to her mother, "Coat of Many Colors." Parton and her husband, Carl Dean, whom she met at a Laundromat just 24 hours after stepping off the bus in Nashville, live on an antebellum estate five miles outside Nashville, and their private menagerie includes 25 Herefords, two peacocks, and a pair of bloodhounds. But Parton, who is unable to have children, is seldom home, because her concert tours take her to some 100 cities each year. Amazingly, her husband has never heard her perform, and Dolly says of Dean, who owns a paving company, "He's sort of shy and quiet. What we have together is so sweet and good that I'd never want it to get jumbled up with my career." Parton upstaged veterans Lily Tomlin and Jane Fonda in her film debut as a pursued secretary in *9 to 5*, but could not save either *The Best Little Whorehouse in Texas* (with Burt Reynolds) or *Rhinestone* (with

Sylvester Stallone). Dolly's fans far preferred to see and hear her in the company of Kenny Rogers. Together they recorded one of the biggest hits of both their careers, "Islands in the Stream." After taking a six-month breather to set up an amusement park called Dollywood, Parton returned to the road. "Hey," she smiled, "I need the money." Parton is known to her small army of adoring nieces and nephews as "Aunt Granny."

Born: January 19, 1946, in Locust Ridge, Tennessee
Height: 5 ft.
Weight: 125 lbs.
Eyes: Blue
Hair: Light brown (but always wears a mammoth blond wig in public)
Measurements: 39–25–39
Zodiac: Capricorn
Education: High school
Religion: Baptist
Marriages: To Carl Dean (1967–)
Children: None
Interests: Animals
Personal Habits and Traits: Is refreshingly candid about her ambitions to become a superstar, a nonsmoker, does not overimbibe, admits to being a hearty eater
Address: Nashville, Tennessee
Income: $10 million

Jane Pauley

"The people who make it in this business have to be tough and super-hyper-ambitious."

Successor to Barbara Walters as the 34th *Today Show* woman after what amounted to a virtual Scarlett O'Hara search, Jane Pauley graduated from Indiana University with honors in political science before landing her first job—reading the news at Indianapolis's aptly named WISH-TV for $13,500 a year. But the honey blond Midwesterner was quickly lured away to become Chicago's first evening news anchorwoman, and a year later found herself up against the likes of Betty Furness and Catherine Mackin for *Today*. Winning the spot opposite Tom Brokaw and Gene Shalit assured cat-fancying, folk-singing Pauley a six figure salary and a nearly total loss of privacy; moving to New York also strained her long-term relationship with *Indianapolis Star* reporter Bill Shaw. In 1980 Pauley, now paired on *Today* with Bryant Gumble, wed Pulitzer Prize–winning *Doonesbury* creator Garry Trudeau, and four years later gave birth to twins.

Born: October 31, 1950, in Indianapolis, Indiana
Height: 5 ft. 3 in.
Weight: 109 lbs.
Eyes: Blue
Hair: Blond
Zodiac: Scorpio
Education: University of Indiana, B.A. in political science
Marriages: Garry Trudeau (1980–)
Children: Twins
Interests: Broadcasting
Personal Habits and Traits: Smokes cigarettes, moderate drinker
Address: New York City
Income: $700,000 (minimum estimate)

Gregory Peck

Eldred Gregory Peck

"I've had my day as a leading man. I'm not fighting tooth and claw to get back to the top of the heap. I am quite happy in the fullness of my years."

Eldred Gregory Peck was movie-struck even as a child in La Jolla, California, but shortly after his parents divorced he was sent off to St. John's Military Academy in Los Angeles. Later while living with his father, a pharmacist, he attended San Diego State College, then transferred to premed at the University of California at Berkeley so he could compete on the rowing team. A back injury altered his plans and he began to focus all his energy on the theater, heading for New York as soon as he graduated. Immediately dropping the name "Eldred," he worked as a carnival barker at the 1939 World's Fair and as a Rockefeller Center tour guide while finding time to perform in regional theater. When Katharine Cornell once forgot her lines he whispered them to her; the great stage star repaid the young novice with a lead role on Broadway in *Morning Star*. RKO's *Days of Glory* heralded his arrival in Hollywood, and his second film, *The Keys of the Kingdom,* cinched his stardom. Some 50 movies followed, including such memorable hits as *Spellbound, The Yearling, Gentleman's Agreement, Twelve O'Clock High, The Snows of Kilimanjaro, Moby Dick,* and *The Guns of Navarone*. After four Academy Award nominations, he won the fifth time for his role as a liberal Southerner in *To Kill a Mockingbird,* but then a professional dry spell occurred between the forgettable *Arabesque* in 1966 and 1977's supernatural spellbinder *The Omen*. His greatest tragedy occurred during this period—the suicide of his eldest son, Jonathan, in 1975 at the age of 30. At his Norman-style estate in the exclusive Holmby Hills district of Los Angeles, Peck begins each day clocking five miles on a stationary bicycle before breakfast and the office. A former president of the Academy of Motion Picture Arts and Sciences and long an outspoken liberal (he made the Nixon enemies list), Peck now contents himself with working on behalf of causes like the regional theater that gave him his start. After a not-so-successful attempt at portraying America's most controversial warrior in *MacArthur,* Peck returned to the screen with fellow trouper Laurence Olivier in the Ira Levin chiller *The Boys From Brazil*—Peck's first try at playing a heavy. His good-guy persona resurfaced when he portrayed none other than Abraham Lincoln in the TV miniseries *The Blue and the Gray*.

Born: April 5, 1916, in La Jolla, California
Height: 6 ft. 4 in.
Weight: 180 lbs.
Eyes: Brown
Hair: Gray-brown
Zodiac: Aries
Education: University of California at Berkeley, B.A. in drama
Religion: Methodist

Marriages:
To Greta Konen (1942–1954)
To Veronique Passani (1955–)
Children: Jonathan (deceased), Stephen, Carey Paul (by Konen); Anthony and Cecilia (by Passani)
Interests: Gardening, promoting regional theater, tennis
Personal Habits and Traits: Early riser, exercise nut
Address: Holmby Hills, California
Income: $800,000 (estimate)

Anthony Perkins

"In the movies, I don't know what I'm doing 75 percent of the time."

This lanky star of stage and screen stunned both Hollywood and New York insiders by suddenly becoming one of the happiest family men in show business. Perkins's roommate for six years, Broadway choreographer Grover Dale, had already moved out by the time Perkins was approached by photojournalist Berry Berenson for an article in Andy Warhol's *Interview* magazine. Their interview expanded into a romance, and after their son, Ozzie, was conceived, Perkins and Berenson, granddaughter of designer Elsa Schiaparelli and sister of actress Marisa, were married in 1974. For the groom, the experience was the result of nine years of analysis, 40 years of often painful living—and an encounter with Victoria Principal that he said opened his eyes to the joys of the opposite sex. The son of matinee idol Osgood Perkins, after whom his son is named, Tony attended a classy prep school in Massachusetts and then Rollins College and Columbia. He commenced his acting career at 15 in summer stock, and just before graduation from Columbia dazzled New York critics in Broadway's *Tea and Sympathy*. After 37 films, from *Tall Story* to *Friendly Persuasion* and *Mahogany,* Perkins is unquestionably best remembered as the knife-wielding psychopath in Alfred Hitchcock's classic *Psycho* (a role he reprised in the 1984 tongue-in-cheek sequel, and again in 1986). After stabs at directing (*Steambath*) and screenwriting (*The Last of Sheila*), Perkins won critical acclaim (though the movie part went to Richard Burton) for his stage portrayal of the tormented psychiatrist in Peter Shaffer's Tony-winning *Equus* and for his part in Bernard Slade's *Romantic Comedy*.

Born: April 4, 1932, in New York City
Height: 6 ft. 1½ in.
Weight: 168 lbs.
Eyes: Brown
Hair: Brown
Zodiac: Aries
Education: Rollins College, Columbia University
Religion: Protestant
Marriages: To Berry Berenson (1974–)
Children: Osgood (b. 1974), Elvis (b. 1975)
Interests: Photography, art, literature, classical music, directing, screenwriting, the theater
Personal Habits and Traits: Quit smoking, drinks little, early riser, homebody, an exercise fiend (runs in place for 20 minutes every morning, bicycles around New York City)
Address: New York City
Income: $300,000+ (estimate)

Bernadette Peters

Bernadette Lazzara

"Just point me in a direction I want to go, and I'm gone!"

With Gibson Girl looks and a Betty Boop voice, Bernadette Peters seemed poorly suited for show business success in the 1970s. But Bernadette Lazzara has parlayed a lifetime of musical comedy experience (she was a regular on the *Horn & Hardart Children's Hour* at age 5 and on Broadway in *The Most Happy Fella* at 11) and oomphed her way to adult stardom in *Dames at Sea,* a spoof of 1930s musicals in which she played a character based on Ruby Keeler, followed by *George M!, Mack and Mabel,* and Stephen Sondheim's Tony Award–winning *Sunday in the Park With George.* A frequent guest on TV variety shows, Peters finally landed her own series in 1973 when producer Norman Lear tapped her for the part of a liberated young news photographer in *All's Fair.* No longer a dyed-in-the-wool New Yorker, she has gradually made the transition to California life, moving into a spacious two-bedroom apartment above Sunset Boulevard. Not that it was all that easy. With characteristic perseverance, she finally earned her driver's license after failing her driving test three times. Peters's main love for years was wild and crazy Steve Martin, with whom she costarred in *The Jerk.* In 1985 she returned to Broadway—and Manhattan living—as the star of Andrew Lloyd Webber's London smash, *Song and Dance.*

Born: February 28, 1948, in New York City
Height: 5 ft. 3 in.
Weight: 120 lbs.
Eyes: Brown
Hair: Blond
Zodiac: Pisces
Education: Professional school
Religion: Roman Catholic
Marriages: None
Children: None
Interests: Meditation
Personal Habits and Traits: Nonsmoker, vegetarian
Address: Sunset Boulevard, Hollywood
Income: $450,000+ (estimate)

Robert Plant

"Zep is the Ultimate Unit."

Led Zeppelin, Britain's high-flying exponent of heavy rock, sold over 25 million albums worldwide—twice as many as the Rolling Stones—spun heavy metal into eight platinum LPs (with single cuts like "Whole Lotta Love" and "Stairway to Heaven"), and broke tour records set by the Beatles. And though critics unanimously dismissed their semidocumentary film *The Song Remains the Same* as being full of hot air, it earned Led Zeppelin a hefty $20 million. The group's unlikely answer to Mick Jagger is lead singer Robert Plant, a Cambridge-educated amateur historian and self-described "medieval freak." Son of a Birmingham civil engineer, Plant headed for a career as an accountant until he was drawn into Birmingham's bohemian circles and several bluesy rock bands. When the popular Yardbirds broke up in 1968 (unleashing Jimmy Page, Eric Clapton, and Jeff Beck), Page set out to form his own group. Perhaps rock's premier guitarist, he collared Plant, drummer John Bonham, and bassist-keyboardist John Paul Jones, and by 1971 Led Zeppelin had become the unchallenged sovereign of nerve-shattering heavy metal. Meanwhile the group built an envied reputation among unruly rock stars for laying waste to hotel suites and groupies on tour, though now when Plant retreats home it is to an 800-year-old stone house on 290 rolling acres in Wales—a working farm (300 sheep and a pig named Madam)—that he shares with Maureen, his Eurasian wife, and their daughter, Carmen. Another child, Karac, died in 1977 from a mysterious infection at age 5—a tragedy that plunged Plant into depression and drink. But after two years and the birth of a new son—Logan Romero—Plant and his musical dirigible once again took flight with sellout concert appearances and a number-one album, *In Through the Out Door*. After the group disbanded, Plant recorded a hit ("Do You Remember") with the Honeydrippers, then took off with a solo smash, "Little by Little." His reunion with the rest of Led Zeppelin on the stage of 1985's historic Live Aid concert coincided with a bestselling account of the group's tours in the mid-1970s, *Hammer of the Gods*.

Born: August 20, 1948, in Birmingham, England
Height: 6 ft.
Weight: 188 lbs.
Eyes: Blue
Hair: Blond
Zodiac: Leo
Education: Cambridge University
Marriages: To Maureen Plant (current)
Children: Carmen, Karac (deceased), Logan Romero
Interests: Medieval history, farming, mathematics
Personal Habits and Traits: Drinks beer, smokes, extroverted
Address: Wales
Income: $2 million (minimum estimate)

Sidney Poitier

"I was born out of joint with the times. If I have not made my peace with the times—they are still out of kilter—I have made my peace with myself."

The first black actor to receive an Academy Award (for 1963's *Lilies of the Field*) grew up on a tomato farm on Cat Island in the Bahamas. At 21, after his 1945 Army discharge, Sidney Poitier walked into Harlem's American Negro Theater to audition for a part but was turned away because of his thick patois. He set out to prove the black casting director wrong, sleeping in public washrooms and working in menial jobs to support himself while "Americanizing" his speech. He was accepted into the theater a year later, and appeared in several small plays before *Anna Lucasta* brought him Broadway stardom in 1948. Two years later, he headed to California and made his first film, *No Way Out*, followed by *Blackboard Jungle, Something of Value, The Defiant Ones, Porgy and Bess, A Raisin in the Sun, To Sir With Love, In the Heat of the Night, Guess Who's Coming to Dinner?, For Love of Ivy, Buck and the Preacher* (which he directed and costarred in with Harry Belafonte), and *Uptown Saturday Night*. He also directed Gene Wilder and Richard Pryor in *Stir Crazy*, one of the most financially successful films in Hollywood history. Unfortunately, he also squandered his talents on the breakdance fiasco *Fast Forward*. Considered one of the most unaffected and articulate of Hollywood's name-over-the-title superstars, Poitier resides in Los Angeles. His memoirs, published in 1982, detailed his longtime romance with Diahann Carroll and his tempestuous friendship with Harry Belafonte.

Born: February 20, 1924, in Miami, Florida
Height: 6 ft. 2 in.
Weight: 180 lbs.
Eyes: Brown
Hair: Black
Zodiac: Pisces
Education: One and a half years of grammar school
Religion: Roman Catholic
Marriages:
To Juanita Hardy (divorced)
To Joanna Shimkus (1975–)
Children: Beverly, Pamela, Sherri
Interests: Acting, directing, producing, politics, art
Personal Habits and Traits: Does not smoke, drinks moderately, is soft-spoken, gets up early, exercises daily
Address: Los Angeles
Income: $800,000+

Priscilla Beaulieu Presley

"Sure, the truth about the way Elvis lived was bizarre, but not as bizarre as the lies people have told about him. That's why I wrote my book.

Although millions of adoring women hurled themselves at him, Elvis Presley chose as his special girl (and later his wife) a quiet, hard-to-get, then-14-year-old beauty, Priscilla Beaulieu. She was the daughter of an Air Force captain stationed in Wiesbaden at the same time that Elvis was serving as a soldier in the U.S. Army and living at 14 Goethestrasse, Bad Neuheim. In the following years, Elvis would create Priscilla in the image of his "ideal woman," teaching her the language of glamour and how to make love his way. But after years of marriage and the birth of a daughter, Lisa Marie, something went wrong. Elvis was often away from home on long road tours, or partying in his bachelor hideaway in Palm Springs while Priscilla single-handedly raised Lisa in Los Angeles and at Graceland, the Presley mansion in Memphis. Priscilla was growing up into an independent modern woman who had her own ideas and whose personality and creativity began to flourish when she studied dance, decorated their homes, and took up karate—a hobby that led to friendships with Chuck Norris and Mike Stone and a life-style that permitted, even welcomed, personal growth. Eventually, she divorced Elvis. Yet they continued to talk every day, to share Lisa, and, at the time of his final decline, to discuss the possibility of reconciliation. Priscilla has not remarried but she has had attractive suitors, such as model Mike Edwards and producer Marco Garibaldi, and she has forged a career as a star on the number-one television series *Dallas*. She is also the author of the blockbuster reminiscence *Elvis and Me*. Priscilla lives on a ranch in Santa Barbara and in an elegant home she designed and decorated in Los Angeles. Often referred to as one of the world's most beautiful women, Priscilla has passed on her looks and good taste to her daughter, blue-eyed, blond Lisa. Under Priscilla's guidance, the once precarious Presley estate is now flourishing—especially Graceland, which has turned a tidy profit ever since Priscilla opened it to the public, delighting residents of Memphis, which now hosts a major tourist attraction.

Born: 1945
Height: 5 ft. 2 in.
Weight: 110 lbs.
Eyes: Blue/green
Hair: Blond
Zodiac: Gemini
Education: When he brought her to America from her home in Germany, Elvis placed her in Immaculate Conception High School, Memphis, and attended her graduation (standing outside the auditorium at her request).
Religion: Scientology
Marriages: To Elvis Presley (1967–1972)
Children: Lisa Marie (b. 1968)
Interests: Decorating her homes, motorcycling, bareback horse riding, roughing it in Africa and Thailand, antiquing, theatergoing, shopping, exploring ethnic cuisines in restaurants all over the world, taking care of her plants, animals (Doberman Willie and kitten Scooter), and spending every Friday night with the large and warm Beaulieu clan
Personal Habits and Traits: Nonsmoker, will take an occasional drink, works out regularly with Jake of Body by Jake
Addresses: Santa Barbara; Beverly Hills; Memphis
Income: $4 million (minimum estimated, from *Dallas* salary, commercials and Presley estate)

Prince

Prince Rogers Nelson

"When a girl can get birth control pills at age 12, she knows about as much as I do. My mom had stuff in her room that I could sneak in and get . . . books, vibrators. I did it. I'm sure everybody does. . . . It could be that I have a need to be different."

His Highness's purple reign began in 1984, just as Michael Jackson's phenomenal *Thriller* began to cool. At one point, Prince boasted the top single in the country ("When Doves Cry"), the top album (*Purple Rain*), and the top movie (*Purple Rain,* which grossed $71 million). At the same time, he played Svengali to a jazz percussionist and transformed her from plain Sheila Escovedo to sexpot singer Sheila (*Glamorous Life*) E., turned Pearl Drops toothpaste model Denise Matthews into the hit-making Vanity, engineered the rise to stardom of protegée (and *Purple Rain* love interest) Apollonia, and pocketed millions more from a

sold-out "farewell" tour with Revolution, his band. When Prince was 7, his jazz musician father moved out of the family's North Minneapolis home; five years later, after an argument with his stepfather, he ran away—first to his father, then to live with an aunt, who soon kicked him out because of his guitar playing. At 13, he finally found a home in the basement of the house owned by Bernadette Anderson, mother of his best friend, Andre Cymone (Anderson became a surrogate mother to Prince, and he still sends her a present on Mother's Day). It was here that Prince taught himself to play 20 instruments by ear, and formed his first bands—Grand Central and Champagne. At 17, Prince became the youngest artist ever granted total control by Warner Bros. Yet his first two albums flopped, and when he opened for the Rolling Stones in 1981 he was booed off the stage. It wasn't until Prince settled on sex as a sales gimmick that he clicked with his third album, the aptly titled *Dirty Mind.* It established him as rock's newest sleaze machine, and he quickly followed up with *1999,* an LP that rode the charts for more than two years. As much a paradox as Jackson is a mystery, Prince professes to be shy, but writhes around onstage clad only in bikini briefs, stiletto heels, and sweat. He is constantly giving thanks to God (as he did when he won his Grammys in 1985 and an Academy Award for *Purple Rain*), but his racy lyrics preach sexual salvation. He is a recluse, too humble even to face the press, but shrewdly controls every facet of his career. Shunning L.A. and New York, he still lives in Minneapolis, in a (surprise) purple house filled with Marilyn Monroe posters and pots of flowers. With friends he still frequents Rudolf's, a favorite rib joint, and the First Avenue Club. But he always returns home to write music with a purple pen on a purple pad into the night (aside from his own hits like "Raspberry Beret" and "Kiss," under the *nom de* purple *plume* "Christopher," Prince has written big singles for other groups, such as the Bangles' "Manic Monday.") A creature of impulse, Prince has on more than one occasion hopped onto his purple bike and—naked—taken a predawn spin around the neighborhood.

Born: June 7, 1958, in Minneapolis
Height: 5 ft. 4 in.
Weight: 120 lbs.
Eyes: Brown
Hair: Black
Zodiac: Gemini
Education: High school dropout
Religion: Protestant
Marriages: None
Children: None
Interests: Writing songs, short stories, arranging, conducting, producing
Personal Habits and Traits: A recluse, seldom speaks, considers himself very religious, a vegetarian, favorite color: purple, surrounds himself with huge, long-haired bodyguards.
Address: Chanhassen, Minnesota
Income: $34 million+

Victoria Principal

"I've probably had fewer relationships than many, but no one will ever believe it."

Unlike the 99.9 percent pure Pam Ewing of *Dallas,* Victoria Principal has done her share of playing around. She had highly publicized romps with Frank Sinatra, football star Lance Rentzel, Desi Arnaz, Jr., her doctor, and a Beverly Hills custom car dealer. She left financier Bernie Cornfeld when he allegedly tried to strangle her, supposedly cured Anthony Perkins of his indifferent attitude toward women, and broke up with eight-years-younger Andy Gibb over his use of drugs. By the mid-1980s, she had apparently settled on plastic surgeon Dr. Harry Glassman. Her career, meanwhile, went through as many changes. An Air Force brat who grew up in Japan and on bases throughout the States, Principal modeled in New York and Europe before moving to L.A. and making *The Life and Times of Judge Roy Bean.* That inauspicious debut was followed by two more turkeys, so she decided to quit acting and become an agent. Then, in 1978, came *Dallas* and the goody-goody role of Bobby Ewing's devoted wife. The series, her bestselling books (*The Body Principal, The Beauty Principal*) and her commercial endorsements (for Jack La Lanne, Vic Tanny, Jhirmack shampoos) have brought Principal fame, wealth—and a security problem. Frightened by threatening phone calls and letters, she decided to turn her Benedict Canyon mansion into a fortress, complete with two attack Dobermans, a half-dozen alarm systems, and a bulletproof bathroom.

Born: January 3, 1950, in Fukuoka, Japan
Height: 5 ft. 6 in.
Weight: 110 lbs.
Eyes: Brown
Hair: Brown
Zodiac: Capricorn
Education: High school
Religion: Protestant
Marriages:
To Christopher Skinner (divorced after 20 months)
To Harry Glassman (1985–)
Children: None
Interests: Arthritis research (her father suffers from the disease), stock-car racing, swimming, chiropractics, backgammon
Personal Habits and Traits: Cautious and tough, loves deal-making, fitness nut
Addresses: Benedict Canyon, California; Palm Springs, California
Income: \$2.5 million annually (estimate)

Richard Pryor

"Everyone carries around his own monsters, but you have to face them and deal with them."

One of the most explosive, self-destructive yet brilliant comic minds in the entertainment world today, Richard Franklin Lennox Thomas Pryor can probably attribute much of his emotional instability to his extraordinary childhood.

Brought up in his grandmother's whorehouse, where his mother worked, Pryor was expelled from a Catholic school when his family background came to light. At 14 he was kicked out of another school for slugging a teacher. After a two-year hitch in the Army, Pryor headed for New York's Greenwich Village and was a frequent stand-up comic on *The Ed Sullivan Show, The Tonight Show,* and *The Merv Griffin Show.* There was a lack of Pryor restraint in his personal life, however. He has been arrested for assault and battery (he was accused of beating a hotel clerk and stabbing his landlord with a fork), and sued for wife beating, but he nonetheless managed to support a $100-a-day cocaine habit. Then he suddenly dropped out of sight, holed up in a Berkeley rooming house, and finally emerged with a cleaned-up act and a major role as Billie Holiday's heroin-addicted piano player in *Lady Sings the Blues.* With the exception of a 10-day jail term for income tax evasion, Pryor's fortunes rose as he starred in a number of box-office hits (*Uptown Saturday Night, Bingo Long, Silver Streak, Car Wash, Greased Lightning, Which Way Is Up?, Stir Crazy*), recorded four gold comedy albums (three of which won Grammys), and cowrote Mel Brooks's blockbuster *Blazing Saddles.* In the fall of 1977 *The Richard Pryor Show* premiered on NBC, and after four weeks during which he waged a public war with the network's censors, the series was torpedoed. Still, his contract called for Pryor to be paid $2 million merely not to appear on another network for five years. Along the way he divorced five wives—two white and three black. An outstanding public display of irrationality occurred in the fall of 1977, when he invited an audience of 17,000 attending a Gay Rights benefit at the Hollywood Bowl to "kiss my happy, rich, black ass." Three years later, he nearly died from burns suffered while freebasing cocaine. Pryor-ity was then given to *Superman III, The Toy, Brewster's Millions,* and *Jo Jo Dancer.*

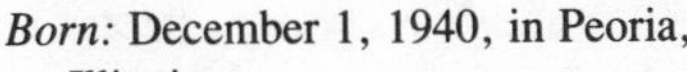

Born: December 1, 1940, in Peoria, Illinois
Height: 6 ft.
Weight: 160 lbs.
Eyes: Brown
Hair: Dark brown
Zodiac: Sagittarius
Education: High school dropout
Religion: Roman Catholic
Marriages: Five
Children: Renee (b. 1957), Richard (b. 1962), Elizabeth (b. 1968), Rain (b. 1969)
Interests: Scriptwriting, music (jazz, rhythm and blues), social problems
Personal Habits and Traits: Once a heavy drinker and cocaine user, he has eliminated both; still erratic, volatile
Addresses: San Fernando Valley, California; Hawaii
Income: $3 million per film

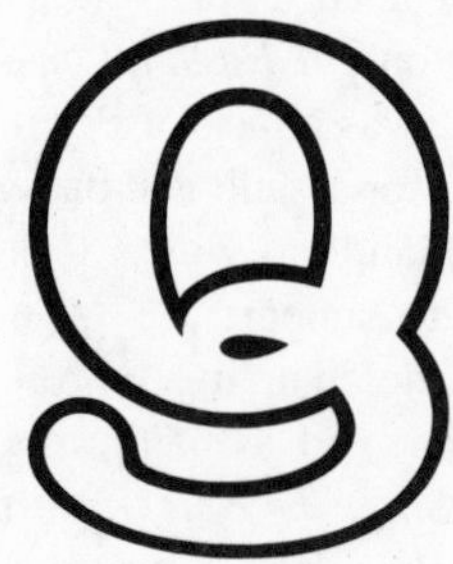

Anthony Quinn

"They said all I was good for was playing Indians."

Not even such a debacle as *The Greek Tycoon,* the ludicrous, thinly disguised film biography of Aristotle and Jacqueline Bouvier Kennedy Onassis, could dent the career of two-time Oscar winner (for *Viva Zapata* and *Lust for Life*) Anthony Quinn. Born in Mexico the son of an Irish-American soldier of fortune and his Mexican bride, young Anthony was smuggled out of the country into Texas at the height of the Mexican Revolution; hidden in a wagon carrying coal, he nearly smothered. Working on the streets of Los Angeles at age 5, he was later employed as, among other things, a dress cutter and a fruit picker, until he formed his own theater company at age 15. His professional stage debut occurred with Mae West in a turkey called *Clean Beds,* and Quinn soon turned to movies, only to lose solid parts because of his swarthy looks. He finally broke through the Van Johnson syndrome by following Marlon Brando into the part of Stanley Kowalski in Broadway's *A Streetcar Named Desire*. Success on film came only after he married Cecil B. DeMille's daughter Katherine. Over the next 40 years Quinn played everything from Barrabas and Attila the Hun to the first Russian pope to a mad Greek named Zorba. Anxious to work for Federico Fellini, he dropped everything to act in the classic *La Strada*. Before fulfilling his longtime friend Aristotle Onassis's request to portray him in the movies (Jacqueline Bisset played Jackie O), Quinn was embroiled in another controversial project. As the star of the Arab-made $17 million epic *Mohammad, Messenger of God,* Quinn emerged as the focal point of hostility among many Moslems who found the film blasphemous. At one point a fanatical Hanafi Muslim sect shot its way into three Washington, D.C., theaters and held 100 people hostage, demanding that the film be shut down. The Hanafis surrendered, but the continuing threat of violence against theaters showing *Mohammad* finally ruined the movie's moneymaking potential. Divorced from DeMille after almost 30 years of marriage, Quinn married the mother of two of his out-of-wedlock sons (he has eight children), Italian wardrobe girl Iolanda Addolori. A confirmed expatriate, he now lives with Addolori in a lavish Roman apartment. Quinn returned to the stage in the hit Broadway musical version of *Zorba the Greek*.

Born: April 21, 1915, in Chihuahua, Mexico
Height: 5 ft. 10 in.
Weight: 170 lbs.
Eyes: Brown
Hair: White
Zodiac: Aries
Education: High school dropout
Religion: Roman Catholic

Marriages:
To Katherine DeMille (divorced)
To Iolanda Addolori (1966–)
Children: Eight
Interests: Painting, sculpture, literature
Personal Habits and Traits: Chain-smokes, drinks, workaholic, early riser
Address: Rome
Income: $829,000

Gilda Radner

"I love tap dancing because you can stamp your little guts out if you're pissed off."

From her parody of newswoman "Baba Wawa" to original creations like Emily Litella and Roseanne Rosanadanna ("Did you ever get somethin' stuck in your teeth and you didn't know what the heck it was?"), Gilda Radner rocketed to stardom along with Chevy Chase on NBC's satirical *Saturday Night Live* series. Born to an upper-middle-class Jewish family in Detroit, she was 14 when her father died. In addition to his encouragement, Radner credits the Liggett School for Girls with steering her toward comedy. Overweight as a child, Radner endured the requisite miserable childhood; at one point she turned down an offer to model for Lane Bryant. After studying for her teaching credentials at the University of Michigan, Gilda ran away to Toronto. While performing with a local *Godspell* musical company and as a member of Toronto's version of the Second City improvisation troupe, she met John Belushi. They joined New York's *National Lampoon Show* in 1974, and Lorne Michaels tapped them both for his new *Saturday Night Live*. When Chevy Chase left in 1976, Radner unofficially took his place as first among equals on the enormously successful show. Gilda left three years later, opened on Broadway in *Gilda Radner Live* and then *Lunch Hour*. Trimmed down to 105 pounds (her 1970 peak was 150), Radner exists largely on a diet of sugarless Bazooka bubblegum and frequently makes herself throw up when she feels she has binged. Sharing a Greenwich Village flat with gay roommate Dale Anglund, Radner carried on intermittent affairs with British actor Peter Firth (*Equus*) and Susan Sarandon's ex-husband Chris before marching to the altar with rock guitarist G. E. Smith. That marriage crumbled two years later, so she tried again, this time with fellow funny person Gene Wilder, her costar in *The Woman in Red*.

Born: June 28, 1946, in Detroit, Michigan
Height: 5 ft. 6 in.
Weight: 105 lbs.
Eyes: Brown
Hair: Brown
Zodiac: Cancer
Education: University of Michigan, B.A. in education
Religion: Jewish

Marriages:
To G.E. Smith (1980–1982)
To Gene Wilder (1983–)
Children: None
Interests: Workaholic (60 hours a week), art, tap dancing
Personal Habits and Traits: Does not smoke, rarely drinks, fanatical dieter
Address: Greenwich Village, New York City
Income: $300,000 (estimate)

Princess Lee Radziwill

Caroline Lee Bouvier

"I'm nobody's kid sister."

Caroline Lee Bouvier and her sister Jacqueline were raised together in a succession of mansions from East Hampton and Manhattan to Newport and Virginia. And though they opted for different colleges—Jackie for Vassar, Lee for Sarah Lawrence—they remained very close until 1953, when Lee married Michael Canfield, a publishing scion, and moved to England. Their marriage lasted five years. In 1959 Lee again took the plunge, this time with Polish nobleman Prince Stanislas ("Stash") Radziwill, a wealthy London-based real estate investor. For a while Princess Lee hobnobbed with an artistic crowd including Rudolf Nureyev and Truman Capote, but she soon grew terribly restless and tried acting onstage in a Chicago production of *The Philadelphia Story,* then on television in *Laura*—bombing in both. She coauthored a childhood memoir with her sister called *One Special Summer* and tried her hand, again unsuccessfully, as host of a CBS talk show. Meantime, Lee divorced Stash in 1974 (he died two years later). That same year she finally seemed to hit on the right career. Renting a Manhattan office from favorite Kennedy architect John Carl Warnecke, she began to decorate suites for the Americana hotel chain, residences in San Francisco, a nightclub in Houston, and a resort in Brazil. "It's no joke," she says. "My decorating business is a tremendous success, and for one reason: I take my work seriously." With children Antony and Anna Christina, Lee makes her home in her own tastefully decorated Fifth Avenue duplex just seven blocks south of big sister Jackie. Lee almost moved to San Francisco for married life with Nob Hill hotelier Newton Cope, but called the wedding off at the last minute.

Born: March 3, 1933, in New York City
Height: 5 ft. 6 in.
Weight: 105 lbs.
Eyes: Brown
Hair: Auburn
Zodiac: Pisces
Education: Sarah Lawrence, B.A. in art history
Religion: Roman Catholic

Marriages:
To Michael Canfield (1953–1958)
To Prince Stanislas ("Stash") Radziwill (1959–1974)
Children: Antony (b. 1959), Anna Christina (b. 1960)
Interests: Decorating, theater, art, ballet
Personal Habits and Traits: Late riser, drinks moderately, is mercurial
Address: Manhattan
Income: $250,000 +

Tony Randall

"What most people probably don't know about me is that I have a terrible, awful temper. I wish I were kinder, less impatient than I am."

An opera and theater fanatic who would much rather have been another Caruso or Olivier, Tony Randall ranks as one of the classier TV funnymen. Irrepressibly droll—"I even enjoyed my parents' divorce"—Randall grew up the son of an art dealer who mainly serviced Tulsa's oil-rich clientele. Randall wound up going to 24 schools when his father hit the road to sell art in Palm Beach and then New York, and was relieved when Dad finally left for good. "It was pleasant for me," concedes Randall, who was 13 at the time. "My rival was gone." To correct his Oklahoma accent Tony attended Northwestern University's School of Speech, then studied acting with Sanford Meisner in New York. During the late 1950s he landed the role of Harvey Weskit in the hit television sitcom *Mr. Peepers.* Some 25 films followed, ranging from the Rock Hudson–Doris Day flick *Pillow Talk* to his favorite effort, *The Seven Faces of Dr. Lao.* But Randall's lackluster screen career prompted him to return to TV, starring as the fussy Felix Unger opposite Jack Klugman's sloppy Oscar Madison in *The Odd Couple.* After five seasons playing Felix, Randall weighed in with *The Tony Randall Show* on ABC in 1976, in which he played a persnickety Philadelphia judge with a mad housekeeper and two outrageously precocious kids. Randall later tried to break down the gay barrier as the homosexual protagonist of the series *Love, Sidney.* Judging by the ratings, the network decided viewers didn't Love Tony in this role. "I am a slob," Randall says of his priggish image. "But nobody will believe it." Between series, Randall kept his income well into the six figures by endorsing photocopiers on television.

Born: February 26, 1920, in Tulsa, Oklahoma
Height: 5 ft. 8 in.
Weight: 150 lbs.
Eyes: Brown
Hair: Brown
Zodiac: Pisces
Education: Northwestern University
Marriages: To Florence Gibbs (1941–)
Children: None
Interests: Opera, ballet, trivia, "mothball music" of the 1920s and 1930s
Personal Habits and Traits: Nonsmoker, beer drinker
Addresses: New York City; Chateau Marmont Hotel, Los Angeles; Malibu, California
Income: $400,000 (estimate)

Dan Rather

"Performing doesn't turn me on. It's an egomaniac business, filled with prima donnas—including this one."

Television's $20 million newsman (his 1980 contract to replace Walter Cronkite as CBS anchorman calls for $8 million spread over five years, but insiders predict that other factors will push it closer to the $20 million mark) is the son of a Houston ditchdigger and his waitress wife. He made it through Sam Houston State Teachers College working as a gas jockey and served a hitch in the Marines before finally landing a job with Houston's KTRH radio station at $67.20 a week. Often paying his own way to report stories, Rather broke through to the network level with his on-the-spot coverage of Hurricane Carla for Houston's CBS affiliate. The assassination of John F. Kennedy was Rather's first big story as a CBS staff correspondent, followed by a lengthy Vietnam tour and an on-camera showdown with Richard Nixon at the height of Watergate. Following Nixon's resignation, Rather was transferred from the White House beat to *CBS Reports,* then to *60 Minutes*—a move that coincided with *60 Minutes'* spectacular and unprecedented (for a news show) rise to the top of the Nielsens. No less successful were his two books—*The Palace Guard* and *The Camera Never Blinks* (the first coauthored with Gary Gates, the second ghosted by Mickey Herskowitz), which shot to number one on national bestseller lists. As dashing as Cronkite was reassuringly rumpled, Savile-suited Rather was appointed the retiring Cronkite's successor in 1980—a decision that came as a blow to longtime heir-apparent Roger Mudd, who promptly defected to NBC. Despite a 110-hour work week, Rather has managed to maintain a solid marriage to Jean Goebel, whom he wed when he was 24. An indefatigable health nut, he jogs down Park Avenue every morning before dawn, scuba dives, fishes, hunts, and diets on yogurt. How does he stack up against his predecessor at the CBS anchor desk? "Walter is believable," explains Rather. "The rest of us are trying to live up to that."

Born: August 31, 1931, in Wharton, Texas
Height: 6 ft.
Weight: 180 lbs.
Eyes: Brown
Hair: Salt and pepper
Zodiac: Leo
Education: Sam Houston State Teachers College
Religion: Baptist
Marriages: To Jean Goebel (1955–)
Children: Dawn Robin and Daniel Martin
Interests: Hunting, fishing, scuba diving, tennis, running
Personal Habits and Traits: Scrupulously polite, nonsmoker, moderate drinker, weight-conscious, given to homey aphorisms ("He's all hat and no cattle")
Address: Manhattan
Income: $5 million annually (minimum estimate)

Lou Rawls

"I had forgotten that you still have to deal with the dude on the street corner. It don't mean nothin' if he can't come up to you and say, 'That's my man.' "

A satin-voiced successor to Nat King Cole, Lou Rawls plummeted from a top supper club and record draw into oblivion, only to stage a remarkable comeback in 1977. Raised on the South Side of Chicago by his grandmother while his mother worked, Lou started singing in his church choir when he was 7, and at 14 formed a gospel group with three other boys, including the late Sam Cooke. After a stint in the Army paratroops, Rawls sang in L.A. with another gospel group called the Pilgrim Travelers and by the early 1960s had become a protégé of Duke Ellington. He cut five hit singles (including the number-one "Dead End

Street") and collected a Grammy, but in 1973 he was abruptly dropped by his record company—and by his wife of 12 years. Four years later his album *All Things in Time* went platinum, and he received an American Music Award for his number-one single "You'll Never Have Another Love Like Mine." A lucrative contract to become the singing spokesman for Budweiser followed, as well as commercials for Blue Cross, Dodge Charger, and Eastern Airlines. But perhaps most important to Rawls, who dazzles when performing live, the MGM Grand Hotel in Las Vegas signed him to a five-year, $1 million contract.

Born: December 1, 1935, in Chicago, Illinois
Height: 5 ft. 8 in.
Weight: 140 lbs.
Eyes: Brown
Hair: Black
Zodiac: Sagittarius
Education: High School
Religion: Baptist
Marriages: One. Ended in divorce in 1973
Children: Lou, Jr. (b. 1964), Louana (b. 1968)
Interests: Charity performances, soccer, Ping-Pong, golf, tennis
Personal Habits and Traits: Smokes occasionally, drinks beer, cool, soft-spoken
Address: Los Angeles
Income: $380,000 (estimate)

Ronald Reagan

"My heart is a hamloaf."

It was 5:35 P.M., November 5, 1980. The former Governor of California was stepping out of the shower when the phone rang in his Century Plaza Hotel suite. Nancy Reagan stood in stunned silence as her husband, wrapped in a towel and still dripping wet, listened to President Jimmy Carter concede defeat and offer his congratulations to the man who was now to succeed him in the Oval Office. After a bitterly fought campaign, Ronald Reagan's election as the fortieth President of the United States was a fittingly dramatic climax to one of the most remarkable careers in American political history. Born in Tampico, Illinois, but raised in nearby Dixon, "Dutch" Reagan was an unspectacular high school football player but a superb swimmer who saved a total of 77 people during the summers he worked as a lifeguard. He graduated from Eureka College (Illinois) and became a regional celebrity as radio announcer for the Chicago Cubs before striking out for Hollywood in 1935. One week after signing a $200-per-week, seven-year contract with Jack Warner, Reagan was appropriately cast as a radio announcer in *Love Is on the Air*—the first of fifty-three movies that included *Knute Rockne, All American* ("Let's win this one for the Gipper!"; Reagan played the dying Gip), *Santa Fe Trail* (with Reagan portraying a callow George Custer), and 1942's *King's Row,* in which he woke up after his leg was amputated and screamed the line that would serve as the title of his 1965 autobiography: *Where Is the Rest of Me*? Reagan was rewarded with a lifetime membership in the Screen Actors Guild after serving as president during six turbulent years, but his politics turned increasingly conservative during the late 1950s and early 1960s, when he served as spokesman for General Electric and hosted the *G. E. Theater* and *Death Valley Days* on television. Officially changing his registration from Democrat to Republican in 1962, he attracted national attention two years later as a rousing speaker on behalf of GOP candidate Barry Goldwater. In 1966, Reagan went up against old pro Edmund G. "Pat" Brown, then seeking a third term as California's Governor, and surprised the experts by winning the election by a 2–1 margin—a feat he repeated four years later when he ran for reelection against state legislator Jesse Unruh. Proving himself a capable administrator, Reagan nonetheless was denied his party's Presidential nomination when he tried in 1968 and again in 1976. But he succeeded handily in his third try, and the Ronald Reagan–George Bush ticket trounced Jimmy Carter and running mate Walter Mondale with 489 electoral votes to the incumbents' 49. Reagan's inauguration marked a number of Presidential "firsts": He was the only divorced man elected to the office, the first former union leader, the first Democrat-turned-Republican, and at 69 the oldest. A devout Californian, President Reagan and his ultrachic First Lady get back as often as they can to their home in Pacific Palisades and their ranch in the Santa Barbara Mountains. They are now cast as America's First Couple, but it is only one of several productions the Reagans have appeared in together, including—believe it or not—a 1958 television play entitled *A Turkey for the President*. On March 30, 1981, Reagan narrowly escaped death when John Hinckley, Jr., shot the President and three others—including press secretary James Brady—as they left the Washington Hilton. President Reagan, who recovered swiftly after the bullet was removed from his left lung, even wisecracked as he was being wheeled into the operating room. "I hope," he told the surgeons, "you are all Republicans." It looked as if practically everybody was Republican on Election Day 1984, when Walter Mondale and running mate Geraldine Ferraro were buried by a Ronald Reagan–George Bush landslide—the largest in U.S. history. Several months later, the President was operated on for colonic cancer, and a second time for a skin cancer on his nose.

Born: February 6, 1911, in Tampico, Illinois
Height: 6 ft. 1 in.
Weight: 180 lbs.
Eyes: Blue
Hair: Brown
Zodiac: Aquarius
Education: Eureka College, B.A.
Religion: Protestant
Marriages:
To Jane Wyman (1940–48)
To Nancy Davis (1952–)
Children: Maureen (by Wyman) and Michael (adopted); Patricia and Ronald (by Davis)
Interests: Horseback riding, astrology, western art
Personal Habits and Traits: Superstitious (overcame a fear of flying, but still bowls an orange down the center aisle for good luck); stuffs pockets with jellybeans that he nibbles throughout the day; has an occasional cocktail; likes to work regular hours and get to bed by 11 P.M.
Addresses: 1600 Pennsylvania Avenue, Washington, D.C.; Pacific Palisades, California; Santa Barbara
Income: $200,000 (Presidential salary)

Nancy Reagan

Anne Frances Davis

"Believing in true love, saving yourself for that true love, and having one husband for all of your life just seems to me how things should be."

"They ought to elect the First Lady and then let her husband be President" is the line she uttered in her prophetically titled high school play *First Lady* back in 1939. Not that Nancy Reagan's values offstage have been anything other than traditional. "My life," she is often quoted as saying, "began when I married Ronnie." Herself the product of a broken home—her New Jersey car dealer father took off when she was 2, and her actress-mother Edith "DeeDee" Luckett spent several months a year on the road—Nancy (a childhood nickname) was sent to live with relatives in Maryland until Mom married wealthy Chicago neurosurgeon Loyal Davis. Legally adopted at 14, young Nancy Davis attended toney Girls' Latin School, at 16 made her debut at Chicago's Casino Club, and topped it all off with a Smith College education. After breaking off a brief engagement to an Amherst student, Nancy decided to head for Lotusland. Spencer Tracy, a friend of the Davises, helped her along by wangling a screen test for Nancy with MGM. In her starlet days, she dated Clark Gable, Cary Grant, and others while she made films like *The Next Voice You Hear* and *Hellcats of the Navy*. In 1952, four years after Reagan divorced Jane Wyman, he and Nancy married. Fittingly, she played Ronnie's love five years later in *Hellcats,* her last movie. The most stylish First Lady since Jackie Kennedy, Nancy Reagan—a member of the Fashion Hall of Fame—favors gowns by Galanos and everyday dresses by the haute-couture likes of Adolfo and Albert Nipon. And she promptly spiced up White House functions by liberally sprinkling guest lists with old Hollywood pals like the Frank Sinatras, the James Stewarts, and the Charlton Hestons, and wealthy Southern Californians like Betsy Bloomingdale and Dart Industries-founder Justin Dart. Unlike her immediate predecessor, Rosalynn Carter, Mrs. Reagan has no pretensions about shaping foreign or domestic policy, focusing instead on a variety of charities and projects like Foster Grandparenting, a program where mentally retarded children are matched with senior citizens. Not that she doesn't have strong political opinions of her own: she opposes abortion, the Equal Rights Amendment, and premarital sex. Even their political opponents concede that the Reagans' enduring relationship is one of the White House's great love affairs. Being with her, muses the President, is "like coming from the cold air into a warm room." He calls her "Mommie." Others call her the power behind the Presidency, and they're right: Nancy wields a tremendous influence not only on her husband's policies, but also on the day-to-day operations of the White House staff. Bearing up bravely in the face of her husband's cancer operation in 1985, Nancy proved herself to be a first-class First Lady. Still, she and Ron were stung when daughter Patti Davis wrote a thinly disguised novel about a presidential daugthter, *Home Front.*

Born: July 6, 1923, in New York City
Height: 5 ft. 4 in.
Weight: 106 lbs. (size 6)
Eyes: Brown
Hair: Light brown
Zodiac: Cancer
Education: Smith College
Religion: Protestant
Marriages: To Ronald Reagan (1952–)
Children: Patricia, Ronald
Interests: Working with handicapped children, fashion, horseback riding
Personal Habits and Traits: Diets, does not smoke, is soft-spoken, does not brook any profanity
Addresses: 1600 Pennsylvania Ave., Washington, D.C.; Pacific Palisades, California; Santa Barbara

Robert Redford

"Other people have analysis. I have Utah."

Hollywood's hottest property of the 1970s, blond-maned, ice-blue-eyed Robert Redford has no peer as a current screen sex symbol (though he returns to earth when his kids chant "Double R, Superstar, who in hell do you think you are?"). Growing up in Southern California Redford seemed the perennial golden boy. A superb athlete in high school, he attended the University of Colorado on a baseball scholarship, then headed for Europe as a roving art student. Once back in the United States he met a strong-willed Mormon named Lola Van Wagenen, whom he married; and in order to make ends meet while he pursued his painting career, Redford grudgingly followed friends' advice and tried acting. The Neil Simon Broadway hit *Barefoot in the Park* launched his career in 1963, and his subsequent avalanche of hit movies included *Butch Cassidy and the Sundance Kid, Downhill Racer, The Candidate, The Great Gatsby, The Way We Were, The Sting, The Great Waldo Pepper, Three Days of the Condor, The Electric Horseman,* and *Brubaker*. Redford played the role of *Washington Post* reporter Bob Woodward opposite Dustin Hoffman's Carl Bernstein in the Watergate saga *All the President's Men,* which Redford also produced. Outside his profession he is an equally multifaceted powerhouse. At Sundance, his resort in the Utah mountains that doubles as a training ground for young actors and filmmakers, Redford skis (his favorite sport), water-skis, rides horseback, fishes, hunts, plays tennis, and pilots his own plane. Not that he shuns the city, for Redford spends most of the year in his Fifth Avenue apartment, and his children attend school in New York. While Lola heads Consumer Action Now (CAN), Redford himself is one of the nation's most outspoken advocates of solar power. He stepped behind the cameras for the first time as director of *Ordinary People,* based on the bestselling novel by Judith Guest. Redford not only won an Oscar for his efforts, but *Ordinary People* grabbed top honors as Best Picture of 1980. After *The Natural* opened to mixed reviews in 1984, Redford began filming the Oscar-winning *Out of Africa* with another blond box-office draw, Meryl Streep, and signed to do another movie with *Butch Cassidy* buddy Paul Newman. R. R. and Debra Winger squared off in court in the 1986 comedy *Legal Eagles.*

Born: August 18, 1937, in Santa Monica, California
Height: 5 ft. 10 in.
Weight: 159 lbs.
Eyes: Blue
Hair: Reddish blond
Zodiac: Leo
Education: University of Colorado (dropped out)
Religion: Protestant
Marriages: To Lola Van Wagenen (current)
Children: Shauna (b. 1961), Jamie (b. 1962), Amy (b. 1970)
Interests: Skiing, water-skiing, tennis, boating, hunting, fishing, the environment, solar energy, American Indian culture, horses
Personal Habits and Traits: Nonsmoker, does drink alcohol, never diets, nonstop worker and athlete, highly competitive
Addresses: New York City; Sundance, Utah
Income: $4 million +

Vanessa Redgrave

"America is gangsterism for the private profit of the few."

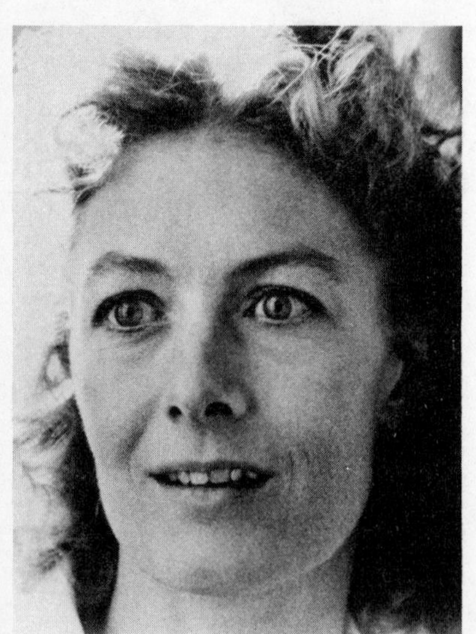

This outspoken member of Britain's legendary theatrical family has a consummate talent for acting—and for provoking controversy. When she finally accepted an Oscar for Best Supporting Actress in *Julia* after an acclaimed movie career that has included *Blow-Up, Morgan, Camelot, The Loves of Isadora, The Devils, The Trojan Women,* and *Mary, Queen of Scots,* Vanessa was virtually booed off the stage for calling those who opposed her pro-Palestinian politics "Zionist hoodlums." Vanessa, whose father Michael was once banned by the BBC for supporting the leftist People's Convention in the 1930s, started promulgating Communist ideology at 14 in school debates. An ardent, vehemently anti-American Trotskyite whose causes range from pacifism to support of Fidel Castro's regime, Vanessa ran twice for Parliament on the Workers Revolutionary ticket and was thoroughly trounced. With the exception of capitalist sister Lynn Redgrave, a star in her own right (*Georgy Girl, Black Comedy, The Happy Hooker*), Vanessa counts on moral support from her mother, actress Rachel Kempson, and from her younger brother, Corin, a fellow Marxist who also ran for Parliament and lost. Meanwhile Ms. Redgrave's personal life has been no less tumultuous: married for five years to British director Tony Richardson, she divorced him in 1967 for adultery with Jeanne Moreau; two years later she became pregnant with *Camelot* costar Franco Nero's child, then announced she had no intention of marrying him. And despite her Trotskyite beliefs, Vanessa nonetheless sent her daughters by Richardson and son by Nero to an expensive English private school. Whatever her offscreen activities, Redgrave once again won critical acclaim for her starring role in *Yanks* and sparked furious debate by appearing in TV's 1981 concentration camp saga *Playing for Time.* When the Boston Symphony canceled an appearance with her, she sued for damages and won. Redgrave was nominated for an Oscar for her role in *The Bostonians,* and was praised for her work in the PBS miniseries *Three Sovereigns for Sarah,*

about the Salem witch trials. She once again received accolades for her unsettling performance in the film *Wetherby*. Redgrave then under took one of the toughest roles of her career as transsexual Renee Richards in the TV movie *Second Serve*. Now mixed doubles is one thing . . .

Born: January 30, 1937, in London, England
Height: 5 ft. 10 in.
Weight: 139 lbs.
Eyes: Blue
Hair: Blond
Zodiac: Aquarius
Education: High school
Religion: Atheist
Marriages:
To Tony Richardson (1962–1967)
Children: Natasha (b. 1964), Joely Kim (b. 1965) by Richardson; Carlo (b. 1969) by Franco Nero
Interests: Communism, the Middle East, pacifism, archeology, documentary filmmaking
Personal Habits and Traits: Smokes and drinks, intolerant, radical
Address: London
Income: $400,000+ (minimum estimate)

Rex Reed

"I love Mexican food, Southern Gothic writers, horror movies, fireplaces, corn on the cob, Dr. Pepper, old movies, and ketchup on my steak. I hate phonies, liver, onions, organized behavior, milk—which I'm allergic to—subways, and writers who write about themselves."

The zappiest and one of the most entertaining of current show business critics grew up the son of an oil company supervisor in Fort Worth, Texas, and continually received straight As in 13 schools as his family moved from one new oil field to another. Sporting the clean-cut good looks of a Hollywood contract player, Reed briefly flirted with an acting career before putting his Louisiana State University journalism training to vitriolic use. Both *The New York Times* and the late *New York Herald Tribune* published his freelanced interviews with stars like Buster Keaton in the mid-1960s. Soon Rex became the darling of the talk shows as he lacerated everyone from Barbra Streisand to Marlon Brando. Amazingly he emerged relatively unscathed from his disastrous movie debut as a would-be transsexual in Gore Vidal's *Myra Breckinridge*. Reed wisely chose to concentrate on his typewriter and subsequently turned out a series of revealing bestsellers—among them *Do You Sleep in the Nude?*, *Conversations in the Raw*, *Big Screen, Little Screen*, and *Valentines and Vitriol*. A perennial bachelor, Reed resides at the Dakota, Manhattan's most chic residential address, and on a farm in Connecticut. He is working on a novel about an aging movie queen.

Born: October 2, 1938, in Fort Worth, Texas
Height: 5 ft. 10 in.
Weight: 159 lbs.
Eyes: Green
Hair: Black
Zodiac: Libra
Education: Louisiana State University, B.A. in journalism
Religion: Methodist
Marriages: None
Children: None
Interests: Movies, art, food
Personal Habits and Traits: Nonsmoker, moderate drinker, partygoer
Address: New York City; Roxbury, Connecticut
Income: $200,000+ (estimate)

Christopher Reeve

"I am overenergetic, a live wire, ambitious, friendly, self-centered—and still at the stage where I'm taking care of my career first."

Plucked from a lineup of 200 hopefuls, this Cornell alumnus shot to stardom faster than a speeding you-know-what with the release of *Superman* in 1978. The part, for which Reeve beefed up 30 pounds (from 188 to 218) by eating four meals a day and pumping iron three hours daily, came none too soon: in the months before landing the role, Reeve had become so depressed by his inability to get his career off the ground that he began "sponging off friends, sleeping on couches, and turning into a vegetable." That phase lasted five months—until Reeve decided to put his Broadway aspirations on hold and don the red cape. Born in Manhattan to poet-translator-creative writing professor Franklin D. Reeve and his journalist wife, Barbara Johnson, Reeve was only 4 when his parents split. (Their bitter divorce has had a lasting influence on Christopher, who remained unmarried even after British model agent Gae Exton gave birth to their two children.) Reeve claims that as a teenager he got around the problem of having to ask Sally for a date by starring in virtually all of the productions at Princeton Day School. After Cornell, a two-year stint on the cast of the daytime soap *Love of Life* helped Reeve pay for his tuition at New York City's Juilliard School of Drama, where John Houseman was one of his teachers. In 1975, he landed his first role on Broadway as Katharine Hepburn's doting grandson in Enid Bagnold's quirky comedy *A Matter of Gravity*. Reeve's performance in *Superman* earned the praise of critics and the moviegoing public alike, and the two sequels—*Superman II* and *III*—brought the total *Superman* take at the box office to a staggering $900 million. He was less successful in other endeavors such as *Somewhere in Time* ("I overacted dreadfully"), *Monsignor,* and *Death Trap,* though he rebounded somewhat in 1984's *The Bostonians*. The quintessentially preppy Reeve shares an apartment on Manhattan's West Side with Exton and their children, and unwinds by biking around the city. The Man of Steel has managed to emerge from his encounters with the tabloid press, well, stainless. "One way you adjust to celebrity," says Reeve, set to star in 1987 in the comedy *Street Smart,* "is to let the sleazy stuff miss you." He barely escaped death in the summer of 1984 when he went up in a parachute at the beach, waved to his family below (upsetting his balance), and plunged into four feet of water.

Born: September 25, 1952, in Manhattan
Height: 6 ft. 4 in.
Weight: 200 lbs.
Eyes: Blue
Hair: Brown
Zodiac: Libra
Education: B.A. in English and music theory, Cornell University
Religion: Protestant
Marriages: None
Children: Matthew (b. 1979), Alexandra (b. 1983)
Interests: Classical piano (practices 90 minutes daily), composing, flying (he owns both a small plane and a glider), sailing, ice skating, skiing, tennis, theater
Personal Habits and Traits: Wears preppy clothes (Hush Puppies, corduroy pants, tweeds), a nonsmoker, driven, self-confident, extremely polite and intelligent
Address: New York City
Income: $3 million

Lee Remick

"The longer I'm away from America the more American I become."

Anything but *A Face in the Crowd* since she played the part of a cracker drum majorette in that 1957 film, Lee Remick earned her star status as Jack Lemmon's alcoholic wife in *Days of Wine and Roses* and as Sir Winston's smoldering mum on the Emmy-winning PBS series *Jennie: Lady Randolph Churchill.* Like the original Jennie, Remick has herself become an expatriate Yankee (Lee's father owned a department store in Quincy, Massachusetts), forging a new life for herself as the wife of an Englishman. First married to American TV producer-director Bill Colleran, Remick became involved with married movie director William ("Kip") Gowans while shooting *Hard Contract* in Brussels. Gowans's wife, British actress Valerie Gearon, named Remick as co-respondent in a divorce suit, and Lee moved to London and married Gowans when his divorce became final in 1970. The Gowanses now share a five-story Georgian town house in London's exclusive St. John's Wood. Following her triumph as *Jennie,* Remick returned to the big screen in the blockbuster *The Omen* and in several made-for-TV movies. Remick turned in spellbinding performances as the shoplifting wife of auto tycoon Rock Hudson in *Wheels* (the TV miniseries based on Arthur Hailey's bestseller), as Margaret Sullavan in the TV movie *Haywire,* in the film version of Henry James's *The Europeans,* television's *The Women's Room,* and, on Broadway, in *Wait Until Dark.* In 1986, she took to the stage in an acclaimed, all-star concert performance of Stephen Sondheim's *Follies.*

Born: December 14, 1935, in Quincy, Massachusetts
Height: 5 ft. 5 in.
Weight: 118 lbs.
Eyes: Ice blue
Hair: Ash blond
Zodiac: Capricorn
Education: High school
Religion: Roman Catholic

Marriages:
To William Colleran (divorced)
To William "Kip" Gowans (current)
Children: Kate (b. 1962), Matthew (b. 1964)
Interests: Embroidery, shopping, antiques, biographies, cooking
Personal Habits and Traits: Smokes, drinks moderately, a homebody
Address: London
Income: $250,000 (minimum estimate)

Burt Reynolds

"I want to lead a quiet pseudo-intellectual life and go out and direct a picture two times a year. You can only hold your stomach in for so many years."

Burt Reynolds is the part-Indian son of the police chief of Riviera Beach, Florida. Kept in line by his strict father (he was thrown in jail by the elder Reynolds one night after a preteen prank), Burt was often made to use the servants' entrance when dating rich girls from nearby Palm Beach. He proved a killer

halfback at Florida State College, then dropped out when a knee injury terminated his playing career. Starting out as a television stuntman in New York, Reynolds played summer stock and even bit parts on Broadway before receiving a Universal Studios contract that secured him roles in *Branded, Gunsmoke,* and then two shows of his own—*Hawk* and *Dan August.* During this period he was briefly married to *Laugh-In*'s Judy Carne, then in 1972 broke out of his confining contract-player mold with his first solid movie performance in *Deliverance* and a sensation-causing, tongue-in-cheek nude centerfold for *Cosmopolitan* magazine that sold out on the newsstands within three days. Yet what really made him a household name was the talk show circuit. Blending a unique brand of machismo with his self-deprecating wit, Reynolds was soon asked to serve as Johnny Carson's substitute host on the *Tonight Show*—a ploy that instantly transformed him into a bankable star capable of comedy as well as action-adventure roles. Surely Reynolds's most memorable talk show appearance was his debut on *Dinah,* which marked the beginning of his lengthy impassioned romance with host Dinah Shore. That dissolved in 1977, and Reynolds squired a number of female personalities, including Tammy Wynette, until settling into a long-term relationship with Sally Field (*Norma Rae*). After that affair cooled, he moved on to Loni Anderson (*WKRP in Cincinnati*). Reynolds's films include *100 Rifles, White Lightning, Sam Whiskey, W. W. and the Dixie Dance Kings, The Longest Yard, The Man Who Loved Cat Dancing, Semi-Tough, Hooper,* and *Starting Over.* Reynolds also directed himself in *Gator* (1976) and *The End* (1978). While his attempt at song-and-dance Fred Astaire-style in *At Long Last Love* and his goofy sidekick performance with Gene Hackman and Liza Minnelli in *Lucky Lady* flopped miserably, Reynolds's *Smokey and the Bandit* raked in over $100 million—more than any other 1977 picture except *Star Wars.* Not immune to scandal, Reynolds was hospitalized for internal bleeding and emotional exhaustion after costar Sarah Miles's manager mysteriously killed himself during the filming of *Cat Dancing* in 1973, but beyond the obvious strain of adverse publicity Reynolds also discovered he suffered from a severe case of hypoglycemia (a blood sugar disorder) and promptly went on the wagon. Still, he continued to suffer from a mystery disease that had the rumor mill grinding away. With flops like *Sharkey's Machine, Cannonball II, The Man Who Loved Women,* and *Stick,* his career was also ailing. Reynolds now divides his time between an elegant Holmby Hills hacienda with a mirrored bedroom ceiling and a sprawling ranch in Jupiter, Florida, not far from the dinner theater that bears his name. After AIDS felled Rock Hudson, Reynolds felt it necessary to go on national television and deny he had the disease, which principally attacks homosexuals. His book was sold to Arbor House for $1 million.

Born: February 11, 1936, in Waycross, Georgia
Height: 6 ft. 1 in.
Weight: 178 lbs.
Eyes: Brown
Hair: Brown
Zodiac: Aquarius
Education: Dropped out of Florida State College
Religion: Protestant
Marriages: To Judy Carne (divorced)
Children: None
Interests: Poetry, football, horses, music, art, directing
Personal Habits and Traits: Nonsmoker, a teetotaler, early riser, articulate, relatively easygoing, always signs autographs, wears lifts and a hairpiece, a hypochondriac
Addresses: Holmby Hills, California; Jupiter, Florida
Income: $5.5 million

Debbie Reynolds

Marie Frances Reynolds

Through *Three Little Words, Singin' in the Rain, Tammy and the Bachelor, The Singing Nun,* and a smash 1973 Broadway revival of *Irene,* Debbie Reynolds has remained as unsinkable as her *Molly Brown* despite a series of career setbacks and two failed marriages. Born Marie Frances Reynolds in El Paso, Texas, on April Fool's Day, 1932, she was named Miss Burbank in 1948 (her talent routine was an imitation of Betty Hutton) and was soon signed to a Warner Studios contract. Producer Jack Warner came up with the name Debbie, then quickly dropped her after a small inane role in one picture. Once in the MGM stable, the nuclear-powered confection had Gene Kelly romping through mud puddles in *Singin' in the Rain.* Married to crooner Eddie Fisher at Grossinger's in 1955, she soon found herself in the highly publicized and humiliating position of the rejected woman when he left her to marry Elizabeth Taylor in 1959. The following year she married shoe mogul Harry Karl, but after 17 years that too ended in divorce. Since her comeback in *Irene,* Reynolds has stayed afloat as one of Las Vegas's top draws, and her daughter, Carrie Fisher, suggested the beginnings of a family dynasty when she starred in the *Star Wars* trilogy. Mom, who marched down the aisle a third time in 1985, jumped on the video bandwagon with her own bestselling exercise tape that had Jane Fonda eating her heart out.

Born: April 1, 1932, in El Paso, Texas
Height: 5 ft. 2 in.
Weight: 110 lbs.
Eyes: Blue
Hair: Blond
Zodiac: Aries
Education: High school
Religion: Roman Catholic
Marriages: Three
Children: Carrie (b. 1956), Todd (b. 1958)
Interests: The Hollywood Hall of Fame, emotionally disturbed children, a variety of charities, painting
Personal Habits and Traits: Smokes, drinks, a dynamo
Address: Beverly Hills
Income: $500,000 (minimum estimate)

Lionel Richie

"Too much is not enough."

Born on the campus of Tuskegee Institute near Montgomery, Alabama, where his grandfather worked in the university business department with Tuskegee founder Booker T. Washington, 1986 Oscar-winner (for "Say You, Say Me" from *White Nights*) Richie grew up the son of an Army captain and an elementary school principal. As a freshman at Tuskegee, Richie was asked by five classmates to join a band they were forming called the Jays. Richie put his plans for a marketing career aside while the Jays toured Canada and Europe, where they were spotted performing on the French Riviera by Ed Sullivan. His show was canceled before they could go on, but the Jays were soon getting plenty of exposure as the opening act for the Jackson 5. Motown signed them, changed the group's name to the Commodores, and with Richie as composer and lead singer, struck platinum in the late 1970s with "Easy," "Brick House," "Three Times a Lady," "Sail On," "Lady (You Bring Me Up)," and "Still." In 1981 the "Endless Love" duet by Richie and Diana Ross went to number one. At this point Richie wanted to pursue a solo career and remain with the Commodores, but the other five members of the group would have none of it. Forced to go it alone, Richie proceeded to churn out hit after hit—"You Are My Love," "Truly," "All Night Long," "Running With the Night," "Hello," and "Penny Lover," just to name a few. By the mid-1980s, he had collected numerous Grammys and other awards, won an American Music Award as Best Pop Vocalist, signed an $8.5 million contract to do commercials for Pepsi, and collaborated with old friend Michael Jackson on "We Are the World," the huge 1985 hit recorded by the superstar-laden USA for Africa group. In his "spare time," Richie also managed to produce Kenny Rogers's biggest hit, "Lady." Richie's personal life has revolved since 1975 around wife Brenda, a former psychiatric social worker who now serves as her husband's production assistant.

Born: June 20, 1949, in Tuskegee, Alabama
Height: 6 ft.
Weight: 150 lbs.
Eyes: Brown
Hair: Brown
Zodiac: Gemini
Education: Graduate of Tuskegee Institute
Religion: Protestant
Marriages: To Brenda Harvey (1975–)
Children: None
Interests: Composing, producing, Ethiopian famine relief, providing scholarships for needy black students
Personal Habits and Traits: A casual dresser, cautious with money, nonsmoker and nondrinker, easygoing, somewhat shy, a confirmed workaholic
Address: Tuskegee, Alabama
Income: $15 million annually (minimum estimate)

John Ritter

"I was the guy who always had 46 girlfriends. I would claim undying love until the question of the altar came up—until I met Nancy."

The Burbank-born son of country music star Tex Ritter, John earned a theater arts degree at the University of Southern California before embarking on a stage career. Going nowhere fast in the theater, he tried his luck guesting on such television series as *The Mary Tyler Moore Show, Hawaii Five-O, Kojak,* and *The Waltons* (he played the minister) before landing in the hit sexcom *Three's Company.* Married in October 1977 to actress Nancy Morgan, Ritter showed up on the *Three's Company* set the morning after his wedding in pajamas to protest the interference of work with his honeymoon; nonetheless, the series has made the Emmy-winning Ritter one of the TV industry's most sought-after and highly paid stars. Ritter gave up his bachelorhood on the air as well when the show was revamped as *Three's a Crowd.* John is an est graduate, a cleanaholic, and a confirmed night owl who nevertheless rises at 7 A.M. to take on his friends in a fierce game of racquetball. The Ritters share a two-story English country–style home in Brentwood with their golden retriever, Bambi.

Born: September 17, 1948, in Burbank, California
Height: 6 ft.
Weight: 180 lbs.
Eyes: Blue
Hair: Brown
Zodiac: Virgo
Education: University of Southern California, B.A. in theater arts
Religion: Protestant
Marriages: To Nancy Morgan (1977–)
Children: Jason (b. 1979)
Interests: Cerebral palsy (his older brother suffers from CP), theater, racquetball, collects Beatles records and memorabilia
Personal Habits and Traits: Nonsmoker, drinks occasionally, night person, needs little sleep
Address: Brentwood, California
Income: $2.5 million +

Joan Rivers

"Can we talk?"

Starting out as "Wimpy with a Hairbow," young Joan Rivers was the overweight, hypersensitive daughter of a successful Larchmont, New York, doctor and his moneyed wife. She graduated Phi Beta Kappa from Barnard College at 19, then fled her first husband and job as a fashion coordinator in 1958 to struggle as a comedienne. For the next seven years, Rivers knocked around "every dump in the country. If a trash can had a bulb, I played it." By 1965 she was long overdue for her big break, and it finally came in the form of a guest shot on the *Tonight Show.* With her rapid-fire sarcasm, she emerged as a curious blend of Woody Allen, Phyllis Diller, and Henny Youngman. By 1973 she had become the top opening act in Las Vegas and decided to move to Beverly Hills to write her own TV sitcom. When that effort failed, she penned a Broadway comedy called *Fun City,* which also promptly flopped. Undeterred, she plunged into her next project—a 1978 movie called *Rabbit Test,* the story of the world's first pregnant man. To make the film, Rivers and her husband Edgar Rosenberg mortgaged a second $300,000 on their house and raised another $700,000 from relatives and friends. Though a critical flop, *Rabbit Test* paid off at the box office. Still a bundle of insecurities, Rivers is most comfortable in her "petite Versailles" in California, surrounded by crystal chandeliers, Louis XVI furniture, and several thousand books. Her daughter, Melissa, was born in 1968, and after two miscarriages and a tubal pregnancy, Rivers said she was thinking of adopting. In 1984 Edgar survived a near-fatal heart attack—just one year after she landed the plum assignment as Johnny Carson's sole substitute host on *Tonight.* That, coupled with her bestselling book *The Life and Times of Heidi Abramowitz*, her MCI commercials and a hit comedy album, got her onto the covers of *Newsweek* and *People* (twice). Ironically, Rivers and longtime target Elizabeth Taylor became fast friends when both began spearheading efforts to raise funds for AIDS research. In mid-1986, Rivers stunned Johnny Carson by announcing she would host her own talk show on the new Fox network.

Born: 1935 in Brooklyn, New York
Height: 5 ft. 2 in.
Weight: 110 lbs.
Eyes: Brown
Hair: Blond
Education: Barnard College
Religion: Jewish
Marriages: Two. Currently to Edgar Rosenberg
Children: Melissa (b. 1968)
Interests: History, directing, writing, reading, needlepoint
Personal Habits and Traits: Does not smoke, drinks, a self-confessed chronic worrier and workaholic
Address: Beverly Hills
Income: $3 million (estimate)

Jason Robards, Jr.

"It's strange, all right, this thing between me and O'Neill. It's like a line from Moon for the Misbegotten: *'There is no present or future—only the past, happening over and over again—now.' "*

Wheeled onstage in a baby carriage shortly after his birth, the foremost interpreter of Eugene O'Neill's anguished roles read his first play by the Nobel Prize winner while serving in the Navy for seven years as a radioman. Decorated with the Navy Cross for valor during World War II, Jason Robards, Jr., son of the famous stage actor, enrolled after the war in the American Academy of Dramatic Arts in New York and survived lean years with a number of odd jobs—including "stretching" applicants too short for the police academy. Jason, Jr., began to outshine his celebrated father in 1956, when he portrayed Hickey in José Quintero's legendary production of O'Neill's *The Iceman Cometh.* He subsequently starred in O'Neill's *Hughie* and triumphed in the stage and movie versions of *Long Day's Journey Into Night,* as well as scoring a similar double triumph in Herb Gardner's *A Thousand Clowns.* Then came a decade-long career hiatus. On December 8, 1972, amid speculation that Robards was distraught over director

John Frankenheimer's decision to cast Lee Marvin as Hickey in his film version of *Iceman,* a drunken Robards smashed his Mercedes into an abutment in the mountains above Malibu. The nearly fatal accident rearranged Robard's features, though after months of painful plastic surgery he was able to return to work. O'Neill's *Moon for the Misbegotten* signaled Robards's auspicious and riveting return to Broadway in 1974, and three years later he successfully tackled *A Touch of the Poet.* At the same time his movie career ignited with Best Supporting Actor Oscars bestowed for his portrayal of *Washington Post* editor Ben Bradlee in *All the President's Men* and writer Dashiell Hammett in *Julia.* Robards also portrayed the antithesis of his *President's Men* role—paranoid U.S. President "Richard Moncton" in ABC-TV's newsmaking miniseries *Washington: Behind Closed Doors.* Along the way, he has endured four tempestuous marriages and fathered six children. His powerful performance as Howard Hughes in 1980's *Melvin & Howard* earned him yet another nomination for an Academy Award for Best Supporting Actor. After conquering his battle with booze, Robards proved that he was still a triple threat in films (*Max Dugan Returns*), onstage (a hit 1984 revival of *You Can't Take It With You* and an '85 revival of *Iceman*), and on television (*The Day After*). He credits Alcoholics Anonymous with saving his life and is one of AA's most ardent and eloquent supporters.

Born: July 22, 1922, in Chicago, Illinois
Height: 5 ft. 9 in.
Weight: 165 lbs.
Eyes: Brown
Hair: Gray
Zodiac: Cancer
Education: High school
Marriages:
To Eleanore Pitman (1948–1959)
To Rachel Taylor (1959–1961)
To Lauren Bacall (1961–1969)
To Lois O'Connor (1970–)
Children: Jason III, Sarah, David (by Pitman); Sam (by Bacall); Shannon, Jake (by O'Connor)
Interests: Fast cars, the theater, Alcoholics Anonymous
Personal Habits and Traits: Smokes, a recovered alcoholic
Addresses: Malibu, California; New York City
Income: $500,000 (estimate)

Harold Robbins

"Hemingway was a jerk."

A perfect character for one of his own torrid novels, Harold Robbins has no idea exactly where he was born or to whom. His birth certificate reads Francis Kane, and he was abandoned on the doorstep of a Catholic orphanage in New York's teeming and crime-infested Hell's Kitchen. Anglicizing the name of one of his foster parents, a New York druggist named Harold Rubin, Robbins dropped out of school at 15 and began to amass the first of his several fortunes. Working as a grocery clerk he recognized a shortage of canned goods, so he took flying lessons, flew a rented plane to Kentucky and proceeded to buy up options on various crops. By 20 he was a millionaire and started speculating on sugar, buying it up by the shipload. But when the price of sugar was frozen by President Roosevelt at a price below what Robbins had paid, Robbins was wiped out. In 1940 he went to work as a $27-a-week shipping clerk for Universal Pictures in New York, and after obtaining a $37,000 refund for the company by proving it had been illegally overcharged for freight, he eventually rose to become Universal's executive director of budget and planning. He soon decided that he could "write better crap" than what was being offered to the studio in the way of scripts, and in 1948 scored with his first bestseller *Never Love a Stranger*. Over the next three decades Robbins spun off 13 more potboilers, including *The Carpetbaggers* (selling over 6 million copies), *A Stone for Danny Fisher, The Betsy, The Pirate, The Lonely Lady, Dreams Die First, Memories of Another Day, Stiletto, Descent from Xanadu, The Dream Merchants, Goodbye, Janette, Spellbinder,* and *The Inheritors*. Every day 25,000 people around the world buy a Harold Robbins novel, making him one of the world's biggest-selling (not to mention highest-paid) living authors. Although he accomplishes most of his writing in New York's nondescript Elysee Hotel ("with the shades drawn so I'm not distracted"), Robbins lives an otherwise lavish life that includes a yacht, estates in Cannes, Acapulco, and Beverly Hills, and a gambling habit that in one night alone at Monte Carlo cost him $150,000.

Born: May 21, 1916, probably in New York City
Height: 5 ft. 9 in.
Weight: 164 lbs.
Eyes: Brown
Hair: Brown and balding
Zodiac: Gemini
Education: High school dropout
Religion: Jewish
Marriages: Two. Currently to Grace Palermo
Children: Two daughters
Interests: Art, finance, his 85-ft. yacht *Gracara*
Personal Habits and Traits: Chain-smokes cigarettes, drinks, gambles heavily
Addresses: Beverly Hills; Cannes; Acapulco
Income: $1.8 million (minimum estimate)

Cliff Robertson

"I pay my own bills. I told Deenie I would never want a relationship remotely resembling a consort."

When his ship was bombed in the Pacific shortly after Pearl Harbor, Merchant Marine Cliff Robertson was reported among the dead. His grieving family back in the Southern California town of La Jolla was ecstatic to remove the gold star from their window when Robertson walked through the front door—alive and healthy. Later he would portray a similar World War II survivor, John F. Kennedy, in the film *PT 109*. Rebelling against the antiwork ethic of his father, who lived off a family trust fund, Robertson supported himself as a stevedore, parking lot attendant, cabbie, and busboy while working off-Broadway. He made it onto the Great White Way opposite Maureen Stapleton in Tennessee Williams's *Orpheus Descending*. After Emmy nominations for *Days of Wine and Roses*

(Jack Lemmon landed the movie part) and *The Two Worlds of Charly Gordon* (he finally won an Emmy for *The Game,* a 1965 *Bob Hope Presents* drama), he bought the rights to the *Charly Gordon* teleplay and brought it to the big screen as *Charly.* Despite its modest budget and controversial theme of mental retardation, *Charly* earned Robertson a Best Actor Oscar in 1969. His other films include *Picnic, The Best Man, Three Days of the Condor,* and *Obsession,* and in 1977 he portrayed an embattled CIA director in ABC-TV's *Washington: Behind Closed Doors.* Robertson became enmeshed in an explosive offscreen controversy when he fingered powerful Columbia studio chief David Begelman in 1978 for having illegally cashed a $10,000 check in the actor's name. That revelation led to Begelman's admission that he had embezzled more than $60,000 from the studio by writing at least three other fraudulent checks. Under tremendous pressure to conceal the information, Robertson confided it to the press only after the shock of Begelman's reinstatement after a brief suspension and a stalled police investigation. As a result, Begelman resigned and was subsequently indicted. Robertson feared for his safety for a time, and there was the possibility that he would be blackballed by Hollywood moguls loyal to Begelman. But the loss of income was never a worry; in 1966 the ruggedly handsome actor married actress Dina Merrill, heiress to the immense Post cereal and E. F. Hutton fortunes. The Begelman scandal was thoroughly aired in the bestseller *Indecent Exposure.* Robertson plodded through a season on TV's *Falcon Crest* and did a creditable job in the TV production of *A Key to Rebecca,* but viewers now know him as the unflappable front man for AT&T.

Born: September 9, 1925, in La Jolla, California
Height: 6 ft.
Weight: 174 lbs.
Eyes: Blue
Hair: Brown
Zodiac: Virgo
Education: Antioch College
Religion: Protestant
Marriages:
To Cynthia Stone (divorced)
To Dina Merrill (1966–split in 1986)
Children: Stephanie (b. 1959) by Stone; Heather (b. 1968) by Merrill
Interests: Flying (he owns six vintage airplanes), fishing, tennis, skiing, swimming, the sea, producing and directing
Personal Habits and Traits: Chain-smokes, drinks, is very family oriented
Addresses: New York City; La Jolla, California
Income: $1 million+

Kenny Rogers

"Music is ever-changing, and you have to go with it."

The son of a Houston dockworker who played the fiddle, Kenny Rogers formed a band in high school called the Scholars and claimed his first national hit, "Crazy Feeling," in 1957. Then came a semester at the University of Houston and a stint

as one of the popular New Christy Minstrels before he broke off to form his own group, Kenny Rogers and the First Edition. He captured the soft-rock market in the late 1960s with a dozen hits, most notably the countrified Vietnam war ballad "Ruby, Don't Take Your Love to Town." The First Edition also broadcast a nationally syndicated TV variety show out of Canada before finally disbanding in 1976. Turning to Nashville, Rogers spun out several country hits, including the Country Music Association's Song of the Year, "Lucille," and "The Gambler," which also earned him a Grammy. "She Believes in Me," "You Decorated My Life," "Lady," "Turn It Around," "Islands in the Stream" (with Dolly Parton), and "What About Me?" (with Kim Carnes and James Ingram) followed. Thus, Kenny Rogers can claim number-one hits on all folk, rock, and country charts. His domestic life has been no less varied. Rogers was married three times before he met *Hee Haw* star Marianne Gordon when he did a guest shot on the show in 1975. They wed in the fall of 1977 and set up house in a $7 million Beverly Hills mansion with gold bathroom fixtures and green onyx floors, where their close circle of friends included John Davidson and Glen Campbell. Rogers, who at one point owned several houses worth tens of millions of dollars, also starred in *The Gambler* and *The Gambler Part II,* and played a key role in the recording of USA for Africa's "We Are the World."

Born: April 21, 1940, in Houston, Texas
Height: 6 ft. 1 in.
Weight: 200 lbs.
Eyes: Blue
Hair: Gray
Zodiac: On the cusp of Aries and Taurus
Education: One semester at the University of Houston
Religion: Protestant
Marriages: Four. Currently to Marianne Gordon (1977–)
Children: Carole Lynne (b. 1958), Kenneth Ray II (b. 1964)
Interests: Photography, boating, composing
Personal Habits and Traits: Nonsmoker, a self-confessed "spendaholic," determined dieter
Address: Beverly Hills
Income: $24 million

Roy Rogers

Leonard Slye

"When my time comes, just skin me and put me right up there on Trigger, just as if nothing had ever changed."

Three decades after his heyday as Hollywood's straightest straight-shooter, Roy Rogers was better known to a whole generation of buckeroos as King of the Double-R-Burger (a cheeseburger with ham) served at the more than 200 restaurants that bear his name. And while Roy Rogers Family Restaurants are actually owned by the Marriott Corporation, Ol' Roy rakes in a hefty percentage—though he hardly needs the money; during a career in westerns that spanned 14 years and 87 films, Rogers has amassed a personal fortune estimated at well over $30 million. Born Leonard Slye in Cincinnati and raised in rural Ohio, Rogers migrated to California in 1930 and worked as everything from truck driver to fruit picker before organizing Gene Autry's backup group of musicians, the Sons of the Pioneers. No sooner did he discover that Autry was threatening to walk out on Republic Pictures than Rogers picked up the reins and convinced the studio to give him a break as its resident singing cowboy. He first starred in *Under Western Stars* in 1938, then cranked out one lucrative western after another at the rate of nine or ten per year. Rogers's first wife Arlene died in 1946 from complications involving the birth of their third child, and the next year he acquired a new wife as well as a new partner—former band singer Dale Evans. Marketing himself shrewdly, Rogers and his sidekicks—Dale, Trigger, Bullet, Dale's buckskin Buttermilk, Gabby Hayes, Pat Brady and his Jeep, Nellybelle—have appeared on everything from pocketknives to pint-sized 10-gallon hats. Trigger died in 1965 and was stuffed (as was Bullet), to be displayed at the Roy Rogers Museum in Apple Valley. Dale turned author of inspirational books after their 2-year-old daughter Robin died in 1952; tragically, since then the Rogerses have lost two more of their other eight children to accidents. In 1975, Rogers made his first feature-length movie in 23 years, *Mackintosh and T.J.*

Born: November 5, 1912, in Cincinnati, Ohio
Height: 5 ft. 10 in.
Weight: 178 lbs.
Eyes: Blue
Hair: Light brown
Zodiac: Scorpio
Education: High school
Religion: Protestant
Marriages:
To Arlene Rogers (until her death in 1946)
To Dale Evans (real name Frances Octavia Smith) (1947–)
Children: Six
Interests: Breeds horses, bowls, (average score 185), rides motorcycles
Personal Habits and Traits: Nonsmoker, teetotaler
Address: Apple Valley, California
Income: $30 million (total net worth)

Linda Ronstadt

"I wish I had as much in bed as I get in the newspapers."

With the exception of Barbra Streisand and Diana Ross, perhaps no female singer has sold more records than Linda Ronstadt, Queen of Torch Rock. In her hometown of Tucson, where her father runs a hardware business, Linda attended parochial school, then came out as a debutante in Tucson and endured a semester at the University of Arizona. At 18, she escaped and headed for Los Angeles, where she formed a group with Bob Kimmel and Kenny Edwards called the Stone Poneys. After their only hit single, "Different Drum," in 1967, the trio dissolved. Under the guidance of rock producer Peter Asher (once half of the Peter and Gordon rock duo), Ronstadt soon became the first recording artist to fuse the country-western sound with driving California rock. With no fewer than six platinum albums to her credit, Ronstadt scored with such singles as "You're No Good," "It's So Easy," "When Will I Be Loved?," "Pitiful Me," "Blue Bayou," and "Heat Wave." Ronstadt has never been married but has been involved with comedian Albert Brooks, several ex-managers and as many rockers, including J. D. Souther, Jackson Browne, and Mick Jagger. By way of her curious relationship with California's offbeat young Governor (and perennial Presidential hopeful) Jerry Brown, Ronstadt, whose $375,000 Malibu beach house provided a second home to the Governor, was for a time the state's closest contender to a First Lady. Ronstadt broke out of the rock rut in 1981 to triumph on Broadway in *The Pirates of Penzance*. When it looked as if there were no surprises left, Ronstadt triumphed with two hit albums of old standards arranged and conducted by Nelson Riddle: *What's New?* and *Lush Life*. What was new in her lush life circa 1985 was a long-term romance with director George Lucas of *Star Wars* trilogy fame. Her opera debut as Mimi in *La Bohème* was jeered by the New York critics.

Born: July 30, 1946, in Tucson, Arizona
Height: 5 ft. 2 in.
Weight: 111 lbs.
Eyes: Brown
Hair: Auburn
Zodiac: Leo
Education: One semester at the University of Arizona
Religion: Roman Catholic
Marriages: None
Children: None
Interests: Running
Personal Habits and Traits: Needs little sleep, is a compulsive eater
Address: Malibu, California
Income: $2.2 million

Diana Ross

"With the Supremes I made so much money so fast all I wanted to do was buy clothes and pretty things. Now I'm comfortable with money, and it's comfortable with me."

The slinky, feline lead singer of Motown's Supremes (the second biggest-selling recording group of the 1960s after the Beatles) and briefly a Hollywood movie star second only in bankability to Barbra Streisand, Diana Ross was brought up in a family of six crammed into a Detroit housing project. Along with Cass Technical High School pals Mary Wilson and Florence Ballard, Ross formed a group called the Primettes—a female counterpart to the all-male Primes, who later emerged as the Temptations—and when they auditioned for Motown Record mogul Berry Gordy, Jr., he told them to come back after graduation. They did, working as backup singers for a number of established Motown names like Smokey Robinson and the Miracles and Marvin Gaye before exploding with their own hit "Where Did Our Love Go?" in 1964. Carefully groomed by Gordy—taught how to walk, sit, talk, hold a cigarette, and shake hands—the Supremes were decked out in sequined costumes and a dazzling variety of wigs. This glossy musical package cut a series of successive number-one hits—including "Baby Love," "Stop, in the Name of Love," "My World Is Empty Without You,

Babe," "The Happening," "Nothing but Heartaches," "Reflections," and "Love Child." The group became officially billed as Diana Ross and the Supremes in 1968, but two years later Diana ("Diane" or "D" to intimates) finally struck out on her own, and her farewell single with the Supremes, "Someday We'll Be Together," proved one of the group's biggest hits ever. As a soloist Ross has obviously not lost the golden touch, and has recorded hit singles ("Reach Out and Touch," "Ain't No Mountain High Enough," "Touch Me in the Morning," "Last Time I Saw Him," "Love Hangover," "Upside Down," "I'm Comin' Out," and "It's My Turn") on a dozen platinum albums. Her first starring movie role as Billie Holiday in *Lady Sings the Blues* brought Ross an Academy Award nomination, and though critics loathed her *Mahogany,* it became one of the biggest-grossing films of 1976 and produced another platinum hit for Ross. She has also starred in several top-rated TV specials, a one-woman Broadway show for which she was awarded a special Tony, and the disappointing film version of *The Wiz*. Although she had conducted an intermittent romance with producer Gordy for years, Ross married real estate man Robert Silberstein and in five years gave birth to three daughters. The Silbersteins were considered a dream match until their abrupt divorce in 1976. Four years later, Ross pulled up stakes and moved to Manhattan with her children, then on to Connecticut. Her 1983 Central Park concert was marred by roving gangs of thugs, but her reputation remained untarnished and in 1985 she released her 69th pop chart hit—the most recorded by any female artist—a tribute to the late Marvin Gaye called "Missing You." Ross's participation in the USA for Africa recording of "We Are the World" brought the number to an even 70. On October 23, 1985, Ross and Norwegian-born Arne Naess were married in a secret ceremony lasting less than 15 minutes in the Madison Avenue offices of her lawyer, then repeated their vows in an elaborate ceremony in Europe.

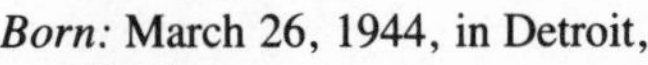

Born: March 26, 1944, in Detroit, Michigan
Height: 5 ft. 4½ in.
Weight: 100 lbs.
Eyes: Brown
Hair: Black
Zodiac: Aries
Education: High school
Religion: Baptist
Marriages:
To Robert E. Silberstein (1971–1976)
To Arne Naess (1985–)
Children: Rhonda (b. 1971), Tracee (b. 1972), Chudney (b. 1975)
Interests: Tennis, skiing, fashion
Personal Habits and Traits: Early to bed, fitness conscious
Address: Connecticut
Income: $6 million (minimum estimate)

Yves Saint Laurent

"Over the years I have learned that what is important in a dress is the woman who's wearing it."

"He was born with a nervous breakdown," Pierre Bergé says of his business partner and longtime companion Yves Saint Laurent. Indeed, as a soldier in the French Army in his early 20s, Saint Laurent spent two months in solitary confinement at a psychiatric hospital. Born in Algeria to a distinguished Alsatian family, Yves entered a contest at 17 sponsored by the International Wool Secretariat, and his design of a low-cut black cocktail dress easily captured first prize. Saint Laurent journeyed to Paris to pick up the award and within a matter of days was hired as a designer for the House of Dior. Shortly after Yves's 21st birthday, Dior died and left his young protégé to hurriedly create a new spring collection, which proved an instant smash. But the draft interrupted his career, and when Yves returned he found his job at Dior had been taken over by Marc Bohan. Flat broke and out of work, Saint Laurent teamed up with financial whiz Bergé and on January 29, 1962, they introduced their first collection. From that triumphant moment on, Saint Laurent has been indisputably acknowledged as the world's most influential fashion designer, while his name has since graced hundreds of products including men's cologne (YSL, for which he posed nude in an ad), scarves, linens, fur coats, sunglasses, luggage, and a string of some 100 Rive Gauche boutiques worldwide, all of which have made the House of Saint Laurent second in size only to Dior. No sooner did the mercurial master of haute couture stand the fashion world on its ear with his daring "peasant look" than he retreated to Es Saada la Zaria (Arabic for "the house of happiness in serenity"), his pink and white villa in Marrakech. When it came time for the fall 1976 collection Saint Laurent holed up in Morocco and within a few weeks sketched the entire line down to the last precise detail. Once back in Paris he collapsed from nerves and spent three weeks recuperating in a hospital. Aside from their five-bedroom Moroccan estate, Saint Laurent and Bergé share a sumptuous apartment on Paris's Rue Babylon filled with the works of Matisse, Leger, and Warhol.

Born: August 1, 1936, in Oran, Algeria
Height: 6 ft. ½ in.
Weight: 169 lbs.
Eyes: Blue
Hair: Blond
Zodiac: Leo
Education: High school
Religion: Roman Catholic
Marriages: None
Children: None
Interests: Art, music, design
Personal Habits and Traits: Chain-smokes, drinks wine, a nervous wreck, practices yoga and meditation
Addresses: Paris, Marrakech
Income: $25 million (personal gross)

Carlos Santana

Devadip Carlos Santana

"I never considered myself the leader of Santana. The musicians' union just required that the group have one. So I was it."

Lead singer and guitarist of the fabled Latino rock group that bears his name, Carlos Santana was born in Autlán de Navarro, Mexico, and started playing the violin at age 5. By 14 he was playing guitar in Tijuana dives for tips, then moved north to San Francisco at the height of the Haight-Ashbury scene. In 1968 he joined with pianist-organist Gregg Rolie and bass guitarist Dave Brown, among others, to form the Santana Blues Band. Blending Mexican, Cuban, and African rhythms with hard rock and blues, the group quickly found an adoring following in San Francisco's Spanish Mission District, and in early 1969 the band broadened its appeal by recruiting Jose Areas on conga drums and trumpet, Mike Carrabello also on congas, and Mike Shrieve on drums. They became billed simply as Santana, and the group's first two albums, *Santana* and *Abraxas,* propelled them to the forefront of the music business. They scored their first *salsa* hit single in 1971 with a raw version of Tito Puente's "Oye Como Va," and later cut their biggest-selling single to date, "Evil Ways." In the mid-1970s, the group's leader became a devout follower of mystic Sri Chinmoy (they parted ways in the 1980s) to the extent that he added the name given to him by Chinmoy—Devadip Carlos Santana. His fiery south-of-the-border sound remained largely the same, however, and he teamed up with folk singer Joan Baez to wow a truly captive audience: some 600 inmates of California's tough Soledad Prison.

Born: 1946 in Autlán de Navarro, Mexico
Height: 5 ft. 9 in.
Weight: 140 lbs.
Eyes: Brown
Hair: Dark brown
Religion: Roman Catholic
Interests: Composing, performing, the teachings of mystic Sri Chinmoy, meditation
Personal Habits and Traits: Chain-smokes, drinks tequila, quiet, semireclusive
Address: San Francisco
Income: $500,000+

Vidal Sassoon

"Before Shampoo *we hairdressers were queens, now we're machos. In truth, we're neither."*

The son of a Sephardic Jew from Turkey who disappeared when Sassoon was a mere infant, Vidal grew up in London's cockney East End, and was placed in an orphanage when his mother could no longer afford to care for him. He left school at 14 and took a job shampooing hair in a beauty salon—the first small step toward eventually ruling his own *haute coiffure* empire. In 1948 he volunteered to fight for Israel, and spent most of the 1950s in London perfecting his geometric approach to haircutting in his tiny third-floor walk-up salon. The advent of the Beatles and the rise of Mary Quant, Carnaby Street, and mod fashion signaled Sassoon's own ascent as a trendsetter, and he is still known today primarily for his clean-lined, unfettered hairstyles. Now his chain of thirty-one salons in six countries employs one thousand people and grosses well over $10 million per year. Sassoon has also branched out successfully into all areas of hair grooming, marketing his own line of cosmetics ("If you don't look good, we don't look good.") and designer jeans, hosting his own syndicated TV talk show, and even writing a bestseller, *A Year of Beauty and Health,* with his exotically beautiful Alberta-born second wife, Beverly. Having moved his corporate headquarters from London to New York in 1968 and then on to California in 1974, Vidal lived with Beverly and their four children—Catya, Elan, Eden, and David—in a $5 million Beverly Hills mansion complete with pool and a Rolls-filled garage. Although that arrangement was disrupted somewhat when Beverly filed for divorce, the ex-Mrs. Sassoon continued to work for the Sassoon organization. (Mrs. Sassoon's subsequent romance with Erik Estrada steamed, then fizzled).

Born: January 17, 1928, in London, England
Height: 5 ft. 6 in.
Weight: 137 lbs.
Eyes: Brown
Hair: Brown
Zodiac: Capricorn
Education: High school dropout (at fourteen)
Religion: Jewish
Marriages: Two. The last to Beverly Adams
Children: Catya (b. 1959), Elan (b. 1960), Eden (b. 1973), David (b. 1973, adopted)
Interests: Yoga, meditation
Personal Habits and Traits: Nonsmoker, does daily calisthenics, keeps early nights, hates red meat, fasts 36 hours each month
Address: Beverly Hills
Income: $10 million annual gross

Telly Savalas

Aristoteles Savalas

"Who loves ya, baby."

The late-blooming superstar with the billiard-ball pate and an insatiable appetite for lollipops sums up his appeal and the tremendous success of the CBS series *Kojak*—in 1974 the number-one show in all of TV—with, "I'm the kind of gorilla people can identify with." Sartorially splendid, tough-talking, and libidinous on and off camera, Telly (for Aristoteles) Savalas qualifies as one of Hollywood's most implausible sex symbols. Growing up in middle-class Garden City, Long Island, with a sister and three brothers named Socrates, Praxiteles, and Demosthenes (otherwise known as George, the obese second banana on *Kojak*), Savalas recalls that his family's lifestyle changed sharply with the fortunes of his Greek immigrant father, who made and lost several of them before Telly left home to join the Army during World War II (he received an honorable discharge for being disabled). Savalas was well on his way to his master's degree in psychology at Columbia when he decided to drop out and work for the State Department in the 1950s, and later as an executive for ABC News he earned a Peabody Award. His 37th birthday had already passed when Savalas decided to audition for an acting job on a lark, and after landing the part and a subsequent apprenticeship on live television he turned his boundless energy to character parts in the movies. By the time he received an Oscar nomination for a supporting role in *Birdman of Alcatraz* (1962), Savalas had become inevitably typecast as a heavy. His second-best-known movie is *The Dirty Dozen* (he first shaved his head to play Pontius Pilate in 1965's *The Greatest Story Ever Told*). *Kojak*, which grew out of the made-for-TV movie *The Marcus-Nelson Murders*, reaped an Emmy for its star before it was finally canceled in 1978. Savalas is now concentrating on producing as well as starring in films, and on his somewhat dubious career as a crooner. In 1985, his 34-years-younger fourth wife, Julie, gave birth to his fifth child, Christopher.

Born: January 21, 1922, in Garden City, Long Island
Height: 6 ft.
Weight: 209 lbs.
Eyes: Brown
Hair: None
Zodiac: On the cusp of Capricorn and Aquarius
Education: Columbia University, B.S. in psychology
Religion: Greek Orthodox
Marriages: Three ending in divorce. To Julie Savalas (1984–)
Children: Three daughters, two sons
Interests: Law, current events, singing
Personal Habits and Traits: Nonsmoker, nondrinker, womanizer
Address: Los Angeles
Income: $750,000 (estimate)

Diane Sawyer

"People assume you can't be shy and be on television. They're wrong."

She is variously described as "the thinking man's Angie Dickinson" and a "wood nymph with a microphone." The daughter of a county judge in Kentucky, Diane Sawyer won America's Junior Miss contest in 1963 at age 17, graduated from Wellesley College in 1967, and spent three years as a poetry-spouting weathergirl on Louisville TV before joining the Nixon White House as a press aide. Rather than depart after Nixon resigned, she stayed with him in San Clemente, assisting the exiled President with his memoirs. Sawyer then landed an on-camera job as a general assignment reporter for CBS and proved her mettle by once digging in at the State Department for an entire week during the Iranian hostage crisis. In 1981, the much-admired Sawyer (she appears to have no detractors) joined the *CBS Morning News,* and though she could not pull the show out of the ratings cellar, she was generally considered to be its strongest asset. In 1984, she became the first woman to join *60 Minutes,* the highest-rated news show in TV history, topped during the 1984–85 season by only three programs—*Dynasty, Dallas,* and *Bill Cosby.* A vintage movie poster showing Lana Turner looking seductive in the role of *Diane* graces one wall of Sawyers *60 Minutes* offices. She has dated Warren Beatty and has had a long-standing relationship with former State Department official Dick Holbrooke, but as she approached the Big 4–0, Sawyer had yet to commit to marriage and children. "I'll probably wake up one morning," Sawyer once said, "and say, 'This is the day. This is the day to get married.' You know, to have a baby, you need to be married."

Born: December 22, 1945, in Louisville, Kentucky
Height: 5 ft. 9 in.
Weight: 120 lbs.
Eyes: Blue
Hair: Blond
Zodiac: Capricorn
Education: Wellesley College
Religion: Protestant
Marriages: None
Children: None
Interests: Poetry, politics
Personal Habits and Traits: Shy, a good listener, loyal friend, drinks moderately, nonsmoker
Address: New York City
Income: $1 million

Charles Schulz

"One day I sat down and drew a boy and a girl sitting on a curb. He said to her, 'I know, Judy, I could learn to love you if your batting average were better.' Charlie Brown was born."

Charlie Brown's alter ego was a 26-year-old teacher at the Art Instruction Schools in his hometown of Minneapolis when he was struck with the idea for *Peanuts* and its motley cast—lovable loser Charlie Brown, rotten-to-the-core Lucy, and the thinking man's beagle Snoopy among them. On October 2, 1950, the comic strip made its debut in eight American newspapers, and 35 years later it had become syndicated to 1,655 newspapers worldwide, while lucrative spin-offs have included television specials (23 by 1981), movies (*A Boy Named Charlie Brown*), a long-running Broadway musical (*You're a Good Man, Charlie Brown*), Hallmark's number-one line of greeting cards, and everything from T-shirts to drinking mugs and stationery. All of which made Charles Schulz, whose own nickname "Sparky" derives from a horse in the *Barney Google* comic strip, the richest cartoonist in history. Actually the lead character in *Peanuts* acquired his name from one of Schulz's coworkers back in Minneapolis, and Schulz battled with the United Features syndicate for years to have the strip named *Good Ol' Charlie Brown* ("I think *Peanuts* is a terrible name"). Pressures ended Schulz's 23-year marriage to Joyce Halverson in 1972, and he lived in his office at 1 Snoopy Place until he married divorcée Jean Clyde a year later. Now residing in a Santa Rosa, California, house that once served as the official residence of an Episcopal bishop, Schulz spends a full workday at the drawing board, beginning with dialogue and then drawing in characters. To unwind, the multimillionaire comic strip artist plays tennis, golfs on his private course, or plays a little hockey at his $2 million Redwood Empire Ice Arena in northern California, one of the biggest rinks in the country. Schulz celebrated *Peanuts*'s 35th anniversary with a traveling exhibition featuring Charlie Brown and the gang in major museums across the country.

Born: November 26, 1922, in Minneapolis, Minnesota
Height: 5 ft. 9½ in.
Weight: 160 lbs.
Eyes: Blue
Hair: White
Zodiac: Sagittarius
Education: High school
Religion: Protestant

Marriages:
To Joyce Halverson (1949–1972)
To Jean Clyde (1973–)
Children: Five
Interests: Golfs occasionally, plays tennis daily, plays hockey three times a week
Personal Habits and Traits: Workaholic, soft-spoken and extremely courteous
Address: Santa Rosa, California
Income: $4.3 million (minimum estimate)

Arnold Schwarzenegger

"I know a lot of athletes and models are written off as just bodies. I never felt used for my body."

Those lats! Those pecs! The "Austrian Oak" was 18 when he went AWOL from the Austrian Army to compete in the Mr. Europe Jr. contest in Stuttgart. Two years later, he flexed his way to his first Mr. Universe championship. Schwarzenegger moved to Venice, California ("a body builder's paradise"), in 1968, sculpted his own body ("I felt like Leonardo da Vinci") with 50-ton-a-day workouts. After going on to win four more Mr. Universe titles and six Mr. Olympia titles, he retired from competitive body building in 1975 to write *Arnold: The Education of a Body Builder,* the first of his three bestsellers. First seen in the documentary *Pumping Iron,* Schwarzenegger won a Golden Globe Award for his

first feature film, *Stay Hungry,* but it was as that lovable barbarian Conan and the less-than-lovable killing machine in *The Terminator* that Schwarzenegger proved his beefcake bankability. At the 1977 Robert F. Kennedy Pro-Celebrity Tennis Tournament, he began a serious relationship with Maria Shriver, the beautiful daughter of former Vice-Presidential candidate Sargent Shriver and Eunice Kennedy, and a cohost, beginning in 1985, of the *CBS Morning News.*

Born: July 30, 1947, in Graz, Austria
Height: 6 ft. 2 in.
Weight: 220 lbs.
Eyes: Blue
Hair: Brown
Zodiac: Leo
Education: B.A., University of Wisconsin
Religion: Roman Catholic
Marriages: To Maria Shriver (1986–)
Children: None
Interests: Working out (an hour each day), tennis, diving, wild boar hunting, archery, business
Personal Habits and Traits: Articulate, scrupulously polite, nondrinker, smokes Cuban cigars
Addresses: Santa Monica, California; Palm Springs, California
Income: $1.5 million (estimate)

George C. Scott

"There is no question you get pumped up by the recognition. Then a self-loathing sets in when you realize you're enjoying it."

The cantankerous, controversial star of *Patton* (for which he won and rejected an Academy Award in 1971) attributes his tumultuous and too often troubled life to an unhappy childhood in Michigan, where his mother died when he was 8 and his father ruled the house with an iron fist. Scott enlisted in the Marines at 17 and was immediately assigned to burial detail at Arlington National Cemetery; though the grim experience triggered Scott's heavy drinking he managed to earn a B.A. in journalism at the University of Missouri and to become a teacher at Stephens College for Women. Marriage to one of his students, Carolyn Hughes, soon followed, but one illegitimate child later Scott took off for New York. He worked as a check sorter in a bank for years, until his portrayal of the villainous king in Joseph Papp's production of *Richard III* immediately earned him recognition as an acting dynamo. He then worked with Colleen Dewhurst in Circle in the Square, and in 1960 they divorced their respective spouses (he had since married actress Pat Reed) to marry each other. Oscar nominations for *Anatomy of a Murder* and *The Hustler* (which he refused) only enhanced his career, and his *East Side, West Side* TV series proved a CBS smash. But he continued to drink and brawl frequently, and on the set of *The Bible* in 1966 he conducted an extramarital affair with Ava Gardner that sent Dewhurst packing. Three years later, Scott joined Alcoholics Anonymous and remarried Dewhurst. But by the time he filmed *Patton* in 1970, Scott was drinking heavily again and at one point went on a two-day binge rather than show up on the set. When he was voted an Oscar for his bravura performance he refused it on the grounds that the Academy Award show was "a meat parade." Since then his career has rollercoastered dramatically, peaking with films like *The Hospital* and plays like *Sly Fox* (in which he starred on Broadway with Trish Van Devere, whom he married in 1972 after he divorced Dewhurst a second time) but plummeting with *The Day of the Dolphin, Islands in the Stream, The Hindenburg,* and *The Formula.* His biggest bomb to date has been *The Savage Is Loose,* which he personally produced and starred in with Van Devere. Still regarded as one of the most explosive stars in Hollywood, at one point Scott's fifth marriage was rocky enough for both to seek help from a Santa Monica gestalt therapist. Scott's stage work was another matter; he made a triumphant return to Circle in the Square in a smash revival of Noël Coward's *Present Laughter.* And on television, he created one of the most memorable Scrooges in memory in a 1984 remake of Dickens's *A Christmas Carol.* The next year, he was planning to star in the title role of *Maigret,* based on the famed Paris police detective created by prolific French author Georges Simenon.

Born: October 18, 1927, in Wise, Virginia
Height: 6 ft. 1 in.
Weight: 180 lbs.
Eyes: Blue
Hair: Gray
Zodiac: Libra
Education: University of Missouri, B.A. in journalism
Religion: Protestant

Marriages:
To Carolyn Hughes (divorced)
To Pat Reed (divorced)
To Colleen Dewhurst (divorced)
To Colleen Dewhurst (remarried and divorced)
To Trish Van Devere (1972–)
Children: Six
Interests: Chess, journalism, golf, tennis, riding
Personal Habits and Traits: Chain-smokes, drinks heavily, temperamental
Address: Greenwich, Connecticut
Income: $600,000 (minimum estimate)

Neil Sedaka

"The nicest part is that there are no theatrics. I sit at the piano and play my songs. That is what I am."

One of the few rock 'n' roll legends from the 1950s to stage a successful comeback a musical generation later, Neil Sedaka was raised in a Sephardic Jewish family in Brooklyn. While still in high school, he was selected by Arthur Rubinstein as New York City's outstanding young classical pianist. But short, squat Neil thought the way to make friends was to write pop tunes, so at 16 he composed his first hit, Connie Francis's "Stupid Cupid." He formed a group called the Tokens, but soon discovered that he worked better alone, and by the time he was 23 he was rich enough to retire with such Top-10 Sedaka hits as his 1959 "Oh, Carol" (a paean to songwriter Carole King), "Breaking Up Is Hard to Do," "Happy Birthday Sweet Sixteen," "I'm Living Right Next Door to an Angel," and "Calendar Girl." Swamped by the invasion of the Beatles and the Rolling Stones in the mid-1960s, Sedaka nonetheless maintained his annual income in the six-figure bracket by penning hits like the Fifth Dimension's "Workin' on a Groovy Thing" and "Puppet Man." But Sedaka yearned to be back on top as a performer, and superstar Elton John obliged by backing his

return. In 1975 alone Sedaka wrote three number-one singles—"Love Will Keep Us Together" for the Captain and Tennille, and two for himself, "Laughter in the Rain" and "Bad Blood." Pudgy, and with a tenor that comes perilously close to resembling Olivia Newton-John, he still managed to make good on his PR slogan "Sedaka's Back"—so much so, in fact, that he was fired as the Carpenters' opening act for upstaging the stars. He returned two months later to the Riviera Hotel—this time as a headliner.

Born: March 13, 1939, in Brooklyn, New York
Height: 5 ft. 6 in.
Weight: 150 lbs.
Eyes: Brown
Hair: Brown and thinning
Zodiac: Pisces
Education: Juilliard School of Music
Religion: Jewish
Marriages: To Leba Sedaka (1962–)
Children: Dara (b. 1963), Marc (b. 1966)
Interests: Classical piano (practices four hours a day on one of his four pianos)
Personal Habits and Traits: Nonsmoker, does drink occasionally, enjoys parties, discos, a dyed-in-the-wool family man
Address: New York City
Income: $400,000 (estimate)

Tom Seaver

George Thomas Seaver

"Pitching involves two questions: How are you going to get the ball there, and how fast are you going to throw it to get it there?"

Baseball's "Mr. Clean" earned his athletic renown by almost single-handedly transforming the New York Mets from a national joke into the World Series champions of 1969. So when Tom Seaver was unexpectedly traded to the Cincinnati Reds, the hottest pitcher in the league was stunned, although he knew the Reds were pennant contenders. Seaver's farewell press conference was so emotionally charged that he was unable to speak at all, instead writing out his thanks to his New York fans, but Seaver and his wife Nancy recovered sufficiently within several months to start building a new life in Cincinnati. Christened George Thomas Seaver, he was raised in a sports-minded upper-middle-class family in Fresno, California, where his father worked as an executive with a fruit-packing company. After meeting his future wife at Fresno City College, Tom studied predentistry at the University of Southern California in Los Angeles while on a baseball scholarship. Following a year in the minors during which he and Nancy were married, Seaver was called up by the Mets in '67 and became an instant favorite of the New York fans, finishing his USC degree while collecting three Cy Young Awards. Although they spend the summers in a condominium outside Cincinnati, the Seavers—Tom, Nancy, and their two young daughters—repair to their $800,000 mansion in Greenwich, Connecticut, for the remainder of each year. Once he does hang up his jersey Seaver will have little trouble selling himself either as sportscaster (he has already delivered commentary for ABC) or TV pitchman; since 1973 the Seavers have appeared on television and in print endorsing everything from Sears menswear to Phillips 66. Seaver rejoined the Mets in 1983. In 1986, after playing for the White Sox, the Hall-of-Famer was traded to the Boston Red Sox.

Born: November 17, 1944, in Fresno, California
Height: 6 ft. 1½ in.
Weight: 208 lbs.
Eyes: Brown
Hair: Brown
Zodiac: Scorpio
Education: University of Southern California, B.S. in dentistry
Religion: Protestant

Marriages: To Nancy Seaver
Children: Sarah (b. 1971), Elizabeth (b. 1975)
Interests: Dentistry, sports commentary
Personal Habits and Traits: Nonsmoker, teetotaler
Addresses: Greenwich, Connecticut; Cincinnati, Ohio
Income: $500,000

Erich Segal

"I am innocent. I believe every word I write."

The Yale classics-professor-turned-bestselling-novelist was born a rabbi's son and raised on Brooklyn's Flatbush Avenue. After obtaining his Ph.D. in 1964 at Harvard, he joined the Yale faculty and soon began moonlighting as a scriptwriter, turning out the screenplays for the Beatles's *Yellow Submarine* and Stanley Kramer's *RPM* before starting work on the script for a movie called *Love Story*. Before the movie was released in December 1970 Segal published his previously drafted novel of *Love Story*. It became an instant smash, while the movie version starring Ryan O'Neal and Ali MacGraw still ranks as one of the Top 10 money-grossers in the history of motion pictures. But Segal's instant celebrity caused him ridicule back at Yale, and he departed in 1973 to guest-lecture in Munich and Tel Aviv, and at Dartmouth and Princeton. An avid runner who began working out at 15 as therapy for a leg severely injured in a boating accident, Segal has competed in every Boston Marathon since 1958—never finishing better than 50th. In 1974 he met a children's book editor named Karen James in London, and after she obtained a divorce from her first husband they were married in 1975. Segal's 1973 novel *Fairy Tale* turned into a critical and commercial disappointment, but his sequel to *Love Story, Oliver's Story,* fetched $1.5 million in paperback rights alone. Now ensconced in a comfortable house in London, insomniac Segal rises at 3 A.M. to begin writing and works straight through until late afternoon, when he embarks on his daily swim in his one-lane (8 feet × 50 feet) indoor lap pool. His *Man, Woman and Child* and *The Class,* his Harvard novel, also climbed the bestseller list despite raspberries from the critics.

Born: June 16, 1937, in Brooklyn, New York
Height: 5 ft. 6½ in.
Weight: 135 lbs.
Eyes: Brown
Hair: Brown and thinning
Zodiac: Gemini
Education: Harvard University, Ph.D. in classical civilization
Religion: Jewish

Marriages: To Karen James (1975–)
Children: None
Interests: Running, writing, the classics, Greek civilization
Personal Habits and Traits: Nonsmoker, teetotaler, insomniac, runs daily
Address: London
Income: $465,000 (minimum average annual income)

George Segal

"The first time I saw myself was in The Longest Day, *in which I was on screen the time it takes to blink. But when I saw this huge head wearing a helmet—it was me, but I couldn't find myself at first—I nearly jumped out of my skin."*

Growing up in the upper-middle-class suburb of Great Neck, Long Island, George Segal started performing magic tricks at birthday parties when he was 8 and in high school played trombone in a band. After graduating from Columbia University and briefly flirting with the idea of teaching English, he formed his own orchestra—Bruno Lynch and His Imperial Jazz Band. Why Bruno Lynch? "I thought that sounded better than 'George Segal and His Imperial Jazz Band,'" he explains. "Besides, I didn't want to shame my family." Actually, Segal resisted efforts to shed his decidedly ethnic name, and it paid off when others like Dustin Hoffman and Elliott Gould finally came in vogue. After five rough years off-Broadway during which he worked as a theater usher and perfected his banjo playing, he finally landed roles in *The Longest Day, The Young Doctors,* and *Ship of Fools.* As the belligerent young husband of Sandy Dennis in *Who's Afraid of Virginia Woolf?,* the wheeling-and-dealing prison camp crumb in *King Rat,* the timid bookstore clerk who falls for hooker Barbra Streisand in *The Owl and the Pussycat,* and Glenda Jackson's very-much-married lover in *A Touch of Class,* George Segal has continually exuded a little-boy charm that makes him one of Hollywood's (at $750,000 per picture) most in-demand properties. Other films in which Segal plays the great schlemiel: *Loving, Where's Poppa?, California Split, Somebody Is Killing the Great Chefs of Europe,* and *Carbon Copy.* A drug habit that began in the 1960s with pot, LSD, and mescaline escalated to a dependence on cocaine that, he concedes, "was destroying my life." He only kicked it after his new wife, Linda Rogoff, spent two weeks with him in a Palm Springs motel room while he went cold turkey.

Born: February 13, 1936, in New York City
Height: 5 ft. 11¾ in.
Weight: 155 lbs.
Eyes: Blue
Hair: Dark blond
Zodiac: Aquarius
Education: Columbia University
Religion: Jewish
Marriages:
To Marion Sobel (1956–1983)
To Linda Rogoff (1983–)
Children: Elizabeth (b. 1962)
Interests: Banjo, trombone, jazz, offbeat songs
Personal Habits and Traits: Does not smoke, punctual, intelligent, wry sense of humor, nervous flier, loves to snack, sleeps in boxer shorts
Address: Los Angeles
Income: $450,000

Tom Selleck

"I'm not Vic Virile."

The sometimes-squeaky voice and aw-shucks manner don't always match the rest of the package, but it may just be those touches of shyness and vulnerability that make the star of CBS's *Magnum, P.I.* the Hunk of the '80s—and the tube's highest-paid actor. A native of Detroit (hence the ever-present Tigers cap), Selleck moved to Los Angeles when he was 4. Like his two brothers and his sister, Selleck abstained from smoking, alcohol, and swearing until he was 21, and was rewarded with a gold watch from his father, a top executive of Caldwell Banker. A star athlete in high school, he went on to win a basketball scholarship to the University of Southern California. To make ends meet while studying business administration, he started making commercials (for Pepsi, Salem, Close-Up and Revlon's Chaz cologne, among other products), and twice appeared as Bachelor Number 2 on *The Dating Game*—both times he was not selected. Selleck landed a recurring role on TV's *Bracken's World* and made his film debut as one of Mae West's handpicked studs in *Myra Breckinridge*. Small roles in *The Seven Minutes* and *Coma* followed, then an 18-month stint on the soap *The Young and the Restless*. Two guest turns playing a practically perfect private detective on *The Rockford Files* led to *Magnum,* the story of an anything-but-perfect Navy-officer-turned-Hawaiian eye. "Magnum is a flawed, self-doubting man who doesn't always get the girl," says Selleck, whose devilish charm is akin to that of fellow macho superstar Burt Reynolds. Propelled by the phenomenal success of *Magnum,* the Emmy-winning Selleck made the leap to leading roles on the big screen with the adventure films *High Road to China, Lassiter,* and *Runaway*. All made money but were dismissed by critics and the industry. Meantime Selleck, who has supplanted *Hawaii Five-O*'s Jack Lord as the islands' Numero Uno booster, lies low in Honolulu, away from the L.A. limelight. His main regret is that his six-day shooting schedule doesn't always allow him time for his stepson, Kevin, the only child of Selleck's wife, Jacquelyn Ray, the actress-model he divorced in 1982 after 11 years of marriage. Amazingly, both Selleck and Kevin walked away after the Jeep Kevin was driving dropped off the top floor of a three-story parking garage.

Born: January 29, 1945, in Detroit
Height: 6 ft. 3½ in.
Weight: 200 lbs.
Eyes: Green
Hair: Dark blond
Zodiac: Aquarius
Education: B.A. in business administration, University of Southern California
Religion: Protestant
Marriages: One, to Jacquelyn Ray (1970–1982)
Children: A stepson, Kevin (b. 1969)
Interests: Volleyball (honorary captain of the U.S. Olympic team, he raised money for them with with a bestselling poster), sailing, swimming, running
Personal Habits and Traits: Neither smokes nor drinks, self-deprecating
Addresses: Los Angeles; Honolulu
Income: $6 million+ ($4.8 million per season for *Magnum,* minimum $2 million per feature film)

Gene Shalit

He admits to being a "classical groupie," and with his chaotic coif and unruly mustache Gene Shalit long looked like Arthur Fiedler's illegitimate son (by the mid-'80s, he got around to trimming his hair). Born in New York City and raised in Morristown, New Jersey, and Urbana, Illinois, Shalit attended the University of Illinois and began writing book and film reviews as a freelancer. On the way to becoming what amounts to a one-man critical conglomerate, he wrote for *Look, Ladies' Home Journal, Newsday,* and *Sport* magazines. Without dropping any of these jobs—with the exception of the demise of the old *Look*—Shalit began his broadcasting career as a commentator on NBC Radio's popular *Monitor* program. Shifting to television, he began giving his witty, stand-up book reviews on *Today* in 1969, and four years later officially replaced Joe Garagiola as a featured regular. Throughout the comings and goings of various hosts and co-hosts, including the late Frank McGee, Barbara Walters, Jim Hartz, Tom Brokaw, Jane Pauley, and Bryant Gumbel, Shalit (who has yet to overcome his fear of flying), remains to tweak viewers with his Perelman-like wit or, worse, pummel them with puns. A sample Shalitism is his review of a 1976 film starring Diana Ross: "*Mahogany* is oke."

Born: 1932, in New York City
Height: 6 ft.
Weight: 183 lbs.
Eyes: Brown
Hair: Brown
Education: University of Illinois
Religion: Jewish
Marriages: One (she died in 1979)
Children: Six
Interests: Bassoon, classical music (he is a closet conductor), books, movies, people, puns
Personal Habits and Traits: A nonsmoker, social drinker, early riser (for *Today*), intensely private, terrified of flying
Address: New York City
Income: $700,000

Omar Sharif

Michael Shalhoub

"Barbra Streisand's problem is that she wants to be a woman and she wants to be beautiful—and she is neither."

Syrian-Lebanese by descent, Omar Sharif was raised in Alexandria, Egypt, and attended Cairo's Victoria College. His life was forever changed when director David Lean cast him in *Lawrence of Arabia* after spotting the swarthy Sharif in the Egyptian film *Goha,* named Best Picture at the 1959 Cannes Film Festival. *Funny Girl* firmly established him as a sex symbol, and his fiery clashes with costar Barbra Streisand were highly publicized. Sharif has also smoldered on screen as the Austrian heir-apparent in *Mayerling* and as the doctor himself in *Dr. Zhivago.* A master at bridge (he coauthors a syndicated bridge column), the generally even-tempered Sharif nonetheless suffers from a nervous stomach, relying on English tea crackers as a staple of his diet. Divorced from Egyptian film star Faten Hamana, he published his autobiography *The Eternal Man* in

1977. Sharif was lured into the cast of the HBO miniseries *The Far Pavilions* by the prospect of working with John Gielgud, acted in the BBC's *The Edge of the Wind,* and hammed it up in the spy spoof *Top Secret!* before sinking his teeth into the four-part TV adaptation of Robert K. Massie's *Peter the Great.*

Born: October 10, 1932, in Alexandria, Egypt
Height: 5 ft. 11 in.
Weight: 178 lbs.
Eyes: Brown
Hair: Brown
Zodiac: Libra
Education: Victoria College
Religion: Moslem
Marriages: To Faten Hamana (1955–1974)
Children: Two
Interests: Bridge, writing
Personal Habits and Traits: Chain-smokes, battles an ulcer, likes to gamble
Address: Switzerland
Income: $400,000 (minimum estimate)

Cybill Shepherd

"I like to get into the scrap, get my nails in."

"Cybill Shepherd," the *Today* show's Gene Shalit said of her performance in the disastrous musical comedy *At Long Last Love,* "cannot sing, dance or act." A full decade later, she was laughing all the way to an Emmy for Best Actress in a dramatic series as the star of the ABC hit in *Moonlighting*. Named for both her grandpa, Cy, and her dad, Bill, Cybill grew up in Memphis, where at 16 she won the Miss Teenage Memphis title (she lost out at the Miss Teenage America pageant but was nonetheless named Miss Congeniality). From there, she went straight to Madison Avenue and a career as one of the hottest models in the business; hers was the fresh young face that sent millions of women rushing to the store to buy Cover Girl cosmetics. Director Peter Bogdanovich spotted her on the cover of *Glamour* and promptly cast her as the lead in *The Last Picture Show.* Their relationship soon evolved into somewhat more than strictly business, and he came to be regarded as her Svengali. *The Heartbreak Kid, Daisy Miller,* and *Taxi Driver* followed, but *At Long Last Love* so traumatized Shepherd that she returned home to Memphis. There she met and married auto parts dealer David Ford, the father of her daughter, Clementine. Still, Cybill grew itchy. A 1982 guest shot on *Fantasy Island* put Hollywood on notice that Shepherd was back in circulation. The following year she was cast as a steel-willed rancher in the short-lived *Yellow Rose*—more exposure that paved the way for her tailor-made Emmy-winning role of the model-turned-private eye in *Moonlighting.*

Born: 1949 in Memphis
Height: 5 ft. 8 in.
Weight: 131 lbs.
Eyes: Blue *Hair:* Blond
Education: High school
Religion: Protestant
Marriages: To David Ford (1978–1982)
Children: Clementine (b. 1979)
Interests: Art, literature, jazz
Personal Habits and Traits: Strong-willed, decisive, brown rice a diet staple, racewalks three times a week (carrying a revolver for protection), unwinds in a hot tub
Address: Malibu
Income: $50,000 per week (estimate)

Brooke Shields

"What does 'good in bed' mean to me? When I'm sick and I stay home from school propped up with lots of pillows watching TV and my mom brings me soup—that's good in bed."

At the age of 1 she was a professional model and by 12 she attracted international attention playing a child prostitute in Louis Malle's controversial movie *Pretty Baby*. Yet Brooke herself, a flawless beauty with brown hair, azure eyes, and lushly dark eyebrows, has remained very much an unaffected little girl. "Brookie," as her friends call her, collects stuffed animals, dolls, and glass; plays football in Central Park; has an insatiable sweet tooth; and seems oblivious to the nature of the material in *Pretty Baby* and the charges that the movie was nothing more than child pornography. Coinciding with the release of the movie was the publication of *The Brooke Book,* a collection of poems, pictures, and schoolwork. The indomitable force behind the Brooke Shields phenomenon that continued with *The King of the Gypsies; Just You and Me, Kid; Wanda Nevada;* and *The Blue Lagoon,* is Brooke's divorced, hard-as-nails stage mother Teri Shields (Brooke was born four months after Teri's marriage to Helena Rubinstein vice-president Frank Shields, a marriage that lasted a matter of weeks). Brooke's father has grudgingly come to accept Brooke's career. Teri, who went on the wagon at Brooke's insistence, has a reputation for being a tough negotiator and has managed to inflate her daughter's per-film asking price from $27,500 for *Pretty Baby* to $300,000 for *Wanda Nevada* to $500,000 for *The Blue Lagoon* and an estimated $750,000 for *Endless Love*. Yet each project she undertook seemed more dreary than the last, from the inept *Sahara* to the soggy TV movie *Wet Gold*. Nevertheless, Shields always seemed to be at the center of some controversy, from her lawsuit to prevent the publication of nude photos of her when she was 10 (she won) to her dating Michael Jackson to the apocryphal story that her publishing contract for her second book called for her to remain a virgin until her clean-living guide for teens came out in late 1985. As a Princeton sophomore, she took time off to celebrate her 20th birthday at Chippendale's, an all-male strip club in New York. Brooke's idol, strangely enough, is Carol Burnett.

Born: May 31, 1965, in New York City
Height: 6 ft.
Weight: 120 lbs.
Eyes: Blue
Hair: Dark brown
Zodiac: Gemini
Education: Private schools, Princeton University
Religion: Roman Catholic
Marriages: None
Children: None
Interests: Horses (Peter Fonda gave her a chestnut bay filly named Magic), movies, television, reading, writing poetry, collecting stars' autographs
Personal Habits and Traits: Is well mannered, unspoiled, gets to bed early, a dedicated actress, loves Japanese food
Addresses: New York City; Englewood Cliffs, New Jersey; Princeton, New Jersey
Income: $1 million +

Dinah Shore

Frances "Fannie" Rose Shore

"I owe everything—my success and happiness—to men. Could anything be finah?"

Fannie Rose Shore had already taken the name Dinah from the song of the same name by the time she landed her own radio show in Nashville. Once in New York in the early 1940s, she began recording hits like *Blues in the Night* and performing regularly on Eddie Cantor's tremendously popular NBC radio show. Her own popularity seemed to peak with the phenomenal success of the Chevrolet-sponsored *Dinah Shore Show* on Sunday nights, which earned her five Emmys. When the show finally went off the air Dinah sat out the 1960s playing tennis and golf, and performing in Nevada casinos while getting divorced from her husband of 18 years, actor George Montgomery, and then marrying a Palm Springs contractor for one year in 1963. A sleeker and younger-than-ever Shore returned to television with a daily NBC talk show called *Dinah's Place* in 1970, and the show's glowing hostess quickly proved that she was as good an interviewer as a singer. With a slightly modified format she launched an expanded 90-minute *Dinah!* in 1975. It was on *Dinah's Place* in 1971 that she first met Burt Reynolds, who spent most of his guest shot trying to coax her to accompany him to Palm Springs. Their meeting launched a much publicized affair—she is 19 years his senior—that lasted until each amicably went his separate way in 1977. Now Dinah also writes cookbooks (*Someone's in the Kitchen With Dinah*), lends her name to the Dinah Shore/Colgate Golf Classic, and gets plenty of television exposure starring in commercials for Holly Farms chicken.

Born: March 1, 1917, in Winchester, Tennessee
Height: 5 ft. 5 in.
Weight: 110 lbs.
Eyes: Brown
Hair: Blond
Zodiac: Pisces
Education: High school
Religion: Jewish
Marriages:
To George Montgomery (1943–1962)
To Maurice Smith (1963–1964)

Children: Melissa (b. 1948), John (adopted 1954)
Interests: Needlepoint, cooking, tennis, golf, politics
Personal Habits and Traits: Does not smoke, drinks moderately, is a fitness fanatic, articulate, soft-spoken, unaffected, intelligent, punctual
Address: Beverly Hills
Income: $600,000+ (minimum estimate)

Carly Simon

"In analysis, I used to make up these dreams about candlesticks . . . but I like myself now, physically, sexually—though not to a narcissistic degree."

As a child Carly Simon stuttered so badly that by the time she entered high school she was resigned to remaining virtually silent around others. At home, however, her mother discovered a way for Carly to communicate without speaking: Carly would sing whatever it was she wanted to say, and her voice emerged clearly and beautifully. No small wonder that she later turned her gift for singing and songwriting into one of the biggest success stories in the music industry, starting with "That's the Way I've Always Heard It Should Be" (inspired by a 1969 run-in with a casting-couch producer in Nashville) and continuing with gold-plated rock hits and ballads like "Anticipation" (later used as the Heinz catsup jingle), "You're So Vain" (ostensibly about ex-lover Warren Beatty), "Mockingbird" (a duet with James Taylor), "Nobody Does It Better," "You Belong to Me," and "Jesse." Above and beyond her stutter, leggy, lush-lipped Carly faced quite a bit of competition within her family. Her father, Richard Simon, cofounded the publishing house of Simon and Schuster, eldest sister Joanna became a mezzo-soprano (with the New York City Opera), second sister Lucy competed as an aspiring rock singer, and little brother Peter fared respectably as a photographer. During Carly's childhood it was not that unusual for Albert Einstein or Richard Rodgers to show up at the dinner table in Manhattan or as a house guest at the Simons' homes in Riverdale and Connecticut. She went into analysis at 9 to deal with her stutter, and the death of her father in 1960 left her emotionally devastated. She managed to pull herself out of her depression by the time she entered Sarah Lawrence College, where she and Lucy recorded a single in 1964 called "Winkin', Blinkin' and Nod." In 1971 she became romantically involved with singer-songwriter James Taylor after a Carnegie Hall concert, and they were married the next year. Simon helped Taylor through his struggle to overcome an addiction to heroin, while he in turn helped her overcome a monumental case of stage fright. In 1978, after six years spent shunning the concert circuit, Simon performed her first live appearances, a modest seven-city tour that nonetheless propelled her *Boys in the Trees* LP into her first platinum album. The following summer, her famous friends flocked to Martha's Vineyard to make a success of Carly's new disco on the island. Taylor and Simon went their separate ways—she straight into the arms of former *Dynasty* cast member Al Corley. She later opted not to become Carly Corley.

Born: June 25, 1945, in New York City
Height: 5 ft. 11 in.
Weight: 138 lbs.
Eyes: Blue
Hair: Brown
Zodiac: Cancer
Education: Sarah Lawrence College
Religion: Jewish
Marriages: To James Taylor (1972–1981)
Children: Sarah (b. 1974), Benjamin (b. 1976)

Interests: Composing, piano, interior design and architecture, clothes, est, meditation, Freudian analysis
Personal Habits and Traits: Has terrible stage fright, still stutters when nervous, gets to bed by 11:30 P.M.
Addresses: New York City; Martha's Vineyard, Massachusetts
Income: $1.8 million

Neil Simon

Marvin Neil Simon

"Too much of a good thing can be—wonderful."

Known to his friends simply as "Doc" because of his boyhood ambition to become one, Marvin Neil Simon collects an estimated $45,000 a week in royalties from more than 30 plays and screenplays penned since *Come Blow Your Horn* trumpeted his arrival as a playwright in 1961. Growing up tough in the Bronx, Neil dropped out of New York University after two years to enlist in the Air Force, then wound up being stationed right back at NYU. Simon and his brother Danny started writing for the *CBS Comedy Workshop,* creating material first for Robert Q. Lewis, then for *Your Show of Shows,* Garry Moore, and Carol Burnett, among others. After a full decade as a highly paid TV comedy writer, Simon began *Come Blow Your Horn* while working for Jerry Lewis. By the time his play was filmed with Frank Sinatra in the lead, *Barefoot in the Park* had exploded on Broadway starring an up-and-coming young matinee idol named Robert Redford. Doc then proceeded to Simonize Broadway with comedies (including *Plaza Suite, The Last of the Red-Hot Lovers, The Sunshine Boys, California Suite, Chapter Two*) and musicals (*Little Me, Sweet Charity, Promises, Promises*), most of which were made into movies. *The Odd Couple,* Simon's most successful play, was converted both into a motion picture and a long-running television series. There were also original comedy screenplays: *Star-Spangled Girl, The Heartbreak Kid, The Out-of-Towners, Murder by Death, The Goodbye Girl,* and *The Cheap Detective*. Simon's 1970 attempt at Broadway drama, *The Gingerbread Lady* starring Maureen Stapleton, received mixed reviews. But his bittersweet *Chapter Two,* chronicling the death of his first wife, Joan, from cancer in 1973 and his subsequent courtship and marriage to Oscar-nominated actress Marsha Mason (*The Goodbye Girl*), was critically touted as the playwright's finest effort. That is, until his autobiographical *Brighton Beach Memoirs,* the Tony-winning *Biloxi Blues* (both starring young Matthew Broderick), and *The Odd Couple,* restaged with Sally Struthers and Rita Moreno in the starring roles, Simonized Broadway again. Mason and Simon called it quits in 1982, and Neil started Chapter Three with agent Ann Bell. One of the many honors accorded Simon: A fine old Broadway theater bears his name.

Born: July 4, 1927, in the Bronx (New York City)
Height: 6 ft. 1½ in.
Weight: 180 lbs.
Eyes: Brown
Hair: Brown
Zodiac: Cancer
Education: New York University (two years)
Religion: Jewish

Marriages:
To Joan Baim (1955 until her death in 1973)
To Marsha Mason (1974–1982)
To Ann Bell (1983–)
Children: Two daughters
Interests: Tennis
Personal Habits and Traits: Suffers from back trouble, thyroid problems, a chronic giggler, quiet, self-effacing
Addresses: Bel Air, California; Manhattan
Income: $45,000 per week

Paul Simon

"The public hungers to see talented young people kill themselves."

Greeting darkness as an old friend, Paul Simon, in the melancholy and moving opening lines of "Sounds of Silence," established himself as a leading troubadour of the 1960s and one of the finest lyricists of his time. A teacher's son who grew up in Queens, Simon teamed up with Art Garfunkel while they were both in the sixth grade, and they separated just long enough to attend college before reuniting in Europe. Although they recorded their first actual hit when they were 15 under the names Tom and Jerry, Simon and Garfunkel surged to the top with the hauntingly beautiful "Sounds of Silence," and over the following years until their final split in 1970, the duo produced such outstanding hits as "Mrs. Robinson," "Scarborough Fair," "The Boxer," "Cecilia," "Baby Driver," "El Condor Pasa," "Keep the Customer Satisfied," and "Bridge Over Troubled Waters." Released in 1970, the *Troubled Waters* album proved far and away Simon and Garfunkel's most successful, racking up six Grammy Awards and selling 9 million copies worth over $40 million: their royalties on the album alone amount to well over $4 million, not counting several million more for publishing rights. As a solo act since 1973 Simon has managed to compose Top 10 singles like "Love Me Like a Rock," "Kodachrome," "Slipsliding Away," and "One Trick Pony" (also the title of the 1980 film in which he starred). Yet it was hard to top his reunion with Garfunkel for their already legendary concert in Central Park. After his divorce in 1975, Simon and Shelley Duvall (*Popeye*) were an item until she was replaced by Carrie Fisher. They were wed in 1983, splitting less than two years later.

Born: November 13, 1942, in Newark, New Jersey
Height: 5 ft. 2 in.
Weight: 131 lbs.
Eyes: Brown
Hair: Brown and balding
Zodiac: Libra
Education: Queens College, B.A. in English literature
Religion: Jewish

Marriages:
To Peggy Simon (divorced in 1975)
To Carrie Fisher (1983–1985)
Children: Harper (b. 1972)
Interests: Baseball, composition, guitar
Personal Habits and Traits: Does not smoke, easily depressed, exercise nut, workaholic
Address: New York City
Income: $3.1 million

O. J. Simpson

Orenthal James Simpson

"Life was so good to me. I had a great wife, good kids, money, my own health—and I'm lonely and bored."

Orenthal James Simpson's parents divorced when he was four, and his mother Eunice supported her four children in San Francisco's seedy Potrero Hill district working as an orderly in the psychiatric ward of San Francisco General Hospital.

Simpson fought to overcome a childhood case of rickets that left him permanently bowlegged and pigeon-toed and as a teenager helped meet the family's bills by unloading freight cars and peddling fish. But he also joined a series of street gangs, leading to three separate arrests. Not until the Giants' Willie Mays invited him to spend a day at his lavish home did Simpson decide that he wanted a different future, and he went on to attend the University of Southern California on an athletic scholarship. At USC he was fired as a truck driver for RC Cola when caught sleeping on the job. Several years later, after he had won the 1968 Heisman Trophy, O.J. signed a six-figure contract to endorse RC. As a running back for the Buffalo Bills he set ten NFL records in nine years, then was traded to San Francisco in 1978, selling his Tudor-style mansion in Buffalo and settling down in his $650,000 Los Angeles home with his college bride, Marguerite. Off the field, "The Juice" collected hefty salaries plugging Hertz, TreeSweet orange juice, Dingo boots, Wilson Sporting Goods, and Hyde Spot-Bilt athletic shoes, as well as acting in *The Towering Inferno, The Cassandra Crossing, Capricorn One,* ABC's *Roots,* and CBS's *A Killing Affair.* Back in his hometown, Simpson's family is much the same as it was before young O.J. hit the big time: his mother is now a hospital supervisor, his father a chef, and his brother a doorman at the Clift Hotel. Coming to the end of one of the most spectacular careers in professional sports, Simpson began to concentrate even more on his promising acting career, sportscasting (for ABC), and endorsements (Hertz)—but at the expense of his marriage. Marguerite and O.J. headed for the divorce courts in the summer of 1979 to put an end to their 13-year marriage. Tragedy struck not long after when his 2-year-old daughter Aaren drowned in a swimming pool. Simpson marched to the altar again in 1984, and a year later became a dad for the fourth time. Daddy's nickname for little Sydney Brooke Simpson: "Sweets."

Born: July 9, 1947, in San Francisco, California
Height: 6 ft. 1 in.
Weight: 210 lbs.
Eyes: Brown
Hair: Black
Zodiac: Cancer
Education: Dropped out of USC two semesters short of a B.A. in public administration
Marriages: To Marguerite (1966–1979)
Children: Arnelle (b. 1969), Jason (b. 1970), Aaren (b. 1977, died 1979), Sydney Brooke (b. 1985)
Interests: Acting, cars, fashion (one of the 10 best-dressed men in America in 1975), fiction, tennis, poker, rock, cooking
Personal Habits and Traits: Carries a Cartier lighter even though he does not smoke, drinks beer, runs five miles every day, works out with weights
Addresses: Los Angeles; San Francisco
Income: $2 million (estimate)

Frank Sinatra

Francis Albert Sinatra

"I detest bad manners. If people are polite, then I am; they shouldn't try to get away with not being polite to me."

Whether known as "Frankie," "Ol' Blue Eyes," or by a number of unprintable expletives, Frank Sinatra can perhaps be called the world's number-one (with the possible exception of Bob Hope) entertainment personality. He was born Francis Albert Sinatra in Hoboken, New Jersey, where his father was fire captain; Sinatra's mother Dolly died tragically in the 1976 crash of a private jet. The skinny youth's first radio appearance was with the Hoboken Four on Major Bowes' Amateur Hour in 1937. After linking up with bandleaders Harry James and Tommy Dorsey he caused bobby-soxers to swoon when he grabbed the microphone at the Paramount to sing such highly romantic ballads as "This Love of Mine" and "I'll Never Smile Again," and over the years he has recorded literally dozens of million-sellers, including "Witchcraft," "High Hopes," "Nancy With the Laughing Face," "One More for the Road," "Strangers in the Night," "My Kind of Town," "Hey, There," "It Was a Very Good Year," "My Way," "That's Life," "Love's Been Good to Me," "Somethin' Stupid" (with his daughter Nancy), and "New York, New York." He has also enjoyed a successful movie career that included an Oscar-winning performance in *From Here to Eternity* (ending a four-year career slump) as well as *Guys and Dolls, Pal Joey, The Manchurian Candidate,* and *The Detective.* But as titular head of the so-called "Rat Pack" Sinatra has also earned a reputation as an arrogant, womanizing brawler who routinely clobbers members of the press, and whose questionable underworld connections have tarnished his image. His alleged friendship with mobster Sam "Momo" Giancana, for example, resulted in his being forced by the government to relinquish his ownership of a Tahoe casino (Sinatra regained his Nevada gambling license in 1981). His first marriage to Nancy Barbato ended in divorce in 1951 and later that year he married Ava Gardner. According to Earl Wilson's biography *Sinatra,* their tumultuous relationship was "a six-year soap opera, with screaming fights heard round the world." One story had Sinatra "firing a revolver into mattresses" when he suspected her of seeing other men, and two weeks before their first anniversary, he had police throw Gardner and her pal Lana Turner out of his Palm Springs mansion. They divorced in 1957, and Sinatra went on to court Lauren Bacall ("He behaved like a complete shit," says Bacall), Juliet Prowse, and Marilyn Monroe. Wife number three was actress Mia Farrow, 28 years his junior, whom he married in 1966. That lasted two years. In 1977 Sinatra wed Zeppo Marx's comely blond widow, Barbara, after a four-year courtship. Regarded by his friends as generous and loyal, and by his detractors as compulsive, egotistical, and even violence-prone, Sinatra is certainly one of the most powerful and enigmatic figures on the American scene—particularly since the election of his good pal Ronald Reagan as 40th President of the United States. Sinatra, who chaired the entertainment committee for both Reagan inaugurations, was awarded the nation's highest civilian honor—the Medal of Freedom—in 1985. It was not an altogether popular decision.

Born: December 12, 1917, in Hoboken, New Jersey
Height: 5 ft. 8½ in.
Weight: 160 lbs.
Eyes: Blue
Hair: Gray and thinning
Zodiac: Sagittarius
Education: High school
Religion: Roman Catholic
Marriages:
To Nancy Barbato (1939–1951)
To Ava Gardner (1951–1957)
To Mia Farrow (1966–1968)
To Barbara Marx (1977–)
Children: Tina, Nancy, Frank, Jr. (all by Nancy Barbato)
Interests: Politics, investments, horse racing, acting, his grandchildren, art, the state of Israel, a wide variety of charities
Personal Habits and Traits: Chain-smokes, an accomplished drinker, volatile
Addresses: Palm Springs, California; Beverly Hills; New York City
Income: $5 million+ (personal worth of $65 million)

Grace Slick

''Alcohol goes better with my body chemistry. I started drinking heavily at 16—anything I could get my hands on. My headmistress thought I was drinking orange juice—actually I was getting smashed on screwdrivers.''

The pilot of the Jefferson Airplane in the mid-1960s and the Jefferson Starship in the 1970s, Grace Slick started out the ungainly daughter of a wealthy northern California family. When flower children hit Haight-Ashbury in 1965, however, Slick and her group of musicians joined Janis Joplin, Jimi Hendrix and The Doors as leading purveyors of the electric, psychedelic rock that filled San Francisco's Fillmore West and Winterland. Slick's sulfur-voiced rendition of ''White Rabbit'' became an anthem to a whole generation of acid freaks, but when the counterculture nosedived in the 1970s, so did the Airplane. The group split up, as did Slick's long-standing relationship with Paul Kantner, the father of her daughter China (Slick had originally named her ''god'' with a small g, but later decided that was pretentious). In 1974, Kantner, Slick, and Airplane founder Marty Balin reunited to form the Jefferson Starship, but as pressures mounted to get Starship airborne Slick switched from drugs to booze and was soon drinking with a vengeance. Arrested twice for drunkenness, she finally went on the wagon, and by 1976 Slick and the Starship were once again in the Top 10. Despite further bouts with the bottle, in 1978 the group's *Earth* album and the single ''Count on Me'' both climbed to number one, giving the acid-rockers their most successful year ever. Now Slick possesses a spacious residence in Mill Valley, California, a 40-foot oceangoing cruiser and a husband 14 years her junior, Skip Johnson. She struck out on her own as a singer just as Barbara Rowes's biography of her was going to press. Slick went New Wave in the early 1980s, but it was not until she rejoined the reformed Starship, *sans* Kantner, that Slick was back on top of the charts with ''We Built This City'' and ''Sara'' from the group's *Knee-Deep in the Hoopla* album. Slick was one of the celebrities who talked candidly about their battle with the bottle in Dennis Wholey's bestselling *The Courage to Change*.

Born: October 30, 1939, in Chicago, Illinois
Height: 5 ft. 7 in.
Weight: 118 lbs.
Eyes: Blue *Hair:* Brown
Zodiac: Scorpio
Education: Finch College dropout
Religion: Protestant
Marriages:
To Jerry Slick (1961–1970)
To Skip Johnson (1976–)
Children: Daughter China, by Jefferson Starship guitarist Paul Kantner
Interests: Composing, performing, boating (owns a $70,000 cruiser)
Personal Habits and Traits: A former alcoholic and drug addict, began in 1978 trying to kick her reliance on liquor, LSD, cocaine, pot and pills
Address: Mill Valley, California
Income: $1.1 million (estimate)

Jaclyn Smith

"Sure, I'm making a bundle now, but this is a fickle business and the trick is keeping *it."*

Charlie's Angel Kelly is a Texas belle, the daughter of a well-to-do dentist. She studied at San Antonio's Trinity University Drama School before moving to New York City, where she lived at the famous Barbizon Hotel for Women while breaking into TV commercials with Listerine mouthwash, Breck shampoo, Wella Balsam shampoo and conditioner, and Max Factor cosmetics (one contract was reportedly worth $250,000). Between takes Jaclyn, a ballet student since the age of 3, managed to set up a ballet school for underprivileged youngsters in New York's Upper West Side slums. When *Charlie's Angels* zoomed to the Top 10 on TV in 1976, Smith's rating as a bankable television actress soared with it. Now earning well in excess of $1 million a year from various sources, Smith has exercised her own considerable talent as a money manager, and her biggest tax shelter is a $500,000 Tara-like estate in the heart of Beverly Hills. A five-year marriage to actor Roger Davis collapsed before the debut of *Angels,* and Smith bemoans the fact that as a star of one of the most successful series in the history of television she only has time to "work, study my lines, and sleep." Nevertheless, she found enough space in her hectic schedule to marry fellow television actor Dennis Cole. That lasted less than two years. A 1979 poll of *People* magazine readers revealed that Jaclyn was considered by the public at large to be *the* most beautiful woman in America. Wed to cinematographer *(Nightkill)* Tony Richmond in 1981, working mom Smith stuck to what she knew best—television. Among her '80s credits: *Rage of Angels, George Washington, Florence Nightingale, Rage of Angels II*—and a line of Jaclyn Smith fashions exclusively for K-Mart.

Born: October 26, 1947, in Houston, Texas
Height: 5 ft. 7 in.
Weight: 110 lbs.
Eyes: Green *Hair:* Brown
Zodiac: Scorpio
Education: Trinity University in San Antonio (one year)
Religion: Baptist
Marriages:
To Roger Davis (divorced after five years)
To Dennis Cole (1978–1980)
To Tony Richmond (1981–)
Children: Gaston (b. 1982)
Interests: Finance (she is a tax expert), ballet, education

Personal Habits and Traits: Nonsmoker and nondrinker, health food fiend

Address: Beverly Hills
Income: $2.5 million

Tom Snyder

"I have never fallen in love with my own voice, but I've always had an attraction for it."

Possessing a manic laugh and a bionic tongue, television's Tom Snyder single-handedly escalated the very late night *Tomorrow* talk show into one of NBC's biggest moneymakers and a tonic for several million insomniacs. Abrasive, contentious and remarkably thin-skinned—he supposedly reacted to criticism from one TV critic by sending the critic's wife 13 yellow roses with the note *You were terrific in the sack*—Snyder launched *Tomorrow* in 1973 from Los Angeles, then took it to New York (where he also anchored WNBC *Evening News* and the 8:57 P.M. *NBC News Update*), returned West in late 1976, and came back again to New York. Beginning in late 1980, Snyder shared the *Tomorrow* spotlight with Rona Barrett. A Milwaukee-raised altar boy who mastered Latin while attending Milwaukee's Jesuit Marquette University, Snyder idolized NBC's John Cameron Swayze back in the 1950s and spent 20 years hopping from one TV station to another as an ambulance-chasing newsman. He has since easily matched wits with such diverse personalities as Jimmy Hoffa and William F. Buckley, Jr., on the air and has become one of the medium's most skillful interrogators. Aside from the dissolution of his 17-year marriage to Mary Ann Snyder, his biggest dilemma to date was defending himself against the persistent public conviction that he was determined to either succeed John Chancellor as NBC's national anchorman or Johnny Carson as host of the *Tonight Show*. That possibility was dealt a blow by the dismally low ratings garnered by his live *Prime Time Sunday*. Snyder returned to local news, collecting an estimated half-million dollars a year as anchorman for ABC's flagship New York station before departing in 1984. One year later, he was negotiating for a return to ABC—this time in the familiar capacity of late-night talk-show inquisitor.

Born: May 12, 1936, in Milwaukee, Wisconsin
Height: 6 ft. 4 in.
Weight: 198 lbs.
Eyes: Brown *Hair:* Gray-brown
Zodiac: Taurus
Education: Marquette University
Religion: Roman Catholic
Marriages: To Mary Ann Snyder (1959–1976)
Children: Anne Marie (b. 1964)

Interests: Broadcasting, politics, antique Lionel toy trains
Personal Habits and Traits: Chainsmokes, drinks Stolichnaya vodka, collects teddy bears, is a workaholic, prefers Jacqueline Susann and Harold Robbins to weightier material
Address: Beverly Hills
Income: $500,000 (minimum estimate)

Suzanne Somers

Suzanne Mahoney

"I've tried so hard to be a good person, but now they're bringing up things out of context in my life. It makes me want to cry."

After nine unsuccessful TV pilots Suzanne Somers scored as the endearingly half-witted bombshell on ABC's number-one situation comedy *Three's Company,* and within a year after the series' 1977 debut she graced the covers of *People* and *Newsweek*—as well as a pinup poster that sold over 500,000 copies. The daughter of a secretary and a high school athletic coach, Suzanne Mahoney was expelled from her Catholic high school for writing notes to her classmates, but she managed to graduate from a public high school and proceeded to San Francisco's Lone Mountain College. At 17 she married Bruce Somers (now a lawyer-psychologist) and within months became the mother of a son, Bruce, Jr. But the marriage lasted only a year, and Suzanne subsequently focused on an acting career, paying the rent by working nights as a cocktail waitress. While in San Francisco she landed bit parts in on-location films like *Bullitt* and *Magnum Force,* and appeared on several game and talk shows. Then came the part of the blond in the Thunderbird who captures the imagination of Richard Dreyfuss in *American Graffiti,* and Somers relocated to Holywood. Contrary to her show business persona, reminiscent of Judy Holliday or even Marilyn Monroe, she also wrote two volumes of poetry—*Touch Me* and a sequel, *Touch Me Again*—at the behest of friend Jacqueline Susann. In 1977 she married Canadian television personality Al Hamel after 10 years together. They live with Bruce, Jr., in a Santa Monica beach house. By her fifth season as *Three's Company* Chrissie, Somers was embroiled with the producers in a bitter dispute over her participation in the series' astronomical profits that resulted in her being dropped from the show. She more than makes ends meet with her $100,000-a-week stage shows in Las Vegas and Atlantic City.

Born: October 16, 1945, in San Bruno, California
Height: 5 ft. 5½ in.
Weight: 111 lbs.
Eyes: Blue *Hair:* Blond
Zodiac: Libra
Education: Lone Mountain College, B.A.
Religion: Roman Catholic
Marriages:
To Bruce Somers (1963–1964)
To Al Hamel (1977–)

Children: Bruce Somers, Jr. (b. 1964)
Interests: Poetry (has published two volumes), language, Cordon Bleu cooking (attended both Le Cordon Bleu and La Varenne schools in Paris)
Personal Habits and Traits: A nonsmoker, nondrinker, contemplative, introspective
Address: Marina Del Rey, California
Income: $1.4 million (minimum estimate)

Stephen Sondheim

''Hummable is a meaningless word, and so is melodic. If a tune is heard often enough, it becomes hummable. When they say my music is not, they're really saying it is not reminiscent of something else. My main goal is to tell a story.''

With his Tony Award–winning *Company, Follies, A Little Night Music, Sweeney Todd,* and *Sunday in the Park With George,* this brilliant word gamesman has radically altered the shape and substance of the American musical. Stephen Sondheim first learned his trade at the feet of theatrical colossus Oscar Hammerstein II. After his mother divorced Herbert Sondheim and moved the family to a farm in Bucks County, Pennsylvania, the Hammersteins were neighbors; young Stephen was friendly with the Hammersteins' son Jamie and wound up spending four summers with them. A lyricist first, Sondheim collaborated with Leonard Bernstein on *West Side Story,* then wrote *Gypsy* with Jule Styne and (for Richard Rodgers) *Do I Hear a Waltz?* No less successful were his efforts at handling both words and music, starting with *A Funny Thing Happened on the Way to the Forum.* His hauntingly beautiful ''Send in the Clowns'' from *A Little Night Music* not only handed folk singer Judy Collins another gold record, but also received the Grammy as Best Song of 1975. In 1976 Sondheim and producer-director Hal Prince, his partner in many musical hits, stretched the boundaries of the ''concept musical'' even further with the provocative *Pacific Overtures,* and then again with the macabre *Sweeney Todd.* Perhaps the truest test of his permanent influence on the theater has been *Side by Side by Sondheim,* a simple tribute that wound up becoming one of the longest-running musicals of the decade. A chain-smoking, vodka-sipping bachelor, Sondheim prefers the company of a few friends like Bernstein, Prince, the Tony Perkinses, and director Arthur Laurents. On any given evening they can be found challenging one another to decipher anagrams in the luxurious sitting room of his five-story town house in Manhattan's Turtle Bay district. *Sunday in the Park With George,* inspired by the Seurat masterpiece, brought Sondheim the one award he had yet to receive: the Pulitzer Prize.

Born: March 22, 1930, in New York City
Height: 5 ft. 10 in.
Weight: 167 lbs.
Eyes: Brown *Hair:* Gray
Zodiac: Aries
Education: Williams College
Religion: Jewish
Marriages: None
Children: None

Interests: Composing, writing lyrics, screenplays, anagrams and word games, antiques
Personal Habits and Traits: A chain smoker, drinks vodka, intensely private but not antisocial
Address: New York City
Income: $750,000

Sissy Spacek

Mary Elizabeth Spacek

''I don't want to live my life to be a movie star. That's a trap. Movie star is not a position in life.''

The role of a harassed and tormented student who wreaks telekinetic revenge on her classmates in *Carrie* reaped freckle-faced Sissy Spacek the National Society of Film Critics Best Actress Award, an Oscar nomination and a highly bankable future on screen. But *Carrie* bore little resemblance to Mary Elizabeth Spacek's real-life girlhood in tiny Quitman, Texas, where at her local high school she shone as a baton-twirling majorette and homecoming queen. She bought a $14 guitar at Sears at age 14 and decided she wanted to break into show business as a folksinger. Her brother Robbie died of leukemia at 19, just before she headed to New York, and in retrospect Spacek concedes that his death compelled her to ''live every moment as if it were the last.'' Rooming in Greenwich Village with her first cousin Rip Torn and his wife, Geraldine Page, she modeled while studying with Lee Strasberg at the Actors Studio and made her movie debut as a stoned teenage prostitute in 1972's *Prime Cut* with Gene Hackman. Her first starring role arrived the next year, as mass-murderer Charles Starkweather's girl in Terence Malick's *Badlands.* Robert Altman then used her in *Welcome to L. A.* and in *Three Women,* where she played a disturbed teenage Texan who frantically tries to assume friend Shelly Duvall's identity. Quick on the heels of *Carrie,* Spacek scored another critical success as the talentless but lovable USO showgirl in PBS Television's *Verna.* Her portrayal of Loretta Lynn in *Coal Miner's Daughter* earned her an Academy Award as Best Actress of 1980. Married since 1974 to movie art director Jack Fisk, she lives in a comfortable Topanga Canyon house complete with redwood hot tub and skylights. One of a trio of actresses Oscar-nominated for their roles in sod sobbers (Sally Field in *Places in the Heart,* Jessica Lange in *Country,* and Spacek in *The River*), Sissy lost out to Field. She played a real-life crusader in her first post-*River* film, *Marie,* and a photojournalist after old beau Kevin Kline in *Violets Are Blue.*

Born: December 25, 1949, in Quitman, Texas
Height: 5 ft. 7½ in.
Weight: 111 lbs.
Eyes: Green *Hair:* Blond
Zodiac: Capricorn
Education: High school
Religion: Prostestant
Marriages: To Jack Fisk (1974–)
Children: A daughter, Schuyler Elizabeth (b. 1982)
Interests: TM, photography, drawing, tap dancing (takes daily lessons), backpacking, the baton, singing
Personal Habits and Traits: Does not smoke or drink, frequently fasts, is a chronic worrier
Addresses: Topanga Canyon, California; Quitman, Texas
Income: $650,000 (estimate)

Steven Spielberg

"If I were just a member of the audience and not part of the craft, I probably would never see Bergman or Zeffirelli or Fellini or Costa-Gavras. I'd probably just see Irwin Allen disaster movies and Lucas films."

While still in grammar school in New Jersey he shot his first movie—a three-and-a-half-minute western. One day he missed a Boy Scout troop excursion on which everybody spotted a UFO. Hearing about the incident prompted him, at 16, to write, direct, and edit a two-and-a-half-hour movie called *Firelight,* an outer-space invasion saga. Those same fantasies would also fuel *Close Encounters of the Third Kind* and the biggest-grossing movie of all time, *E.T.*, years later, but in the meantime he was signed by Universal Studios to a seven-year director's contract at the age of 21 on the basis of his short called *Amblin'*, made as a film student at California State College at Long Beach. Spielberg directed a number of episodes of TV's *Marcus Welby* before his Emmy-winning made-for-television movie *Duel,* in which Dennis Weaver portrayed a hapless motorist terrorized by the unseen driver of a mammoth truck. His first feature film, *The Sugarland Express* starring Goldie Hawn, was hailed by critics and led to his directing *Jaws,* which held the title as the biggest money-grossing film in history between 1975 and the arrival of *Star Wars* in 1977. Within months after *Star Wars'* release, Spielberg sprang his own *Close Encounters* on the public; it also became an outlandish box office success, though it did not break *Star Wars'* record. Along with *Star Wars* director George Lucas, Francis Ford Coppola, and John Milius, Spielberg remains part of a Hollywood conglomerate in which all four directors share ideas, assist in one another's projects and even share in one another's profits. The results: blockbusters like *Poltergeist, Raiders of the Lost Ark, Indiana Jones and the Temple of Doom, Gremlins,* and *Goonies*. Bachelor Spielberg was caught by a roving camera at the 1978 Academy Awards ceremony mouthing the words "I love you" to actress Amy Irving *(The Competition),* his longtime housemate. Before she gave birth to their child, Spielberg signed a contract with Irving agreeing to support the tyke, regardless of what happens to their relationship. Spielberg's highly touted *Amazing Stories* anthology series on NBC was anything but amazing in the Nielsens; Angela Lansbury's *Murder, She Wrote* proved stiff competition. Steven Spielberg and Amy Irving wed in late 1985.

Born: December 18, 1947, in Cincinnati, Ohio
Height: 5 ft. 10½ in.
Weight: 174 lbs.
Eyes: Brown *Hair:* Brown
Zodiac: Sagittarius
Education: California State College at Long Beach
Religion: Jewish
Marriages: To Amy Irving (1985–)
Children: Max Samuel (b. 1985)

Interests: Gadgetry (pinball machines, etc.), finance, television
Personal Habits and Traits: Bites his fingernails, occasionally smokes, drinks, procrastinates, is nonetheless a perfectionist and workaholic
Address: Los Angeles
Income: $100 million+ (minimum estimate of net worth)

Bruce Springsteen

"I can't describe that feeling onstage. It's livin', that's all."

His "Glory Days" began as a Catholic growing up in Asbury Park, New Jersey, when Bruce Springsteen was asked to draw a picture of Jesus and handed a nun his personally prophetic drawing of Christ crucified on a guitar. In 1975, his galvanic *Born to Run* album catapulted the street rocker onto the covers of both *Time* and *Newsweek,* though what followed were three years of legal battles between Springsteen and his former manager, a severe case of celebrity anxiety, and a punishing creative dry spell. In the spring of 1977 he emerged after more than 10 months closeted in the recording studio with producer Jon Landau and set the music world on its ear with "Darkness on the Edge of Town," which struck platinum within weeks of its release. More hits ("Hungry Heart") and SRO concerts in Madison Square Garden and coliseums across the country attest to Springsteen's stature as a Dylan-sized rock poet, but "the Boss," as he is called by his friends, is far from secure with his new superstar status; on a stopover in Los Angeles he once defaced his own billboard above Sunset Strip with a can of spray paint. Springsteen beefed up with weights, cut his hair, and emerged with his triple-platinum *Born in the U.S.A.* album (including the hit singles "Dancing in the Dark," "Glory Days," and "My Home Town") as a powerful yuppie–blue-collar hybrid. Not long after adding his distinctive growl to USA for Africa's "We Are the World," Springsteen replaced his gold earring with a gold wedding band in 1985, when he married leggy model-actress Julianne Phillips.

Born: September 23, 1949, in Freehold, New Jersey
Height: 5 ft. 9½ in.
Weight: 141 lbs.
Eyes: Brown *Hair:* Brown
Zodiac: Libra
Education: High school
Religion: Roman Catholic
Marriages: Julianne Phillips (1985–present)
Children: None (as of 1986)
Interests: Composing, swimming
Personal Habits and Traits: A procrastinator, anxious, a workaholic, reclusive
Address: Asbury Park, New Jersey
Income: $24 million + (minimum estimated income for 1985)

Sylvester Stallone

Michael Sylvester Stallone

"Reality, that's the main event."

The "Italian Stallion" who turned his movie *Rocky* into the Horatio Alger story of 1976 (he wrote, starred in and fought for the film that walked away with the Best Picture of the Year Oscar), Stallone was a feisty scrapper long before he exploded on Hollywood as a new Brando. Stallone was raised in New York's Hell's Kitchen; his mother was an ex-Billy Rose chorus girl and his father owned a chain of beauty parlors. Stallone was bounced from a dozen schools—including one for hairdressers—then quit a job as a dorm bouncer and gym instructor at a Swiss boarding school for girls to study acting at the University of Miami. Stallone, who made his stage debut on Broadway in a nudie musical called *Score,* appeared in a soft-core porno flick called *A Party at Kitty and Stud's* and the cult movie *The Lords of Flatbush* to make ends meet while he spent years working on his *Rocky* script. He was offered $300,000 for the story on the condition that a name actor play the part—an offer that Stallone absolutely rejected, and when he finally brought the movie to the screen himself, "Sly" stood to collect a cool $5 million from his victory. Stallone followed up with *F.I.S.T.,* the story of a Hoffa-style labor boss, then his autobiographical *Paradise Alley,* both critically panned. Yet by the time he started shooting his blockbuster sequel *Rocky II* in the fall of 1978, his asking price per film had become a flat $2 million—the top fee then for any box-office titan. Such head-spinning success threw this normally soft-spoken family man off balance, and Stallone found himself involved in a much publicized extramarital affair with his costar in *Paradise Alley,* Joyce Ingalls. However, at the Los Angeles opening of *F.I.S.T.,* Stallone dramatically announced that he and his wife, Sasha, were reuniting, and the Stallones and their son, Sage Moonblood, moved to a veritable chateau (complete with an indoor waterfall) in exclusive Pacific Palisades. Leggy, Muriel Cigar Girl Susan Anton evidently proved irresistible, however, and in the summer of 1979 Sasha and Sly called it quits—only to reconcile a year later. Stallone's boomerang marriage seemed over for good in the mid-1980s, and Sasha filed for divorce in 1985. Stallone was left free to pursue his romance with Danish model-actress Brigitte ("Gitte") Nielsen, whom he called after she sent him a letter with her picture enclosed. Still, Stallone shares with Sasha the heartbreak of their son Seargeoh's autism. Stallone managed to smash box-office records with his pectorially perfect *Rocky III, First Blood* and *Rambo: First Blood II,* but while filming *Rocky IV* was hospitalized with severe chest pains—not a heart attack, but a bruised heart muscle, the result of chronic overwork. That won't keep him from climbing into the ring for more *Rockys,* or perhaps filming his pet project, a screen bio of Edgar Allan Poe. Nude stills from early porno days graced the pages of *Playgirl* in 1985. In the same year, Sylvester Stallone managed to top *Rambo*mania with the phenomenally successful *Rocky IV*, and *Cobra* struck in '86.

Born: July 6, 1946, in New York City
Height: 5 ft. 10 in.
Weight: 185 lbs.
Eyes: Brown *Hair:* Dark Brown
Zodiac: Cancer
Education: University of Miami
Religion: Roman Catholic
Marriages: To Sasha Stallone
Children: Sage Moonblood (b. 1976), Seargeoh (b. 1979)

Interests: Painting, criminology, astrology (Sage was conceived only after consulting astrological charts to ensure his birth under the sign of Taurus), weight training, most sports, screenwriting, directing, acting
Personal Habits and Traits: Neither smokes nor drinks, a health nut, is articulate, shrewd, drives a smoke-colored Mercedes
Address: Pacific Palisades, California
Income: $25 million a year

Jean Stapleton

"One of the biggest ovations I ever received was when I did Hello, Dolly! *in a summer production and ad-libbed some lines! 'Wow, wow, wow, fellas—look at the dingbat now, fellas.' "*

America's number one "dingbat" (a 1979 *People* magazine readers' poll rated her the country's top female TV star), scribbled for a short time as a secretary in Manhattan before trying her luck as an actress on Broadway. Musically inclined—her mother was an opera singer—Stapleton appeared in *Damn Yankees* and *Bells Are Ringing* on both the stage and screen. For 13 seasons she ran the Totem Pole Playhouse near Gettysburg, Pennsylvania, in a modest Mom-and-Pop arrangement with her husband, producer-director William Putch (as in "much"). Then, in 1971, Mom landed the landmark *All in the Family* role of Archie Bunker's wife, Edith. Although Stapleton never had any complaints about the part, she nonetheless avoided similar sweet-but-not-quite-all-there roles. When she performed seriously in the movie *Klute,* more than a few fans in the audience had to suppress giggles, yet she was able to lend intelligence and a natural dignity to her portrayal of an aging Eleanor Roosevelt in a 1978 television biography. The Putches were separated half of each year while she worked on the *All in the Family* set in Hollywood, but the biggest problem they faced was Putch's long-running fight against lymphatic cancer. In 1979, Stapleton stunned CBS by announcing her intention to retire from what may be considered the most successful comedy series in the history of the medium. *All in the Family* was replaced shortly afterward by *Archie Bunker's Place,* and Stapleton went on to portray, among others, Eleanor Roosevelt and Agatha Christie's Miss Marple. In 1983, Putch was directing his wife in a touring production of *The Show-Off* in Syracuse, New York, when he suddenly died of a heart attack. Hours later, Stapleton went on as scheduled because "That's what he would have wanted."

Born: January 19, 1923, in New York City
Height: 5 ft. 7¾ in.
Weight: 140 lbs.
Eyes: Green *Hair:* Brown
Zodiac: Capricorn
Education: High school
Religion: Christian Scientist
Marriages: To William Putch (1957–until his death in 1983)
Children: Pamela (b. 1959), John (b. 1962)
Interests: Graeffenberg (the 1740s inn she runs in Gettysburg), musical comedy, reading history and biographies
Personal Habits and Traits: Does not smoke, avoids the party circuit
Addresses: Gettysburg, Pennsylvania; Los Angeles
Income: $400,000+

Ringo Starr

Richard Starkey

"I always thought we were five. Us four—and we weren't the greatest players—and something else: magic!"

The fourth Beatle was raised by his grandmother while his barmaid mum worked; his father, a house painter, left when Richard Starkey was 3. He spent much of his childhood recuperating from one serious ailment after another—at various times he endured pleurisy, peritonitis, and a smashed pelvis. Young Starkey dropped out of school at 14 to work as an engineer's apprentice, though he actually considered becoming a hairdresser until his mother bought him a set of drums. Later, while in Hamburg playing a date with his group, Rory Storme and the Hurricanes, he caught a new act called the Beatles, and they became friends. When their drummer Pete Best left the group two years later, they asked Ringo to replace him. Ringo (so named because he wore numerous rings on his fingers, and now wears them through his ears) recorded several solo hits after the Beatles broke up in 1971—"It Don't Come Easy" and "You're Sixteen" among them—and acted in such movies as *Candy, The Magic Christian,* and *Sextette.* His marriage to Maureen Cox ended in 1975 after 10 years and three children, and Starr moved in with striking American model Nancy Andrews the following year. That lasted until he hooked up with actress Barbara *(The Spy Who Loved Me)* Bach on the set of their 1981 movie *Caveman.* Maintaining a two-bedroom apartment overlooking the Mediterranean in Monte Carlo, Starr need pay no income taxes so long as he is a legal resident of the principality; nonetheless he spends up to six months a year at his Beverly Hills home—without having to answer to the IRS. Undaunted by the lukewarm receptions to TV's *Princess Daisy* and the movie *Give My Regards to Broad Street* with fellow Beatle Paul McCartney, Ringo signed to do a takeoff on the old Bob Hope–Bing Crosby vehicles titled *Road to Australia.*

Born: July 7, 1940, in Dingle, England
Height: 5 ft. 8 in.
Weight: 150 lbs.
Eyes: Blue *Hair:* Gray-brown
Zodiac: Cancer
Education: High school dropout
Marriages:
To Maureen Cox (1965–1975)
To Barbara Bach (1981–)
Children: Zak (b. 1965), Jason (b. 1967), Lee (b. 1970, a girl)
Interests: Acting, science fiction, old films
Personal Habits and Traits: Has given up smoking, drinks, wears earrings, seldom goes out but often jams at home with friends like Peter Frampton and Eric Clapton
Addresses: Monte Carlo; Hollywood Hills, California
Income: $4 million (minimum estimate)

Rod Steiger

"Acting is an immediate reward and an immediate death."

A Method acting disciple responsible for gripping performances as the possessed concentration camp survivor in *The Pawnbroker,* the maniacal Napoleon in *Waterloo,* the potbellied redneck sheriff in *In the Heat of the Night* (for which he copped a 1967 Best Actor Academy Award), and crazy W.C. himself in *W.C. Fields and Me,* Rod Steiger has few equals in his profession. At 16 he discarded a comfortable life in Westhampton, New York, to join the Navy during World War II; stationed in the Pacific, he commenced his acting career performing *Shadow* tales over his ship's loudspeaker. Once discharged, he enrolled in New

York's Actors Studio and landed several choice roles on live TV, making his mark in the title role of *Marty* on television (Ernest Borgnine claimed the Oscar when the teleplay was translated to the big screen); Steiger in turn conquered the movies playing Marlon Brando's rotten older brother in *On the Waterfront*. Married first to Sally Grace and then to comely British actress Claire Bloom, he wed Sherry Nelson in 1973. The breakup of his marriage to Nelson six years later and a triple coronary bypass pushed him to the brink of despair. After months of psychiatric counseling, he was well enough to resume his screen career playing the exorcist-priest in *The Amityville Horror* and to start part-time counseling of patients himself. Steiger's more recent film roles include the part of a crusading Senator trying to nail labor boss Sylvester Stallone in *F.I.S.T.*

Born: April 14, 1925, in Westhampton, New York
Height: 5 ft. 10½ in.
Weight: 190 lbs.
Eyes: Brown *Hair:* Gray
Zodiac: Aries
Education: High school dropout
Religion: Jewish

Marriages:
To Sally Grace (divorced)
To Claire Bloom (divorced)
To Sherry Nelson (1973–1979)
Children: Anna (b. 1960, by Bloom)
Interests: Literature, music, politics
Personal Habits and Traits: Smokes, tends to overeat
Address: Los Angeles
Income: $400,000 (minimum estimate)

Gloria Steinem

"This is what 50 looks like."

Destined to become America's leading feminist, Gloria Steinem was 11 when her resort-operating father divorced her mother, Ruth, who worked as a newspaper reporter while Gloria was growing up. Despite mediocre grades in high school, Gloria fared well enough on her entrance exams to enter Smith College, and she graduated *magna cum laude* in 1956. Seven years later she capitalized on her leggy good looks by securing a job as a Playboy bunny and then writing a colorful exposé based on her innumerable "sexist" experiences. From then on Steinem was in demand as a freelancer for *Glamour, McCall's, Look, Life, Cosmopolitan,* and *Vogue*. It was not until 1969 that she plunged headlong into the feminist movement, joining forces with the likes of cofounders Betty Friedan and Bella Abzug. Three years later, she launched a new liberated-women's magazine called *Ms.*, which has flourished commercially under her astute leadership as a first-among-equals editor. Throughout her campaign on behalf of the Equal Rights Amendment and against American machismo, Steinem also popularized rimless aviator glasses, and though she has never married ("Marriage makes you legally half a person"), she has nonetheless dated such diverse personalities as director Mike Nichols, saxophonist Paul Desmond, Olympic decathlon-winner Rafer Johnson, and, most recently, financier Mort Zuckerman.

Born: March 25, 1934, in Toledo, Ohio
Height: 5 ft. 8¾ in.
Weight: 118 lbs.
Eyes: Brown *Hair:* Streaked blond
Zodiac: Aries
Education: Smith College
Religion: Protestant
Marriages: None
Children: None
Interests: ERA and the feminist movement, consumerism, show business, politics
Personal Habits and Traits: Chain-smokes, drinks moderately, seldom cooks, parties a great deal
Address: New York City
Income: $5 million net worth

James Stewart

"I don't act. I react."

One of the few Hollywood legends of the 1930s and 1940s still very much in the public eye, James Maitland Stewart was the son of a Scottish hardware store owner in Indiana, Pennsylvania. At Princeton University he could not attain the grades in mathematics necessary to become an engineer, so when pal Joshua Logan—later to become one of the theater's most accomplished writer-directors—suggested the idea of breaking into summer stock, Stewart jumped at the chance. Rooming with Logan and Henry Fonda in New York while they all struggled to make it on Broadway, Stewart finally caught the eye of a Hollywood talent scout in 1934's *Yellow Jack* and headed west. Perennially underwhelmed, Stewart developed his "aw shucks" style on the screen in such varied movie hits as Kaufman and Hart's *You Can't Take It With You, Mr. Smith Goes to Washington, It's a Wonderful Life, The Philadelphia Story* (for which he won an Oscar in 1940), *Harvey, Rear Window,* and *The Spirit of St. Louis.* More recently he brought *Harvey* and *Right of Way* (with Bette Davis) to television and has starred in disaster films like *Airport '77* and *The Swarm,* in which he shared top billing with old roommate Hank Fonda. The highest-ranking show business figure in the military, Stewart enlisted in World War II as a private and eventually led bombing missions over Bremen, Berlin and Frankfurt before the war was over, retiring in 1968 with the rank of Brigadier General. His homey commercials for Firestone tires long supplemented his retirement pay, and by the late 1980s Stewart seemed to spend most of his time picking up rewards, from Hollywood's coveted Life Achievement Award to a Kennedy Center award presented to him by longtime friend Ronald Reagan.

Born: May 20, 1908, in Indiana, Pennsylvania
Height: 6 ft. 4 in.
Weight: 170 lbs.
Eyes: Blue *Hair:* White
Zodiac: Taurus
Education: Princeton University
Religion: Protestant
Marriages: To Gloria McLean (1949–)
Children: Judy and Kelly (twins)
Interests: Flying, photography, painting
Personal Habits and Traits: Does not smoke, a social drinker, early to bed, very superstitious (he takes a lucky tie with him at all times)
Address: Los Angeles
Income: $300,000 (minimum estimate)

Rod Stewart

"I'll be dead by the time I'm 40."

The raspy-voiced legend of 1970s rock 'n' roll grew up in a working-class Scottish-English family in the gritty Highgate section of London. A talented soccer wing, he signed with a semipro league after graduation from high school and augmented his income by working part time as a gravedigger. Stewart soon quit soccer and instead hooked up with a succession of bands—Jimmy Powell's Five Dimensions, the Hootchie Coochie Men, the Steampacket Band, the Jeff Beck Band, the Small Faces, the Faces, Rod Stewart and the Faces, and finally his own Rod Stewart Band. Playing harmonica and wailing in the strained voice that made him a male counterpart to Janis Joplin, Stewart growled out a number of suggestive hits ("Every Picture Tells a Story," "Maggie Mae," "Tonight's the Night," "Hot Legs," "Do Ya Think I'm Sexy?") while earning a reputation in the music industry as a raunchy trasher of hotel rooms and a groupie collector. In 1975, however, he met Swedish actress Britt Ekland backstage after one of his concerts at the Los Angeles Forum, and began a long-running and much publicized nonmarital relationship that made headlines two years later when she filed suit against him for $15 million—what she claimed to be her share of his earnings made while they lived together. The issue was settled out of court, and the unabashed Beau Brummell who dyes his hair pale blond and prefers baggy white suits worn without a shirt spends more than half of each year on the road away from his elegant, art nouveau–filled Holmby Hills Home. In 1979, he married George Hamilton's ex, Alana—just in time for the birth three months later of their daughter Alana Kimberly. After the acrimonious breakup of his marriage to Alana, Stewart fretted about no longer being a "Young Turk" but was not beyond another "Infatuation"—this time with blonde model Kelly Emberg. Not long after he reached the age he never thought he'd survive to see—40—Stewart appeared to have dumped Emberg for another Kelly: *Woman in Red* knockout Kelly LeBrock. "Some Guys Have All the Luck," indeed.

Born: January 10, 1945, in Glasgow, Scotland
Height: 5 ft. 7½ in.
Weight: 135 lbs.
Eyes: Hazel *Hair:* Blond
Zodiac: Aquarius
Education: High school
Religion: Protestant
Marriages: To Alana Hamilton (1979–)
Children: Alana Kimberly (b. 1979)
Interests: Soccer, clothes, art, automobiles
Personal Habits and Traits: Smokes, heavy drinker, rowdy, promiscuous
Address: Holmby Hills, California
Income: $2.7 million (estimate)

Sting

Gordon Matthew Sumner

"There's something about playing to 90,000 people that pumps you up like the most exquisite drug."

It may be due to an early addiction to black-and-yellow striped sweaters or simply because of his buzzing energy, but the nickname stuck even before The Police became rock's most arresting group. Born to a hairdresser and a Newcastle, England, milkman, and educated at Warwick University, Sting was the only male teacher at St. Mary's Convent School in his native city. Married to Frances, who played the Virgin Mary opposite him in a university production of Tony Hatch's *Rock Nativity,* Sting moved to London in 1976 and was spotted playing double bass at a jazz club by American drummer Stewart Copeland. They teamed up with British guitarist Andy Summers to form The Police and find their distinct sound, a fusion of rock and reggae. They did not go over instantly; at one joint in Poughkeepsie they played before a bartender and two customers. Another one of their early jobs was a television commercial for Wrigley's gum that was never aired because the networks deemed it too raunchy. In 1978 Sting wrote "Roxanne," a song about a prostitute. Banned by the BBC, it quickly became their first hit. Soon The Police had locked up hit singles (including "Don't Stand So Close to Me," "Every Breath You Take," "King of Pain") and platinum albums *Regatta de Blanc* and *Synchronicity.* A fractious group ("like kids at the dinner table arguing over who's got more Rice Krispies"), The Police have nevertheless provided their sullenly sexy lead singer with a springboard to the movies. Critically acclaimed for his nonsinging role in *The Who's Quadraphenia,* Sting dropped his Police escort to star in *Brimstone and Treacle,* don a leather jockstrap in the sci-fi film *Dune,* play Dr. Frankenstein in a 1985 remake of *The Bride of Frankenstein* called *The Bride,* act opposite Meryl Streep in *Plenty,* and play himself in *Bring on the Night.* When his second daughter, Kate, was only a few months old, the Chief of Police went to live with his pregnant girlfriend, Trudie Styler. Their child, a girl they named Michael, was born in early 1984. A year later she gave birth to a boy, Jake. Sting's first solo smash: "Set Them Free," quickly followed by "Fortress Around Your Heart."

Born: October 2, 1951, in Newcastle, England
Height: 5 ft. 9 in.
Weight: 150 lbs.
Eyes: Blue *Hair:* Blond
Zodiac: Libra
Education: Graduated Warwick University
Marriages: To Frances Tomelty (1976–1984)
Children: Joe (b. 1976) and Kate (b. 1982) by Tomelty; daughter Michael (b. 1984) and son Jake (b. 1985) by Trudie Styler
Interests: Acting, composing, psychology, racehorses (he owns three)
Personal Habits and Traits: A vegetarian, relaxes listening to favorites Beethoven, Prokofiev, Ravel, and Ralph Vaughan-Williams, articulate, melancholic
Addresses: Ireland; Hampstead, London
Income: $3.3 million + (estimated)

Meryl Streep

Mary Louise Streep

"I've got plenty of people gunning for me, but as long as I can keep working, it really doesn't matter. The work will stand, no matter what."

As a little girl in Summit, New Jersey, she had a bossy streak that made her "a Lucy to neighborhood Charlie Browns." But when her parents discovered that their little angel with the hideous glasses and permed hair had a beautiful singing voice, they took her to Beverly Sills's voice teacher, Estelle Liebling, who promptly accepted her as a pupil. She gave up her voice lessons four years later and plunged headlong into high school life; she peroxided her hair, chucked her braces, traded in her specs for contacts, joined the swim team, became a cheerleader, and—signifying the ultimate in adolescent acceptance—was crowned Homecoming Queen. At Vassar, Meryl acted in Strindberg's *Miss Julie* but did not become hooked on acting until she enrolled in the Yale School of Drama. She played 40 parts in three years and upon graduation was instantly snapped up by Joseph Papp for his Public Theater, where in Central Park, she turned in a brilliant, bombastic performance as Shakespeare's violent termagent Kate in *The Taming of the Shrew,* opposite Raul Julia. Streep went virtually unnoticed in her first screen appearance, as a flightly socialite in 1977's *Julia,* but the following year won an Academy Award nomination for *The Deer Hunter* and an Emmy for the searing NBC miniseries *Holocaust.* Hailed from that point on as "The Actress for the '80s" and "Magic Meryl," Streep, who alternates between blond madonna and almond-eyed ice maiden, proceeded to earn more accolades with her roles in *The Seduction of Joe Tynan, Kramer vs. Kramer* (a Best Supporting Actress Oscar), *The French Lieutenant's Woman,* the riveting *Sophie's Choice* (another Academy Award, this time as Best Actress), and *Silkwood.* She also chalked up a couple of turkeys—chiefly *Still of the Night* and *Falling in Love.* After the tragic death in 1978 of her lover, actor John *(The Godfather, Dog Day Afternoon)* Cazale, from bone cancer, Meryl married New York sculptor Donald Gummer. She backburnered her career to start a family, and one year later, little Henry Gummer was born by cesarean. Critics were in ecstasy over Streep's flawless portrayal of a woman slowly going mad in the film version of *Plenty,* even more lavish in their praise for her Oscar-nominated work opposite Robert Redford in *Out of Africa* and Jack Nicholson in *Heartburn.*

Born: June 22, 1949, in Summit, New Jersey
Height: 5 ft. 6 in.
Weight: 115 lbs.
Eyes: Blue *Hair:* Blond
Zodiac: Gemini
Education: Vassar, Yale Drama School
Religion: Protestant
Marriages: To Donald Gummer (1978–)
Children: Henry (b. 1979), Mary Willa (b. 1983), Grace (b. 1986)
Interests: Reading, art, women's rights (ERA supporter)
Personal Habits and Traits: Straightforward, no-nonsense, candid, fights for her turf, rides the subways
Address: New York City; Litchfield County, Connecticut
Income: $2 million per film

Barbra Streisand

"When I sing, people shut up."

"The greatest star by far" endured a typical Brooklyn Jewish girlhood steeped in endless talk about the Dodgers and young doctors who would make good catches. But the aggressively determined Streisand went to work in a Chinese restaurant so she could escape and study acting, then broke through easily in the supporting role of Miss Marmelstein in Broadway's *I Can Get It for You Wholesale*. In her very first leading stage role as Fanny Brice in *Funny Girl,* a superstar was born, and La Streisand was on her way to becoming the number-one performer of her generation, with hit recordings ("Happy Days Are Here Again," "People," "Sam You Made the Pants Too Long," "Second-Hand Rose"), and Emmy-winning television specials *(My Name Is Barbra).* Then Streisand set out to conquer Hollywood, and beginning with her Academy Award-winning performance in the 1967 *Funny Girl* screen version (she shared her Oscar with Katharine Hepburn, who tied for *The Lion in Winter),* she climbed to the country's number-one movie box-office attraction through such a fare as *Hello, Dolly!, On a Clear Day You Can See Forever, The Owl and the Pussycat, Up the Sandbox, The Way We Were, What's Up, Doc?,* and *For Pete's Sake*. By the time hairdresser Jon Peters arranged to meet her in 1973, Streisand had long since shed husband Elliott Gould and finished her dalliances with Canadian Prime Minister Pierre Trudeau and *What's Up* costar Ryan O'Neal. Peters, three years her junior, became Streisand's man and together they plotted the movie project on which both their careers would ride—a rock 'n' roll remake of the classic *A Star Is Born,* with Kris Kristofferson as her costar. The film was released in December of 1976 and was invariably panned, but nonetheless managed to turn a handsome profit for odd couple Streisand and Peters, as well as land Barbra her second Oscar—this time as the composer of the movie's love theme, "Evergreen." After a lengthy absence from the Top 40, Streisand had returned by spinning out gold records like "The Way We Were," and "My Heart Belongs to Me." Teaming up with O'Neal once again in *The Main Event,* Streisand had another box-office smash on her hands—as well as a disco hit with the title tune. Her collaborations with Neil Diamond and Donna Summer produced number-one hits ("You Don't Bring Me Flowers" and "No More Tears," respectively), but they paled in comparison to the success she shared with Barry Gibb on their album *Guilty*. The LP spun off several smash singles, most notably "Woman in Love." Streisand's live-in relationship with Peters provided plenty of grist for the rumor mill as she set out to film *Yentl.* But she shrugged off gossip that his Svengali-like hold on her bound them together: "I'll settle for people enjoying my work—and my friends enjoying me." Indeed, Peters's hold proved temporary; after her critically and commercially successful *Yentl* (which she co-wrote, produced, directed, and starred in) was frozen out of the running for an Academy Award, Streisand dumped Peters for Baskin-Robbins ice cream heir Richard Baskin, a composer-arranger *(Nashville)* eight years her junior. Returning to her roots,

Streisand pleased her fans once again by releasing *The Broadway Album* containing the ethereal hit single, "Somewhere."

Born: April 24, 1942, in Brooklyn, New York
Height: 5 ft. 4½ in.
Weight: 124 lbs.
Eyes: Blue *Hair:* Reddish blond
Zodiac: Taurus
Education: High school
Religion: Jewish
Marriages: To Elliott Gould (1963–1969)
Children: Jason (b. 1967)
Interests: Directing, acting, producing, antiques, health foods, gardening
Personal Habits and Traits: Does not smoke, drinks wine, a perfectionist, up by 6 A.M.
Address: Malibu, California
Income: $12 million+

Sally Struthers

"Acting is cheap group therapy, being a schizo 50 different ways. And we're paid!"

Sally Struthers grew up in Portland, Oregon, the daughter of a doctor and his Norwegian-American wife. Despite the fact that she sported a silver front tooth, needed to wear corrective shoes and suffered from a kidney ailment that required her to carry a thermos of medicine to class, she excelled in almost everything at high school. Struthers was an excellent student, the captain of the cheerleading squad and founder of the girls' track team—but the lingering effects of her parents' traumatic divorce left her unwilling to enroll in college and pursue her girlhood dream of becoming a physician. Instead "Samantha Featherhead," as Sally's mother called her, joined the fabled Pasadena Playhouse and was promptly voted best all-around actress. To make ends meet she scrubbed washrooms, sold popcorn in a movie theater and played a musical pogo stick with the Spike Jones, Jr., Band until guest shots on the *Smothers Brothers Comedy Hour* secured her several small movie parts. In her third film, *Five Easy Pieces,* Struthers turned in a scene-stealing if torrid performance that caught the eye of Norman Lear. Cast as Gloria opposite "Meathead" Michael Stivic (Rob Reiner), Struthers soon became a favorite on America's number-one television show. In 1974, after four seasons and one Emmy (a tie with Valerie Harper), she spread her professional wings and tackled a Las Vegas nightclub act. Four seasons later the Stivics moved out of Chez Bunker so that Reiner could pursue his own series on ABC and Struthers would be free to do the same on CBS. As she wound up her last season in 1977, Struthers married Dr. William C. Rader, psychiatrist and noted authority on teenage alcoholism, then stepped out of character long enough to play a gun moll in Sam Peckinpah's *The Getaway*. Struthers shed Rader at about the same time her own series first aired. It lasted two seasons, and Struthers then plunged into her work for the nondenominational

Christian Children's Fund. Struthers scored her first Broadway hit in the 1985 revival of Neil Simon's *The Odd Couple*.

Born: July 28, 1948, in Portland, Oregon
Height: 5 ft. 1½ in.
Weight: 110 lbs.
Eyes: Blue *Hair:* Blond
Zodiac: Leo
Education: High school
Religion: Protestant
Marriages: To Dr. William C. Rader (1977–)
Children: Samantha (b. 1979)
Interests: Singing, acting, psychiatry, the Christian Children's Fund
Personal Habits and Traits: Chain-smokes, drinks moderately, a junk food junkie
Address: Brentwood, California
Income: $470,000 (minimum estimate)

Donna Summer

La Donna Andrea Gaines

''My objective is simple: to make people feel warm.''

Donna Summer moaned and groaned her way to gold on the explicitly erotic ''Love to Love You Baby'' (22 climaxes—count 'em) and the equally orgasmic ''Theme from The Deep,'' but the Queen of Disco has also proved that her talents extend far beyond the prurient with ''I Feel Love,'' ''The Last Dance,'' the sizzler ''Hot Stuff,'' ''Bad Girls,'' ''Dim All the Lights,'' ''On the Radio,'' and ''The Wanderer.'' One of a Boston butcher's six daughters, Summer was 10 when she subbed for the soloist at her church and discovered that she could sock it to the congregation with her mighty vocal chords. Later appearing in the Munich company of *Hair,* she decided to remain in Germany when she failed to land a job replacing Melba Moore in the Broadway production. Over the next seven years she recorded a few European hits and scored as a successful model, though it took her outrageous, banned-on-the-BBC ''Love to Love You'' to capture the attention of American audiences. Following a brief marriage to the Austrian who fathered her daughter, Mimi, Summer moved into a hilltop Beverly Hills estate with German surrealist painter Peter Mühldorfer on her return to the U.S. in 1976, then two years later left him for guitarist Bruce Sudano of the group *Brooklyn Dreams.* Among her biggest-selling singles: ''The Last Dance,'' which Summer performed in the *Saturday Night Fever* rip-off *Thank God It's Friday,* and her smash disco version of Jimmy Webb's unusual ''MacArthur Park.'' Her *Bad Girls* album was one of the decade's most successful, and Summer made recording history by teaming with Barbra Streisand on the single ''No More Tears (Enough Is Enough),'' the first female duet ever to make it to number one. ''She Works Hard for the Money,'' but Summer surprised many fans who remember the orgasmic ''Love to Love You'' by becoming a vocal born-again Christian.

Born: December 31, 1948, in Boston, Massachusetts
Height: 5 ft. 7 in.
Weight: 115 lbs.
Eyes: Brown *Hair:* Black
Zodiac: Capricorn
Education: High school
Religion: Baptist
Marriages:
To Helmut Sommer (divorced in 1974)
To Bruce Sudano (1980–)
Children: Mimi (b. 1973)
Interests: Astrology, singing, acting, dancing, art, clothes
Personal Habits and Traits: Independent, ambitious, hates housework, enjoys partying, born-again Christian
Address: Beverly Hills
Income: $1.5 million (minimum estimate)

David Susskind

"After years of dealing with their tantrums and their egos, I have come to one conclusion: actors are children."

David Susskind was born in Brookline, Massachusetts, and was a straight-A student who became president of his high school debating team and went on to graduate *cum laude* from Harvard in 1942. He spent World War II in the Navy, and later worked as a press agent for Universal, Warner Brothers and MCA. In 1952 he broke away and set up his own production company that over the years evolved into Talent Associates Ltd., a venture that more than justified its name under Susskind's direction by bankrolling films *(A Raisin in the Sun, Network),* plays *(Rashomon),* and television shows (dramatic specials like *Harvey, All the Way Home, The Power and the Glory,* Arthur Miller's *The Price,* and hit sitcoms like CBS's *On Our Own).* In 1977 Time Incorporated bought Talent Associates, and Susskind moved his headquarters to the Time-Life Building in Rockefeller Center (that arrangement lasted barely three years). However, to most people, the gray-haired Susskind is known as the host of his own absorbing television talk show, grinning incredulously as he listens to the famous (like Nikita Khrushchev and Dean Rusk) and obscure (criminals revealing prison conditions, physicians discussing malpractice, nutritionists, astrologers, etc.). After being married for 25 years to Phyllis Briskin, Susskind divorced her in 1965 to marry Canadian broadcaster Joyce Davidson in 1966. That lasted not quite as long—a mere 16 years.

Born: December 19, 1920, in Brookline, Massachusetts
Height: 5 ft. 7 in.
Weight: 150 lbs.
Eyes: Blue *Hair:* White
Zodiac: Sagittarius
Education: Harvard University, B.A. in 1942
Religion: Jewish
Marriages:
To Phyllis Briskin (1940–1965)
To Joyce Davidson (1966–1982)
Children: A son, two daughters (by Briskin); a daughter (by Davidson)
Interests: Producing, literature, politics, art, music
Personal Habits and Traits: Does not smoke, a social drinker, is impatient, a fiendish worker
Address: New York City
Income: $400,000+ (minimum estimate)

Donald Sutherland

"Early in my career I was in my dressing room making up. Suddenly, I turned around and there was this totally naked woman. 'What's the matter, darling?' Tallulah Bankhead said. 'Haven't you ever seen a blond before?'"

From the wiseacre surgeon in *M*A*S*H* to Karen Black's florid and ineffectual husband in *The Day of the Locust* to the legendary lecher in Fellini's monumental *Casanova,* Donald Sutherland has managed to overcome his early antihero image as just another not-so-pretty face through tackling demanding and varied roles. A native of St. John, New Brunswick, the lanky, bellows-voiced Sutherland studied engineering at the University of Toronto, then acted in theater workshops before *M*A*S*H* propelled both him and Elliott Gould to stardom in 1969. Other Sutherland efforts: *Act of the Heart, Kelly's Heroes, Little Murders, Alex in Wonderland, Klute,* the chilling *Don't Look Now, The Eagle Has Landed, 1900, A Bridge Too Far, Ordinary People, Invasion of the Body Snatchers,* and *The Eye of the Needle*. Onstage, he thrilled some and outraged others as Humbert Humbert in Edward Albee's adaptation of the Vladimir Nabokov novel *Lolita.* Now, after two failed marriages, he lives with dark-haired French-Canadian actress Francine Racette six months of the year; his home is in Los Angeles and hers in Paris. They have a young son named Roeg (after film director Nicholas Roeg) and have occasionally worked together in films like *Alien Thunder* and *The Disappearance*.

Born: July 17, 1934, in St. John, New Brunswick
Height: 6 ft. 4 in.
Weight: 185 lbs.
Eyes: Blue *Hair:* Blond
Zodiac: Cancer
Education: University of Toronto, B.A. in engineering; Academy of Music and Dramatic Art, London
Religion: Protestant
Marriages: Two. Both ended in divorce. Currently lives with Francine Racette.
Children: Three by his previous wives; one by Racette
Interests: Politics (he's far to the Left), literature, music
Personal Habits and Traits: Chain-smokes, not a teetotaler
Addresses: Los Angeles; Paris
Income: $400,000 per film

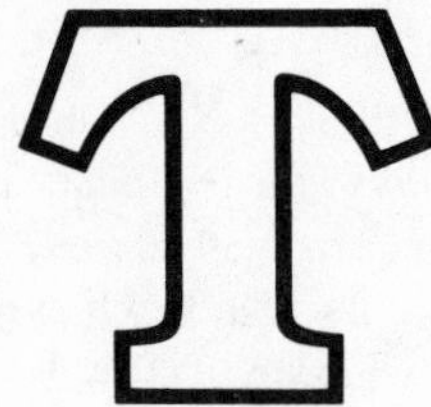

Mr. T

Lawrence Tureaud

"I don't do Shakespeare. I don't talk in that kind of broken English."

Pity the fool who doesn't recognize the Mandinka hairdo, the scowl, and the muscles draped in 23 pounds of gold chains. Lawrence Tureaud was only 15 when his father walked out, leaving his mama to raise Lawrence and her other 11 children in the Chicago ghetto—which explains why he is a devoted daddy to his own daughter Lesa, born out of wedlock in 1971. During his childhood, Tureaud says, "the only meals I remember were oatmeal, miss a meal, and no meal." A football star in college, he attended Texas A&M on an athletic scholarship but was expelled after less than a year because, he claims, he wouldn't identify classmates who had taken part in a campus riot. After serving in the National Guard as an MP, he billed himself as "Mr. T, the World's Greatest Bodyguard," and charged between $2,000 and $10,000 a day to look menacing standing next to Michael Jackson, Mick Jagger, Muhammad Ali, and other celebrities. Spotted by Sylvester Stallone participating in a "World's Greatest Bouncer" competition, Mr. T was cast as Sly's nemesis in 1981's *Rocky III,* and was soon costarring in NBC's T-rashy *A-Team* series (the bloodiest on TV) and the film *D.C. Cab.* Amazingly, Mr. T somehow managed to become a role model for kids, urging them in public service announcements, through his Saturday morning *Mr. T* cartoon show and during personal appearances around the country to play by the rules, stay in school, avoid drugs, and obey their parents. His siblings, however, were mightily T-eed off by his 1984 autobiography and claimed that he had reneged on public promises to help his mother out of her dilapidated rental house and that "he tells lies every time he's interviewed." With an annual income that easily topped $1 million by the mid-1980s, Mr. T divides his time between a high-rise apartment in Chicago and another in Westwood that he decorated himself. "All my life," he told *People,* "I always wanted a canopy bed."

Born: May 31, 1952, in Chicago
Height: 5 ft. 11 in.
Weight: 219 lbs.
Eyes: Brown *Hair:* Black
Zodiac: Gemini
Education: Texas A&M, one year
Religion: Protestant
Marriages: None
Children: One, Lesa (b. 1971)
Interests: Spreading the gospel (Mr. T is a born-again Christian), children, wrestling
Personal Habits and Traits: Goes to bed early, sleeps late, starts his days with 100 situps, 100 pushups and weight training, nonsmoker, teetotaler, wears more than 20 pounds of gold chains, 10 rings, and seven earrings, all reportedly worth over $300,000
Addresses: Westwood; Los Angeles; Chicago
Income: $1 million+

Elizabeth Taylor

"I don't think of John as Husband Number Seven. He's Number One all the way—the best lover I've ever had." (About John Warner shortly before their divorce)

Life magazine's champion cover girl (11 times over 25 years) launched her career as the angelic child star of *National Velvet* and wound up acquiring six husbands, two Academy Awards (for *Butterfield 8* and *Who's Afraid of Virginia Woolf?*), and the most public private life in the world. Born in London, Liz actually appeared in several films including *Jane Eyre* before Enid Bagnold's tale about the high-spirited young girl who takes the Grand National established her stardom on screen. After studying for eight years at MGM's famous studio school she graduated from Westwood's University High at eighteen. Soon touted as the most beautiful woman in the world, the raven-haired, lavender-eyed actress proved that she could also act in such movies as *A Place in the Sun* (1950), *Cat on a Hot Tin Roof* (1958), *Cleopatra* (1962), *The Taming of the Shrew* (1967), and *Night Watch* (1973). Yet Taylor's frail health (she has endured slipped discs, a tracheotomy, and a hysterectomy) was viewed by many as the primary reason she received her first Oscar; she almost succumbed to pneumonia shortly before the Academy rewarded her for the leading role in *Butterfield 8* in 1960. However, there was no doubt seven years later about bestowing an Oscar on Taylor for her brilliant performance as the self-destructive shrew Martha in *Who's Afraid of Virginia Woolf?* Still, Taylor's professional career cannot compete with her riotous marital life. Conrad Hilton's playboy son Nicky became Mr. Elizabeth Taylor Number 1, followed by British actor Michael Wilding, producer Michael Todd (it ended when he died in a plane crash), crooner Eddie Fisher, Richard Burton (twice), and finally Virginia Republican politician John Warner. Her explosive relationship with Burton kept tongues wagging for 15 years—from the time they carried on a scandalous extramarital affair on the set of *Cleopatra* to their second and final divorce in 1976. During their marriage Burton and Taylor lived like royalty, collecting yachts, $50,000 sable coats, palatial homes in Mexico, Switzerland and on the French Riviera, and a king's ransom in jewelry that included the $1.2 million pear-shaped Cartier diamond (at that time the highest price in history for such a single privately owned gem). When Burton suddenly married English model Suzy Hunt, Taylor turned to pal Henry Wynberg, but wound up marrying Virginia aristocrat Warner. After another of her screen disasters, 1977's *A Little Night Music,* Liz decided to settle down back on the Warners' Virginia estate and ease into the low-key life of a Southern politician's helpmate. Taylor's skills as a campaigner apparently paid off, for Warner was elected to the U.S. Senate by the slimmest of margins in 1978. Liz soon grew restless; she starred onscreen in *The Mirror Crack'd* and on Broadway in the smash 1981 revival of Lillian Hellman's *The Little Foxes.* Taylor then jettisoned the Senator, and was engaged to Mexican millionaire Victor Luna before going back to playing the field with the likes of Carl Bernstein and New Yorker Dennis Stein. She also managed to get in a little work between romances: a stint on her favorite soap, *General Hospital;* an HBO movie, *Between Friends* (with Carol Burnett); the made-for-TV movie *Malice in Wonderland* and the miniseries *North and South.* Before taking on the *Malice* assignment, Liz checked into the Betty Ford clinic in Palm Springs to get control of her drinking, and emerged not only sober but svelte—and with a new pack-a-day habit. Nor had she broken another habit; with buddy George Hamilton cast in the role of matchmaker, Liz fell in love yet again—this time with Sir Gordon White.

Born: February 27, 1932, in London, England
Height: 5 ft. 6 in.
Weight: 125 lbs.
Eyes: Lavender *Hair:* Black
Zodiac: Pisces
Education: High school
Religion: Jewish (a convert)
Marriages:
To Nicky Hilton (divorced)
To Michael Wilding (divorced)
To Michael Todd (widowed)
To Eddie Fisher (divorced)
To Richard Burton (divorced)
To Richard Burton (remarried and divorced)
To John Warner (divorced)
Children: Michael Wilding (b. 1953), Christopher Wilding (b. 1954); Liza Todd (b. 1957); Maria Burton (b. 1961, adopted); one grandchild
Interests: Horses, jewels, art, music, dance, fashion, politics, cooking
Personal Habits and Traits: On the wagon, but long given to eating and dieting binges, has an explosive temper, chain-smokes
Address: Beverly Hills
Income: $1 million (minimum estimate)

James Taylor

''I like success almost as much as I dislike it. I find comfort in earthquakes and eclipses—in fatalism and inevitablity.''

Rock's Sweet Baby James survived an addiction to heroin and a grueling bout with suicidal despair before rebounding to the top with his *Handy Man* album in 1978. The son of an independently wealthy, Scottish Southern doctor and his Yankee, lyric soprano wife, James, along with brothers Livingston and Alex and

his sister Kate, studied violin, cello and piano while growing up near Chapel Hill, North Carolina, and on Martha's Vineyard. At 15 James won a hootenanny contest and throughout his teens performed with Livingston on harmonica and guitar at local community center square dances. Miserable at Milton Academy, his depression devolved into suicidal psychosis and at 17 he signed himself into a mental hospital, eventually graduating from the hospital high school. After nine months he headed for New York, where he knocked around Village bars and cafes as composer-vocalist and lead guitarist for a band called the Flying Machines. He also became dependent on heroin and fled again, this time to London, where he was spotted by singer-turned-producer Peter Asher (formerly of Peter and Gordon) and signed to a contract with Apple Records. A year later he switched to Warner Brothers and upon his return to the United States promptly landed in another mental hospital. Asher helped pull him through that crisis, and the result was the landmark album *Sweet Baby James,* containing a string of hit singles like the poignant and autobiographical "Fire and Rain," "Don't Let Me Be Lonely Tonight," and "Mockingbird" with Carly Simon. After a highly publicized affair with folk singer Joni Mitchell, Taylor married Simon in 1972, then began a long slide back into heroin addiction. And not until seven years later, with Carly's help, did he fully overcome his drug dependence and resurface professionally with his *JT, Handy Man* and *Flag* albums. His hit single "It Used to Be Her Town" told the poignant story of his 1981 divorce from Simon. Taylor appeared headed for the altar once more in 1985, this time with actress Kathryn Walker—at about the same time his career rebounded with the long-awaited *That's Why I'm Here* album. The first cut from the album to make the charts: a remake of the Buddy Holly classic "Every Day" followed by *Only One*. James Taylor wed Kathryn Walker in December 1985 just as "Every Day" climbed the charts.

Born: March 12, 1948, in Boston, Massachusetts
Height: 6 ft. 3 in.
Weight: 157 lbs.
Eyes: Brown *Hair:* Brown
Zodiac: Pisces
Education: High school
Religion: Protestant
Marriages: To Carly Simon (1972–1981)
Children: Sarah (b. 1973), Benjamin (b. 1976)
Interests: Carpentry (he built his own Cape Cod house on 65 acres at Martha's Vineyard), composing, ecology, American Indians
Personal Habits and Traits: Chain-smokes, drinks, has kicked his heroin habit, irritable, generally quiet
Addresses: New York City; Martha's Vineyard, Massachusetts
Income: $300,000 (together, Taylor and Simon were show business's highest-paid married couple at $2.5 million)

Marlo Thomas

Margaret Thomas

"It's very appealing when a man takes charge of his own life. It should be just as appealing for a woman."

Marlo Thomas finally emerged from her famous father's shadow after conceiving and starring in her own hit TV show *That Girl,* setting up her own production company and building a reputation as one of Hollywood's most formidable personalities. Born in Detroit, she sat in on father Danny's script conferences when still a kid, attended a series of Catholic schools, and then the University of Southern California with the idea of becoming an English teacher. She graduated *cum laude* with a teaching certificate only to plunge headlong into an acting career (aided by a bit of cosmetic surgery that rid her of the Thomas nose) and six years later, after scores of bit parts in summer stock, she was approached by Mike Nichols and offered the lead in the London production of Neil Simon's *Barefoot in the Park.* She returned to America and launched *That Girl* in 1966. When *That Girl* went off the air four seasons later, she immersed herself in liberal Democratic politics as a George McGovern supporter in 1972 and concentrated on producing Emmy-winning specials like *Free to Be . . . You and Me* and 1977's *It Happened One Christmas* (a remake of the Jimmy Stewart tearjerker *It's a Wonderful Life*—with Thomas in the Stewart role). She also starred in the Broadway and movie versions of *Thieves,* an urban comedy by Marlo's love of five years, Herb Gardner. While promoting *Thieves* in 1976, she appeared on the *Phil Donahue Show,* and within a few weeks Chicago-based Donahue and Californian Thomas were conducting a passionate cross-country romance. Yet although she was enthusiastic about their relationship, Thomas was cautious when the subject turned to marriage, an attitude that she admitted stemmed from her mother's decision to forsake her budding career as a radio singer to raise her children. "I like to think," she once said, "that I'm my mother's revenge." In 1980, she threw caution to the wind and married Donahue, and four years later they relocated to Manhattan. That girl delivered a riveting portrayal of a women battling mental illness in the made-for-television movie *Nobody's Child.*

Born: November 21, 1938, in Detroit, Michigan
Height: 5 ft. 5 in.
Weight: 96 lbs.
Eyes: Brown *Hair:* Dark brown
Zodiac: Scorpio
Education: University of Southern California, B.A. in English
Religion: Catholic
Marriages: To Phil Donahue (1980–)
Children: None
Interests: Women's rights, childhood education, filmmaking, Democratic politics
Personal Habits and Traits: Works until dawn, does not cook but is always trying to gain weight, nearly always wears glasses, is a social creature
Addresses: Beverly Hills; New York
Income: $250,000 (minimum estimate)

Cheryl Tiegs

"What if I want to be taken seriously? There's a Farrah Doll, but there's no Phyllis George Doll."

The daughter of an Alhambra, California, undertaker, Cheryl Tiegs always escorted the rest of the family to Sunday Quaker meetings, proved a good student, a fair violinist and—not surprisingly—a luscious high school pom-pom girl. A talent agent visited her school when Cheryl was just 16, and soon she graced the covers of *True Romance, Teen* and *Seventeen.* At 19 Tiegs abandoned college—and her plans to major in English at Cal State's Los Angeles campus—for New York City. Far from becoming an instant modeling superstar, Tiegs quit the business and returned to Los Angeles after she married adman-turned-film director *(Love at First Bite)* Stan Dragoti (who in 1979 was busted for cocaine possession). Leading a housewife's life, her weight quickly ballooned to 155. Suddenly spurred on by a photograph of a model in a bathing suit she resolutely dropped 35 pounds within a year and signed up with model agent Eileen Ford. Farrah Fawcett's prime challenger as queen of the California look, Tiegs has become one of the most sought-after and highest-paid (more than $700,000 a year) models in history. Her marriage was not as solid as her career, however, and while filming an ABC special in Africa she fell for photographer Peter Beard. Still, Tiegs steadfastly stood behind Dragoti during his cocaine ordeal. In May 1981, Tiegs married Beard. Their marriage soon collapsed, and Tiegs took up with Gregory Peck's handsome young son Tony.

Born: 1947 in Alhambra, California
Height: 5 ft. 10 in.
Weight: 120 lbs.
Eyes: Blue *Hair:* Blond
Education: California State at Los Angeles, dropped out after two years
Religion: Quaker

Marriages:
To Stan Dragoti (1970–1980)
To Peter Beard (1981–1984)
Children: None
Interests: Tennis, swimming
Habits: Nonsmoker, moderate drinker, perpetual dieter
Address: Bel Air, California
Income: $700,000 (minimum estimate)

Lily Tomlin

Mary Jean Tomlin

"Reality is just a crutch for people who can't deal with drugs."

She is America's reigning female comic genius—and, as Edith Ann would say, "that's the truth." Mary Jean Tomlin was the daughter of a heavy-drinking factory worker in Detroit. She studied English at Wayne State University before moving to New York and a job as a secretary to a casting director. Tomlin broke

in her unique comedy routines at Upstairs at the Downstairs, the now defunct Manhattan nightclub, while appearing off-Broadway in *Arf* and *The Great Airplane Snatch*. Then, after guesting on Merv Griffin, she landed a part on *Laugh-In* in 1969. Over the next four years Tomlin's characters—Ernestine, Ma Bell's snorting switchboard emissary ("Is this the party to whom I am speaking?"), as well as sassy 5-year-old Edith Ann and pompom-wielding Suzy Sorority—transformed the unknown comedienne into a national phenomenon. Turning down a flat $500,000 offer from Bell Telephone to "buy" Ernestine for TV commercials, Tomlin has collected Emmys for her TV specials, flourished on the big screen in *Nashville* and *The Late Show* (for which she won an Oscar nomination), and scored a solo triumph on Broadway in *Appearing Nightly,* which earned her a special Tony and grossed about $2 million in box-office receipts after a five-city tour. But *Moment by Moment,* a tearjerker in which she played the older woman in John Travolta's life (supposedly mirroring his romance with the late Diana Hyland), was unanimously panned by critics and audiences alike. She fared better in *9 to 5,* and her sci-fi sendup *The Incredible Shrinking Woman*. Tomlin's most memorable movie portrayal was that of the deceased spinster, Edwina Cuttwater, who occupies half of Steve Martin's body in *All of Me*. In 1985 she opened on Broadway in *The Search for Intelligent Life in the Universe*.

Born: September 1, 1937, in Detroit, Michigan
Height: 5 ft. 9 in.
Weight: 118 lbs.
Eyes: Brown *Hair:* Dark brown
Zodiac: Virgo
Education: Wayne State University
Religion: Protestant
Marriages: None
Children: None
Interests: Writing, acting
Personal Habits and Traits: Smokes, drinks socially, likes to stand on her head, is as crazy as she seems
Address: Beverly Hills
Income: $1.5 million (estimate)

Daniel J. Travanti

"Everything's come out all right despite me, thank God."

This King of the *Hill Street Blues,* the son of Italian immigrants, is a recovered alcoholic who used to guzzle a bottle of vodka a day. A superachiever in his early years—straight-A student, high school football star, Phi Beta Kappa at the University of Wisconsin, a fellowship to Yale Drama School—Travanti started boozing because underneath it all he was "deeply insecure." It didn't help that he could only get bit parts on TV series or supporting roles on stage. He finally hit the wall in Indianapolis in 1973 while touring with Sada Thompson in *Twigs*. He actually began shaking in the middle of the scene, apologized to the audience, and walked off before bursting into tears. He joined Alcoholics Anonymous and started afresh. Having beaten the bottle, he earned his masters at L.A.'s Loyola Marymount University, and then tried acting again—this time as Spence Andrews in the soap *General Hospital*. Travanti brought his own experience to the role of hard-nosed Captain Frank Furillo in *Hill Street Blues;* Furillo is also a recovered alcoholic. Gritty *Hill Street* was nearly canceled its first season due to competition from *Fantasy Island,* but the series went on to become one of the most popular and honored shows in television history. Along the way, Travanti, often romantically (but inaccurately) linked with costar Veronica Hamel, picked up two Emmys and found time to deliver a shattering performance in the TV movie *Adam,* based on the disappearance and brutal murder of a 6-year-old Florida boy, Adam Walsh. *Adam* focused national attention on the problem of missing children, and actually led to the discovery of several.

Born: March 7, 1940, in Kenosha, Wisconsin
Height: 6 ft.
Weight: 188 lbs.
Eyes: Brown *Hair:* Black
Zodiac: Pisces
Education: Master's degree, Loyola Marymount University
Religion: Roman Catholic
Marriages: None
Children: None
Interests: Gardening, cooking, reading, writing short stories, entertaining
Personal Habits and Traits: Gregarious, talkative, obsessed with fitness (spends hours cycling, running and lifting weights; has rowing machine), eschews fried foods, sugar, and salt but is a voracious eater who devours oranges with their peels, apples with their cores, and chickens with their bones
Address: Santa Monica, California
Income: $50,000 per episode (estimate)

John Travolta

''Before I was famous, I had what you would call one-night stands. But I found these are much more exciting in my fantasies than in reality.''

Dubbed the ''street Tyrone Power'' by Hollywood producer-promoter Alan Carr, John Travolta first claimed national attention as sweat hog Vinnie Barbarino in ABC-TV's *Welcome Back, Kotter*—a role that coincided with his success as a recording artist. But Travolta had been striving toward stardom practically his entire life. His mother, Helen, who died from cancer in November 1978, sang as one of the Sunshine Sisters on Hackensack radio during the Depression and joined a local stock company in Englewood, New Jersey, after marrying Salvatore Travolta, a semipro athlete who sold tires to support his wife and six children. The baby of the family, John—whose five siblings are all in show business—was soon imitating Jimmy Cagney in *Yankee Doodle Dandy* to a rapt audience in the Travolta family garage. At 16 he dropped out of high school to shoot commercials, tour (in a minor role) with the road company of the Broadway musical *Grease*—six years later he starred in the screen version for a neat $1 million—and spend eight months in the Broadway production of the Andrew Sisters' hit *Over Here!* As a fledgling trying to break into films, Travolta lost out on a part in *The Last Detail* and settled for a secondary role in the telekinetic hair-

raiser *Carrie,* but when he stepped before the cameras to portray a dead-end disco king in *Saturday Night Fever* the result was instant superstardom and international sex symbol status. His much publicized relationship with Diana Hyland, an accomplished actress 18 years his senior, ended tragically when she died in Travolta's arms after losing her battle with breast cancer while he was filming *Saturday Night Fever* in 1976. *Fever* also brought its 22-year-old star a Best Actor Academy Award nomination (Richard Dreyfuss wound up snagging the prize for *The Goodbye Girl).* Travolta then tried to shed his street-kid image also evident in *Grease* (the top grosser of 1978 with box office receipts of over $125 million) by acting opposite Lily Tomlin in the disastrous *Moment by Moment.* Two years later, he was ready to rebound in *Urban Cowboy.* Now ensconced in a West Hollywood penthouse and on his 17-acre Santa Barbara ranch, Travolta has replaced his model airplanes with the real thing—a Constellation, a Citation, and a 550-mph Lockheed JetStar 731. Ironically Travolta, who began taking flying lessons at 16, can no longer pilot a plane while he is working on a movie; his insurance company thinks he is far too precious a commodity—and they're right. On the ground, Travolta tools around in a Jaguar, a Cadillac, a Mercedes, a Thunderbird, a limo or a Rolls. For the *Fever* sequel *Staying Alive,* director Sylvester Stallone helped Travolta develop a physique that was very near *Perfect*—though his next movie of the same name was anything but.

Born: February 18, 1954, in Englewood, New Jersey
Height: 6 ft.
Weight: 168 lbs.
Eyes: Blue *Hair:* Dark brown
Zodiac: Aquarius
Education: High school dropout
Religion: Roman Catholic
Marriages: None
Children: None
Interests: Airplanes
Personal Habits and Traits: Nonsmoker (except for an occasional cigar), nondrinker, a junk-food junkie (favorite foods: guacamole, tuna melt sandwiches, hot fudge sundaes), starstruck, loves to impersonate male and female stars, no known romantic interests
Address: West Hollywood, California
Income: $2 million (minimum estimate)

Ted Turner

"One summer I made $50 a week, and my father charged me $25 a week rent. I asked him if that wasn't a little high. He said that if I could do better than that for food and lodging seven days a week I could move out."

Even before he made an unsuccessful power play for CBS in 1985 (and a successful one for MGM in 1986), the "Mouth of the South" has every right to brag about his accomplishments: after his father shot himself in despair over his declining fortunes, Ted inherited the family billboard business at age 24 and pyramided it into a conglomerate that includes the Cable News Network, numerous radio and television stations, the Atlanta Braves baseball team, and the Atlanta Hawks basketball team. A champion yachtsman, he also managed to win the America's Cup in 1977. Turner was a standout even back at Brown University, where he was kicked out of his fraternity for burning down the homecoming display; he finally left the school altogether following two suspensions. A bombastic, tobacco-chewing good ole boy, Turner once attended a conference on arms control in Atlanta alongside Jimmy Carter and other dignitaries, and when he became bored, pulled a tiny TV from his pocket and switched on a Braves game. Despite his tremendous success, Turner still seems haunted by the memory of his father, who often used a wire coat hanger on him ("to get my attention") and charged his student son rent for the time he spent at home during summer vacation. He is also obsessed by the violence of Turner, Sr.'s violent death. "He talks about death incessantly," says a friend. "Over the years, killing himself was a high-priority topic of conversation. Most of the time he was flippant about it. He would talk in this joking way about how, if things did not work out, he could always sell the business, how all he needed was a roof over his head and some food. Then he would say, 'If things get really bad, I can always kill myself.' He could not go several days without talking about suicide."

Born: November 19, 1938, in Cincinnati, Ohio
Height: 5 ft. 11 in.
Weight: 175 lbs.
Eyes: Blue *Hair:* Gray
Zodiac: Scorpio
Education: Brown University
Religion: Baptist
Marriages: Twice. Currently to Jane Smith (1964–)
Children: Laura Lee, Robert Edward 4th, Beauregard, Rhett, and Jennie
Interests: Baseball, basketball, yachting, broadcasting, conservative political causes
Personal Habits and Traits: Drinks beer, aquavit, chews tobacco, smokes cigars, workaholic, can be loud, raucous
Address: Marietta, Georgia
Income: $300 million (estimate of net worth)

Tina Turner

Anna Mae Bullock Turner

"Physical strength in a woman—that's what I am."

Rock's soul survivor and comeback queen grew up the daughter of a Brownsville, Tennessee, sharecropper. After her parents' divorce, she eventually went to live with her mother in St. Louis. There, while still in high school, she started singing with a young Missisippian named Ike Turner and his Kings of Rhythm band. Soon she was pregnant—not by Ike, but by another band member who promptly split. Anna Mae supported herself and her infant son with a hospital job and weekend gigs, until Ike persuaded her to change her name to Tina and join his band on the road full-time. By the time they were married in 1964, they had a son of their own; Ike's two sons by a previous relationship were also raised by Tina. Over the next several years, the Ike and Tina Turner Revue became a pop phenomenon, largely due to Tina's gyrating, mane-tossing wild-woman onstage persona. She taught Mick Jagger how to move when the ITT Revue toured with the Rolling Stones in 1966, and recorded such hits as "River Deep Mountain High," "Proud Mary," and "Come Together." But at home her life with Ike, who had also become involved with one of the "Ikette" backup singers, was marred by violence. After one particularly severe beating that took place in the back of a limo, Tina sneaked out of their Dallas hotel room with only 36 cents in her pocket and a Mobil credit card in her wallet. She spent the next eight years building a new life for herself, singing in Las Vegas and at suburban supper clubs to pay off hundreds of thousands of dollars of debt that resulted from the duo's broken concert dates. She was broke and actually on food stamps for a time, but by 1983 Tina was pumping those nonstop legs alongside the Stones and Rod Stewart during their concert tours. She scored a hit with "Let's Stay Together" in early 1984, yet it would take the updated, toned-downed sound of her *Private Dancer* album to propel Tina Turner to the top of the charts. One of the cuts off the album, the ballad "What's Love Got to Do With It?," gave the singer her first number-one hit, quickly followed by "You Better Be Good to Me" and the single "Private Dancer." Turner walked away with two Grammys in 1985, as well as a whole new audience for her videos. A full decade after her auspicious movie debut as the Acid Queen in *Tommy,* Turner was also getting another chance at movie stardom playing Auntie Entity, proprietress of a post-apocalyptic Dodge City, opposite Mel Gibson in *Mad Max III* (from which she spun off her hit single "We Don't Need Another Hero"). The Tina behind the raunch is a devout Buddhist and, to quote her tongue-in-cheek ads for a ladies magazine, "one of the drab Homebodies who reads *McCall's.*"

Born: November 26, 1938, in Nutbush, Tennessee
Height: 5 ft. 4 in.
Weight: 118 lbs.
Eyes: Brown *Hair:* Reddish
Zodiac: Sagittarius
Education: High school
Religion: Buddhist
Marriages: To Ike Turner (1964–1976)
Children: Four
Interests: Buddhism, astrology, and the occult, reading
Personal Habits and Traits: Chants at least a half-hour most days at her home Butsudan shrine, a vegetarian, nonsmoker, nondrinker, anti-drug
Address: Los Angeles
Income: $5 million+

Peter Ustinov

"I've always been too intrigued by life itself to shut any of the windows. The point of living, and of being an optimist, is to be foolish enough to believe the best is yet to come."

This protean actor, novelist, playwright, producer, director, wit, and bon vivant was born in London to a distinguished German correspondent of Russian descent and his artist wife—nine months to the day after their wedding. Not a "particularly happy child," young Peter spent his years at the exclusive Westminster School mimicking his teachers and employing his ample girth to block soccer goals before enrolling at Michel St. Denis's London Theatre Studio. There he wrote, directed and acted in plays before joining the Army in 1940 for service in World War II. He remained a private for four and a half years, but nonetheless worked with the likes of David Niven and Garson Kanin on propaganda movies. Appropriately, Ustinov's first big hit was *The Love of Four Colonels,* which won the New York Drama Critics' Award as Best Play of 1952. Four years later he made his Broadway acting debut in the equally well received *Romanoff and Juliet* (earning two Tonys for Best Play and Performance). Taking on Hollywood, the corpulent actor starred with Humphrey Bogart in *We're No Angels,* fiddled as Nero in *Quo Vadis,* bagged two Oscars for his supporting roles in 1961's *Spartacus* and 1964's *Topkapi,* received an Emmy for his portrayal of Dr. Samuel Johnson on television's *Omnibus,* and even copped a Grammy for his narration of the LP *Peter and the Wolf.* Though his first love is still writing (to background music with a felt pen), Ustinov has not forsaken his acting career. He was a despicable Herod in TV's controversial *Jesus of Nazareth,* kept movie audiences doubled over as the one-legged Foreign Legion sergeant in Marty Feldman's spoof *The Last Remake of Beau Geste,* and sleuthed as Hercule Poirot in *Death on the Nile.* Fluent in English, German, French, and Italian, and passable in Russian and Spanish, he retains a British passport but lives in Paris and Switzerland with his third wife, Paris-born Hélène du Lau d'Allemans.

Previously married to Isolde Denham, Angela Lansbury's half sister, and French-Canadian actress Suzanne Cloutier, Ustinov owns a vineyard at his Geneva estate that yields 4,000 bottles of wine each year, drives a 1968 Maserati and a 1934 Hispano-Suiza, and cruises the Mediterranean in a 58-foot yacht christened *Nitchevo* (Russian for "nothing"). Ustinov's 1977 autobiography, *Dear Me,* proved an instant international bestseller. Ustinov turned increasingly to interviewing; Prime Minister Indira Gandhi of India was walking to her interview with Ustinov when she was assassinated by her Sikh bodyguards in 1984.

Born: April 16, 1921, in London, England
Height: 5 ft. 11½ in.
Weight: 222 lbs.
Eyes: Brown *Hair:* Gray-white
Zodiac: Aries
Education: High school dropout
Religion: Agnostic (Lutheran-Catholic background)
Marriages:
To Isolde Denham (1940–1947)
To Suzanne Cloutier (1954–1971)
To Hélène du Lau d'Allemans (1972–)
Children: Tamara (b. 1946) by Denham; Pavla (b. 1954), Igor (b. 1957), Andrea (b. 1959) by Cloutier
Interests: UNICEF and UNESCO, tennis, swimming, yachting, art, languages and dialects, Mozart
Personal Habits and Traits: Smokes one or two Havana cigars each day; an oenophile (wines and wine-making)
Addresses: Geneva; Paris
Income: $400,000 (estimate)

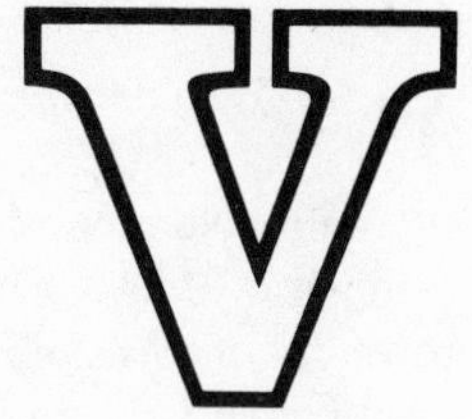

Abigail Van Buren

Pauline "Popo" Esther Friedman

"It's a sad commentary on our times when our young must seek advice and counsel from 'Dear Abby' instead of going to Mom and Dad."

She began writing her advice column just a few months after twin sister Ann Landers began hers, and ever since their competition has been professionally fierce. On a personal level, however, Pauline "Popo" Esther Friedman and her sister Esther "Eppie" Pauline are as close as they were back in grammar school when they subbed for each other in class—depending on who had done the homework. Now married to millionaire Morton Philips, Abby is syndicated by more than 800 newspapers, marginally fewer than her sister, and—just like her sister—she is against drinking, smoking, and premarital sex. Friedman, who took the name Abigail from the Old Testament and Van Buren from eighth President Martin Van Buren, has a staff of eight to help her handle 10,000 letters per week.

Born: July 4, 1918, in Sioux City, Iowa
Height: 5 ft. 5½ in.
Weight: 121 lbs.
Eyes: Brown *Hair:* Dark brown
Zodiac: Cancer
Education: Morningside College (1936–1939)
Religion: Jewish
Marriages: To Morton Phillips (current)
Children: Two
Interests: Drug abuse, alcoholism, health, teenagers, human relations
Personal Habits and Traits: Nonsmoker, nondrinker, workaholic
Address: Beverly Hills
Income: $500,000 (estimate)

Gore Vidal

Eugene Vidal

"Most writers write books that they wouldn't read. I ought to know; I've done it myself."

Whether getting slugged by archenemy Norman Mailer at a cocktail party, exchanging verbal sniping with William F. Buckley, Jr., or suing Truman Capote for stating that he had been thrown out of a White House party, Gore Vidal can certainly lay claim to being one of the most contentious figures on the American literary scene. Born in West Point, New York, Eugéne Vidal (he changed his first name to Gore in honor of his uncle, Senator Thomas Gore of Oklahoma) was educated at Phillips Exeter and served in the Army for three years before causing a national furor with the publication of his homosexual novel *The City and the Pillar*. The next three decades yielded more bestsellers, including *Washington, D.C., Julian, Blood Kin, Myra Breckinridge, Two Sisters, Myron, Burr, 1876, Khalki, Creation* and *Dubuque*. He also has managed to run unsuccessfully for Congress in New York, experience a brief engagement to actress Joanne Woodward (before she married Paul Newman), and enrage his old friends the Kennedys. Nor did he spare his vitriol when serving up Lyndon Johnson in his 1968 play *Weekend* or another President four years later with Broadway's *An Evening With Richard Nixon*. And in 1978 Vidal decided to reveal that he was the man behind the pseudonym that graced a number of widely read mystery novels, Edgar Box. Having publicly defended bisexuality—Buckley called him a "queer" on television in retaliation for Vidal's labeling him a proto-Nazi—as well as reportedly undergoing a face-lift, Vidal now divides his time between a spacious villa near Rome and a house in Los Angeles, where he announced his intention to run for the Senate in 1982. Instead, he pulled out and wrote another bestseller, *Lincoln*.

Born: October 3, 1925, in West Point, New York
Height: 5 ft. 10 in.
Weight: 185 lbs.
Eyes: Blue *Hair:* Graying
Zodiac: Libra
Education: Phillips Exeter

Marriages: None
Children: None
Interests: Politics, literature, music
Personal Habits and Traits: Nonsmoker, healthy drinker
Address: Rome
Income: $550,000 (minimum estimate)

Jon Voight

"I've learned from my mistakes. Popularity is not the answer. Good honest work is the answer. Then success is real."

Voight grew up in the affluent suburb of Scarsdale, New York, where his father was a golf pro at the Westchester Country Club. He attended Catholic University in Washington, D.C., then studied at New York's Neighborhood Playhouse where he initially hoped to score as a comedian. Gravitating toward straight drama off-Broadway, he met and teamed up with Dustin Hoffman for *Midnight Cowboy.* No sooner did he conquer the screen in 1969 with his Oscar-nominated performance in *Midnight Cowboy* than Voight's career began to unravel, and with the exception of *Deliverance,* Voight seemed to be getting nowhere—until he ran into Jane Fonda at a fund raiser for the California senatorial campaign of her activist husband Tom Hayden. Sharing Fonda's anti-Vietnam war sentiments, Voight was approached by the actress to star with her as her Marine captain husband in a project to which she was deeply committed, *Coming Home.* But upon reading the script Voight insisted on portraying the male lead, Jane's paraplegic lover, and after badgering Fonda and the film's director, Hal Ashby, he finally landed the extraordinarily challenging role. His choice turned out to be well worth the struggle, for at 39 the young blond actor netted a Best Actor Oscar and was back on top as leading man and sensitive sex symbol. To master the role in *Coming Home,* Voight spent 11 weeks at the Rancho Los Amigos Hospital near Los Angeles interviewing 500 paraplegics to learn how they conducted sexual relations, and the resulting graphic love scene with Fonda became one of the most talked-about couplings in recent movie history. As for his own love life, Voight was married for five years to actress Lauri Peters, whom he met on Broadway when they both had small parts in 1962's *Sound of Music.* He lived with actress Jennifer Salt after his success in *Cowboy,* then married Marcheline Bertrand. That lasted for six years until Voight left to live with Stacey Peckrin. Still, he shares child-rearing responsibilities for his son and daughter by Marcheline and assists Peckrin with cooking and household chores. Although he trained furiously for his role in Franco Zeffirelli's remake of *The Champ,* the 1979 tearjerker bombed with the critics. He got his career back on track with 1986's *Runaway Train* (for which he was Oscar-nominated), soon followed by *Desert Bloom.*

Born: December 29, 1938, in Yonkers, New York
Height: 6 ft. 1 in.
Weight: 180 lbs.
Eyes: Blue *Hair:* Blond
Zodiac: Capricorn
Education: Catholic University, B.A. in art
Religion: Roman Catholic
Marriages:
To Lauri Peters (1963–1968)
To Marcheline Bertrand (1971–1978)
Children: James (b. 1972), Angelica (b. 1974)
Interests: Women's liberation, ecology, gay rights, solar energy, liberal Democratic politics
Personal Habits and Traits: Does not smoke, drinks little, does household chores, is superconscientious, an exercise nut
Address: Los Angeles
Income: $450,000 (minimum estimate)

Diane Von Furstenberg

"A woman should dress for men. She should show a little leg!"

She was one half of the Beautiful People's "perfect couple" (the other half was Prince Egon von und zu Fürstenberg) until they separated, and then she set out to conquer the world with her "perfect little dress." In 1972 she borrowed $30,000 to manufacture her design in Italy and market it in the United States, and by 1975 she was commanding a $300,000 salary while her firm was selling an estimated $150 million worth of her trademark wraparounds and shirtwaists—not to mention such spinoff items as linens and cosmetics. A native of Brussels, Diane attended schools in Spain and in England before majoring in economics at the University of Geneva, where she met Prince Egon. Soon the two commenced their six-year reign as the darlings of the international jet set, which included being photographed nude from the waist up for the cover of *Town & Country* (though the picture was cropped). Her overnight success landed Von Furstenberg on the cover of *Newsweek,* but her empire began to unwrap with the decline of her perfect little dress. In 1978, she licensed the dress business to the giant Puritan Fashions Corporation but in 1982 terminated that contract (which guaranteed her $1 million annually) and took control of her dress line again. It was the right move—her Liquid Assets line sold and DVF was back on top. Now as queen of a global fashion empire she has kept her old pals like Andy Warhol (whose silkscreen portrait of her hangs in von Furstenberg's apartment), Marisa Berenson, and Twentieth Century-Fox chief Barry Diller. Most important, von Furstenberg is a tireless worker who not only designs most of her dresses and selects all her fabrics, but also cuts the exacting patterns herself.

Born: December 31, 1946, in Brussels, Belgium
Height: 5 ft. 3 in.
Weight: 100 lbs.
Eyes: Brown *Hair:* Black
Zodiac: Capricorn
Education: University of Geneva, B.A. in economics
Religion: Jewish
Marriages: To Prince Egon Von Furstenberg (1969–1978)
Children: Alexandre (b. 1970), Tatiana (b. 1971)
Interests: Design, finance, art, health and beauty
Personal Habits and Traits: Chain-smokes, social drinker, workaholic, speaks in a monotone
Addresses: New York City; Paris
Income: $2 million (estimate)

Robert Wagner

"All these years, I've just been a young leading man. The studios always thought of me as the boy next door—the smooth-talking and great-with-the-chicks-type guy, but no actor."

The only son of a wealthy Detroit metals manufacturer, "R.J." Wagner was a young rebel who, after being expelled from several fashionable prep schools, landed a job at Warner Brothers as an extra. Bit parts in over 40 films followed, and Spencer Tracy took the young actor under his wing in the mid-1950s. A studio product whose off-and-on marriage to Natalie Wood was an obsession of fan magazines for two decades, Wagner made such movies as 1960's *All the Fine Young Cannibals* (with Wood) and *The Mountain* (with Tracy) before scoring in three hit television series. In *It Takes a Thief* the slim, perennially youthful Wagner re-created the urbane Cary Grant role on TV in 1968 and 1969, and five years later returned as Eddie Albert's reformed con man–sidekick in the CBS series *Switch.* Without breaking stride, he then portrayed a tycoon moonlighting as a detective in *Hart to Hart*. Throughout, Wagner and Wood remained behind-the-scenes powers in television; their partnership with Aaron Spelling to produce shows like *Charlie's Angels* was tested when they sued for profits they charged had been denied them. Still, with the exception of his charming debut in *Titanic,* Wagner's career has been consistently and dramatically overshadowed by his turbulent private life. Married to Wood in a splashy Hollywood-style 1957 ceremony, Wagner divorced her after four years in the spotlight, married Marion Donen (with whom he fathered a daughter), then divorced her to remarry Natalie Wood in 1972. Wagner was shattered by Wood's tragic drowning in 1982, but he was comforted by longtime friend Jill St. John; there was frequent speculation that they would eventually marry. Wagner's short-lived return to the tube in *Lime Street* was marred by yet another tragedy when his young costar, Samantha Smith, was killed in the crash of a small plane.

Born: February 10, 1930, in Detroit, Michigan
Height: 6 ft.
Weight: 170 lbs.
Eyes: Blue *Hair:* Brown
Zodiac: Pisces
Education: High school dropout
Religion: Protestant
Marriages:
To Natalie Wood (1957–1962)
To Marion Donen (divorced)
To Natalie Wood (1972–until her death in 1982)
Children: Courtney (by Wood); Kate (by Donen)
Interests: Tennis, yachting, skiing
Personal Habits and Traits: Smokes, moderate drinker, homebody, avoids parties, generally in bed by 11 P.M.
Address: Beverly Hills
Income: $3 million (minimum estimate)

Irving Wallace

Irving Wallechinsky

"Writing a bestseller instantly makes an author suspect in the eyes of critics."

Patriarch of the writing Wallace family—wife Sylvia, son David, and daughter Amy are all bestselling authors—Irving Wallechinsky (the original name was later readopted by David) spent his boyhood in Kenosha, Wisconsin, then started stringing for a Milwaukee newspaper. After a brief stint in the Army, Wallace tried his luck as a screenwriter but discovered as soon as he was handed his first assignment—*The West Point Story* starring Doris Day and James Cagney—that Hollywood was definitely not for him. So Wallace turned to writing novels and in 1960 produced his first bestseller, the explicit, Kinseyesque *The Chapman Report*. Over the next 25 years his books *(The Seven Minutes, The Man, The Prize, The Word, The Second Lady, The Almighty* among them) sold around 100 million copies and were translated into over 30 languages. While Sylvia penned her own novel about a health spa called *The Fountains,* Wallace collaborated with son David on the number-one nonfiction bestseller *The People's Almanac* (I and II), with Amy on *The Two,* and with David and Amy on *The Book of Lists* (I and II) and *The Intimate Sex Lives of Famous People*.

Up around 11 A.M. at his Beverly Hills home, Wallace breakfasts, jogs, begins to write around 1 P.M., lunches at 3:30, then returns to work before winding up at 6 P.M. After dining or partying he usually returns to writing—often until dawn. Earning well over $1 million (not counting the rest of the family), Wallace can easily afford the gas for his Rolls-Royce and vintage Bentley.

Born: March 19, 1916, in Chicago, Illinois
Height: 6 ft.
Weight: 180 lbs.
Eyes: Blue *Hair:* Gray
Zodiac: Pisces
Education: High school
Religion: Jewish
Marriages: To Sylvia Kahn (1941–)
Children: David Wallechinsky (b. 1948), Amy (b. 1956)
Interests: Handicapping horse races
Personal Habits and Traits: Smokes a pipe, a social drinker
Address: Beverly Hills
Income: $1 million+

Mike Wallace

"TV is a no-win business."

Myron Wallace

Night Beat established this Massachusetts-bred TV broadcaster with the sledgehammer delivery in the 1950s, and the show flourished until Wallace's grilling of racketeer Mickey Cohen resulted in the latter calling an L.A. policeman a "degenerate"—a comment that sparked $3 million in libel suits and a $67,000 out-of-court settlement. He then hosted the oustanding *Biography* series, but that lasted only one season. In 1962, while Wallace was between jobs, his son Peter died tragically in a fall while mountain-climbing in Greece. Reordering his life, Wallace switched from talk shows to straight news at the age of 45. A decade later Wallace was perhaps the nation's toughest television reporter as a co-host (along with Dan Rather, Morley Safer, and Harry Reasoner) of the most popular news program in the medium's history: *60 Minutes*. Zipping around the globe (he averages 200,000 miles a year), Wallace is as equally adept at cross-examining heads of state such as the Shah of Iran and Anwar Sadat as he is at uncovering exposés on auto safety and diploma mills. Divorced twice (he once shared billing with his second wife, Buff Cobb, on the *Mike and Buff* radio and TV shows), Wallace met abstract painter Lorraine Perigord when he bought a $250 canvas at a gallery she was running in Puerto Rico. They married in 1955 and maintained lavish residences in New York City and Haiti before they separated, 29 years later. Since taking charge of the *60 Minutes* hot seat, four-time Emmy winner Wallace claims that he received the strongest backlash of his career when he presented a program relatively sympathetic to Syria. The response perplexed the veteran reporter, the son of Russian Jewish immigrants. In November 1979, in the midst of the Iranian student occupation of the U.S. Embassy in Teheran, Wallace was able to secure an interview with the Ayatollah Khomeini himself. Wallace found himself at the eye of the storm that would make his Syria experience mild by comparison: a libel suit by General William Westmoreland that charged *60 Minutes* with falsely stating that Westmoreland had lied about enemy troop strength during the Vietnam War. CBS won, but the strain on Wallace was so great he was hospitalized for exhaustion.

Born: May 9, 1918, in Brookline, Massachusetts
Height: 5 ft. 10 in.
Weight: 150 lbs.
Eyes: Brown *Hair:* Black
Zodiac: Taurus
Education: University of Michigan
Religion: Jewish
Marriages:
To Norma Kaplan (1940–1948)
To Buff Cobb (1949–1955)
To Lorraine Perigord (1955–1984)

Children: Peter (died in 1962), Chris (b. 1948)
Interests: Art, tennis
Personal Habits and Traits: Chain-smokes, workaholic
Address: New York City
Income: $900,000

Barbara Walters

On her debut as television's first anchorwoman: *"It will be my luck to flub the first four words."*

The 33rd *Today Show* host and television's first $5 million newscaster, Barbara Walters grew up surrounded by the rich and famous in New York, Boston, and Palm Beach. Her father, Lou Walters, owned Manhattan's famous Latin Quarter, and as a child Barbara hoped to tap-dance her way to stardom under the stage name "Babs Elliott." She attended Sarah Lawrence and summered regularly in Europe. Suddenly her father went bankrupt and suffered a massive heart attack, forcing Barbara to support both her parents. Starting out as a newswriter for CBS, she worked for an advertising agency, wrote material for Jack Paar and Dick Van Dyke, and finally landed a job on *Today* in 1961. After two years of toiling in the background, Walters seized the opportunity to work in front of the camera. Ill at ease in the beginning—a slight speech impediment that eventually led to Gilda Radner's "Baba Wawa" parody on NBC's own *Saturday Night Live* turned off some viewers—Walters spent the next dozen years proving she is one of the most astute interviewers in TV history. In addition to conducting lengthy and newsmaking interviews with every President since Lyndon Johnson, she aggressively pursued such eminent politicos as Henry Kissinger, Golda Meir, Menachem Begin, and Anwar Sadat. Her assignments for NBC have also included the China visits of Presidents Nixon and Ford, the Shah's prophetic 2,500th birthday gala for the Persian empire at Persepolis in Iran, and the investiture of Charles as Prince of Wales. Five of those *Today* years were spent hosting her own tremendously popular syndicated series *Not for Women Only* and writing the bestseller *How to Talk to Anybody About Practically Anything*. Walters had already made the cover of *Newsweek* and been named by *Time* as one of the 100 most influential leaders in America by the time she signed her million-dollar-a-year, five-year contract to co-anchor the *ABC Evening News* with Harry Reasoner. "I do not know whether people want to watch a woman giving the news," she admitted at the time, and her doubts proved well founded—the uneasy format lumbered along for only 18 months, though during that period Walters shone at what she did best (as she continued to do as part of the ABC news team)—special prime-time interviews with subjects ranging from Barbra Streisand and her boyfriend Jon Peters to Dolly Parton and Reggie Jackson. No longer stuck with *Today's* in-bed-at-10-P.M.-and-up-by-5-A.M. regimen, the twice divorced Walters partied into the night with constant companion Alan Greenspan, the White House economist, and with friends like designer Molly Parnis. She then joined ABC's *20/20* opposite old *Today* buddy Hugh Downs. Walters wed Merv Adelson, president of Lorimar Productions, in 1986, and embark on a bicoastal marriage—two weeks in New York alternating with two weeks in Los Angeles. Walters admits to being driven by her career, but is far from pompous when it comes to herself and her profession. She jokingly told a wide-eyed David Frost on his own TV talk show that the way she succeeded in the tough TV business was by hard work, determination and "sleeping with the producer."

Born: September 25, 1931, in Boston, Massachusetts
Height: 5 ft. 4 in.
Weight: 118 lbs.
Eyes: Hazel *Hair:* Light brown
Zodiac: Virgo
Education: Sarah Lawrence College
Religion: Jewish
Marriages: Three. Currently to Merv Adelson
Children: An adopted daughter, Jacqueline (b. 1968)
Interests: Broadcast journalism, writing, fashion
Personal Habits and Traits: Rarely smokes, drinks moderately, a confirmed workaholic, hates to shop (friends like Parnis or Halston send clothes to her, she picks out what she likes)
Addresses: New York City; Beverly Hills
Income: $2 million

Andy Warhol

Andrew Warhola

''Sex is the biggest nothing of all time.''

Born Andrew Warhola in 1927, the celebrity patriarch of American pop art was one of three sons born to Czechoslovakian immigrants who settled in McKeesport, Pennsylvania. Andy's construction worker father died when Warhol was 14. After several nervous breakdowns in his childhood, Warhol attended Pittsburgh's Carnegie Institute of Technology (now Carnegie-Mellon University) and graduated with a B.A. in art in 1949. Warhol peddled vegetables from the back of a station wagon and worked as a soda jerk in a local drugstore before heading for New York City, where he achieved solid success as a fashion illustrator until his Campbell's soup can became the most famous pop art emblem of the 1960s. At The Factory, Warhol's Union Square studio in Manhattan, Warhol has turned out underground films like *Sleep, Bike Boy, Nude Restaurant, Chelsea Girls, Lonesome Cowboys, Trash, Andy Warhol's Frankenstein,* and *Bad*—as well as *Interview* magazine and the Polaroid silkscreen portraits (President Jimmy Carter and the Empress of Iran are among those who have posed) that have made the white-thatched perennial boy wonder perhaps the world's most highly paid commercial artist. The Velvet Underground, a group founded by Warhol in 1967, became the springboard for '70s New Wave stars Lou Reed, John Cale, and Nico. Reality finally imitated the dubious art of Warhol's lurid films, however, when at 4:20 on the afternoon of June 3, 1968, Valerie Solanas, propagandist for the Society for Cutting Up Men (SCUM) and a Warhol ''superstar,'' stalked into his office and shot him with a revolver. Two .32-caliber bullets plowed through his spleen, liver, stomach, esophagus, and lungs; Solanas told police that she did it because Warhol had ''too much control'' over her life. Fully recovered, Andy is now one of New York's most ubiquitous celebrities and can be seen almost nightly milling around any number of discos.

Born: August 6, 1927, in Pittsburgh, Pennsylvania
Height: 5 ft. 8½ in.
Weight: 140 lbs.
Eyes: Blue *Hair:* White (a wig)
Zodiac: Leo
Education: Carnegie Institute of Technology
Religion: Roman Catholic
Marriages: None
Children: None
Interests: Painting, photography, filmmaking, publishing (founder of *Interview* magazine), fashion, dogs
Personal Habits and Traits: Chain-smokes, drinks, nearly always wears dark glasses, tends to drift off in conversation, extremely low-key
Addresses: New York City; Montauk, Long Island
Income: $800,000+ (estimate)

Raquel Welch

Raquel Tejada

''I love being a world-famous sex object. But I had to do a live show to show everybody I was more than just a cash register with glands.''

Asked to identify her ''most erogenous zone,'' Raquel Welch stunned and delighted the television audience with her response: ''The brain.'' Nevertheless, as Hollywood's leading Body Beautiful, voluptuous Raquel is heir to sex goddesses Jean Harlow, Marilyn Monroe, Rita Hayworth, Lana Turner, and Ava Gardner. Unlike previous sex symbols, however, Welch is so tough that around Hollywood she is known to hard-edged deal makers as ''Rocky.'' Almost from the time she danced in a school play at the age of nine, Welch has assiduously pursued a show business career. The daughter of a Bolivian-born aeronautical engineer, Raquel Tejada was briefly married to James Welch, then headed for Hollywood in 1963 with her two young children (she denies rumors that she has since been virtually remade by plastic surgery). Determined to be abreast of the competition, a scantily clad Welch pranced through such fluff as *One Million Years B.C., The Fantastic Voyage, Myra Breckinridge,* and *Kansas City Bomber*. She showed considerable acting talent in *Mother, Juggs and Speed,* but soon became a boob-trap victim and by the mid-1970s was desperately trying to convince producers to gamble on her in a musical comedy. When no takers materialized (''Everybody just laughed''), Welch decided to launch her own one-woman stage show to prove herself more than just an empty-headed sex object. She spent $200,000 and three months assembling an act, yet when she finally opened in Acapulco she did not exactly bring down the house. Unwilling to accept defeat, she plugged away at singing and dancing lessons and tried again. This time she broke the house record set by Frank Sinatra at the Paris Palais de Congrès, then went on to conquer Las Vegas where she now packs 'em in as a regular headliner. Somewhat fickle in her taste for men, she divorced her second husband, producer Pat Curtis *(Leave it to Beaver),* in 1972, then dated Henry Kissinger and soon lived with costume designer cum producer Ron Talsky until her 1976 reign as Queen of the Carnival in Rio. It was then that she met Brazilian music impresario Paulo. She and Paulo shared her Beverly Hills mansion. That lasted for two years before Raquel met and eventually married French film writer and director André Weinfeld. Welch proved she was more than an aging sex symbol when she replaced Lauren Bacall as the star of Broadway's *Woman of the Year* and later jumped on the fitness bandwagon with her own beauty book and hot-selling exercise tape. Welch's daughter Tahnee, meanwhile, got her career off to an auspicious start as one of the stars of Ron Howard's sci-fi blockbuster *Cocoon*.

Born: September 5, 1940, in Chicago, Illinois
Height: 5 ft. 6 in.
Weight: 118 lbs.
Eyes: Brown *Hair:* Reddish blond
Zodiac: Virgo
Education: High school
Religion: Roman Catholic
Marriages:
To Jim Welch (1959–1962)
To Patrick Curtis (1967–1971)
To André Weinfeld (1980–)
Children: Two
Interests: Ballet, jazz dancing, reading
Personal Habits and Traits: Nonsmoker, moderate drinker, has penchant for seven-inch heels
Addresses: Beverly Hills; New York; Mustique
Income: $600,000+

Gene Wilder

Jerome Silberman

''My quiet exterior used to be a mask for hysteria. After seven years of analysis, it just became a habit.''

To cheer up his mother, who suffered a heart attack when he was 6 years old, Jerome improvised comedy skits, and at age 13 made his acting debut at the Milwaukee Playhouse as Balthazar in *Romeo and Juliet*. He went on to study at England's Old Vic Theatre School but was drafted before he could get his career off the ground; so it wouldn't be a total waste, he asked to be assigned to work in the psychiatric ward of the Valley Forge Military Hospital (''I chose the job because it seemed most applicable to acting. I've always been drawn to roles of emotional cripples''). Wilder apprenticed in a few less-than-sensational Broadway plays, but it was not until he was in his mid-30s that the frizzy-haired actor became an ''overnight'' success as the hysteric accountant Leo (''My blue blanket! My blue blanket!'') Bloom in Mel Brooks's *The Producers*. Wilder's manic talent was showcased in two other Brooks blockbusters: *Blazing Saddles* and *Young Frankenstein*, which he cowrote with Brooks. Wilder made his bow as a director in 1975 with *The Adventures of Sherlock Holmes' Smarter Brother*, added producer to his list of credits on *The World's Greatest Lover*, and continued to prove his worth as an onscreen clown as the star of *Silver Streak, Stir Crazy,* and *The Lady in Red.* In 1984, the screen's most lovable *shlemiel* married Gilda *(Saturday Night Live)* Radner in Saint-Paul-de-Vence in France.

Born: June 11, 1935, in Milwaukee
Height: 5 ft. 9 in.
Weight: 150 lbs.
Eyes: Blue *Hair:* Blond
Zodiac: Gemini
Education: B.A., University of Iowa
Religion: Jewish
Marriages:
To Mary Mercier (1960–1966)
To Mary Joan Schutz (1967–1980)
To Gilda Radner (1984–)
Children: Katharine Anastasia
Interests: Bridge, tennis
Personal Habits and Traits: Quiet, serious, smokes, moderate drinker
Address: Los Angeles
Income: $500,000+ (estimate)

Andy Williams

Howard Andrew Williams

As an alto-voiced teenager, Howard Andrew Williams, the youngest offspring of a choir director in Wall Lake, Iowa, dubbed Lauren Bacall's singing voice for a Hollywood film in the early 1940s. He then joined his brothers Bob, Dick, and Don to back up Kay Thompson in a successful nightclub act. In 1954 young, velvet-voiced Andy struck out on his own as a Steve Allen regular on the old *Tonight Show* and launched his own variety series in 1962. Until 1968 Williams's mellow style and endless wardrobe of turtlenecks rendered him the prime time successor to crooner Perry Como, while his recording career flourished in the 1960s with 15 gold records. Several were the songs of composer Henry Mancini—Williams's trademark ''Moon River'' (from *Breakfast at Tiffany's),* ''Days of Wine and Roses,'' ''Charade,'' and ''Dear Heart.'' Among his other memorable soft-pop hits are ''Love Is Blue,'' the ''Theme From Love Story,'' and ''Happy Heart.'' The same year he started his own series he married French singer Claudine Longet, and though separated in 1970, they continued to appear together with their children on Williams's annual television Christmas show. That came to an abrupt end in 1977, however, when Longet was found guilty of ''negligence'' and sentenced to six months in jail for the shooting death of her lover, professional ski champ Spider Sabich (Williams stuck by his ex-wife throughout the entire ordeal). A longtime consort of Robert Kennedy's widow Ethel, Andy nonetheless played the field with a number of much-younger women.

Born: December 3, 1928, in Wall Lake, Iowa
Height: 5 ft. 6 in.
Weight: 145 lbs.
Eyes: Blue *Hair:* White
Zodiac: Sagittarius
Education: High school
Religion: Protestant
Marriages: To Claudine Longet (1962–1970)
Children: Three
Interests: Golf (his Andy Williams San Diego Open helps the Salk Institute), art, basketball (a major stockholder in the Phoenix Suns of the NBA), liberal Democratic politics
Personal Habits and Traits: Quit smoking, cut down on his drinking, diets, prefers tinted aviator glasses, wears pink Christian Dior boxer shorts
Address: Beverly Hills
Income: $1 million (estimate)

Cindy Williams

"Growing up in the country, you're left in the wilds of your imagination. I remember being alone a lot as a child, and I still love to be alone."

The Lucy-like half of ABC-TV's sitcom *Laverne and Shirley* was born the daughter of an electronics technician in the San Fernando Valley and grew up in a Dallas suburb. Moving back to California in the mid-1960s, she was encouraged at Van Nuys' Birmingham High School to follow in the footsteps of upperclassman Sally Field. Two years at Los Angeles City College and a stint as an antiwar activist kept Williams busy while she searched for movie and TV roles and commercials. Her first film role was a bit part in *The Blob* (a 1950s sci-fi classic that starred a young actor named Steve McQueen), followed by *Travels With My Aunt, The Conversation,* and finally the part of Ron Howard's girlfriend in *American Graffiti.* The hit movie spawned the Howard-Henry Winkler sock-hop superhit *Happy Days,* which in turn gave birth to *Laverne and Shirley.* Cast with Penny Marshall as roommates working on the assembly line of Milwaukee's Shotz Brewery, Williams at one point stomped off the set when it appeared that Marshall, whose father and brother happen to produce the show, was hogging air time. She was eventually promised equal treatment, and the rivalry between the two costars ceased. Later, Williams developed hypoglycemia and a case of bronchitis serious enough to require injections of antibiotics on her lunch breaks. On the brink of nervous collapse by the end of the 1977 season, she headed for the desert to recuperate. Long an intractable single, Williams ricocheted from romances with Richard Dreyfuss to writer-producer Harry Gittes (with whom she lived for three years) to actor Barry Newman (TV's *Petrocelli)* to Henry Winkler to David Lander (who plays Squiggy in her series) to pop sculptor Larry Shapiro before marrying Goldie Hawn's ex, Bill Hudson.

Born: August 22, 1948, in San Fernando, California
Height: 5 ft. 4 in.
Weight: 104 lbs.
Eyes: Blue *Hair:* Brown
Zodiac: Leo
Education: Two years at Los Angeles City College
Religion: Roman Catholic
Marriages: To Bill Hudson (1983–)
Children: A son (b. 1982)
Interests: Spiritualism, reincarnation, art, psychology (in psychoanalysis for two years), fencing, tennis, swimming, the desert
Personal Habits and Traits: Smokes, does not drink, exercise nut, diets continually, drives a Ford Granada
Address: Los Angeles
Income: $1 million

Paul Williams

"I always knew what I wanted to be when I grew up. Trouble is, I never did."

Randy Newman notwithstanding, this composer-lyricist-performer stands head and shoulders above most of his competition—even though he is only five feet tall. Nebraska-born Williams headed for Hollywood at 21 determined to make it as an actor, but aside from a part in *The Loved One* (he played a 10-year-old) and small roles in *The Chase, Watermelon Man,* and *Planet of the Apes,* he was forced to housepaint to pay his rent. So he picked up his guitar and began writing ballads that were promptly turned into million-selling hits by other artists. The Carpenters' "Rainy Days and Mondays" and "We've Only Just Begun," Helen Reddy's "You and Me Against the World" and "Just an Old-Fashioned Love Song" by Three Dog Night established Williams as a pint-sized Burt Bacharach. Emboldened by his behind-the-scenes success, Williams began to make frequent appearances on television talk shows. With his offbeat and self-deprecating humor he became an immediate celebrity who soon opened in Las Vegas, and although he had never recorded his own hits, Williams proved an instant hit and now commands a reported $70,000 per week as a Vegas headliner. In 1977 Williams and Barbra Streisand both picked up Oscars for "Evergreen," the love theme from *A Star Is Born,* for which she wrote the music, he the lyrics. Then Williams finally got his chance to star in a movie when he played the Faustian villain in Brian De Palma's rock horror spoof *Phantom of the Paradise.* He was nominated for another Oscar in 1980—this time for "The Rainbow Connection" (from *The Muppet Movie)*—but lost to "It Goes Like It Goes" from the film *Norma Rae.*

Born: September 19, 1940, in Omaha, Nebraska
Height: 5 ft.
Weight: 140 lbs.
Eyes: Blue *Hair:* Blond
Zodiac: Virgo
Education: High school
Religion: Protestant
Marriages: Two. Currently to Katie Clinton
Children: None
Interests: Songwriting, art, films, trivia
Personal Habits and Traits: Incessant dieter, junk-food junkie, does drink occasionally
Address: Hollywood
Income: $400,000 + minimum

Robin Williams

"TV or not TV. Whether 'tis nobler to do kiddie crap at 8 o'clock or sweat my ass off in small clubs."

It all started when Scotti Marshall asked her dad Garry, producer of *Happy Days* and *Laverne and Shirley,* to work an alien into the plot of a *Happy Days* episode. No one fit that description better than loony Robin Williams, who handily won the part in an open audition. Within weeks Williams's Mork, a wacky extraterrestrial with a penchant for sitting on his head and talking to sandwiches, was spun off into a series of his own, *Mork and Mindy*. The show easily became the biggest new hit of the 1978–1979 season, rocketing to number-one in the Nielsens for a time. A rich kid brought up in a 30-room mansion in the exclusive Detroit suburb of Bloomfield Hills, Williams was a chubby child and was taunted by his fellow students at the Detroit Country Day School until he dieted off 30 pounds and took up wrestling. After his father retired and moved to Marin County (near San Francisco), Robin experienced the psychedelic-and-gestalt period of the 1960s before finally becoming interested in theater at a junior college, the College of Marin. Williams won a scholarship to Juilliard and later spent three years training with John Houseman *(The Paper Chase)*. He picked up $150 a day miming on the steps of the Metropolitan Museum of Art in New York on weekends, and back in San Francisco tried improvisation while making ends meet by tending bar. By 1980, he pocketed more than $1 million portraying the sailor man himself in the film version of *Popeye,* followed by *The World According to Garp, The Survivors, Moscow on the Hudson,* and *Club Paradise*. Williams and his wife, Valerie Velardi, weathered early storms in their marriage and now share a ranch in northern California's breathtaking Napa Valley with their son, Zachary, and a private menagerie that includes an iguana and a parrot he's taught to squawk "Birds can't talk." Williams, who joined with Whoopi (*The Color Purple*) Goldberg and Billy Crystal to raise money for the homeless, stole the 1986 Academy Awards show with, among other antics, his on-the-money impression of Jack Nicholson.

Born: July 1952 in Chicago, Illinois
Height: 5 ft. 8 in.
Weight: 142 lbs.
Eyes: Blue *Hair:* Brown
Education: College of Marin, The Juilliard School
Religion: Roman Catholic
Marriages: To Valerie Velardi (1978–)
Children: Zachary (b. 1983)
Interests: Rollerskating, yoga, dance exercises, swimming, backgammon, electronic games, reading (J.P. Donleavy and Isaac Singer are favorites)
Personal Habits and Traits: Does not smoke, a vegetarian, runs three miles a day
Addresses: Beverly Hills; Zuma Beach, California
Income: $2 million

Vanessa Williams

"I am not a lesbian and I am not a slut, and somehow I am going to make people believe me."

The first black Miss America was also, unfortunately, the first to ever relinquish her title when *Penthouse* published nude photographs of her in graphic lesbian poses. The daughter of two public school music teachers, Vanessa and her younger brother, Christopher, were raised as Roman Catholics in suburban Millwood, New York. In addition to playing the French horn and piano, Williams became the singing star of Horace Greeley High in nearby Chappaqua. Williams, who had been handpicked by *People* magazine the week of the pageant as a likely winner, walked away with the crown after winning the talent competition with her throaty rendition of "Happy Days Are Here Again." Williams' happy days were short-lived; just weeks before her reign was to end, *Penthouse* publisher Bob Guccione printed the controversial photos (Hugh Hefner had first crack at them for *Playboy,* but declined). It seems that one year before that magic coronation night in Atlantic City, Williams had posed nude with another woman for Mount Kisco, New York, photographer Tom Chiapel. Her motive: "curiosity." When pageant chairman Albert Marks saw the pictures, he demanded she turn in her crown within 72 hours. As a man, a father, a grandfather, as a human being, he said, "I have never before seen anything like these photographs. *Ugh.* I can't even show them to my wife." Williams, who was succeeded by runner-up Miss New Jersey, Suzette Charles, lost more than just the Miss America title: she lost something in the neighborhood of $2 million in endorsements for Proline hair products, Avon, Hawaiian Punch, and Canada Dry, Kona Kai of Hawaii, and Gillette—not to mention a job as host of the Macy's Thanksgiving Day Parade, two Bob Hope specials, and a starring role in Broadway's *My One and Only*. By the close of 1985, Williams was trying to piece together the remnants of her singing career with a role in an Off-Broadway show.

Born: March 18, 1963, in New York City
Height: 5 ft. 6 in.
Weight: 112 lbs.
Eyes: Hazel *Hair:* Light brown
Zodiac: Pisces
Education: High school
Religion: Roman Catholic
Marriages: None
Children: None
Interests: Music (plays piano, French horn), acting
Personal Habits and Traits: Drinks wine, nonsmoker, very articulate and determined
Address: New York City
Income: $30,000 (estimate)

Flip Wilson

Clerow Wilson

"Being a comedian is like being a con man."

One of 18 children born to a Jersey City janitor, Clerow Wilson worked as a San Francisco bellhop before he cracked up his fellow enlisted men in the Air Force with his audacious sense of humor. He was so successful that Flip, as he came to be called, was sent on a tour of the Pacific to boost morale. Like so many of his contemporaries, Wilson later got his first break on the *Tonight Show,* bringing the house down with his imitation of Queen Isabella sending Christopher Columbus to discover America ("I ain't jivin'. We gonna discover *Ray Charles!").* Wilson used the same Butterfly McQueen voice and donned a honey-blond wig and miniskirt for his most popular routine—the sassy black bombshell Geraldine on his top-rated *Flip Wilson Show.* During the run of the program from 1970 to 1974 Wilson, the first black comedian ever to host his own prime time variety show, added a couple of indelible phrases to American jargon: "When you're hot, you're hot (and when you're not, you're not!)," and "What you see is what you get!" The father of four, Wilson was sued in 1979 by two of his former roommates, Kayatana Harrison and Rosylin Taylor; each wanted a chunk of his $5 million net worth. Flip now lives in Malibu, where he can be spotted tooling around in his Rolls-Royce with license plates bearing the name of Geraldine's unseen boyfriend "KILLER." He teamed up with Gladys Knight for 1986's CBS comedy series *Charlie & Co.*

Born: December 8, 1933, in Jersey City, New Jersey
Height: 5 ft. 8 in.
Weight: 155 lbs.
Eyes: Brown *Hair:* Black
Zodiac: Sagittarius
Education: High school dropout
Religion: Baptist
Marriages: One, 1957—divorced in 1967
Children: Four
Interests: Community affairs and charities, directing (keeps a two-inch-thick guidebook of his "Laws of Comedy")
Personal Habits and Traits: Smokes, drinks, late sleeper, bit of a night owl, tends to overeat, is a perfectionist
Address: Malibu, California
Income: $300,000+ (minimum estimate)

Debra Winger

"I have a thing *with the camera. The lens is unconditional. It doesn't judge you."*

At the age of 18, while working as a guide at Magic Mountain amusement park near Los Angeles, she was thrown from a pickup on New Year's Eve, 1973—a near-fatal mishap that left her blind and paralyzed for several months. Debra Winger, whose mother was an office worker and whose father ran a kosher frozen-food business, emerged from the experience determined to pursue an acting career: "I decided in the hospital that when I got out I'd just take my chances out there." Not that her life had exactly been humdrum before the accident; after graduating from high school in 1971 and a brief tour of Europe, she settled on a kibbutz and applied for Israeli citizenship. After three months of military training, she changed her mind and returned to the United States to study criminology and sociology at California State University at Northridge. Winger dropped out after three years and apprenticed on such TV shows as *Police Woman* and *Wonder Woman* (playing Lynda Carter's younger sister, Drusilla) before taming both John Travolta and a mechanical bull in *Urban Cowboy.* Her next feature film, *Cannery Row,* smelled, but she got her first Oscar nomination playing Richard Gere's girl in the weepy *An Officer and a Gentleman.* Winger was not entirely happy with *Officer;* she describes the filming of her nude scene with Gere "the most uncomfortable day of my life." She was nominated a second time for her portrayal of Shirley MacLaine's daughter in *Terms of Endearment* but lost out to MacLaine. Although the two actresses had battled on the set, during her acceptance speech MacLaine praised Winger's "turbulent brilliance." *Terms* marked a personal as well as professional turning point in Winger's life; while on location in Lincoln, Nebraska, she began a long-term romance with Nebraska Governor Robert Kerrey. Much to the abject surprise of friends and fans, Winger wed Timothy (*Ordinary People, The Falcon and the Snowman*) Hutton in early 1986. Winger's voice, which sounds like coal rumbling down a metal chute, was one of three electronically blended to create the voice of E.T.

Born: May 16, 1955, in Cleveland, Ohio
Height: 5 ft. 4 in.
Weight: 110 lbs.
Eyes: Brown *Hair:* Brown
Zodiac: Taurus
Education: Three years at California State College at Northridge
Religion: Jewish
Marriages: To Timothy Hutton (1986–)
Children: None
Interests: Writes verse (e. e. cummings is her favorite poet), Democratic Party politics
Personal Habits and Traits: Drives fast (often with her German shepherd, Pete, beside her), smokes, is tempermental, diets constantly (a "former fatty," she once weighed 135 pounds)
Addresses: Malibu, California; Santa Fe, New Mexico
Income: $2 million per film

Henry Winkler

"In a way, I've created a monster."

As "The Fonz," a leather-jacketed greaser who fights off swooning girls on TV's hit series, *Happy Days,* Henry Winkler created one of the most popular characters in the history of television—and in the process nearly created a Frankenstein that threatened to destroy his career. Nonetheless, his punk role brought the struggling young actor from New York a seven-figure bank account and instant superstardom. Winkler's parents, refugees from Nazi Germany, wanted him to join the State department. He attended private schools in Manhattan and Switzerland, but majored in drama at Boston's Emerson College and went on for a master's at Yale University School of Drama. He supported himself shooting TV commercials for everything from pizza to toothpaste, and later fashioned his trademark "duck's ass" haircut for the first time as a star (along with another unknown of the time, Sylvester Stallone) of the cult screen hit *The Lords of Flatbush.* Once in Hollywood he appeared on various sitcoms prior to beating out more than a dozen competitors for the role of Arthur Fonzarelli, and in a single season he brought *Happy Days* from 48th place in the Nielsens to number one. Off camera, the diametric opposite of The Fonz, Winkler is overly analytical and self-absorbed—something he realizes and tries hard to overcome. In 1977 he allayed his fears of being typecast by scoring two film successes: *Heroes,* in which he played a Vietnam vet, and a tongue-in-cheek wrestling saga called *The One and Only.* Winkler married longtime roommate Stacey Weitzman in 1978 and they share a modest Hollywood Hills house with Jed, Stacey's son by a previous marriage, their own children Zoe and Max, and two Yorkies. When not acting in films like *Night Shift* or producing (TV's *McGiver*), Winkler is involved in a variety of causes, from Toys-for-Tots to the Epilepsy Foundation to the Starlight Foundation, which tries to grant the last wishes of terminally ill children.

Born: October 30, 1945, in New York City
Height: 5 ft. 6½ in.
Weight: 140 lbs.
Eyes: Hazel *Hair:* Dark brown
Zodiac: Scorpio
Education: Emerson college, B.A. in drama; Yale University, M.A. in drama
Religion: Jewish
Marriages: To Stacey Weitzman (1978–)
Children: Zoe Emily (b. 1980), Max (b. 1983)
Interests: Shakespeare, working with dyslexic students at Glendale grade school, United Friends of the Children, his rock garden
Personal Habits and Traits: Smokes cigarettes when at home; a partygoer, he nonetheless prefers to watch TV at home with non-show-business friends; quiet, introspective, prone to stuffiness
Address: Toluca Lake, California
Income: $1.1 million

Jonathan Winters

"I'm still a little boy, and I don't know a man who isn't."

Having personally gone crazy—Winters spent eight months in a California sanitorium after a complete nervous breakdown—this undisputed comic genius has created a battery of mad characters from Maude Frickert to the Hefty trashbag garb*ahge* man. He grew up in a broken family; and he was raised by his radio actress mother in Ohio. Winters was always the class clown. After he dropped out of the Dayton Art Institute in 1949 (they gave him his degree 27 years later for "life experience"), Winters develped his comic talents at New York's Blue Angel and on the Jack Paar and Steve Allen television shows. After his breakdown in the early 1960s and a bout with whiskey that sent him to Alcoholics Anonymous, he starred in Stanley Kramer's wacky *It's a Mad Mad Mad Mad*

World and *The Loved One*. But television is Winters's forte, and in various incarnations he has spent five good seasons on the tube. Now he is generally confined to an occasional prime time special. For nearly a decade he was the star of TV commercials for Hefty trash bags. One-sixteenth Cherokee, he is active in Indian causes and is also an accomplished surrealist painter who greatly admires the work of Magritte and Dali.

Born: November 11, 1925, in Dayton, Ohio
Height: 5 ft. 10 in.
Weight: 200 lbs.
Eyes: Brown *Hair:* Brown
Zodiac: Scorpio
Education: Dayton Art Institute
Religion: Protestant
Marriages: To Eileen Winters (1949–)
Children: Jonathan, Jr. "Jay" (b. 1950), Lucinda (b. 1956)
Interests: The American Indian, painting
Personal Habits and Traits: A former drinker, he now carries a six-pack of Diet Pepsi wherever he goes; an incurable workaholic
Addresses: Toluca Lake, California; Malibu, California
Income: $200,000+ (estimate)

Shelley Winters

Shirley Schrift

"Nudity on the stage? I think it's disgusting, shameful and unpatriotic. But if I were 22 with a great body, it would be artistic, tasteful, patriotic and a progressive, religious experience."

Peppered with the names of famous friends (Marilyn Monroe, Jimmy Dean), coworkers (Ronald Coleman, Montgomery Clift, Lee Strasberg, Charles Laughton), bosses (Harry Cohn, George Stevens, George Cukor, Howard Hughes), and lovers (Marlon Brando, Errol Flynn, Adlai Stevenson, Burt Lancaster, Farley Granger, John Ireland, Robert Walker, and—only on Christmas Eves—William Holden), Shelley Winters's nothing-left-to-the-imagination memoirs, *Shelley: Also Known as Shirley,* shot to the top of the bestseller lists. This "epic of vindictive triumph," as *The New York Times* labeled it, actually begins in St. Louis, where Shirley was born into a Polish immigrant family. Raised in Brooklyn, she experienced her first seduction at 15—and her first abortion shortly thereafter. As a teenager, she worked as a Seventh Avenue model while attending drama school before finally finding work as an actress in a touring company of *Meet the People*. Taking Shelley ("my favorite poet") as her first name and her mother's maiden name (Winter) for her last—Universal Studios would later add the "s" and make her plural—the Brooklyn bombshell exploded on Broadway in *Rosalinda* and then promptly headed for Hollywood. There she found herself trapped in dumb blonde roles—a mold she was at last able to break out of in 1947 playing opposite Ronald Coleman in *A Double Life* (even though she set a record doing 96 takes before getting her first scene right). Winters's first Oscar nomination for Best Actress came in 1949 when she was murdered by

Montgomery Clift in *A Place in the Sun*. She copped the gold statuette a decade later in *Diary of Anne Frank* and chalked up another victory in the Oscar sweepstakes in 1965, this time for *A Patch of Blue*. A Strasberg-trained master of Method, Winters also established herself as a formidable acting talent on stage in *A Hatful of Rain* and *Night of the Iguana*. She has tried her hand at playwrighting—*One Night Stand of a Noisy Passenger* brought Robert DeNiro to public attention. But she is better known for her film work, which includes *Lolita, Alfie,* and *The Poseidon Adventure*. Ironically, Winters's five decades in the theater and on movie screens has probably accounted for only a fraction of the exposure she now receives as a perennial Peck's Bad Girl on the TV talk-show circuit; an entire new generation is discovering the brash ex-bombshell as a worthy opponent for the likes of Johnny Carson and Merv Griffin. After a first marriage to Air Force Captain Mack Paul Mayer, Shelley went on an Italian binge, marrying actor Vittorio Gassman and later taking Anthony Franciosa as Spouse No. 3. Single since her divorce from Franciosa, Winters divides her time between New York, where she teaches at the Strasberg Institute, and the sound stages of Hollywood, London, Berlin, Israel, and Italy.

Born: August 18, 1924, in St. Louis, Missouri
Height: 5 ft. 5 in.
Weight: 130–170 lbs.
Eyes: Green *Hair:* Blond
Zodiac: Leo
Religion: Jewish
Marriages:
To Mack Paul Mayer (divorced)
To Vittorio Gassman (divorced)
To Anthony Franciosa (divorced)
Children: Victoria Gina (b. 1953) by Gassman
Interests: Politics (a passionate Kennedy Democrat), French impressionism, playwrighting, teaching, swimming, urban renewal
Personal Habits and Traits: Nonstop talker, nervous eater and routine crash-dieter, perfectionist, irrepressibly candid
Addresses: New York City, Los Angeles
Income: $250,000 (estimate)

Wolfman Jack

Bob Smith

"I never prayed for no money and I never prayed for no fame. Dat's de whole trip in life, ya know."

Brooklyn native Bob Smith, alias Wolfman Jack, has been "comin' atcha" with his outrageous jive patter since he was 16, when he quit school and landed his first job at a Newport News, Virginia, radio station. Two years later he was "Big Smith with the Records" at Shreveport's KCIJ. In the early 1960s he became "Wolfman Jack"—from the early rock jock Dr. Jive's "What's up, Jack?" and a cartoon of a wolf sent to him by a fan in 1962. He started zapping American listeners all over the country from the 250,000-watt XERF just across the Mexican border (out of reach of U.S. wattage restrictions) and grossed an astronomical income. But rival factions tried to take over the lucrative station by force, and in 1964 after several attempts on his life, Wolfman Jack (he legally changed his name) left XERF for another Mexican station, 50,000-watt XERB just across the L.A. market in Rosarita Beach. Wolfman found himself $500,000 in the hole when U.S. authorities managed to force him out of business, and he turned to drugs. L.A.'s KDAY finally hired him in 1972 at $18,000 annually (he had been raking in almost that much per month during his stint across the border), but his appearance in the movie *American Graffiti* and a song written about him by Burton Cummings called "Clap for the Wolfman" (performed by The Guess Who) sparked new interest in the ghetto growl (the result of nodules on his vocal chords) that most listeners were convinced belonged to a black man. After a $300,000 stint at WABC in New York ended in 1975 he decided to set up shop for himself; his Howl Productions now controls the syndicated *Wolfman Jack Television Show* and Wolfman's two-hour, five-times-a-week syndicated radio show broadcast over some 2,200 stations in 43 countries. With a weekly audience of over 100 million, he is easily the most successful disc jockey of all time. Yet his face was best known to the American public through his weekly appearances as host of NBC's *Midnight Special,* and his *Wolf Rock TV* show for kids on ABC.

Born: January 21, 1938, in Brooklyn, New York
Height: 6 ft.
Weight: 185 lbs.
Eyes: Brown *Hair:* Brown
Zodiac: Aquarius
Education: High school
Marriages: To Lucy ("Lou") Lamb (1960–)
Children: Joy (b. 1961), Tod (b. 1964)
Interests: His family (he reserves at least 20 weekends a year for them), broadcasting, rock, swimming, cars, chess, backgammon, horror films, acting
Personal Habits and Traits: Chain-smokes, drinks little, a workaholic, he no longer takes drugs
Addresses: Beverly Hills; North Carolina; France; England; Japan
Income: $700,000 (minimum estimate)

Stevie Wonder

Steveland Morris Hardaway

"Eyes lie if you look into them for the character of a person."

Blind at birth, Steveland Morris Hardaway was already a virtuoso on the piano, bongos, guitar and harmonica by the time he was 10. That was the year a friend's older brother—a member of the Miracles—introduced Stevie to Motown. By 12, he recorded his explosive *Fingertips,* and soon Little Stevie Wonder reigned as the crown prince of R&B, cranking out Top 40 singles like "I Was Made to

Love Her," "My Cherie Amour," and "Uptight" at the rate of one a year. Blending the insistent Motown sound with hard rock, jazz and various other influences, Wonder followed his landmark *Music of My Mind* album by joining the Rolling Stones on their 1972 U.S. tour. *Innervisions, Fulfillingness' First Finale* and *Songs in the Key of Life*—the last one a year overdue—all claimed Grammys as Best Album of the Year. Ranging from reggae *(Boogie On, Reggae Woman)* to solid rock *(Superstition)* to political protest *(You Haven't Done Nothin')* to soulful ballads *(All in Love is Fair),* Wonder's ingenious outpouring is unmatched by any Motown graduate. It may have been propelled in part by his brush with death in 1973, when the car in which he was riding slammed into the back of a logging truck. A log crashed into Wonder's forehead, and he lay unconscious for a week. Friend and aide Ira Tucker sat by Wonder's bedside mumbling the inspiration for Wonder's "Higher Ground" for hours on end and Stevie pulled through. Amicably divorced from singer Syreeta Wright, Wonder has been living with Yolanda Simmons since 1973. The arrival of their daughter Aisha, prompted Wonder to write his upbeat "Isn't She Lovely?," and two years later his album *The Secret Life of Plants* bloomed on the charts. Wonder continued to grind out hits—"Ebony and Ivory" with Paul McCartney, "Up and Away"—and picked up an Academy Award for "I Just Called to Say I Love You" from *The Woman in Red.* Wonder waged a one-man campaign against South Africa's apartheid policies and was a moving force behind USA for Africa's "We Are the World" single, not to mention "That's What Friends Are For," (for AIDS research), "Part-Time Lover" and "Overjoyed."

Born: May 13, 1950, in Saginaw, Michigan
Height: 6 ft.
Weight: 179 lbs.
Eyes: Brown *Hair:* Black
Zodiac: Taurus
Education: High school
Marriages:
To Syreeta Wright (1970–1973)
Wonder has been living with Yolanda ("Londie") Simmons since 1973
Children: Aisha (b. 1975) by Simmons
Interests: Crusading against apartheid, bowling, swimming, rollerskating, air hockey
Personal Habits and Traits: Nonsmoker, teetotaler
Addresses: Manhattan; San Fernando, California
Income: $3 million (estimate)

Joanne Woodward

"I'm always asked what it's like to be married to Paul. I just can't smile and cope with that role any more. I resent it."

The green-eyed wife of the most famous pair of baby blues in the country—belonging to her husband, Paul Newman—Joanne Woodward has been a star in her own right since *The Three Faces of Eve* won her an Oscar back in 1958. Since marrying Newman, however, Woodward has settled into something of a homebody, devoting most of her time to raising six kids (three of theirs and three by his first marriage) on a three-acre estate near Westport, Connecticut. The daughter of a high school mathematics teacher, Miss Woodward (as she prefers to be called) spent a small-town girlhood in Thomasville, Georgia, then met Newman while he was the second lead in *Picnic* on Broadway and she was a struggling understudy. His first marriage to actress Jacqueline Witte was already dissolving and her engagement to Gore Vidal had foundered, and although Woodward thought at first sight that Newman was merely a typical Hollywood pretty boy, their romance blossomed along with their separate careers. They appeared together in eight movies, most notably *The Long, Hot Summer,* but their most successful collaboration occurred in the 1970s when Newman directed her in *Rachel, Rachel* and the riveting *The Effect of Gamma Rays on Man-in-the-Moon Marigolds.* A balletomane since 1965, Woodward works out at the barre daily in her own informal practice studio and raises money for two Manhattan dance groups. She experienced a bit of *déjà vu* portraying the psychiatrist to Sally Field's umpteen personalities in the gripping made-for-TV psychodrama *Sybil.* In 1975 both Newman and Woodward were honored by the Film Society of Lincoln Center—a tribute accorded previously only to Alfred Hitchcock, Fred Astaire, and Charles Chaplin. Woodward, who worries about the risks her race-car driver husband persists in taking, retired from TV drama after turning in one of her most moving performances, as an Alzheimer's victim in the Emmy-winning *Do You Remember Love?* Woodward knows the devastating impact of the disease all too well—her mother suffers from Alzheimer's symptoms.

Born: February 27, 1930, in Thomasville, Georgia
Height: 5 ft. 7 in.
Weight: 120 lbs.
Eyes: Green *Hair:* Blond
Zodiac: Pisces
Education: Louisiana State University
Religion: Protestant
Marriages: To Paul Newman (1958–)
Children: Nell (b. 1959), Lissie (b. 1960), Clea (b. 1964)
Interests: Ballet, Planned Parenthood, women's rights, needlepoint, cooking, jazz, poetry, liberal Democratic politics
Personal Habits and Traits: Smokes, drinks, does much of her own shopping
Address: Westport, Connecticut
Income: $350,000+

Robert Woodward and Carl Bernstein

"I suppose we were a contributing factor, but we didn't bring down the President. I think there must be an adversary situation in any case of investigative reporting. They kept saying we were liars. We had to prove them wrong. The only way we could do it was with solid fact."

"I had grave doubts about all sorts of things. As it became more and more and more serious and you saw more and more where it was going, you would say to yourself, 'Jesus, are we being fair? Is there something we might have missed? Is there an explanation for this we don't understand?' We don't perceive ourselves as heroes. We just did our job."

Carl Bernstein was assigned to the Virginia desk of the *Washington Post* and Bob Woodward had just finished a story on rat droppings in Washington restaurants when a man known as "Deep Throat" began feeding them the clues that would eventually unravel "Watergate," the American political scandal of the century. By the time it was over, Richard Nixon would resign the Presidency, several of his top aides would be convicted and sent to prison, and Woodward and Bernstein would become the nation's two most celebrated—and perhaps richest—journalists. Their account of the Watergate break-in and subsequent cover-up, *All the President's Men,* became a number-one bestseller and a tremendously successful film, with Robert Redford playing Woodward and Dustin Hoffman playing Bernstein. Amazingly, they managed to top themselves with their sequel, *The Final Days.* In fact, Woodward and Bernstein are an unlikely duo. As the son of a Republican judge from Wheaton, Illinois, Yale-educated Woodward served as a Navy officer and contemplated a law career before signing on with the *Post.* As a University of Maryland dropout, the shaggier Bernstein started out as a copyboy and worked his way up. While neither is a particularly noted writer, both are indefatigable reporters. Their tenacity earned them a Pulitzer Prize and a permanent place in American history. Now both working on their own projects, they have had to cope with major personal changes since landing in the public eye. Woodward is separated from his second wife, while Bernstein shed his first wife and married writer Nora *(Crazy Salad, Scribble, Scribble)* Ephron. Seven weeks after the birth of their second son, Max, Ephron stormed out of the Bernsteins' Washington condominium amid published rumors that Carl was having an affair with Margaret Jay, leggy blond daughter of former British Prime Minister James Callaghan and wife of ex-British Ambassador to the United States Peter Jay. Ephron later recycled the marital comedy of errors as a bestselling novel, *Heartburn.* Meanwhile, Woodward and Scott Armstrong's controversial account of the internecine machinations on the Supreme Court, *The Brethren,* shot to number one on the bestseller lists in a single week. Woodward was at the center of another controversy after publication of his sordid, tell-all biography of John Belushi, *Wired,* in 1983. Bernstein, for his part, took an unfortunate detour into television as an ABC correspondent and was seen about town squiring the likes of Elizabeth Taylor before turning back to the typewriter as a freelancer.

Robert Woodward

Born: March 26, 1943, in Geneva, Illinois
Height: 5 ft. 9½ in.
Weight: 174 lbs.
Eyes: Brown *Hair:* Brown
Zodiac: Aries
Education: Yale University, B.A. in history and English literature
Religion: Protestant
Marriages: Two. Both ended in divorce.
Children: None
Interests: Reporting, history, a voracious reader of nonfiction
Personal Habits and Traits: Does not smoke, drinks little, describes himself as boring, shuns the party circuit
Address: Georgetown, Washington, D.C.
Income: $700,000 (estimate)

Carl Bernstein

Born: February 14, 1944, in Washington, D.C.
Height: 5 ft. 8 in.
Weight: 150 lbs.
Eyes: Brown *Hair:* Dark brown
Zodiac: Aquarius
Education: University of Maryland dropout
Religion: Jewish
Marriages:
To Carol Ann Honsa (1968–1970)
To Nora Ephron (1976–1980)
Children: Jacob (b. 1978), Max (b. 1979)
Interests: Rock and classical music (has extensive tape collection), American history, bike racing
Personal Habits and Traits: Chain-smokes, does not abstain from alcohol, affects a disheveled appearance, shuns interviews but cultivates publicity
Addresses: Washington, D.C.; New York City
Income: $400,000 (estimate)

Andrew Wyeth

''Mood is what I'm after.''

His *Christina's World* is America's favorite painting, with over 300,000 reproductions sold, and he may well be the nation's most celebrated living artist. But realist Andrew Wyeth, whose bleak, unpeopled landscapes and moody still lifes fetch up to $200,000, has often been branded by critics as ''the rich man's Norman Rockwell.'' Son of famed illustrator N. C. Wyeth and father to painter Jamie, Andrew was born at Chadds Ford, Pennsylvania, and began exhibiting his work at age 20. Reflecting the pastoral life of Pennsylvania's Brandywine region, Wyeth's paintings are so exact in their detail that they exude an indefinably photographic yet surreal quality. In 1976, *The Two Worlds of Andrew Wyeth,* an exhibit focusing on two American families (the Olsons of Maine and the Kuerners of Chadds Ford), drew the largest audience of any living artist to New

York's Metropolitan Museum of Art. Preferring to stay close to Chadd's Ford with his wife, Betsy, and the rest of the clan (Jamie lives nearby), Wyeth has restored several buildings in the area, but had to give up his favorite hobby, fencing, after he seriously injured his right arm in a fall. Wyeth summers in Cushing, Maine, but seldom travels outside the Northeast. He made an exception in the spring of 1977, when he hopped a Concorde to Paris to be installed by the French Academy of Beaux Arts—the first American so honored since John Singer Sargent.

Born: July 12, 1917, in Chadds Ford, Pennsylvania
Height: 5 ft. 9 in.
Weight: 165 lbs.
Eyes: Brown *Hair:* Brown
Zodiac: Cancer
Education: High school
Religion: Protestant
Marriages: To Betsy Wyeth (1940–)
Children: Jamie, Nicholas, and Carolyn
Interests: Miniatures, fencing, farming, restoring old farmsteads
Personal Habits and Traits: Nonsmoker, drinks very little, goes to bed early, is semireclusive
Addresses: Chadds Ford, Pennsylvania; Cushing, Maine
Income: $500,000+

Jamie Wyeth

James Browning Wyeth

"I doubt things. Being satisfied by something is a real danger for me. I hope I never lose that. That would be death."

A third-generation painting Wyeth (his grandfather N. C. Wyeth was the great artist-illustrator who settled in Pennsylvania's lush Brandywine Valley; his father is the legendary Andrew), Jamie is unquestionably the most commercially successful artist of his generation. Brought up in Chadds Ford, coonskin cap-wearing Jamie was 6 when he posed for one of his father's famous portraits, *Faraway*. At 11, he quit school to study painting with his older sister Carolyn. At the age of 20 he was asked by the Kennedy family to paint a posthumous portrait of JFK. Wyeth, whose uncle Peter Hurd had painted an unflattering portrait of Lyndon Johnson that infuriated LBJ, threw himself into the Kennedy project, working from photographs of the late President and—to capture the family resemblance—from life studies of Bobby and Teddy. By the time he was in his mid-20s he was commanding at least $7,500 for his watercolors and $30,000 for his oils. The young Wyeth's naturalistic, realistic style is strongly suggestive of his father's but comparisons do not bother Jamie; he views them as a form of flattery. Married since 1968 to Phyllis O. Mills, a member of the DuPont dynasty who worked as a White House secretary during the Kennedy administration, Jamie lives just a few miles from his parents' old farmhouse and the Brandywine Museum, where the works of N. C., Andrew and Jamie make up virtually the entire collection.

Born: July 6, 1946, in Chadds Ford, Pennsylvania
Height: 6 ft.
Weight: 151 lbs.
Eyes: Blue *Hair:* Blond
Zodiac: Cancer
Education: Dropped out of school at 11, then tutored at home
Religion: Protestant
Marriages: To Phyllis O. Mills (1968–)
Children: None
Interests: Art, farming, horses
Personal Habits and Traits: Seldom smokes, occasionally drinks, a furious worker, spends more than 10 hours per day in the studio
Address: Chadds Ford, Pennsylvania
Income: $300,000 (minimum estimate)

Jane Wyman

Sarah Jane Fulks

''If you asked Ronnie the time, he'd tell you how to make a watch.''

A queen of the four-hankie tearjerker (most notably in her 1948 Academy Award–winning role of *Johnny Belinda),* Ronald Reagan's first wife is known to a whole new generation of fans as scheming Angela Channing of the *Falcon Crest* TV series. Growing up in St. Joseph, Missouri, little Sarah Jane was the daughter of the chief of detectives and started in show business as a bit player. Her big break occurred in the Norman Krasna movie *Princess O'Rourke,* which caught Billy Wilder's eye. Wilder then cast her opposite a perpetually pickled Ray Milland in *Lost Weekend,* followed by 85 more movies, including *The Blue Veil, Miracle in the Rain, Magnificent Obsession,* and *The Yearling*. Her eight-year marriage to Reagan, which she refuses to discuss, ended because she did not share his consuming interest in politics. When Louella Parsons asked him why his marriage wound up on the rocks, Reagan, who called Jane ''Nuts,'' ''Monkeypuss,'' and ''Little Miss Button Nose,'' replied: ''I think Jane takes her work too seriously. Jane says she loves me but is no longer 'in love' with me and says this is a fine distinction. I think she is nervous, despondent, and therefore feels our life together has become humdrum.'' Said Jane at the time: ''We're through, we're finished and it's all my fault.'' Wyman hosted her own TV show in the mid-1950s, but retired from the business for nearly 20 years—coming out in 1981 for the part of *Falcon Crest*'s deliciously evil mistress (''Once I read the script, I was hooked''). During a portion of the 1983 season, sparks flew on the *Falcon Crest* set when Lana Turner was brought in to play Angela Channing's rival.

Born: January 4, 1914, in St. Joseph, Missouri
Height: 5 ft. 6 in.
Weight: 112 lbs.
Eyes: Blue *Hair:* Reddish brown
Zodiac: Capricorn
Education: High school
Marriages: Five. To an unnamed musician, to dress manufacturer Myron Futterman, to Ronald Reagan, and to bandleader Freddie Karger, whom she married and divorced twice
Children: Michael (adopted) and Maureen Reagan
Interests: Reading, clothes, knitting, painting, arthritis research
Personal Habits and Traits: Chain-smokes low-tar cigarettes, a teetotaler, wears a wig, watches little television and dislikes the theater, very energetic, a difficult interview
Address: Los Angeles
Income: $100,000 per episode ($2 million+)

Tammy Wynette

Wynette Pugh

''Sometimes I wish I weren't famous.''

The nightmare began in September 1978, when country singer Tammy Wynette and her fifth husband George Richey returned to discover eight X's scrawled across the back door of their palatial Nashville home. The next day a kidnaping attempt on Wynette's youngest daughter, Tamala Georgette, was aborted. Then, just one week later, Wynette felt a gun jabbed in her ribs as she climbed into her yellow El Dorado. The man, wearing a stocking over his head, held her captive on an 80-mile ride before strangling and beating her savagely. Abandoned in the backwoods she managed to find her way to a house and called an ambulance. The reason for the abduction remains a bizarre mystery, for Wynette was neither sexually molested nor robbed. But it was not the first sensational melodrama to befall the onetime beautician whose real name is Wynette Pugh. Since fighting her way from the cotton fields of Mississippi to the recording studios of Nashville, she has been named the Country Music Association's Female Vocalist of the Year three times and recorded no less than 32 straight number-one country hits, including ''Stand by Your Man'' (the biggest-selling country single in history) and ''D-I-V-O-R-C-E.'' In addition to her five husbands, she experienced a much-publicized fling with Burt Reynolds—though Wynette is still most often linked by her fans with third husband George Jones, a C&W star in his own right; they reigned as the self-appointed ''Mr. & Mrs. Country Music'' for six years, until their bitter D-I-V-O-R-C-E in 1975. Actually, the abduction was only one in a series of disasters to befall Wynette within a period of a few months. During that time her home was broken into 15 times, and on one of those occasions ''SLUT'' was scrawled across her TV screen and on the mirrored ceiling above her bed. The bedroom wing of her mansion was then set ablaze and burned to the ground, and her tour bus was also torched while Tammy and her musicians were asleep inside; miraculously, they all managed to escape. A plane crash subsequently took the life of her pilot, and Wynette herself wound up in the hospital with severe bronchitis. Once recovered from the shock of being nearly killed at gunpoint during her abduction, Wynette resumed her usual touring schedule of more than 160 performances a year. When she isn't on the road, Wynette sticks close to her 17,500-square-foot home with its 15 bathrooms and new three-man security force. Her biography, *Stand by Your Man,* was published in 1979.

Born: May 5, 1942, in Red Bay, Alabama
Height: 5 ft. 7 in.
Weight: 121 lbs.
Eyes: Brown *Hair:* Brown
Zodiac: Taurus
Education: High school
Marriages: Five. Currently to George Richey (1978–)
Children: Gwen, Jackie, Tina, Georgette
Interests: Cars, clothes
Personal Habits and Traits: Somewhat fatalistic, a perfectionist and tireless worker, avid television-watcher, drinks moderately
Address: Nashville, Tennessee
Income: $475,000 (estimate)

Michael York

On his role in *The Island of Dr. Moreau: "I looked in the mirror and growled, 'You beast.'"*

He was transmogrified into a beast in *The Island of Dr. Moreau* and made light of his almost-too-pretty looks in Marty Feldman's *The Last Remake of Beau Geste*. But for the most part, Oxford-educated Michael York has (despite a twice broken nose) made a career for himself as a sexy matinee idol in such films as *Romeo and Juliet, Justine, Something for Everyone, The Taming of the Shrew,* the musical remake of *Lost Horizon,* and Richard Lester's two hit *Musketeer* sagas. Admitted to the National Theatre of Great Britain after Oxford, York got his first minor stage part in Franco Zeffirelli's production of *Much Ado About Nothing*. Several years later, when the Italian director was casting for *The Taming of the Shrew,* he decided that the dewy-eyed young Englishman would make a perfect Lucentio. York has a not inconsiderable flair for comedy, but his best role to date was as the brainy bisexual in Bob Fosse's Oscar-winning *Cabaret*. He has been married to former *Glamour* photographer Patricia McCallum, an American, since 1968. After grunting his way through the embarrassing *Island of Dr. Moreau,* York channeled most of his energies into such television fare as the miniseries *Space* and the ill-fated occult soap *Dark Mansions*.

Born: March 17, 1942, in Fulmer, England
Height: 6 ft.
Weight: 168 lbs.
Eyes: Blue *Hair:* Blond
Zodiac: Aries
Education: Oxford University, the National Theatre
Religion: Protestant
Marriages: To Patricia McCallum (1968–)
Children: None
Interests: Literature, art, music, soccer, rugby, cricket, photography
Personal Habits and Traits: Smokes, drinks Scotch, avoids parties
Address: London, England
Income: $420,000 (minimum estimate)

Z

Pia Zadora

"I have known exactly what I wanted since I was 8 years old. My husband chased me until I caught him."

At 6, she was cast by Burgess Meredith in a Broadway play starring Tallulah Bankhead. From there, she was pushed by her wardrobe-mistress mother into nine more plays on the Great White Way, including *Fiddler on the Roof* and *Dames at Sea* (she took over the lead from Bernadette Peters). Yet when, at 22, she married 53-year-old billionaire Meshulem Riklis, pouty-lipped Pia Zadora was instantly portrayed in the press as a gold-digging Lolita. In fact, it is Riklis who seems determined to make his nubile young wife a sex symbol for the 1980s. So determined that he poured millions into her first film, the kinky sexpic *Butterfly,* and the international publicity that led to her winning a Golden Globe Award. "Pia's is the perfect body," says Riklis of his former Dubonnet Girl. "Her legs are not too long, her torso is not too wide, her bottom is not too big." The Rapid-American chairman continued to pump money into her movie career, financing two more bombs, *Fake Out* and *The Lonely Lady.* He also pushed his surprisingly prudish ("I was a virgin when I met my husband") wife into doing a *Penthouse,* er, spread. Nevertheless, shortly after the birth of her daughter, Kady (named after the character Mom played in *Butterfly),* Zadora did manage to record her first hit single, a duet with Jermaine Jackson called "When the Rain Begins to Fall," and to carve a niche for herself belting out standards of the 1930s and '40s. Critics praised her unembellished style, and Pia gained enough confidence to appear on the TV program for which she had inadvertently supplied so much material: *The Tonight Show* starring Johnny Carson. Her husband, meantime, was less fortunate: his fortune declined to a paltry $150 million.

Born: 1955, in Brooklyn, New York
Height: 5 ft.
Weight: 97 lbs.
Eyes: Brown *Hair:* Blond
Education: High school
Religion: Roman Catholic
Marriages: To Meshulem Riklis (1978–)
Children: Kady (b. 1984)
Interests: Music, art, the theater
Personal Habits and Traits: Does not cook (the Riklises eat out every night), does not smoke, drinks moderately, loves chocolate, hates opera, bossy, shopaholic
Address: Manhattan
Income: $500,000 (independent of Riklis's income)

PICTURE CREDITS

ASYLUM RECORDS
p. 76

ATLANTIC RECORDS
pp. 16, 160, 172, 299, 313

BUDDAH RECORDS
p. 254

CAPITOL RECORDS
pp. 301, 308

CBS
pp. 31, 34, 79, 211, 305, 315, 328, 379

CHRYSALIS
p. 65

ALFRED EISENSTAEDT
p. 450

EPIC RECORDS
p. 219 (top)

JAY BEE
pp. 60, 73, 130, 151, 154, 214, 227, 259, 280, 301, 334, 335, 338, 364, 374, 375, 394, 396, 398

MCA
p. 123

THE MEMORY SHOP
pp. 7 (all photos), 8 (left, center), 10 (left), 11 (left, right), 36, 37, 46, 49, 62, 67, 68, 70 (top), 81, 82, 83, 87, 90, 98, 100, 103, 105, 106 (top), 106 (bottom), 108, 112, 113, 115, 120, 125, 140 (top), 140 (bottom), 141, 145, 148, 152, 157, 162, 166, 169, 170, 179, 180, 182, 183, 184, 195, 197, 220, 223, 228, 231, 234, 238, 247, 252, 255, 262, 263, 266, 267, 269, 270, 271, 273, 275, 276, 284, 285, 290, 293, 303, 304, 306, 307, 309, 312, 314, 320, 326, 339, 347, 348, 352, 359, 366, 367 (bottom), 372, 382 (bottom), 386, 387, 390, 391, 392, 393, 404, 405, 411, 412, 413, 418, 424, 425, 426, 427, 444, 445, 447, 453, 458, 459, 462

MGM
p. 65

MOVIE STAR NEWS
pp. 9 (all photos), 10 (center), 18, 22, 39, 47, 57, 70, 71, 72, 80, 94, 99, 102, 110, 118, 122, 128, 131, 133, 134, 143, 153, 176, 177, 178, 187, 188, 192, 194, 200, 202, 206, 210, 215, 216, 218, 219 (bottom), 235, 241, 242, 273, 277, 279, 287, 289, 291, 294, 295, 296, 298, 319, 330, 349, 354, 360, 363, 367, 369, 384, 403, 410, 417, 419, 421, 433, 442, 449, 461

PHOTOREPORTERS
pp. 8 (right), 10 (right), 29, 42, 45, 59, 74, 77, 86, 91, 92, 93, 109, 149, 158, 163, 164, 165, 186, 207, 229, 236, 244, 272, 274 (bottom), 282, 316, 331, 333, 341, 400, 440, 443

PICTORIAL PARADE
p. 356

ROBIN PLATZER
pp. 11 (center), 78, 80, 261, 286

WARNER BROTHERS RECORDS
pp. 65, 161, 204